THE TRAIL DRIVERS OF TEXAS

GEORGE W. SAUNDERS
President and Organizer Old Time Trail Drivers' Association

THE
TRAIL DRIVERS
OF TEXAS

Interesting Sketches of Early Cowboys and
Their Experiences on the Range and on
the Trail during the Days That Tried Men's
Souls—True Narratives Related by Real
Cowpunchers and Men Who Fathered the
Cattle Industry in Texas

Originally Compiled and Edited by
J. MARVIN HUNTER
and
Published under the Direction of
GEORGE W. SAUNDERS
PRESIDENT OF THE OLD TIME TRAIL DRIVERS' ASSOCIATION

Introduction by
B. BYRON PRICE

UNIVERSITY OF TEXAS PRESS, AUSTIN

International Standard Book Number 0-292-78076-1;
0-292-73076-4 (pbk.)
Library of Congress Catalog Card Number 84-52817
Copyright 1924 by George W. Saunders
Copyright 1925 by Lamar & Barton, *Agents*
Copyright © 1985 by the University of Texas Press
All rights reserved
Printed in the United States of America

Fourth University of Texas Press Hardcover Printing, 1992
First University of Texas Press Paperback Printing, 1992

Requests for permission to reproduce material from this work should
be sent to Permissions, University of Texas Press, Box 7819, Austin,
Texas 78713-7819.

⊗ The paper used in this publication meets the minimum
requirements of American National Standard for Information
Sciences—Permanence of Paper for Printed Library
Materials, ANSI Z39.48-1984.

*This edition is taken from the second edition revised (two volumes
in one) published in 1925 by Cokesbury Press.*

INTRODUCTION

An estimated 25,000 to 35,000 men trailed six to ten million head of cattle and a million horses northward from Texas to Kansas and other distant markets between the end of the Civil War and the turn of the century. Judging from the literary remains housed in range archives and libraries, memories of the experience lingered far longer in the minds of the men and boys involved than did the tracks of bovine hooves upon the landscape of the Great Plains and beyond. Besides drudgery and hardship, the long drive promised excitement and danger for some; for many, a trip across the prairie behind a herd of Texas Longhorns was the most unforgettable experience of their lives. Years later, memories of raging rivers, unpredictable stampedes, and sudden violence still stirred the blood of these now older and wiser men as they clustered together at old settlers' days and county fairs recounting days that would never pass again and yearning for a simpler life in a world grown complex. "Cowboys," observed one novelist descended from a long and distinguished line of Texas cowpunchers, "are romantics, extreme romantics, and ninety-nine out of a hundred of them are sentimental to the core. They are oriented to the past and face the present only under duress, and then with extreme reluctance."[1] The trail drivers of Texas were no exception. As their numbers steadily declined, the history and folklore created by these drovers threatened to disappear as well.

---

1. Larry McMurtry, *In a Narrow Grave* (Austin: Encino Press, 1978), p. 149.

Alarmed at this prospect and determined to preserve for posterity the historical contributions of the trailriding cowboys, George W. Saunders, himself a veteran of the cattle trail, founded the Old Time Trail Drivers' Association in 1915. The new organization and the heavily attended annual reunions that it sponsored provided members with a sense of community and family as well as a place to reminisce. G. O. Burrow, an active member of the association, remarked that in his old age "the only real enjoyment I have is our reunions of the Old Trail Drivers." Many others apparently felt the same, for during its first year of operation membership in the Old Time Trail Drivers' Association rose to 375 and represented several states. By 1921 the organizational rolls had swelled to more than 1,000.

At the annual convention held in San Antonio in 1917, a crowd estimated at between seven hundred and eight hundred individuals listened eagerly as George Saunders, president-elect of the body, unveiled a plan to publish a book compiled from the members' own recollections of droving. Saunders had been soliciting narratives for at least two years and many in the assembly enthusiastically volunteered to add their stories for publication. Responsibility for editing the volume was offered to A. C. Williams of Fort Worth, who was the assistant secretary of the Cattle Raisers' Association of Texas and editor of the *Cattleman*.

Problems that "would have tested the patience of Job," as Saunders later put it, plagued the enterprise from the beginning. Few drovers responded quickly, and most had to be cajoled into submitting their stories with follow-up telephone calls, telegrams, and letters. Moreover, neither Williams nor his successor, a columnist for the *San Antonio Express*, was able to complete the project. World War I intervened and, even more disastrous, the San Antonio firm hired to print the volume went bankrupt and disappeared with virtually all of the previously edited source material.

Undaunted, the determined Saunders embarked afresh on his task, soliciting orders at the 1920 convention for

a five-hundred-page volume to be delivered in August.
Remembering J. Marvin Hunter, a newspaperman who
had shown an earlier interest in the project, Saunders approached him on April 21, 1920, to complete the work.
Hunter was dubious about his ability to finish the book in
only three months' time. Besides, he had never been a cowboy, although his father had once driven the trail. He took
the job, nevertheless, but only because he realized that "it
would be a wonderful contribution to the historical annals .
of Texas, and that the time was ripe for its publication, as
the older fellows are passing off the stage of action at an
alarming rate and that within a few years not many would
be left to tell the tale."

Not only was the time schedule incredibly tight but also
the source material was almost wholly lacking. Beginning
with thirty-five historical sketches that had arrived too late
to be considered for the earlier planned book, Hunter went
to work editing and lining up a competent printer while
Saunders sought additional reminiscences. Routinely working late into the evening and never getting more than three
or four hours' sleep a night, Hunter compiled and edited
the steady stream of manuscript material brought him
by Saunders. Each day he delivered his previous night's
work to the Jackson Printing Company, where he picked up
finished proofs to be read and corrected that night. Amaz-
ingly, Hunter met his deadline and delivered the completed
book to Saunders on July 21. The $500 he received for
his efforts paid the mortgage on the Hunter home in San
Antonio.

The Trail Drivers of Texas was issued in an edition believed to have numbered a scant one thousand copies. Its
favorable reception by association members encouraged
Saunders and Hunter to produce an additional volume of
perhaps five hundred copies in 1923. By this time Hunter
had moved to Bandera, where he had established a small
print shop with a linotype machine. "I printed this second
volume," he would later write of the crudely produced

work, "but it was a piece of printing I was always ashamed of."[2] Following the issuance in 1924 of a corrected and revised version of the first volume with a second-edition imprint on the title page, the whole was combined in 1925 into a single volume of 1,060 pages by Cokesbury Press of Nashville, Tennessee, and presented as the second edition revised. This edition, which is reproduced here, contains information not included in the earlier volumes and thus comprises the best and most complete version to date.

Saunders intended that *The Trail Drivers of Texas* preserve the role played by the drovers in fulfilling the manifest destiny of the nation. "These pages sparkle," boasted the foreword to the work, "with the lustre of deeds well done by a passing generation, and it is our purpose to keep bright that lustre, that it may not pale with the fleeting years." Saunders vigorously defended the cowboys and drovers with whom he had been associated and frequently commented upon the sterling quality of their characters. Reacting to pulp portrayals of cowboys as wild and lawless brigands, he argued that only a small percentage actually became criminals and that the number was not proportionally greater than one from a comparable sample of college graduates would be. Similar sentiments permeate the volume. Typical was C. S. Broadbent's characterization of the cowboy as "generous, brave and ever ready to alleviate personal suffering, share his last crust, his blanket and often more important, his canteen. He spent his wages freely and not always wisely, and many became an easy prey to gambling and other low resorts. Some among them became leading men in law, art and science—even in theology, proving again that it is not in the vocation but in the man, that causes him to blossom and bring a fruitage of goodness, honor and godly living."

Despite the facts that as many as six thousand former drovers may still have been living at the time *Trail Drivers*

---

2. J. Marvin Hunter, *Peregrinations of a Pioneer Printer* (Grand Prairie, Tex.: Frontier Times Publishing House, 1954), p. 172.

was being prepared and that a drovers' organization of more than a thousand members supported its publication, fewer than 350 individual entries comprise the largest edition of the book. First-person narratives of cattle droving account for less than half of the total number of articles while the rest of the contents can be divided into several broad categories. A number of first-person accounts, for example, relate various frontier experiences but do not touch on trail driving. Several other entries are reprinted from other published sources, including books and newspapers. A few poems also are sprinkled throughout the work. To this list may be added the various individuals who authored tributes to relatives or friends who drove north from Texas. By far the largest number of entries, however, were prepared by Hunter, who concerned himself primarily with portraying the lives of successful cowmen and businessmen rather than the average drover. Many of his subjects already had died. In order to stimulate reader interest, Hunter frequently tagged articles with exotic or sensational titles. For the same reason he included a number of colorful tales of Indian fighting and outlaws having little or nothing to do with droving.

A careful examination of the contents of the Cokesbury Press combined edition reveals some additional insights about the hurried conditions under which the volume was conceived and produced. The vast majority of first-person respondents lived in Texas with only about 6 percent residing outside the state and another 3 percent of unknown origin. Over 60 percent of the residents of the Lone Star State lived within 150 miles of San Antonio and only about 14 percent lived north of a line drawn east and west through Austin. Not surprisingly, the largest number of first-person droving narratives, about 21 percent of the total, came from persons living in San Antonio. Lockhart provided the next-largest number, just over 5 percent, followed by the towns of Del Rio, Pearsall, and Bartlett. The remainder were scattered throughout twenty-one other communities.

Trail Drivers contains many omissions and inaccuracies

and must therefore be used with caution as a historical re-source. For example, George Saunders once estimated that one-third of the men who went up the trail were black or Hispanic, yet little attention is given in the volume to the contributions of these ethnic drovers. Rarely are they men-tioned by name and relatively few Hispanics and only one black, George Glenn, figure prominently in any of the in-dividual accounts. Most of the minor errors of fact are matters of questionable spelling and inconsistent dates. A few, however, are more serious. Perhaps the most stinging illustration occurs in the associational sanctioning of an er-roneous identification of the route of the Chisholm Trail. Further problems exist in inconsistent organization, which J. Frank Dobie appropriately characterized as "chaotic."[3] The quality and the informational content of the articles also vary considerably. Some articles cover only a single trail drive while others are more detailed and compre-hensive. Most tend to dwell on a few particularly colorful or otherwise memorable incidents. Despite these short-comings, *The Trail Drivers of Texas* offers an interesting glimpse of trail life as well as some intriguing possibilities for cliometricians and prosopographers. By eliminating su-perfluous narratives and sampling the 157 legitimate first-person accounts of droving, a profile of the men who en-gaged in this occupation begins to emerge.

The birthplaces of slightly over 40 percent of the sample are unknown. Of those listing a place of birth, just over 40 percent were born in states other than Texas. Of these, Mississippi sired the largest number, followed by Mis-souri, Alabama, Tennessee, Ohio, Arkansas, and Ken-tucky. Foreign-born drovers numbered only four, Germany being the homeland of two and Poland and France one each. The Texas-born part of the sample hailed from twenty-five different counties, led by Caldwell, Travis, Montgomery,

---

3. J. Frank Dobie, *Guide to Life and Literature in the Southwest* (Dallas: Southern Methodist University Press, 1943), p. 65.

and Gonzales. Nearly 60 percent of the first-person narratives mention a year of birth. The range of dates extends from 1833 to 1871, with over 80 percent occurring during the decades of 1840 and 1850. Perhaps surprisingly, only slightly more than 10 percent of the men mentioned their Civil War service and only one of these, Joseph Cotulla, identified himself as a Union Army veteran. These figures do not, however, count a significant number of individuals who may have served on the Indian frontier during the conflict.

C. W. Ackerman remembered that, on his first drive to Kansas in 1873, the oldest man in the crew was twenty-five while the rest ranged between the ages of eighteen and twenty-two. Indeed, trail drivers enjoyed a rigorous occupation full of privation and physical hardships that demanded the vigor of youth. While it is not possible to determine with any degree of reliability the age at which nearly half of the first-person cases took the trail north for the first time, about three out of four of the rest appear to have first taken the trail between the ages of sixteen and twenty-two. Another 20 percent embarked on their first drive at an older age, while only about 6 percent started younger. Many of the old drovers spoke of engaging in range work almost as soon as they could sit a saddle and one, A. D. McGehee, actually drove from Belton to Abilene in 1868 at the ripe old age of eleven.

The first-person accounts contained in *Trail Drivers* do not seem to bear out George Saunders' estimate that only about one-third of all drovers repeated the experience. Nearly three-quarters of those responding acknowledge participation in more than one drive and nearly 60 percent mention going up the trail more than twice. Only about 20 percent drove five years or longer and this number dwindled steadily to less than 5 percent at the end of a decade. William B. Slaughter reported the most trips, logging more than twenty.

Men or boys, these drovers regularly pushed Longhorn herds to dozens of different trail termini located in several western states. Many of these cattle were destined for shipment to the beef packeries and butcher stalls of the industrial midwest and northeast. Other herds supplied Indian reservations and military posts through government contracts. Parts of a single drive might be sold or delivered at several different points. As might be expected, mention of Kansas trail heads dominates the accounts in *Trail Drivers*. Nebraska, Wyoming, Colorado, New Mexico, Indian Territory, and the Dakotas also are frequently listed, followed by Louisiana, Montana, Arizona, Oregon, Idaho, Missouri, Mississippi, Iowa, and Mexico.

As deliveries of cattle accelerated during the two decades that followed the Civil War, the droving labor force expanded rapidly to keep pace. Detractors seeking to debunk the mythical cowboy hero point out that the real puncher was merely a hired man on horseback. Indeed, on the range or trail the wages of cowhands rarely exceeded $30–$40 per month and most of the time were less. W. T. Bright reminisced that he had gathered many of the herds that eventually made their way north but that he never went himself because range work paid better than trailing. Besides, he reasoned, "I never liked to get up and herd cattle at night, so never had any desire to go to Kansas." Yet the cowboy experience was only a transient one for most before other jobs beckoned. Said F. M. Polk, another disgruntled ex-drover with loftier aspirations after his last trip up the trail, "On my way home I reviewed my past life as a cowboy from every angle and came to the conclusion that about all I had gained was experience, and I could not turn that into cash, so I decided I had enough of it, and made up my mind to go home, get married and settle down to farming."

Just under half of the first-person accounts in *Trail Drivers* reveal facts concerning drovers' posttrailing employment and occupational patterns. In an article written about the Old Time Trail Drivers' Association in 1921, the *Cattleman* boasted, no doubt with some exaggeration, that "hundreds of them are now millionaires," adding perhaps more truthfully, "but luck has not been with all of them."[4] There is, nevertheless, ample evidence that many trail drivers achieved some degree of upward mobility and that a few enjoyed a measure of real financial success. A survey of these narratives also reveals considerable diversity in occupational pursuits. Of those who mention their lives after droving a sizable percentage remained in ranch-related activities, from hand to manager to owner, or engaged in stock farming. Some ex-drovers, such as "Lead Steer" Jack Potter, ended up with substantial holdings in land and cattle. Perhaps a greater number emulated the experience of E. L. Brouson, who, after quitting the trail in the 1880s, acquired a small herd of his own. Brouson went broke in 1903 and repeated the experience so many times that he eventually lost count. Several former cowboys transferred their skills and experience to the stockyards, where they became commission merchants and livestock shipping agents for railroads. At least one put his talents to use in the show arena, where he performed with a wild west show.

The pursuits of those who left the range for jobs in cities and towns were even more diverse. A fuel dealer, a marble yard operator, a ginner, and an undertaker may be counted besides the more common occupations, such as merchant, hotel owner, and butcher. Several trail drivers eventually became financiers. This group included men like J. B. Pumphrey, who made five trips up the trail during the 1870s, and George F. Hindes, a Confederate veteran who delivered herds to Kansas and Wyoming for a decade after 1872. A number of others were like S. H. Woods, Duval County judge between 1896 and 1915, and held such public offices as district attorney, county commissioner, sheriff, marshal, postmaster, city councilman, and Texas Ranger.

The paucity of marriage statistics in *Trail Drivers* makes it difficult to arrive at any meaningful conclusions as to the effects the institution may have had upon the lifestyle of the

---

4. "The Story of the Old Trail Drivers," *Cattleman* 7 (March 1921): 216.

drovers. Nearly 70 percent of the first-person accounts do
not mention a wife. From the relatively small sample of
those remaining, it appears that the economic and social re-
sponsibilities of that institution curtailed many droving careers. About one-half of the married men quit droving before or during the year of their marriage. And while only
about 20 percent continued droving some did so for more
than a decade. The status of the rest is uncertain.

George Saunders, in summarizing the accomplishments
and strong character of his droving associates, pauses to acknowledge the contributions of women to the winning of the
West. At one point in *Trail Drivers* he quotes several pages
from J. M. Hunter's book *A Pioneer History of Bandera
County*, which noted, ". . . it is only proper that we should
record some encouraging word to her aspirations and advocate her claims to a just and proper place in the history of
our great state." Women are treated with reverence and
respect throughout *Trail Drivers*. Several females contributed articles about life on the frontier or wrote tributes
to loved ones. Others figure prominently in such stories.
Hunter, for example, included the story of Mrs. Lou Gore,
the operator of Drover's Cottage, an Abilene, Kansas, hotel
frequented by Texas cowboys during the heyday of the
town as a cattle shipping point. The popular Mrs. Gore became an honorary member of the Old Time Trail Drivers'
Association and was invited to the 1924 reunion. Hunter
also wrote several short biographical sketches of the wives
and daughters of well-known cattlemen.

Not all the trail drivers of Texas were men. The accounts
of several women who took the trail also grace the volume.
Samuel Dunn Houston recounted the story of a girl who,
dressed as a man, joined his trail crew for four months in
1888 on a drive between New Mexico and Colorado. Association member Amanda Burks of Cotulla provided a detailed description of a trip up the trail with her husband's
herd to Newton, Kansas, in 1871, and Mrs. William B.
Slaughter wrote ably of an 1896 trail excursion between
Fort Sumner, New Mexico, and Liberal, Kansas. (Else-

where in the volume, her husband remembered the same trip as having taken place in 1901 between Clifton, Arizona, and Liberal.) Mrs. Sallie M. Redus also briefly mentioned a journey she and her baby made with a trail crew.

In *Clio's Cowboys*, a volume critical of the historiography of the range cattle industry, author Don Walker calls *The Trail Drivers of Texas* the "richest storehouse of historical information"[5] about droving and cowboy life written by the participants themselves. He notes the tendency among stockmen during the late nineteenth century, when "moved by a sense of the past,"[6] to reflect on their past lives. He warns, however, that a sense of the past and a sense of history are two different things and cautions that "what purports to be a history of the trail and ranch life is often a selective, nostalgic memory."[7] Walker encourages historians to penetrate the myths of sentimentality, lore, and legend in order to get closer to the truth.

Certainly, *The Trail Drivers of Texas* reeks of "good old days" sentimentality. Part of the nostalgia most probably stems from the disorientation that some drovers may have felt at the passing of their way of life. C. H. Rust of San Angelo, who drove the trail during the 1870s, spoke for many of his genre when he wrote: "I turn my face west. I see the red lines of the setting sun, but I do not hear the echo come back, 'Go west, young man, go west.' I turn my face east and I hear the dull thud of the commercialized world marching west, with its steam roller procession, to roll over me and flatten me out." Not all expressed such pessimism about the future. One greeted the rapid advances in communications and transportation affecting twentieth-century Texas almost eagerly when he remarked, "May we not venture to predict that in another sixty years somebody will have established a trail to Mars or other

---

5. Don D. Walker, *Clio's Cowboys* (Lincoln: University of Nebraska Press, 1981), p. 101.
   6. Ibid., p. 47.
   7. Ibid., p. 102.

planets, and our descendents may be signalling the latest market quotations to the cowmen of those parts?"

Despite its many weaknesses, historians, bibliographers, and cowboys themselves have always rated *The Trail Drivers of Texas* as one of the finest works ever produced on the cattle industry. Shortly after the publication of the second edition of the first volume, the *Cattleman* called it "a book that is destined to become a classic of its kind" and "the 'Bible' of every old time Texas cowpuncher."[8] More recently, one bibliographer termed it "an essential foundation book for any range library."[9]

George Saunders hoped that the sales of the volume would help fund the erection of a major granite monument in Brackenridge Park in San Antonio, commemorating the early Texas pioneers. Although he believed that the necessary funds could be raised as early as 1924, Saunders' campaign to raise $30,000 for the marker still was incomplete at the time of his death following a lengthy illness on July 3, 1933. The year before, the seventy-eight–year–old cowman had led about twenty-five of his old comrades to the site of Doan's Crossing of the Red River, where they placed a marker commemorating the old trail drivers. Saunders' body lay in state in the Municipal Auditorium at San Antonio before funeral services commenced at the First Baptist Church. A multitude of floral arrangements, one of them from Will Rogers, covered and surrounded the casket. Spurs, a quirt, a rope, and a bandana replaced the flowers at the graveside services as the old trail driver went out in style to the strains of "Rounded Up in Glory," a favorite cowboy hymn.

George Saunders never lived to see the marble-and-granite monument of his dreams. A smaller one honoring

---

8. "The Story of the Old Trail Drivers," p. 218.

9. William S. Reese, *Six Score: The 120 Best Books on the Range Cattle Industry* (Austin: Jenkins Publishing Company in Cooperation with Frontier America Corporation), p. 45.

him and the others who "pointed them north" eventually
was placed at a site in front of what is now the Old Trail
Drivers' Museum in San Antonio. But in a sense it does not
matter. Saunders and his publishing partner, J. Marvin
Hunter, already had left a far more substantial legacy embodied in *The Trail Drivers of Texas*.

B. Byron Price
Panhandle-Plains Historical Museum
Canyon, Texas

FOREWORD

This volume is brought forth to present a link in the long chain of Texas history that cannot well be spared if the record is "kept straight," and posterity is given a true account of the deeds of daring and heroism of the early pioneers of our great state. The characters mentioned in this book are men of sterling worth and integrity, as has been proven in every instance wherein they came in contact with the problems and difficulties that made for the development of an empire so vast in its possibilities as to excite the envy of the world. These pages sparkle with the lustre of deeds well done by a passing generation, and it is our purpose to keep bright that lustre, that it may not pale with the fleeting years.

The men and women, the pioneers who blazed the way for the present-day civilization, happiness and prosperity in Texas, are looked upon with the greatest respect and veneration. Fifty years ago the Indian, the buffalo and the deer roamed at will over the Texas prairies. A half century now intervenes, but today prosperous cities dot the green distances and men and women who thirty-five and forty years ago drifted to the great and boundless West with hardly a penny are today wealthy and "in the saddle" in the State's affairs. They endured many privations. They fought for what they believed was right. They blazed the trail. The people of today, the younger generation, are not unmindful of what the early settlers

did for them, and as they enjoy the splendid prosperity
that is theirs they silently thank the earlier ones.

To the memory of the old trail drivers, the Texas
pioneers—to the heroic mothers, fathers—to the young
and the brave who fought manfully for proud, imperial
Texas, this volume is lovingly dedicated.

CONTENTS

CONTENTS xxiii

CONTENTS

PAGE

THE TRAIL DRIVERS OF TEXAS

THE TRAIL DRIVERS OF TEXAS

Before the advent of railroads the marketing of cattle
was a problem that confronted the man who undertook
the raising of cattle in Texas. The great expanse of unsettled domain was ideal for the business. No wire fences
were here to limit the range, grass was knee high, and
cattle roamed freely over the hills, valleys and prairies
of Texas. The long-horn was in the hey-day of his glory.
The limitless range, broken by no barrier, extending from
the Gulf to Kansas, offered ample opportunities for the
man with nerve and determination in this great out-of-
doors. There being no fences he allowed his cattle to
scatter over the range, but at times he would round them
up and throw them back in the vicinity of the home ranch
when they strayed too far away. In the spring the big
"round-ups" usually took place, when all of the cowmen
of each section would participate, coming together at a
stated time, gathering all of the cattle on the range, and
branding what was rightfully theirs. Be it said to their
credit, those early cowmen seldom claimed animals that
belonged to a neighbor. If a cow was found unbranded,
and there was any evidence that she belonged to some
cowman not present, or who lived over in the "next
neighborhood," the owner was notified and usually got
his cow. There was a noticeable absence of greed in
those days in the cattle business, for the men who chose
that means of livelihood were of that whole-souled, big-

hearted type that established a rule of "live and let live," and where a man was suspected of being a thief he was watched and if the suspicions were realized that man found that particular neighborhood to be a mighty unhealthy place to live in. Being sparsely settled in those early days, the ranches being from ten to fifty miles apart, counties unorganized and courts very few, every man in a way was a "law unto himself," so that speedy justice was meted out to offenders whose deeds were calculated to encourage lawlessness.

Gradually the country began to settle up with people, some coming from other states to establish homes in the great Lone Star State, and in the course of time the cattle industry became the leading industry in this region. Farming was not thought of, more than to raise a little corn for bread. Beef was to be had for the asking, or wild game for the killing. Mustangs furnished mounts for the cowman, and these horses proved their value as an aid to the development of the cattle industry. A good rider could break a mustang to the saddle in a very short time, and for endurance these Spanish ponies had no equal. Then loomed the problem of finding a market for the ever-increasing herds of cattle that were being produced in South and Southwest Texas. In this state there was no demand for the beef and hides of the long-horn, but in other states where the population was greater the beeves were needed. Then it was that some far-seeing cowman conceived the idea of getting his cattle to where the demand existed, so it was that trail-driving started. A few herds were driven to Abilene, Kansas, on the Atchison, Topeka and Santa Fé Railroad, and the venture proved so successful financially that before a great while everybody began to send their cattle "up the trail." These drives were not unattended by many dangers, as a great portion of the route was through a region infested by hostile Indians, and many times the redskins carried off the scalps of venturesome cowboys.

For many years the trail-driving continued, or until those great arteries of commerce, the railroads, began to penetrate the stock-raising region, and then gradually the cowpuncher, whose delight was to ride his pony "up the trail," was deprived of that privilege, and now instead he goes along with a trainload to "tail 'em up" when the cattle get down in a stock car.

With the passing of the trail came a better breed of cattle, the long-horn gave place to the short-horn white face Hereford, less vicious and unruly. The free range passed away, wire fences came as a new era set in, with the encroachment of civilization. The Texas cowmen formed an association with regular annual conventions, where ways and means for the improvement and betterment of their business were devised. These gatherings are a source of much pleasure to the old-time stockmen, and it was at one of these conventions a few years ago that George W. Saunders suggested that an auxiliary association of old-time trail drivers be formed, to be composed of men who "went up the trail" in those early days. But inasmuch as such an association would detract from the usual business transacted at the meetings of the parent association it was eventually decided to form a separate association with a different time for its meetings, and thus the Old Trail Drivers' Association sprang into existence, and met with popular favor, so much so that within a year from its organization it had a membership of over five hundred.

The ranks of the old trail drivers are becoming thinner each year, but there still remain many who knew the pleasures and hardships of a six and eight months' trip to market with from fifteen hundred to three thousand head of cattle. They are scattered from Texas to the Canadian border and from California to New York. Many are rated in Dun and Bradstreet's in the seven-figure column, while others are not so well off financially. The stories some of these old fellows could tell would make your hair stand on end, stories of stampedes and Indian raids, stories with dangers and pleasures intermingled and of fortunes made and lost; they made history which the world does not know a thing about.

To perpetuate the memory of these old trail drivers, who blazed the trail to greater achievement, is the aim of every native-born Texan who knows what has been so unselfishly accomplished. To stimulate it, and keep it alive in the hearts of our Texan youth, will inspire a spirit of reverence and gratitude to their heroic fathers for the liberty which they have given them—for the free institutions which are the result of their daring.

                                        J. R. BLOCKER.

ORGANIZATION OF THE OLD TIME TRAIL DRIVERS' ASSOCIATION

The following, taken from the Secretary's record, gives an outline of the first steps that were taken toward organizing the Old Trail Drivers' Association:

"A number of the old time trail men in San Antonio met in the Chamber of Commerce hall on the afternoon of February 15, 1915, for the purpose of organizing an association to include in its membership those surviving who had shared the dangers, vicissitudes and hardships of the trail.

"After a general discussion it was unanimously resolved to perfect the organization and prepare for the enrollment. George W. Saunders outlined the plan of formation, and the following officers were elected: J. R. Blocker, president; George W. Saunders, vice-president; Luther A. Lawhon, secretary, and Colonel R. B. Pumphrey, treasurer."

At that time it was suggested that the Association affiliate with the Texas Cattle Raisers' Association, and hold joint meetings with that organization. At the Cattle Raisers' convention on March 9th and 10th, 1915, a great many members were added to the new association, and in March, 1916, the Old Trail Drivers had their first roundup when the Cattle Raisers' convention met in Houston. We give below the complete proceedings of the Old Trail Drivers' meeting, in which is included the report of the Secretary, and a list of the officers and directors of the association:

Minutes of the First Annual Convention of the Old Time Trail Drivers' Association Held in the City of Houston, Texas, March 21, 22, 23, 1916

In accordance with the date and place selected by the Texas Cattle Raisers' Association, with which the Old Time Trail Drivers' Association is affiliated, these two organizations convened in the city of Houston on Tuesday, March 21, 1916, in annual convention.

Headquarters for the Old Time Trail Drivers' Association was established in the lobby of the Rice Hotel, with Vice-president and Organizer George W. Saunders, Secretary Luther A. Lawhon and C. D. Cannon in charge. Badges and buttons, furnished by the association, were distributed to the members, of whom quite a large number were in attendance, and the books of the association were opened for the enrollment of new members.

At 10 o'clock A.M. Tuesday, 21st, the two organizations—the Texas Cattle Raisers' Association and the Old Time Trail Drivers' Association, met jointly in the city auditorium for the opening exercises, which were associately conducted, the Hon. Joe Jackson, President of the Texas Cattle Raisers' Association, presiding.

After preliminary prayer and introductory speeches by the Hon. Pat Garrett, the Hon. Ben Campbell, mayor of the city, delivered the address of welcome. This was responded to on behalf of the Texas Cattle Raisers' Association by the Hon. G. W. Armstrong, of Fort Worth, and on behalf of the Old Time Trail Drivers' Association, by Secretary Luther A. Lawhon. The joint preliminary exercises having been concluded, the Old Time Trail Drivers' Association recessed until 2:30 P.M.

Afternoon Session

Promptly at 2:30 the members of the Old Time Trail Drivers' Association assembled in the ballroom of the Auditorium, which had been kindly placed at the disposal of the Association by the city of Houston. Owing to the absence of President John R. Blocker, who was indisposed, Vice President and Organizer George W. Saunders presided. In calling the Association to order, Vice President Saunders in a forcible address, reviewed the history of the organization, its aims and its purposes, and dwelt with especial pride upon the cordial and hearty endorsement which had been given the Association by the "Old Trailers" throughout the country, as evidenced by the many applications for membership which the Secretary had received during the current year.

At the conclusion of Vice President Saunders' address, Secretary Luther A. Lawhon presented the following annual report, which was unanimously adopted:

Hon. John R. Blocker, *President,* Old Time Trail Drivers' Association:

Sir—I have the honor to herewith submit to you for the benefit of the Old Time Trail Drivers' Association my annual report as Secretary of the Association. I congratulate the membership upon the rapid growth of the Association, and for the deep and fraternal interest which has been unanimously manifested for its maintenance and welfare.

Assembled as we are in our first annual convention, I trust it will not be deemed inappropriate to refer briefly to the origin of our Association—an organization which has taken such a strong hold upon the hearts of the old-time trail men, and the motives and the influences which called it into being.

As is well known to most of the membership, the name of George W. Saunders, our vice president, is indissolubly linked with that of the Old Time Trail Drivers' Association. Mr. Saunders, an old-time cowboy, and one of the first to go up the trail, had urged through the press, as well as orally, the desirability and importance of an organization that would include and perpetuate the names of those survivors who had shared the dangers and the hardships of the trail—a condition and a society long since passed away. The proposition awakened a responsive chord in the hearts of the old-time trail drivers through a call published in the San Antonio *Daily Express,* a number of prominent cattlemen residing in San Antonio, with others of nearby counties, met in the rooms of the San Antonio Chamber of Commerce on the afternoon of February 15, 1915, and formally organized the Old Time Trail Drivers' Association with the election of the following officers and board of directors:

John R. Blocker, President.
George W. Saunders, Vice President.
Luther A. Lawhon, Secretary.
R. B. Pumphrey, Treasurer.

J. M. Bennett, Sr., W. J. Moore, George W. West, J. H. Presnall, W. H. Jennings, T. A. Coleman, Ike T. Pryor, J. D. Houston, San Antonio, Texas; D. H. Snyder, Georgetown, Texas; John Pumphrey, Taylor, Texas; W. B. Blocker, Austin, Texas; P. B. Butler, Kenedy, Texas; R. B. Masterson, Amarillo, Texas; J. B. Irving, Alpine, Texas; John Holland, Alpine, Texas; J. H. Paramore, Abilene, Texas; Clabe Merchant, Abilene, Texas; T. D. Wood, Victoria, Texas; George W. Littlefield, Austin, Texas; M. A. Withers, Lockhart, Texas; Charles Schreiner, Kerrville, Texas; Jim Scott, Alice, Texas.

By resolution all those are eligible for membership who went up the trail with cattle or horses during the years from 1865 to 1896. A membership fee of One Dollar was authorized to be assessed.

The Cattle Raisers' Association of Texas, at its annual convention held in San Antonio, March 9th, 10th, 11th, 1915, generously extended its fraternal recognition of the Old Time Trail Drivers' Association, by passing a resolution inviting the latter to meet with the former in its annual convention. In this connection I desire to return thanks to the editor, A. C. Williams of *The Cattleman,* the official organ of the Cattle Raisers' Association of Texas, and Assistant Secretary of that organization for the courteous consideration which he persistently extended to the Old Time Trail Drivers' Association.

In May, 1915, your secretary addressed to each member of the Association a letter signed by Vice President George W. Saunders, asking that the parties addressed would write their reminiscences, incidents and adventures of the Trail for the benefit of the Association. In response to these letters the Secretary has received a number of communications, which are not only highly interesting, but are valuable contributions to the frontier history of Texas. It is expected that at this convention the Association will take such steps as it may deem proper to have these chronicles edited and properly arranged for the press, that they may be ultimately published in book form for sale to the general public, and for the benefit of the Association.

On February 5th, 1916, at a meeting of the Executive Committee composed of the officers and Board of Directors, held in San Antonio, a resolution was passed making the sons of the old time trail drivers eligible for membership. This was done at the urgent solicitation of many of the younger cattlemen of Texas, whose fathers had been trail men, and who felt an interest in, and a desire to become identified with the organization.

In addition to appreciating the interest shown by the

sons of the old-time trail men, the Executive Committee recognized that in a few years at best, the old-time trail men will have passed away, and the incorporation of the young cattlemen would be the means of perpetuating our organization. We now have a membership of 375, scattered through the states of Missouri, Oklahoma, Arizona, New Mexico and Texas.

The Executive Committee, also at this meeting, decided to have a button manufactured for the members to wear permanently in the buttonhole of the lapel of their coats. Vice President Saunders was authorized to select the design and arrange for the manufacture. In obedience to this, Mr. Saunders designed and has had manufactured a button which is artistic, appropriate and worthy to be worn by the membership of the Old Time Trail Drivers' Association. He also had badges printed for distribution to the members attending this convention.

I regret to have to report that since our last meeting death has taken from our midst the following members:

J. H. Winn, Pleasanton, Texas; William Choate, Beeville, Texas; S. R. Guthrie, Alpine, Texas; O. C. Hildebrand, Brownsville, Texas; T. D. Woods, Victoria, Texas. In the death of these members, our Association has suffered a severe loss, and I submit that this convention pass appropriate resolutions to their memories.

In conclusion I desire to return my sincere thanks to the officers and members of the Association for their cordial cooperation in behalf of the Association, and for the uniform courtesy and consideration which they have extended to me. For the past twelve months I have, as Secretary, served the Association to the best of my ability, and I trust that the interest of our honored Association will continue to advance for the future as it has in the past.

LUTHER A. LAWHON, *Secretary.*

The Secretary's report having been adopted, the Association went into discussion of the origin, start, route and terminus of the "Old Chisholm Trail." There was found to be a considerable difference of opinion as to details pertaining to this famous historic highway, and it was finally decided to leave the subject for further discussion at the 1917 convention, the Secretary, in the meantime being instructed to correspond with as many of the original trail men as possible, that the origin and route of this famous trail might be definitely established at the succeeding annual convention. To this end, the Secretary was especially instructed to write to the following "Old Trail" men for such data and information as they might be able to furnish: Bud Daggett, Fort Worth, Texas; John Coffee, Knoxville, Texas; Eli Baggett, San Angelo, Texas.

Acting President Saunders appointed a committee to draft appropriate resolutions on death of deceased members. The committee in due time reported, and the resolutions were unanimously adopted. On motion of Acting President Saunders, the Association unanimously voted a monthly salary of Thirty Dollars to Secretary Luther A. Lawhon for the succeeding year, or for such time as he should continue to act as Secretary for the Association.

After disposing of further routine matters as claimed the immediate attention of the convention, there was a general interchange of old-time reminiscences, incidents and experiences. A number of ladies were in attendance on the convention, who were interested listeners, and who evinced a deep and patriotic interest in the proceedings of the Association. Having disposed of all business to be transacted, the convention adjourned sine die.

LUTHER A. LAWHON, *Secretary.*

The second annual reunion of the Old Trail Drivers' Association was held in San Antonio, Texas, July 2 and

3, 1917. It was estimated that fully two hundred and fifty of the old trail men were in attendance. The meeting place was in the ballroom of the Gunter Hotel. Addresses of welcome were delivered by Hon. Dave Woodward as representative of Mayor Sam C. Bell, by Hon. J. H. Kirkpatrick, representing the Chamber of Commerce; Col. Ike T. Pryor, President of the American Live Stock Association, and Vice President George W. Saunders of the Old Trail Drivers' Association, who responded on behalf of the Association. Following is Secretary Lawhon's report as adopted at this meeting:

HON. JOHN R. BLOCKER, *President,* Old Time Trail Drivers' Association.

SIR—I have the honor to herewith submit to you, and through you to the members of this Association, my annual report as Secretary for the years 1916–17.

Assembled as we are in our second annual reunion, I am proud to be able to congratulate the Association upon its continued growth in membership, and upon the loyalty and zealous interest which has been manifested by the membership at large. This is an incentive and an encouragement to further effort on our part, individually and collectively. Therefore, judging the future by the past, I believe I am not indulging in an unwarranted assumption when I say the Old Time Trail Drivers' Association is destined to take its place as one of the permanent and popular associations of our country.

Within a few days after adjournment of our reunion at Houston last year, your Secretary addressed a letter to each of those members who were not in attendance on the Houston reunion, and enclosed a badge and the Association button with concise mention of the meeting. With this effort I am persuaded that the members at large have received their badges and buttons to be worn in the lapels of their coats. There are, however, some exceptions to this assertion. A few of the letters so

addressed were returned to your Secretary "unclaimed."
I assume that the members in question had changed their
residence after enrollment at San Antonio in 1915, and
had neglected to acquaint me with the change.

While our Association is not yet two years old, we
have in the neighborhood of five hundred members'
names upon the Association's books, or, to be exact, 488
members are now actively identified with the Association.
Eight of these are sons of the old-time trail drivers.
This list is being rapidly augmented by new accessions,
and our membership as it stands today shows the names
of members resident in Missouri, Oklahoma, Kansas,
Arizona, New Mexico, Texas and other states.

During the past twelve months, so far as your Secretary has been able to ascertain, the hand of Providence
has lain lightly upon the membership of our Association.
Since our last meeting, death has claimed but two of our
members, Jesse Presnall and M. Standifer, both of San
Antonio. The former was well and favorably known
throughout the state as one of the old-time cowmen, while
the latter, though not actively engaged in the livestock
industry, was one of the "old trailers," and took a deep
interest in the organization. In the death of these
two members our Association has suffered a grievous
loss.

After the reading of the Secretary's report a general
discussion of the origin and terminus of the Old Chisholm Trail was indulged in. A letter on this subject,
written by W. P. Anderson, was read in which the writer
gave many facts concerning the origin and route of this
famous highway, stating that this trail was named for a
half-breed, John Chisholm, who ranched in the Indian
Territory, and who in the early sixties had driven a herd
of cattle through the Indian Territory to the government
forts on the Arkansas River, and that subsequently when
the great drives from Texas commenced these herds
would intersect and follow for a considerable distance

this Chisholm Trail in the Indian Territory, and for this reason became familiarly known as "The Chisholm Trail." This version of Mr. Anderson's was unanimously adopted by the Association as being authoritative and authentic:

Origin of the Old Chisholm Trail

Mr. LUTHER A. LAWHON, *Secretary,* Old Time Trail Drivers' Association, San Antonio, Texas.

DEAR SIR—Your letter of April 13th came to hand after following me through the Cattle Convention to the Northwest and was finally received at El Paso, Texas, last week on my way here from San Antonio.

In reference to the Old Chisholm Trail I notice that you spell the name "Chism." Another version is "Chissum," but probably the correct one is "Chisholm." As I understand the history of these trails, the original Chisholm Trail was named after John Chisholm, who was a Cherokee cattle trader, who supplied the government frontier posts with their cattle supply in the early part of the occupation of frontier posts and during the Civil War.

Among the first herds that started north from Texas was that of Smith and Elliot, and their guide was a gentleman who was formerly a soldier with Robert E. Lee, who had to do with the civilized tribes of the Indian Territory and used the old military trails, which were supposed to run from Texas to Sedalia, Mo., and crossed the Red River at Colbert's Ferry, and who afterwards was a citizen of San Antonio and whose children reside here now. The name I do not recall at present.

The first diversion from this trail was where the trail left the Sedalia trail for Baxter Springs. It was originally used by this same John Chisholm, the Cherokee Indian cattle trader, to supply Fort Scott, Kan. The basic ground for the commencement of this trail was probably about the mouth of the Grand River where it emptied into the Arkansas. The most prominent branch of this trail runs directly up the Arkansas River as far as Fort Zarah, which was about a mile east of where Great Bend, Kan., now stands. From along this trail there were diversions made by these cattle that went into the army supply at Fort Riley, Fort Harker, near Ellsworth; Fort Hays, near Hays City; Fort Wallace, now Wallace, Kan., the main base being in the Arkansas bottom on what is now called Chisholm Creek near the present city of Wichita, the trail continuing on west as far as Fort Bend and Fort Lyon in Colorado, for the delivery of these cattle, hence all cattle trailed from Texas across the Arkansas River would, perforce, strike at some point the old Chisholm Trail, and hence practically all cattle, whether by Colbert's Ferry, Red River Crossing or Doan's Store or elsewhere intermediate, would naturally use some part of the original Cherokee Indian Chisholm Trail on some part of its journey to Western Kansas.

In about the late 60's or early 70's, Mr. Charles Goodnight went the western route up the Pecos into the Colorado country, establishing what was known as the Goodnight or the Goodnight & Loving Trail, afterwards trailing the "Jingle Bobs" or the John Chissum cattle north, laying the old Tascosa route out to Dodge City, Kan., which became famous as the Chissum Trail and naturally produced the confusion as to the identity of the original Chisholm cattle trail. Nominally every man that came up the trail felt as though he had traversed the old Chisholm Trail. The facts hardly establish the original of either the New Mexican John Chissum Trail or the John Chisholm Cherokee Trail leading to western frontier army posts as originating in Texas.

In reference to Mr. Goodnight's allusion to my "blazing" the trail for the Joe McCoy herd, my recollection of the first herd that came to Abilene, Kan., was that of J. J. Meyers, one of the trail drivers of that herd now living at Panhandle, Texas. A Mr. Gibbs, I think, will ascertain further on the subject. The first cattle shipped out of Abilene, that I recollect, was by C. C. Slaughter of Dallas, and while loaded at Abilene, Kan., the billing was made from memorandum slips at Junction City, Kan.

The original chapters of Joe McCoy's book were published in a paper called *The Cattle Trail,* edited by H. M. Dixon, whose address is now the Auditorium building, Chicago. It was my connection with this publication that has probably led Mr. Goodnight into the belief that I helped blaze the trail with McCoy's cattle herd. This was the first paper I know of that published maps of the trails from different cattle-shipping points in Kansas to the intersection of the original Chisholm Trail, one from Coffeyville, Kan., the first, however, from Baxter Springs, then from Abilene, Newton, then Wichita and Great Bend, Dodge City becoming so famous obviated the necessity for further attention in this direction.

There are many interesting incidents that could still be made a matter of record connected with the old cattle trails that I could enumerate, but I will reserve them for another time.

Yours truly, W. P. ANDERSON.

Election of Officers

Then followed the election of officers for the ensuing year. George W. Saunders was elected president; J. B. Murrah, vice president; Luther A. Lawhon, secretary, and R. B. Pumphrey, treasurer. On motion of Mr. Murrah the following resolution was unanimously adopted:

"Resolved, That in his voluntary retirement from the presidency of the Old Time Trail Drivers' Association, we extend to Hon. John R. Blocker our sincere appreciation of the able and patriotic manner in which he has presided over the destinies of the Old Time Trail Drivers' Association, and we extend to him our sincere wishes for his future health and happiness.''

Vacancies in the Board of Directors occasioned by death were filled by the election of John Doak of Del Rio, J. M. Dobie of Cotulla, Texas, and W. S. Hall of Comfort, Texas.

The wives and daughters of members of the Association were made eligible for membership.

It was resolved that all communications intended for the proposed book of trail and frontier reminiscences must be received by the Secretary of the Association on or before January, 1918.

San Antonio was selected as the place for the next reunion. The convention adjourned, after passing a number of resolutions which are of but little concern to the readers of this book.

During this convention the members of the Association, with their wives, daughters and friends, were given an automobile ride through the city and out to the Saunders ranch on the Medina River, where an old-fashioned barbecue which had been prepared by George W. Saunders and T. A. Coleman was tendered the visitors.

Owing to the World War, which was in progress at the time scheduled for the meeting in 1918, no reunion was held that year, and the funds which had been appropriated for the reunion were used in the purchase of $500 worth of Liberty Bonds. But on September 10th and 11th, 1919, the Association again met in San Antonio, and following is the report of the proceedings of that meeting, as furnished by the Secretary:

**Minutes of the Annual Reunion of the Old Time Trail Drivers'
Association, Held in San Antonio, Texas,
September 10th and 11th, 1919**

After a recess of two years on account of the World
War, the members of the Old Time Trail Drivers' Association met in annual reunion September 10th, 1919, in
the ballroom of the Gunter Hotel, in the city of San
Antonio. The meeting had previously been called by the
Board of Directors for September 10th and 11th.
Promptly at 10 o'clock A.M., President George W. Saunders rapped for order, and declared the annual reunion
of the Old Time Trail Drivers' Association to be in session. Chaplain J. Stewart Pierce, who was elected chaplain of the Association at a former reunion, and who is
also chaplain of the 15th Field Artillery, U. S. A., delivered an impressive invocation, after which Luther A.
Lawhon, secretary of the Association, as the representative of Mayor Bell, delivered the address of welcome.
Secretary Lawhon was followed by Judge S. H. Wood
of Alice, Texas, who in an eloquent address, which was
frequently applauded, responded in behalf of the membership of the Association. Addresses were also made
by J. D. Jackson of Alpine, Texas, ex-President of the
Texas Cattle Raisers' Association, and by Nat M.
Washer, prominent merchant and citizen of San Antonio.
Mr. Washer's eloquent and patriotic sentiments were
frequently loudly cheered. In the interval between the
addresses the orchestra played popular and patriotic
songs. After the morning's program had been concluded, the reunion took a recess until two o'clock P.M.

On reassembling, the afternoon's session was devoted
to a general discussion of business matters affecting the
interests of the Association, and the passage of resolutions. President Saunders appointed J. D. Jackson, J. B.
Murrah and Luther A. Lawhon a committee to draft suit-

able resolutions on the death of deceased members. The committee reported as follows:

"Whereas, It has pleased Divine Providence to remove by death from our midst the following members of the Old Time Trail Drivers' Association: E. E. Rutledge, John Hoffman, Maxey Burris, John H. Meads, W. J. Moore, Joe Farris, Walter J. Dunkin, B. M. Hall and E. R. Jensen, all of San Antonio; W. B. Houston of Gonzales, J. A. Martin of Kenedy, John B. Pumphrey of Taylor, Tom Perry of Bracketville, J. H. Jaroman of Abilene, S. R. Guthrie of Alpine, W. M. Choate of Beeville, J. H. Winn of Pleasanton, T. D. Wood of Victoria, J. A. Kercheville of Devine, Henry Rothe of Hondo, W. T. Mulholland of Jourdanton, C. C. Hildebrand of Brownsville, W. D. Crawford of Dilley, R. D. Peril of Jewett, Hart Mussey of Alice, A. H. Allen of Eagle Pass and Ed Dewees, Wilson County; therefore be it

"Resolved, That we deplore the loss of these old pioneers. We feel that their families have suffered an irreparable loss and we extend to them our heartfelt sympathies; and we further recognize that in the death of these members the state has lost some of its worthy citizens and this Association some of its most active, zealous and worthy members."

At the close of the afternoon session of the first day's meeting it was announced that there was free admission for every member of the Association for the evening performance at the Princess Theater. On motion of President Saunders the members of the Albert Sidney Johnston Camp of Confederate Veterans, were made honorary members of the Association.

The morning session of the second day of the reunion (September 11th) was devoted to a general discussion or old-time "pow-wow," as some of the boys termed it. These interesting proceedings continued until eleven o'clock, when the members entered automobiles and were driven to the Saunders ranch, some twelve miles from the city, where, upon the banks of the beautiful Medina River, an old-time barbecue had been prepared for the "Old Trailers" and their friends. After partaking of the bountiful repast, speech-making was indulged in and old-time reminiscences were recounted, after which the members and friends returned to the city for the closing session of the reunion.

On reassembling in the ballroom of the Gunter Hotel, the election of officers was the first to be considered. This resulted in the re-election of the following officers: George W. Saunders, president; J. B. Murrah, vice president; R. F. Jennings, secretary, and R. B. Pumphrey, treasurer. Rev. J. Stewart Pierce was unanimously re-elected chaplain. On motion of J. D. Jackson the annual dues, which had been put at one dollar, were raised to two dollars, in accordance with the expressed wish of the Association that the Secretary should be paid a salary of thirty dollars per month—a part of which sum was to be expended by the Secretary for postage, stationery, etc. The following resolutions were unanimously adopted before final adjournment:

"Resolved, By the Old Time Trail Drivers' Association, that we, each and every one, appreciate the warm hospitality which has been accorded by the city of San Antonio, and we look forward with pleasure to our visit here next year.

"Resolved, That the thanks of the Old Time Trail Drivers' Association are hereby extended to Percy Tyrell, manager of the Gunter Hotel, for the many courtesies which he has extended to this Association during this reunion.

"M. W. S. Parker, J. D. Jackson, J. B. Murrah, M. A. Withers, committee."

At the close of the afternoon session of the second day (September 11th) the annual reunion of the Old Time Trail Drivers' Association, was declared at an end. This concluded two days of solid enjoyment, in which

some three hundred "Old Trailers," many of them with
their wives and daughters, took part. These old pioneers
had gathered from all sections of Texas and neighboring
states to renew old friendships and recount the incidents
of frontier life and dwell once more upon the hardships
and adventures of the old trail days.

ORIGIN AND CLOSE OF THE OLD-TIME
NORTHERN TRAIL

(Compiled by George W. Saunders and Read at the Reunion
of the Old Time Trail Drivers' Association)

The following, prepared by President George W.
Saunders, was read at the 1917 reunion of the Old Time
Trail Drivers' Association. Embodied in the article are
statistics regarding cattle movements in early days,
which are graphically portrayed by Mr. Saunders, and
worthy of preservation:

Very few people realize at this late date the important part played by the old-time trail drivers towards
civilization and development of the great State of Texas.
At the close of the Civil War the soldiers came home
broke and our state was in a deplorable condition. The
old men, small boys and negroes had taken care of the
stock on the ranges and the state was overstocked, but
there was no market for their stock. In 1867 and 1868
some of our most venturesome stockmen took a few small
herds of cattle to New Orleans, Baxter Springs, Abilene,
Kansas, and other markets. The Northern drives proved
fairly successful, though they experienced many hardships and dangers going through an uncivilized and
partly unexplored country. The news of their success
spread like wildfire, and the same men and others tackled
the trail in 1869. At that time it was not a question of
making money; it was a question of finding a market for

their surplus stock at any price. There was very little money in the country, and no banks or trust companies to finance the drives. In this great undertaking some of them drove their own stock and others buying on credit to pay on their return, giving no other security than a list of brands and amounts due. The 1869 drives proved successful, which caused many other stockmen to join the trail drivers in 1870. By this time going up the trail was all a rage; 1870 was a banner year at all the markets. The drivers came home and began preparing for the 1871 drives. Excitement ran high; there was never such activity in the stock business before in Texas. Drivers were scouring the country, contracting for cattle for the next spring delivery, buying horses and employing cowboys and foremen. Many large companies were formed to facilitate the handling of the fast growing business. Capital had been attracted from the money centers and financial arrangements to pay for the stock as received in the spring were made. Thus opened the spring of 1871, also all the drivers increasing the number of herds previously driven and many companies and individuals driving ten to fifteen herds each. Imagine all the ranchmen in South, East and Middle Texas at work at the first sign of spring, gathering and delivering trail herds.

This work generally lasted from April 1st to May 15th. The drivers would receive, road-brand and deliver a herd to their foremen, supply them with cash or letters of credit, give the foremen and hands instructions and say "Adios, boys, I will see you in Abilene, Dodge, Ellsworth, Ogallala, Cheyenne," or whatever point was the destination of the herd. Then riding day and night to the next receiving point, going through the same performance, then on to the next until all herds were started up the trail. Some of the drivers would go on the trail, others would go by rail or boat to the markets, lobby around waiting for their herds, sometimes going down the trail several hundred miles to meet their herds, often bringing buyers with them. I made my first trip up the trail in 1871 for Choate & Bennett. John Bennett, Sr., was a member of the firm. They sent fourteen herds up the trail that year. Dunk Choate, now deceased, counted and delivered this herd to Jim Byler, our boss, on the Cibolo near Stockdale, Wilson County, pointed our herd north and left, saying, "You boys know the rest, I must leave you and receive other herds."

The first few years there was no market for cow ponies at the cattle markets. In 1871 we brought back over the trail 150 cow ponies and several chuck wagons from Abilene, Kan., belonging to Choate & Bennett and W. C. Butler; but later, after ranches were established throughout the Northwest those ranchmen learned that our Spanish ponies were better for the range work than their native horses, and after that cow ponies were ready sale and the cowboys came home by rail or boat. Later there was a demand for Texas brood mares. This proved a bonanza for Texas ranchmen, as our ranges were over-stocked with them and they were almost worthless. I drove 1,000 in two herds to Dodge City in 1884. It was claimed that 100,000 went up the trail that year and more than 1,000,000 went up the trail from the time the horse market opened until the trail closed.

1871 was not a successful year, but it did not prevent a grand rush for the 1872 drive. Some of the drivers had made government contracts to supply Indian agencies, some had contracts with Western ranchmen for stock cattle and young steers; others driving on the open market. 1872 proved a successful year which caused a great rush for the 1873 drive. Those that sold early, had contracts or got tips from the money centers, did fairly well, but a panic clogged the wheels of commerce. Some sold at heavy losses, some wintered herds, 'thinking a steer in good condition could live where a buffalo could;

a cold winter and a sleet-covered range caused many losses. The 1874 drive was lighter and profitable, which caused a larger drive in 1875. Those losers in 1873 patched up weak places and were on the trail again; such men would not stay broke. By this time the drivers had become acquainted with the Western ranchmen. Large companies were formed and many large ranches were established in the Indian Territory and the Northwestern ranges. The drives continued, but they did not always have smooth sailing. The market fluctuated, some had heavy losses from losing stock on the trail on account of drouths, late spring, cold weather and many other causes. During all these years the Texas ranchmen were not idle. With the proceeds of cattle sold to trail men they were able to improve their stock, establish new ranches, all the time pushing west and forcing the savages before them. At the close of the war all the country west of an air line from Eagle Pass to Gainesville was uncivilized and sparsely settled. Every ranch or village above this line was subject to an Indian raid every moon. The government had a string of posts across the state above this line, but the Indians made many raids between these posts, murdered men, women and children, stole stock and made their escape without seeing a soldier. The soldiers did their best, but the cunning savages generally outwitted them. The trailers and ranchmen were the most dreaded enemies of the Indians and Texas Rangers next, most of them being cowboys. The savages were forced back slowly but surely by the trailer and ranchmen and were finally forced into the mountains of New Mexico, Old Mexico and Arizona, their number being reduced to a small band led by the notorious Geronimo, chief of the Apaches, which was captured by the government troops in 1885. This ended Indian depredations in Texas. The co-operation of the trailers, ranchmen and rangers with the government troops accomplished this great feat, but the most credit belongs to the old-time trail driver, the starter and finisher of the destiny of this great state, and the men that blazed the way that led to many great commercial enterprises, besides stocking and causing to be stocked the ranges from the Rio Grande to British possessions that before that time were a desert (not bringing a cent of revenue to the state's treasury) inhabited by wild animals and savages. From 1885 the drives were lighter up to 1895, when the trail which had been used twenty-seven years was closed. Nothing like it and its far-reaching accomplishment ever happened before and will never happen again. It is estimated by the most conservative old-time trail drivers that an average of 350,000 cattle were driven up the trails from Texas each year for 28 years, making 9,800,000 cattle at $10 a head received by the ranchmen at home making $98,000,000; 1,000,000 horse stock at $10 per head received by the ranchmen at home, making $10,000,000, or a total of $108,000,000. This vast amount sounds like a European war loan, but it was not. It was all caused by a few fearless men making the start in 1867 or 1868. No one had any idea that the cattle, the staple product, would blossom out thus and bring such prosperity to our state and heap so much glory on the heads of the old-time trail men. The circulation of the billions of dollars produced by the industry, passing as it did, directly into channels that were opened to receive it, produced the prosperity that has been in evidence in Texas for so many years, the cowman, the merchant, the farmer, the day laborer, profited thereby, and the vast volume of gold that flowed through these channels is absolutely incomprehensible.

Had these old-time trail drivers not looked for and found this market our vast herds would have died on the ranges and the vast unstocked ranges would have lain dormant and unproductive. Our ranchmen would have left Texas disgusted and broke, and it would have been a difficult matter to re-inhabit our state; therefore development would have been checked for many years; possibly no iron horse would have reached the Rio Grande up to this time as the inducement would not have been attractive. No one knows what would have happened had the Northern trail never existed, but it is plain that all commercial achievements, civilization, good government, Christianity, morality, our school system, the use of all school and state lands making them revenue-bearers, the expansion of the stock business from the Rio Grande to the British possessions, which is producing millions of dollars; the building of railroads, factories, seaports, agricultural advancement and everything else pertaining to prosperity can be traced directly to the achievements of the old-time trail drivers. The many good things accomplished by the untiring efforts of these old heroes can never be realized or told just as they were enacted, and it would be the father of all mistakes to let their daring and valuable efforts be forgotten and pass to unwritten history. Our Association now has 500 members and by resolution we made the sons of the old-time trail drivers eligible to membership. There are many old-timers that have not joined, but I believe every one will when the importance of perpetuating the memory of the old-timers is fully understood by them. It is our purpose to write a history dealing strictly with trail and ranch life and the early cattle industry. This book will consist of letters written by trail drivers only, giving the minutest details of their experiences of bygone days at home and on the trail, and will contain facts and be full of thrills. Such a book has never been written; all the books published on this subject have been by some author who spent a few months on some ranch, then attempted to write a book, understanding very little about stock or the stock business, and consequently having them pulling off stunts that have never been pulled off anywhere else but in the fertile imagination of some fiction writer. We are now assessing the old members $5.00 each and are charging $5.00 each for the enrollment of new members. This fund will be used for compiling and printing our history and paying the necessary expenses of the Association. Each member will get a book free. If there is any more left it will stay in the treasury to be used with the proceeds of the sale of our history as directed by the directors or by the Association as a whole. I am in favor of building a monument somewhere on the old trail, between San Antonio and Fort Worth, to the Old Time Trail Drivers.

THE PUMPHREY BROTHERS' EXPERIENCE ON THE TRAIL

By J. B. Pumphrey of Taylor, Texas

I am glad that the Old Trail Drivers' Association is making up a collection of letters and stories of the "Boys Who Rode the Trail," and it will be fine to read them and recall the old days. I am pleased to hand you a brief sketch of myself and some of my experiences.

My mother was a Boyce, one of the old pioneer families of Texas, and my father came from Ohio as a surgeon with General Taylor during the war between the United States and Mexico, and afterwards settled in Texas. My oldest uncle, Jim Boyce, was killed and scalped by Indians on the bank of Gilleland's Creek, near Austin.

I was born at old Round Rock on the 10th of November, 1852, and had the usual schooling of that time, when the "Blue Back Speller" and "Dog-wood Switch" were considered the principal necessities for the boy's education.

All of my life I have been engaged in the cow business, taking my first job in 1869 at $15.00 a month, for eighteen (18) hours a day if necessary, with horses furnished.

In February, 1872, I made my first trip on the long trail helping to gather a herd at the old Morrow Ranch, about two miles from Taylor, and from there we went through to Kansas, and then rode back, making about a four months' trip in all, and then I felt like I was a real graduated cowboy. I would like to see this ride in '72 compared with the longest ride that was ever made. My wages on the trail were $60.00 per month, I furnishing six head of cow ponies. This trip was made while working for Cul Juvanel, who was from Indiana and had a lot of Indiana boys with him, whom we called "Short Horns." Myself and two others, Beal Pumphrey, my brother, and Taylor Penick, were the only Texans in the bunch. When we reached the South Fork of the Arkansas River it was night, and about five o'clock in the morning, after waking the cook, I was on my way back to the herd when I saw our horses were being hustled, and was afraid they would stampede the herd, when just then the cook yelled "Indians," and sure enough they had rounded up our horses and were going away with them. A heavy rain was falling and the boss said, "You Texas boys follow the Indians and get those horses." The two others and myself rode one day and night, having to swim rivers and creeks with our clothing fastened on our shoulders to keep them dry, making the hardest ride of my life, but we did not overtake the Indians; and I am now glad that we did not. We were left with but one horse each, with this herd, but had another herd near by and, throwing the two together, making about six thousand head, we took them through to Kansas.

I remember one trip later in the year with Dave Pryor and Ike Pryor, when we were working for Bill Arnold of Llano County. We got back home on the night of December 24th, and rolling up in our blankets, slept in the yard, where the folks found us in the morning.

In 1873 I made another trip to Kansas with Bill Murchison of Llano County, and in later years took two other herds through to Kansas.

I have handled cattle in Mexico, South and Central Texas, Oklahoma, and once had a herd in Wyoming. I was director and vice president of the Taylor National Bank for twenty-four years, president of the McCulloch County Land & Cattle Company about twenty-five years, and now have ranches in McCulloch and Stonewall Counties.

I have never forgotten the feel of the saddle after a long day, the weight and pull of the old six-shooter, and what a blessing to cowmen was the old yellow slicker. Those were the days when men depended upon themselves first, but could rely on their friends to help, if necessary. Days of hard work but good health; plain fare but strong appetites, when people expected to work for their living and short hours and big pay was unknown.

In conclusion, I wish to say any movement that will preserve the memories of the old trail days is valuable, for in a few years most of those who "Rode the Trail" will have crossed the great divide. All honor to the Old Timers who have gone before, and good luck to all of you who are left.

By R. B. Pumphrey of San Antonio

In offering this, a small sketch of my life, to be published in the book that is to be published by the Old Trail Drivers' Association, I find it will be necessary for me to quote the same things that are written by my brother, J. B. Pumphrey.

"My mother was a Boyce, one of the old pioneer families of Texas, and my father came from Ohio as a surgeon with General Taylor, during the war between

the United States and Mexico, and afterwards settled in
Texas. My oldest uncle, Jim Boyce, was killed and
scalped by Indians on the
bank of Gilleland's Creek
near Austin.''

Like my brother, I, too,
was born at Old Round Rock,
on April 3rd, 1854. Our education was very much alike,
the principal studies being
''Blue Back Speller'' and the
''Dog-wood Switch.''

I have been in the cattle
business practically all of my
life, beginning when I was
sixteen or seventeen years
old, and finally in February,
1872, my brother and I

R. B. PUMPHREY

assisted in making up a herd for the Trail. This herd
was sold to a man by the name of Cul Juvanel and our
experiences on this trip were practically the same. We
went through to Kansas, riding back, making about a
four months' trip in all. My wages on the trail were
$60.00 per month. This trip was made while working for
Cul Juvanel, who was from Indiana and had a lot of Indiana boys with him, whom we called ''Short Horns.''
Myself and two others, John Pumphrey, my brother, and
Taylor Penick, were the only Texans in the bunch. When
we reached the South Fork of the Arkansas River it was
night, and about 5 o'clock in the morning, after waking
the cook, was on my way back to the herd when I saw
our horses were being hustled, and was afraid they
would stampede the herd, and just then the cook yelled
''Indians,'' and sure enough they had rounded up our
horses and gone away with them. A heavy rain was
falling and the boss said, ''You Texas boys follow the
Indians and get those horses.'' The two others and my-

self rode one day and night, having to swim the rivers
with our clothing fastened on our shoulders to keep them
dry, making the hardest ride of my life, but we did not
overtake the Indians; and I am now glad that we did not.
We were left with but one horse each, with this herd, but
had another herd near by and, throwing the two together,
making about 6,000 head, we took them through to
Kansas.

In 1873 I made another trip to Kansas with W. T.
Avery. On this trip, just north of the Arkansas River,
we had another experience that I think is worth relating.
There were about four or five big herds camped near together and we had a very severe storm, consequently
our herds were badly mixed and it took us all the following day to separate them, each fellow getting his own
cattle. After we had separated the cattle we counted
ours and found that we were about fifteen head of cattle
short. So Mr. Avery and myself and one other man that
we could rely on made a circle around where the cattle
were lost to see if we could find the trail where they had
gone off. We finally found the trail and followed it for
ten or fifteen miles, when my horse was bitten by a rattlesnake and, of course, we knew it would not do to attempt
to go further on a snake-bitten horse, so we retraced our
steps to the camp, finally getting this snake-bitten horse
into the camp about 12 o'clock at night. During the
absence some of the neighbors told the bosses that we
had been killed by the Osage Indians and our men, of
course, all thought we had been killed until we arrived
at camp, or else we would not have stayed out so late.
Early the next morning we reported to our foreman, telling him that we had found the trail and that they were
being driven off by the Indians—so he reinforced our
party by one man and sent us off again to see if we could
get the cattle. We did not lose much time in following
the cattle, but as they had two days the start of us, we
were never able to overtake them, which perhaps was a

good thing, as we were poorly armed and perhaps would have been three men against ten or fifteen Indians. We rode our horses so hard the first day that we were unable to get back for two days and we and our horses were worn out and almost starved when we reached our camp. It was not thought advisable to trail the cattle any further.

After this second year's experience on the trail I, with my two brothers, went to Llano County, where we associated ourselves with the Moss boys, who were our first cousins, and for ten years I ranched in Llano County. In '84 my brother, Mr. Kuykendall and myself moved about 12,000 cattle to Wyoming Territory, where I spent two years on the range. This proved not to be a very successful move for me, as we lost practically everything we put in that country. After that I did not attempt any trail driving until '84 and '85. My brother, Kuykendall and myself had established a ranch in Greer County and drove several herds from Central Texas to Greer County to stock this ranch with.

While those were hard old times, I never have regretted for a minute that I underwent the hardships, as it was the kind of a life that I loved at that time and I only wish that I was young enough to engage in the same life again. Many of the old boys who were on the trail have passed away, but I want to wish for the few that are left that they will always "graze with the lead cattle."

(EDITOR'S NOTE.—J. B. Pumphrey died at Taylor, Texas, July 21, 1917. R. B. Pumphrey died at Austin, May 4, 1920.)

DODGING INDIANS NEAR PACKSADDLE MOUNTAIN

By E. A. (Berry) Robuck, Lockhart, Texas

I was born in Caldwell County, Texas, September 3, 1857, and was in my sixteenth year when I entered the trail life. My father came to this state from Mississippi in 1854, when he was sixteen years old. He enlisted in the Confederate Army and died in 1863 of pneumonia while in the service. I was the oldest of three brothers, one of them being Terrell (Tully) Robuck, who went to North Dakota with Colonel Jim Ellison's outfit in 1876. He was then sixteen years old. Emmet Robuck, who was assassinated at Brownsville in 1902 while serving as a state ranger, was my son.

I made my first trip up the trail to Utah Territory with old man Coleman Jones, who was boss for a herd belonging to Colonel Jack Meyers. This herd was put up at the Smith & Wimberly ranch in Gillespie County. I gained wonderful experience on this trip in the stampede, high water, hailstorms, thunder and lightning which played on the horns of the cattle and on my horse's ears. We suffered from cold and hunger and often slept on wet blankets and wore wet clothing for several days and nights at a time, but it was all in the game, and we were compensated for the unpleasant things by the sport of roping buffalo and seeing sights we had never seen before.

On one occasion my boss sent me from the Wimberly ranch to another ranch twenty miles away to get some bacon. At the foot of Packsaddle Mountain, in Llano County, I passed about fifty Indians who had killed a beef and were eating their breakfast, but I failed to see them as I passed. When I reached my destination a man came and reported the presence of the Indians. I had to return over the same route I had come, so I took the best horse I had for my saddle horse and put the packsaddle and bacon on another horse, for I was determined to go back without being handicapped by that bacon. I dodged the Indians and got back to the Wimberly ranch in safety.

On one of my trail trips we had a trying experience between Red River and the Great Bend of the Arkansas River on the Western trail, when we had to go without water for twenty-four hours. When we finally reached water about 600 head of the cattle bogged in the mud and we worked all night pulling them out.

At another time I was on the Smoky River in Kansas when 2,800 beeves stampeded. I found myself in the middle of the herd, while a cyclone and hailstorm made the frightened brutes run pell-mell. The lightning played all over the horns of the cattle and the ears of my horse, and the hail almost pounded the brim of my hat off. I stuck to the cattle all night all alone, and was out only one hundred head the next morning. Another time I ran all night, lost my hat in the stampede, and went through the rain bareheaded.

On one trip myself and a negro, Emanuel Jones, ran into a herd of buffalo in the Indian Territory, and roped two of them. The one I lassoed got me down and trampled my shirt off, but I tied him down with a hobble I had around my waist. One day my boss told me we were going to make a buffalo run, and asked me to ride my best horse. The horse I rode was a red roan belonging to George Hill, who was afterward assassinated at Cotulla, Texas. Myself and Wash Murray rode together, and when we got into the chase I caught a five-year-old cow. My horse was "Katy on the spot" in a case of that kind, and helped me to win the championship on that occasion. I was the only man in the party that succeeded in roping a buffalo.

I met Mac Stewart, Noah Ellis, Bill Campbell and several other old Caldwell County boys in Ellsworth, Kan., on one of my trips. Stewart served three years in

F. A. (Perry) ROBUCK

the Confederate Army, after which he took to trail life and followed that for several years, then going to Mexico, where he became involved in a difficulty with an officer and killed him. He was in prison for over ten years with the death sentence hanging over him, but through the influence of friends in this country, he was finally released and returned to Texas, dying shortly afterward.

After meeting this bunch in Ellsworth, a number of us returned home together with the saddle horses. We came back the old Chisholm Trail. While returning through the Indian Territory we were caught in a cyclone and hailstorm one night while I was on guard. The wind was so strong at times it nearly blew me out of the saddle, and the hail pelted me so hard great knots were raised on my head. Next morning I found myself alone in a strange land with the horses, for I had drifted with the storm. Picking up the back trail, I started for camp, and before long in the distance I saw some people coming towards me. I thought they might be Indians, but it turned out to be Mac Stewart and others who had started out to search for me. The horse I was riding that night was raised by Black Bill Montgomery, and had been taken up the trail that year by Mark Withers. Three days later we reached Red River, which was on a big rise. We were out of grub, but had to remain there for three days waiting for the river to run down, but it kept getting higher, so we decided to attempt the crossing. We put into the stream, and with great difficulty got the horses across. Mac Stewart's horse refused to swim, and as Mac could not swim, I went to his rescue. The horse floated down the river, and Mac told me he had $300 in money and his watch tied on his saddle. Sam Henry and I then swam to the horse and took the saddle off, and came out under a bluff. We had a pretty close call, but reached the bank, where we had a big reunion and something to eat.

There is one incident which I feel I ought to add, as

perhaps it did not fall to the lot of many of the boys to have a similar one. I am the chap who caught the blue mustang mare. This was while we were range herding cattle in Kansas on the Smoky River, near the King Hills, about fifteen miles from old Fort Hayes. This blue mustang would come to our saddle horses at night, and also to the river for water. The boys were all anxious to get her, had set snares made of ropes at the watering places, hoping to get her by the feet, but she always managed to avoid this danger. One day the boys found her with the horses and, on seeing them, she stampeded. I was on the range about the foot of the hills, saw her coming and made for her with my rope ready. To get back to her herd she had to go through a gap in the hills. I was riding a good sorrel horse, an E P horse, raised by Ed Persons of Caldwell County. I made for the gap, getting there just in time and as she started to enter, running at breakneck speed, just in the nick of time I threw my rope; it went true and fell securely around her neck. When the rope tightened, she jerked my horse fully thirty feet, and both animals went down together, not more than ten feet apart. I scrambled to my feet, getting out of the mixup, but I had my mustang. Manuel Jones and Dan Sheppard, two of the cowboys on the range, coming up about this time, helped me to further secure her and we got her safely back to camp. In time she responded to good treatment, made a fine saddle animal, and, with her long black mane and tail, she was a beauty of which I was justly proud. Good saddle horses could be had cheap at that time, but I sold her near Red River for $65.00.

FOUGHT INDIANS ON THE TRAIL

By Henry Ramsdale of Sabinal, Texas

I came to Texas in 1876, and have been handling cattle nearly ever since. Made my first trip with Joe Collins and had a pretty good time. My next trip was from Llano and Mason Counties. Was attacked by Indians several times and on one occasion we lost all of our horses except the ones we were riding, and one man was killed by the redskins. Had to make the drive from the head of the Concho to the Pecos River, a distance of eighty miles, without water for ourselves or cattle. From there we had a very good trip, but saw Indians nearly every day. I stayed with this outfit until the next spring, when I came back to Texas and settled in Uvalde County, and have been here ever since.

LOCATION OF THE OLD CHISHOLM TRAIL

By C. H. Rust of San Angelo, Texas

I will state that from my own knowledge, and from short stories by 35 old early day trail men, most of whom went up the old Chisholm Trail, indicating the Trail by naming rivers and towns, showing same on maps, so, with the long drawn-out investigation, and with all this information from different sources, I believe the old Chisholm Cow trail started at San Antonio, Texas, and ended at Abilene, Kan. Forty-five years have passed since I went over the Trail, and I am using my memory to aid me, especially on the Texas end of the Old Cow Trail.

This old Trail that I attempt to tell you about, begins at San Antonio, and from there leading on to New Braunfels, thence to San Marcos, crossing the San Marcos River four miles below town, thence to Austin, crossing the Colorado River three miles below Austin. Leaving Austin the Trail winds its way on to the right of Round Rock, thence to right of Georgetown, on to right of Salado, to the right of Belton, to old Fort Graham, crossing the Brazos River to the left of Cleburne, then to Fort

C. H. RUST

Worth, winding its way to the right of Fort Worth just about where Hell's Half Acre used to be, crossing Trinity River just below town. Fort Worth was just a little burg on the bluff where the panther lay down and died.

From Fort Worth the next town was Elizabeth, and from there to Bolivar; here the old Trail forked, but we kept the main trail up Elm to St. Joe on to Red River

Station, here crossing Red River; after crossing Red River I strike the line of Nation Beaver Creek, thence to Monument Rocks leading on to Stage Station, to head of Rush Creek, then to Little Washita, on to Washita Crossing at Line Creek, from there to Canadian River, to the North Fork, on to Prairie Spring, from there to King Fisher Creek; thence to Red Fork, on to Turkey Creek, to Hackberry Creek; thence to Shawnee Creek, to Salt Fork; to Pond Creek, from there to Pole Cat Creek, to Bluff Creek; thence to Caldwell, line of Kansas River on to Slate Creek to Ne-ne-squaw River; thence to Cow Skin Creek to Arkansas River to head of Sand Creek; on to Brookville; thence from Solomon to Abilene, and from there on to Ellsworth.

I have no definite information as to what year this old Trail was laid out, and if this is not the old Chisholm Cow Trail, then there is no Chisholm Trail. It is just what we call the Old Chisholm Trail, and when the cowboy reached his destination, weary and worn, he forgot all about the rainy nights he experienced while on the Trail, in the companionship of the other Long and Short Horns.

Now, let me test my memory as to distance. I will call the distance from one town to another as the old wagon road runs. From San Antonio to New Braunfels is thirty miles, from New Braunfels to San Marcos, twenty miles; from San Marcos to Austin, thirty miles; from Austin to Round Rock, seventeen miles, from Round Rock to Georgetown, nine miles; from Georgetown to Salado, twenty-four miles; from Salado to Belton, twelve miles; from Belton to Fort Graham, sixty-five miles; from Fort Graham to Cleburne, forty miles; from Cleburne to Fort Worth, twenty-eight miles.

I note that I do not find in John Chisum's history where he ever drove a herd of cattle from Texas to Kansas, but he drove thousands of cattle into the Pecos Country and New Mexico, about 1864 and 1866.

It is stated that one Jess Chisholm drove cattle to the
Nation and Kansas before and during the war, crossing
the Red River at Choke Bluff Crossing below Denison.
Mr. Sugg also states that this Jess Chisholm was half
Indian, and that his ranch was located near the Canadian
River. In later years he crossed his herd higher up near
Gainesville, so as to reach his ranch on the Canadian.

I note again the Old Cow Trail forked at Bolivar.
The route of this right-hand trail crossed the Red River
below Gainesville, thence to Oil Springs, on to Fort Arbuckle, crossing Wild Horse Creek, and intersecting the
main trail at the south fork of the Canadian River. The
last main western trail ran by Coleman, Texas, on to Bell
Plain, thence to Baird, on to Albany, from there to Fort
Griffin, to Double Mountain Fork, crossing Red River
at Doan's Store.

Now here I have one more old trail, and I have a
printed map of same. They call it the McCoy Trail. It
started at Corpus Christi, leading from there to Austin,
thence to Georgetown, on to Buchanan, to Decatur, from
there to Red River Station, on to the Red Fork of the
Arkansas River; thence to Abilene, Kan. A short story
of the life of Wild Bill Hickok goes with the map. I do
not think there ever was a cow trail in Texas called the
McCoy Trail, but I will state that I am somewhat acquainted with Wild Bill Hickok. He was city marshal
of Wichita, Kan., in 1870. I think they are trying to put
the "kibosh" on us.

The Old Chisholm Cow Trail varied in width at river
crossings from fifty to one hundred yards. In some
places it spreads out from one mile to two miles in width.
The average drive in a day was eight to ten and twelve
miles, and the time on the Trail was from sixty to ninety
days, from points in Texas to Abilene or Newton, or
Ellsworth, Kan.

What happened on the Old Cow Trail in those days
of long ago is almost forgotten, and it is a sad thought

to us today that there is no stone or mile post to mark the Old Trail's location. The old-time cow puncher that followed the Trail, his mount, his make-up, the old Trail songs that he sang, what he did and how he did it, is left yet to someone to give him the proper place in history.

What he was then and what he is now, I hope to meet him over there in the Sweet Bye and Bye, where no mavericks or slicks will be tallied.

WHAT HAS BECOME OF THE OLD-FASHIONED BOY?

C. H. Rust, San Angelo, Texas

What has become of the old-fashioned boy that went in his shirt tail until 10 or 11 years old, that being about the only garment he possessed during the summer months?

He could step up to an old rail fence and if he could hang his chin on the top rail, he would step back and leap over it and his shirt tail would make a kind of a fluttering noise as he went over.

What has become of the old-fashioned boy that used to run away from home on Sunday to the old swimming hole on the river five or six miles from home, where the alligators were lying round on the banks of the river, seven and eight feet long, and, when he returned home in the evening, what has become of the old-fashioned mother that called him up for a reckoning and when she began to pry into his private affairs and became convinced that he was lying? When she got through with him, he went off behind the old ash hopper and got himself together as best he could, then he meditated and resolved to ask his mother's pardon, and the big swimming hole on the river was a closed matter.

What has become of the old-fashioned boys and girls

that danced the square dance to the tune of "Cotton Eyed Joe," "Old Dan Tucker," "Black Jack Grove," "Hogs in the Cornfield," "Cackling Hens," and the "Old Gray.Horse Came Tearing Through the Wilderness?"

What has become of the old-fashioned boy and girl that became one in wedlock when they went just across the spring branch from the old folks on the slope of the hill and built a house under the shadow of the old oak tree and raised a family and lived for God and humanity?

CYCLONES, BLIZZARDS, HIGH WATER, STAMPEDES AND INDIANS ON THE TRAIL

By G. H. Mohle, Lockhart, Texas

In April, 1869, I was employed by Black Bill Montgomery to go with a herd of 4,500 head of stock cattle

GEO. H. MOHLE

on the drive to Abilene, Kansas. We started from Lockhart and crossed the Colorado River below Austin, out by way of Georgetown, Waxahachie and on to Red River, which we found very high. We were several days getting the herd across this stream. The first day I crossed over with about a thousand head and came back and worked the rest of the day in the water, but could not get any more of the cattle across on account of the wind and waves. Two of the boys and myself went across with grub enough for supper and breakfast, but the next day the weather was so bad the others could not cross to bring us something to eat and we were compelled to go hungry for forty-eight hours. The next night about twelve o'clock we heard yelling and shouting, but thinking it might be Indians, we remained quiet and did not know until noon the next day that it was some of the boys of our outfit who had brought us some grub, which we found hanging in a tree. The third day the balance of the herd was crossed over without further trouble. Flies and mosquitoes were very bad, and kept us engaged in fighting them off.

When we reached the North Fork of the Canadian River it was also pretty high, on account of heavy rains. The water was level with the bank on this side, but on the far side the bank was about six feet above the water and the going out place being only about twenty feet wide. We had trouble getting the cattle into the water, and when they did get started they crowded in so that they could not get out on the other side, and began milling, and we lost one hundred and sixteen head and three horses. When we arrived at the Arkansas River we found it out of its banks and we were compelled to wait several days for it to run down. We were out of provisions, and tried to purchase some from a government train which was camped at this point. This wagon train was loaded with flour and bacon, en route to Fort Sill. The man in charge refused to sell us anything, so when the guard was absent we "borrowed" enough grub to last us until we could get some more. When the flood stage had passed we crossed the river and reached Abilene, Kansas, the latter part of June, camping there a month, and finally sold the cattle to Mr. Evans of California for $25 per head, with the understanding that Black Bill Montgomery, Bill Henderson, myself and Gov, the negro cook, were to go along with the cattle. Mr. Evans also bought the horses.

About the first of August we started for California.

When we reached the Republican River a cyclone struck
us, turned our wagon over, and scattered things generally. Mr. Evans had a large tent. It went up in the air
and we saw it no more. We next reached the Platte River.
where we camped for several days to allow the cattle to
graze and rest. On account of quicksand in the river we
had to go up the stream about twenty-five miles to make
a crossing. At Platte City we purchased a supply of
provisions, and went on up the northwest side of the
river about a hundred miles, to where about five hundred
soldiers were camped. We camped about a quarter of a
mile above the soldiers' camp, and thought we were
pretty safe from Indian attack, but one night about three
o'clock we were awakened by an awful noise. We thought
it was a passing railroad train, but instead it was our
horses being driven off by Indians right along near our
camp. As they passed us the Indians fired several shots
in our direction, but no one was hit. We had sixty-three
horses and the red rascals captured all of them except
five head. Mr. Evans sent one of the hands to notify the
soldiers of our loss and get them on the trail of the Indians. It was nine o'clock the next morning before the
soldiers passed our camp in pursuit, and as the Indians
had such a good start, they were never overtaken. We
remained there all day, and the next morning we started
out afoot. For about a week we felt pretty sore from
walking, as we were not used to this kind of herding.
When we reached Cheyenne we secured mounts and laid
in a supply of grub and traveled up Crow Creek to
Cheyenne Pass, where we had our first blizzard and
snow.

The next morning the snow was six inches deep and
the weather was bitterly cold. Our next town was Fort
Laramie, and from there we went on to Elk Mountain
on the Overland Immigrant Trail to California, where we
stopped for three days because of the heavy snow. We
had very little trouble until we reached Bitter Creek,

called Barrel Springs on account of many barrels having been placed in the ground and served as water springs. Here we cut out five hundred of the cattle because they were not able to keep up. Five of us were left to bring them on, and we traveled down the creek for a distance of about twenty miles. One day at noon we camped and some of the cattle drank water in the creek, and within twenty minutes they died. I drank from a spring on the side of the mountain, thinking the water was good, and in a short while I thought I was going to die too. An Irishman came along and I told him I was sick from drinking the water, and he informed me that it was very poisonous. He carried me to a store and bought me some whiskey and pretty soon I was able to travel. We went up Green River and crossed it at the mouth of Hamsford, and then crossed the divide between Wyoming and Utah. The temperature was down to zero, and when we reached the little town of Clarksville, Utah, we remained there two weeks. Mr. Evans sent the cattle up into the mountains, and we took stage for Corrine, just north of Salt Lake City, where we boarded the train for home.

(EDITOR'S NOTE.—Mr. Mohle, the writer of the above sketch, died at his home in Lockhart, Texas, October 11, 1918, aged 71 years.)

MISTAKEN FOR COLE YOUNGER AND ARRESTED

By S. A. Hickok, Karnes City, Texas

I was born at Columbus, Ohio, December 8th, 1842, and moved to Mattoon, Illinois, when I was about twenty-four years old and engaged in buying chickens, turkeys, ducks and geese and shipping them by carload to New Orleans, Louisiana.

When I would go to New Orleans with my shipment

of poultry I heard a great deal about Texas, and the money that was to be made in sending cattle up the trail, so I decided to move to Texas. I met a man by the name of Couch who was making up a party to go on an excursion train to Dallas, Texas, and made arrangements to meet him in Saint Louis and join the excursion party there. My brother accompanied me to Saint Louis, and a short while after our arrival we passed a man on the street and he said, "Hello, Younger." I told him he was mistaken, that my name was not Younger. He asked me if I was not from Marshall, Missouri, and I told him that I was not. We went to a cheap boarding house and made arrangements to stay all night. We went to the Southern Hotel that night to see if Couch had arrived. While we were there a man came in and asked me if I was from Marshall County, and I replied, "No; I have been asked that question twice today." He then called me aside and asked me several questions, and just then motioned a policeman to come near. They asked me if I was armed and I told them that it was none of their business, but as they insisted on searching me I told them to proceed, but be sure they had the proper authority for their action. They found a small six-shooter, a draft for $1,000, and about $100 in cash on me, and the policeman said he would have to take me down to the police station. When we arrived there I learned that they thought that they had Cole Younger, one of the Jesse James desperadoes. I told them to telegraph the First National Bank of Mattoon, Illinois, and they could get all the information they needed to establish my identity. But they locked me up in a cell and kept me there over night. Next day they released me, and returned my pistol and money to me.

I reached Dallas in the Spring of 1875, and went to Fort Worth, which was then a small place. My brother and I purchased a pair of Mexican ponies, a new wagon and camping outfit and started for San Antonio. Near

Burnett we met a man who had a ranch and some sheep
in Bandera County, and we went with him and bought
six hundred head of sheep, thus embarking in the sheep
business, doing our own herding, shearing, cooking and
washing. We had hard sledding for a long time, but
finally achieved success. We moved our herd from Bandera County to the southeast corner of Atascosa County,
near the line of Live Oak and Karnes Counties, where I
located a ranch of 15,000 acres in 1877 or 1878. There I
engaged in sheep raising for several years, finally selling
out and buying horses and cattle. I went to the border
on the Rio Grande, and bought many horses and mares
and drove them to Kansas. The next year I went over
into Mexico and bought several hundred horses, which I
kept on the ranch for about a year and then shipped them
and many more which I had bought at different times to
Ohio, New York, Nebraska, Tennessee, Arkansas and
Mississippi.

A THORNY EXPERIENCE

By S. B. Brite of Pleasanton, Texas

Like most of the boys of the early days, I had to sow
my wild oats, and I regret to say that I also sowed all
of the money I made right along with the oats. I went
up the trail in 1882 with a herd belonging to Jim Ellison
of Caldwell County, delivering the cattle at Caldwell,
Kansas. I went again in 1884 with Mark Withers, starting
from the Tigre ranch in LaSalle County, where Mr. J. M.
Dobie now lives. When we reached the Canadian River
it was on a rise, and we drowned a horse which was
hitched to the chuck wagon. While making this crossing
a negro's horse sank in the middle of the river and left
the rider standing on a sandbar. After we crossed the
cattle over I swam my horse out and allowed the negro

to swing to his tail, and thus ferried him across. The
negro thanked me and said
that horse's tail was just like
the "hand of Providence."
We delivered the cattle on the
Platte River and I returned
to the Tigre ranch, where I
worked for seven years.
While on this ranch one day
Gus Withers, the boss, picked
out a fine bay horse and told
me that if I could ride him
I could use him for a saddle
horse. I managed to mount
him, but after I got up there
I had to "choke the horn and
claw leather," but to no avail,
for he dumped me off in the middle of a big prickly
pear bush. When the boys pulled me out of that bush
they found that my jacket was nailed to my back as
securely as if the job had been done with six-penny
nails.

S. B. BRITE

I went up the trail twice, and drove the drag both
times, did all the hard work, got all the "cussin'," but
had the good luck never to get "fired."

A TRIP TO CALIFORNIA

By Jeff M. White of Pleasanton, Texas

I was born in Palmyra, Marion County, Missouri,
October 20th, 1831. In the spring of 1852 a bunch of us
were stricken with the gold fever. We rigged up three
ox wagons, five yoke to a wagon, and started on the 13th
day of April, 1852, for the California gold mines. We

crossed the Mississippi River at Savannah, Holt County, Missouri, on the 3rd day of May. At this time this country belonged to the Sioux Indians, being their hunting grounds. However, we had no trouble with them. The first white people we saw after leaving the Missouri River were a few soldiers at Fort Karney on the Platte River. Regarding these soldiers will say they were in no condition to protect anyone, as it looked as though they had not washed their faces in months. However, they were good card players. We forded the South Platte and went across to the North Platte and proceeded up that stream to Fort Laramie. We also found a few soldiers here in about the same condition as the others, and we did not look to them for any protection. We crossed the middle fork of the Platte above Fort Laramie on a bridge and from there we went north to the North Platte. We traveled up this stream to the Mormon Ferry. Before reaching this Mormon Ferry we passed some two or three times a big black Dutchman rolling a wheelbarrow. The Mormons put him across ahead of us, giving him a bottle of whiskey and some buffalo meat, and this is the last we ever saw of him.

The next water we found was the Sweetwater River, but will say the water was not sweet, but as fine as I ever drank. The first curiosity we found was the Chimney Rock. This was on the south side of the North Platte. The base of this rock covered some five or six acres of the ground and extended in the air to a height of approximately four hundred feet, and from this there extended a smaller stem some ten or twelve feet in diameter and must have been eighty or more feet high and was soft sand rock.

After crossing the Sweetwater River we found another curiosity called the Independence Rock. This rock is on the Old Fremont Trail and this is where Fremont ate his Fourth of July dinner on July 4th, 1847, hence the name Independence Rock. Where the Sweetwater

River comes out of the Rocky Mountains is a solid rock gap claimed to be three hundred feet deep. I know it was so deep we couldn't look over into it without laying down flat on our stomachs. From here we proceeded to what is called the South Pass, a low flat place in the Rocky Mountains, and some two days' travel brought us to a place where the roads forked. At this place we held an election to determine which road to take, the left road going to Salt Lake City and the right-hand road was the Fremont Trail going west. The majority voted to go by Salt Lake City. Will say, before reaching the forks of this road, we had overtaken another party, called the Priest Train, making a total of seven wagons and twenty-eight men.

On our road to Salt Lake City we had to go into what is called Echo Canyon. The Mormons, on going down into this canyon, let their wagons down by putting ropes and chains around trees that grew upon the side of the canyon and fastening same to rear of wagon. When we reached this place the trees were all dead, so we took all the oxen loose except the wheel team and fastened them to the rear axle and let the wagon down into the canyon. It required half a day to let our seven wagons down. After getting down into this canyon the road travels down same into the Salt Lake Valley.

Will also add that our principal fuel on this trip was buffalo chips, but west of the Rocky Mountains there were no buffalo so we used cow chips.

It is eight hundred miles from Salt Lake City to California and there were only two different tribes of Indians, the Utahs and Piutes. In the summer time the Piutes live mostly on roasted lizards and grasshoppers, there being no game in this part of the country to amount to anything, only a few scattering black tail deer.

We arrived in Salt Lake City a day or two before the Fourth of July, 1852, and spent the Fourth there. About

all the celebration was a few horse races on the main
street of the city. At this time it was a small town, there
being only two good houses in the town, the Mormon
Temple and Brigham Young's Temple. At this time it
was told by the Mormons that Brigham Young had some
sixty-odd wives and, of course, it required a large house
to hold them.

We were never bothered by the Indians, as we watched
them day and night, and an Indian is good only when he
is watched. I never saw one with a gun or pistol on the
entire trip. Their fighting weapons were bow and
arrows, tomahawk and scalping or bowie knives.

After leaving Salt Lake City we crossed the River
Jordan and the next water was a good spring at the head
of the Humbolt River. This river, however, is three
hundred and thirty miles long, running through a flat
alkali country, and the worst water a human or beast
ever tried to drink. It spreads out and sinks into the
earth, not emptying into any other stream. While traveling down this stream one of our men took sick and we
had no good water for him. While nooning one day, on
this stream, one of the boys went fishing with a little fly
hook not larger than a sewing thread and caught four or
five fish. When he returned he found an old Piute Indian in camp. This Indian wanted to see what our boy
had caught the fish with and when the boy showed him
the hook he examined it very closely and, from his actions, it seemed this was the first hook he had ever seen.
He had on an old ragged coat and from the tail of this
he unwound a string and brought out a Mexican dollar
and gave it to the boy for the fish-hook. This old Indian
having a Mexican dollar was as much a curiosity to us
as the fish-hook was to him. He was four hundred miles
from Salt Lake City and about the same distance from
California or any white settlement, and the question was
"Where did he get the Mexican dollar?" Where this
Humbolt River sinks into the earth we cut grass and

filled our wagons to feed our stock on, as we had to cross a desert fifty miles wide, and filled all of our water kegs so as to give stock water that night, and this was all the water they had until we crossed the desert. The last twelve miles of this trip was deep white sand. It took a day and night to cross this desert and we fed our stock one time and gave them one drink. This brought us to Carson River, where our sick man died. We rolled him in his blankets, as we had no coffin, and buried him under a large elm tree, covering him the best we could with timber and dirt. We traveled up the Carson River, the worst road we had on the entire trip, crossing the Sierra Nevadas and followed the slope to Hangtown, California, the first mining town we struck. There we sold out everything we had in the shape of teams and wagons. We arrived there the 27th day of August, 1852. This being Dry Diggings, meaning no gold to be found, after resting a few days we all scattered and went to the South Fork of the American River and four or five of the boys I have never seen or heard of since. I know they never came back home. After staying about two years and a half I returned home. I was the youngest of the outfit, being only 20 years old, and was called a 20-year-old boy.

RAISED ON THE FRONTIER

By Walter Smith, Del Rio, Texas

It made me feel twenty-five years younger to attend the reunion of the Old Trail Drivers in San Antonio, for I met so many of my old boyhood friends, many of them I had not seen in forty-five years, boys that I had been associated with during the early days of the frontier.

I was born at Corpus Christi, May 8th, 1856, and

moved to San Antonio when I was six years old. Went to school at the old Free School house which stood on Houston Street in that city. San Antonio was then only a small adobe town. In 1869 I landed in Uvalde in an ox-wagon owned by Bill Lewis of the Nueces Canyon. There were only six ranches in the canyon at that time, but lots of Indians were there to harass the few settlers, We had many narrow escapes, but we were a happy and seemingly contented people. I have lived on the Western frontier ever since I reached manhood, and have had many thrilling experiences and hard trials, but have lived through all down to this day of the high cost of everything. We lived then on the fat of the land, and that was not a luxury. Our food was plain but wholesome, and if the people of today would be content with the table comforts we had in those days the doctors' signs would soon disappear.

I went up the trail six different times, the last herd being driven from Uvalde County in 1882 for the Western Union Beef Company to the South Platte River, Colorado. I have had so many ups and downs that if I were to undertake to tell all of them it would more than fill this volume.

Was married at Uvalde, Texas, May 8th, 1879, to Sarah A. Fulgham, and we have had eleven children, eight of whom are still living.

DROVE A HERD OVER THE TRAIL TO CALIFORNIA

By W. E. Cureton of Meridian, Texas

I was born in the Ozark Mountains of Arkansas, in 1848; came to Texas with my father, Captain Jack Cureton, in the winter of 1854–55; settled on or near the Brazos River below old Fort Belknap in what is now

Palo Pinto County, and began raising cattle. The county was organized in 1857.

W. E. CURETON

In 1867 we (my father and John C. Cureton) drove a herd of grown steers from Jim Ned, a tributary of the Colorado of Texas, now in Coleman County, up the Concho at a time when the Coffees and Tankersleys were the only inhabitants there. That year the government began the building of Fort Concho, which is now a part of the thrifty little city of San Angelo. The Indians killed a Dutchman and scalped and partly skinned him a little ahead of us, and Captain Snively, with a gold hunting outfit, had quite a skirmish along the Concho with them.

From the head waters on the Concho we made a ninety-six-mile drive to Horsehead Crossing on the Pecos River without giving the cattle a good watering. Our trail was the old military stage route used by the government before the Civil War. The Indians had killed a man and wounded a woman ahead of us at the old adobe walls at Horsehead Crossing on the Pecos, and captured a herd of cattle belonging to John Gamel and Isaac W. Cox of Mason, Texas. A few miles above Horsehead Crossing the Indians stole eleven head of our horses one night; only having two horses to the man, we felt the loss of half our mounts very severely. A little further up the river the Indians wounded Uncle Oliver Loving, the father of J. C. and George B. of the noted Loving family of the upper Brazos country and the founder of the great Texas Cattle Raisers' Association. The old man died at Fort Sumner of his wounds. They also killed Billy Corley, one of Lynch & Cooper's men, from Shackleford County, the same drive.

We left the Pecos near where now stands the town of Roswell, and traveled up the Hondo out by Fort Stanton over the divide to San Augustine Springs, near the Rio Grande, and wintered the cattle and sold them in the spring of 1868 to Hinds & Hooker, who were the United States contractors to feed the soldiers and Indians, as they were pretending to subdue and keep the Indians on reservations, but in reality were equipping them so they could depredate more efficiently on the drovers and emigrants.

In the summer of 1869 I sold a bunch of grown steers in Palo Pinto County, Texas, to Dr. D. B. Warren of Missouri, and we trailed them to Baxter Springs, Kansas. We swam Red River at the old Preston Ferry. We camped near the river the night before and tried to cross early in the morning. The river was very full of muddy water, and the cattle refused to take the water. After all hands had about exhausted themselves Dr. Warren, who was his own boss, said to me: "William, what will we do about it?" I answered him that we had better back out and graze the cattle until the sun got up so they could see the other bank, and they would want water and go across. "You should know that you can't swim cattle across as big a stream as this going east in the morning or going west late of an evening with the sun in their faces." About one P.M. we put them back on the trail and by the time the drags got near the river the leaders were climbing the east bank. The doctor looked at me and said, "Well, I'll be damned—every man to his profession."

In the spring of 1870 my father took his family along, and turned over more than eleven hundred cattle to us boys, John C. and J. W., to drive to California. We went out over the old Concho Trail to the Rio Pecos, up the

river to the Hondo, out by the Gallina Mountains, crossing the Rio Grande at Old Albuquerque, over to and
down the Little Colorado of the West; through New
Mexico into Arizona, by where Flagstaff is now; on the
Santa Fé Railroad, parallel to the Grand Canyon on the
south side of the Colorado; crossed the Colorado at
Hardyville above the Needles; crossed over the California desert; climbed over the Sierra Nevadas and
wintered the cattle between San Bernardino and Los
Angeles in California, a fifteen-hundred-mile drive. In
the spring of 1871 we drove the cattle back across
the Sierras, north up the east side of the mountains to
the head of Owens River, where we fattened them on the
luxurious California meadows; then drove them to Reno,
Nevada, five hundred miles from our wintering grounds,
and sold them, and Miller & Lux, the millionaire butchers
of San Francisco, shipped them to their slaughtering
plant in San Francisco, California—and, by the way, the
firm still controls the California market there. We paid
ten dollars for grown steers in Texas; got thirty dollars
after driving them two thousand miles and consuming
two years on the trip. After all, I honor the old long
horn; he was able to furnish his own transportation to
all the markets before the advent of railroads.

I made many other trips, but think these will give a
fair idea of the hardships of the pioneers.

I have been interested in cattle raising for sixty years,
ranching in Texas, New Mexico, Arizona and California
during that time, but always claimed Texas as home; was
a schoolboy with the late Colonel C. C. Slaughter of Dallas and George T. Reynolds of Fort Worth more than
sixty years ago.

PARENTS SETTLED IN THE REPUBLIC OF TEXAS

By Joseph S. Cruze, Sr., San Antonio, Texas.

MRS. M. K. CRUZE   JOSEPH S. CRUZE, Sr.

My parents, William and Isabella Cruze, came to the Republic of Texas in 1840 and located on the Brazos River in Washington County. There I was born July 27th, 1845, and when I was three months old father placed a buffalo hair pillow on the horn of his saddle, placed me thereon, mounted his horse and was ready to emigrate west with his family. He settled on Onion Creek, nine miles south of Austin, near the Colorado River, where he remained for several years, then in 1854 we moved to the central part of Hays County, where father died in 1856.

I enlisted in the Confederate Army in 1862, received my discharge in 1865, and returned home to my widowed mother. On July 24th, 1865, I was married to Miss Mary Kate Cox of Hays County.

In the years 1870 and 1871 I drove cattle to Kansas over the old Chisholm Trail. I remember the killing of Pete Owens, who was with the same herd I was with. We had reached the Cross Timbers of Texas, and passed a ranch where booze was sold. There was a row and Pete was shot and killed. He was a good friend to me, we had been soldier comrades for nearly three years, worked cattle together, and I loved him as a brother. Billie Owens, known to many of the old trail drivers, was his brother. The Owens boys were good soldiers, upright, honest and brave men.

In those days the cowmen underwent many hardships, survived many hair-breadth escapes and dangers while blazing our way through the wilderness. My comrades yet living have not forgotten what we had to endure. Everything was then tough, wild and woolly, and it was dangerous to be safe.

In September, 1866, I settled on Loneman Creek, in Hays County, near the Blanco River, and established the Cruze Ranch, which I sold to my son, S. J. Cruze, in 1917, and moved to San Antonio with my wife and two daughters, Margaret and Addie, and my grandson, Forest Harlan. I have a nice little home in Los Angeles Heights, and would be glad to hear from any of my old friends at any time.

My address is Route 10, Box 101a, Los Angeles Heights, San Antonio.

COMING UP THE TRAIL IN 1882

By Jack Potter of Kenton, Oklahoma.

In the spring of 1882, the New England Livestock Co. bought three thousand short horns in Southwest Texas, cut them into four herds and started them on the trail to Colorado, with King Hennant of Corpus Christi in charge of the first herd, Asa Clark of Legarta the second herd, Billie Burke the third herd, and John Smith of San Antonio in charge of the fourth. When they reached a point near San Antonio, Smith asked me to go with the herd at $30 a month and transportation back. Now, friends, it will not take long to tell my experiences going up the trail, but it will require several pages to recount what I had to endure coming back home.

JACK POTTER

There was no excitement whatever on this drive. It was to me very much like a summer's outing in the Rocky Mountains. We went out by way of Fredericksburg, Mason and Brady City, and entered the Western trail at Cow Gap, going through Albany near Fort Griffin, where we left the Western trail and selected a route through to Trinidad, Colorado, via Double Mountain Fork of the Brazos, Wichita and Pease Rivers to the Charles Goodnight ranch on the Staked Plains. We had several stampedes while crossing the plains.

En route we saw thousands of antelope crossing the trail in front of the herd. We crossed the Canadian at Tuscosa. This was a typical cowboy town, and at this time a general roundup was in progress, and I believe there were a hundred and fifty cow-punchers in the place. They had taken a day off to celebrate, and as there were only seven saloons in Tuscosa they were all doing a flourishing business. We had trouble in crossing the river with our herd, as those fellows were riding up and down the streets yelling and shooting.

Our next point was over the Dim Trail and freight road to Trinidad, Colorado, where we arrived the tenth of July. Here the manager met us and relieved two of the outfits, saying the country up to the South Platte was easy driving and that they would drift the horses along with two outfits instead of four. The manager

and King Hennant made some medicine and called for
the entire crews of John Smith and Asa Clark, and told
Billie Burke to turn his crew over to Hennant, who was
to take charge of the whole drive. I was disappointed,
for I did not want to spoil the summer with a two months'
drive. They called the men up one at a time and gave
them their checks. However, King Hennant arranged
with the manager for me to remain with them, and then
it was agreed to send me with some of the cow ponies
tc the company's cattle ranch in the Big Horn Basin
later on.

The drive up the South Platte was fine. We traveled
for three hundred miles along the foothills of the Rockies,
where we were never out of sight of the snowy ranges.
We went out by way of La Junta, Colorado, on the Santa
Fé, and then to Deer Trail. We would throw our two
herds together at night and the next morning again cut
them into two herds for the trail. We arrived at the
South Platte River near Greeley, Colorado, about the
tenth of August.

The itch or ronia had broken out on the trail and in
those days people did not know how to treat it successfully. Our manager sent us a wagon load of kerosene
and sulphur with which to fight the disease.

When we reached Cow Creek we turned the herds
loose and began building what is known as the Crow
Ranch. I worked here thirty days and it seemed like
thirty years. One day the manager came out and gave
instructions to shape up a herd of one hundred and fifty
select cow ponies to be taken to the Big Horn Ranch,
and I was chosen to go with the outfit. This was the first
time I had seen an outfit fixed up in the North. I supposed we would get a pack horse and fit up a little outfit
and two of us hike out with them. It required two days
to get started. The outfit consisted of a wagon loaded
with chuck, a big wall tent, cots to sleep on, a stove, and
a number one cook. We hit the trail, and it was another

outing for me, for this time we were traveling in new fields.

After leaving Cheyenne we pulled out for Powder River and then up to Sheridan. The weather was getting cold and I began to get homesick. When we reached the Indian country I was told that it was only one day's drive to Custer's battleground. I was agreeably surprised the next morning as we came down a long slope into the Little Big Horn Valley to the battleground. I was under the impression that Sitting Bull had hemmed Custer up in a box canyon and came up from behind and massacred his entire army. But that was a mistake, as Sitting Bull with his warriors was camped in the beautiful valley when Custer attacked him in the open. It seems that the Indians retreated slowly up a gradual slope to the east and Custer's men followed. The main fight took place at the top of the rise, as there is a headstone where every soldier fell, and a monument where Custer was killed.

The balance of that day we passed thousands of Indians who were going the same direction we were traveling. When they go to the agency to get their monthly allowance they take along everything with them, each family driving their horses in a separate bunch. When we arrived at the Crow Agency the boss received a letter from the manager instructing him to send me back to Texas, as the company were contracting for cattle for spring delivery, and I would be needed in the trail drives. The next morning I roped my favorite horse and said to the boys: "Good-bye, fellows, I am drifting south where the climate suits my clothes." That day I overtook an outfit on the way to Ogallala, and traveled with them several days, and then cut out from them and hiked across the prairie one hundred and fifty miles to the Crow ranch, where I sold my two horses and hired a party to take me and my saddle to Greeley, where I expected to set out for home.

Coming Off the Trail

Now, reader, here I was, a boy not yet seventeen years old, two thousand miles from home. I had never been on a railroad train, had never slept in a hotel, never taken a bath in a bath house, and from babyhood I had heard terrible stories about ticket thieves, money-changers, pickpockets, three-card monte, and other robbing schemes, and I had horrors about this, my first railroad trip. The first thing I did was to make my money safe by tying it up in my shirt tail. I had a draft for $150 and some currency. I purchased a second-hand trunk and about two hundred feet of rope with which to tie it. The contents of the trunk were one apple-horn saddle, a pair of chaps, a Colt's 45, one sugan, a hen-skin blanket, and a change of dirty clothes. You will see later that this trunk and its contents caused me no end of trouble.

My cowboy friends kindly assisted me in getting ready for the journey. The company had agreed to provide me with transportation, and they purchased a local ticket to Denver for me and gave me a letter to deliver to the general ticket agent at this point, instructing him to sell me a reduced ticket to Dodge City, Kansas, and enable me to secure a cowboy ticket from there to San Antonio for twenty-five dollars. Dodge City was the largest delivering point in the Northwest, and by the combined efforts of several prominent stockmen a cheap rate to San Antonio had been perfected for the convenience of the hundreds of cowboys returning home after the drives.

About four P.M. the Union Pacific train came pulling into Greeley. Then it was a hasty handshake with the boys. One of them handed me my trunk check, saying, "Your baggage is loaded. Good-bye, write me when you get home," and the train pulled out. It took several minutes for me to collect myself, and then the conductor came through and called for the tickets. When I handed him my ticket he punched a hole in it, and then pulled out a red slip, punched it, too, and slipped it into my hatband. I jumped to my feet and said, "You can't come that on me. Give me back my ticket," but he passed out of hearing, and as I had not yet learned how to walk on a moving train, I could not follow him. When I had become fairly settled in my seat again the train crossed a bridge, and as it went by I thought the thing was going to hit me on the head. I dodged those bridges all the way up to Denver. When I reached there I got off at the Union Station and walked down to the baggage car, and saw them unloading my trunk. I stepped up and said: "I will take my trunk." A man said, "No; we are handling this baggage." "But," said I, "that is my trunk, and has my saddle and gun in it." They paid no attention to me and wheeled the trunk off to the baggage room, but I followed right along, determined that they were not going to put anything over me. Seeing that I was so insistent one of the men asked me for the check. It was wrapped up in my shirt tail, and I went after it, and produced the draft I had been given as wages. He looked at it and said, "This is not your trunk check. Where is your metal check with numbers on it?" Then it began to dawn on me what the darn thing was, and when I produced it and handed it to him, he asked me where I was going. I told him to San Antonio, Texas, if I could get there. I then showed him my letter to the general ticket agent, and he said: "Now, boy, you leave this trunk right here and we will recheck it and you need not bother about it." That sounded bully to me.

I followed the crowd down Sixteenth and Curtiss Streets and rambled around looking for a quiet place to stop. I found the St. Charles Hotel and made arrangements to stay all night. Then I went off to a barber shop to get my hair cut and clean up a bit. When the barber

finished with me he asked if I wanted a bath, and when
I said yes, a negro porter took me down the hallway and
into a side room. He turned on the water, tossed me a
couple of towels and disappeared. I commenced undress-
ing hurriedly, fearing the tub would fill up before I could
get ready. The water was within a few inches of the
top of the tub when I plunged in. Then I gave a yell
like a Comanche Indian, for the water was boiling hot!
I came out of the tub on all fours, but when I landed on
the marble floor it was so slick that I slipped and fell
backwards with my head down. I scrambled around
promiscuously, and finally got my footing with a chair
for a brace. I thought: "Jack Potter, you are scalded
after the fashion of a hog." I caught a lock of my hair
to see if it would "slip," at the same time fanning myself
with my big Stetson hat. I next examined my toe nails,
for they had received a little more dipping than my
hair, but I found them in fairly good shape, turning a
bit dark, but still hanging on.

That night I went to the Tabor Opera House and saw
a fine play. There I found a cowboy chum, and we took
in the sights until midnight, when I returned to the St.
Charles. The porter showed me up to my room and
turned on the gas. When he had gone I undressed to
go to bed, and stepped up to blow out the light. I blew
and blew until I was out of breath, and then tried to fan
the flame out with my hat, but I had to go to bed and
leave the gas burning. It was fortunate that I did not
succeed, for at that time the papers were full of accounts
of people gassed just that way.

The next morning I started out to find the Santa Fé
ticket office, where I presented my letter to the head man
there. He was a nice appearing gentleman, and when he
had looked over the letter he said, "So you are a genuine
cowboy? Where is your gun and how many notches have
you on its handle? I suppose you carry plenty of salt
with you on the trail for emergency? I was just reading

in a magazine a few days ago about a large herd which stampeded and one of the punchers mounted a swift horse and ran up in front of the leaders and began throwing out salt, and stopped the herd just in time to keep them from running off a high precipice." I laughed heartily when he told me this and said, "My friend, you can't learn the cow business out of books. That yarn was hatched in the brain of some fiction writer who probably never saw a cow in his life. But I am pleased to find a railroad man who will talk, for I always heard that a railroad man only used two words, Yes and No." Then we had quite a pleasant conversation. He asked me if I was ever in Albert's Buckhorn saloon in San Antonio and saw the collection of fine horns there. Then he gave me an emigrant cowboy ticket to Dodge City and a letter to the agent at that place stating that I was eligible for a cowboy ticket to San Antonio.

As it was near train time I hunted up the baggage crew and told them I was ready to make another start. I showed them my ticket and asked them about my trunk. They examined it, put on a new check, and gave me one with several numbers on it. I wanted to take the trunk out and put it on the train, but they told me to rest easy and they would put it on. I stood right there until I saw them put it on the train, then I climbed aboard.

This being my second day out, I thought my troubles should be over, but not so, for I couldn't face those bridges. They kept me dodging and fighting my head. An old gentleman who sat near me said, "Young man, I see by your dress that you are a typical cowboy, and no doubt you can master the worst bronco or rope and tie a steer in less than a minute, but in riding on a railway train you seem to be a novice. Sit down on this seat with your back to the front and those bridges will not bother you." And sure enough it was just as he said.

We arrived at Coolidge, Kansas, one of the old land-

marks of the Santa Fé trail days, about dark. That night
at twelve o'clock we reached Dodge City, where I had to
lay over for twenty-four hours. I thought everything
would be quiet in the town at that hour of the night, but
I soon found out that they never slept in Dodge. They
had a big dance hall there which was to Dodge City what
Jack Harris' Theater was to San Antonio. I arrived at
the hall in time to see a gambler and a cowboy mix up
in a six-shooter duel. Lots of smoke, a stampede, but no
one killed. I secured a room and retired. When morning came I arose and fared forth to see Dodge City by
daylight. It seemed to me that the town was full of cowboys and cattle owners. The first acquaintance I met
here was George W. Saunders, now the president and
chief remudero of the Old Trail Drivers. I also found
Jesse Pressnall and Slim Johnson there, as well as several others whom I knew down in Texas. Pressnall said
to me: "Jack, you will have lots of company on your
way home. Old 'Dog Face' Smith is up here from
Cotulla and he and his whole bunch are going back tonight. Old 'Dog Face' is one of the best trail men that
ever drove a cow, but he is all worked up about having
to go back on a train. I wish you would help them along
down the line in changing cars." That afternoon I saw
a couple of chuck wagons coming in loaded with punchers,
who had on the same clothing they wore on the trail, their
pants stuck in their boots and their spurs on. They
were bound for San Antonio. Old "Dog Face" Smith
was a typical Texan, about thirty years of age, with long
hair and three months' growth of whiskers. He wore
a blue shirt and a red cotton handkerchief around his
neck. He had a bright, intelligent face that bore the
appearance of a good trail hound, which no doubt was
the cause of people calling him "Dog Face."

It seemed a long time that night to wait for the train
and we put in time visiting every saloon in the town.
There was a big stud poker game going on in one place,

and I saw one Texas fellow, whose name I will not mention, lose a herd of cattle at the game. But he might have won the herd back before daylight.

I will never forget seeing that train come into Dodge City that night. Old "Dog Face" and his bunch were pretty badly frightened and we had considerable difficulty in getting them aboard. It was about 12:30 when the train pulled out. The conductor came around and I gave him my cowboy ticket. It was almost as long as your arm, and as he tore off a chunk of it I said: "What authority have you to tear up a man's ticket?" He laughed and said, "You are on my division. I simply tore off one coupon and each conductor between here and San Antonio will tear off one for each division." That sounded all right, but I wondered if that ticket would hold out all the way down.

Everyone seemed to be tired and worn out and the bunch began bedding down. Old "Dog Face" was out of humor, and was the last one to bed down. At about three o'clock our train was sidetracked to let the westbound train pass. This little stop caused the boys to sleep the sounder. Just then the westbound train sped by traveling at the rate of about forty miles an hour, and just as it passed our coach the engineer blew the whistle. Talk about your stampedes! That bunch of sleeping cowboys arose as one man, and started on the run with old "Dog Face" Smith in the lead. I was a little slow in getting off, but fell in with the drags. I had not yet woke up, but thinking I was in a genuine cattle stampede, yelled out, "Circle your leaders and keep up the drags." Just then the leaders circled and ran into the drags, knocking some of us down. They circled again and the news butcher crawled out from under foot and jumped through the window like a frog. Before they could circle back the next time, the train crew pushed in the door and caught old "Dog Face" and soon the bunch quieted down. The conductor was pretty angry and threatened to have us transferred to the freight department and loaded into a stock car.

We had breakfast at Hutchinson, and after eating and were again on our way, speeding through the beautiful farms and thriving towns of Kansas, we organized a kangaroo court and tried the engineer of that westbound train for disturbing the peace of passengers on the eastbound train. We heard testimony all morning, and called in some of the train crew to testify. One of the brakemen said it was an old trick for that engineer to blow the whistle at that particular siding and that he was undoubtedly the cause of a great many stampedes. The jury brought in a verdict of guilty and assessed the death penalty. It was ordered that he be captured, taken to some place on the western trail, there to be hog-tied like a steer, and then have the road brand applied with a good hot iron and a herd of not less than five thousand long-horn Texas steers made to stampede and trample him to death.

We had several hours' lay-over at Emporia, Kansas, where we took the M., K. & T. for Parsons, getting on the main line through Indian Territory to Denison, Texas. There was a large crowd of punchers on the through train who were returning from Ogallala by way of Kansas City and Omaha.

As we were traveling through the Territory old "Dog Face" said to me: "Potter, I expect it was me that started that stampede up there in Kansas, but I just couldn't help it. You see, I took on a scare once and since that time I have been on the hair trigger when suddenly awakened. In the year 1875 me and Wild Horse Jerry were camped at a water hole out west of the Nueces River, where we were snaring mustangs. One evening a couple of peloncias pitched camp nearby, and the next morning our remuda was missing, all except our night horses. I told Wild Horse Jerry to hold down the camp and watch the snares, and I hit the trail of those peloncias which headed for the Rio Grande. I followed it for about forty miles and then lost all signs. It was nightfall, so I made camp, prepared supper and rolled up in my blanket and went to sleep. I don't know how long I slept, but I was awakened by a low voice saying: "Dejarle desconsar bien por que en un rato el va a comenzar su viaje por el otro mundro." (Let him rest well, as he will soon start on his journey to the other world.) It was the two Mexican horse thieves huddled around my campfire smoking their cigarettes and taking it easy, as they thought they had the drop on me. As I came out of my bed two bullets whizzed near my head, but about that time my old Colt's forty-five began talking, and the janitor down in Hades had two more peloncias on his hands. Ever since that night, if I am awakened suddenly I generally come out on my all fours roaring like a buffalo bull. I never sleep on a bedstead, for it would not be safe for me, as I might break my darn neck, so I always spread down on the floor."

It was a long ride through the Territory, and we spent the balance of the day singing songs and making merry. I kept thinking about my trunk, and felt grateful that the railroad people had sent along a messenger to look out for it. At Denison we met up with some emigrant families going to Uvalde, and soon became acquainted with some fine girls in the party. They entertained us all the way down to Taylor, where we changed cars. As we told them good-bye one asked me to write a line in her autograph album. Now I was sure enough "up a tree." I had been in some pretty tight places, and had had to solve some pretty hard problems, but this was a new one for me. You see, the American people go crazy over some new fad about once a year, and in 1882 it was the autograph fad. I begged the young lady to excuse me, but she insisted, so I took the album and began writing down all the road brands that I was familiar with. But she told me to write a verse of some kind.

1 happened to think of a recitation I had learned at school when I was a little boy, so I wrote as follows: "It's tiresome work says lazy Ned, to climb the hill in my new sled, and beat the other boys. Signed, Your Bulliest Friend, JACK POTTER."

We then boarded the I. & G. N. for San Antonio, and at Austin a lively bunch joined us, including Hal Gosling, United States Marshal, Captain Joe Sheeley and Sheriff Quigley of Castroville. Pretty soon the porter called out "San Antonio, Santonnie-o," and that was music to my ears. My first move on getting off the train was to look for my trunk and found it had arrived. I said to myself, "Jack Potter, you're a lucky dog. Ticket held out all right, toe nails all healed up, and trunk came through in good shape." After registering at the Central Hotel, I wrote to that general ticket agent at Denver as follows:

San Antonio, Texas, Oct. 5th, 1882.

Gen. Ticket Agt. A. T. & S. F.,
    1415 Lamar St., Denver, Colo.:

DEAR SIR—I landed in San Antonio this afternoon all O. K. My trunk also came through without a scratch. I want to thank you very much for the man you sent along to look after my trunk. He was very accommodating, and would not allow me to assist him in loading it on at Denver. No doubt he will want to see some of the sights of San Antonio, for it is a great place, and noted for its chili con carne. When he takes a fill of this food, as every visitor does, you can expect him back in Denver on very short notice, as he will be seeking a cooler climate. Did you ever eat any chili con carne? I will send you a dozen cans soon, but tell your wife to keep it in the refrigerator as it might set the house on fire. Thank you again for past favors.

Your Bulliest Friend,
                        JACK POTTER.

(EDITOR'S NOTE.—The foregoing will be read with much interest by
the old cowboys who worked the range and traveled the trail with Jack
Potter.   Mr. Potter is now a prosperous stockman, owning large ranch
interests in Oklahoma and New Mexico. He is the son of Rev. Jack Potter,
the "Fighting Parson," who was known to all the early settlers of West
Texas.   The above article is characteristic of the humor and wit of this
rip-roaring, hell-raising cow-puncher, who, George Saunders says, and other
friends concur in the assertion, was considered to be the most cheerful
liar on the face of the earth. But he was always the life of the outfit in
camp or on the trail.)

WHEN A GIRL MASQUERADED AS A COWBOY AND SPENT FOUR MONTHS ON THE TRAIL

By Samuel Dunn Houston, San Antonio, Texas

My first trip was from Southern Texas, in the spring
of 1876. Mac Stewart was foreman. The cattle belonged
to Ellison & Dewees.   In the
spring of 1877 and 1878 I was
on the trail with Bill Green
with the Ellison & Dewees
cattle. In the spring of 1879
I was on the trail with Len
Pierce, but when we crossed
the Cimarron, the boys all
went to the Longhorn Roundup and got too much whiskey,
went to camp, made a rough
house and fired Mr. Pierce.
He went to Dodge City and
we put John Saunders of

S. D. HOUSTON

Lockhart in charge of the herd.   Pierce was no good.   In
the spring, 1880, I was on the trail with Henry Miller,
with the Head & Bishop cattle.   In the spring, 1881, I was
on the trail with Monroe Hardeman, Head & Bishop
cattle.   In 1882 I went with George Wilcox, Head &
Bishop cattle.   In 1883 I worked for Captain B. L. Crouch
in Frio County.   In 1884 I went on the trail with two

herds for Captain Crouch, spring herd and fall herd. In the fall, 1884, I was ordered to Seven Rivers, New Mexico, by Captain Crouch to help deliver the Joe Crouch cattle which the Captain had sold to the Holt Live Stock Company, after Joe Crouch had died.

I was on the range during the year 1885.

In the spring, 1886, I went to work for the Holt Live Stock Company and was promoted trail foreman and drove my first herd for that company in the spring of 1886, and was trail boss for the company until 1893. I would take off the spring herd and drive from one to two feeder herds to the Corn Belt country down on the Cimarron. That year I was on the trail almost the year around. One winter I didn't get back from the third trip until the last of January. I expect I have made more trips over the cow trail from Southern Texas and New Mexico than any man in the country.

In the fall of 1893 I came back to my old home to die, but I am still living and able to do a man's work every day. I live in San Antonio with my good wife and three nice daughters, and keep my gun at the head of my bed to keep the young, up-to-date cowboys away.

Now I am going to write a sketch of a trip I made while I was with the Holt Live Stock Company of New Mexico, in the spring, 1888.

I was hiring men for the spring drive and they were not very plentiful in that country, but as luck was on my side, I heard that there were four men at Seven Rivers who had come up from Texas and wanted work. I got in my chuck wagon, went to Seven Rivers and found what I was looking for, so that completed my outfit.

In a few days I went up the Pecos to the spring round-up and took charge of the steer herd of twenty-five hundred three's and up. George Wilcox, the ranch boss, counted them out to me and said, "Sam, they are yours."

I lined up my men, drifted over toward Roswell, and did fine the first night. We passed around town the next morning, and camped that night on Salt Creek. I picked the wrong place to bed the herd, so about nine pin they broke, and we didn't get them stopped until four o'clock in the morning. I told the boys we had lost half of the herd. Just as soon as daylight came I had everything in the saddle to move the herd off the bed ground. I counted them and I was out six hundred and thirty-five head of steers. I left four men with the herd and cut for sign. I found where they had struck the Pecos River and went down that stream. We struck a gallop and found the entire bunch, six miles down the river. They showed they had been in a stampede for they were as green as the grass itself.

When I got back to camp I found the cause of the stampede. I had failed to go over the bed ground the evening before and I found I had bedded the herd on high ground and on the worst gopher holes I could have found in that country. I was out only four or five head and they were close to the range.

I had a boy with me by the name of Gus Votaw. He was about twenty years old, and was the son of Billie Votaw, who all the old-timers knew in San Antonio. Gus made a good hand.

That day while drifting along up the Pecos River I went ahead to hunt a watering place and when I rode up on a gyp hill overlooking the herd I saw six or seven men in a bunch. I went down to the herd to know the cause and hand out a few orders. When I got to them I found the four men I had secured at Seven Rivers were gunmen and had been playing pranks on Gus Votaw. I told them they would have to cut that out and they didn't say yes or no, so I kept my eyes open from there on. In a few days I caught one of them at the same thing and I read the law to him and when I got them all in camp I told them that I was going to run the outfit and such

things as that must be cut out right now. I also told
Gus that if they worried him any more to let me
know.

I will leave off now from here to Fort Sumner, New
Mexico, which was less than a month.

I arrived at Fort Sumner in less than a month and
had to stop and write some letters, so I told the cook and
horse rustler to take the wagon and camp it up the river
and for the cook to have dinner early, for I would be
there about ten o'clock.

I finished my job at the postoffice, mounted my horse
and pulled out for camp. When I got up within two hundred yards of camp I looked up and saw what I thought,
every man in camp and only one man with the herd.
When I rode up every man had a gun in his hand but
Gus Votaw. I got off my horse and, of course, knew the
cause. The cook said, "Boss, there is going to be hell
here. I am glad you came."

I went to the front of the wagon, got my gun off of
the water barrel and told the men that I would play my
trump card, that I had to have every gun in camp. I
didn't expect to live to get the last one, but I did. I got
six of them, knocked the loads out, threw them in the
wagon, got out my time and check books and gave the
four men their time. I told the cook and horse rustler
to hitch up the mules and we would move camp. I left
the four bad men sitting on their saddles under a cottonwood tree and felt that I had done the right thing. I
went up the river about two miles and camped.

After all this occurred, right here my troubles began.
I had to leave the Pecos River and drive across the
Staked Plains, ninety miles without water. The next
water was the Canadian River. Being short handed, I
had to put my horses in the herd, put the horse rustler
with the herd and made a hand myself. I held the herd
over that day and rested, raised the men's wages five
dollars, and made my plans. The next day we had dinner

early, filled my water barrel and left the old Pecos at eleven o'clock for a long, dry drive.

That evening at sundown we reached the top of the mesa, fifteen miles up hill all the way. We rounded up the herd on the trail, got a bite to eat, changed horses and drove until daybreak, bedded on the trail again and had lunch. The cattle were getting very dry and men were worn out. We kept this up until we reached the Canadian River, which was fifty-two hours from the time we left the Pecos River. I didn't lose a steer.

I could not let the herd string out in making the trip. If I had we would have lost cattle. I kept them in a bunch and when I reached the Canadian River I laid over three days to let the men, horses and cattle rest. I would run off the range cattle in the evening and turn everything loose at night except one horse for each man.

It was only a few miles to Clayton, New Mexico, a small railroad town ahead, so I struck camp, left the boys with the herd and I went to town to see if I could get two or three trail men.

When I got there I found there were no men in town, but I met an old friend of mine and he told me that there was a kid of a boy around town that wanted to get with a herd and go up the trail, but he had not seen him for an hour or so. I put out to hunt that kid and found him over at the livery stable. I hired him and took him to camp, and put him with the horses and put my rustler with the cattle. I got along fine for three or four months. The kid would get up the darkest stormy nights and stay with the cattle until the storm was over. He was good natured, very modest, didn't use any cuss words or tobacco, and always pleasant. His name was Willie Matthews, was nineteen years old and weighed one hundred and twenty-five pounds. His home was in Caldwell, Kansas, and I was so pleased with him that I wished many times that I could find two or three more like him.

Everything went fine until I got to Hugo, Colorado,

a little town on the old K. P. Railroad, near the Colorado and Wyoming line. There was good grass and water close to town, so I pulled up about a half a mile that noon and struck camp. After dinner the kid come to where I was sitting and asked me if he could quit. He insisted, said he was homesick, and I had to let him go.

About sundown we were all sitting around camp and the old herd was coming in on the bed ground. I looked up toward town and saw a lady, all dressed up, coming toward camp, walking. I told the boys we were going to have company. I couldn't imagine why a woman would be coming on foot to a cow camp, but she kept right on coming, and when within fifty feet of camp I got up to be ready to receive my guest. Our eyes were all set on her, and every man holding his breath. When she got up within about twenty feet of me, she began to laugh, and said, "Mr. Houston, you don't know me, do you?"

Well, for one minute I couldn't speak. She reached her hand out to me, to shake hands, and I said, "Kid, is it possible that you are a lady?" That was one time that I could not think of anything to say, for everything that had been said on the old cow trail in the last three or four days entered my mind at that moment.

In a little while we all crowded around the girl and shook her hand, but we were so dumbfounded we could hardly think of anything to say. I told the cook to get one of the tomato boxes for a chair. The kid sat down and I said, "Now I want you to explain yourself."

"Well," she said, "I will tell you all about it, Mr. Houston. My papa is an old-time trail driver from Southern Texas. He drove from Texas to Caldwell, Kansas, in the '70's. He liked the country around Caldwell very much, so the last trip he made he went to work on a ranch up there and never returned to Texas any more. In two or three years he and my mother were married. After I was ten or twelve years old, I used to hear papa talk so much about the old cow trail and I made up my mind that when I was grown I was going up the trail if I had to run off. I had a pony of my own and read in the paper of the big herds passing Clayton, New Mexico, so I said, now is my chance to get on the trail. Not being far over to Clayton, I saddled my pony and told brother I was going out in the country, and I might be gone for a week, but for him to tell papa not to worry about me, I would be back. I had on a suit of brother's clothes and a pair of his boots. In three or four days I was in Clayton looking for a job and I found one. Now, Mr. Houston, I am glad I found you to make the trip with, for I have enjoyed it. I am going just as straight home as I can and that old train can't run too fast for me, when I get on it."

The train left Hugo at 11:20 o'clock in the evening. I left one man with the herd and took the kid and every man to town to see the little girl off. I suppose she was the only girl that ever made such a trip as that. She was a perfect lady.

After I got through and returned to the ranch on the Pecos River, I had many letters from the little girl and her father also, thanking me for the kindness toward Willie and begging me to visit them.

The trip I made that year was for the Holt Live Stock Company of Denver, Colorado. They also had large ranches in New Mexico.

The next morning I went to Hugo and secured three more men and hit the trail for Pole Creek, Wyoming, about fifty miles from the Montana and Wyoming line, where I turned over the big herd to the Russell Brothers Ranch, and that was the end of this drive.

A TRYING TRIP ALONE THROUGH THE WILDERNESS

By Samuel Dunn Houston, 2206 South Presa Street,
San Antonio, Texas

In 1879 I went through Southern Texas with a big herd of cattle to the Northern market, Ogallala, Nebraska. This herd belonged to Head & Bishop.

We reached Ogallala August 10th, 1879, and there we met R. G. Head, who gave the boss, John Sanders, orders to cross the South Platte the next morning and proceed to the North Platte. He said he would see us over there and would tell us where to take the herd.

On August 11th we crossed the South Platte and went over on North River about ten miles and camped. Dick Head came over to camp for dinner and told our boss to take the herd up to Tusler's Ranch on Pumpkin Creek and Mr. Tusler would be there to receive the cattle. He said it was about one hundred miles up the Platte. After dinner we strung the herd out and drove them up there. We rushed them up because we were anxious to get back to Ogallala to see all of our old cowboy friends get in from the long drive from Texas.

We reached the Tusler Ranch on August 19th and on the 20th we counted the old herd over to the ranch boss and started back to Ogallala, making the return trip in four days.

The next morning as we were going through town, I met an old trail boss, and he wanted me to go with him to Red Cloud Agency, Dakota, with four thousand big Texas steers that belonged to D. R. Fant. They were Indian contracted cattle, so I told the boss I was ready to make the trip. Tom Moore was the foreman's name and he was a man that knew how to handle a big herd.

I went to camp with Tom that night and he got all the outfit together and on August 28th we took charge

of the big herd. They were one of the old King herds
which had come in by way of Dodge City, Kansas, from
the old coast country down in Southern Texas.

They wanted to walk, so we strung them out and
headed for the old South Platte. When the lead cattle
got to the bank of the river the boss said, "Now, Sam,
don't let them turn back on you, and we won't have any
trouble." We landed on the other side all O. K. and
went through the valley and on through the town. Everybody in town was out to see the big King herd go through.
I threw my hat back on my head and I felt as though
the whole herd belonged to me.

When the lead cattle struck the foothills I looked
back and could see the tail end coming in the river, and
I told my partner, the right-hand pointer, that we were
headed for the North Pole. We raised our hats and bid
Ogallala good-bye. When the lead cattle got to North
River it was an hour and ten minutes before the tail end
got to the top of the hills. My partner and I threw the
range cattle out of the flats and we had it easy until the
chuck wagon came over and struck camp for noon, then
four of us boys went to camp.

We had a highball train from there on.

We didn't cross the North Platte until we got to Fort
Laramie, Wyoming. The snow was melting in the mountains and the river was muddy and no bottom to the
quicksand. I was looking every night for a stampede,
but we were lucky. The night we camped close to the
Court House Rock, they made a jump off the bed ground,
but that didn't count. I think they got wind of the old
negro cook. This herd had come from the old King
Ranch, away down in Texas with a Mexican cook. I told
the boss that the next morning and he said he was almost
sure that was the cause.

The North Platte River in places is more than a mile
wide and it seemed to me when we reached the place we
were to cross, it was two miles wide. The range cattle

on the other side looked like little calves standing along the bank.

When we reached Fort Laramie we made ready to cross. I pulled my saddle off and then my clothes. Tom came up and said, "Sam, you are doing the right thing." I told him I had crossed that river before and that I had a good old friend who once started to cross that river and he was lost in the quicksand. His name was Theodore Luce of Lockhart, Texas. He was lost just above the old Seven Crook Ranch above Ogallala. Tom told all the boys to pull off their saddles before going across. When everything was ready we strung the herd back on the hill and headed for the crossing. Men and steers were up and under all the way across.

We landed over all safe and sound, got the sand out of our hair, counted the boys to see if they were all there and pulled out to the foothills to strike camp.

About ten o'clock that night the first guards came in to wake my partner and I to stand second guard. I got up, pulled on my boots, untied my horse and then the herd broke. The two first guards had to ride until Tom and the other men got there. Three of us caught the leaders and threw them back to the tail end, then run them in a mill, until they broke again. We kept that up until three o'clock in the morning, when we got them quieted.

We held them there until daylight, then strung them towards the wagon and counted them. We were out fifty-five head, but we had the missing ones back by eight o'clock. We were two miles from the grub wagon when the run was over. The first guards said that a big black wolf got up too close to the herd and that was the cause of the trouble.

Our next water was the Nebraska River, which was thirty miles arcoss the Laramie Plains. We passed over that in fine shape. From there our next water was White River. The drive through that country was bad, because the trail was so crooked and such deep canyons. We reached White River, crossed over and camped. About the time we turned the mules loose, up rode about thirty bucks and squaws, all ready for supper. They stood around till supper was ready and the old negro cook began to get crazy and they couldn't stay any longer. They got on their horses and left.

An Indian won't stay where there is a crazy person. They say he is the devil.

The next morning the horse rustler was short ten head of horses. He hunted them until time to move camp and never found them, so Tom told me that I could stay there and look them up, and he would take the herd eight or ten miles up the trail and wait for me. I roped out my best horse, got my Winchester and six-shooter and started out looking for the horses. I rode that country out and out, but could not find them, so I just decided the Indians drove them off during the night to get a reward or a beef. I thought I would go down to the mouth of White River, on the Missouri River in the bottom where the Indians were camped. When I got down in the bottom I saw horse signs, so I was sure from the tracks they were our horses. I rode and rode until I found them. There was no one around them, so I started back with the bunch.

When I had covered three or four miles, I looked back and saw a big dust on the hill out of White River. Then I rode for my life, because I knew it was a bunch of Indians and they were after me. I could see the herd ahead of me, and never let up. I beat them to camp about a half mile.

When they rode up and pointed to the horses, one Indian said, "Them my horses. This man steal 'em! Him no good!" We had an old squaw humper along with us, and he got them down to a talk and Tom told them he would give them a beef. Tom went with them out to the herd and cut out a big beef and they ran it off a short distance and killed it, cut it up, packed it on their ponies and went back toward White River. If those Indians had overtaken me I am sure my bones would be bleaching in that country today. The Indians were almost on the warpath at that time and we were lucky in that we did not have any more trouble with them.

A week longer put us at the Agency. Tom went ahead of the herd and reported to the agent. We camped about four miles this side that night and the next morning we strung the old herd off the bed ground and went in to the pens at Red Cloud Agency, Dakota. There I saw more Indians than I ever expected to see. The agent said there were about ten thousand on the ground.

It took us all day to weigh the herd out, ten steers on the scales at one time. We weighed them and let them out one side and the agent would call the Indians by name and each family would fall in behind his beef and off to the flats they would go.

After we got the herd all weighed out the agent told us to camp there close and he would show us around. He said the Indians were going to kill a fat dog that night and after they had feasted they would lay the carcass on the ground and have a war dance.

All the boys wanted to stay and see them dance. A few of the bucks rode through the crowd several times with their paint on. In a little while a buck came up with a table on his head and set it down in the crowd and then came another with big butcher knives in his hand and a third came with a big fat dog on his shoulder, all cleaned like a hog. He placed it on the table, then every Indian on the ground made some kind of a pow-wow that could be heard for miles, after which the old chief made a speech and the feast began. Every Indian on the ground had a bite of that dog. They wanted us to go up and have some, but we were not hungry, so we stood back and looked on. "Heap good," said the chief, "heap fat." About ten o'clock they had finished eating and two squaws took the carcass off the table and put it on the ground and the dance began. Every Indian was painted in some bright color. That was a wonderful dance.

The next morning we started back over our old trail to Ogallala. It was about October 16th and some cooler and all of the boys were delighted to head south.

Seven days' drive with the outfit brought us back to the Niobrara River and we struck camp at the Dillon Ranch.

The Dillon Ranch worked a number of half-breed Indians. I was talking with one about going back to Ogallala, as I was very anxious to get on the trail road and go down in Texas to see my best girl.

He told me he could tell me a route that could cut off two or three hundred miles going to Ogallala. So I wrote it all down. He told me to go over the old Indian trail across the Laramie Plains, saying his father had often told him how to go and the trail was wide and plain and it was only one hundred and seventy-five or two hundred miles. Right there I made up my mind that I would go that way and all alone. There were only two watering places and they were about forty miles apart. The first lake was sixty-five or seventy miles.

I had the best horse that ever crossed the Platte River and if I could cut off that much I would be in Texas by the time the outfit reached Ogallala.

I asked Tom to pay me off, saying that I was going back to Texas over the old Indian trail across the Laramie Plains. I knew if an Indian crossed that country I could also.

He said, "You are an old fool. You can't make that trip, not knowing where the fresh water is, you will starve to death." I told him that I could risk it anyway, and I knew I could make it.

Next morning I was in my saddle by daylight, bade the boys good-bye and told them if they heard of a dead man or horse on the old Indian trail, across the plains, for some of them the next year to come and pick me up, but I was sure I could make the trip across.

The first day's ride I was sure I had covered sixty-five or seventy miles. I was getting very thirsty that evening, so I began to look on both sides of the trail for the fresh water lake, but was disappointed. I was not worried. Just as the sun went down I went into a deep basin just off the trail where there was a very large alkali lake.

I had a pair of blankets, my slicker and saddle blankets, so I made my bed down and went to bed. I was tired and old Red Bird (my horse) was also jaded. I lay awake for some time thinking and wondering if I was on the wrong trail. The next morning I got up, after a good rest, ate the rest of my lunch, and pulled down the trail looking on both sides of the trail for the fresh water lake, but failed to find it. I then decided that the half-breed either lied or had put me "up a tree." Anyway, I would not turn back. I had plenty of money, but that was no good out there. I could see big alkali lakes everywhere, but I knew there would be a dead cowboy out there if I should take a drink of that kind of water.

I rode until noon, but found nothing. The country was full of deer, antelope, elk and lobo wolves, but they were too far off to take a shot at. When I struck camp for noon I took the saddle off my horse and lay down for a rest. Got up about one-thirty and hit the trail.

That was my second days' ride and my tongue was very badly swelled. I could not spit any more, so I began to use my brain and a little judgment and look out for "old Sam" and that horse.

About the middle of the afternoon I looked off to my left and saw a large lobo wolf about one hundred yards away and he seemed to be going my route. I would look in his direction quite often. He was going my gait and seemed to have me spotted. I took a shot at him every little while, but I kept on going and so did he. I rode on until sundown and looked out for my wolf, but did not see him. The trail turned to the right and went down into a deep alkali basin. I rode down into it and decided that I would pull into camp for the night, as I was very much worn out. I went down to the edge of the lake, pulled off my saddle and made my bed down on my stake rope so I would not lose my horse. The moon was just coming up over the hill.

I threw a load in my gun and placed it by my side, with my head on my saddle, and dropped off to sleep. About nine o'clock the old wolf's howls woke me up. I looked up and saw him sitting about twenty feet from my head just between me and the moon. I turned over right easy, slipped my gun over the cantle of my saddle and let him have one ball. He never kicked. I grabbed my rope, went to him, cut him open and used my hands for a cup and drank his old blood. It helped me in a way, but did not satisfy as water would. I went down to the lake and washed up, went back to bed and thought I would get a good sleep and rest that night, but found later I had no rest coming.

I was nearly asleep when something awakened me. I raised up and grabbed my gun, and saw that it was a herd of elk, so I took a shot or two at them. As soon as I shot they stampeded and ran off, but kept coming back. About twelve o'clock I got up, put my saddle on my horse and rode until daylight. I was so tired, I thought I would lay down and sleep awhile. Riding that night I must have passed the second water lake. After sleeping a little while I got up and broke camp and rode until twelve o'clock, when I stopped for noon that day. That being my third day out, I thought I would walk around, and the first thing I saw was an old dead horse's bones. I wondered what a dead horse's bones were doing away out there, so I began to look around some more and what should I see but the bones of a man. I was sure then that some man had undertaken to cross the

plains and had perished, so I told old Red Bird (my
horse) that we had better go down the trail and we
pulled out.

That evening about four o'clock, as I was walking
and leading my horse, I saw a very high sand hill right
on the edge of the old trail. I walked on to the top of
the sand hill and there I could see cottonwood trees just
ahead of me. I sat down under my horse about a half an
hour. I could see cattle everywhere in the valley, and I saw
a bunch of horses about a mile from me. I looked down
toward the trees about four miles and saw a man headed
for the bunch of horses. I didn't know whether he was
an Indian or not. He was in a gallop and as he came
nearer to the horses I pulled my gun and shot one time.
He stopped a bit and started off again. Then I made two
shots and he stopped again a few minutes. By that time
he had begun to round up the horses, so I shot three
times. He quit his horses and came to me in a run. When
he got up within thirty of forty feet of me he spoke to
me and called me by my name and said, ''Sam you are
the biggest fool I ever saw.'' I couldn't say a word for
my mouth was so full of tongue, but I knew him. He
shook hands and told me to get up behind him and we
would go to camp. He took his rope and tied it around
my waist to keep me from falling off, for I was very
weak. Then he struck a gallop and we were at camp
in a very few minutes. He tied his horse and said, ''Now,
Sam, we will go down to the spring and get a drink of
water.''

Just under the hill about twenty steps was the finest
sight I ever saw in my life. He took down his old tin
cup and said, ''Now, Sam, I am going to be the doctor.''
I was trying all the time to get in the spring, but was
so weak he could hold me back with one hand. He would
dip up just a teaspoonful of the water in the cup and
say, ''Throw your head back,'' and he poured it on my
tongue. After a while he increased it until I got my fill

and my tongue went down. When I got enough water
then I was hungry. I could have eaten a piece of that
fat dog if I'd had it.

My friend's name was Jack Woods, an old cowboy
that worked on the Bosler ranch. Jack and I had been
up the trail from Ogallala to the Dakotas many times
before that.

Jack said, "Now, Sam, we will go up to the house and
get something to eat. I killed a fat heifer calf yesterday
and have plenty of bread cooked, so you come in and
lay down and I will start a fire quickly and cook some
steak and we will eat some supper." Before he could
get it cooked, I could stand it no longer, so I slipped out,
went around behind the house where he had the calf
hanging, took out my pocket knife and went to work
eating the raw meat, trying to satisfy my appetite. After
fifteen or twenty minutes Jack came around hunting me
and said, "Sam, I always thought you were crazy, now
I know it. Come on to supper." I went in the house and
ate a hearty supper.

After finishing supper, I never was so sleepy in my
life. Jack said, "Sam, lay down on my bed and go to
sleep and I will go out and get your horse and treat him
to water and oats." He got on his horse and struck a
gallop for the sand hills, where my poor old horse was
standing starving to death.

Next morning Jack told me that a man by the name
of Lumm once undertook to cross those plains from the
Niobrara River to the head of the Little Blue over that
same Indian trail. Jack said, "He and his horse's bones
are laying out on the plains now. Perhaps you saw them
as you came along." I told him I saw the bones of a
man and the horse, but didn't remember how far back it
was. It seemed about 25 miles.

I remained there five days and every morning while
I was there, Jack and I would get on our horses and go
out in the valley and round up the horses he was taking

care of, rope out the worst outlaw horse he had in the bunch and take the kink out of his back. The five days I was there I rode four and five horses every day.

On October 29th I saddled my horse and told Jack I was going to Texas. He gave me a little lunch, and I bid him good-bye and headed for the North Platte.

I reached Bosler's Ranch at 12:20 o'clock, had dinner, gave the boss a note from Jack Woods, fed my horse, rested one hour, saddled up, bade the boys good-bye and headed for Ogallala on the South Platte, forty miles below.

I reached Ogallala that night at 9:30 o'clock, put my horse in the livery stable, went up to the Leach Hotel and there I met Mr. Dillon, the owner of the Niobrara Ranch, sold my horse to him for $80, purchased a new suit, got a shave and haircut, bought my ticket to Texas, and left that night at 11:30 o'clock for Kansas City.

On November 6th I landed in Austin, Texas, thirty miles from my home, and took the stage the next morning for Lockhart. That was where my best girl lived, and when I got there I was happy.

This was the end of a perfect trip from Nebraska on the South Platte to Red Cloud Agency, North Dakota.

FIRST CAMP MEETING IN GRAYSON COUNTY

From "Fruits and Flowers," by Z. N. Morrell

At the end of the conference year, 1847, the Rev. Mr. Brown, assisted by the Presiding Elder, Rev. Mr. Custer, held a camp meeting at Warren, in Grayson County. Rev. Mr. Duncan, a missionary from the Indian Territory, also assisted in the meeting. A camp meeting in those days was a most important event, and anticipated with intense interest by the settlers far and near. Different motives actuated people to attend camp meetings, and the same rule will apply to all such occasions of later date. Some go out of courtesy, to see and be seen, others regard it as a season of rest and diversion, while many embrace the occasion to gossip, exchange news, see the latest fashions, and make new acquaintances. A few, a chosen few, anticipate the event in God's natural temples, the leafy groves; they feel the "outpourings of the spirit," or experience the magical change of heart, granted through the efficacy of prayer to those who earnestly seek the Divine blessing. But we will go as spectators, mere lookers-on, and take a bird's-eye view of this panorama in the midst of nature. We first see a large shed covered with brush and limbs of trees; this is to shelter the large audience; while heavy boards or logs are to serve as seats. Another slab upheld by stakes driven in the ground and covered by a bearskin is the pulpit; a number of chairs, some split bottom and some covered with rawhide, the hair left on, are for the stewards and ministers expected to be present. The "mourner's bench" has not been forgotten, nor has the straw which is scattered around with a liberal hand. Little brush shanties have been erected all around in convenient places for the camps, and soon the occupants began to arrive. They came "afoot and horseback," riding single or double. On carts and wagons are loaded bedding, cooking utensils and children. Dogs have not been invited, but they come anyway, and make themselves too familiar for comfort, and are all sizes and breeds, from the long-eared deerhound to the common cur. The camp ground begins to assume the appearance of a picnic on a large scale; horses neigh as the newcomers arrive, babies cry, children shout and play and a hum of good-natured conversation, inquiries and greetings all combine to make a vivid and realistic picture in its setting of living green. I said something about fashions, but it was a far-fetched allusion. I wonder if our forefathers and mothers in their coonskin caps and slat sunbonnets worried about the "latest styles" or in their primitive simplicity ever imagined that succeeding generations would lose sight of their humble origin, forget what the foundation of American aristocracy really is, and run to vanity, selfishness, patent spring bottom pants, "rats" and false hair?

It is now approaching the time when the meetings are to commence and to blast or toot the horn which brings the scattered congregation together. Those men who from long habit, carry their rifles with them, lean them against a tree and divest themselves of shot pouch and powder horn. A dog fight or two is settled and the yelping curs sent off to crouch under the wagons; then all gather in and seat themselves on the rough boards. A few youngsters who are habitually thirsty at meeting take a last long drink out of the bucket near the pulpit, put the gourd dipper down rather noisily, then make their way to their mothers, who unceremoniously yank them into a seat and bid them all sit there and be quiet. At last all is still and solemn. Brother Brown raises up his tall form threatening to bring the top of his head and the brush above in violent collision. He casts a searching glance over his audience and finally all are attentive as the occasion requires and he commences in a sonorous voice to line out the hymn:

"Children of the Heavenly King,
As we journey sweetly sing,"—

Here we leave them, confident that Brother Brown, in his fervid zeal, will faithfully warn his interested hearers to flee from the wrath to come.

Thus was the foundation of Methodism in Grayson and adjoining counties. Brother Brown was succeeded by Jefferson Shook and he by Andrew Davis and others, all earnest workers in the cause. The Baptist faith was ably upheld by two brothers by the name of Hiram and James Savage. One lived on Caney Creek and the other on Bois d'Arc, as farmers. They tilled the soil during the week, preaching on Sundays, accomplishing great good on the frontier of Grayson.

The Fourth of July, 1847, was the occasion of a grand barbecue and barn dance at Sherman, and to a great many who attended the festivities this was their first view of the new county seat. A log house about 20 feet square, used for a court house, and a few rods of plowed ground comprised the metropolis from one end to the other. I will leave my readers to picture the contrast of the city then and now. For the barbecue a large brush shed was built, under which were tables loaded with all the delicacies of the season, welcome to all, to eat, drink and be merry without money and without price. The refreshment stand, a rail fence partly built around a barrel of whiskey stood near at hand, while a tin cup did frequent duty for a thirsty crowd. The court house was thrown open to accommodate dancers. Justice took off her spectacles, laid aside her scales, and for once in her life gave herself up to the intoxicating pleasures of the hoedown. Music was furnished by a stalwart darkey perched on a barrel; when he gave out another stood ready to take his place until he could visit the refreshment stand and counteract the effect of the heat and his violent exertions by looking for the bottom of his tin cup.

When we stop and think of the advancement made in every direction since this period of Texas' early settlement, the time seems longer than it really is. When we remember that those pioneers had no newspapers, magazines, or any kind of communication with the outside world, save as came by word of mouth; no telegraph, telephone or railroads, that churches and schools barely struggled into existence after long years of patient waiting, it makes one imagine a pre-Adamite sort of existence and not of a time of sixty years ago. Think of having no thread except that manufactured at home; no matches, a flint their only dependence and a stump in the field set fire to by its spark was their reserve when the fire at the house would accidentally go out; the neighbors literally coming to borrow a shovel of coals.

The faithful historian of the Lone Star State cannot ignore, if he is a loyal chronicler, the honor due early settlers for services rendered as advance guards to the great time of immigration that peopled a prosperous land. It has not been in my power to mention but a very few of the pioneers of Grayson County, but however small the number, they help swell the grand total, and I bespeak their recognition in the annals of the State. The pioneers of a country are deserving a niche in the country's history, and the pioneers who became martyrs to the development of an almost unknown land deserve to have a place in the hearts of its inhabitants. None but the brave and venturesome, energetic and courageous dare penetrate the pathless wilderness and trackless forests, and Texas, with her cultivated fields, untold wealth and beautiful homes, may well enshrine the memory of her noble-hearted pioneer pathfinders, martyrs.

SEVEN TRIPS UP THE TRAIL

By J. F. Ellison, Jr., Fort Cobb, Okla.

J. F. ELLISON

My first trip up the trail was in the year 1869, over the old Fort Arbuckle Trail. I made seven trips in all. In 1876 I worked for Ellison, Dewees, Willett and Maberry, and was on the trail for six months. These men drove out that year fully one hundred thousand cattle. We had our hardships, boys, but when we look back and reflect over those good old times spent in each other's company, and compare those old days to the present time, we

conclude that we had our share of the good things of
life and played well our part in the development and
transformation of a wild country into one of peace,
plenty and prosperity. There are hundreds of the old
boys yet living that we knew in the trail days, and to all
of them I send greetings and good wishes.

THE OLD TRAILERS

Recited by Luther A. Lawhon at the conclusion of his
address, when as representative of Mayor Bell, he wel-
comed to San Antonio the members of the Old Time
Trail Drivers' Association, who had assembled for their
annual reunion, September 9th and 10th, 1919:

You recollect, though white your hair,
    When you came up to see the sights,
And pike a little here and there,
    And wager on the badger fights?

Around the plazas, then alive,
    And found an ample feedin' trough;
You smoked 'em with your forty-five,
    And stood the stern policeman off.

But joys like these will soonest pale;
    The eagle will not long be bound;
So pretty soon you hit the trail,
    That led you to the stampin' ground.

"Back to the ranch—to hell with the towns!"
    You shouted with a savage yell;
You told the boys your ups and downs,
    And some things that you didn't tell.

But, ah, today—alas, the change!
  Those good old times have faded out;
'Tis strange—indeed, 'tis passing strange,
  How all these things have come about.

Now "Coke" and Tango run a race,
  For the honors in the social cup,
And golf and baseball take the place
  Of poker, dice and seven-up.

And when we stroll in friendly way
  To read the signs and see the town,
The jitneys mark us for their prey,
  And aeroplanes may knock us down.

The city's lit with 'lectric lights
  That blaze and blind us as we pass;
No more we note, in rooms at nights,
  The warning, "Don't blow out the gas."

But we still have John Blocker here,
  And Ike T. Pryor, good and stout;
And they'll come down—you never fear—
  With what we need to help us out.

And we've George Saunders, too, today;
  He'll hand us up the welcome ten,
Which we'll remit without delay,
  And which he'll never see again.

Sweet are the whispered words of love;
  And sweet the poet's honied rhymes;
But sweeter far, where'er we rove,
  The memories of those good old times!

Such are the scenes that we recall;
  And still, perchance, for them we mourn;
But have a good time—one and all,
  For, fellers, San Antonio's your'n.

—By courtesy of Jos. G. McCoy, the Pioneer Western Cattle Shipper—Published in 1874.

KILLING AND CAPTURING BUFFALO IN KANSAS

By M. A. Withers of Lockhart, Texas

I was born in Monroe County, Missouri, September 23, 1846. I came to Texas with my parents and settled in Caldwell County in November, 1852 or 1853, and have lived in the same county ever since.

M. A. WITHERS

In 1859, when I was only thirteen years old, I made my first trip on the trail. I went with a herd of cows and calves from Lockhart to Fredericksburg, Tex. The cattle were sold to Tom and Sam Johnson by George Haynes at $3.00 per head.

My next trip, in 1862, was from Lockhart, Texas, to Shreveport, La., with a herd of steers for the Confederate States government. George Haynes was the contractor and S. H. Whitaker was the boss. After arriving at Shreveport a herd of steers, too poor for Confederate soldiers to eat, was delivered to us to be driven to the Brazos River and turned loose on the range. I rode one horse on this entire trip. I was to get two dollars per day and board. I got the board, consisting of cornbread, bacon, and sometimes coffee, but I never got the two dollars per day promised me. On my return to Lockhart I joined the Confederate Cavalry and served to the end of the war in Company I, 36th Texas Cavalry.

I left Lockhart, Texas, April 1, 1868, with a herd of 600 big wild steers. The most of them belonged to my father, brothers and myself. I bought some of them at

$10.00 per head to be paid for when I returned from the drive. I had eight hands and a cook, all of whom are dead except myself. We crossed the Colorado River at Austin, the Brazos River at Waco, the Trinity River where Fort Worth now is. Only one or two stores were there then. We crossed the Red River where Denison now is, and the Arkansas River at Fort Gibson, then traveled up the north side of the Arkansas River to Wichita, Kansas, which then consisted of a log house used for a store.

Before we reached Wichita I went several miles ahead of the herd and stopped at a large lake to get a drink of water and water my horse. Suddenly my horse became restless and when I looked up I saw seven Osage Indians coming helter-skelter straight for me. Maybe you think I wasn't scared, but I surely was. I could not run for the lake was on one side and the Indians on the other. I thought my time had come. They ran their horses up to me and stopped. All had guns, and I thought they were the largest ones I had ever seen. There I was with my back to the lake and with only my horse between me and the Indians, who were looking at me.

After looking at me for a few minutes, the big chief held out his hand and said "How," and then asked for tobacco. I did not give my hand, but I gave him all the tobacco I had. It was a great relief to me when I saw them whirl their horses and leave in as big a hurry as they came.

A few days later we killed and barbecued a beef. Early the next morning one of the boys, who was with the herd, came running into camp and shouting, "Indians! Indians!" We looked up and saw about thirty Osage Indians coming as fast as their horses could run straight for our camp. Each Indian gave the customary greeting, "How," and all placed their guns around a tree. They made short work of our barbecued meat, and then began to pick up the things scattered about the wagon.

They asked us to give them a beef and we gladly gave them a "stray." They butchered it and immediately began to eat it. While they were thus engaged we moved the herd away as quickly as possible.

We continued our journey to Abilene, Kansas, reaching there about July 1, 1868. Between Wichita and Abilene we found the skull of a man with a bullet hole in the forehead. Whose skull it was we never knew. After reaching Abilene we established our summer camp on the Chatman Creek, twelve miles north of Abilene, Kansas. We discharged four hands and kept the others to range-herd the cattle until fall, when I sold the steers to W. K. McCoy & Bros. of Champagne, Illinois, for $28.00 per head. The cattle were worth from $8.00 to $10.00 per head in Texas and the expenses were about $4.00 per head. The steers were not road-branded and we reached there with a full count. I received $1,000 in cash and the remainder in drafts on Donald Lawson & Co., of New York City, signed by W. K. McCoy & Bros. One of these drafts for a small amount was never paid and I still have it in my safe. I would like to collect it now with compound interest.

On our trip from Lockhart, Texas, to Abilene, Kansas, we found plenty of grass and water. The cattle arrived in Abilene in fine condition and were rolling fat when sold.

After selling out we bought new wagons and harness and made work horses out of our cow ponies. We sent the boys through Arkansas and loaded the wagons with red apples. After reaching Texas they placed an apple on a twig on the front end of the wagon and began to peddle them. They received a fine price for those that they did not eat or give away to the girls along the road.

I went from Abilene, Kansas, to St. Louis, Mo., and took the last steamer down the Mississippi River which would reach New Orleans before Christmas. It took eleven days to make the trip, for the boat stopped at every landing and added chickens, turkeys, ducks, etc., to her cargo. There was a dance on deck each night except Sunday night. I came from New Orleans to Galveston, Texas, by steamer; from Galveston to Columbus by train, and from Columbus to Lockhart by stage, and arrived at home on Christmas day, 1868.

In the summer of 1868 I was chosen to go with Joe G. McCoy and a party to Fossil Creek Siding on the Kansas Pacific Railway for the purpose of roping buffalo bulls to be sent East as an advertisement. It had been found that by advertising a large semi-monthly public sale of stock cattle to take place at the shipping yards at Abilene, Kansas, a ready market had been found for the stock cattle. Buyers were also needed for grown cattle. The plan adopted to call attention to the fact was to send East a carload of wild buffaloes, covering the side of the car with advertisements of the cattle. But how to get the buffaloes was the next point to be considered.

The slats of an ordinary stock car were greatly strengthened by bolting thick planks parallel with the floor and about three feet above it to the side of the car. One-half dozen horses, well trained to the lasso, were placed in one car and in the other were six men with supplies. Both cars departed for the buffalo region. In the party chosen were four Texas cowboys, Jake Carroll, Tom Johnson, Billy Campbell and myself, also two California Spaniards, all experts with the rope.

On the afternoon of our arrival on the buffalo range we started out to capture our first buffalo. After riding for a short while, we saw a moving object in the distance which we supposed was the desired game. We followed and saw that it was a man after an animal. We thought it was an Indian after a buffalo.

All of us, with the exception of Tom Johnson, who rode away to the right, started in pursuit of the desired game. We soon discovered what we supposed was an

Indian and a buffalo was a white man driving a milch cow to the section house. He ran to the section house and told them that the Indians had chased him and were coming straight to the house. He said that one long-legged Indian riding a white horse tried to spear him. The supposed Indian on the white horse was none other than Tom Johnson, who was about four hundred yards away from the man. When we reached the section house, the men had barricaded themselves in the dugout await-ing the arrival of the Indians. They supposed we were Indians until we were close enough for them to tell we were white men. They came out and told us what the frightened man had told them.

During our hunt we had to guard our horses at night from the savages. We saw three small parties of In-dians, and one bunch gave some of us a little chase over the prairie.

The next morning after our arrival we spied seven buffalo bulls on the north side of the Saline River and preparations were made to capture them. Two of them refused to cross the river, and when I attempted to force one to cross he began to fight and I shot him with my Navy six-shooter. This was the first buffalo I ever killed. The others were started in the direction of the railway and when in several hundred yards of it two of them were captured. The two Spaniards roped one and Billy Campbell and I roped the other one. The buffalo charged first at one and then the other of us. He would drop his head, stiffen his neck, and await for us to come near him, then chase one of his captors until there was no hope of catching him, then turn and go after the other.

When he was near the track a third rope was placed around his hind legs and in a moment he was laying stretched out on the ground. Our well-trained horses watched his movements and kept the ropes tight. After he ceased to struggle his legs were tied together with short pieces of rope, then the lariats were taken off and the buffalo was lifted into the car by means of a block and tackle. One end was fastened to the buffalo's head and the other to the top of the car on the opposite side. After his head was securely bound to a part of the car frame his feet were untied. Sometimes the buffalo would sulk for hours after being loaded and show no desire to fight.

In about a week we captured twenty-four buffalo bulls. Some of them died from heat and anger caused by capture, others became sullen and laid down before they were gotten near the cars, and only twelve were successfully loaded and started on the road to Chicago.

It was very interesting to see how well trained were the horses. They seemed to know what movements to make to counteract those of the captured animal. It was almost impossible to entangle them in the rope, for they knew by experience the consequences of being entangled.

After hanging upon each side of the cars an advertisement of the cattle near Abilene, they were sent to Chicago via St. Louis, causing much newspaper comment. Upon reaching Chicago the buffalo were sent to the Fair Grounds, where the two Spaniards, Billie Campbell and I roped them again to show the people how it was done. This advertisement feat was followed by an excursion of Illinois cattlemen to the West. The people were taken to the prairie near Abilene and shown the many fine herds of cattle. Several people invested in these cattle, and in a short time the market at Abilene assumed its usual life and activity. The year of 1868 closed with Abilene's success as a cattle market of note. Soon Texas cattle became in great demand for packing purposes.

Later in the fall of the same year, 1868, I went on a hunt with a party about seventy-five miles south of Abilene to the valley between the Big and Little Arkansas Rivers, where we saw countless numbers of buffalo. As far as we could see the level prairies were black with buffaloes. The grass was eaten off as smooth as a floor behind these thousands of animals. We killed all we wanted in a very short time.

In 1872 on the Smoky River near Hays City, Kansas, while with a herd of cattle we had a big stampede. While running in the lead of the steers I saw by a flash of lightning that I was on the edge of a big bluff of the river. There was nothing left for me to do but jump, so I spurred my horse and landed in the river, which had three or four feet of water in it. Neither my horse nor I was hurt, although some of the steers were killed and many crippled.

While riding that same horse that fall in Nevada, he fell into a prospector's hole full of snow, and both of us had to be pulled out.

On this same trip between Fort Steele on the North Platte River and Independence Rock on the Sweetwater, we crossed a desert which was seventy miles across. There was no grass or water except some alkali lakes, which were not good for man or beast. On the banks of one of these lakes I found what I thought were pretty rocks. I picked up a few and later showed them to a jeweler, who told me that they were moss agates and that they made fine sets for rings or pins and were very valuable.

Soon after crossing the desert two of our men quit, and as we were far from any human habitation and in an Indian country, I have often wondered what became of them. We found game of all kinds, fine grass and water on this trip. The Indians made two attempts to get our horses, but they did not succeed. I sold this herd of 3,400 two-year-old steers and heifers to Tabor & Rodabush at $20.00 per head, delivered at Humbolt Wells, Nevada. I also sold the horses to them at the same price. Our horses gave out and we walked most of the last five hundred miles. Bart Kelso of Pleasanton, Texas, was with me on this trip.

While following the trail I was in a number of storms.

During a storm in 1882, while I was delivering cattle to Gus Johnson, he was killed by lightning. G. B. Withers, Johnson and I were riding together when the lightning struck. It set Johnson's undershirt on fire and his gold shirt stud, which was set with a diamond was melted and the diamond was never found. His hat was torn to pieces and mine had all the plush burned off of the top. I was not seriously hurt, but G. B. Withers lost one eye by the same stroke that killed Johnson.

I followed the trail from 1868 to 1887. I bought cattle in Texas and New Mexico and drove them to Kansas, Colorado, Nebraska, North and South Dakota, Montana, Oregon, Wyoming, Utah, Idaho and Nevada. My first herd numbered 600 Texas steers. The largest herd I ever drove from Texas was 4,500 steers, which I drove from Fort Griffin, Texas, to Dobie Walls in what was then known as "No Man's Land." These cattle were sold to Gus Johnson.

At different times while driving cattle to Northern markets I had as partners Bill Montgomery, George Hill, Dr. John G. Blanks, Dick Head and Jesse Presnall. Some years we had five or six herds, each herd numbering from 2,000 to 3,000 steers. At first we could buy cattle in Texas on time and sell them in Kansas and the territories for cash, but the last few years I drove we had to pay cash for cattle and sell to Northern buyers on credit, and then I quit the trail.

I had a number of flattering offers to remain North in the cattle business, but I loved Texas so well that I always returned after each drive.

ON THE TRAIL TO NEBRASKA

By Jeff D. Farris of Bryan, Texas

I was born in 1861 on a farm in Madison County, Texas. My parents had moved to the country from Walker County in 1858. They originally came from Tennessee to Texas in 1850. When my father located in Madison County there were only seven white men in the neighborhood where he located. My wife's father hauled the first load of iron that was put on the ground to build up our state penitentiary, which now covers twenty acres of ground. As I grew up I remained on the small farm we cultivated, and in the spring I gathered wild horses and helped brand cattle until 1881, when I went to Bryan with a bunch of cattle, where I found an outfit going to Kansas with a herd belonging to Colonel Jim Ellison of San Marcos. Tom Taylor was the boss and I decided to go along with this outfit and see some of the country that I had heard so much about. I have been told that Tom still lives at Uvalde.

We had 2,500 head to drive and a force of ten men, some of whose names I can't recall. One was named Hamby, and a one-armed boy named Hugh Strong. We went north from Bryan to Cleburne and Fort Worth, and crossed the Red River in Montague County. Just below old Fort Sill we struck the trail for Fort Dodge, Kansas, and passed through the Indian Territory. There was no Oklahoma in those days. When we reached Fort Dodge we continued north until we came to the South Platte River, and from there to Ogallala, Nebraska, on the north side of the river, where I quit the outfit and came home. Ogallala was the town where Sam Bass, the noted outlaw, made his headquarters after holding up the Union Pacific. He later came to Texas and was killed by the Rangers at Round Rock.

I remained at home until the spring of 1883, when I went to Hearne, Texas, and struck out with an outfit going to San Angelo, in Tom Green County. We left Hearne about the 10th of May and reached San Angelo the later part of July.

In 1885 I married the sweetest woman in all the country and to our union were born five boys and three girls, all of whom are living except one. I am living within half a mile of where I was born.

ECHOES OF THE CATTLE TRAIL

By Jerry M. Nance of Kyle, Texas

I left Hays County, Texas, on April 15th, 1877, bound for Cheyenne, Wyoming, with 2,100 cattle, forty head of ponies and two yoke of oxen with the chuck wagon. The country was open, no fences to bother us. We crossed the Colorado about four miles below Austin, and went through Belton. We camped one night near Belton, and while there it came a heavy rain. From here we moved out several miles the next morning to where there was grass, and where we stopped for breakfast. After we had been there about an hour I saw a man ride up and begin looking over the herd. After he had looked through closely he came over to the camp and I asked him if he found any of his cattle in the herd. He said no. I asked him to get

JERRY M. NANCE

down and have breakfast with us, explaining that our breakfast was late on account of leaving Belton so early that morning to get out where there was grazing for the cattle. He said he lived where we had camped the night before, and when we got up the next morning he did not see his small bunch of cattle and thought we had driven them off with our herd. He probably found them when he returned home. We crossed the Brazos above Waco. The river was on a rise and it was so wide that all of the cattle were in the river swimming at the same time, and it looked as if I had no cattle at all, for all we could see was the horns. A boat helped us get the chuck wagon across. One of the boys was taken sick the next day, and went back home. When we reached Fort Worth, then a small village, we bought enough supplies from York & Draper to carry us through to Dodge City, Kansas.

We crossed the Red River at Red River Station, into the Indian Territory. After leaving this point we saw no more white people, except those with herds, until we reached Dodge City. When we reached the Washita River it was up and hard to cross. There I met Joel Collins of Goliad. He had just crossed and had made a raft of three big logs tied together with ropes. I exchanged some of my ropes for his raft and used it in ferrying my stuff across. The next day I put the cattle to swimming the river, which had a very swift current. At first they would not take the water, but I cut off bunches of about seventy-five to a hundred and put them to moving Indian fashion and shoved them right off into the water. Some of them would turn and try to come back, but the swift current had carried them down to where the steep banks on this side kept them from coming out, and they had to go across. I crossed the whole herd in this manner. We had but little trouble in getting the horses across. One of the boys had a mule in the outfit which had a pair of hopples tied around his neck, and in swimming the mule passed near a willow limb that had

been broken off by the cattle, and this limb had caught
the hopples on the mule's neck and held him there swimming in the water. I told the man who owned the mule
that unless the hopples were cut loose the animal would
drown. It was a dangerous undertaking, but he plunged
in and cut the hopples, and the mule swam across. From
here we made the trip all right until we reached the North
Canadian, which was also on a rise and all over the bottom lands. We waited for several days for the flood
waters to subside, but all to no use. In the meantime
other herds had come in sight and, for fear of bad nights
and a mix-up, I decided to make a raft and go across.
The cattle were started across and were going fine, when
it came up a terrific hailstorm, which interrupted the
proceedings. One man was across on the other side of
the river, naked, with his horse and saddle and about half
of the herd and the balance of us were on this side with
the other half of the herd and all the supplies. There was
no timber on our side of the river, and when the hail
began pelting the boys and myself made a break for the
wagon for shelter. We were all naked, and the hail came
down so furiously that within a short time it was about
two inches deep on the ground. It must have hailed considerably up the river, for the water was so cold we could
not get any more of the herd across that day. We were
much concerned about getting help to the man across the
river. We tried all evening to get one of the boys over,
to carry the fellow some clothes and help look after the
cattle, but failed in each attempt. We could not see him
nor the cattle on account of the heavy timber on the other
side, and the whole bottom was covered with water so
that it was impossible for him to come near enough to
hear us when we called him. The water was so cold that
horse nor man could endure it, and in trying to cross over
several of them came near drowning and were forced to
turn back, so the man on the other side had to stay over
there all night alone and naked. I was afraid the Indians

would run the cattle off, but they did not molest them. Next morning everything was lovely and our absent man swam back to us after he had put the cattle in shape. He had a good saddle blanket which he said had kept him comfortable enough during the night. While we were getting the balance of the cattle across one of my Mexican hands suffered three broken ribs and a fractured collar bone by his horse falling with him. Some movers who were waiting for the river to fall, agreed to convey the Mexican to Fort Reno, twenty miles away, for me. At Fort Reno an army surgeon patched him up, and he remained there until the following September, when he came back home.

On the 8th of June, while we were on the Salt Fork, a cold norther blew up, accompanied by rain, and it soon became so cold we had to stop driving about three o'clock in the afternoon and gather wood for the night. We undertook to hold our cattle that night in the open, but it was so cold that we finally drifted them close to the river where there was a little protection, and kept a man on guard to look after them. About daybreak they stampeded, but we soon caught them without loss of a single head. Eight ponies belonging to other herds near us froze to death that night.

We crossed the Arkansas River at Dodge, but stopped there one day only, for supplies. At this place we saw a number of Texas cattlemen who were waiting for their herds.

We crossed the Platte River at Ogallala, Nebraska, and still had a long stretch to cover to reach Cheyenne. Near Julesburg we came to a stone dam across a little creek. There was no sign of a habitation near this dam, and why it was placed there, and who constructed it, was beyond my comprehension.

We reached Cheyenne some time in July, after having been on the trip for about three months. We sold our cattle and ponies and took the railroad for home.

I also drove another herd of two thousand head of cattle from Hays County in 1880 to Dodge City, Kansas. We crossed the Colorado at Webbersville, and after crossing Brushy Creek near Taylor, we struck camp. Just before sundown two men drove up in a wagon, and one of them, who had been drinking, ordered us to move on, saying we could not camp there. I told him he had arrived too late, for we were going to remain right there. He said he would get the sheriff to come and move us, and as he was standing up in the back end of his wagon he fell out when the driver started the team. He turned a complete somersault and fell hard upon the ground. If he had been sober I am sure he would have broken his neck. Picking himself up, he clambered back into his wagon and drove on amid the yells and whoops of my boys. That was the last we saw of him.

After we crossed Gabriel, the other side of Taylor, we turned west and went by Lampasas, and quit the trail on account of water. We passed through Comanche and struck the trail again in Brown County. When we reached Fort Griffin we purchased supplies to last us until we reached Dodge, Kansas. We crossed the Brazos high up where there was not much water in it, and the water it did contain was so salty our cattle would not drink it. At Doan's Store we crossed Red River when it was very low, and I was glad of it. We drove on through the Territory until we reached Dodge. We were bothered some by Indians on this trip.

In 1881 I sold a herd of two thousand head of cattle to be delivered at Ogallala, Nebraska, on the Platte River. I did not go up the trail with this herd that year.

In 1883 I became part owner in a ranch in Jeff Davis County. I shipped my cattle out there and ranched them ten years with the Toyah Land & Cattle Company. In 1885 I drove three thousand steer yearlings out there, which I bought at Columbus, Texas. We went by way of Blanco, Fredericksburg, Mason, San Angelo, up the

Main Concho and across the plains to Fort Stockton. We also had ninety ponies along. That was too many cattle to have in one herd, and they did not do well. Water was scarce and, being late in the season, one sixty-mile drive from the head of the Concho to the Pecos River without water, was a pretty hard trip, worse than going to Kansas.

In 1887 we shipped two thousand head from the ranch to Big Springs, and drove them across to Coolidge, Kansas, where we sold them out. Part of them were shipped west to Pueblo, Colorado, and part of them were driven back to Fort Sill in the Indian Territory, and delivered there.

In 1888 we drove two thousand head to Panhandle City. We sold some of them to be delivered above Amarillo, and the remainder were driven on to Kiowa and sold there. In driving this herd across the plains from the Pecos River to Warfield, a station ten miles west of Midland, I had made arrangements with a ranchman at Warfield to have enough water pumped up for two thousand head of cattle. He had a windmill and troughs for watering and charged five cents per head. We could water only about one hundred and fifty head at a time, so it took some time to water them all. When we had the last bunch in the pen late that evening a heavy hailstorm and rain came up and scattered our herd. Everybody stayed with the herd, which began to drift with the storm's course. Some of the boys used blankets and heavy gloves to protect their heads. We had one bald-headed man in the outfit, and when the hailstorm was over he was a sight to behold. He had welts and bruises all over, and lots of hide had been peeled off. The hail had beaten the grass into the ground and killed lots of jackrabbits in the vicinity. We lost about a hundred head of cattle during the storm, and they were the last ones to water in the pen. We found them the next day several miles away.

In the fall of 1888 we shipped about two thousand head to Colorado City and Sweetwater to winter on account of no grass at the ranch, and in the spring of 1889 we gathered them to ship out. Those at Colorado City were put in a small five-section pasture for a few days before shipping them north. While they were in this little pasture a cyclone came along and killed about one hundred and fifty, two to five-year-old steers and crippled about a hundred others for us. The cyclone was only about one hundred yards wide and went through about a mile of pasture, leaving everything trimmed clean in its path. Even the mesquite switches had all the bark pulled off. Deer, rabbits, owls, snakes, and many other animals were to be found in its wake.

REMINISCENCES OF OLD TRAIL DRIVING

By J. M. Hankins, 2923 South Presa Street,
San Antonio, Texas

I was born in 1851 near Prairie Lea, in Caldwell County, Texas, and remember when the Civil War began and the many hard trials experienced during that period.

It was in 1868 that I recall the first herd of cattle driven from Prairie Lea "up the trail," though possibly Colonel Jack Myers and others at Lockhart had driven earlier. That year Baker & Duke, merchants, bought some steers and exchanged merchandise for them. Father and others put in a few head, and I put in a five-year-old steer, for which I received a pair of shoes, a straw hat and a linen coat, the value of all being about ten dollars, but I was fully rigged out for Sunday wear, and was satisfied with the deal.

After 1868 the drives became general and large herds could be seen on the Lockhart trail from March to August. I very often helped local buyers get up bunches of Kansas cattle, as they were called, and in 1871 I was employed by Smith Brothers at Prairie Lea to go "up the trail." I furnished my own mounts, three corn-fed horses, which they agreed to feed until grass came. We left Prairie Lea the latter part of February for San Miguel Creek, went to San Antonio, and expected to be absent about thirty days. We failed to gather the cattle we expected to on the San Miguel, so we were ordered to move on to the Nueces River, where Jim and Tobe Long and others put up a herd for them. We got back to the San Marcos River about the 15th of May, without having had a bushel of corn for our horses after leaving San Antonio. The country was very dry, no water from one river to the other, no grass nearer than three miles out. Those who worked soon got afoot. Between the Cibolo and Guadalupe Rivers I swapped horses twice in one day, the last time with a negro, and got a small pony which seemed to be fat. That was all I saw until he took his saddle off, when a foot of hide stuck to the blanket. The boys set up a big laugh, but I "scaffold" up, threw my "hull" on and galloped around the herd. It beat walking and punching the "dogies" at the rear. I was promoted right then to the flank.

That night I experienced the first stampede. Early in the night it had rained, and I was on the watch. The herd began drifting, and the boss and several others came out to help with the cattle, and after the rain ceased we got them stopped, when Rany Fentress, a negro who had been in stampedes before, came to where I was in the lead and told me to move further away. About that time some of the boys struck a match to light a pipe, and the flare frightened the big steers and they began to run. I was knocked down three times, but managed to stay with the pony, and came out with the drags, which I stayed with until daylight.

After we crossed the San Marcos River the boys began leaving for home, but I remained until the boss said

I could not go until the others returned. At this I re-
belled, "cut my bedding," rounded up my "crow bait"
and pulled out for home, where I stayed two days.
Father insisted that I go back. I told him I had nearly
killed three horses, which they never fed as they agreed
to. But I went back with a fresh mount and got "fired"
just as the herd was ready to start on the trail. Smith
Bros. went "busted" that year.

In 1874 I left home again in February with Ellison &
Dewees, with young Jim Ellison as boss. We went to
San Antonio, where we received a bunch of cow ponies,
and then established camp near the Cibolo, where the
Lowe cattle were received and started. Our camp was
the catch and cut-out for all the other bosses. Young
Jim Ellison took the first herd with all negro hands about
the 9th of March. Jim Rowden took the second herd,
and so on, until all the Lowe cattle were received and
started. Our outfit then went to Burnett County and
received our herd from Oatman, mostly wild mountain
steers.

When we were nearing Red River we threw in with
Peter Smith, making one large herd, with which I stayed
until we arrived at Dodge City, Kansas. Our trip was
like most others, sometimes good, and at other times
pretty tough, especially when the cattle stampeded during stormy nights and mixed with other herds, causing
no end of worry and trouble and often forcing us to go
without our breakfast until 10 or 11 o'clock the next day.
But as soon as we were filled with frijoles and black
coffee, and the sun shone clear, we were jolly and happy
again.

One little incident during a run on a stormy night was
amusing. The cattle had been running most of the night,
but at last they had quieted down. We saw a light a
short distance away swinging around, and heard a voice
calling out to us. We supposed it was the cook, and the
boss said some ugly words about the cook screaming at

us, and sent a man into the herd to find out what he wanted. It turned out to be a man standing on the top of his dug-out, and he was in great distress. The cattle had crushed in the roof of his domicile and one had fallen through his bedroom and disturbed his peaceful slumbers.

The country was wild and unsettled then, and from the Red River to the Kansas line was known as the Indian Territory. Montague was the last town I saw until we reached Great Bend, Kansas. I might add incidents, but as short sketches for this book are expected, will say to all the old cow-punchers and trail drivers of Texas that I will be glad to meet any of you and talk about the old times and the pioneers of Texas.

GOT "WILD AND WOOLLY" ON THE CHISHOLM TRAIL

By J. N. Byler of Dallas, Texas

I was raised in East Texas and worked cattle back in the piney woods and canebrakes of that region. Went West after the Civil War and worked cattle there. The range was at that time somewhat overstocked with beef cattle and bulls. A great many of the old bulls were shipped over to Cuba, and supplied the natives there with beef. In getting them ready to ship the cowboys would rope them on the range, throw them down, and chop the points of their horns off with an axe to keep them from hurting each other on the boats. In those days beef cattle on the range were worth about $10 per head. A few were driven to Lousiana.

In 1866 Monroe Choate and B. A. Borroum drove a herd to Iowa to find a market. They crossed Red River at Colbert's Ferry, went by way of Boggy Depot, crossed the Arkansas at Fort Gibson, and then struck west of the settlements of Kansas.

In 1867 Butler, Baylor & Rose drove a herd to Abilene, Kansas, as did also Pucket & Rogers.

In 1868 the drives were pretty heavy, but further west, crossing Red River at Gainesville. In 1869 and 1870 they were heavier still, most of the herds crossing at Red River Station, passing east of old Fort Sill and west of the Indian and negro settlements, over which route water and grass were plentiful. This was known as the old Chisholm Trail. When we reached Kansas we usually found plenty of buffalo. When these animals were disturbed they would begin to travel northward. That is where the expression "wild and woolly" originated. When the boys reached Abilene or some other Kansas town, they were usually long-haired and needing a barber's attention, as there were no barbers on the trail. Upon being asked how they got there, they would sing out: "Come the Chisholm trail with the buffalo wild and woolly."

WITH HERDS TO COLORADO AND NEW MEXICO

By G. W. Scott of Uvalde, Texas

I was born at Comfort, Texas, September 3, 1871, and was raised on a ranch. In 1876 my father moved to Coleman County, but in 1877 he moved to Frio County and bought a farm. In 1888 I came to Uvalde, and in the spring of 1890 I hired to Paul Handy of Colorado to drive a herd to that state. We left the Plank Pens on the Leona Ranch south of Uvalde on March 10 with our herd, numbering 2,221 two-year-old steers, sixty-four horses and eleven men, including the cook. We crossed the Nueces and camped the first night in the Moore & Allen pasture. After six or eight days our herd was easily controlled, especially at night. Grass and water were plentiful, and we had an easy time until we reached

Fort McKavett, where I accidentally caused the cattle
to stampede one moonlight night. From here we drove
to San Angelo and stopped one night near that town,
which at that time was a wide-open place. Several of
the boys went in to see the sights and have a good time.
We drove our herd across the plains to Quanah, where
we were quarantined for several weeks on account of
Texas fever. While we were here holding our cattle it
came up a severe rainstorm one night and we had another
stampede, the steers going in all directions, running over
wire fences and going across creeks that happened to be
in their course. We had thirteen steers killed by lightning that night. When daylight came I was about four
miles from camp with four hundred head of the steers.
We held these steers at Quanah for seven weeks before
being allowed to proceed on to Colorado.

In 1881 I went with a herd to White Lake, New
Mexico, for James Dalrymple, starting from the Leona
Ranch. Most of the boys in this outfit were from the Frio
Canyon, and I recall the names of Sam Everts, George
Leakey, Tobe Edwards, James Crutchfield, Os Brown,
Allison Davis and Tip Davis. We drove 2,178 two-year-
old steers this trip, crossing the Nueces River at Eagle
Pass crossing. We headed north toward Devil's River,
which we crossed above Paint Cave. At this time the
range was dry and water scarce, and many of our cattle
gave out and had to be left on the trail. We reached
the Pecos River, at the mouth of Live Oak, where we
rested for a few days. We were in the Seven D range
at this time, and Taylor Stevenson was foreman of the
Seven D Ranch, and he brought his outfit and helped us
work up the Pecos from the mouth of Live Oak to Horse
Head Crossing, where we left the thinnest of our cattle
and proceeded on our journey. Our next point was Midland, where we found plenty of fine grass and water.
After leaving Midland we again found a dry range with
no grass. When we reached the Colorado River that

stream was very low. Here I saw my first buffalo, but
it was a tame animal and was branded a long S on each
side. Ed Hagerman of Kimble County was ahead of us
with a herd of the Half Circle L C cattle. After a great
deal of hard luck and trouble we reached Yellow Horse
Draw about ten miles from Lubbock, where we encountered a heavy hailstorm. We had lost a great many
of our cattle on the trip, and the sudden change chilled
a number of others to death as well as five saddle horses.
We left camp at this point with only 1,072 head. We
reached White Lake, New Mexico, on June 21, and delivered to Mr. Handy. Here we found Ham Bee and
his outfit and accompanied them back to Midland, where
we took the train for Uvalde.

RECOLLECTIONS OF OLD TRAIL DAYS

By B. A. Borroum of Del Rio, Texas

My first experience on the
trail was in the year 1870.
About the first of April of
that year I started from Monroe Choate's Ranch in Karnes
County with a herd of cattle
belonging to Choate & Bennett. E. B. Rutledge was the
boss and part owner. Among
the hands were Jesse Mc-
Carty, Drew Lamb, George
Blackburn, John Strait, and
one or two others whose
names I have forgotten. Go-

B. A. BORROUM

ing north all the time, we crossed the Guadalupe at Gonzales, the Colorado at Austin, the Brazos at Old Fort
Graham, the Trinity at Fort Worth, Red River at Red

River Station, the Washita at Dr. Stearn's, the Red Fork near Turkey Creek Stage Stand in Kaw Reservation, the Salt Fork at Cow Creek Station, the Arkansas at Wichita, the Smoky at Abilene, Kansas, which was our destination, and where we arrived about July first.

Like many others, when I had work for the time being I did not think I would ever make another trip up the trail, but also like many others, when the next drive came I was " 'rarin'' to go. In the spring of 1871 I again went up with a herd belonging to Choate & Bennett, with Jack Scroggin as boss and part owner. The hands on this trip were W. M. Choate, John Paschal, Monroe Stewart, Joe Copeland, John Ferrier, myself and John Sumner, the cook. We started from Rock Creek, Atascosa County, about the first of April and traveled the same trail after coming into it at Gonzales through to Abilene. We went into the Chisholm Trail about three miles below Red River Station, and just as soon as we crossed Red River all our stock seemed to go wild, especially our horses, although we did not come into contact with any buffalo until we reached a point between the Red Fork and the Salt Fork of the Arkansas River. Several herds lost heavily at that time by cattle and horses getting into the buffalo drifts, which were at that season drifting northward. These animals were in countless numbers; in fact, the whole face of the earth seemed to be literally covered with them, all going in the same direction. The drovers were compelled to send men on ahead to keep them from stampeding their herds. On a plain about halfway between the Red Fork and the Salt Fork we had to stop our herds until the buffalo passed. Buffalo, horses, elk, deer, antelope, wolves, and some cattle were all mixed together, and it took several hours for them to pass, with our assistance, so that we could proceed on our journey. I think there were more buffalo in that herd than I ever saw of any living thing, unless it was an army of grasshoppers in Kansas in July, 1874. Just after we crossed the Red Fork I went on ahead of the herd to the Trinity Creek Stage Stand, a distance of about six miles, and at this place I found the present president of the Old Trail Drivers' Association, George W. Saunders, surrounded by a big bunch of Kaw Indians. George was mounted on a little gray bob-tailed pony, his saddle had no horn, and one stirrup leather was made of rawhide and the other was a grass hopple. He was trying his best to trade those Indians out of a buffalo gun, as he was in the buffalo range. And he made the deal. I never saw him again until after we reached Kansas, when the drovers made up an outfit to bring their horses back to Texas. George and I were in this outfit and we came back the trail we had gone up, except we crossed Red River at Gainesville instead of at Red River Station.

I went up the trail again in 1874, starting from Druce Rachel's ranch on the Nueces Bay in San Patricio County, March 25th. This herd also belonged to Choate & Bennett, with D. C. Choate as boss. We followed the same trail as previously mentioned. After crossing Red River we stopped on the Ninnesquaw for the summer, and shipped out in the fall from Great Bend. The Osage Indians being on the warpath, we had to detour our horses in bringing them back to Texas, crossing the Arkansas River near Coffeyville into the Cherokee, Creek, Choctaw and Chickasaw nations, crossing Red River at Colbert's Ferry near Sherman into Texas.

In the '80s I drove several herds up the western trail to Dodge City, Kansas, for the firm of Borroum & Choate. I think everyone of the boys that went up with the herds mentioned above have passed beyond the Divide from which no mortal returns, except Brown (A. B.), Paschal and myself.

HIGH-HEELED BOOTS AND STRIPED BREECHES

By G. O. Burrows of Del Rio, Texas

I had my share of the ups and downs—principally downs—on the old cattle trail. Some of my experiences

G. O. BURROWS

were going hungry, getting wet and cold, riding sore-backed horses, going to sleep on herd and losing cattle, getting "cussed" by the boss, scouting for "gray-backs," trying the "sick racket" now and then to get a night's sleep, and other things too numerous to mention in this volume. But all of these were forgotten when we delivered our herd and started back to grand old Texas. Have often stopped a few days in Chicago, St. Louis and Kansas City, but always had the "big time" when I arrived in good old Santone rigged out with a pair of high-heeled boots and striped breeches, and about $6.30 worth of other clothes. Along about sundown you could find me at Jack Harris' show occupying a front seat and clamoring for the next performance. This "big time" would last but a few days, however, for I would soon be "busted" and would have to borrow money to get out to the ranch, where I would put in the fall and winter telling about the big things I had seen up North. The next spring I would have the same old trip, the same old things would happen in the same old way, and with the same old wind-up. I put in eighteen or twenty years on the trail, and all I had in the final outcome was the high-heeled boots, the striped pants and about $4.80 worth of other clothes, so there you are.

SIXTY YEARS IN TEXAS

By William J. Bennett of Pearsall, Texas

My father moved to Texas in 1848 from Randolph County, Missouri, and settled on the Trinity River about five miles from Fort Worth, which was at that time an Indian Reservation with Lieutenant Worth in command of the post. There was only one store there then. The Indians often came to my father's house and were friendly to the few white settlers there. Game was plentiful, deer, turkey, buffalo and prairie chickens, as well as the fiercer animals. We lived near Fort Worth four or five years, until father sold out to a man named Parker, and we moved above Fort Worth some twenty miles to Newark. After remaining there a few years we then moved down to Frio County in the fall of 1858 and located on the Leona River, where we found a fine country, with wild game and fish galore. We brought with us about four hundred head of cattle, which were allowed to roam at will over the excellent range, there being no fences to keep them confined to the immediate vicinity of our ranch. But they did not get far away from us for some time, or until other ranchers began to locate around us, when the cattle began to mix with other cattle and then began to stray off, some drifting as far as the Rio Grande or the coast. Soon the settlers began to organize cow hunts and work the cattle. I have been on cow hunts when there were as many as one hundred men working together from different counties. Stockmen of today do not know anything about the hard work and the strenuous times we encountered in those days. Sometimes we would be out for weeks at a time, starting every morning at daylight, and probably not getting in before dark, tired and hungry, and having to do without dinner all day. Our fare consisted of cornbread, black coffee and plenty of good beef.

We were not bothered by the Indians very much until the Civil War, when the troops were largely withdrawn from the frontier posts, and the country was left unprotected. The Indians came in great numbers then, killing many settlers and driving off a great many of their stock. Also Mexican cattle thieves became troublesome, and stole thousands of cattle off the range, which they would drive across the Rio Grande into Mexico. Many of the ranchmen were compelled to take their families back to the settlements for protection. After the Civil War cattle soon became plentiful on the range, and Sam Allen of Powder Horn soon had a monopoly on the shipping by chartering every boat from there to New Orleans. He sent men out all over the country to buy fat cattle, which made times pretty good for a while, but as no one could ship by water except Allen, the demand was soon filled, and in order to reach the market for their stock the cattlemen began driving their cattle to Kansas. In 1872 I took my first herd, starting from Uvalde and going up that long and lonesome trail to Wichita, Kansas. We had a pretty good time going up, with only a few storms and stampedes, and lost no cattle. We crossed the Red River at Red River Station, then took the old Chisholm Trail and went out of the Indian Territory at Caldwell, Kansas. After holding my herd at that point about three months I sold to A. H. Pierce, and came home by way of Kansas City, St. Louis, New Orleans, Galveston, and then to Austin on the new railroad, and from Austin by stage to San Antonio and Uvalde.

In 1873 I took another herd of steers up the trail. Had a pretty hard time that trip and lost many head of cattle and about all I received for them. Nearly all of the Texas cattlemen went broke that year, as it was the year of the severe panic, when silver was demonetized.

During the years 1874 and 1875 occurred what is still remembered by the old-timers as the "Big Steal." Cattle were driven off and the country was left bare. They drove them off in all directions, some to Kansas, Wyoming, Colorado, New Mexico, Arizona and California.

Then came the sheep men with large flocks, and prosperity again smiled upon us. With the advent of the man with the plow, the sheepman moved further west, and the scream of the panther and the howl of the wolf began to give place to the whistle of the locomotive and the hum of the cotton gin. It would require volumes to record all of the hardships and dangers we went through during the sixty years I have lived in the West, and I merely contribute this brief sketch to add my testimony to that of the other pioneers that helped to blaze the trail through the wilderness.

During the Civil War, and for many years after the war, the people of this station hauled their supplies out from San Antonio in ox wagons, and in looking back to those times and comparing them with the present we cannot but discern the great change that has been wrought. Our manner of travel was necessarily slow in those days. Sometimes we were on the trail for four and five months. It usually required three months to take a herd to the Red River. Only a few days ago the papers gave an account of an aviator flying from San Antonio to Oklahoma City, a distance of over six hundred miles, in the short space of three hours! Such a feat was undreamed of in those old days, and if even a prediction of such things happening had been made no one would have believed it would ever come to pass. May we not venture to predict that in another sixty years somebody will have established a trail to Mars or other planets, and our descendants may be signalling the latest market quotations to the cowmen of those parts?

THE GOOD OLD COWBOY DAYS

By Luther A. Lawhon

My fancy drifts as often, through the murky, misty maze
Of the past—to other seasons—to the good old cowboy
  days,
When the grass wuz green an' wavin' an' the skies wuz
  soft and blue,
And the men were brave an' loyal, and the women fair
  an' true!
The old-time cowboy—here's to him, from hired hand to
  boss!
His soul wuz free from envy and his heart wuz free from
  dross,
An' deep within his nature, which wuz rugged, high and
  bold,
There ran a vein uv metal, and the metal, men, wuz gold!

He'd stand up—drunk or sober—'gin a thousand fer his
  rights;
He'd sometimes close an argument by shootin' out the
  lights;
An' when there was a killin', by the quickest on the draw,
He wern't disposed to quibble 'bout the majesty uv law;
But a thief—a low-down villain—why, he had no use for
  him
An' wuz mighty apt to leave 'im danglin' from a handy
  limb.
He wuz heeled and allers ready—quick with pistol or
  with knife,
But he never shirked a danger or a duty in his life!

An' at a tale uv sorrow or uv innocence beguiled
His heart wuz just as tender as the heart uv any child.
An' woman—aye, her honor wuz a sacred thing; an'
  hence
He threw his arms around her—in a figurative sense.

His home wuz yours, where'er it wuz, an' open stood the
   door,
Whose hinges never closed upon the needy or the poor;
An, high or low—it mattered not—the time, if night or
   day,
The stranger found a welcome just as long as he would
   stay.

Wuz honest to the marrow, and his bond wuz in his word.
He paid for every critter that he cut into his herd;
An' take your note because he loaned a friend a little
   pelf?
No, sir, indeed! He thought you wuz as worthy as him-
   self.
An' when you came and paid it back, as proper wuz an'
   meet,
You trod upon forbidden ground to ask for a receipt.
In former case you paid the debt (there weren't no intres'
   due),
An' in the latter—chances wuz he'd put a hole through
   you!

The old-time cowboy had 'is faults; 'tis true, as has been
   said,
He'd look upon the licker when the licker, men, wuz red;
His language weren't allers spoke accordin' to the rule;
Ner wuz it sech as ye'd expect to hear at Sunday school.
But when he went to meetin', men, he didn't yawn or
   doze,
Or set there takin' notice of the congregation's clothes.
He listened to the preacher with respect, an' all o' that,
An' he never failed to ante when they passed aroun' the
   hat!

I call to mind the tournament, an' then the ball at night;
Of how old Porter drawed the bow an' sawed with all his
   might;

Of how they'd dance—the boys an' girls; an' how that
   one wuz there
With rosy cheeks, an' hazel eyes, an' golden, curly hair;
An' I—but here I'm techin' on a mighty tender spot;
That boyhood love, at this late day, had better be forgot;
But still at times my heart goes back agin' and fondly
   strays
Amidst those dear remembered scenes—the good old cow-
   boy days!

The old-time cowboy wuz a man all over! Hear me, men!
I somehow kinder figger we'll not see his like agin.
The few that's left are older now; their hair is mostly
   white;
Their forms are not so active, and their eyes are not so
   bright
As when the grass wuz wavin' green, the skies wuz soft
   an' blue,
An' men were brave, an' loyal, and the women fair and
   true,
An' the land wuz filled with plenty, an' the range wuz
   free to graze,
An' all rode as brothers—in the good old cowboy days!

COURAGE AND HARDIHOOD ON THE OLD
TEXAS CATTLE TRAIL

Sol West, one of the best-known cattlemen in Texas,
who is a part owner of a ranch of 30,000 acres in Jackson County, worked a whole year for 75 cents and board,
when a young man. Mr. West belongs to the old school
of cattlemen. He received his business training in the
early days in Texas when the chief occupation of its
citizenship was raising cattle, but the more difficult proposition was to find a market for them. Texas had no rail-

ways then except in the eastern portion of the state, and
these were not available, for
the reason that they did not
go to Kansas and the Northwest. Men were forced to do
some farming, for they had to
raise corn in order to have
bread.

In the early days an occasional buyer who resided in
Southwest Texas would purchase a herd of 8,000 or 10,000
steers on time. There was no
payment made at the time of
the purchase, for the reason
that the buyer needed all the
money at his disposal to de-

SOL WEST

fray the expense of the drive. The seller did not even
take his note for the purchase price, because he knew he
was dealing with an honest man. The only evidence of
debt was the tally of the cattle, giving the numbers in
each class, including the mark and brand they bore. The
purchaser would head north with them. Sometimes he
would go to Ellsworth, Abilene or Dodge City, Kansas,
or some other point at the southern teminus of railroad transportation where the chief occupation of the
cowboy at times was to see that his shooting irons were
in good working order. Sometimes the herd would be
headed for Montana, Dakota or Nebraska. The seller
did not exact any promise from the purchaser to pay
for the cattle at a certain time, for neither of them
knew whether it would take one, two or three years
for the buyer to dispose of his holdings, and get back to
Texas again. There was always a satisfactory settlement, however, when he returned. If he had the money
to pay for them it was all right, but if he had lost half
of them in a blizzard, the seller did not take his note

for the balance due and insist on its being secured by
a mortgage. The slate was wiped clean and work
began again shipping up another herd on the same
terms.

The trite old saying that "man's inhumanity to man
makes countless thousands mourn" had no place in
the lexicon of the Texas cattlemen in those days. He
was then, as he is now, ready to lend a helping hand to
a deserving fellowman, and he could shed tears as easily
as a woman when his friends were bowed in grief.

It was amid such surroundings that the firm of
McCutcheon & West of Lavaca County, composed of the
late Willis McCutcheon of Victoria and George W. West,
was preparing another herd of cattle to go North. Sol
West, now a resident of San Antonio, was a younger
brother of George W. West. While still a mere stripling
he had made three previous trips up the trail, and the
firm made a deal with him in 1874 to take a herd to
Ellsworth, Kansas, for half the profits. He was the
youngest man who ever "bossed" a herd up the trail.

"It was a trip fraught with some adventure, considerable responsibility, and very little cash," said Mr. West
a few days ago, while he was in the reminiscent mood.
"I was the first man to reach Ellsworth that spring, notwithstanding the trials and tribulations which beset us,
and as a mark of their appreciation, the business men
of the town presented me with a suit of clothes, hat, boots
and, in fact, a new outfit entirely. I stayed around up
there all year, selling a few steers here, a few there.
There never had been such a spree of weather as greeted
us in the Indian Territory on our way up. Myself and
the men got back to Lavaca County about December 1st.
My brother George was the bookkeeper for the firm of
McCutcheon & West, and when I turned over to him the
list of my receipts and expenditures, and what cash I
brought back with me, he proceeded to figure up results.
I had to check it up very carefully to be sure that he made

no mistake. We had agreed on a price for the cattle when I started with them, and I was to have one-half of all they brought over that price, after deducting the expenses incident to the trip. The net profit on the year's work was $1.50, and when my brother handed me the 75c he made some jocular inquiry as to whether I expected to buy a herd of my own, or start a bank with it.

"I left Lavaca County on February 27th, 1874, with the herd, and on the night of the 28th reached Gonzales Prairie, in Gonzales County. On the 1st day of March we crossed the Red River into the Indian Territory without any mishap, having had a splendid drive, with clear, open weather all the way. But this was not to last long. We pushed on north, and late in the afternoon of April 6th we reached Rush Creek, where the two prongs came together just above the trail. The range had been burned off by the Indians and was black, but, being protected by two streams, the grass between these prongs was fine. We stayed there for two days, and on the morning of the 8th took an early start for a camp on Hell Roaring Creek, about fifteen miles further north, which I had selected because grass and water were plentiful there. The cook, with the wagon, had preceded us, but we got in sight of camp about three o'clock in the afternoon. The day had been a bad one, misting rain and snowing lightly all day, with a brisk wind from the north. Just as the head cattle came within about one hundred yards of camp at the foot of some high hills the blizzard broke forth with increased fury. The cattle at once turned their heads to the south and began to drift with the wind. I knew we were in for a bad night of it, and there was not a man in the outfit over 20 years old. We held them back as best we could until after dark. In the meantime the horses ridden by the boys had actually frozen to death, and their riders on them during our progress of about five miles. My horse was the last to go down.

"I had instructed the boys that when the horses went

down they should go back to camp. When I was forced to leave my horse there were two men with me, both on foot, of course. One of them was Charles Boyce of Goliad County, who is now a prosperous stock farmer, and who will easily recall that fearful night. The other was Jake Middlebrack of Lavaca County, who returned to that county with us, but of whom I have lost sight for many years. We finally got the cattle checked, after the wind had subsided a little, and as we had not touched a bite to eat since early morning, we began to cast about for something to break our fast. We had each a box of matches, but our hands were so numb that we could not strike one, even if we could have gotten the box out of our pockets.

"Presently I saw a light in the hills about two miles away. We started for it and reached the dug-out, for such it proved to be, after a weary trudge of an hour or more. The dug-out had two rooms and the men took us in after we told them our hard luck story. They gave us a fine supper and put us to bed in the spare room, with plenty of good warm bedding. The next morning at the peep of day I roused out the boys. I found a dun pony under a shed on the outside with a bridle and saddle convenient and I appropriated it and told the boys to follow me down in the direction of the herd, provided it was where we had left it. They followed me down and I found the herd intact, just where we had left it the night before, after one of the coldest nights I ever experienced.

"Soon after I reached the herd the other boys hove in sight and we started the cattle back towards the camp, the snow, sleet and ice being a foot and a half deep. Hell Roaring Creek and all the other streams in that section were frozen hard. We had traveled a couple of miles down the creek when I discovered a man on foot coming toward us. He proved to be Al Fields of Victoria. He was what was known as my neighbor on the trail, having a herd just behind me. He was overjoyed to see me, as he feared we had all frozen to death that night before. All of his horses and work oxen had frozen to death and his herd was scattered to the four winds. When we finally reached the camp Jim Taylor, the man who had entertained us in the dug-out the night before, and about fifteen of his men, were there.

"Charles Boyce had told me previously that he was not in a very good humor about the plan I had adopted to borrow his horse. I proved to be a good talker, however, and when I got through Jim said he guessed $1.50 would be enough for the use of the horse. I told him that the price was cheap enough, but I didn't tell him there was only ten cents in cash in the whole outfit. I traded him some steers for three horses and a mule, and included the $1.50 in the trade. Our troubles were not to end here, however.

"Two men were behind with the 'remuda' of 65 horses used by the men on alternate days in coming up the trail. I sent two of the boys back to meet them, and led them into camp. Going back about eight miles, they met the men coming toward camp on foot, as the whole 65 head had frozen to death the night before in a space not larger than an ordinary dwelling house, and the boys had only saved themselves from a like fate by building a fire in the blackjack timber and keeping it going all night. We held the herd there for a couple of days with the three horses and the mule, and I traded some steers to the Indians for three more horses. We then started on north and reached Ellsworth on May 20th. This heavy loss of horse flesh was a prominent factor in the hindrance which cut the net profits of the drive down to $1.50. Not a single one out of 78 head of horses survived the terrible blizzard of four or five hours' duration."

Mr. and Mrs. Sol West now reside at 422 Pershing Avenue, San Antonio, Texas. Their two sons, George W. West, Jr., and Ike West, are ranching in Zavalla County, Texas. Their daughter, Mrs. Alfred Pierce

Ward, lives in San Antonio—all enjoying good health and prosperous.

Mr. West made twelve successive trips over the trail from the coast of Texas to Colorado, Kansas, Nebraska and other Northern markets with large herds of Texas cattle. His first trip was in 1871—a good many trips for a boy to make without break, and he didn't ride in any automobiles on these trips.

LIVED ON THE FRONTIER DURING INDIAN TIMES

By Joe F. Spettel, Rio Medina, Texas

I was born in the Haby Settlement in 1856, and have lived in Medina County all my life. My parents were

JOSEPH SPETTEL

Castro colonists and came to this country in 1844, locating in the Haby Settlement. My father, John Spettel, was a "Forty-niner," and went to seek his fortune in the California gold fields. He, with two companions, made quite a lucky strike, but in returning homeward they were overtaken by a band of robbers, his companions were killed and father received a bullet wound which eventually caused his death, although he lived for several years afterward. He came home and remained a while, and again went to California, but did not find mining so successful as on his former trip. However, he brought back some gold nuggets that are still in the possession of our family.

In 1852 he married Miss Mary Haby, and of this union

were born three children, respectively, John B., Mary
and Joseph F. Spettel. My father died in 1857, his early
demise being due to the wound he received while prospecting. My sister became the wife of my partner, Louis
Schorp, and she died in 1905. My brother died in 1909,
so I am the sole survivor of one of the most courageous
men that ever resided in this vicinity, who overcame all
obstacles to penetrate the unknown Western land to accumulate a fortune.

After my father's death my mother had to depend
on hired help, as we were not large enough to take care
of the farm and stock. At this time we had but one horse,
and the Indians stole him. As time went on we began
to prosper, our cattle increased and we had a fine bunch
of saddle horses, but fate was against us, it seemed, for
in 1866 the Indians made another raid in our settlement
and drove off every cow pony we owned. We did not let
this misfortune discourage us, but purchased more horses
and soon were able to take the proper care of our cattle.

During the Civil War we were troubled a great deal
by the soldiers, who would come into the community and
gather up all the able-bodied men and boys. But the
settlers would keep out of their way as much as possible
and hide out their work oxen and horses to keep the soldiers from taking them.

In 1870 the Indians made another raid in our neighborhood, but failed to take any of our horses, as we had
heard of their approach and penned our stock. My uncle
had two horses in a small pasture which he trained to
come home when he whistled to them. That night he
called them up and staked them near the house, armed
himself with a shotgun, concealed himself behind a tree
and waited the results. About one o'clock the horses
began to snort and caper around, and he knew Indians
were near. Looking around he saw three Indians coming along the rail fence in a trot. Just as the Indians
were opposite him the foremost put his head inside the

fence between the upper and second rails, and my uncle
cut down on him with that old shotgun, which was loaded
with buckshot. The Indian dropped in his tracks and his
companions instantly vanished. The following full moon
another raid was made, probably by the same band, but
they did not steal any horses this time. They went into
a field about three hundred yards from home and cut up
many melons. One of our dogs came home with an arrow
sticking in his neck.

During the seventies two companions and myself
drove a hundred fat steers from Medina County to Luling, the nearest railway station, from where they were
loaded and shipped to New Orleans.

In the spring of 1873 I assisted in driving five hundred aged steers from Haby Settlement to a place above
San Antonio, where we delivered them to John F. Lytle
and Bill Perryman, and were met by another herd owned
by the same men, who drove them up the Kansas trail
to Northern markets.

In 1875 Julius Wurzbach, my brother and I put up a
herd of eleven hundred steers for the the firm of Lytle &
McDaniel. It was in charge of Gus Black, who now
resides in Kinney County. We continued to gather herds
for Lytle & McDaniel for several years.

In 1878, while on a round-up near the Medina and
Uvalde county line, one night the Indians made a raid
and tried to steal our horses, but succeeded in getting
only four.

From 1878 to 1887 my brother and I looked after our
stock and sold steers near our home. In 1883 Louis
Schorp married my sister, and we formed a partnership,
and our ranches are still known as the Schorp & Spettel
property. In 1887 we purchased a ranch in Frio County
and drove our aged steers there every fall and shipped
them to market each following June.

MADE A LONG TRIP TO WYOMING

By H. D. Gruene of Goodwin, Texas

In the spring of 1870 William Murchison, who was living on the Colorado River, told me that William Green of Llano and Colonel Myers of Lockhart were getting ready to take a herd of cattle to Kansas, and asked me to go along as he had hired to them. I secured the consent of my father, as I was only nineteen years old at that time, and Bill and I pulled out for Llano, where I was engaged by Mr. Green at $30.00 a month. After several days gathering the cattle we started on our trip with two wagons carrying grub and luggage, going by way of Burnett and Belton, where we had an awful rain one night and all of our cattle got away. We finally succeeded in getting them together without loss of a single head. When we reached Fort Worth the Trinity River was on a rise, and we were compelled to drive our cattle some distance up the river to swim them across. From there we had good going and crossed Red River at Red River Station into the Indian Territory. In the Territory during the rainy nights we had several stampedes, and they came so often we soon got used to them. When we reached Abilene, Kansas, where we were to deliver the cattle, we held the herd for several weeks and were surprised to learn that the cattle would have to be driven to Cheyenne, Wyoming. All of the Texas boys quit the herd and returned home, with the exception of four, myself being one of the number who consented to remain with the outfit. Brace Lincecum of Lockhart was the boss of the bunch that was to take the cattle to Cheyenne. After many days' hard driving we reached our destination. There the cattle were sold to another party who wanted them delivered at Bear River, 110 miles above Salt Lake City, Utah, and our boss, Mr. Lincecum, was

employed to take them there. I went along on condition
that I was to receive $60 per month and that I would
not have to work at the rear of the herd. John Riggs of
Lockhart was my companion on this drive.

We had to take the cattle through the Rocky Mountains, and we found the nights so cold we had to burn
sagebrush to keep warm.

After the cattle were delivered all of the boys were
paid off, and I received my wages in twenty-dollar gold
pieces. We boarded a train to Ogden, where we stopped
off and went to Salt Lake City. There we bought some
new clothes and had a general "cleaning-up," for we
were pretty well inhabited by body lice, the greatest pest
encountered on the trail. The next day we took the train
for Abilene, Kansas, and there we each bought a horse
and rode as far as Baxter Springs, Missouri, where we
met up with some people named Wilks, who were living
at Mountain City, Hays County, Texas. They were returning to Texas, and as they had four wagons, we made
arrangements to travel with them. For our passage and
board we agreed to do the cooking for the crowd. We
finally reached home after a trip that covered nine
months.

The following year (1871) I made another trip, but
went only as far as Kansas City. I had 335 head of
cattle which I put in with a bunch belonging to William
Green. When we reached the end of our trip we found
cattle were selling very cheap, and we had to sell on
credit. The party to whom I sold went broke and I lost
all that was due me. This was my last trip. After a
year at home I married and settled at Goodwin, my present home, where, with much hard labor, in which my wife
bore more than her part, we have prospered and are
living very contented. I am in the mercantile business
and handle lumber and implements as well, besides having a cotton gin, and own some good farms. We have
four children, two boys and two girls, and they are all

right here with me helping to conduct my business. Our place is better known as Gruene's, and any time any of my old friends come this way I will appreciate a visit.

PLAYED PRANKS ON THE TENDERFOOT

By Henry D. Steele, San Antonio, Texas

Early in the spring of 1882 I was employed by Mark Withers of Lockhart, to go up the trail with a herd to Kansas. Before starting on the trip I went to San Antonio and purchased a complete cowboy equipment, broad-brimmed hat, leggins, Colt's pistol, scabbard, cartridges, and the usual trimmings. We went down into McMullen County to get the cattle, and I was selected as horse-wrangler for the outfit. The cattle were bought from a man by the name of Martin. While we were at Tilden, George Hill came up with some of the boys and helped

HENRY D. STEELE

to gather the herd. I was pretty much of a "tenderfoot," just a slip of a boy, and the hands told me this man Hill was a pretty tough character and would steal anything he could get his hands on, besides he might kill me if I didn't watch him. They loaded me up pretty well on this kind of information, and I really believed it. They would steal my matches, cartridges, cigarette papers and handkerchiefs, and tell me that Hill got them. I reached the time when I was deprived of almost everything I had and even had to skin prickly pears to get wrapping for my cigarettes, believing all the while that the fellow Hill had cleaned me up. Things were getting serious and I was desperate, and if Hill had made any kind of a break the consequences would probably have been disaster. At last Hill, who was fully aware of the game that was being played on me, called me aside and told me that it was all a put-up job, and said it had been carried far enough. We all had a good laugh and from that time forward harmony reigned in camp.

John Story was our cook until we reached Coleman County, but there he left us and returned to Lockhart, to engage in the blacksmith business. After Story left us I had to do the cooking some time, and, getting tired of that work, I quit the herd and returned home, George Hill accompanying me as far as Austin.

In the spring of 1883 I was employed by Dick Head of Lockhart to go with a herd. Monroe Hardeman was boss. We gathered the cattle in Mason and Coleman Counties. The cattle were pretty thin, as the range was dry and had little grass. We passed through McCulloch County, through North Texas, and into the Indian Territory. Crossed the Washita River when it was on a big rise. That night we had a severe thunderstorm and I lost my hat during the rain.

When we reached Dodge City, Kansas, we remained there several days to allow the herd to rest, and from here we proceeded to Ogallala, Nebraska, where Mr. Head sold the cattle, and most of the crew came home, but Joe Lovelady, Pat Garrison, myself and Charlie Hedgepeth, a negro, went on with the herd to Cheyenne, Wyoming, where we arrived in August. When we started back we bought our tickets for Austin, and the price was $33.35 each.

It has been just thirty-seven years since I went over the trail. I do not know what has become of the men who went with me on that trip. One of the hands, Charlie

Hedgepeth, the negro, was hanged at Seguin by a mob some years ago. I saw Mark Withers at the Old Trail Drivers' reunion in San Antonio in 1917.

WHEN A MAN'S WORD WAS AS GOOD AS A GILT-EDGED NOTE

By George N. Steen, Bryan, Texas

Taking the advice of Jake Ellison, in 1867 I decided to go into the cattle business. I had no money, but the people let me take their cattle on credit, and I gathered enough to start a herd from San Marcos, Texas, to Abilene, Kansas, in the spring of 1868. I had six cowboys and only one hundred dollars to start on the trip with, but I knew I would get through somehow. When we reached Gainesville my money was all gone, and our stock of grub was low. I went into the town to see if I could buy enough groceries to last until we could get through the Indian Territory. I was a perfect stranger there, and did not know a man in the town. I went into George Howell's store, told Mr. Howell my circumstances, and asked if he could credit me for what I needed. He looked me straight in the eye for a few seconds and said he would do so. And he didn't ask for a mortgage or a note or anything to hold me bound except my word to pay.

Our bread gave out before we got through the Indian Territory, and I started foraging. One of the boys in my outfit had a ten dollar gold piece and loaned it to me to use in buying flour. I struck a small trail and followed it until it led me to a little old log cabin. I got off my horse and went inside and found an old Indian who could not speak very much English, and did not seem to understand what I wanted. Looking around the room I saw a sack of flour and said to him, "How much take?" He said "Ten dollars," so I gave him the gold piece and went back to camp rejoicing."

Capt. Bill George of Seguin joined me while going through the Indian Territory. We had some trouble with Indians on the trip. One night our herd was stampeded and we discovered that it was a ruse played by the Indians to get possession of our horses. I heard them rustling about and put after them, with the result that I captured a horse and bridle. Next morning when we started the herd we tied the horse at the edge of a mot of timber, and I concealed myself in the thicket to watch for developments. Pretty soon an Indian came to the horse and I covered him with my gun. He thought his time to depart to the happy hunting grounds had arrived. After giving him a good scare I made him promise to quit thieving and to never again attempt to steal horses from trail drivers. Then I let him go.

I was in Abilene when Tom Bowles and Wild Bill, the city marshal, had a shooting scrape and a policeman was killed by a stray bullet. While we were there one night a man was drinking at a bar in a saloon, and somebody fired in from outside, the bullet striking him in the mouth and instantly killing him. Later one of the boys with a Texas herd was shot and killed by one of the Mexican hands. The Mexican skipped out. A reward was offered for his capture dead or alive, and Wesley Hardin got the reward.

MY EXPERIENCE ON THE COW TRAIL

By F. M. Polk of Luling, Texas

My first experience on the cow trail was in 1872. I went with Joe Tennison and Warnell Polk, my father. We traveled the trail known as "the Old Chisholm Trail." We left for Lockhart, Texas, on the first of

April and went by way of Fort Worth. Fort Worth was a new town then and, of course, we had to stop over and see the sights. After leaving Fort Worth we made good time until we reached Red River, which we crossed at Red River Station. The river was swollen by the heavy spring rains and we were forced to swim our cattle through very deep and swift water. We lost a few, but felt lucky in getting off light.

We were a care-free bunch, had lots of fun and also lots of hard work. It was the spring of the year and the woods were very beautiful. We would pitch our tents at night, get our work all done, and after supper would light our pipes and sit or lounge around the campfire and listen to the other men spin their hair-raising yarns, of their earlier trips. We would then make our beds, using our saddles for pillows, stretch our tired limbs and soon be sound asleep and know nothing else until morning, unless something happened to disturb the cattle, when we would bound up and be ready for action.

I recall one stampede especially on this trip. We had camped on the south side of the North Canadian River one stormy night and after retiring we heard a big noise and we were up and out to the cattle in a very few minutes. We soon realized that we had our hands full, for the cattle had scattered everywhere and it required two days to get them back together again.

As we went through the country, it kept us busy looking out for Indians and buffalo. One man was always sent ahead to keep the buffaloes out of the herd and scout for Indians, for they were very savage at this time and we never knew when they would attack us. We landed in Wichita, Kansas, some time near the middle of July without serious mishaps or the loss of very many cattle.

I decided I would take it easier coming back, so bought a wagon and left Wichita the middle of August. I came down through Arkansas and the edge of Missouri and landed at home the 20th of September with five head of horses.

As I was only eighteen years old, my father thought I was too young for such a strenuous life and persuaded me to farm a few years before returning to the trail, but I did not like farming and after two years' trial of it, I was more than ready to go back to the wild, care-free life of a cowboy. In 1875 I went to work for J. W. Montgomery, better known among the cowmen as "Black Bill." He moved his cattle to Lampasas County and I worked for him three years, 1875, 1876 and 1877. I returned home then and worked on a ranch until the spring of 1881, when I went to work for W. H. Jennings and John R. Blocker. I bought cattle over Caldwell County until the first of April.

We left the ranch near the San Marcos River on the first day of April for Kansas. We landed at the Blocker ranch in five days and received twenty-eight head of outlaw horses. Blocker and Jennings always took several herds up the trail at the same time. On this trip they bought 200 head of Spanish horses from someone on the Rio Grande. Bob Jennings, the boss of our herd, and I, were sent after this bunch of horses. They were the worst horses we ever handled. We had lots of fun and lots of falls trying to ride them. It was Ab and Jenks Blocker's job to rope, down and put shoes on them, and let me tell you it was a worse job than some ladies have in trying to put a No. 3 shoe on a No. 5 foot.

We made our way to Taylor, Texas, and received 300 head of steers. It was then the 18th day of April and it required several days to put the road brand on this bunch before we were ready for the long, long trail. The boys had a rough time, but we certainly had lots of fun. Nothing ever happened that we didn't get a good laugh out of it. We had one "greener" with us on this trip and we never missed a chance to play a prank on him.

His name was Joe Hullum. Cal Tuttle, Charlie Roberts
and I all knew him well and, of course, delighted in teas-
ing him. When we reached Lampasas County we told
him we were getting into a country where the Indians
were very bad and that they didn't mind wearing a few
scalps on their belts. He pretended not to care, but before we had gone very much further he bid us farewell,
saying that he didn't care anything about being buried
on the lone prairie for the wild coyotes to howl over his
grave and, besides he was getting too far away from
"dear old Caldwell County." He bade us good luck and
the last we saw of him he was taking the newly
traveled end of the trail, and he wasn't slow about it,
either.

For the next few days everything went on fine, the
weather was fair, the cattle were quiet, and we began to
say to each other: "Cattle driving is just about the
easiest job I know of," but, alas, peace never lasted long
on the cattle trail. I don't remember just where we
struck the Western Chisholm Trail, but as we neared
Little River we had a terrible storm and rain. The cattle
became frightened and pulled off a big show. It took
us three days to get them all together again, and when
we reached the river we had to swim the cattle. They
were restless and unruly and it took us two days to get
them all across. We had a fellow by the name of Rufe
Fuller taking care of the horses, and in crossing the river
he drowned the horse he was riding and one of the bunch
he was driving. We made pontoons and fastened them to
our wagons to float them across. We made good time
after that until we reached Pease River, but here we had
a big stampede and had to lay over two days to gather up
our cattle. The country was lined with antelope and
prairie dogs and we found great sport killing them.

We crossed the Red River into the Indian Territory
at Doan's Store, and here we struck the Indians by the
thousands. We kept our eyes open and managed to keep

peace by giving them a beef every day. They would come to us fifty and one hundred at a time. Some would ride with us all day and they always asked for a cow, which they called "Wahaw," and, of course, we acted like we were glad to give it to them, but we were not very badly frightened. We all had our guns and knew how to use them if we got in a tight. As we went through this part of the country we had great sport roping buffalo and elk. You could look across the prairie and see hundreds of them in droves.

J. R. Blocker and W. H. Jennings overtook us at Bitter Creek. They were to deliver the cattle at Mobeetie, a little town in the Panhandle. I quit the herd at Bitter Creek. Mr. Blocker sent Will Sears and I on to overtake Givings Lane, one of Blocker & Jennings' bosses. We overtook Mr. Lane in three days at Bluff Creek, and while camped there we had a big rainstorm, which put the creek up and caused a big stampede among our cattle. We stayed with Mr. Lane until he got the cattle rounded up and across the creek, when we decided to go to La Junta, Colorado. I had a cousin there running a ranch for J. J. Jones. We left Dodge City the first of August and traveled up the Arkansas River horseback. We reached the Jones ranch on the fifth of August. I rested one day and went to work. J. J. Jones was at that time the biggest cattleman in Colorado, so you may guess that we had lots of work to do. I worked here until the first of December, and as it was getting very cold up there by that time, and we were having some heavy snowfalls, I decided I would strike for a warmer climate, and back to Texas I came.

I hired to M. A. Withers on April the first, 1882, and struck the trail again. He sent several herds this time and I went with a bunch under Gus Withers. We had lots of hard work and plenty of bad horses to ride. They were the worst bunch I ever saw with the exception of the Blocker bunch. The stampedes were so numerous that I could not keep track of them, but we had a well-trained bunch of men and lost no cattle, but had to work hard and sleep with one eye open.

There was so much rain and the cattle were so restless, we never knew what to expect. Lots of times I never pulled off my boots for three days and nights. After one of these strenuous times, we would lay over some place and rest for a few days. We would have lots of fun trying to prove who was the best rider, but oftentimes the horse would prove that he was on to his job better than any of us.

At Pease River we had a big stampede and would have lost a great many cattle if we had not been near Millet's Ranch. Millet worked only desperadoes on this ranch, but they were all good cattlemen and came nobly to our rescue. We ran across one boy in that crowd from Caldwell County. He had decided quite a while ago that Caldwell County was getting too warm for him and his cattle rustling and had struck for a cooler climate. It seemed awfully good to us to see anyone from home, even a cattle rustler. He enjoyed our stay very much, as he learned of lots that had happened at home since he left. We rested here a few days and struck out again.

We crossed the Red River at Doan's Store and there we found a large number of Indians camped, but they were peaceable, for they were fast finding out that it didn't pay to molest cattle drivers. M. A. Withers overtook us here and sent Gus Withers on with his herd, which was going to Dodge, while he went ahead to get Mr. Johnson, who had bought these cattle for an English syndicate, to come to Mobeetie to receive our herd. He put Tom Hawker over us and also changed my brother, Cal Polk, to our bunch, which pleased me very much. We had been separated for quite a while and had lots to tell each other.

After leaving Doan's Store we traveled up Bitter

Creek for forty or fifty miles and then turned west to Mobeetie, when we turned our herd over to John Hargroves to hold on the L. X. Ranch until fall, as we could not take them on to Tuscosa until after frost on account of a quarantine they had on at that time.

After Mr. Johnson received our bunch he and M. A. Withers returned to Dodge to receive the herd he had sent there. After reaching Dodge and counting the cattle, Mr. Johnson was struck and killed by lightning while returning to camp. Mr. Withers was knocked from his horse, but wasn't hurt further than receiving a bad fall and shock.

About the first of October, the boss and I had a row and I decided I was ready for the back trail. I took the buckboard for Dodge, which was about 300 miles from Mobeetie. On reaching Dodge, I bought a ticket for San Antonio. On my way home I reviewed my past life as a cowboy from every angle and came to the conclusion that about all I had gained was experience, and I could not turn that into cash, so I decided I had enough of it, and made up my mind to go home, get married and settle down to farming.

PUNCHING CATTLE ON THE TRAIL TO KANSAS

By W. B. Hardeman of Devine, Texas

I was just a farmer boy, started to church at Prairie Lea one Sunday, met Tom Baylor (he having written me a note several days before, asking if I wanted to go up the trail) and the first thing he said was, "Well, are you going?" I said, "Yes," so he said, "Well, you have no time to go to church." So we went back to my house, got dinner and started to the "chuck wagon and remuda," which was camped some six miles ahead. There

I was, with a white shirt, collar and cravat, starting on
the trail. You can imagine just how green I was.

We put the herd up below Bryan. We were gone
seven months, so I had plenty
of time to learn a few things
in regard to driving cattle.
We were a month putting up
the herd. I was always left
to hold the cattle, and when
we finally drove out of the
timber and reached the prairie, the grass was ten inches
in height, green as a wheat
field and the cattle were poor
and hungry, so went to chopping that grass as though
they were paid. There was
a nice little shade tree right
near, so I got off my horse

W. B. HARDEMAN

to sit in the shade for a few minutes and watch the cattle.
The first thing I knew Tom Baylor was waking me. I
thought, "Well, I have gone to sleep on guard. I had
just as well put my hand in Colonel Ellison's pocket and
take his money." I never got off of my horse any more
when on duty, though I have seen the time when I would
have given five dollars for one-half hour's sleep. I would
even put tobacco in my eyes to keep awake. Our regular
work was near eighteen hours a day, and twenty-four if
a bad night, then the next day, just as though we had
slept all night, and most of us getting only $30.00 per
month and grub, bad weather making from twenty-four
to forty-eight hours, never thinking of "time and over-
time," or calling for shorter hours and more pay.

In Kansas one day for dinner we bought some pies,
eggs and milk from a granger. He informed Baylor that
a certain section of land that had a furrow plowed around
it, did not belong to his neighbor, but was railroad land

and the number was 115. When I came to dinner Baylor told me about the section. He also told me we would not strike any more water that evening. This creek on Section 115 had fine water, and he asked me if I thought best to water there. I said, "Yes," knowing I had to herd that afternoon. Ham Bee protested, and said we should not treat that old man that way, but Ham did not have to hold the herd that evening, so I insisted, and Baylor said, "Get your dinner and fresh horses, I will start to the water." The old man lived in a dug-out on the side of a hill where he could see everything, so when he saw the cattle cross that furrow he came out with a shotgun, rolling up his sleeves, waving his arms and shouting, "Take those cattle off my land or I will have every damn one of you arrested." Baylor, being in the lead, came in contact with him first. He said, "Old man, there must be a mistake; we have some fat cattle and the agent of the railroad (some four miles to the depot) said he had no stock cars and for us to throw the cattle on Section 115." Well, sir, you should have heard that old man curse that (innocent) agent, as well as the country in general, stating he had moved his family out there, the drouth came and it looked like starvation, so he was trying to save that little grass for winter. Baylor compromised by telling him he had a family and knew how it was, and would be willing to water on one-half of the section and would give him a dogie calf that had got into the herd several days before and we did not want it. The old man got in a fine humor, had us to send the wagon by the house to get a barrel of spring water—that was the kind of a neighbor the old man had.

While in the Indian Territory one day at noon, about a dozen head of range cattle got in the herd. We did not discover them until we threw the herd back on the trail, so we had to cut them out and run them back some three miles. Some time during the night they trailed us up and came into the herd, and we did not discover it until we

were out of that range. After we got up into Kansas
I saw two men riding around the herd with Baylor and
when he left them he came to me and said, "Bud, those
men are butchers, and said they would give us $300.00
for those range cattle and do not want a bill of sale."
I said, "Tell them the cattle are not ours, so we can't
do that; we will turn them over to Colonel Ellison and
he can find the owner," and we took them on. We delivered that herd at Ogallala, Nebraska, took another
from there to the Bell Fourche in Wyoming—a 60-mile
drive without water for the cattle. We were just twelve
miles from the buffalo. By the time we branded out the
herd we were short of grub, so did not go buffalo hunting, and right there I lost my only chance to kill buffalo.
We were five hundred miles from a railroad, but I wish
I had gone anyway.

Tom P. Baylor was a son of General John R. Baylor.
He died some twenty-one years ago. He was as fine a
man as I ever knew. Ham P. Bee is now in San Antonio,
express messenger on a railroad.

In 1883 I went on the trail with W. T. Jackman of
San Marcos. We started the herd from Colorado County
at "Ranches Grande," owned by Stafford Brothers.
While in the Indian Territory one evening two Indians
ate supper with us. I was holding the herd while first
relief was at supper. Dan, a fifteen-year-old boy, was
holding the "remuda" (saddle horses). We really had
two herds with one wagon, had three thousand cattle,
four hundred horses and one hundred saddle horses, fifteen men in all, and only three six-shooters in the outfit.
Just as I went to eat my supper and the horse herders
were going to relieve Dan, we heard him give a distress
yell and shoot several times. Jackman and Lee Wolfington mounted their horses, drew their guns and started
in a run for Dan. That was one time I wished for a gun.
Twelve men and nothing to defend ourselves with. So
you know I was like the little negro, "Not scared, just a

little frightened,'' knowing four hundred Indians were
in camp, just three miles away. Those two Indians that
had eaten supper with us had mounted their horses and
ostensibly started for their camp, but slipped around and
drove off two saddle ponies. Dan discovered them by
skylight, hence the alarm. Jackman and Wolfington followed them and recovered the horses, but did not see the
two Indians. W. T. Jackman is postmaster at San Marcos. He was sheriff there for twenty years, and as good
as Texas ever had.

In 1886 I went with J. C. Robertson. We drove for
Blocker, Davis & Driscoll. They drove forty thousand
head of cattle, and had fourteen hundred horses. We
started for Uvalde, went up the East Fork of the Nueces
River, the roughest trail I ever went. We could not see
all of the cattle, only at bedding time. When nearing
the Territory one evening, a young man and young lady
came galloping by us. The girl was well mounted, and
had on a handsome riding habit. We had not seen a
woman for months, so we were all charmed and thought
she was the most beautiful object we had ever beheld.
All wanted to see more of her. Joe Robertson being the
boss, found out we would pass near where the family
lived the next evening and there was a fine spring of
water where they lived, so that noon he had me to trim
his hair and whiskers, his intention being to take the
chuck wagon by to get a barrel of spring water. Of
course we all knew it was just an excuse to get to see
that pretty girl once more. Sandy Buckalew called out
to me to "fix the boss right," and I did my best. Sandy
was pointing the herd and had a chance to pass right
near the house before Robertson could get up there, so
he galloped over to the house to get a drink of water.
The old mother, who was a very kind and nice lady,
brought him some water. He thanked her and began to
brag on the beautiful country, to all of which she agreed,
but deplored the fact that there was no school. Sandy

saw his chance and said, "Well, that can be arranged, I think, as our boss is married and his wife is a splendid school teacher, and he is well pleased with the country, so I feel confident that you will have no trouble in having him to locate here. He will be by to get a barrel of water and you can mention it to him." You can imagine how the boss felt when the good mother did all the entertaining all the time, urging him to bring his fine little wife and teach their school. I don't think he even got a glimpse of the girl. We had lots of fun out of it, anyway, though none of us ever laid eyes on that most beautiful woman again. Joe has never married, but has more children to look after than any of us, as he has charge of the San Pedro Springs Park in San Antonio and looks after the children there, and a better man can't be found. In the final roundup, may we all meet again

---

EXCITING EXPERIENCES ON THE FRONTIER AND ON THE TRAIL

By C. W. Ackermann of San Antonio

I was born in the year 1855 on the Salado Creek four miles east of San Antonio, Bexar County, Texas.

My first adventure I can remember was when I was six years old. One day my brother, ten years old, asked me to go with him to hunt some cows. We both rode on one horse. After we had ridden for several miles we found a cow with a young calf. My brother told me to stay with that cow while he hunted others, then he would return for me. While he was gone the cow and calf rambled off and I got lost from them in the high grass. I kept on hunting the cow and in the meantime my brother returned for me, but could not find me. After hunting for me a while he concluded I had followed the cow home, so he went on home.

C. W. ACKERMANN

My parents immediately began to search for me.

In the meantime I kept on walking in the direction the cow went, believing I was going home, till night came. The wolves began to howl and scared me so I climbed up a little tree, where I remained till they stopped howling. Then I crawled down and slept soundly under the tree till the sun woke me up. I got up and started off again.

I walked all day with nothing to eat but chaparral berries and I was fortunate enough to find a small pool of water that afternoon. By night I had not reached home, so I made my bed under a tree as I had done the night before.

That night there was a big thunderstorm and rain. I was completely drenched. But my courage never failed, so in the morning bright and early I started out.

I heard some roosters crowing, so I went in that direction, thinking I had at last found home. But, to my disappointment, it was only a Mexican house. The dogs began to chase me, but the old man called them back, then took me in his house where they were just ready to eat breakfast.

I was scared almost lifeless, for I could neither speak nor understand Spanish. I could picture them roasting me for dinner and all kinds of horrible things they might do with me. Nevertheless, I greedily drank the cup of coffee and ate the piece of bread they gave me and asked for more, because I was almost starved, but they would not give me any more.

Immediately after breakfast the old "hombre" saddled his horse, tied a rope around me and put me behind him on his horse. Then he rode to an American family and got a written note from the white man that he (the Mexican) had not kidnaped me, but was taking me home.

The old Mexican took me on home and received a generous reward from my father.

Afterward I learned that I had roamed to Chipadares, a distance of about twenty miles from my home. At that time that was the nearest settlement southeast of home.

During the Civil War I was just a mere boy of nine years. Nevertheless, I recall some thrilling adventures.

My father was exempted from the army on account of owning a flour mill. This mill was located on the San Antonio River about sixteen miles from our farm. Father had to run the mill himself, so he and mother moved there and left my older brother, 13 years old, and I at the farm to take care of the stock and everything.

One day while I was alone the Confederate soldiers came around gathering up horses. They threatened to take mine and had me scared to death. I begged hard for my horse and I told them that I needed him to get supplies with. After frightening me real good they told me I could keep my horse. I was the only one they left with a horse around that neighborhood.

The schools in those days were very much different to the schools of today. We only had private schools and these lasted the entire year. Our only vacation was two weeks in August.

The only subjects they taught were reading, writing, arithmetic, spelling, history, geography and grammar. On Monday, Tuesday and Wednesday we studied reading, writing, spelling and arithmetic. On Thursday and Friday we had history, grammar and geography.

I started to school when I was eleven years old and attended three years. After that I was sent to San Antonio, where I studied surveying.

When I was a boy, rounding up cattle was a very exciting event. In those days people did not have their pastures fenced, so the cattle often wandered many miles from home.

About the beginning of spring we would start on the round-up. Three or four neighborhoods would send out ten to fifteen men together. Out of these one man was selected as captain. I was just fourteen years old when I went out on my first round-up. My father put me in the care of our captain and from him I learned how to rope and brand cattle and many other important things one should know about round-ups.

I often roped and branded as many as eight or ten calves by myself in a day. Branding was not a very easy task, either, for we had to run the brand. We had no ready-made brands as now. Many times we had to gather the wilder cattle at night. When they went out on the prairie we would sneak a tame bunch of cattle in with them and thus drive them in a corral. Sometimes we would build a stockade around water holes, leaving only one opening for the cattle to get in. Even with such a trap we were often unable to hold the wildest ones in.

Licenses permitting one to carry arms was unheard of in my earlier days. Every man always carried his "six-shooter" buckled to his side. This was necessary on account of there being so many robbers. There were about forty or more highway robbers scattered over the country in squads of 5 or 6 men.

I remember one time as three of the other boys and myself were coming from the market in San Antonio we were waylaid by some robbers. Fortunately we spied them in time and each of us galloped off in different directions. They fired at us, but we all escaped unharmed.

When I was sixteen years old I had a little experience with horse thieves.

My father noticed a suspicious looking man riding

around our place one day, so he told us boys we had
better watch the horses. My brother and I went out to
guard the horses that night and just about midnight the
thieves came in two or three different squads. How
many there were we never knew. We watched them give
signals to each other with the fire of their cigarettes.
Then we fired at them and scared them away. We hit
one of them, but never knew if we killed him or not.
After that we were never bothered with horse thieves.

The robbers were certainly skillful. I recall one day
when my brother and I were out on a hunt, we laid down
to rest. We used our saddles for pillows and put our
belts and "six-shooters" under them. And while we
were resting someone sneaked up and stole my belt and
"six-shooter" right from under my head. I suppose
whoever it was thought I had money in the little money
pouch on my belt, but they sure got fooled.

In 1872 we were not allowed so much liberty. A law
was passed which prohibited men from carrying concealed arms.

In 1874 horse thieves and highway robbers were so
bad something had to be done. The ranchmen formed
an organization known as the "Stock Association" to rid
the country of these marauders. I was one of the fifty
deputies elected. After a year's time we had Bexar
County clear of robbers.

My first trip up the old cow trail to Kansas was in
the year 1873, when I was just a boy of eighteen. My
father decided to take some of his cattle to the Kansas
market, as they sold so cheap here. At that time one
thousand-pound beeves sold in San Antonio for $8.00
per head and in Wichita, Kansas, for $23.80 per head.

Father asked a bunch of young cowboys if they
thought they could take his cattle to Kansas. As we were
all young fellows, between the ages of eighteen and
twenty-two, eager for adventure, we willingly consented.
So on the first day of February we began gathering our

cattle and finished rounding up a herd on March 14th. Early next morning we started on our journey. We traveled all day and that night made our first camping place where Converse, Bexar County, now stands, but at that time it was only an open country.

That first night was one never to be forgotten. It rained all night long and our cattle stampeded eighteen times. During one stampede they ran into one of our men. His horse was run over by the cattle and crippled, while the man was carried off about a fourth of a mile on top of the cattle. He escaped with only a few bruises. We were lucky not to lose any cattle that night, but fifteen head were crippled.

The next morning we bought a two-wheeled cart to carry our bedding and provisions in. Then, with a yoke of oxen hitched to it, we began our journey again and made our next stop on the Santa Clara, where now stands the little town, Marion. That night there was an electric storm which was followed by cold weather and frost. After a few days' rest we resumed our trail. When we reached the Guadalupe River it was up about six feet. Our cattle had to swim across and our cart was taken on a ferryboat.

At our next camping place we had another stampede and lost thirty-five head of cattle, which we never found.

When we reached the Colorado River it also was up about four feet. After swimming that we kept on the trail to Round Rock, where our yoke of oxen was stolen, so we had to rope and hitch two wild steers to the cart. When we reached Fort Worth, at that time a small town of one hundred inhabitants, we sold our cart and bought a wagon and team of horses.

It was a very rainy year and every river we came to was up; however, we crossed them all without loss. When we reached Washita River, in Indian Territory, we had to stay there eight days on account of heavy rains. There I had my hardest time of the trip. For six nights I slept only about one and a half hours and never pulled off my slicker and boots.

Upon reaching the Canadian River we found that so high we could not cross for two days.

Our next stop was on Bluff Creek, on the line of Kansas. There one of our men, Joe Menges, roped a buffalo calf which we carried with us to Wichita and sold it to "Buffalo Joe," who was running a beer garden for the amusement of the trail men.

We camped on the river called Ninnesquaw for three months in order to fatten our cattle for the market. Then my father came to Kansas by train and sold them.

On the seventh of September we began our return trip, bringing with us forty-five head of saddle ponies. It took us twenty-seven days to make the return trip to San Antonio. Only five of us made the return trip, Hartmann, Eisenhauer, Markwardt, Smith, and myself.

On my journey I saw many buffalo, but killed only one great big one. I also killed seven antelopes.

One morning while I was eating breakfast one of the boys came running up and said, "Chris, come on quick, buffalo ran in the herd and they have stampeded." I jumped on my horse and went with him. The first thing I saw was one of the boys, Philip Prinz, galloping after some buffaloes trying to rope one. When he spied me he came and asked me for my horse. I would not give it to him and told him to let the buffalo alone if he didn't want to get killed. He got a little sore at me, but we rode on back to camp together.

I think we were the youngest bunch of trailmen on the "Trail" that year. The oldest man, Ad. Markwardt, our cook, was only twenty-five years old, and the rest were between eighteen and twenty-two years. Those that rode the "Trail" with me were Alf. Hartmann, Steve Wooler, Joe Menges, Phil Prinz, Louis Eisenhauer, Ad Markwardt, Henry Smith, a negro, and my brother, Fred.

Besides making trips over the "Trail" to Kansas, I often made trips to the coast.

Years ago there were no trains we could ship our cattle on as nowadays. Whenever we wanted to take cattle to the seaport we had to drive them. We usually drove them in herds of about two hundred head.

In the spring of the year we usually began rounding up our cattle, as the beef buyers usually came in the early fall. Our captain would give us orders for the trip, then we would start out, each man with his pack-horse and two saddle horses.

There were large stock pens scattered over the country. We would each go in different directions and all meet at one of the pens. At night when we went into camp we would hobble our tamest horses with buckskin hobbles and staked the wilder ones. We hung our "grub" up in a tree so nothing could bother it.

After we had all the cattle together we would start for home. As we came near to each man's house he would cut his cattle out of the herd.

Then came the beef buyer. After he bought as many as he wanted he would get ready for the drive to the seaport. I helped him out many times just to take the trip.

We would often lose cattle on these trips, for they would stampede and, of course, we seldom found those that got lost. At one of our camping places an Irishman had built a pen on rollers. When the cattle stampeded in that pen there was no danger of losing any. When they would run the pen went right with them. It was often carried as far as fifty yards.

In the year 1874 I had another very thrilling experience. On account of such a dry year my father decided to move to a different location. He did not know where to go, so he gave me the job of hunting a suitable place.

In August of that year I started out with two saddle horses and one pack horse. I went in a northwestern direction, then turned toward the Concho country. I went as far as the New Mexico boundary line, then started back home.

The country I traveled through was very wild. There were just a few small settlements scattered here and there and the people even seemed uncivilizd.

I saw antelope and buffalo by the thousands. It was that year the government was trying to kill out the buffalo. I passed many mule teams loaded with buffalo hides. Even though the country was wild I found some excellent locations for a ranch, especially in the Concho country.

When I returned home and told father about the wild country and people he decided not to move so far away. So he bought a ranch close to where now stands Wetmore. Later he gave me this ranch. I moved up there in 1877 and lived a bachelor's life till I married Emma Bueche in 1882.

We lived on that same ranch until 1905. Then I bought a small farm of 500 acres at Fratt, about nine miles from San Antonio, and left one of my sons in charge of the ranch.

I am now living a quiet, peaceful life on my farm. Every time I go up to my ranch memories of those old wild, happy days come back to me.

Now I am 65 years old and have a clear record of never being arrested and never was involved in any kind of lawsuit.

OBSERVATIONS AND EXPERIENCES OF BYGONE DAYS

By Louis Schorp of Rio Medina, Texas

In the spring of 1873 John Vance, a merchant of Castroville, decided to drive a herd of cattle up the Kansas Trail. In company with my neighbors I helped to round up and deliver steers to Mr. Vance, this being my first work along this line.   Bladen Mitchell, a pioneer of

LOUIS SCHORP

Bandera County, was engaged by Mr. Vance as trail boss.   All of the cattle were received by Mr. Mitchell and driven to Bandera County, to a point about two miles north of the Mormon Camp, where Mr. Mitchell had his herding pens, and what was known as the Mitchell Crossing.   This property was purchased during the early eighties by the firm of Schorp & Spettel, but at the present time it is entirely covered by the Medina Lake, a vast body of water impounded by a great concrete dam.   After delivering my bunch of steers I went over to Elm Creek, a tributary to the Medina River, where I found a crowd rounding up cattle for Perryman & Lytle, among whom were the Spettel, Habys and Wurzbachs.   The following day five men out of this crowd, including myself, were going to Bandera to see the Vance cattle inspected and road branded.   As we were getting ready to start the steers became frightened and stampeded.   I was the only one horseback, and one of the men yelled to me to "turn the leaders toward the bluff and mill them."   I did not understand the meaning of this, for I had never seen a stampede before.   I knew how to turn the crank of a coffee-mill, but when it was necessary to "mill" a bunch of outlaw steers I did not know where to look for the crank.   I turned the lead cattle from running into camp and crowded them against the bluff, but they did not mill, and when I looked back I saw that most of the cattle had turned behind me.   By this time all of the men in camp

were on their horses and it took about an hour to get all
of the cattle together again. Every steer had his tongue
out, and an ox tongue never looked so cheap to me before
or after.

The next day I went with the boys to take the herd
out to graze, and when several miles southwest of Bandera one of the men pointed to a large live oak tree and
said six men were hung to its branches during the Civil
War by Confederate soldiers. The next day the cattle
were inspected by a man named Pue. During the inspection a dispute arose about a certain steer belonging to
a Frenchman named Cordier at Castroville. I had delivered this steer to Mr. Mitchell, and knew it by the
flesh marks, and it was branded R I, but the party calling
the brand called it B I. The inspector asked for water
with which to dampen the brand and, finding the bucket
empty, he took out a bottle of whiskey, wet the brand
with the liquor, smoothed the hairs, and the brand showed
R I very plainly. Thus twelve dollars were saved for
the old Frenchman.

I rounded up steers every spring thereafter and delivered most of them to Lytle & McDaniels of Medina
County.

During the year 1874, while riding over the range
one day looking after stock, I noticed a cow running
about and bellowing and rode over to see what was the
matter with her. I found she had a very young calf by
her side and three wolves were trying to get the calf.
I chased the wolves away and drove the cow toward shelter. The calf had been wounded, and had I not happened
along when I did the wolves would have killed it I am
sure. I have been on the range more or less since 1870
and this is the only time that I ever saw wolves attack
a calf.

During the winter of 1878 and 1879 grass in the
Medina Valley was very short and many of the stockmen lost heavily. My father at this time owned about

five hundred cattle, and I remember that I skinned seventy head of father's cattle that winter. In the fall of 1879 I moved the remainder of our cattle to San Miguel, in Frio County, to where the Keystone pasture is now located. In the spring of 1880 I purchased all of the stock belonged to my father. I sold the steers to John Lytle and delivered them to him in the Forks Pasture at the mouth of the Hondo. This was the last bunch of steers I sold and delivered to go up the trail.

In the fall of 1882 the land in this particular part of Frio County where I ranched was purchased by a company from Muscatine, Iowa, known as the Hawkeye Land & Cattle Company. I sold all my land and stock to this company and moved back to Medina County, where I have resided ever since.

In the spring of 1884 I formed a partnership with Ed Kaufman, who now resides in San Antonio, and we drove a herd of horses to Pueblo, Colorado. In the outfit were George Gerdes, now with the Schweers-Kern Commission Company; John Saathoff of Hondo, Eames Saathoff of New Fountain, and a cook whose name I have forgotten.

MET QUANAH PARKER ON THE TRAIL

By John Wells of Bartlett, Texas

I was born in Gordon County, Georgia, July 19, 1859. My father died when I was three years old. I left home in July when only ten years of age, and from that time on earned my way. The family moved to Texas in 1866 and in the winter of 1867 to Bell County. First started on the trail when I was 23 years of age with thirteen men, including boss, cook and horse rustler. Worked for Hudson, Watson & Co. in spring of 1883. Gathered about eight thousand cattle from Lampasas, Burnet, Llano,

ALEX WEBB   J. L. WELLS
South Dakota
        Actual Photo Taken on the Trail

Williamson, Gillespie and San Saba Counties. The company sold three thousand cattle to Bob Johns and two thousand cattle to Bill Shadley, also eighty-five horses, chuck wagon and trail outfit, drove them to Taylor and shipped to Wichita Falls. Alex Webb and I were sent to San Antonio to receive and bring two thousand cattle and twenty-four horses to Wichita Falls. This bunch was then unloaded and thrown with the Burnet County herd, making a total of about four thousand cattle and one hundred and fifteen horses. The cattle ranged from one-year-olds to seven. We held them fifteen miles from the town between Wichita and Red River for a rest period of ten days to fit them for the trail. While crossing at the mouth of Pease River we had ten steers to bog in the quicksand, and after digging them out we threw the herd on the prairie and camped for the night. The boys were all thirsty, having nothing to drink but gyp and alkali water. I saw a settlement down the draw, a mile away, and went down and asked the people for a drink of water. They told me to ride to the spring, where I would find a cup and help myself. I went and found a bubbling spring as clear as crystal, which on tasting was gyp water too. So I went to the house and asked if they had some buttermilk they would sell. They sold me about two gallons for fifty cents. I took it back to the herd and I and four other boys drank it. We were very glad to get our thirst quenched. The next evening we camped near Doan's Store and there we saw our first Comanche braves. The next day the range men cut the herd. We crossed the South Fork of Red River that evening where thirteen steers bogged and had to be dug out. One steer was bogged and I and Henry Miller, the boss, went to dig him out. The boss hobbled his horse. I told him he had better hitch to the horn of my saddle, as the steer might catch him before he could unhobble his horse. I hitched my horse to his saddle, but, being boss, I guess he thought he needed no advice. He had the spade in his hand and we walked down and dug out some sand from the animal. The steer began to lunge and I thought he was going to get out, and so I got my horse in between the steer and my boss in time to keep him from being run over by the steer.

We continued up Red River for four or five days' drive. Had plenty of grass and a good supply of fresh lakes of water until we came to Wichita Mountains, where we crossed the North Fork of Red River. There we found Quanah Parker and his friend waiting for us. He wanted a yearling donated, and said, "Me squaw heap hungry." After the boss and five of the boys had gone to dinner I and four of the others were left on herd. I rode around the herd to where I came up to Quanah Parker and his friend. Quanah was dressed like a white man. His friend wore breech clout and hunting skirt with a Winchester to his saddle. Quanah had on a hat and pants with a six-shooter in cowboy style. I made friends with Quanah, but I didn't like the looks of his friend. When the boss returned to the herd after dinner he gave Quanah a yearling and by that time four or five other warriors had appeared. They drove the yearling to their camp.

We passed through a gap of the Wichita Mountains and camped on the east side of the trail. After we had bedded our cattle and eaten our supper we saw a prairie fire in the foothills on the west side of the trail. The first relief was on herd. The boss was afraid the fire might cross the trail and burn out over camp or cause a stampede, so he called the boys up and told them to get their horses and named two to go to the herd, the remainder to go with him. Alex Webb was to go to the herd, but the cook asked Webb if he was going to leave his six-shooter with him. Webb told him no, he needed it. But Cook says, "By Jacks, when it begins to thunder and lightning you fill 'this wagon full of six-shooters, but when the Indians are around the guns are all gone, and

who is going to protect me?'' The men rode far enough
to find out that there was no danger of fire crossing the
trail, then they returned to camp and all spent a peaceful night.

We saw no more of the Comanches and the next tribe
was Kiowas, who were frequent visitors to the camp.
There were seventeen for dinner one day. Three squaws
sat down together, and two or three papooses went to
looking for lice on each mother's head and eating them.

While passing through the Kiowa Indian country one
of our men at Alverson had a close brush with one of
the warriors which might have resulted seriously had it
not been that the boss was close at hand with his six-
shooter. The Indian, after being forced to put up his
Winchester, ran into the herd and killed two steers before
he stopped.

I was riding with the herd in the Cheyenne country
when a brave asked for a cartridge from my belt. I told
him my cartridges were forty-fives and his gun was a
forty-four. He made signs to show me how he would
reload it, and I had to give him one. Then he wanted to
run a race. Our horses were not at all matched, mine
being far superior, but I managed to hold him in for a
short distance alongside the herd, so the brave could join.
The Indian parted with me saying, ''Me heap hungry.''
I told him to come to Po Campo at night. He came,
bringing three friends, one of them a youngster from
college, out in full war paint, breech clout and hunting
shirt. He traded quirts with Jim Odell, giving him a
dollar to boot. The Indian wanted the quirt to ride races
with. About that time Frank Haddocks rode up and was
mistaken by a two-hundred-pound warrior for one of
their tribe. He began talking to Frank in Cheyenne, at
the same time advancing for a friendly bout. The college
Indian, acting as interpreter, called him aside and told
him that a family in their tribe had lost a baby years
before and they believed Frank was this child. They

concluded then that Frank had been stolen from the Kiowas and that white people had stolen him before he learned to talk. Nothing seemed to shake their belief that he was an Indian. They urged him to go to their camp. Frank asked me to go with him and I believe he would have gone had I consented.

While we were at supper the Indians were sitting on piles of bedding which the cook had thrown from the chuck wagon. One of the boys said, "Those damned Indians will put lice on our beds." The cook heard this and, angry at having extra company, said, "I'll get the fireshovel and get them off." The young Indian of course understood, and at a word from him they moved and sat on the grass nearby. Early next morning the Indian who supposed himself to be Frank's brother, came and for an hour or more tried to persuade him to come and live with them. Frank asked me again to go along, and finally refused, when he saw I couldn't be persuaded. Looking back I can see we might both have been benefited by staying.

We reached Dodge City, Kansas, about six weeks after leaving Wichita Falls. There the boss bought provisions and after crossing the Arkansas River threw the cattle out on the tableland and camped for the night. One incident broke into the regular trail life between this place and Buffalo which it might be well to relate. A Kansas jayhawker had been in the habit of exacting toll from the herds crossing his land at Shawnee Creek. The boss, riding ahead, found out that he asked a cent apiece for the cattle, and decided to put one over on the gentleman. At noon the boss came back to us with instructions to get the cattle across as quickly as possible and not tell the Kansas man how many head we carried. To say about twenty-five hundred if he pressed us. The next morning the boss wrote a check for twenty-five dollars and proceeded at once to Buffalo, where he wired Bob Shadley, the owner, not to honor the check.

The trail led through Buffalo and on beside the grave of two of Sam Bass' men, Joel Collins and his partner, who were killed by officers at that place some years before.

Through Kansas and Nebraska we had good water, plenty of grass, and the cattle thrived. Reaching Ogallala our cook quit and his cloak fell on my shoulders as the only one of the bunch qualified to fill it. We crossed the South Platte River and hiked out up the North River about sixty miles, where we stopped to brand for nearly ten days. We proceeded to Sydney Bridge and crossed below the Block House. From this place we took the right-hand trail and went to Fort Robertson on the White River, past the famous Crow Burke Mountain—through the Bad Lands of Dakota and crossed the Cheyenne River three miles below Hot Springs, at the foot of the Black Hills. We proceeded seventy-five or a hundred miles further to the Company Ranch on Driftwood Creek. Webb and Odell stayed at the ranch. The remainder went to Julesburg, Nebraska, with the provision wagon, where we bought tickets and came back to Texas.

Should any of my companions read this sketch I would be glad to have them write John Wells at Bartlett, Texas, or better known on the range as John Arlington.

TEXAS COWBOYS AT A CIRCUS IN MINNEAPOLIS

By S. H. Woods of Alice, Texas

I was born in Sherman, Grayson County, Texas, January 29th, 1865, and left home in Sherman in the spring of 1881, when a lad sixteen years of age, and worked for Suggs Brothers on the IS ranch, near the mouth of Beaver Creek, in the Chicksaw Nation, about 25 miles north of Montague, in Montague County, Texas.

In the month of July, 1881, we left the IS ranch for
Wyoming with about 3,000 head of Southern steer yearlings. I was second boss—the horse rustler. We started
from the Monument Hills, about 15 miles north of Red
River Station on the old Chis-
holm Trail, which was known
at that time as the Eastern
Trail. About the third night
out the Indians stampeded
our herd at the head of Wild
Horse Creek, which delayed
us for a few days. Leaving
this point, we had fine
weather and moved along
rapidly until we left the Eastern Trail at Red Fork Ranch,
on the Cimarron River, to intersect the Western Trail.
Here we had some trouble,
but nothing serious. When

S. H. WOODS

we arrived within eight or ten miles of Dodge City, Kansas, a beautiful city, situated on the north bank of the
Arkansas River and about one month's drive from Red
River, we could see about fifty different trail herds grazing up and down the valley of the Arkansas River. That
night we had a terrible storm. Talk about thunder and
lightning! There is where you could see phosphorescence
(fox fire) on our horse's ears and smell sulphur. We saw
the storm approaching and every man, including the
rustler, was out on duty. About 10 o'clock at night we
were greeted with a terribly loud clap of thunder and a
flash of lightning which killed one of our lead steers just
behind me. That started the ball rolling. Between the
rumbling, roaring and rattling of hoofs, horns, thunder
and lightning, it made an old cow-puncher long for headquarters or to be in his line camp in some dug-out on the
banks of some little stream. After the first break we

were unable to control the cattle longer, for just as soon as we could get them quiet, some other herd would run into us and give us a fresh start. Finally so many herds had run together that it was impossible to tell our cattle from others. When lightning flashed we could see thousands of cattle and hundreds of men all over the prairie, so we turned everything loose and waited patiently for daybreak. The next morning all the different outfits got together and we had a general round-up. It took about a week to get everything all straightened out and trim up the herds. We then crossed the Arkansas River just above Dodge City and traveled northwest across the State of Kansas and struck North Platte River at Ogallala, Nebraska. Following the North Platte River, we passed Chimney Rock, old Fort Fetterman and Fort Laramie and camped on the north bank of the North Platte River, where we rested one day grazing cattle, bathing and washing our saddle blankets. We then started on a four days' drive without water (about sixty miles) across the mountains from the North Platte River in Nebraska to Powder River in Wyoming. When we arrived on the divide or the backbone, between the two rivers, we passed along where a train of emigrants had been murdered by the Cheyenne Indians about two years before. For about the distance of half a mile the trail on both sides was strewn with oxen bones, irons and pieces of wagons where they had been burned, but did not see any human bones because I didn't take time to make a close examination. From the appearance of the surroundings there must have been twenty-five or thirty wagons and ox teams. We were told by old Indian fighters that there were 150 persons in the train, including the women and children, all murdered—none left to tell the tale.

By this time the cattle were getting dry. They had been two days without water, and these little Southern steers began to look like race horses. All the men were in front of the cattle except myself, the drag driver and the cook. Of course, we had to take good care of the grub wagon and cook. This was in the evening about 4 o'clock, and we did not see the men nor the lead cattle until the next day about 5 o'clock in the evening. The boys reported that the lead cattle reached Powder River about 10 o'clock, while we did not arrive until about 5 o'clock. After resting two or three days we proceeded down Powder River to the mouth of Crazy Woman, a small stream that empties into Powder River, and then up Crazy Woman River to near the foot of the Big Horn Mountain to our Wyoming headquarters. It took us just exactly three months and twenty days to drive a herd of Southern "dogies" from Red River and deliver them at the Wyoming ranch. We rested a few days while the Wyoming outfit gathered a beef herd for market and delivered it to us, and then we continued our northward drive with the beef herd to a station on the Northern Pacific Railroad called Glendive, on or near the Yellowstone River in Montana. When we loaded our cattle on the railroad for Chicago all the Texas outfit, numbering about twelve, took the cow trail for Texas by the way of Chicago.

Our first stop was at St. Paul, in Minnesota, to feed and water the cattle, and while the cattle were resting we all took the interurban street car for Minneapolis, about five miles from St. Paul, to see the Barnum & Bailey circus. We arrived at the circus, still wearing our trail garb, just a short time after the performance had begun. Of course we were feeling good by this time, and just as we entered the clown had his trick mule in the ring and was offering anyone $5.00 that could ride him. Twelve Texas cowboys fresh from the range, thought that was easy money, and all wanted to win the $5.00, so, we selected one of our party to earn the money. (He is now one of the wealthiest and most prominent stockmen of Texas, but I won't tell his name.) The clown let out his mule and we let out our Texas cowboy. One of the boys had a pair of Texas spurs in his pocket and we fastened them on the boots of the party that was to pull off the Wild West stunt. The mule was blindfolded and our man got on, and when the word was given one of our boys pulled off the blindfold, halter and all, and left the two in the ring ready for business. The rider fastened his spurs in the mule's shoulders and struck him in the flank with his Texas hat and that started the performance. There were thousands of people in the audience to witness the stunt. The mule made two or three jumps and roared like a mountain lion and our rider yelled like a Comanche Indian; the mule would pitch and roar, but our rider stuck to him like a postage stamp. As the rider could not be dismounted, the mule laid down on the ground and rolled over like a ball. Our rider stood by, and when the mule would get on his feet he would find our rider again on his back until, finally, the mule sulked and just stood in the middle of the ring with our rider still on him spurring and whipping him with his hat. The audience went wild and uncontrollable and the police had to interfere and pull our rider off the mule. The $5.00 was given the rider, and after the performance we returned to St. Paul, reloaded our cattle and continued our journey for Chicago, where we delivered them and left for Texas.

I stopped at Sherman and went to school that fall and winter and the next spring I returned to the IS ranch in the Indian Territory.

For six years I worked for Suggs Brothers during each spring and summer, returning in the late fall to Sherman, where I attended school during the winter months. After those six years spent on the trail and the range I returned to Sherman and attended one full term of school, after which I took up the study of law in the office of Woods & Brown, of Sherman, was admitted to the bar in the year 1888, then left for the West to grow up with the country. I first located in Haskell, Haskell County, Texas, but in the spring of 1890 one of those blizzards struck me and I drifted south, and as there were no wire fences to stop me, I landed in Laredo, Webb County, Texas, on the Rio Grande River, where I remained a short time, then moved to San Diego, in Duval County, Texas, where I hung out my "shingle" and commenced the practice of law. In the spring of 1893 I was appointed county judge of Duval County, but in the spring of 1894 I resigned as county judge to accept the appointment of district attorney for the old 49th Judicial District of Texas (a warm district about that time), composed of the counties of Webb, Duval and Zapata. I received this appointment from the Hon. C. A. Culberson, then governor of Texas. I served as district attorney for one term and in 1896 I was again elected county judge of Duval County, which office I held continuously until August, 1915, when I resigned and moved to Alice in Jim Wells County, Texas, where I am now practicing law.

THE REMARKABLE CAREER OF COLONEL IKE T. PRYOR

A history of the trail drivers of Texas would not be complete without a sketch of the career of Colonel Isaac Thomas Pryor, whose achievements during the past sixty years have been remarkable, to say the least. His life story reads like a romance, for it is made up of thrills and pathos, struggles and hardships, failures and triumphs that befell but few men who successfully overcame such obstacles that Colonel Pryor met and conquered. A pioneer of the early days of the unfenced range, he has become the most widely known cattleman of America, and his reminiscences, if ever written, would afford a complete panorama of the cattle industry of the United

States. From the early days of the grass trails, when the great herds of the Texas longhorns were driven thousands of miles to market, down to the present, with its bred cattle, its modern marketing system and rail transportation, he has been an active participant. At all the various stages that mark this period of Texas' development his has been an important part. His has been the directing mind in determining many of those steps where the decision meant either the advancement or downfall of the live stock industry. At these times of peril he became the trusted leader, just as in the earlier days of his young manhood he was looked upon to lead and direct when brawn and courage were needed to assure right by might.

Born at Tampa, Florida, in 1852, the third child of three boys, the subject of this sketch was left fatherless in 1855 at the age of three years, through his father's death. Shortly after his father's death, Mrs. Pryor took her three boys to Alabama, where two years later she passed away. She gave one each of the boys, ranging in age from five to nine years, to her three sisters. Ike, the last one, being with an uncle at Spring Hill, Tennessee.

At the age of nine years he ran away from the home of his relative and boldly struck out into the world for himself. He plunged at once into some of its most awesome and thrilling scenes. It was in the year 1861 with the Civil War just beginning its devastating reign. Into the midst of it he entered. Attaching himself as a newsboy to the Army of the Cumberland, he lived among the hardships of the campaign. He witnessed the scenes enacted at Murfreesboro, Chickamauga, Lookout Mountain and other desperately fought actions of the war between the States in which the loyal sons of the North and of the South fought to the end, each for what they held was right.

It was in such environment that tried the very souls

COL. IKE T. PRYOR

of men, that an impressionable boy not yet in his teens, had the early molding of his character. In it was seasoned the courage that had sent him, inexperienced and frail, to challenge for life and fortune. In these scenes in which were born the reunited nation with its brilliant future he imbibed the spirit of empire, the broadness of vision and the inspiration of immensity that determined the wide bounds his later activities in life were to reach.

In addition to helping mold his character, the great maelstrom into which he had thrust himself had a decisive effect upon determining his immediate life and actions. The little newsboy, unafraid where many a man knew fear, won numerous friends among both enlisted men and officers. So personal was the interest they took in him that after his pony had been shot from under him in one of the sharpest engagements, an army surgeon decided it was no place for a boy of his years and had him sent to his home in Ottawa, Ohio, where he arrived in 1863.

As a background to this remarkable part of Colonel Pryor's boyhood there is a story of a kind woman's influence over a motherless boy and her persevering search for him that ended in a manner that cannot but be considered providential.

In one of the former homes to which the boy was sent he found an elder cousin, a beautiful young girl just entering into womanhood, who felt the warmest sympathy for the orphaned boy brought into the home of her sisters and brothers. She was his defender in the reckoning over childish scrapes and his comforter in times of childish grief. Following his transfer to the home of his uncle at Spring Hill, this girl had married Mr. John O. Ewing and removed to Nashville, Tenn. The orphan boy frequently thought of her in his new home and longed for her comforting. It accordingly happened that when he was severely, and, as he felt, unjustly punished for a prank in which he had played an unwilling part, he determined to leave his uncle's home and go to Mrs. Ewing, who, he felt, would gladly give him a home with her.

He was resolutely making his way toward Nashville when a sudden advance of Federal forces passed beyond him and left him within the Union lines, thus determining his further wanderings. Incidentally, the sudden shifting of battles around interrupted the pursuit of the runaway and prevented his being returned to Spring Hill, Tennessee.

More remarkable still was the manner in which eventually he was found by Mrs. Ewing. Never losing faith that ultimately he would be located, she religiously asked every person who came from the Union lines for information of him. One day a Federal forage party reached the country home where she was living outside Nashville. The commanding officer, after taking the supplies wanted, courteously offered to issue a receipt for the property taken so that later claim might be made for the amount. He approached Mrs. Ewing to give her the document and, pursuing her usual course, she asked him if by chance he knew aught of a boy she described who was thought to be among the Federal troops. To her unbounded surprise and joy the officer not only knew the boy; he had frequently shared his couch with him, bought papers from him and assisted him. More important still, he knew of his being sent to Ottawa, Ohio, by the Federal surgeon. Means were at once adopted to get in communication with the boy in his new home. It was just in time, for the adventurous lad, thus placed on the very shores of Lake Erie, had determined upon a maritime career. He had even selected the vessel upon which he was to embark and had made overtures to her captain. Only the strong love he felt for the good woman who had protected him in his earlier childhood deterred him from becoming a seaman.

President Johnson, himself, became interested in the story of the boy, which reached him, and in 1864 had him returned to his relatives in Tennessee. He remained with them until 1870, when he took the step that was the real determination of his future career. At that time he turned his steps to the wide expanse of Texas. His first employment was as a farm hand. For this he received $15 a month. The next year he entered the cattle industry. His first connection with it was as a trail hand, driving his cattle to Coffeyville, Kansas. This was but the first of a number of trips he made over the now almost forgotten trails upon which are found today some of the greatest cities of the country as successors of the hamlets of those times. In 1872 he helped to drive a herd of cattle from Texas to Colorado. From then on his activities for many years were uninterrupted in the raising and marketing of live stock as practiced in those years. In 1873 he was employed on the Charles Lehmberg ranch in Mason County and there he really began his upward climb in the cattle business. Within a short time he had become ranch manager and in 1874 he had the responsibility of driving the cattle to Fort Sill, then Indian Territory, in fulfillment of contracts for their delivery to the Indians. The following year he was engaged largely in driving cattle to Austin for sale to the butchers there.

In 1876 he became a ranch owner, buying land and cattle in Mason County. The next year he again had charge of a herd of cattle driven overland, this drove including 250 head of his own cattle, which, together with those of John W. Gamel, were taken to Ogallala, Nebraska. Each season he reinvested and as the years passed in succession he drove ever-increasing herds of his own to the Northern markets. In 1878 he drove 3,000 head on his own account, in 1879 he drove 6,000 and in 1880 he drove 12,000. About that time he formed a partnership with his brother in Colorado and by 1881 he had so increased his drive that the total that year was fifteen herds of 3,000, making a total of 45,000 head in

a single year. These were taken to the North and Northwest over the much-discussed Chisholm Trail, being
marketed in Kansas, Nebraska, Wyoming and the Dakotas. Profits of from $3 to $5 a head were reckoned for
the enterprise, but a period of reverses came with the
winters of 1884 and 1885, and despite the large operations that had been carried on, Pryor Brothers showed
a loss of half a million dollars and their liquidation
resulted.

Nothing daunted, Mr. Pryor again resumed his operations, centering his activities again in the Texas field,
where he had achieved his first successes. By this time
the innovation of the railways and barb wire fencing had
greatly changed the conditions that existed in the earlier
days of the open range and the trails. Adapting himself
to the new conditions, Colonel Pryor again achieved success, and this time a lasting one.

The Texas Cattle Raisers' Association had been organized by leading cattlemen of the State in order to
afford themselves mutual protection for their cattle.
Colonel Pryor early became identified with the organization and in 1887 he was elected a member of its executive committee. This was the beginning of a long and
distinguished service in the interest of organized cattle
industry. In 1902 Mr. Pryor was elected first vice president of the Texas Cattle Raisers' Association and in 1906
he became its president under conditions which made the
honor one especially great. This was due to the fact
that Colonel Pryor was one of the heads of one of the
largest live stock commission firms in the country (the
Evans-Snider-Buel Company). Some opposition developed in the convention to electing as president a man
who was so prominently engaged in the commission business, where it was felt that there might arise conditions
in which the interests of the cattle raisers and the commission merchants would be at variance. Those who
knew him personally and therefore trusted him to the

limit, were sufficiently strong to bring about his election. During his administration for the year the others became so thoroughly convinced of his unfaltering devotion to their interests that the 1907 convention witnessed the dramatic and touching incident of his re-election without opposition by unanimous consent, attested by a rising vote. It was thus he was recognized by an organization that had grown to a membership of 2,000 cattlemen, owners of an aggregate of 5,000,000 head of cattle. Even this tribute was not the full measure of their reliance upon him. The succeeding year the members of this organization, which had grown to be one of the most important in the commercial life of the nation, broke the time-honored rule of limiting the presidency to two terms. They passed an amendment to the constitution permitting a longer term and enthusiastically named him for his third term. In 1909 he was again importuned to stand for re-election, but resolutely declined.

In the meantime, Colonel Pryor had also been elected president of the Texas Live Stock Association, which included all classes of interest in the live stock industry of the State. He was importuned to accept another term as its head, but declined re-election. Later he was chosen to head the National Live Stock Shippers' Protective League, which was organized at Chicago for the purpose of protecting the interests of live stock shippers all over the United States.

On January 8, 1917, at the convention held at Cheyenne, Wyo., there was added to the other honors conferred upon him by the live stock interests of the country, the presidency of the American National Live Stock Association. Again at the convention held in January, 1918, at Salt Lake City, Utah, he was elected to succeed himself. A speech made by Colonel Pryor before that convention made definite recommendations to Congress for national legislation affecting the cattle and meat-packing industry and attracted nation-wide interest and indorsement. This was perhaps the beginning of the active campaign in behalf of the Kendrick or Kenyon bill, as it is generally known. In 1919 Colonel Pryor retired from the presidency of the American National Live Stock Association, being succeeded in that office by Senator J. B. Kendrick. Last September Colonel Pryor went to Washington and testified before the Senate Agricultural Committee favoring the Kendrick or Kenyon bill. This testimony was given wide publicity through the American press at that time and is believed to have exerted a wide influence.

While centering his greatest efforts in the live stock business, Colonel Pryor has not attained prominence in it alone. He was first chairman of the Texas Industrial Congress. In 1908 he was elected president of the Trans-Mississippi Commercial Congress at Denver, Colo., and it was in a large measure through his instrumentality that San Antonio was selected for the 1909 session of that great body. In 1909 he organized and accepted the presidency of the City National Bank of San Antonio. He was at the same time vice president of the R. E. Stafford & Co., bankers, of Columbus, Texas, and vice president and one of the managers of the Evans-Snider-Buel Company.

Keeping constantly in touch with all conditions affecting the cattle market, he has been able successfully to manage affairs that many would deem impossible. At the outbreak of the Spanish-American War he sent a special agent to Cuba to keep him advised as to the cattle conditions on that island. This foresight and enterprise resulted in his sending the first shipload of beeves that arrived in Cuba after the blockade had been lifted. Other shipments followed in quick order until 7,000 head in all had been landed at Havana, bringing the unusually high prices that they could command. Interested with Colonel Pryor in this bit of enterprise was J. H. P. Davis of Richmond, Texas.

Such is his character that it is his great fortune not to be envied in his success and honors. This is because in his rise to prominence and wealth he has never been other than the same true-hearted man of the plains. To this day his office in San Antonio is the gathering place of the greatest of that great clan of Texas empire-builders, the early cattlemen.

HABITS AND CUSTOMS OF EARLY TEXANS

By L. B. Anderson, Seguin, Texas

I was born in Amite County, Mississippi, March 24, 1849. Came overland with my parents to Texas in the

L. B. ANDERSON

spring of 1853. Our outfit consisted of two wagons and a buggy, and we also brought several of our negro slaves. My mother and the youngest children rode in the buggy, which was drawn by an old mule. We crossed the Mississippi River on a ferryboat. I do not know how long it took us to make the trip, but we must have made very slow progress, for the older children walked almost all of the way and drove an old favorite milch cow that we called "Old Cherry." I remember one amusing incident about that old cow. She had a growing hatred for a dog, and never failed to lunge at one that came near her. One evening about dusk as we were driving her along the way we came to a large black stump by the roadside, and "Old Cherry," evidently thinking it was a dog, made a lunge at it and knocked herself senseless.

The one thing that stands out most vividly in my recollection of that trip is the fact that I was made to wear a sunbonnet all the way. I hated a bonnet as much as "Old Cherry" hated a dog, and kept throwing my bonnet away and going bareheaded, so finally my mother cut two holes in the top of the bonnet, pulled my hair through them and tied it hard and fast. That was before the days of clipped hair, and as mine was long enough to tie easily, that settled the bonnet question, and I had to make my entrance into grand old Texas looking like a girl, but feeling every inch like a man.

We stopped in Williamson County, near Georgetown, then in the fall of the same year we came to Seguin, Guadalupe County, where I have lived ever since, except when I was following the trail. My father bought a tract of land west of Seguin for $1,000 cash. As it had not been surveyed by either the buyer or the seller neither of them knew how much land the tract contained. Twenty years later father sold it for just what he had paid for it, and when it was surveyed it was found to be several hundred acres, and is now worth $100 per acre.

There was but little farming carried on in those days, the settlers depending on grass for feed for their work teams and other stock. The crops of corn and cane were made with oxen. Many times I have seen the heel flies attack a yoke of oxen and they would run off, jump the rail fence and get away with the plow to which they were attached, and sometimes it would be several days before they were found. Of course we did not make much farming after that fashion, but we did not need much in those days. We lived care-free and happy until the outbreak of the Civil War, when father and my older brother went into the service to fight for the South, leaving me, a lad of only 11 years, the only protection for my mother and younger brothers and sisters, but mother was a fearless woman and the best marksman with a rifle I ever saw, so we felt able to take care of ourselves. My duties during the war were many and varied. I was mail carrier and general errand boy for all of the women in the neighborhood. Among other things it was my duty to look after the cattle. During this trying time the cattle accumulated on the range and after the war when the men returned cow hunting became general. From ten to twenty men would gather at some point, usually at old man Konda's, in the center of the cow range, and round up the cattle. Each man would take an extra pony along, a lengthy stake rope made of rawhide or hair, a wallet of cornbread, some fat bacon and coffee, and plenty of salt to do him on the round-up. Whenever we got hungry for fresh meat we would kill a fat yearling, eat all we wanted and leave the remainder. On these trips I acquired my first experience at cow-punching. Our route usually would be down the Cibolo by Pana Maria and old Helena to the San Antonio River, and up Clate Creek, gathering all the cattle that belonged to our crowd and some mavericks besides. The drives would generally wind up at old man Konda's, from where he had started, and here division was made, each man taking his cattle home, where they would be branded and turned out on the range again. Some of the men who went on these trips were Gus Konda, considered the best cowman in Guadalupe County, John Oliver, Frank Delaney, Dud Tom, Whit Vick, W. C. Irvin, John and Dud Jefferson, Pinkney Low and sons, and General William Saffold.

There was no local market for the cattle, and the Kansas drives started about that time. Eugene Millett and his two brothers, Alonzo and Hie, engaged in buying beeves and work oxen to send up the trail in 1869. My father sold them several yoke of oxen which he had freighted to Mexico with, and I helped deliver them to Mr. Millett at the Three Mile Water Hole north of Seguin. I was already a cowboy in my own estimation, those hunts on the range having given me a taste of the life. Hearing Millett's men tell of their trips up the trail, I decided at once that that was the life for me, so I told my father I wanted to go with the herd. He very reluctantly gave his consent, but made me promise that if I was going to be a cowman that I would be "an honest one." He then proceeded to give me a lot of advice, and presented me with a ten-dollar gold piece for use on the trip. My mother sewed that money in the band of my trousers (breeches, we called them in those days) and I carried it to Kansas and back that way, and when I returned home I gave it back to my father.

The next fall and winter I worked for Pinkney Low, gathering cattle on the range to be taken up the trail in the spring. I went on the trail every year thereafter until 1887, when the trail was virtually closed. I went twice as a hand and sixteen times as boss of the herd. I drove over every trail from the Gulf of Mexico to the Dakotas and Montana, but the Chisholm Trail was the one I traveled the most. The men I drove for were E. B. Millett, Alonzo Millett, Hie Millett, Colonel Seth Maberry, W. C. Irvin, Tom and John Dewees and Jim Sherrill. The places I most often delivered cattle to were Baxter Springs, Great Bend, Newton, Abilene, Ellsworth and Dodge City, Kansas, Ogallala and Red Cloud Agency, Nebraska, Fort Fetterman, Wyoming and Dan Holden's ranch in Colorado on Chug River. Some of the most prominent cattlemen I knew in those days were Pressnall and Mitchell, John Blocker, Jim Ellison, D. R. Fant, John Lytle and Dick Head.

My experiences on the trail were many and varied, some perilous and some humorous. I remember one exciting time in particular, when I was taking a herd for Millett & Irvin from the Panhandle ranch to Old Fort Fetterman in the Rocky Mountains. The Sioux Indians made a raid on us, got off with most of our horses and all of our provisions. We had nothing to eat except buffalo and antelope meat until we reached North Platte City, a distance of two hundred miles.

In 1871 I went up the trail with T. B. Miller and Bill
Mayes. We crossed at Red River Station and arrived at
Newton, Kansas, about the time the railroad reached
there. Newton was one of the worst towns I ever saw,
every element of meanness on earth seemed to be there.
While in that burg I saw several men killed, one of them,
I think, was Jim Martin from Helena, Karnes County.

One fall after I returned from Wyoming, Millett sent
me to the Indian Territory to issue beef to the Indians
on a government contract. I was stationed at Anadarko
on the Washita River, and issued but once a week at
Fort Sill and Cheyenne Agency on the Canadian River.
There I saw my first telephone. It was a crude affair,
and connected the agent's store and residence, a distance
of several hundred yards. The apparatus consisted of
one wire run through the walls of the store and house
with a tube at each end through which you had to blow
to attract attention of the party called, and then you
could talk over it as well as any phone of the present time.

I was in Abilene when Wild Bill Hickok had full sway
in that town and it was dangerous for a man to walk
the streets. I was there when he killed Phil Coe.

Some of the old cowboys who followed the trail from
this country were the twin brothers, Cap and Doc Smith,
Dud Tom, Joe Ellis, Haynes Morgan, Mit Nickols, John
and Fenner Jefferson, Whit Vick, Bill Coorpender,
Frank Rhodes, Leroy Sowell, Billie McLean, Billie
Thompson, Pat Burns, Tom Terrell, John and Tom Lay
and many others.

The journeys up the trail were beset by many dangers
and difficulties. Savage Indians often attacked the herd
in attempts to cause a stampede. Few outfits were strong
enough to repel the Indians by force and were compelled
to pay them tribute in the form of beef. To do the work
required on those drives took men of strong nerves, iron
bodies and alert brains.

The last trip I made was in 1887, when I drove horses.

I bought them from Redman and his partner through Mr. George Saunders. They were a bunch of Spanish mares just from Mexico, and I remember a squabble I had with two other buyers over a big white paint stud that happened to be in the bunch. I got the stud, all right, and made big money on him as well as all of the other horses.

In 1888 I married and settled down on my farm, but never could quite give up the cattle business, and on a small scale have handled some kind of cattle ever since, but the Jersey or any other kind of milch cow has never appealed to me as the Texas longhorn did. After thirty years of settled life the call of the trail is with me still, and there is not a day that I do not long to mount my horse and be out among the cattle.

HIT THE TRAIL IN HIGH PLACES

By Jeff Connolly of Lockhart, Texas

I was born at Prairie Lea in 1863 and moved to Lockhart in 1876. My experience in the good old days gone by was as follows:

Drove on the trail for old Captain King of Nueces County in 1880 with a man by the name of Coleman as boss, and when I got as far as Taylor, King sent me back and I helped another brother of this man Coleman drive another herd of the King cattle to Red River. The only white men with the herd were Coleman and myself, the balance of the bunch being Mexicans. All the old-timers know how King handled the Mexicans—he had them do the work and let the white men do the bossing.

I was on the trail that year about three months and drew a salary of $1.50 per day and board was furnished me.

During the winter of 1881 and spring of 1882 I drove

cattle for George W. Littlefield of Austin, who I am sure all the old-timers remember and regard very highly. I went with A. A. Woodland, who all the old-timers in Lockhart knew very well and who lived here during his latter days. When we got to old Fort Griffin we cut the stock cattle all out, which amounted to about 1,000 cows at that time. Myself and two other men held these at Foil Creek, this side of Fort Griffin, until another herd reached us, which was about thirty days. Then we turned them in with another herd of Littlefield's cattle that was being handled by a man by the name of McCarty, another Irishman who looks about like I do. From there we went on to the Pecos River, where the L F D ranch of Littlefield was established, known to be one of the foremost ranches in that part of the country. We had plenty of good horses on this drive and McCarty and Littlefield bought fifty more when we reached Fort Griffin from a Mexican at that place. These last horses they bought had a colt every once in a while as we were mounting them in the mornings.

This herd of cattle McCarty was looking after was bought from Jim Ellison, a noted cowman in Caldwell County in the seventies, who owned what was then known as the Ellison ranch, where these cattle were delivered to Littlefield.

Last time I was in Austin, about six years ago, I went into the American National Bank with a friend of mine and I asked the teller of the bank where the Major was. He told me he was back in his private office. This friend of mine wanted to know why I was asking about Major Littlefield and asked me if I knew he was a millionaire? I told him that I knew that, but that I used to drive on the old trail for him and was anxious to see him. I went back and told the Major who I was and he treated me as fine as any man was ever treated. If I had been a millionaire myself he could not have treated me any better, and that's what makes us common fellows like him. He is just as plain as if he didn't have any more than we have. We talked about old times when the other fellows like Bud Wilkerson, Phelps White, Tom White, some of his men, used to work with me for him. He told me these three fellows were still with him on the ranch and making good.

In 1884 I drove a herd of horses from Banquette in Nueces County, for a man by the name of Frank Byler. Right at the edge of Lockhart, where we camped that night, and from where we started to town next morning we were arrested by Sheriff Allie Field for trespassing. We had no money and Frank did not know what in the world to do, and I told him to go to Dr. Blanks of Lockhart, a great friend of the old trailers, and he would loan us the money to pay the fine. We borrowed $50.00 in money and bought $50.00 worth of grub on credit, and when we got to Onion Creek we sold two horses for $100.00 and in a few days sent the money to Lockhart, and from that time on we had plenty of money to do us.

When we got to Hillsboro it was very cold and raining and we broke our wagon down and had to stop. Our horses stampeded all over that country and twenty-seven froze to death that night.

We remained there about four days waiting for it to thaw out, and when it did we sold about forty-five saddle horses to an old cowman of the Red River country. We headed from there to Red River, and when we got there the river was up and we got a little of that stuff that livens up. The herd attempted to stampede, but we held them and put them across all right.

Everything went well until we got to the Washita, where the herd stampeded again and we were two days crossing the river. One night I stayed over there with the Indians. This side of Okmulgee we went out hunting a place to camp one evening and came across a little clump of trees where we saw a man hanging there by the neck with a sign on him, "Death to the one who cuts him down.'' We saw he was dead and we did not cut the rope. We went on further to camp that night.

We reached the Arkansas River in a few days, where we had to lay four days on account of the river being up. Just before we crossed we found that the Indians had stolen a lot of blankets from our Mexicans. I made our bunch of Mexicans go up to their camp and steal some of the Indians' blankets and slickers, and the next day when we crossed the river the Indians were pointing at the Mexicans, noticing that they had stolen their blankets and slickers. They were talking Indian and our Mexicans did not know what they were talking about. We had no further trouble until we got to Baxter Springs, Kansas. The first night we were camped on the state line we had a big stampede. The Indians were there to count us up for grass fee, and we run them through so fast they could not count them and lost count. They accepted our count and, of course, we guessed them low enough to take care of ourselves.

We did very well, selling these out to people all over the United States, as there were traders there from everywhere.

In 1885 I drove cattle with Bill Jackman of San Marcos, the herd belonging to Hez Williams and Bill Goode of Kyle. This herd was put up at Rancho Grande, in Wharton County, by Bob Stafford of Columbus. When we got to old Texarkana we had a big stampede that night and whipped them in and ran them over one another trying to hold them until they looked like they had been in a wreck. They had "run" on the brain all the way until we got to Kyle. When we reached there every fellow was about on foot, as our horses had played out, so we put the herd in Desha Bunton's pasture and stayed there several days to get a new outfit of horses, and had them all shod up to go through the mountains and get a new outfit of men also, as the boys all quit except Fisher, Jackman and myself. We pulled out from there with a new set of men and horses headed for Deer Trail, Colorado, south of Cheyenne. A few nights after we left Kyle we had a big rain and the cattle drifted pretty well all night, and Tom Fisher and myself came upon a man camped in a wagon and told him to get up, for it was daylight. When he got up we both crawled in with our wet clothes on and went to sleep and left him on the outside. When morning came we got up and began rounding up the herd and none of the bunch had missed us. We traveled along all right then until we reached Bell Plains one evening. There a Dutchman came out and told us to move on, and we told him to hunt a warmer climate, that we were going to camp there that night. About twelve o'clock that night he and the sheriff came to our camp hunting the boss and couldn't find him. They went away and next morning before breakfast they came back and wanted to know where the boss was, and we told him we didn't have any. He wanted to stop our herd of cattle, but we told him if they did they would have to give a $30,000 bond, as these cattle were mortgaged and could not be stopped without somebody giving bond. The sheriff called us off and talked with us a while and told us he would see us about it, and this was the last we ever heard of the matter.

Everything went all right from here until we got up to Doan's Store, when one night the wagons caught fire and burned the wagon sheet. We got busy just at this time trying to save our coffee and a little meat we had picked up from the 3 D cattle.

From there we had to rustle a wagon sheet to keep everything dry when the rains came up. We got along all right from here until we got to Wolf Creek at old Camp Supply, where they quarantined us, and we had to go down to No Man's Land, a strip between the Panhandle and Kansas, now a part of Oklahoma. Crossing the plains it drizzled very nearly every night, just enough to make the cattle walk till about eleven o'clock at night.

When we got to Beaver, this side of the Arkansas River, in Colorado, we sold the cattle. After we turned them over Bill Jackman and myself came back over the trail and met Alex Magee and his cattle and stopped him for a few days to let his cattle rest up, as we knew the people that had contracted his cattle were waiting for him, and we wanted his bunch to look good when he got there. Wanted them to show up all right so there would be no kick. When we brought the cattle up to turn them over to the buyers they received them with the understanding that we had to brand them. We carried them up Beaver Creek for about 40 miles, where we branded them, and after we had done this they asked us to carry a bunch of about three hundred white-face Herefords, the first I ever saw, up in the Rocky Mountains and put them in winter quarters. When we got them there he fitted us up with fresh horses and everything and started us for West Los Angeles to ship us back home.

In 1886 I started to go up with Bill Jackman again, but when I got to the Hutcheson ranch near San Marcos, Jackman was there and told me he had sold the cattle to John Blocker, who would be there directly with his outfit to receive them. When they came he recommended me to the man who was in charge of the cattle—a man by the name of Murchison, who was also in charge of the horses and outfit. Next day we rounded up the pasture, but they didn't take the cattle, and we went from there on to Kyle to the Vaughn pasture. Arch Odem in a few days bought about 1,500 head of cattle down on the Guadalupe River and brought them up to where we were and turned them over to us. We went on up in a few days to the Hez Williams ranch and got about 800 more steers. In a few days we got about 700 head more from places near there, then pulled out for the trail, being the first herd of the Blocker cattle for that year. When we got between Runnels and Abilene we laid in wait there until ten more herds of the Blocker cattle caught up with us. Then we shaped up ten herds to go on to Colorado, and I and my bunch cut cattle all the way until we got to Red River. At Red River we took the lead cattle out of two herds and put them together in one herd and left the drags together in another herd.

When we reached the Wichita Mountains, in Indian Territory, the Indians met us there and wanted beef. I had a big black range steer I had picked up in Texas, and when I got up in the roughest part of the mountains I cut this steer out and told them to go after him. The steer outran them and got away and directly I saw them coming back, one after another, like they travel, but without any beef. The next day the trail cutters looked us up and did not find anything. Then we went on until we got to Camp Supply, where we had to go across the plains again, and it was very dry. The first evening we struck the plains we drove right square until night and I held up the lead cattle and the wagon was not in sight at this time. We camped there that night and there came the hardest rain I ever saw fall, and it was so cold we nearly shook ourselves to death. It rained all the time from there on to Hugo, Colorado, where Blocker turned these cattle loose and where they were rebranded and turned loose again.

From Hugo I helped take about 1,000 head of saddle horses and put them in winter quarters, and when that was done I came back home.

THE MEN WHO MADE THE TRAIL

By Luther A. Lawhon, San Antonio, Texas

We can scarcely estimate the debt which we owe to the men who made the Trail. Lest we forget—those pioneer settlers and ranchmen were not only empire builders, but were also the "mudsillers" upon which has been erected that superb structure of productive wealth

—the American live stock industry as it exists today west of the Mississippi. It is indeed a far stretch from the domesticated, gentle thoroughbred to the wild, untamable "longhorn." But is it not well that at times we take a

LUTHER A. LAWHON

retrospective view, and contrast the present with the past? By so doing we may the better determine the extent to which this all important industry h a s progressed with our geographical development, and also incidentally keep alive the memories and the traditions of a bygone age.

By a degree of good fortune it fell to me to be reared from infancy to m a n h o o d in Southwest Texas in the midst of that favored section when it was one vast breeding ground for cattle and horses, and from which was afterward to be driven those herds that, moving across the prairies of Texas and through the Indian Territory, from 1869 to 1886, poured into the wild and unsettled area from Kansas to the British Dominions. In the days and in the section of which I treat the railroad, the telegraph and the telephone were unknown. A greater part of the land still belonged to the State and was prized in the main for the grasses which grew upon it; fencing wire had not been invented, and in consequence the entire country, except where dotted with ranches, was unfenced and uncontrolled—a common pasture in which thousands of horses and cattle roamed at will.

In imagination reverting again to those bygone scenes, I shall endeavor to describe briefly some of the conditions which surrounded the old-time Texas ranchman, his peculiarities and his customs. The country at large was sparsely settled. In a majority of the counties there was barely sufficient population for county organization. The largest and, in most instances, the only town in the county, was the county seat village, with its rock or lumber court house, which was rarely of two stories, and near by, as an adjunct, a one-cell rock or lumber jail. Around the public square were built the few unpretentious storehouses, that flaunted the proverbial signs, "Dry Goods and Grocers," or "Dry Goods, Boots and Shoes," as the case might be. That the weaknesses as well as the social predelictions of the sturdy citizenship might be readily and conveniently catered to, a saloon or perhaps several, could always be found on or near the public square. Clustered about the commercial center, and growing further apart as the distance increased, were private residences which went to make up the hamlet. After the court house and jail, the hotel—generally a two-story building—was considered the most important, as it was frequently the most imposing structure in the village. In addition to the official and business edifices, there was always a well-constructed school house (there were no free schools in those days) and a commodious, comfortable church house at convenient distances. I purposely use church house in the singular, for in the days under consideration the tabernacle of the Most High was a union structure, erected by the joint contributions of the various and divergent church members, as well as of philanthropic citizens who made no "professions," and in which those pioneer men and women with their families, irrespective of denomination, met together with good and honest hearts and worshiped God in spirit and in truth.

Such, in brief, was the frontier village. Beyond its

confines the country, as stated, was unfenced and uncontrolled. Luxuriant grasses and fragrant wild flowers covered prairie, hill and valley for two-thirds of the year. Herds of cattle and horses grazed in every direction, and each ranchman, by his mark and brand, was enabled to identify his stock and secure its increase. Trained to the range and keen of eye as they were, the old-time ranchmen and their cowboys would necessarily fail to find some of the year's increase when they worked this vast territory. As a result there was a small percentage, yearly, of unmarked and unbranded calves. These animals, after being weaned from the mother cows, would thenceforth be abroad on the prairies, the property of whomsoever found and branded them, and in cowboy parlance were called "mavericks." This name had its origin in the fact that Mr. Sam Maverick, now deceased, an honored and wealthy citizen of San Antonio, was the owner of a large brand of cattle that ranged throughout Southwest Texas. During the Civil War he was unable to "brand up" the increase in his stock, and in consequence there was a marked augmentation of unbranded and unmarked cattle on the range from San Antonio to the coast. This fact, and the cause of it, was a matter of general knowledge throughout this section. Therefore, when the old-time ranchman and his cowboys in this territory found an unmarked and unbranded yearling or two-year-old on the range, it was assumed that the animal had at one time been the property of the San Antonio citizen. Hence the term "maverick" soon became universal as a designation for an animal whose owner could not be definitely determined, and has now become a permanent fixture in our English nomenclature. The "roundup," with its chuck wagon, its high-priced chef and bill of fare à la carte, had not as yet been introduced. Those old-time ranchmen were content to simply cow hunt twice a year and brand their calves. As a rule those whose ranches were the nearest hunted together and thereby made up an "outfit." Their provisions, flour, coffee and dried beef, with the beddin', was loaded on a pack horse, which was driven with the saddle ponies. They worked the country and branded through the day and camped at night where water was in abundance and where grass was good.

There was an unwritten law, recognized by the good women of the towns as well as of the country, that whenever a party of cow hunters rode up and asked to have bread baked, it mattered not the time of day, the request was to be cheerfully complied with. Not from fear of insult in case of refusal—for each and every cowboy was the champion defender of womanhood, and would have scorned to have uttered a disrespectful word in her presence—but from an accommodating spirit and a kindness of heart which was universally characteristic in those frontier days. My father was a lawyer and therefore my boyhood home was in the village, but I remember the many times that cow hunters rode up to my father's house, and telling my mother they were out of bread, asked that she would kindly bake their flour for them. Everything was at once made ready. The sack was lifted from the pack horse and brought in, and in due time the bread wallets were once more filled with freshly cooked biscuits, and the cowboys rode away with grateful appreciation. These acts of consideration on the part of my mother were entirely gratuitous, but the generous-hearted cowboys would always leave either a half sack of flour or a money donation as a free-will offering.

One of the cardinal virtues of the old-time ranchman was hospitality. This commendable trait was not alone possessed by him, but was an attribute of his entire family. The cordial welcome was not restricted to nearby neighbors, friends and acquaintances, but was as freely extended to "the stranger within the gates." The way-worn traveler was never turned aside, and while a guest at the ranch, did illness overtake him, the watchful vigils and tender hands of the ranchman's wife and daughters ministered to his sufferings as though he was one of the family, until health was restored, and he was sent on his way rejoicing. The wife of the old-time ranchman! How kind, how considerate she was! It mattered not that at the approach of every full moon the saddle horses were rounded up and more closely guarded, and the guns and pistols on the ranch were overhauled and minutely inspected in anticipation of an Indian raid—there was no excitement or complaint on her part! Amidst the dangers and the deprivations of frontier environment, she gathered her little ones closer about her, and with faith in God and reliance on the strong arm of husband, neighbors and friends, went forward uncomplainingly with the stern duties of life. All honor to those noble mothers in Israel!

The methods of business were in keeping with the primitive conditions of society. There were no banks in the country. Owing to this fact every ranch home was the depository of more or less money. The coin, if of considerable amount, was put in saddle bags, morrals, etc., and secreted in remote corners of the house or up under the roof, or buried on or near the premises, and was brought forth from its hiding places as occasion demanded. A somewhat ludicrous incident arose from this peculiar custom. One of the "old-timers," whose ranch was near the line of Karnes and Goliad Counties, finding himself with considerable money on hand, and having no immediate use for it, decided to bury it. Choosing an especially dark night, he went down to his cowpen and, removing one of the posts of the fence, dropped his bag of gold in the posthole. He then replaced the post and returned, satisfied that he had put his treasure where moth and rust could not corrupt nor thieves break through and steal. After considerable time had elapsed he found himself in a position to use his secreted fund. But, unfortunately, he had failed to note the particular post under which he had buried his money, and all signs of his former visit having been obliterated, he was compelled to dig up one-half of his cowpen before he secured the coveted deposit. When the ranchmen bought stock of any kind they brought the money in gold and silver to where the animals were to be received and paid it out, dollar for dollar. They generally carried the money in leather belts buckled around their waist, but the silver, being more bulky, was placed in duckin' sacks, and was loaded on a pack horse or mule. It was necessary in those days to know the weight as well as the value of money, and therefore it was a matter of current knowledge that one thousand dollars in silver weighed sixty-two and one-half pounds. Robbery was a crime unknown among those rugged and honest old pioneers.

Brave, hospitable and generous, the old-time ranchman believed in justice, simple justice, stripped of all technicalities of law. According to his ethics, the man "who'd forsake a friend or go back on his word," was a scoundrel, and the thief, it mattered not who he was, had forfeited his right to live. But those nice distinctions of judicial import, murder in the first or second degree, manslaughter, etc., did not appeal to him. In the enforcement of the code he did not subscribe to the theory that an accused could be morally innocent and at the same time legally guilty of a crime. When a killin' occurred he asked, "Was ther a grudge between 'em, and wuz it a fair fight?" If so, he could not understand why, when the best shot or the coolest nerve had slain his adversary, the great state of Texas should want to prosecute and punish the survivor. And as a juror he would not be a party to such prosecution and punishment. In illustration of his personal application and influence in the enforcement of law, I am reminded of the following occurrence: One of the old-time ranchmen and forceful characters in Southwest Texas was a certain Captain Blank. He had been at the head of a vigilance committee which had hung a number of men under his personal supervision. He was well known throughout his section as a firm, fearless and implacable leader. During the progress of a murder trial in his home county he was summoned to attend as a special venireman. In due time he was called to the stand, and on *voir dire* the district attorney propounded the statutory question, "Have you any conscientious scruples in regard to the infliction of the punishment of death for crime?" To the surprise of the district attorney, as well as of all those present, Captain Blank replied, "I have." Then noting the incredulous smile on the faces of the audience, he turned to the court and said, "Jedge, it's this a-way. I don't want to hang a man unless I've got somethin' agin' 'im."

The old-time ranchman never turned a deaf ear to a worthy appeal. His generosity and his warm-heartedness knew no bounds. On the other hand, he would not tamely submit to what he considered an unjust imposition. With a Hampden spirit, it was not the amount, but the principle for which he was ever ready to fight, if need be to the death. The following will perhaps serve to illustrate this phase of his character: One of the cowboys on a Southwest Texas ranch in the olden time, when gas was the principal municipal illuminant, decided to go up to San Antonio for a few days and see the sights and, incidentally, "pike" a little at the Bull's Head or the White Elephant gambling tables. In due time he returned to the ranch. The boys gathered around him to learn what had been his experiences in the big town. After recounting at some length the incident of his sojourn, he casually remarked, "Fellers, I come damn near havin' to kill a hotelkeeper." "Why, how was that, Bill?" queried his auditors. "Well, it wuz this a-way," explained Bill. "The fust night I wuz thar, when I got ready to go to bed a nigger showed me up to my room an' lit the light. On lookin' around, I saw a great big sign tacked to the wall, sayin', 'Don't Blow Out the Gas.' Of course then

I didn't blow it out, bein's as they said not to. I jest let the light burn, an' by pulling my hat over my face managed to sleep tolerable well. The next mornin' when I went to settle my bill, that low down hotelkeeper tried to charge me two dollars extra, because I didn't blow out the gas. He shore did. An' I jest looked that hotelkeeper in the eye, an' I told him that I'd fight him till hell froze over, an' then skate with him on the ice, before I'd pay one cent of that two dollars. And I meant jest what I said.'' The boys all unanimously agreed that if Bill had killed that hotelkeeper, under the circumstances it would have been a clear case of justifiable homicide. Such were some of the conditions, characteristics and peculiarities of a society now long since passed away.

To conclude: In 1880 a combination of circumstances gave me the long-coveted opportunity to go up the trail. I was one of Mr. Cal Mayfield's ''outfit'' with a herd of one thousand head of ML horses. Our party, with but one exception, was composed of Karnes County boys. We left the Hill pasture in Live Oak County for the long and arduous drive to Dodge City, Kansas. After a halt of three days in the vicinity of Fort Worth, where the chuck wagon was replenished with food sufficient to sustain us to our destination, we virtually bade adieu to civilization, and moved into the wild section of Northeast Texas, and on, on, through the Indian Territory (crossing Red River at Doan's Crossing), until at last, after many hardships and exciting experiences, we again enjoyed the comfort of ''God's land,'' in the frontier town of Caldwell, Kansas. The year above mentioned was one of the worst ever known on the trail. Storms, rain and lightning. We had our first stampede in the Blue Mounds country, north of Fort Worth, and from there on it was a run night after night, with but short intermissions. When we had crossed the Cimarron River, out of the Indian Territory, and came to where the Dodge and the Caldwell trails forked, Mr. Mayfield decided to follow the latter trail, as

Caldwell was somewhat nearer. After resting at Caldwell for a few days, the herd was "split up" and I was assigned to go with a bunch which was loaded on the cars and shipped to Kansas City. From there, back to Texas —and home.

In closing this article, I crave the reader's pardon for what may be an unwarranted intrusion of personal feeling. But the old-time ranchman, his bravery, his rugged honesty and his nobility of character, is a theme which is near and dear to me. The purest, sweetest draughts of happiness that I have quaffed in this life, were drawn in those good old days, when as a boy and as a young man, I dwelt in the little village of Helena, the then county seat of Karnes County, in Southwest Texas, in the midst of a noble pioneer people, among whom were many of the men who made the trail. Time's cruel hand has wrought many changes. The silken ties of early association have been severed for years, but the treasured memories of that golden time have kept green in my heart throughout every change and vicissitude of fortune. These hallowed recollections have walked with me thus far and will continue so to do to the end of the chapter. Then:

"Let Fate do her worst, there are relics of joy,
Bright dreams of the past, which she cannot destroy;
Which come in the nighttime of sorrow and care,
And bring back the features that joy used to wear.
Long, long be my heart with such memories filled,
Like the vase in which roses have once been distilled—
You may break, you may shatter the vase if you will,
But the scent of the roses will cling 'round it still."

A FEW THRILLING INCIDENTS IN MY EXPERIENCE ON THE TRAIL

By L. B. Anderson of Seguin, Texas

One trip I drove for Dewees, Ervin & Jim Ellison. I got the herd at Rockport, in Coleman & Fulton's pasture, and drove to the Millett & Irvin ranch in the Panhandle, camping right where the town of Seymour is now located, and remained there several months helping to round up several thousand head of cattle. Among those who were with me there on the range were Tom Peeler, Billie Bland, Sam and John Wilson, Billie Gray, Charlie Reed and Whit Vick. We started from that point with three thousand yearlings for Major Wolcott's ranch in the Rocky Mountains. Had good luck all the way until we reached Fort McPherson on the North Platte River, where our horses stampeded and ran right through our herd, causing the yearlings to stampede also, going in every direction, several hundred running into the river. We finally rounded all of them up and delivered the herd in fine shape.

I took one herd of cattle up into Colorado for John and Tom Dewees to a man named Cheatem. We killed many buffalo on this trip, but in Kansas in 1874, on the Ninnisquaw River, I saw more buffalo than I ever saw anywhere else. As far as the eye could see over the plains was a solid mass of moving buffalo, all drifting northward. I remember my first experience in trying to kill one of these animals. I did not know the huge hump on their backs was a row of ribs, and that I could not kill one unless I shot below that hump, but I learned that much while trying to shoot my first buffalo. I had an old cap and ball pistol and, taking careful aim at a bull's hump, I began to shoot, but the only effect my shots had was to make him run faster. I kept up with him, firing as we ran. Sometimes all six loads would go off at the same time and I would reload, going at full speed. I ran him several miles before I finally killed him.

Besides buffalo, deer and antelope, we used to kill ducks, geese, prairie chickens and other wild fowl, which were plentiful in the uncivilized part of the state. I always enjoyed hunting, and I guess I killed as many deer as the average man. Speaking of deer, reminds me of a peculiar thing that happened in Atascosa County one day. The outfits of Dudley Tom and myself were gathering cattle on Dewees' ranch, when one morning a negro and myself were rounding up a bunch of cattle, when several deer jumped out of a thicket directly in front of us. Of course we gave chase and ran them so close one of the bucks ran against a tree and broke his neck.

At another time, when we were camped near John Tom's ranch in Atascosa County, we were driving a herd of old Mexican beeves down a long lane, and they stampeded, turned around and started back up the lane. A man and woman had just passed us, riding horseback. When they heard the noise of the stampede and saw the herd coming they began to ride for dear life to get out of the way of the frightened cattle. The woman was riding sideways, as was the custom in those days, and it seemed to us that the cattle were surely going to overtake her. Looking back and seeing the cattle gaining that woman suddenly swung herself astride of the horse she was riding and pulled off a race that beat anything I ever saw. She outdistanced everything in that herd and rode safely away.

Stampedes were very common occurrences. Sometimes they were just tame affairs, but at other times they afforded all the excitement anyone could want. It was hard to tell sometimes the cause of a stampede. Often during a clear, still night, when the cattle were contentedly bedded and the night riders were dozing in their saddles, a sudden run would take place and the remainder of the night would be spent in trying to keep the herd together. One of the worst stampedes I ever witnessed was at Kilgore's ranch near Hondo. Tom Lay was having some fun with a negro boy and the cattle became frightened at the noise the boys made and the stampede that followed cost us several days' hard work and some money to get them together again.

Another bad stampede in which I had to do some tall riding occurred while I was taking a big herd of the Millett beeves to Paul's Valley. When we reached the Devil's Backbone, between Cash Creek and Washita River, we found the country had been burned off except a small scope of ground between the creeks where fire could not get to the grass, and on that ground I camped at the edge of a strip of timber. I think every prairie chicken in that whole country came there to roost. They were there by the thousands. The next morning, when these chickens began to leave the noise they made frightened the cattle and caused them to stampede. The three thousand beeves ran over that rough country in every direction, and they went several miles before we were able to check them. Several were killed and about a hundred got away.

During the eighteen years that I followed the trail life I was never arrested for any infraction of the law, but on two occasions I came very near being arrested; the first time just before we crossed a herd at Red River Station. I had started a herd of the Millett cattle to the Indian Territory to turn them into the cornfields to fatten. Mr. Millett said he thought I could make it for a day or two without inspection papers, saying he would overtake me in a few days and bring the papers with him. I got as far as Red River Station without interference, and while we were stopped there for dinner a cattle inspector rode up and demanded my papers. When I told him Mr. Millett would come with them in a few days he said nothing, but turned and rode away towards the county seat. I knew he was going to get the officers

and arrest me, so we hastily rounded up our cattle and
rushed them across the river. Just as I succeeded in getting the last hoof across the inspector came with the
officers, but he was too late, for I was out of their reach.
Mr. Millett arrived in a few days and everything was all
right.

The next encounter I had with an officer of the law
was near Fort Worth. My outfit had encamped near a
settlement. The boys, in a spirit of fun, caught two or
three hogs that were foraging about the camp and the
squeals of the swine led the settlers to believe that we
were stealing the hogs. Early the next morning just
after we had strung the herd out on the trail and the
cook was getting the chuck wagon in shape to start, the
officer rode up, threw a villainous looking gun down on
me and told me I was under arrest, accused of stealing
hogs. He said he would have to search the wagon, and
I told him to proceed, and gave orders for the cook to
unload the chuck wagon. When the officer was satisfied
we had no hog in the wagon he told us we were free to
continue on our trip. Then I sent him off on a "wild
goose chase" by telling him that there was another herd
several miles ahead of us, and the cowboys of that outfit
were the fellows who had stolen the hogs.

My experience with the Indians were like my other
experiences—some laughable and others serious. The
friendly Indians would sometimes follow us for days and
torment us with their begging. Old Yellow Bear, a chief,
came to our camp one day at noon and wanted bread. · I
told the cook not to give him anything, and this made the
old chief so mad he stamped his foot right down in the
dough the cook was working up to make bread for our
dinner.

The Indians at the Red Cloud agency in Dakota did
not bury their dead under the ground, but would erect
a scaffold some eight or ten feet high, place the body
thereon and cover it with a red blanket, besides placing

a bow and quiver of arrows, with a pot of food on the scaffold for the deceased Indian to use on his journey to the "happy hunting grounds." Every animal the dead Indian owned was brought to the scaffold and killed. I have seen as many as twelve dead horses at one scaffold and several dead dogs.

One of the most perilous things encountered on the trail in those days was the electrical storm. Herds would always drift before a storm and we would have to follow them for miles, while vivid lightning and crashing peals of thunder made our work awesome and dangerous. Only one who has been in a Kansas storm can realize what it means. Sometimes several head of cattle or horses were killed by one stroke of the lightning, and many of the cowboys met their death in the same manner.

MEMORIES OF THE OLD COW TRAIL

By C. H. Rust of San Angelo, Texas

As one of the old cowpunchers that enjoyed the life on the Chisholm cow trail that led from Texas to Kansas between 1867 and 1885, the object, as you will readily see, is to keep alive the memories of those early pioneer days. My own interest in these matters is no more than that of any other old-time cowboy who enjoyed the life of those days, but I would like to see in my own day and time some record left to perpetuate the memories of the life of the old cowboy on the trails and the men that followed them.

What happened on these old trails betweeen 1867 and 1885 is history, but at this present time there is no milepost or stone to mark their location.

I wish to call your attention to the information I can give of those days, the conditions that led up to them, the effect they had on the men who experienced them and on the development of the great Southwest.

In fact, it is not too much to say the reclamation of the Southwest created a class of men that have made and will make a deep and permanent impression on our government. The conditions under which they lived prevented their being bound by conventionalities of an established community. They were creators of a new society. For nearly a hundred years, some in Texas, men have been solving problems that required courage, self-reliance, willingness to assume responsibility and the peculiar quality called long-headedness, which is the ability to foresee the effect of untried experiment. The proof is shown in the influence, out of all proportion to their number, that Texas representatives or delegates exercise in legislative or deliberative bodies outside their own state. The causes that produced this power should be preserved for the study and instruction of those who come after us and who will have to carry on our work. The preservation is surely worth while, and for that reason I am willing to give my own experience, much as I dislike recalling part of it.

I was born in the old red hills of Georgia in 1850. My father and mother emigrated to Texas in 1854. In 1863 my father pushed far out, almost to the danger line, to where the Caddo Peaks and Santa Anna Mountains stand as silent sentinels overlooking the valley of the Colorado River and the great Concho country to the west, far out where countless thousands of buffalo roamed at will, where deer, antelope and wild turkey seemed to have taken possession of the whole country. This wonderful panorama loomed up to me, as a boy, as the idle and happy hunting ground that I had long dreamed of, with the silvery watered streams, like narrow ribbons, winding their way toward the Gulf of Mexico.

I am so tempted that I cannot refrain from quoting from Chapter 1, *The Quirt and the Spur,* by Edgar Rye, it fits so well in the time and condition: ''Far out beyond the confines of civilization; far out where daring men took possession of the hunting ground of the Indians and killed herds of buffalo to make a small profit in pelts, leaving the carcass to putrefy and the bones to bleach on the prairies. Far out where cattlemen disputed over the possession of mavericks and the branding iron was the only evidence of ownership. Far out where a cool head backed the deadly six-shooter and the man behind the gun, with a steady aim and a quick trigger, won out in the game where life was staked upon the issue. Far out where the distant landscape melted into the blue horizon and a beautiful mirage was painted on the skyline. Far out where the weary, thirsty traveler camped over night near a deep water hole, while nearby in the green valley a herd of wild horses grazed unrestrained by man's authority. Far out where the coyote wolves yelped in unison as they chased a jackrabbit in a circle of death, then fought over his remains in a bloody feast. Far out where the gray lobo wolf and the mountain lion stalked their prey, killed and gorged their fill until the light in the east warned them to seek cover in their mountain lairs. Far out where bands of red warriors raided the lonely ranch house, killing, burning and pillaging, leaving a trail of blood and ashes behind them as a sad warning to the white man to beware of the Indian's revenge. Far out into this wonderful country of great possibilities, where the sun looked down upon a scene of rare beauty.''

The sad thought to this writer is the passing out of those scenes so well portrayed in the above by its author; the old free grass, saddle farmer and line rider and range, through mystic regions, it is strange.

I turn my face west. I see the red lines of the setting sun, but I do not hear the echo come back, ''Go west, young man, go west.'' I turn my face east and I hear the dull thud of the commercialized world marching west, with its steam roller procession, to roll over me and flatten me out.

I ring my Ford car's neck, and go off down the street.

I drifted down into San Antonio, Texas, in the winter of 1869. I was about nineteen years old, long lank and lean; my height was full six feet. My weight was about one hundred and forty. I had no business in San Antonio. I just went there. I found board and room with a Mrs. Hall on Alamo Street.

This being the largest town I ever was in, I was somewhat "buffaloed," but Mrs. Hall and her husband were old Texas folks. Mrs. Hall was good to me, tried to advise me, but I knew it all. About all I did during my stay in San Antonio was loaf around such places as the Old Bullhead Saloon that faced south on Main Plaza, piked at monte some, saw big old grizzly gamblers get rich, and poor, in a few hours.

When the spring of 1870 opened up I found work with Myers and Roberts. They had just recently bought out the old NOX Ranch, seventy miles west of San Antonio, on the Frio River, thirty-five miles north of Uvalde. I believe it was about the first of April when Meyers and Roberts sold fifteen hundred head of mixed cattle to Ewing and Ingrams of California. We began to put the cattle up at once. About the middle of May we delivered the fifteen hundred head near San Antonio, five miles west of the Alamo.

Ewing and Ingrams made me an offer to lead the herd up the trail to Kansas. This offer I accepted. We held the cattle up a few days to organize, as the outfit was all new hands—green. Some of them had never seen a horse or a cow, much less ridden one. Will say here, I had never been over the trail as far north as Fort Worth. My duty was to look out for good places to camp, bed grounds and crossing of streams. We made only one drive a day, eight to ten miles. We followed the old cow trail from San Antonio to San Marcos, Austin, Round Rock, Georgetown, Salado, Belton, Cleburne, Fort Worth, Boliver, crossing the Red River near Gainesville, through

Nation to Oil Springs, Fort Arbuckle to Wild Horse and Washita.

Here we met forty Comanche Indians. Every one of the redskins had a parasol. I asked them where they had been. One spoke up, in fairly good English, and said they had been in on the Arkansas River making a treaty with another tribe.

We went through the Osage Nation, striking the line of Kansas at Caldwell Bluff Creek. At Ninnisquaw we turned to the left up the Ninnisquaw to the Sand Hill, crossing the Arkansas River at Rayman, Kansas, to Great Bend. Out ten miles north, on Walnut Creek, we held the cattle up, cut out all the steers to fatten, leaving about eight hundred cows—one, two and three-year-olds. They were taken on to Nebraska and put on a ranch.

Here I left the outfit. Traveled down the Arkansas River about ninety miles to Wichita, Kansas, all alone. Wichita was then about a mile long, one hundred yards wide and an inch thick. Here is where the Long and Shorthorns met and fought it out right. I remained here about ten days, struck an outfit bound for Texas with a bunch of old trail horses and chuck wagon. We traveled slowly back down the trail, easy gait, telling each other our experiences on the trail going up.

My last trail and range work was in 1877, around old Fort Griffin.

I have been a citizen of San Angelo, Texas, for over thirty years. It is not what I might have been, it is what I stand for today. I believe I have made good. I was all wrong at one time in my life. I am all for the right now. My business is dealing in fuel. I have been right here in one place for twenty years, handling coal and wood, and belong to the old M. E. Church South, and I am proud of her record as a church. I am thankful for my own record that I have lived to get right and do something. I know there are hundreds of the early-day trail hitters doing well and living good, clean lives.

It might be that the old trail driver has something buttoned up in his vest that he won't tell. Well, he is not supposed to tell all he knows, but will tell all he can. I was a grown-up man before I ever saw a Sunday School, but I owe much to my mother for the lesson she taught me at her knee. I departed from her advice in early manhood, but I came back. She and my father are buried side by side here in Fairmont Cemetery, in the great Concho Valley, having lived to a good, ripe old age, over eighty years.

The boys that have passed over the Divide, I do not know where they are, but I hope they got right.

ESTABLISHED THE FIRST PACKING PLANT IN TEXAS

Sketch of W. S. Hall of Comfort, Texas

Mr. W. S. Hall was born in Athens, Maine, December 17, 1829, and came to Texas by boat in 1858, landing at

W. S. HALL

Indianola. He proceeded by stage to San Antonio to seek his fortune in the cattle business. That same spring he purchased a stock of cattle from Saul Childers and also made a deal for the Hornsby stock, which had branded a thousand calves the year previous, and also secured several smaller herds. Thus he entered the stock business on an extensive scale and became one of the most prominent cattlemen of his time. At one time he owned forty thousand cattle, which ranged over a vast scope of country. With characteristic foresight and wonderful business

acumen Mr. Hall saw the opening of a new industry in
the South, and accordingly established a packing plant
at Rockport, Texas, and for eight years successfully
operated the plant. In those days artificial ice and modern preservatives were unknown, but, with the aid of salt,
he prepared his products in such a manner as to preserve
and ship to New Orleans and New York and even to
European ports. During the time he was engaged in the
packing industry he slaughtered more than forty thousand cattle, one year alone slaughtering over eleven
thousand head and marketing more than one thousand
barrels of meat in New Orleans. The tallow was shipped
to various countries, a thousand hogsheads going to New
York. The net weight of each of these hogsheads was
eleven hundred pounds. The product brought eight and
one-half cents per pound, which netted the packer a good
profit. Mr. Hall had no difficulty in securing animals for
his packing plant, paying from $7.00 to $12.50 per head
for the beeves, $5.00 to $9.00 for cows, and $3.00 to $4.00
for yearlings. Quite a difference in the price of prime
stuff is to be seen by comparison with present-day market
values.

The only trip Mr. Hall ever made up the trail was in
1872, when he started 4,200 head of cattle from Atascosa
County and drove to Wichita, Kansas, where he sold
them.

While engaged in the packing business his brother
was interested in the industry with him, but the brother
died in the early sixties and Mr. Hall conducted the business alone. In 1865 he had seven thousand head of cattle
stolen from him by Mexicans, and he followed them into
Mexico, where he found some of them, but the cost of
bringing the cattle back to Texas was so great he did not
bring them. The Mexican government required certain
conditions and terms, and it would have cost more than
the cattle were worth to get them out of Mexico. The
United States government sent the Robb Commission to

adjust claims in 1872 for cattle stolen by Mexicans, and when all differences had been settled between the two countries the indemnity claims were pigeonholed in Washington, D. C., and are probably there yet.

Mr. Hall has two sons engaged in the cattle business, W. S. Hall, Jr., and James Beck Hall.

This venerable character, now in his ninety-first year, is quite feeble, the services of a nurse being constantly required to minister to his infirmities. With his wife he lives at Comfort, Kendall County, Texas, where he is spending his declining years, surrounded by all the comforts that loving hands can bestow.

Thus, in brief, we have the history of one of Texas' most useful citizens. He contributed to the making of the history of the state and, with the names of many others, his achievements will be emblazoned on the scroll of Texas' glory and renown.

TRAIL DRIVING TO KANSAS AND ELSEWHERE

By W. F. Cude of San Antonio, Texas

There has always been history from the beginning of the world. It is the duty of the cattle drivers to do their bit in giving to the people of the great state of Texas some important facts that happened more than two score and ten years ago.

In the year 1861 war broke out between the States and it lasted four years, and during all this time there was no market, so the country was beginning to be overrun with cattle so much that thousands died. Some people went out with a wagon and an ax and killed and skinned them for their hides, which sold for one dollar apiece, though there was not much killing of animals for the hides except where the animal was down on the lift or in a bog hole. This was in 1869 and 1870.

Up until 1872 there was not over 150 miles of railroad in the state; that was from Galveston to Houston, and a short line from Houston to Brazoria, twenty-five miles in length, and one road from Harrisburg to Alleyton, three miles east of Columbus.

So the cattle driving to Kansas was the only hope at that time, and it proved to be a great help before the railroads got around. Trail driving to Kansas lasted from 1866 to 1886, and it was estimated that fully eight million head of cattle and horses were driven and sold during the twenty years above mentioned to Kansas, the drivers paying for the cattle on an average of $10.00 per head, although most of the horses came back to Texas and were used the next year. There were all sizes of herds, from five hundred to twenty-five hundred cattle in a drove, usually seven or eight men to the small herds and twelve to fifteen men with the large herds.

My first trip to Kansas was in the year 1868. I went with men by the name of Forehand and C. Cockrell. The cattle were steers, six hundred in number, and were gathered near Cistern Postoffice, in Bastrop County. There were eight hands besides the owners and the cook. After we passed Dallas lightning struck the boys in camp, killing one, and three others were so badly burned that one of them quit, so we only had six all the way to Kansas. We were told by the citizens of Dallas that we would reach the Chisholm Trail a few miles north of Dallas, and we followed it through Fort Worth, a small town, then through the Chickasaw Nation on to Wichita, Kansas, and thence to Solomon City on the Kansas Pacific Railroad, nine miles west of Abilene.

There were but few settlements on the way after we passed Dallas, and when we reached the settlements in Kansas we were all joyful again. We passed through many prairie dog towns and over rattlesnake dens, and lost only one horse from rattlesnake bite. Many kinds of wild animals were to be seen along the way, such as antelope, elk and buffalo, and we killed one buffalo calf and brought it into camp, though I did not like the meat as well as that of our cattle.

The country was one vast stretch of rich land, no timber except on creeks or rivers, and when we came in sight of timber we knew there would be water. In some instances we had to haul our wood to cook with, but generally we would have to gather buffalo chips (dry dung) for that purpose.

In the fall of 1869 I drove a herd of cattle to Shreveport, Louisiana. We made some money, but the buffalo flies were so bad we never went any more to Shreveport. Sometimes we would get farms to put the cattle in at night and the farms were stocked with cockleburrs and the cattle's tails would get full of burrs, and when the buffalo flies would get after them they would lose their tails fighting flies. Their tails would become entangled in small pine trees and there they would stand and pull and bellow until they got loose. You could hear them bawl a mile. Some of the cattle would run off and lay down, crazed with misery, and it was hard to drive them back to the herd. We sold the cattle in Shreveport and down Red River some fifteen miles distant. This herd was gathered in Gonzales County near where Waelder is now.

In the fall of 1870 I gathered another herd near the town of Waelder, Gonzales County, and went to New Orleans. On this trip we had many rivers and bayous to swim. Ferrymen wanted five to ten dollars for their services. The largest stream was Burwick's Bay at Brazier City, nine hundred yards wide straight across. Here a man led an ox to the edge of the stream and drove him into swimming water, when two men in canoes, one on each side, pointed the herd across. I shipped a carload from Brazier City to New Orleans and drove the rest, selling to plantations until I reached the Mississippi River. There I sold the balance, getting a much better price than I received for those I shipped to New Orleans, many of the farmers giving me checks on banks and merchants in New Orelans, very few paying the money down. Another herd of cattle went along at the same time, owned by Col. Fred Malone of Beeville, Texas, and Capt. Gibney of New Orleans, and as the latter knew the city well, I got him to assist me in locating the banks and merchants. One of the merchants had moved, however, so we went to the city register to find his location. When I reached this place I found it to be a house made of beeswax and tallow, and I began to think that fellow could not pay a check for $500.00, but it was all paid.

I also drove another herd that same year to Natchez, Mississippi, and sold to two men by the name of John McKen and James Gainer, who lived on Black River, thirty miles from Natchez. We made some money on this herd of cattle. Some of the hands came back with the horses and wagons, myself, Charles Edwards and Henry Crozier taking a steamboat on Black River, thence down to Red River and on down to the Mississippi River to New Orleans. This boat took on board sugar and molasses all along the way. It was a very pleasant trip and somewhat amusing to see the hands load on the barrels of sugar and molasses. They loaded that boat until the deck was right down to the water's edge. At New Orleans we took a train to Brazier City, there we took a ship to Galveston and from there came by train to our home in Gonzales County.

In the year of 1871 I saddled up "Old Ball," my favorite horse, and rode away to Kansas, this time for N. W. Cude, whose herd was gathered in Gonzales, Caldwell and Bastrop Counties. When we reached North Texas I found the Old Chisholm Trail had been abandoned and went far to the west to cross Red River. One morning about 11 o'clock I rode on ahead of the herd to some timber, where "Old Ball" stopped very suddenly, and then I saw an Indian standing near the road. The

Indian had a gun, and I suppose he was out on a hunt, but I gave my horse more slack on the bridle and passed on, and neither of us spoke. A few days later two Indians came up to the herd and wanted beef, but I told them that I had bought these cattle and had none to give away. They talked some English and asked to see my gun. I gave it to one of them and they looked it all over and soon rode away as fast as their horses could carry them. The cattle market was very low that year, so I failed to sell out all, wintering the balance in Nebraska, but they turned out bad. In crossing the Missouri River, it being frozen over, the cattle milled out on the ice and broke through, and we lost sixteen. The expense of wintering was so heavy we came out behind that year.

The first cattle I ever drove to a market was in 1867, to Houston, Texas, for a man by the name of Tumelson, from Gonzales County, and the last herd was in 1872, for a man by the name of O. J. Baker. R. D. Cude and myself bought the cattle from a Mr. Wimberly, in Hays County. We drove to Kansas and stopped our herd about fifteen miles west of Ellsworth, near the Kansas Pacific Railroad. Everything went well except when we got into Kansas, Bluff Creek being the line. We lay over a day to rest and clean up. Next morning just about sunup, I heard a gunshot down the creek and in a few minutes we saw two Indians running two mules as fast as they could go. They had shot a white man with a gun and arrows. He came dragging up to our camp with one arrow still sticking in him and one of the boys pulled it out and we carried him to a tent not far away.

The trail drivers had many narrow escapes and were exposed to many storms, cyclones, hail and all kinds of weather, stampedes of cattle, running over ditches and bluffs at night. Some few never came back, but were buried along the lonely trail among the wild roses, wrapped only in their bed blankets; no human being living near, just the coyote roaming there.

WHEN LIGHTNING SET THE GRASS ON FIRE

By George W. Brock of Lockhart, Texas

I was born in Caldwell County, Texas, three miles west of Lockhart, January 25, 1860. Beginning at the age of nine years, I commenced to handle stock, but at that time I was too small to get on a horse unaided and my father told me not to get off, but every time I saw a rabbit I would get off and throw rocks at it and then I would have to be helped back on my horse.

About 1871 or 1872 I started on my first trip on the trail, going with my father. When near Fort Worth father concluded I was too young to go on account of the danger of Indians, and he sent me back home.

I continued to work with cattle until 1876, and at this date I went to work for M. A. Withers, herding 300 cows, penning them at night, sleeping at the pens and doing my own cooking.

In 1878 M. A. Withers took a bunch of boys to Fayette County, Texas, and bought about 800 head of cattle. At the crossing on the Colorado, at Judge L. Moore's ranch, we had a great experience in two or three ways. We tried first to swim the cattle across the river, but we only succeeded in getting about ten head across that way and had to rope and drag them. We then crossed the others on the ferryboat. Here I saw my first Jersey. She was a heifer and belonged to Judge Moore, and it was a hard matter to keep her out of our herd. Judge Moore thought very much of this heifer and would watch everybody passing there with cattle. When he came out and found the thing in our herd he threatened to prosecute us for attempting to steal her.

In January, 1879, Blanks and Withers began buying cattle and pasturing them, preparing for a drive in the spring. On the first day of April we rounded up the pasture to start the herd north. On the second we left the pasture and went about three or four miles and camped for the night. We had so few men with us that night we lost about 3,200 out of 3,500 head. They just simply walked off and everyone seemed to take a different direction, and, being short of men, they went their way, with the result as stated.

The next morning G. W. Mills (Pap) and myself held the 300 until the others ate breakfast. When we went to camp there were two horses tied up for us. Not one of us knew anything about these horses, but the general opinion of the camp was that one of them was bad. The cook said, ''Withers left instructions for Brock to ride the one supposed to be bad and for Mills to ride the other one.'' So ''Pap'' had lots of fun while eating breakfast at the thought of seeing Brock thrown and losing his saddle. Breakfast over, Brock saddled the bad horse and mounted him and he walked off perfectly quiet, but it was entirely a different case with ''Pap's'' horse. ''Pap'' was the one that went heavenward and had to call for poultices, which was so often the case on the trail, for the fun did not always show up just where you were expecting it. Going back to the herd, we got them all together by the next day, moved back into the pasture and for four or five nights these cattle would walk off; so the first night we held them we put them on the trail proper the next morning and drove them as far as possible. We had no other happenings except an occasional storm or high water stampede, which belonged to the business.

In the edge of the state of Kansas the cook accidentally set the grass on fire and we had to move into rough country.

One night Mark Withers cautioned me to tie my horse good so that if anything happened I would be ready. About 12 o'clock the cattle stampeded, and when I got to where my horse had been he was gone. I told Mark my horse was gone and he said, ''Durn it! I told you to tie that horse good.'' And when we went to where his horse was tied he was gone also, and I said, "Durn it! Why didn't you tie him good?" We could do nothing but listen to the running of the cattle, and every once in a while Mark would exclaim, "If I only had a horse!"

After I returned from this trip I worked on the ranch until 1883 and then went to La Salle County for Blanks and Withers and worked on the ranch for four or five months. In 1884 we left home for the Blanks and Withers ranch in La Salle County. The first herd prepared was turned over to G. B. (Gus) Withers, numbering 4,000 3's and 4's. I started to help Gus with this herd to Uvalde County, but we had a stampede just above Cotulla and lost 400 or 500 head. Willis Hargis and myself were left to gather them up. We got all but 200 head of the cattle and most of the horses. Some of the horses went back to the ranch before stopping. In this stampede my horse ran into a ditch that night. The cause of him doing this was because I was trying to point the cattle away from the ditch and a negro (Russ Jones) was on the opposite side of the herd trying to do the same thing, and the result was that instead of pointing them away from the ditch, we drove them straight into it. The banks of this ditch were five or six feet high, and I was fortunate in escaping unhurt.

The stampede occurred in a very brushy place and the men next morning all looked like they had been to an Irish wake, all bloody and bruised.

In this drive we rounded up one of those notorious outlaw steers which were to be found in the country at that time. Withers said if there were any two or three men in the outfit that had the nerve to rope that steer and lead him to a good place he would kill him for beef. Well, I caught him, but if I had not have had others close at hand who came to my rescue and also roped him and spread him out, so to speak, I might not have been writing this story. But between us we killed him and enjoyed his carcass.

The outlaw steer above referred to was rounded up
while we were on the ranch after Hargis and I turned
over the cattle we gathered after the stampede. I went
back to the ranch and we gathered another herd and
shipped them to Wichita Falls, Texas. Drove from there
to Julesburg, Colorado, San Childress being the boss.
We crossed the Red River at Doan's Store, where we
laid in supplies to last us until we reached Dodge City,
Kansas. They told us at the store that someone was
stampeding horses across the river and driving them
off. So when we camped at night after crossing the
river, Childress and myself tied our horses to the wagon
and examined our six-shooters to see that they were in
working order. After we had gone to sleep the cook
jumped up and said, "The horses are running." Childress and I jumped on our horses with our pistols in
our hands, but just then the cook discovered that it was
only a pot of beans boiling which he had built a big fire
around before going to bed.

After crossing North Red River in the Wichita Mountains, we met a Comanche chief, who said he had 300
bucks besides the women and children. I gave him five
crippled yearlings to keep his bunch away from our outfit, and he kept his promise. After we got to the top
of the ridge I looked down in the valley of Washita River
and the whole face of the country was alive with herds.
I went back and stopped the herd until I could survey
the route, and found that by going above the trail and
crossing about five miles up and swimming the river
we could get ahead of everything, so we proceeded to
swim the river and get ahead in the lead of all other
herds.

Monroe Hardeman was just behind us with another
herd for Blanks and Withers, and he helped us swim
our herd and we in turn helped him. After we got both
herds across I found that the sun had taken all the skin
off my back. Swimming the river and an occasional

stampede was about the only excitement until we reached Kansas.

Childress at one time had been shot all to pieces by a bunch of soldiers who mistook him and others for horse thieves, causing him to have a natural hatred toward all soldiers, and at Bear Creek he spied about 300 negro soldiers coming toward us. He squared himself with gun in hand and was ready to open fire. I tried to stop him, but saw there was no use to talk to him, so I roped his horse and pulled him around and led him off. I think that was all that saved our whole outfit, as we were so badly outnumbered it would have meant suicide to have started anything like that. However, we had just left Longhorn Roundup and Childress had been celebrating considerably, and that might have had something to do with his display of nerve that he exhibited there.

From there to Dodge City everything went well. At Dodge City every man, including the boss, except myself, celebrated in great style, while I was left to handle and hold the outfit.

After disposing of our lame cattle we shaped up and moved on to Ogallala. About four or five days' drive out of Dodge City, Tobe Swearingen came to our herd to count the cattle, and he and I did the counting. According to my count the cattle were all there, but he made a mistake of 100, making us out that number, and, it being too late to recount, I spent an awful restless night. I couldn't understand how we could lose that many cattle in a prairie country like that. The next morning we recounted and found that my count was correct. Then my nervousness left me.

Several days later we had to make a long drive for water. We watered at the North Republican. The lead cattle struck the Frenchman about sundown, and from then until next morning about 10 o'clock they kept coming in, and every once in a while a man would show up.

The morning we started this particular drive I ate breakfast at daylight and the next meal I ate was at 10 o'clock the next day.

For the next day or two we grazed along the stream, so appropriately named Stinking Water. When crossing the Frenchman the cook broke down the wagon tongue, and we fixed it by wrapping it with ropes so that it held out for the balance of the trip.

After leaving Stinking Water for Ogallala everything went nicely. Leaving Ogallala we went up the south side of the Platte River to Julesburg Junction, where we delivered our cattle to Governor Rout and ex-Governor Brush of Colorado.

Going up the river our only trouble was to keep our stock off the farmers. They had no fences and it took very careful watching to keep them out of those patches. To let your stuff get on those patches meant the highest price grazing that a Texas horse or steer ever got. One night I woke up and heard the horse bell and I knew it was in the wrong direction, so I got up and found them grazing on one of those high-priced corn patches. I quietly drove them to camp, woke up everybody and moved everything away that night. I believe that corn actually did the horses good; at least they seemed that night to travel stronger than usual.

After reaching Julesburg Junction we crossed the Platte and began delivering.

I was then sent to meet Gus Withers, who had not yet come up with us. I had three horses, riding one and leading the others. When crossing the Platte my horses were so weak from the trip from Texas, and the quicksand so very bad, they could not carry me, so I led them, wading water up to my chin. After crossing the river and about the middle of the evening, I met with something entirely different from anything I had ever before been up against. I had thought up to this time that I knew what a Kansas storm was, but that evening I was shown that I had never been in one before. The lightning would strike the ground and set the grass on fire, then the rain would put it out. I got off my horse and tied the three together, took off my spurs, six-shooter and pocket knife, laid them down and moved away. After the storm was over the sun came out and it looked as though nothing had ever happened, so I moved on. At night, not knowing where I was, I stopped at a good hole of water, but I had nothing to eat. After lying down I heard the lowing of cattle. I saddled up, putting my bedding in front of me, and started in the direction of the cattle I had heard and, to my good luck, it was Gus' herd. The boys were all very glad to see me, as I had heard from home and they had not. They had been in the same storm that I had just passed through and the lightning killed one steer for them. Very shortly after I reached them their herd stampeded, but they did not lose anything, and Gus said, "The cattle did that to show they were glad to see Brock." I then piloted them back to Julesburg the same route I had traveled in going to them.

After all our cattle had been delivered we naturally felt that we could sleep as long as we cared to. So Childress and myself slept until 10 o'clock the next morning. The sun was unusually bright and, we both being without whiskers on the top of our heads, the boys said our heads made very good mirrors.

The dinner that Mark Withers gave us at the station when we were ready to come home paid me fully for all the meals I had lost on the trip.

The balance of my work with cattle has been on ranches at home.

Old age and parting of ways in life
  Will not erase the cowboys' strife.
In after years let come what will,
  He proves to be a cowboy still.

"BIG COWBOY BALL"

The cowboys of Springer, New Mexico, gave their fourth annual ball in that city. They sent something like eight hundred invitations at home, and abroad, inscribed with appropriate verse, as follows:

"Caller, let no echo slumber,
    Fiddler sweatin' like a steer,
Huffs a-poundin' at the lumber,
    Makin' music the stars could hear;
Hug the gals up when we swing 'em,
    Raise them plum off their feet.
Balance, all ye saddle warmers,
    Rag a little, shake your feet,
    On to next 'un, and repeat it,
    Balance to the next in waitin',
Promenade, and off you go,
    Seat your pards, and let 'em blow."

DID YOU EVER DO THE SQUARE?

Get yo' little sagehens ready,
Trot 'em out upon the floor.
Line up there, you cusses! Steady!
Lively, now. One couple more.
Shorty, shed thet old sombrero!
Broncho, douse thet cigarette;
Stop thet cussin', Casimero,
'Fore the ladies! Now, all set!

S'lute your ladies, all together!
Ladies opposite the same—
Hit the lumber with your leathers!
Balance all, an' swing your dame!

Bunch the heifers in the middle;
Circle, stags, and do-se-do;
Pay attention to the fiddle!
Swing her 'round and off you go!

First four forward! Back to places!
  Second fellow, shuffle back!
Now you've got it down to cases—
Swing 'em till their trotters crack!
Gents all right a'heel and toeing!
Swing 'em, kiss 'em if you kin—
On to next and keep a-goin',
Till yer hit yer pards agin!

Gents to center, ladies 'round 'em,
Form a basket, balance all!
Whirl yer gals to where you found 'em;
Promenade around the hall!
Balance to yer pards and trot 'em.
'Round the circle double quick,
Grab an' kiss while you've got 'em,
Hold 'em to it if they kick!

Ladies, left hand to your sonnies!
Alaman! Grind right and left!
Balance all an' swing yer honeys—
Pick 'em up an' feel their heft!
Promenade like skeery cattle—
Balance all an' swing yer sweets!
Shake yer spurs an' make 'em rattle!
Keno! Promenade to seats.

                    —JAMES BARTON ADAMS.

EXPERIENCES "TENDERFEET" COULD NOT SURVIVE

By G. W. Mills of Lockhart, Texas

My father and mother were both born in Somerset, state of Kentucky. I first saw the light of day on June 2, 1857, and in the fall of 1872 my father, with his family, including myself, emigrated to Texas. Our mode of

transportation was by way of wagons, there being no railroads convenient at that early date. My father came to look after some land somewhere in the broad domain of Texas (he knew not exactly where) that had been left him by an older brother, Henry P. Mills, who died while serving as a soldier in the Texas War for Independence. We settled near Lockhart in 1874, and at the age of about seventeen I went to work on the M. A.

G. W. MILLS

Withers ranch, one of the biggest ranches of this section at that time, which was due west of Lockhart about four miles, as the crow flies.

I think it would be of interest to the reader to have some idea of the appearance of that ranch as it appeared to me, then a mere lad. It was located on a little flowing stream known as Clear Fork and abundantly fed by many springs. This creek was fringed with timber, pecan, walnut, elm, hackberry and wild plum on either bank, and dipping into its crystal waters were the weeping willows. The creek abounded with an abundance of fish, such as bass, channel cat and the silver perch. The old ranch house stood back about three hundred yards east of the creek, on the summit of a gradual sloping hillside which commanded a view of the beautiful stretch of valley country roundabout and where it was swept by the gentle southern breeze.

About one hundred and fifty yards from the house were the corrals, covering about four acres of ground, and these corrals were divided into various pens, in which we "rounded up" from time to time the great herds for marking and branding. As a matter of course these pens were built to endure and were very strong, as cattle in those days were wild, and in this exciting work none but well-built pens would hold them. The uninitiated will probably be interested in knowing just how these corrals, as we termed them, were built, when material was not so plentiful as now. The material was largely postoak rails, which we had cut and hauled by ox teams about five miles from the timbered country of Caldwell County. The posts were of fine cedar timber obtained from old Mountain City in Hays County. These corrals had to be much higher than the ordinary fence, as the infuriated longhorns would, in their desperation to be free, try to go over the top or break them down. Once the material was on the ground, we dug deep, wide holes, about seven feet apart, and in these we placed two of the cedar posts in such juxtaposition as to hold the long rails which we piled one on top of the other until they reached the top of the high posts. That being done, some of the old-timers bound the ends of the posts together with wire or stout strips of rawhide, but at about the time of which I write we began to bind them with smooth wire. The subdivisions spoken of above were divided into branding pens and horse corrals. We would not be true to the picture we are now attempting to paint in words if we fail to mention the singularly attractive feature of the setting of these particular corrals. They were shaded by large spreading liveoaks, hoary with age, where we hung up our saddles and leggins and various and sundry camp equipage, under which we slept on our blankets and saddle pillows, and partook of our frugal fare. Some of these grand old monarchs of the forest still stand—the pride of the Texas cowboy.

It must be realized that we had no fences arbitrarily deciding the bounds of our little empire, and our cattle and horses roamed at will over the hills and valleys, covered with the rich, luxuriant curly mesquite grass, upon which they grew sleek and fat.

After three years' work on this busy ranch none but the life of a cowboy appealed to me. Around the old campfires at night I heard the tales of the older men of their exciting life on the trail, and naturally I felt like going the route that those I knew, admired and trusted had gone. Right here I want to put in that, fortunately for me, I was associated with a few of the grand old stockmen of early days, to whose fine, though rugged characters, I am indebted for that training which carried me safely through many trying times.

In March, 1877, as our boss was not to drive that year, I secured employment with Ellison and Dewees, who were going to drive about six herds up the trail from this section to Ogallala, Nebraska, on the South Platte River. In the six herds there were about fifteen thousand head of mixed cattle, being about 2,500 head to the herd, each herd having its boss and trail outfit, which we will now attempt to briefly describe. The boss is the man in charge of the herd; then there were eight cowboys, one "horse wrangler" and cook, who drove the wagon, drawn by two yoke of oxen—the wagon containing our provisions and bedding, the provisions being replenished from time to time from the "outposts," sometimes hundreds of miles apart. We received our herd in the western part of Gonzales County, the herd being in charge of N. P. Ellison, a cousin of Col. J. F. Ellison, a grand old cowman, who owned the cattle.

On this trip we had with us the following boys, not a one over twenty-three years of age: W. M. Ellison, son of the boss; E. F. Hilliard, W. F. Felder, E. M. Storey, Albert McQueen, Ace Jackson, myself, two negro cow hands and a negro cook.

We left the Lockhart pasture about the first of April, took the Chisholm Trail and "lit out." My first stampede was on Onion Creek; as usual, this occurred at night, about 12 o'clock. The herd was bedded about one hundred yards from the wagon, two men on guard. In their fright the cattle broke for the wagon, and we asleep at the camp, being aroused by the roar of tramping hoofs, scrambled up on the wagon. One of the older men jumped up and shook a blanket before them and turned them off the other way. The first thing I remember was the boss calling out, "Boys, get down and get your horses." It was then that I discovered that I had quit my pallet and was astride one of the hind wheels. Of course, we hurriedly got our horses, went around the cattle, after about a mile's run, held them, and they quieted down. Old hands at the business will know that we slept no more that night. This trip was marked by excessive rainfall, big rains falling at night, and one hailstorm, adding greatly to the hardship of the cowboy's lot; but we didn't mind it much and, with songs and jokes, kept up our spirits.

When we arrived at old Red River Station, where the old Chisholm Trail crossed, we found the river up and several herds waiting to cross. We stopped on the east side of Panther Creek and pitched camp. I want to say here that that stream was rightly named. We killed a fat yearling—I won't say whose it was—tied a rope to one end of the front bow of the wagon, the other to a small tree; the cook hung the beef on the rope. When the boys came in at 12 o'clock to wake up the third guard he discovered a panther standing on his hind feet eating the meat off of the rope, just on the opposite side of the wagon from where we were sleeping. He opened fire with his forty-five on the panther. We thought "horse rustlers," now commonly called horse thieves, had attacked the camp. The noise of the firing stampeded the cattle. As the boys sprang out of their blankets some had their forty-fives ready and some made for the horses, where it took but a moment to saddle and then off for the cattle. In the rush E. M. Storey sang out, "What is that? If you don't speak out I'll cut loose at you," and then we recognized the voice of E. F. Hilliard, calling out in the inky darkness from the direction of the firing in excited tones, "It's a damned panther; he's eating our meat off the rope." This was about twenty feet from where we were sound asleep, sleeping as only Texas cowboys can. By that time the herd had gotten a good distance away. We made a run to overtake the herd; finally rounded up a part of them that night, and the man on guard checked another part further away. The balance we found next morning in the valley of Red River; rounded all up and started back to camp about five miles away. We counted them—always a part of the program—to see if we had lost any. To show that our work was not all "rough work," and that we had our "bookkeeping" department, though ever so simple, I shall tell how this counting was done. The herd was allowed to string out; two men went on ahead, some distance in width between them, the others pointed the herd in their direction and so that they would slowly go between them; then they counted, and with a knot on the saddle string or some other convenient method, tallied them by hundreds, each calling out to see if they had agreed; then knowing the number that we started with, we knew if our roundup had been complete.

We bedded the cattle on the same bed ground that night; I and my pal stood guard from two o'clock in the morning until day. On guard, one rides one way and the other the opposite direction around. As I got on the round on the side next to the creek I heard the most horrifying yell, or more of a scream, that I had ever heard in all my life. This blood-curdling scream came from a bending tree about sixty yards from the herd. My thick hair went straight up and has never thoroughly settled down since that memorable night. The cattle jumped up, and about that time I met my pal coming toward me. Instantly I said, "What's that?" His reply betrayed his fright also, although he had been up the trail before. In language picturesque and accurate he replied, "The scream of a panther," with some adjectives before that name which assured me that my hair was not standing on end for nothing. From then on until daylight we just rode around together. Next morning we told the boss that we had rather swim Red River (then three hundred yards wide in swimming water) than to stand guard assisted by panthers ready to spring on man or beast. A conference was held among the bosses and it was decided to cross some of the herd that very day. We hit the water about 10 o'clock and crossed our herd first, four other herds following. Of course, the outfits assisted one another in this hard and dangerous work. In this crossing one of the boys had a horse which refused to swim, and the man had to jump off onto a wild steer's back, but with pluck made a safe landing on the other side. This put us into the Indian Territory and new precautions had to be taken to save us from attack by the Indians, the several herds keeping close together to be of mutual help in case of a surprise attack. The next river was Washita, and we had to swim that also; narrow but deep and very swift. About a hundred miles further on we came to the North Canadian River, swimming also, narrow, deep and swift. When I swam across and came out on the opposite side on the second bank I got down to pull off my boots to let the water out, and wring my socks. A few scattering elm trees were ahead and about the time I got my boots off I looked up toward the trees and saw my first Indian, who looked about six and one-half feet tall to me, standing backed

up against one of those elm trees, with the eagle feathers
in his head, a long rifle standing up in front of him. He
had on buckskin clothes with a dandy fringe on them.
My hair rose again very suddenly, so I lit straddle of my
horse and ran out to the front cattle. The other two
boys thought I was just seeing things because I was badly
scared. They did not believe there was an Indian down
there, but when they finished crossing the herd and came
on up with the wagon there were about fifteen Indians
showed up with the one I had first seen acting as chief,
who claimed that he was the noted chief, "Spotted Tail."
He told the boss he wanted "Wa-ha," meaning beef.
Then I had it on the boys and it was their time to get
scared. The boss knew it was best to use a little diplo-
macy, and so he told us to cut out four or five of the
"drag yearlings" and turn them over to them. The
Indians had just as soon have these lame or given-out
cattle as any. Of course, Indian-like, they wanted more,
but we outtalked them, telling them there were more
herds behind and they would gladly give them some of
theirs. Then the chief put up his spiel for "chuck,"
meaning flour, bacon, etc. And they talked like they
meant to have it. We explained that our supply was
short, but just to wait on the big supply coming on behind. They left us and went on to meet the other herds,
so we moved on out of their zone that evening. We saw
no more Indians on that trip, and we did not look for
any. On Salt Fork there came up a rain and lightning
storm, and I saw unbelievable doings of the lightning;
it beat anything I ever saw. The lightning would hit the
side of those hills and gouge out great holes in the earth
like a bomb had struck them, and it killed seven or eight
head of cattle in the herd back of us and two horses out
of the "remuda," which, being interpreted, means the
saddle horses. Nothing more eventful occurred and in
about a week we arrived at the famous and renowned
Dodge City, Kansas, a familiar name to all cowmen in

that day. Then we provisioned and started on the tail-end of the journey to Ogallala, about three hundred miles. We arrived there about August 1st, our cattle all in good shape—in better condition a long ways than when we left. They were there delivered to the various purchasers, who removed them to their respective ranches in that great cow country. Our faithful saddle horses, wagons and all were disposed of with the cattle. On the night of August 20, this being 1877, I went to call on Col. J. F. Ellison, he being indisposed and stopping at the Gass House, and also to get my "time," which really means wages, about $180.00, then a small fortune for a young cowboy. Upon this visit to Colonel Ellison I was introduced to two guests who had called to pay their respects. They were two brothers, Joel and Joe Collins, handsome young men, products of the West. About a week afterwards, in that very neighborhood, the Union Pacific was held up eighteen miles west of Ogallala and the robbers rifled the express car, taking $100,000 in gold, but scorning to take a huge amount of silver, which perhaps was too heavy to take with them in their hasty flight. Joel Collins was in this very holdup, being with the notorious Sam Bass gang, who successfully did the trick. About a week afterward Joel and George Hereford were killed by a detachment of United States soldiers and their part of the loot recovered, about three miles south of what was known then as Buffalo Park, on the K. P. Railroad. Upon getting my time I lit out for home over the U. P. Railroad. On the way back I fell in with some wild and woolly green cowboys making their first trip on a train, just like myself. At Grand Island the train stopped for breakfast; we got off and on the way to the eating place a negro suddenly came around the corner of the house, beating one of those huge gongs, making a most terrific din of noise. We were sacred senseless, and it was all I could do to keep one of those boys from shooting that darkey. He contended that he would let

no d——n nigger stampede him by beating on a tin can.
It is hard for you who have always traveled and become
accustomed to the ways of the city to understand just
how puzzling civilization is to a boy raised up on the
Texas frontier, whose life is very simple, and who knows
cow trails far better than he does paved streets and the
campfires the only hotels he ever saw until forced out into
the world.

We arrived at Austin on time and there I took one of
those old-fashioned stages to Lockhart, feeling like I had
seen the world, and with much pride telling the boys all
that I had seen and been through. The younger boys
looked upon us fellows who had been up the trail as
heroes, and of course this very thing incited others to
want to go. It was the life ambition of many a one to
make such a trip. You were not a graduate in the cowboy's school until you had been.

In 1878 I was back on the comfortable old Withers
ranch. In 1879 my old friend and boss, M. A. Withers,
took through a herd and I went with him. We crossed
the Colorado at Webberville and arrived at Taylor about
the 22nd of April. A rain, a terrible rain, came up about
four o'clock in the evening, raining all evening and all
night. It was very cold and we came very near freezing
to death. At that springtime period several horses and
cattle died of the cold. Every horse that we rode that
bitter night was unfit for service the balance of the trip,
so dreadful was the exposure. You understand cattle
drift before wind-driven rain, and by morning we were
at Hutto, eight miles away; we had had no supper and
no breakfast, and not until noon did we have anything
to eat. When these "drifts" take place every man and
the boss is in front of the herd, holding them as much
as possible; there are no shifts then, but every man to
his post all night long; and the nights are long, too. On
this memorable night I well recall my associates: M. A.
Withers, in charge; G. B. Withers, G. W. Brock, A. N.

Eustace, C. W. Pope, W. M. Ellison, Joe Lewis, the scout; Barney Roland, better known as "Pard"; and Edmundo Martinez, the Mexican horse wrangler. Next day it was still bitterly cold, but the rain had let up, leaving that country covered with water. About noon we got back to camp and our appetites, always good, were now ravenous, and we looked forward to boiling coffee and hot grub of some kind. Instead, imagine our disappointment at finding the trifling cook housed up in the wagon covered in his blankets, and hadn't prepared a thing—hadn't even started a fire. Mr. Withers, always mindful of his men, was outraged and hauled him out of there with a demand to know why he didn't have the boys something to eat. He evasively replied that he couldn't build a fire in that water. Mr. Withers gave him his time and told him to "light a shuck." I can see that cook now making it over those hog-wallows, filled with water, to the nearest town. Under a camp wagon is usually suspended an old cowhide called the "caboose," and in that we throw stray pieces of wood, etc., as long as we are in a country where it can be had, just for use in such emergencies. It came in handy that time, sure, and some of the boys got it out, and with a lavish use of the oil can, we soon had things going, some of the boys doing the cooking. We were not particular and after a hearty meal our spirits were up again ready for any turn of fate in the cowboy's lot. The next day we picked up a boy from old Gonzales County, filled with the spirit of adventure, by the name of Joe Knowles, and he cooked the balance of the way up. He was a good lad and some of the boys have seen him since, just lately, and he is doing well, we are glad to know.

We went the old Chisholm Trail and crossed the river at Red River Station. Nothing exciting occurred until we got to Turkey Creek, Indian Territory. There the trail had been changed to turn northwest and hit the western trail at the Longhorn Roundup on the Cimarron.

The new trail had been marked out by a buffalo head set up about every half of a mile.

It was a hundred miles from Turkey Creek to Longhorn Roundup. We arrived at Dodge City early in July, sold our steer yearlings there to the well-known cattle firm of Day Brothers, moved on up to the Smoky River, sold the cows to J. R. Blocker, then lit out for Ogallala, Nebraska. At about thirty miles from the last named place we pitched camp about a mile from the spring, which, curiously enough, opens up right in the bald prairie and forms the head of the stream known as Stinking Water. Here I had an experience with lightning that I know rivals the experience of any man who ever went up the trail. How we escaped death I have never understood. The storm hit us about 12 o'clock at night. There was some rain, and to the northwest I noticed just a few little bats of lightning. Then it hit us in full fury and we were in the midst of a wonderful electrical storm. We had the following varieties of lightning, all playing close at hand, I tell you: It first commenced like flash lightning, then came forked lightning, then chain lightning, followed by the peculiar blue lightning. After that show it rapidly developed into ball lightning, which rolled along the ground. After that spark lightning; then, most wonderful of all, it settled down on us like a fog. The air smelled of burning sulphur; you could see it on the horns of the cattle, the ears of our horses and the brim of our hats. It grew so warm we thought we might burn up with it, and M. A. Withers and Joe Lewis, old-timers, told me afterwards that they never had seen the like in all of their experiences. Needless to say, we were all on guard that night. The cattle did not give us so much trouble as the constant flashes keeping them moving so much. We delivered at Ogallala and lit out for Texas.

Under the same leadership we drove two herds in 1880 to Fort Griffin, going what was known as the Western

Trail. We threw them together at Fort Griffin, M. A. Withers taking full charge. There were about 4,500 mixed cattle in that herd. It looked like a "roundup" when turning them off of the bedding ground. When we arrived at Beaver Creek, near Pease River, we had a terrible rain, a veritable cloudburst; raining all day, all night and all next day. The ground got so soft it was belly deep to a horse, and they would give out in a short distance, as tough as they were. For two days and nights we were without sleep. We were in the saddle all of the time except when we snatched a bite to eat, and to change saddle horses. The prairie was simply covered with prairie dogs, which had been run out of their homes in the ground by the water.

On this trip when we left Washita, we were expecting to find plenty of water at the South Canadian, and found it as dry as a powder house. That was nearly thirty miles through the hot sun dunes to Wolf Creek—sixty-five miles without any water. The cattle milled all night, suffering for water, and "lowed" piteously. Next morning we hit the trail early. Late that evening we arrived at the brow of the old slope, down to Wolf Creek, with six men ahead to hold the lead cattle back. They made a run for the water, which they had smelled for some distance, ran through an Indian camp, stampeding the Indians and their horses. Cattle and men all went off in the river together.

Here we sold the cows—about five hundred—cutting them out of the great herd. Then we mosied along up to Dodge on the Arkansas, camped just opposite old Fort Dodge, five miles down the river. Held there for ten days. On the Fourth of July, 1880, about two o'clock in the evening, the awfulest hailstorm came up a man ever saw. The hailstones nearly beat us to death; it knocked over jackrabbits like taking them off with a rifle. It even killed a few yearlings and many fleet antelopes, but the cow hands had to stick to their posts, although we nearly froze to death—on the Fourth of July. We had knots and scars all over our hands and backs. The ice lay about four inches deep on the ground next morning. Ten miles back, at Mulberry, next morning we found ourselves when day broke. It was so dark during that storm, in the daytime, that you could not see a man ten feet away. We had no supper nor breakfast; getting back to camp next morning at ten we found the cook fixing to leave, thinking surely that all the men had been killed. We were a hardy lot or we should have been, no doubt. No wonder "tenderfeet" did not survive those experiences.

I guess this about concludes my story. I met many brave and fearless men during those times. I want to say in conclusion that many of these men were tender-hearted and as gentle as a woman; they were rough outside but refined in heart and soul. Of all of them I shall always remember Mark Withers, who was always thoughtful of and devoted to his men.

KILLING OF "BILLY THE KID"

By Fred E. Sutton of Oklahoma City, Okla.

I received a letter from your president, Mr. George W. Saunders, asking for a little story of the most exciting incident that I can recall, which occurred during our cowboy days. As I was at an excitable age and working out of Dodge City, Kansas, which, to put it mildly, was an exciting town, it is a little hard to decide which particular incident to tell about. But one that was indeed interesting to me I believe will be of some interest to you and your readers. It took place in the fall of '81, when fifty other punchers and myself were rounding up some thirty thousand head of cattle for Jesse Evans, in New Mexico, during which we had considerable trouble with a bunch of outlaws and cattle rustlers headed and controlled by the notorious "Billy the Kid."

For the information of those who are not familiar with his history, I will say that his name was William H. Bonney. He was born in New York City on July 9, 1859, and at the age of twelve he killed a boy companion with a pocket knife, after which he escaped and went to Kansas, stopping near Atchison (where the writer then lived), where he worked on a farm for a year and a half. Leaving there he went to New Mexico and went to work on a ranch. He stayed until the fall of '79, when, after a fancied slight, he fell out with a rancher, whom he killed, and from that day on he was an Ishmaelite—his hand against every man and every man's hand against him.

After killing the rancher he surrounded himself with a bunch of the toughest characters to be found on the frontier. His stronghold was the Pecos Valley, where he drank, gambled, stole cattle and murdered all that he fell out with until, at the age of twenty-two, his victims numbered the same as his years.

In the latter part of 1880, a then noted frontier officer by the name of Pat Garrett was detailed to bring "The Kid" in, dead or alive, and as he knew our boys had been bothered a great deal and had lost several cattle, he came to our camp for help. I was detailed as one of the posse to go with Garrett, and we finally located the outlaw in a ranch house about forty miles from White Oaks. After surrounding them a halt was called for a parley, during which "Billy the Kid" sent out word by a Mexican outlaw by the name of Jose Martinez, one of his leaders, that if Garrett would send the writer, who was known as "The Crooked S Kid," and Jimmy Carlyle, a young cowboy, to the house he would try and come to some kind of an agreement. Garrett readily consented to this, as he knew his men and those of "The Kid," and he knew a battle meant death to many. Leaving our guns behind, Jimmy and I went to the house, where we found as tough a bunch of outlaws, gun fighters, and cattle thieves as ever infested a country, or were ever congregated in a space of that size. After an hour spent in propositions and counter-propositions, we agreed to disagree, and started back to our own crowd with the promise of not being fired on until we reached them. But we had only traversed about three-fourths of the distance when there was an avalanche of lead sent in our direction, and poor Jimmy, Sheriff William Bradley, and a ranchman by the name of George Hindman, were instantly killed. Our posse then withdrew.

The killing inflamed the whole Southwest, as all of the dead men were fine men and, with the exception of Jimmy, all had families.

After a few days of rest, Garrett started out with the avowed intention of staying on the trail until he got "The Kid," either dead or alive, and in the summer of 1882 he located him at Sumner, New Mexico, and killed him first—reading the warrant to him afterwards.

Pat Garrett was one of the bravest of frontier officers, and one who never took advantage of an enemy, no matter what the circumstances or provocation. A short time later he was killed by an outlaw by the name of Wayne Brazel, at Las Cruces, New Mexico, where his grave is now marked by a monument erected by the people of that state, who knew and loved him.

I do not know of a more exciting time for yours truly than when "Billy the Kid" and his grand aggregation of murderers and cow thieves opened fire on poor Jimmy Carlyle and me, and do not know why I was not killed, but such is the case, and in a few weeks we were on our way to Dodge City by way of the Chisholm Trail with thirty thousand head of cattle rounded up in New Mexico and Texas.

If this little story comes to the eye of any of the old-time boys who were on this drive with me, I would certainly be glad to have them drop me a line.

HIS FATHER MADE FINE "BOWIE" KNIVES

By John James Haynes of 308 Arden Grove,
San Antonio, Texas

I was born in the Republic of Texas, August 6, 1843, where Gonzales is now located. My father, Charles Haynes, who arrived in Texas some ten years previous, risked his life in helping Texas to gain her independence from Mexico. I was raised in Llano County, then on the frontier. When I was quite small I was taught to ride, shoot, hunt and run wild cattle, and all the other things necessary to withstand the requirements of those strenuous times. At a very early age my father presented each of his three sons with a gun, and as he was a mechanic and smith by trade, he made for each of us a long "Bowie" knife, and gave instructions how to use it. The rule in those days was to use the "Bowie" knife and save powder and shot. I have been in many close quarters when that knife came in mighty handy, for in my time I have killed every kind of wild animal that roamed in this wild country. Besides the wild animals we had worse foes to contend with—the savage Indians, who often made raids upon the white settlements. But as this writing is for our experiences with cattle on and off the trail, I will confine myself to those experiences.

When I was eighteen years old I joined the Confederate Army and was sent out of the State. I served the entire four years of that desperate struggle, and came home with a crippled arm. When we were discharged we were given transportation home, as far as the train went, and it didn't go far into Texas in those days. We came by water to Galveston, and while our "high up" officers were having a "peace treaty" somewhere in town, we "high up privates of the rear ranks" decided we had been away from home long enough, and as we did not see anything of special interest or excitement to

us there, we concluded to leave the "peace subject" with
the officers, so we captured a waiting train and ordered
the engineer to "charge," which order was promptly
obeyed. When any of the boys reached a point anywhere
near a bee-line to his home, he would pull the bellcord
and drop off. I fell off at Brenham, which was the end
of the road at that time. From Brenham I went by stage
to Austin and from Austin I took the "ankle express"
for my home in Llano County, seventy-five miles away.
After a tramp, tramp, tramp with the boys in gray for
four long years, I was alone now, but the thoughts of
getting home spurred me on, and I did not mind the
fatigue as I covered the distance. One night I stopped
at what was known as "Dead Man's Water Hole," so-
called from the fact that the body of an unidentified man
was once found there. I used a soft log that night for
my pillow, and slept to the tunes of the hoot owls and
the coyote wolves. When I reached home I found my
neighborhood was still being raided by hostile Indians.
I was soon rigged out with a new saddle, horse and gun,
and ready to defend my home against the red men. But
I realized that I must seek a livelihood, so, in company
with my younger brother, Charlie Haynes, and Harve
Putman, we decided to go out and round up mavericks
and drive them up the trail. Each of us having secured
two ponies and a pack horse and other equipment for a
long camping trip, we started out, establishing our camp
in the forks of the North and South Llano Rivers where
Junction City now stands. At that time there were no
fences and very few ranches in that region. The cattle
from the open country of the north and northwest had
drifted into that wild and unsettled wilderness without
being sought after and naturally had become very wild.
But we came with the intention of securing our herd,
despite the wildness of the brutes. At a point near our
camp we found a natural trap that was of material assistance to us. It consisted of a long strip of land about

twenty-five feet wide, with a deep hole of water on one side and a very high bluff on the other. This was the watering place for the cattle of that particular range. We built a pen and fenced in one end of this natural chute, leaving the other end open so that when a bunch of cattle came down for water we crowded in on them and ran them into our pen through the trap. We often started after them out on the range, and in order to get away from us, they would make for the water hole, and right into our trap they would go. We usually kept them in this pen without water or grass until they became tame enough to drive to our other pens some distance away, when, of course, they were then driven regularly for water and grazing. We kept this up until we had about a thousand head of maverick yearlings.

Harve Putman and my brother, Charlie, decided to sell their undivided interest in these yearlings, and John Putnam and myself bought them for $2.50 per head, on credit, to be paid for on our return from the Kansas market. We drove the herd by way of Fort Worth and crossed the Texas line at Red River Station. We put a bell on an old cow for a leader, and when a yearling got lost from the herd, and came within hearing of that bell it generally came back to the herd. We reached Abilene, Kansas, with our yearlings in good shape, and we sold them for eight dollars per head. We found ourselves in possession of $8,000, and had started out without a dollar. But any old trail driver who found himself rich in Abilene, Kansas, in 1871, knows the rest.

In 1872 my brother, Charlie, and I took a mixed herd of about a thousand head up the trail. This time we made a general round-up. It was the custom in those days for the party or parties getting up a round-up to take along cattle belonging to people they knew. Owners were glad to have them driven to market and sold. The distance between ranches was so great that a consultation was not possible every time, and it was usually left

to the driver's own judgment. Be it said to the credit
of those early cowmen, every one was honest with his
neighbor and trusted each other absolutely. The only
requirement of the law was that the cattle be inspected
by the county inspector, the marks and brands being
recorded, and it was agreed among the stockmen that
certain value be placed on certain grades, ages, etc., as
assessed by the assessor. After driving the cattle up the
trail to market, we then, on our return home, paid for
cattle as the claimants appeared, according to the assess-
ment, our profit being the selling price, together with
those not claimed or unknown.

Our second trip was somewhat different from the first
one on account of having so many mixed cattle in the
herd. They were easily stampeded by the smell of buffalo, and other things encountered on the trail. We had
several storms on this trip. The lightning during these
storms seemed to be playing all over the heads and horns
of the cattle, and the loud claps of thunder greatly disturbed them, and often caused a stampede. When cattle
stampede they all move in one direction, with the exact-
ness and swiftness of one body. During a storm we
would ride among them, doing our best to get them settled, but in the darkness of the night, the blinding rain,
loud peals of thunder, with vivid flashes of lightning to
keep them excited, our efforts were often of no avail.
When we saw that they were going, in spite of all we
could do, we left two of our Mexican cow hands to "tough
it out" with them. No matter how many miles away we
found the herd the next day, the faithful Mexicans were
still with it.

In a mixed herd many calves were born on the trip,
and it was the custom to kill them before starting the
herd each morning. Some outfits tried taking along a
wagon for the purpose of saving the calves, but it did
not pay.

We drove this second herd to Council Grove, Kansas,

on the Indian reservation, and as we did not find ready sale, the business men of that place secured permission for us to hold them there until the market opened. While we were in camp here an incident occurred that was a bit interesting to us. We had two Indian blankets which my brother had captured during a fight with Indians in Blanco County, Texas, some years before. In this fight the chief of the tribe had been killed. We used the blankets for saddle blankets, and one day we hung them out to dry, when an Indian on the reservation came along and saw them. He called others, and they had a general pow-wow over them, and the result was that they exchanged us two new government blankets for the Indian blankets. That night the Indians all got together and had a big war dance around those blankets. We found out later that the two blankets in question had belonged to their chief. Although we anticipated trouble with the redskins on this account, we were not molested, and we remained here for some time. As the market was crowded, we had to take our time and sell as the demand came for our cattle. In one deal we got a new wagon and a span of good mules. These mules were afterwards stolen by Indians from my brother's home in Blanco County, during a raid when the Indians killed a man named Hadden.

I was still in the cattle business in Edwards and Uvalde Counties as late as 1893. My brand was JOHN (connected), my first name, easily remembered by all who saw one of my cattle in these or adjoining counties. My daughters, Violet and Susie, had their own brands, JOHN (connected) and SUE, respectively.

Long live the Old Trail Drivers and their descendants.

THREE TIMES UP THE TRAIL

By W. E. Laughlin of Bartlett, Texas

I made my first drive in 1877 with John Ellis from Live Oak County to Fort Worth.

W. E. LAUGHLIN

In 1870 I made a drive with the Durant cattle from Williamson County to Taylor County.

I made my third drive in 1880 with Soules and Armstrong f r o m Williamson C o u n t y to Ogallala, Nebraska. We began making up this herd in February, started the drive in April, and reached our destination the following July. The drive was made from Williamson County to Callahan; there the International Trail was taken up and we went by way of Fort Griffin, thence west of Fort Sill, across the Indian Territory, going into Kansas just east of Fort Elliot, and across the state by way of Fort Dodge, and on to Ogallala.

WILL BUILD A TEN-STORY MARBLE HOTEL IN SAN ANTONIO

Sketch of John Young of Alpine, Texas

John Young was born at Lockhart, Texas, February 12, 1856, in a log cabin. He was raised in Bee and Refugio Counties, and went up the trail five times, with Simpson, Jim Reed, Jim Hall, Goodnight and Claire. He was married to Miss Lizzie Drake at Tilden, Texas, November 28th, 1883, and has seven children living. Mr. Young has had many thrilling experiences on the range and on the trail, about the most exciting of which occurred on the Colorado River. He says:

"I have swam every river from the Rio Grande to the Platte, and came near losing my life while crossing a herd on the Colorado in 1880. The river was on a rampage and about four hundred yards wide. When in midstream a drifting treetop brushed me off my horse and sent me to the bottom. When I came to the surface my horse had gotten away and there was nothing for me to do but rely on myself, and although I was badly hurt from the contact with the limbs of the tree, I struck out for the shore. My old friend, Gus Claire of Beeville, had witnessed the accident and started to me on his horse, but I had drifted several hundred yards down stream before he reached me. As he passed by I caught the horse by the tail, when suddenly we got into a swift eddy, which carried us under a bluff, where we could not land, and so we had to drift down stream until the eddy changed, and then swim back to the opposite side of the river."

Mr. Young has occupied a prominent place in cattle affairs in West Texas for many years. He is still the same old John Young the boys of the trail knew in those bygone days. It is his ambition and lifelong dream to at no distant day erect a cattlemen's hotel in San Antonio, on the site of the old Southern Hotel, which for many years was the headquarters for all visiting cowmen. With D. J. Woodward and T. A. Coleman, he owns a mountain of the finest marble in the world near Alpine, and these three gentlemen are endeavoring to secure title to the entire Southern Hotel block, where they propose to build a ten-story marble hotel to be used exclusively by cowmen, and where the Old Trail Drivers' reunions

JOHN YOUNG

would be held with all the pomp and ceremony of a royal
fete. Negotiations are progressing, and it is safe to predict that this ambition of an old comrade will soon be
realized.

WHEN AB. BLOCKER CLIMBED A FENCE

By G. M. Carson of Rocksprings, Texas

I was raised at Blanco City, and at the age of twenty
I started out to be a cowboy and go "up the trail" in
company with my brother, R. P. Carson, J. J. Cage and
Felix Stubbs. We went to Round Mountain, where
Johnnie Blocker was receiving cattle, and he employed
us at $30.00 per month and agreed to furnish us. He
instructed us to meet him at the old Bundick ranch on
the Perdinales River the 10th of March, 1878, to begin
branding. We were right there on time, and found
plenty to do. One day while engaged in branding, a four-
year-old cow refused to go into the chute, but made a
run for Ab. Blocker, who lost no time in climbing to the
very top of the high fence. She then turned in my direction, and I downed her with a stone which I threw with
all my might. I thought I had killed her, and felt that I
would be given a hasty discharge. I looked around to
see Johnnie Blocker standing near, and he said in a very
pleasant way, "Don't throw rocks at the cattle, boys,"
and I knew right then that my job was still secure. The
cow recovered in a few minutes, and when she got to her
feet again she made a bee-line for the chute. We put
the reversed seven brand on her and gave her a free
pass to Cheyenne. When we had finished branding we
drove the cattle across the country between Austin and
Lockhart and met another herd, where we cut the cattle
and shaped up for the trail about the 15th of March.
John Golden was boss, and we had about sixteen men in
the crew. We pointed the herd, numbering about 3,000

head, north, crossing the Colorado River below Austin, and hit the long, lonesome trail for Cheyenne, Wyoming.

After being on the trail for some time the horse wrangler quit us, and the boss put me in charge of the horses, which I drove until we reached North Kansas.

During this drive, somewhere in the Indian Territory, we had a stampede one dark night and Felix Stubbs and a negro named Joe Tasby got lost from the herd and did not get back to us until late the next evening.

This being a good year for driving, everything moved along nicely until we reached Northern Kansas, where we waited for another herd, and when it came, we found there was a surplus of hands, so eight of us came back to Texas, reaching Austin about the first of July. After this I made several short drives, going with one herd from Frio County to Colorado City, Texas.

I have been engaged in the mercantile business at Rock Springs the past fifteen years

---

FOUND A LOT OF SNUFF ON THE TRAIL

By J. A. Blythe of Del Rio, Texas

I went up the trail in 1876, 1877 and 1878. The first two trips were short, one to Fort Worth and one to Fort Dodge, but the last trip was long, starting on the 4th of March and ending on the 4th of July, when we were paid off in Cheyenne, Wyoming Territory. I traveled along the trail side by side with John R. Blocker, and was just below him when he had four horses killed by lightning in Sydney, Nebraska.

I remember one incident in particular that happened on this trip. A negro named Thad found a box containing a lot of snuff the other side of Fort Worth. It had probably fallen off a freight wagon. He was afraid to sell it as we passed through the Cross Timbers, although

I venture to say that at least nine women out of ten in that region used snuff in those days. But he finally disposed of it at Red River Station. At this point we had a big stampede one night, and a fellow tried to steal our remuda. Nothing further happened until we reached Dodge City, where we crossed the Arkansas River. It was my night off, and I went into Dodge with the boss, Sol West, to "whoop 'em up, Liza," but a big cloud came up after I had paid $1.25 for a haircut and shave, and I had to go back to the herd and stand guard all night during a severe storm. The next place we passed was Buffalo Station, where we delivered four hundred steers to Sparks and Taylor, then headed north to Ogallala, Nebraska, crossed the South Platte River, followed the Union Pacific Railroad to Big Springs, the point where Joel Collins had robbed the U. P. train and secured $80,000 in $20.00 gold pieces, and was later killed. We left the North Platte River and went up Pole Creek, but nothing of note happened until we reached Sydney, Nebraska, where a big storm came up and lightning killed the four horses for John R. Blocker. No one was hurt except the cook, who was slightly stunned by the shock. We delivered the cattle within twenty miles of Cheyenne, and all of the boys came back to Texas, except myself. I decided to remain with the same cattle, and we went to Powder River to locate a ranch, but the weather got so cold we located on the North Platte River. I spent the winter there, got homesick and came back to Texas.

EIGHT TRIPS UP THE TRAIL

By A. N. Eustace of Prairie Lea, Texas

I made my first trip up the trail in 1879, starting from Lockhart, Caldwell County, with M. A. Withers. We crossed the Colorado River at Webberville, and at Hutto we encountered a terrible hailstorm and rain, during which our cattle drifted several miles, many of them getting across a little creek, which soon got on a rampage, after Green Mills, "Pard" Roland and I had crossed and were gathering the scattered herd. Green was riding his well-known pony, "Grunter." We were wet, cold, and hungry, but we had to stay with those cattle until the next morning before we could get back to the main herd. This was my first real experience with trail driving, and if I could have gone home right then I would not have been easily persuaded to go on that trip.

From Hutto we continued our course to Belton and Fort Worth. At this time Fort Worth was the terminus cf the Texas & Pacific Railroad. Crossing the Red River at Red River Station, we traveled the old Chisholm Trail until we crossed the Canadian River. Here we quit the Chisholm Trail, going west and intersecting the Western Trail at Cimarron River, and thence to Dodge City, Kansas, where we delivered a part of our herd, taking the remainder to Buffalo, Kansas, on the K. P. Railroad. From here I returned home.

Our outfit was composed of M. A. Withers, Joe Lewis, Green Mills, Rus Withers, George Brock, Cal Polk, Barney Roland, Walter Ellison and myself.

In 1880 I made the second trip. This time we went the Western Trail, out by old Fort Griffin. We crossed the Red River at Doan's Store, going from there to Wolf Creek, Indian Territory, where we divided our herd, putting a part of the cattle with a herd belonging to W. T. Jackman. We delivered this herd at Ogallala, Nebraska.

In 1881 I made my third trip up the trail with J. R. Shanklin of Prairie Lea. We received a part of our herd at George Hindes' ranch in Atascosa County, completing it at Ellison's ranch in Caldwell County. This time we followed the Western Trail through to Ogallala, Nebraska.

In 1882 I was trail-bound again, and made my fourth trip with J. R. Shanklin. We received our herd in Wharton County from Bob Stafford, and came out by Gonzales and Lockhart, from whence we traveled the Western Trail to Throckmorton County. Here I was taken with chills and had to return home.

In 1883 my fifth trip was made with R. W. Robinson, whose herd was received at Pearsall. We went out by Bandera and Kerrville to Runnels County, where we delivered a part of the herd to Doc Grounds, who lived about eighteen miles west of Abilene, Texas. From here I delivered the balance of the herd to J. R. Blocker in the Indian Territory, and returned to San Antonio with the outfit.

My next trip was in 1884, when I went with Giles Fenner. This year we shipped our herd from Austin County to Wichita Falls, driving from there to Ogallala, Nebraska. From Ogallala we went to Wyoming and delivered the herd to Dater Brothers on the Cheyenne River. From there I went with Captain Ellison to Running Water, Wyoming, to deliver another herd to Durgin Brothers and then came back home.

In 1886 I went with Giles Fenner, Joe Blocker, Driscoll and Davis. This herd we received at Texiketa ranch, twenty miles south of Stafford Station. We struck the west prong of the Nueces River at Kickapoo Springs, and continued up the river to its head, passed over the divide to the head of the Llano River, traveled down the Llano about forty miles to Green Lake, and from there went to Fort McKavett, where we crossed the San Saba River. This herd we delivered at Hugo, Colorado.

My last trip was made in 1887. I went with W. T. Jackman from Jeff Davis County. We shipped our herd from Toyah to Big Springs, and from there we went the extreme Western Trail across the plains to Trails City, Colorado. Our crowd was composed of W. T. Jackman, Mac Randle, John Street, Lum Hunt, Dick Craft, the cook, our Mexican hostler, Chapa, and two negroes, George Crunk and Burrel Moore.

Of course the life of a trail driver was made up of many hardships, but now as I recall the happy associations with those good old friends I can certainly say that my hardships were far outnumbered by the good old times spent on the trail.

A LONG TIME BETWEEN DRINKS

By Sam Neill, La Pryor, Texas

SAM NEILL (and horse)

In the spring of 1880 I made my first trip up the trail, starting from old Mount Woodward ranch on the Leona River, in Frio County. We had 3,200 mixed cattle in the herd, which belonged to Captain John Lytle. Billy Henson was our corporal, or boss. We drove through to Ogallala, Nebraska, on the South Platte River, and delivered them to Jim Ellison. It took us five months and ten days to make the trip, and I was the only man that started with the herd and stayed with it until delivery was made. The boss was taken sick and had to quit. Near Dodge City, Kansas, one of our men, Otis Ivey, was killed by lightning, and within a very few days afterward the last of the men who started with the herd left, but I continued on the job.

With the exception of being badly frightened several times, we did not have much trouble with the Indians on this trip. I was just a mere boy at the time, but I believe this was the hardest trip I ever made. I missed going on herd only one single night during the entire journey. My guard was from two o'clock until daylight. From the time we started I was not inside of a house after we left Frio Town until we reached Ogallala. The last house I was in before I left was Tom Bibb's saloon in Frio Town, and the next was Tuck's saloon in Ogallala. This was a mighty long time between drinks.

I made several trips after this, the longest one being to the Cheyenne River, South Dakota. Gus Black was our boss on this trip. Gus is still living, rides horseback as well as he ever did, and looks after his cattle as actively as a young man.

I am now an old broken-down cow-puncher, and am working for Colonel Ike Pryor, one of the finest men in the world, on one of his ranches in Zavalla County. My postoffice address is La Pryor.

SCOUTING AND ROUTING IN THE GOOD OLD DAYS

By J. M. Custer, Alias Bill Wilson

I was born in 1865 and got my first experience on the cow range in 1876. Captain Hall was moving cattle to West Texas from the Colorado River coast country, and as they passed through Live Oak County I joined them and worked with them through the fall of 1876. In 1877 I went to work for Dillard Fant, and John Dumant was my boss. When Fant sold out to George West I worked in the Mustang Camp on Spring Creek catching wild horses and breaking them. In 1879 I went up the trail

with horses for Mr. Neall, and we delivered at Dodge
City, Kansas. On our way up we had several stampedes,
but had no trouble with the Indians. In 1880 I again
went up the trail, this time to Ogallala, Nebraska, and
we had skirmishes with the redskins. One night I was
on herd north of Doan's Store on Red River, near the
mouth of Cold Water Creek, and had for a night mare
a small Spanish mule. That mule smelled the Indians,
his tail went right up against his belly, and it was impossible to hold him. In fact, I did not try to hold him,
just let him take the lead through the darkness, and we
traveled all night. Next morning I found myself about
twenty miles from camp. When I got back to the bunch
we were short thirty-three head, so we started out to
look for the lost horses. The boss sent me up the creek
to the divide where there was no timber to hide in in
case a fellow should get after a bunch of Indians. After
riding about twenty-five miles up the creek, and reaching
a point not far from the Indian Territory line, I discovered several Indians at a distance of about 200 yards
coming toward me, but we did not meet, for their guns
looked as long as the Chisholm Trail, and I did not care
for them to get in closer range. At that time I weighed
only ninety-five pounds, but I picked up my pony on my
spurs and when I let him down I went down his hind leg
with my quirt. I pointed him back down the creek, with
the yelling red devils in full chase, and I working in the
lead. My boss had often told me that in a stampede I
should stay in the lead, and I was bent on carrying out
his instructions. Finally, after I had raced them for
several miles, I came to a crossing in the creek, which
was about forty feet wide and in deep sand. Here my
horse gave up and refused to go further. I shook him
up, but he had done his best, and that was all he could
do. It was then up to me and the Indians to do the rest.
So I went into a small ravine, took the cartridges out of
my belt and put them in my hat, and waited for a fight,

but the red rascals went out of my sight, leaving me as mad as a hornet and wanting to scrap, for I had not had time to fight them during the chase.

I went back to South Texas in the fall of 1881, and worked on the mustang range again in 1882, when I got into trouble and had to leave that region, and was "on the dodge" for twelve years during which time I "fought" cattle for nine years almost night and day. My little case of trouble caused a "moving" disposition to take a hold on me, and for two years it seemed that everywhere I went the officers were after me. During those two years I went under my own name, from place to place, and state to state, but they chased me out, so I returned to the plains, changed my name to Bill Wilson, and went up the trail several times, until 1892. During one of these drives I was in an Indian fight on the Canadian River. We had a stampede one night and lost a few head of cattle, and next day I was sent out to hunt for them. While riding down the river a bunch of Indians jumped me. We had a short race for a thicket of cottonwood trees. As usual, I worked in the lead, and when we got to the thicket I went into it like a rabbit. There were seven Indians in the party, and they immediately surrounded the thicket. I had dismounted, and had my Winchester ready, so when I saw one of the redskins standing up on his horse, I raised old "Betsy" and cracked down, and there was a dead Indian. For about thirty minutes we had a pretty lively time. The battle ended with five dead Indians and one scalp scratch on my head.

In 1885 I took a herd for Chadman Brothers to Butte, Montana. I delivered the herd, shot up the town, and rode out to camp. The next morning I went back and asked the amount of damage I owed for shooting a saloon glass to pieces. The bartender said $1,500.00. We asked him to take a drink. We took one more, and then took off down the trail.

The next year, 1886, I had charge of a herd of stock cattle and started from Las Vegas, New Mexico, to Nebraska. On this trip I killed a smart Mexican in a shooting scrape. I went out of there under fire, but I held my ground, as all of the Mexicans in that region were on my drag. But a boy raised on the frontiers of Texas always had a way to beat that kind of a game. As George Saunders said about Jack West: "If it did not go right, we always had a machine to make it go right." The kind of a machine the cow-puncher had was sometimes called a "cutter," and sometimes it was called a "hog-leg," but it was better known as a six-shooter gun, and we frequently had a use for it, for it was a "friend in need" in those days. The Western boys always stood pat—no draw pat or show-down.

I ran a maverick brand on the head of Double Mountain Fork, on the OO Range. O. J. Warren was the owner. It got so big I lost my job and had to change my brand. That was my headquarters in winter after I got off the trail.

A great many so-called cowboys nowadays think it is fun to work cattle. It is really play, for they have nothing to do. In the early days we had no pens or railroads or wire fences. When we gathered cattle it was to hold them. Sometimes they would run all night. The boss would yell out to us, "Sing to 'em, boys," and we would sing a song as only a cowboy can sing, but something would go wrong and they would be off on a rampage once more. The worse the weather the closer we would have to stay, for then was the time they gave the most trouble. Once I was on guard six days and nights without going to bed.

This was written in September, 1919, just after I had passed through a great Gulf storm, in which we lost everything, house washed away, and everything lost. There are nine in my family, but I did not lose any of them. We were in the storm for twenty hours and during that fearful period I thought of the old times on the trail, when the rain, hail and thunderstorms used to play such havoc with us. Those were strenuous times, and we endured many hardships that will never be recorded for the perusal of oncoming generations, but, just the same, we had our day, and the world is better for it.

CATCHING ANTELOPE AND BUFFALO ON THE TRAIL

By A. Huffmeyer of San Antonio, Texas

My first trip up the trail was in 1876 with a herd of 1,600 steers belonging to Woodward and Oge of Frio County, the man in charge being Dick Crews. We left the ranch on the Frio River, four miles above Frio town, on the 14th of March and delivered the herd at Fort Sill in the Indian Territory to the agent at the fort seven weeks after we left the ranch. We had considerable trouble just after starting until we got out of the brush, after which we got along nicely. The weather was fine, no severe storms or cyclones to contend with. These cattle were purchased

A. HUFFMEYER

by the government for the Tonkaway tribe of Indians. After delivering we started back home with our entire outfit, eleven men and the cook. We reached home safely and immediately went to work on the ranch.

In the spring of 1877 we commenced rounding up another herd, and were ready to make the start by the 15th of March. Gus Black, who now lives at Eagle Pass, was in charge of this herd, and we had, as on the previous drive, eleven men in the outfit. We had the same trouble with the cattle as on our first trip, but as soon as we reached the open country they moved along well. This herd was headed for Dodge City, on the Arkansas River, and we reached our destination about the 20th of the following July, with our cattle in better shape than when we started. Mr. Oge, who was in Dodge City awaiting our arrival, came out to meet us and remained with us until we delivered. Dodge City was then a wide-open town. Gambling and fandangoes were in full blast. While we were there two men were killed in a saloon row.

The cook and horse wrangler started back over the trail with our saddles and outfits with them, and the balance of us returned on the train.

The next year, 1878, we gathered our herd early and were ready to start by the first of March. This herd was taken through by Virgil Johnson, who died several years ago. We had about two thousand head of mixed cows and steers. It happened to be a wet season and we lost a great deal of sleep from the very start until we reached Red River, on account of the excessive rains. At Red River Station we found about a dozen herds scattered over the country waiting for the rise in Red River to run down so they could cross that stream. While we were here a severe thunderstorm came up and rain fell in torrents. While it was in progress I could see the lightning playing on the brim of my hat and the tips of my horse's ears. Suddenly a terrific bolt of lightning struck right in our midst and killed nine of our best cattle. It stunned my horse and he fell to the ground, but was up in an instant and ready to go. The cattle stampeded and scattered and it was all that we could do to keep ahead of them. After running them for a mile or more, every man found that he had a bunch of his own to look after, they were so badly scattered and frightened. I managed to hold 236 head the balance of the night, and

when daylight came we worked the bunches back together
and made a count and found that we had lost over three
hundred head, which meant some tall rustling for the
boys. Before night we had rounded up all of the strays
except about forty head, which we lost entirely. We
waited a couple of days longer for the river to fall, but
it seemed to keep rising, so Mr. Johnson decided to ferry
our chuck wagon over and swim the herd across. When
we struck the stream it was bank full, with a sandbar
(quicksand) showing in the middle of the river. In order
to get the cattle to take the water we brought our work
oxen down and started them across. They seemed to
know just what we wanted, for when they reached the
edge of the water they walked right out into the deep
current and began swimming across, the balance of the
herd following. Four of our steers stopped on the bar
of quicksand and bogged down and we had to swim out
and extricate them after we had all the others on the far
side. Every one of them showed fight when we pulled
him out of the quicksand, and took right after us, and
we had to hustle to keep out of reach. On the other side
of the river we found the bottoms full of ripe wild plums
and enjoyed quite a treat.

When we took the trail again we could see the Wichita
Mountains in the distance, about seventy-five miles away.
We knew the trail passed along the foot of those mountains, but on account of water the trail made a big curve
to the right, which made it a longer drive, so in order to
save time, Mr. Johnson decided to try to go straight
through on a bee-line to the foot of the Wichitas, and
thus save several days. It proved to be a bad venture,
for we traveled without water for two days, not a drop
for the cattle to drink or with which to quench our thirst.
We had to keep traveling, and by noon the third day
our herd was strung out for fully two miles, with the big
steers in the lead going like race horses, and the old
dogies bringing up the rear. I happened to be on the

point and about noon I saw the leaders throw up their heads and start to run. Mr. Johnson said, "They smell water," and, sure enough, after crossing a ridge we found a little stream of clear sweet water. We camped right there that day and all of the next to allow our stock to rest. The country was open and was covered with the finest grass I ever saw. We reached the Wichita Mountains and got back on the old trail. While traveling along we permitted our herd to scatter and graze, and as we were proceeding slowly we discovered a brown bunch of something on a ridge about a mile away. It turned out to be a herd of buffalo, which were the first I had ever seen. We decided to go forth and kill some of the animals and, accordingly, several of us mounted fresh horses and put out to go around them and head them toward our herd so the other boys could get a chance to kill some of them. But when within two hundred yards of the buffalo they saw us coming and struck a bee-line for the north pole. We yelled and fired at them without result, they kept on traveling. I gave out of ammunition and was determined not to go back empty-handed, so I took down my lariat and selected a young bull about two years old, and soon had him lassoed, but found out that I was not fooling with a two-year-old cow brute. I think I let that bull run over my rope a dozen times and threw him each time, but he would be up in an instant, and I just could not hold him. I called Shelby to my assistance, and the two of us finally managed to get him down and cut his throat. Shelby went back to the herd while I remained and skinned the buffalo and had him ready to load into the wagon when it came along. This same young man (Shelby) began bragging about the fine young horse he owned and said he would bet any man $10.00 that he could catch an antelope on him, so one of the boys took the bet, and the next day the race came off. We espied a bunch of antelope on a ridge 400 or 500 yards away, and Shelby put out in their direction. As soon as they saw him coming they scampered away due north. The country was almost a level plain, but there were a few ridges, and for quite a while we could see the race, but finally Shelby passed out of sight. We kept grazing the herd along, all the time watching for Shelby, and after a long time he hove in sight away off to the north and coming in our direction on the right side of the herd with the antelope leading the race by some 300 yards. It is said that antelope as well as other wild animals have a certain range, and it seemed so in this case, for when Shelby struck out after this one it made a big circle and came right back to where we first saw it. We could see that Shelby was losing ground, and the antelope was about all in, for its tongue was hanging out of its mouth when it came by us, and it was panting furiously. It did not seem to pay any attention to our herd or the men around it, so Johnson told a Mexican to go out and lasso it. He succeeded in doing so in a very few minutes. Poor old Shelby came back with his horse completely fagged out, and lost the ten dollars. His horse did not fully recover from the chase for over two weeks.

While we were in the Osage Nation an Indian chief and four bucks came to our camp one day and wanted us to give them a steer or two for allowing us to graze our cattle through their reservation. Mr. Johnson refused to give them any, and the Indians went away in an ugly humor, threatening to come back and stampede our herd that night and get one anyhow. Mr. Johnson told them to just try that trick and pointed to our Winchesters. Of course we expected trouble, but the Indians failed to carry out their threat.

Everything went along smoothly after that. It rained on us frequently, but only showers. As we were going along through a little creek bottom after a shower one morning we discovered a lot of wild turkeys, and I decided to catch a gobbler, and gave chase after a big fellow. After running him for quite a while I managed to hit him on the head with the butt end of my quirt. That night we had stewed wild turkey on our menu for a change.

We crossed over the line into Kansas, and now and then we could see a little 14 x 16 box house where some farmer had located his pre-emption, and near it would be a few acres in a field, but no trees, fences or other improvements. These squatters were not very friendly toward the Texas cowboys.

We reached Nebraska in the early part of June, and one morning a regular blizzard came upon us, and for about two hours we had sleet striking us in the face. Our overcoats were rolled up in the wagon, so we just had to grin and bear it. We reached the American River that day and found a few cottonwood trees, but the limbs we gathered with which to make a fire and warm our chilled bodies would not burn, and we had to "tough it out." When we reached the Platte River we found protection for our herd in the draws or ravines there. We delivered the herd at Ogallala and my uncle, Mr. Oge, sold all of the cow ponies and outfit and all hands took the train for home.

This was my last experience on the trail. After reaching San Antonio I went to Bandera and joined my brother in the mercantile business in 1878.

THE OLD TRAIL DRIVER

May his life's future pathway with roses be strewn,
    Whose thorns have all been pruned away;
May sunshine abide when its shadows have flown—
    Is the blessing I wish him today.

—BRANCH ISABELL, Odessa, Texas.

DROVE A HERD TO MISSISSIPPI AND ALABAMA

By W. D. H. Saunders, 721 Rigsby Avenue,
San Antonio, Texas

I was born in Yalobusha County, Mississippi, March 1, 1845, and came to Texas with my parents in 1850, locating in Gonzales County. Although quite small at that time, I remember when crossing the Mississippi River at Vicksburg, a fire started on the boat and there was great excitement on board. The passengers and crew succeeded in extinguishing the fire before it gained much headway. We moved to Goliad County in 1859.

I was married June 27, 1866, to Miss Annie New in Bee County, Texas. To us were born twelve children, eleven of whom are yet living. I was engaged in the mercantile business in Bee County several years, later moving to Sayers, Bexar County, in 1884, where I was postmaster and merchant for twenty years. I moved to San Antonio in 1919. T. B. Saunders, a prominent business man of Fort Worth, is my son.

In October, 1862, I left Goliad with Jim Borroum and Monroe Choate with eight hundred beeves for Mississippi.

We crossed the Guadalupe River at Clinton and went to Sweet Home, in Lavaca County, where we rented a field in which to pen our cattle. In this field was a large haystack. The cattle became frightened at this haystack and stampeded. Next morning we were eight miles from camp and lost three hundred of the beeves. We remained there several days to round up our cattle, and then started on our trip, crossing the Colorado at Columbus, the Brazos at Richmond, the Trinity at Liberty, the Natchez at Beaumont, the Sabine near Orange, and then passed into Louisiana, after which we crossed the Culeshoe River and passed through Opelousas, where we met Crump and Fleming, who bought half interest in our herd, and put in three hundred more, making eleven hundred in all.

When we were near the Mississippi River the Confederate soldiers arrested all of our crowd, thinking we were trying to get the beeves to the Yankees. They took the owners of the herd to Alexandria and held the rest of us four or five days, but as they could not prove anything, we were all released and permitted to pursue our journey. When we reached the Mississippi a thousand of the beeves took the water and easily swam across, but we had to sell one hundred on this side of the river, as we could not get them across. We had an old negro with us who was very excitable, and was always uneasy for fear the Yankees would get him, and we had a great deal of difficulty in keeping him with us.

We found sugar mills at all of the large plantations and whenever we stopped at a mill our boys were told to "help themselves," which they usually did, with the result that they often ate too much and were sick from the effects of it.

After we crossed the Mississippi the Confederate soldiers arrested us again, and took our men to Fort Hudson, where they kept them several days, but, as in the former case, they found nothing against us and turned us loose. At Woodville, Mississippi, the cattle were divided, and Borroum and Choate sold theirs to parties there. Crum and Fleming went on to Mobile, Alabama, where they sold their cattle.

At Woodville we stayed at a plantation owned by Dr. Simms. The fence around this plantation was made of hedges. One night Dr. Simms persuaded Upshur Brookin and myself to go bird hunting. We had to carry a light and kill the birds with a stick. We succeeded in killing but one bird, and the next morning at breakfast Upshur found that bird on his plate. Dr. Simms had a large canebreak on his farm where he kept his mules and horses. The doctor had never seen a hair rope, so while we were there he drove up all of his horses and had us trim their manes and tails to get hair and make a rope for him.

Upshur Brookin, J. B. New and myself came home together. We crossed the Mississippi with our horses on a ferry boat. The water came within two inches of the top of the boat and I almost knew we would sink before we got across. I reached home in January and enlisted in the army at Corpus Christi, February 23, 1863, when I was just seventeen years old.

"TRAIL LIFE"

Below is a short sketch of some of the incidents of trail life as related and experienced by Mr. James Gibson of Alice, Texas.

James Gibson, born in Maryland and reared in Virginia, came to Texas as a young boy in the early seventies.

It was solely for the love of adventure that he came, seeking what the new country might have in store for him. And, although his father was adverse to having him come to a strange new country, he gave him means for the trip and a letter of introduction to Major Hutchinson of San Marcos, who had been a law student under an uncle in Charleston, Virginia.

JAMES GIBSON

Mr. Gibson and a distant relative by name of Oscar Flagg made the trip together. They landed at Galveston, Texas, and from there made their way to San Marcos, but, wanting to be without restriction, the letter to Major Hutchinson was never presented; and as the means for the trip had become exhausted, these boys went about seeking whatever employment they might find. Their first work was with Mr. H. C. Story of San Marcos, now a prominent stockman.

The first position with a "trip up the trail" was made with Coon Dunman of Refugio, Mr. Gibson driving the remuda. This position he liked, as he was relieved of night herding, except in nights of storm, when all hands were called upon to hold the cattle. This herd was driven to Coleman City, and delivered to an English syndicate, after which he returned to Sweet Home, Lavaca County, and worked on the Willis McCutcheon ranch.

Later, while working as ranch foreman for D. R. Fant, on his Live Oak ranch, Mr. Gibson was one evening "held up" by two bandits upon returning home from doctoring horses in a lower pasture. The outlaws demanded his gun, and when told that he had none, then demanded his new saddle, but after they had been made to see that they already had possessed themselves of all else he had except that, they decided to let him keep it, and started on their way.

Upon entering the ranch it was found to have been stripped of all its choicest possessions. Mr. Gibson then set out for the nearest camp to find help, but being unable to get any, borrowed from George S. Fokes his gun and fourteen cartridges (all he had) and returned to the ranch. Imagine his surprise upon entering the home pasture to find camping beside the gate the same men who had caused him so much trouble the day before. They again demanded the saddle, evidently censuring themselves for their generosity of the day before, but being now in possession of a gun, he refused, which, as the usual thing, brought the guns of both sides into play. Mr. Gibson, seeing a big tree nearby, gained that and, shooting from behind its protecting trunk, finally succeeded in putting them to rout. As soon as possible he set out for the nearest ranch, owned by John Edwards, and there found that Dave Walton, at that time sheriff of Bee County, had the day before tried to arrest the same parties for like depredations. Edwards joined him and later a posse composed of Ed and Tom Lasater, the Coker boys and a number of others, surrounded the house of the bandits, but found that they had moved on. This raid and its subsequent excitement led to the acquaintance of Doss and Garrett Van Meter and their widowed mother, Mrs. E. V. Van Meter, of that place.

It was in the later years to their home and its associations that Mr. Gibson looks back as being one of the very brightest spots in the memory of his young manhood.

The following spring, however, being unable to resist the tinkle of the old bell-mare, Mr. Gibson made the second trip up the trail, this time with Nance and Mitchell, driving cattle. He pointed herd all the way with a boy by the name of John Williams guarding the opposite point. They had a great deal of rain and hail during this trip, and one day as they were passing through the Indian country near the Wichita Mountains, a funny incident took place.

A bunch of Indians rode up behind Mr. Gibson and grunted in their Indian fashion, "How John?" and after lingering a while asked such questions as, "No cara swap horses?" "Dimme Cartuches" and "Unde Campo?" went over to Williams and hailed him by "How John!" As soon as they rode away Williams came over and said, "Jim, those d——ned Indians know me," and when Mr. Gibson expressed surprise and asked where he had met them, said, "I never seen the d——d fools before, but they called me John." Later this circumstance was related in camp to the old trail hands, who whooped and yelled and seemed to consider it a good joke, and when they had quieted enough so as to be understood, told them that Indians saluted all white men by, "How John!"

The next year Mr. Gibson's work was with the Boyce Bros., and as soon as the grass was green they proceeded to Cuero, there to procure the outfit for the trail. This consisted of wagons, harness, saddles, etc., and were bought from John Stratton, who at that time had the largest outfitting store in this part of the country.

The trip was with horses, some five hundred head of which had been bought from Ed Corkill of Conception. These horses were delivered at Dodge City, Kansas, going by way of San Antonio, Kerrville, Soleman City, Vernon and Doan's Store, an Indian trading store on Red River. There the trails forked, one going to Mobeetie and the other by the Wichita Mountains. The delivery of horses took three months, while that of cattle took four.

It was on this trip one night that a severe thunderstorm came up. The horses had been turned loose on the tableland when, just before the storm started, a deer jumped up in front of the herd and caused them to stampede. They ran directly by camp, causing the remuda to join them and, as they had not been hobbled for the night, came near leaving the cowboys all afoot, the remuda man's horse being the only one staked. And as one of the boys ran to mount him he, catching the contagion of fright, pulled up his stake and went rushing by camp. The negro cook, taking in the seriousness of the situation, grabbed the rope and went bumping along for about a hundred yards before he could stop him. He then mounted and assisted in trying to stop the herd that had by this time crossed the creek. The storm, however, growing in intensity, compelled an early return to camp with only a few saddle horses.

Everyone spent a very restless night confronted with the thought that these few horses constituted their all and that it was two hundred miles to the nearest pasture fence south, and all stampeded horses on the trail go back south towards Texas.

Daylight found them in their saddles eagerly searching for tracks and after two days hunting found all but three head. The following spring, however, Jim Mussett, a friend, found the three missing horses in the general roundup with the Indians, and after selling them sent the money to the owners. This was considered a very lucky stampede.

Mr. Gibson made eight trips with horses. Horses in those days were driven by the thousands and sold to early settlers in job lots in Western Kansas and Nebraska.

Jim Dobie, Frank Byler and Boyce Bros. were among some of the most important horse trail drivers. When applying to any of the above mentioned men for a trail job, it was useless to ask what horse one might ride, for the reply would invariably be "Throw your rope and whatever it falls on, fork him." On one of these trips a laughable thing took place. The cook had quit for the good reason that his pay had stopped and that necessitated the finding of another. A young man just arrived from the East was chosen for this position. After he had convinced the boys that, although he was no expert cook, he could boil water without burning it, the boss told him to cook for dinner red beans, bacon, coffee and dried apples. The cook, not knowing the habit of apples, filled the pot full and covered them with water. When they began to swell the pot began to overflow, and it was a funny sight witnessed by one of the boys in passing to see the tenderfoot frantically digging a hole in the sand and burying the surplus supply. At first the coffee was all grounds, the bread like leather and the beans rattled down one's throat, but, being a persevering kind of a fellow, by the next roundup he had become a really good cook.

One year the outfit had a mascot in the form of a little

rooster that had been presented by Ben Jones of Oakville, now deceased, to Mr. Gibson. It was a source of
pleasure and amusement to the whole camp, and the
Indians en route were astonished to see a chicken with
a cow outfit, so far from civilization. His early morning
crowing brought no response, as the nearest ranch was
over two hundred miles away. He had the misfortune
once to hang by one foot all night from the hound of the
wagon, his roost. A storm coming up during the night
had blown him off and when morning came he looked as
if he had been to an Irish wake. He was tenderly cared
for by the boys and the cook and before long was his
normal bright self again, making the trip to Dodge City
and back to Cuero with the cook.

Mr. Gibson's last trip was with horses in 1888, and
he found it very difficult to get through as the man with
the hoe had taken the country, and the old trail had all
been fenced up, so the drive overland from Texas to
Kansas was over and the cattle then, as now, must be
routed by way of the iron horse.

It has been in this manner for the past twelve years,
having holdings in two ranches, that Mr. Gibson, in partnership with Richard King, Jr., grandson of Mrs. H. M.
King of Santa Gertrudes ranch, has conducted his cattle
business and still classes himself as "one of the cowboys."

AN INDIAN BATTLE NEAR THE LEONA RIVER

By L. A. Franks of Pleasanton, Texas

In 1865 occurred one of those sad frontier tragedies
where the settlers were unable to sustain themselves in
an Indian battle, and wives and mothers were made to
mourn for loved ones who never returned except as man-
gled or inanimate bodies. This noted fight occurred on

the 4th day of July in the above named year near the
mouth of the Leona River in Frio County. The settlers
in the vicinity at that time were the Martins, Odens,
Franks, Bennetts, Hays,
Parks, Levi English and Ed
Burleson. These were all in
what was known as the Martin Settlement.

L. A. FRANKS

On the morning in ques-
tion Ed Burleson went out a
short distance from his ranch
to drive up some horses. He
was unarmed and riding a
slow horse. Suddenly and
unexpectedly to him he was
attacked by two Indians, who
ran him very close, one on
foot and the other mounted.
The one on foot outran the
horseman and came near catching Burleson, but he ran
through a thicket and, coming out on the side next his
ranch, arrived there safely. Quite a lot of people had
collected at his house, men, women and children, to celebrate the Fourth and wind up with a dance. Ere the sun
went down on that day, however, the festivities were
changed into mourning. Instead of the gay tramp and
joyous laughter of the dancers, wailing and the slow
tread of a funeral procession was heard. Excitement
ran high when Burleson dashed in and gave the alarm.
Most of the men mounted in haste to go in pursuit and
others were notified. When all the men had congregated
who could be gotten together on short notice, they numbered eleven and were as follows: Levi English, L. A.
Franks, G. W. Daugherty, Ed Burleson, W. C. Bell,
Frank Williams, Dean Oden, Bud English, Dan Williams,
John Berry and Mr. Aikens. Levi English, being the
oldest man in the party and experienced to some extent

in fighting Indians, was chosen captain. When the main trail was struck the Indians were found to be in large force, and going down the Leona River. They crossed this stream near Bennett's ranch, four miles from Burleson's. They then went out into the open prairie in front of Martin's ranch, ten miles further on. The settlers first came in sight of them two miles off, but they went down into a valley and were lost to sight for some time. Suddenly, however, they came into view again not more than two hundred yards away. They were thirty-six Indians, mounted two and two on a horse. The Indians now discovered the white men for the first time and at once commenced a retreat. The white men were all brave frontiersmen and made a reckless and impetuous charge and began firing too soon. The Indians ran nearly a mile and, thinking likely they had well-nigh drawn the fire of the settlers, checked their flight at a lone tree at a signal from their chief, and each Indian who was mounted behind another jumped to the ground and came back at a charge, and for the first time commenced shooting. The mounted ones circled to right and left and sent a shower of arrows and bullets. Some of the Indians went entirely around the white men and a desperate battle at close quarters ensued. The redmen had the advantage of the whites in point of numbers and shots. The latter, having nearly exhausted their shots at long range, had no time to reload a cap and ball pistol or gun in such a fight as was now being inaugurated. Captain English in vain gave orders during the mad charge, trying to hold the boys back and keep them out of the deadly circle in which they finally went. Dan Williams was the first man killed and when he fell from his horse was at once surrounded by the Indians. English now rallied the men together and charged to the body of Williams, and after a hot fight drove them back, but in so doing fired their last loads. The Indians were quick to see this, and came back at them again, and a retreat was ordered. Frank Williams, brother to Dan, now dismounted by the side of his dying brother and asked if there was anything he could do for him, and expressed a willingness to stay with him. "No," said the stricken man, handing Frank his pistol, "take this and do the best you can—I am killed—cannot live ten minutes. Save yourself." The men were even now wheeling their horses and leaving the ground, and Frank only mounted and left when the Indians were close upon him. The Comanches came after them yelling furiously, and a panic ensued.

Dean Oden was the next man to fall a victim. His horse was wounded and began to pitch and the Indians were soon upon him. He dismounted and was wounded in the leg, and attempted to remount again, but was wounded six times more in the breast and back, as the Indians were on all sides of him. Aus Franks was near him trying to force his way out, and the last he saw of Oden he was down on to his knees and his horse gone. The next and last man killed was Bud English, son of the late captain. His father stayed by his body until all hope was gone and all the men scattering away. The Indians pursued with a fierce vengeance, mixing in with the whites, and many personal combats took place, the settlers striking at the Indians with their unloaded guns and pistols. In this fight all the balance of the men were wounded except Franks, Berry and Frank Williams. Captain English was badly wounded in the side with an arrow; G. W. Daughtery was hit in the leg with an arrow; Ed Burleson also in the leg; Aikens in the breast, and W. C. Bell in the side. In this wounded and scattered condition the men went back to the ranch and told the news of their sad defeat. Other men were collected and returned to the battleground to bring away the dead, led by those who participated but escaped unhurt. The three bodies lay within a hundred yards of each other and were badly mutilated. The Indians carried away their dead; how many was not known, but supposed to be but few, on account of the reckless firing of the men at the beginning of the fight. Bud English was killed by a bullet in the breast, and there was also one arrow or lance wound in the breast. The head of Dan Williams was nearly severed from the body, necessitating a close wrapping in a blanket to keep the members together while being carried back. Oden and Williams were brothers-in-law, and were both buried in the same box. Eight out of eleven were killed or wounded.

This is a very good description of the early day life in Texas.

JACK POTTER, THE "FIGHTING PARSON"

Written by John Warren Hunter

No name was more familiarly known thirty-five years ago in West Texas than that of Andrew Jackson Potter, the "Fighting Parson." His name was a household word from the Panhandle to the Gulf; from the Colorado to the Rio Grande, and the stories of his wit, prowess and adventures were sent abroad in the nation by press and pulpit. While the question of frontier protection was being considered in the United States Congress in 1872, a Texas member said in his speech: "Remove your regulars from the garrison on the Texas border; commission Jack Potter, a reclaimed desperado and now a Methodist preacher and Indian fighter, instruct him to choose and organize one hundred men and Indian depredations along the Texas border will cease."

A. J. Potter was born in Charlton County, Missouri, April 3, 1830, and was one of seven children—four boys and three girls—Andrew being the third son. His father, Joshua Potter, was one of those rugged Kentucky marksmen who stood behind the breastworks at New Orleans, January 8, 1815, and helped defeat the flower of the

British army under Packenham. It was on account of his love and veneration for "Old Hickory" that he named his son Andrew Jackson. While quite young the boy's father moved to Grand River, near Clinton, where the lad spent his boyhood. Clinton was at that time a border county and educational facilities were very limited. Three months in school covered the entire period of Andy's scholastic experience, and during this time he learned to read after a fashion, but did not acquire the art of writing.

At the age of ten, Andrew was an orphan, without home, friends or heritage, and became a race rider, and his skill, courage and daring soon won the high regard of his employer to the extent that he taught him to write, play cards and shoot straight; three of the most important branches of a frontiersman's education during those early days. For six years Andrew followed the occupation of race rider, his daily associates being jockeys, gamblers, drunkards and blasphemers—six years of perilous paths that led over hills, mountains and deserts from St. Louis to Santa Fé. In 1846, when hostilities broke out between the United States and Mexico, Mr. Potter then being about 16 years of age, enlisted in Captain Slack's company of volunteers and, under command of General Sterling Price, took up the line of march for Santa Fé, New Mexico. A few days' march demonstrated the fact that Andrew was too small to carry a haversack and musket and endure the fatigue of a soldier. He was detailed as teamster, where he learned his first lesson in driving oxen.

The expedition left Leavenworth, Kansas, in September, 1846, and the route led up the Arkansas. Before reaching Bent's Fort the entire train of 40 wagons was captured by the Cheyenne Indians. Not apprehending danger, it seems the main body of troops had passed on far in advance, leaving the train without an escort. Under the cloak of friendship, two Indians came into the

camp early in the morning and were given food and remained. When the train moved out two others came up;
other squads joined them and then still larger bands,
then three hundred savages rushed upon the teamsters.
No attempt at violence was made by the Indians. The
chief gave the wagonmaster to understand that he only
wanted provisions, not scalps, and if he had to fight to
obtain the provisions he'd take scalps also. The wagonmaster agreed to give him a certain amount of provisions,
and while this was being given out a cloud of dust was
seen rising far in the rear and the teamsters shouted,
"Soldiers! The soldiers are coming!" Seizing their
plunder, the Indians mounted and fled. The cloud of
dust was caused by an approaching wagon train.

At Bent's Fort, young Potter was seized with an attack of "camp fever," and it was thought necessary to
leave him at that post, but his wagonmaster, who had
become greatly attached to the lad, made arrangements
to take him along. It was yet three hundred miles to
Santa Fé, winter was at hand and the Raton Mountains
were before them. After enduring untold hardships,
they reached Santa Fé in January, 1847. For five years
young Potter remained with the army in that region, operating in New Mexico and Arizona, fighting, trailing and
routing the vengeful Apaches and other dangerous tribes.
It was during this period that he became an adept in all
the arts of Indian warfare. He was an apt student in
their school of cunning and strategy. Mr. Potter leaves
on record his impressions made by the sufferings of
Price's men in the hospital at Santa Fé. He says:

"In the latter part of 1847 I was employed as a nurse
in the hospital at Santa Fé. On entering that place I saw
an affecting scene; a large number of men sick of scurvy,
measles and pneumonia, were lying on narrow bunks so
closely crowded together that there was just room to pass
between them. My time of nursing came on in the first

part of the night, and it was an awful half night to me. Many of the sufferers in their fevered delirium would rise up and gather their blankets, saying they were going home. By the time I would get them quieted, others would be crying out: 'Good-bye, I am going home!' at the same time making efforts to get up. Never shall I forget those dreary half nights I spent there with the dead and dying. Oh, the sweet thoughts of home, sweet home! They came as a dream charm over the fevered brain when visions of wife, babes and loved ones at home entered the mind.

"At length a train set out for Fort Leavenworth to carry home all the sick who were able to stand the trip across the plains. I was one of the attendants. As our ox teams slowly moved up the hill I took my last lingering look at the old adobe town of Santa Fé, with eyes dimmed by unshed tears, as I gazed for the last time on the graves of so many brave soldiers who lay side by side on the tomb-covered hill beyond, not to arise until Death's long reign is passed. Many of our sick died in the great wilderness and we rolled them up in their blankets and hid them in earth's cold clay at intervals in our long journey from Santa Fé to Fort Leavenworth. Their unmarked graves are in the unsettled wilds of Nature's solitude. Friends and dear ones at home know not the place of their rest. When we wrapped their cold bodies in their soldier shrouds and shaped the grave mound over them, the hardy soldier would perchance moisten the earthen monument with a pitying tear. To me it was a terribly gloomy thought to leave them alone in savage lands, to be trodden under foot by the wild, roving bands of Nature's untamed children in their merry dances over the dust of their vanquished foes."

After six years' service as a soldier, Mr. Potter came to Texas, reaching San Antonio in 1852, and from there he went to visit a brother then living on York's Creek in

Hays County. Shortly after his arrival at his brother's he was stricken with typhoid fever and came near dying. When he recovered he found himself penniless and a big doctor's bill to pay. His first employment was driving an ox team at $15 a month, hauling lumber from Bastrop County to San Marcos, and by saving up his wages he was soon able to pay off all indebtedness. About this time Rev. I. G. John, a Methodist preacher, came along and filled an appointment on York's Creek. Potter went out to hear him, more for the novelty of the meeting and a spirit of curiosity. The text, ''Who is the wise man?'' pierced his soul, and from that day he became a regular attendant at preaching, even denying himself the pleasures of a Sunday race in order to hear Rev. John preach.

John preached at a great religious revival held at Croft's Prairie, in 1856. Mr. Potter was converted, joined the church and the horse racer, gambler and saloonkeeper tough was completely transformed and became one of the most useful men West Texas ever knew.

The new life inspired Mr. Potter with a desire to learn and he became a devoted Bible reader. He learned to write, and soon began to preach. In 1859 he sold out in Bastrop County and located on a place nine miles east of Lockhart, where he was licensed to preach and from there began his wonderful career as an itinerant preacher.

In 1861 he was seized with a desire to visit the old home in Missouri, but had no money to defray the expenses of the journey. Mr. Miller, of Lockhart, was getting ready to start a herd of cattle to Kansas. Mr. Potter hired to him as a herder and after 47 days' travel, reached a point 100 miles from the home of his boyhood, which he traversed in a few days. His sister only remained to greet him and those who had known him as the reckless race rider and gambler were astounded to learn that Andy Potter had come to life and was a preacher! He preached to a great concourse the Sunday following his arrival, and this was the beginning of a great revival that continued three months.

In February, 1862, Mr. Potter enlisted as a private in Captain Stoke Home's Company at Prairie Lea. This company was assigned to Wood's Regiment, Thirty-second Texas Cavalry. The command was first stationed at Camp Verde, Kerr County, and later near San Antonio, where Rev. Potter was appointed chaplain of De-Bray's regiment. From San Antonio the command went to Brownsville, where the fighting parson whipped the editor of the local paper for having published what Potter conceived to be a libel on his regiment, and was on the eve of throwing the printing plant into the river, but was prevented by General Bee.

Mr. Potter was in all of the battles of the Red River campaign in 1864, one of unspeakable hardships to the soldiers of the Confederacy—hunger, sickness, toils, battle strife, death. Bread, sugar and berries were the chief articles of food. The good chaplain shared all these hardships with the common soldiers, passing through all the daily drills and marches, preaching, praying and exhorting the men.

When in battle array and ready for the order to advance, Chaplain Potter could be seen with hat in one hand and Bible in the other, walking back and forth in front of his regiment exhorting the men to repentance. "Boys, some of you may fall in this battle," he would say; "in a few minutes you may be called to meet your Maker. Repent now and give your heart to Christ. He is waiting to receive you. Oh, men, it's a solemn moment! You are facing death and eternity!" And when the order "forward" was given, Mr. Potter seized a musket, fell in rank and fought side by side with his men. At the close of battle Potter seemed endowed with the power of ubiquity. Everywhere, praying with the dying, administering to the wounded, writing last messages to friends at home, day and night, scarcely pausing to take food

or rest. This is the testimony of his comrades, many of
whom are yet living who will confirm the statement.

In the fall of 1865 Mr. Potter was appointed as a
supply to the Prairie Lea circuit and at the annual conference held at Seguin in the fall of 1867, he was sent
to the mountain frontier and took station at Kerrville.
This threw him in the region where, on each light moon,
the Indian left his trail of blood along some mountain
side or valley. But the Comanche yell had no terrors
for Potter; he had heard it before and had been schooled
in all their wiles and methods. In 1868 Mr. Potter bought
a place near Boerne and moved his family to it. In
1871 he was sent to the Uvalde circuit, which bordered
on the Rio Grande, where Indians could cross any day,
and their depredations, killing and stealing, were almost
of daily occurrence. Uvalde, at that time, was known
as one of the wickedest places on the border and never
before had preaching. In addition to his ministerial
work, Mr. Potter had been appointed colporteur, and
over this vast territory he distributed among rich and
poor alike a great number of Bibles.

During the first year of his work in the mountain
region the Indians made a raid on Curry's Creek. Dr.
Nowlin, an old frontiersman, knew the Indians were in the
country and stationed two men in his corncrib to guard
his horses, which were loose in the lot. The moon was
at its full and along about midnight two Indians were
seen to stealthily approach, and as they began to let
down the lot fence, one of the men in the crib took good
aim and fired, killing the Indian in his tracks, the other
man was so scared he could not shoot and the other
Indian got away.

While on his rounds in the Uvalde work, on the road
between the Frio and Sabinal Canyon, Mr. Potter met a
squad of four Indians. He was traveling in an ambulance drawn by two small Spanish mules and while passing through a lonely defile in the mountains he came up

almost face to face with these four redskins. He saw there was going to be a fight and, seizing his Winchester, he leaped out of his ambulance and securely tied his mules to a sapling and then, under cover of a thicket, he reached a slight elevation, where he could better command a full view of the enemy. Getting in a good position, the parson took good aim and pulled the trigger, but the gun failed to fire and the "click" of the hammer revealed his whereabouts. Two Indians had citizen rifles and blazed away at him, but without effect. The parson fired at the same instant, wounding one of the Indians and knocking the gun out of his hands. The wounded Indian was taken up by his comrades and carried off.

Potter might have killed all four before they got out of reach, but he was afraid to risk his cartridges, as they had been on hand some time. Returning to his ambulance, he drove off some distance from the road and came to the foot of a mountain and drove into a dense thicket. He knew there were more than four Indians around, and that they were likely to lay in ambush somewhere ahead. When he had secured his team in the thicket he carefully cleaned his gun, selected the best cartridges, got his pistol in fighting trim, and began to look around. He discovered two Indians watching for him from the summit of the hill above him and when they saw that he had seen them, they blazed away, but missed their mark. Mr. Potter pumped several shots at them as they scampered over the hill out of sight. He then re-entered his vehicle and drove away without seeing that bunch of redskins again.

One instance out of many, will give the reader an idea of the person, the men and the times of which we write. While on this frontier work, late one evening he reached a military outpost. It might have been Fort Clark. The soldiers had just been paid off and the little village near the post was crowded with gamblers, sharpers, crooks and other disreputable characters. Many of these knew Mr. Potter and when he rode up they set up a shout, "Here comes the fighting parson!" "Hold up, there, old pardner! Can't you give us a gospel song an' dance tonight?" When told he would preach to them if they would provide a place, one sang out, "Sure, Parson, we'll make way for ye, if we have to rent the saloon!" A saloon gallery was provided with rude seats, kegs, barrels and a few chairs from dwellings nearby, and as the word had gone abroad that a strange preacher was in town, people began to assemble early. One man who was the worse for drink, insisted on acting the part of usher and town crier. He mounted a barrel and for some time kept up the cry, "O yes. O yes. O yes! There is going to be some hellfired racket here, right here on this gallery by fightin' Parson Potter, a reformed gambler, but now a regular gospel shark. The jig will begin now in fifteen minutes, and you old whiskey soaks and card sharpers, come over and learn how to mend your ways, or the devil will get you quicker'n hell can scorch a feather."

A great crowd assembled—one of the hardest looking sets of human beings Potter had ever preached to, but they kept good order, and when service concluded they wanted to "set 'em up" to the parson, but when he declined that mark of their respect they passed an empty cigar box and all "chipped in." He preached the next day and was pressed by those rude Western men to come again and come often.

In 1878 or 1879 Mr. Potter began his labors at Fort Concho. San Angelo was a small frontier village and, like all post towns along the border, had a record not the best along the lines of morality. The saloons and gambling halls were popular resorts. They were open day and night, and every man went heavily armed. Mr. Potter visited the families, preached to the gamblers, soldiers and plainsmen.

In 1883 Mr. Potter moved his family to San Angelo, but continued his ministerial work wherever assigned.

In 1894 he was sent to the Lockhart circuit. Here it was on this same circuit that he began his ministry. On October 21, 1895, he preached his last sermon prior to going to conference. It was the close of his year's work, and proved to be the closing scene of his life work. This was at Tilden, and while delivering his peroration with uplifted hands with the words, "I believe," he fell in the pulpit and when tender hands lifted the limp form the great soul had gone home to the Father who gave it. To the writer who knew him and loved him as a brother for many years, he had expressed a wish to die in harness, in the pulpit.

As has been stated, no man who ever lived in Southwest Texas was more widely known than A. J. Potter. That he acquired the title of the "fighting parson" was in no wise derogatory to his character as a man, a Christian gentleman or a preacher. He was a man absolutely without fear. He was never the aggressor, and when a difficulty was forced upon him he always acted on the defensive and vanquished his assailant. His personal combats with Indians and desperadoes would fill a volume. It is a notable fact that when he had overcame an assailant in a fist fight or otherwise, if he chanced to be a white man, he always gave him fatherly counsel and offered him his hand.

It was said of him that he knew every road, trail and landscape throughout all West Texas. He had visited nearly every home in all this vast region, administered to the sick, officiated at weddings and funerals, and received a frontier welcome everywhere.

SWIMMING THE NORTH PLATTE RIVER   From a Painting by Warren Hunter

THE CHISHOLM TRAIL

By Fred Sutton of Oklahoma City, Okla.

The meeting of "The Old Time Trail Drivers' Association," of which the writer is a charter member, held at Houston, Texas, calls to mind many interesting bits of history of the early-day cow business and of the drives made over the romantic and historic Chisholm Trail. And I wonder what has become of all of those good boys who blazed the way from San Antonio to where it crossed the Red River near Gainesville, thence through what is now Love, Carter, Garvin, Grady, Canadian, Kingfisher, Garfield and Grant Counties in Oklahoma.

This trail was started in 1868 by John Chisholm, for whom the trail was named. One of the principal watering places was at what was called the government spring, and which is now a beautiful park in the city of Enid. In 1872 the terminus was shifted to Ellsworth, Kansas, and in that year the Santa Fé built into the Great Bend country and Dodge City was laid out as a townsite, and in 1874 the head of the drive was located at that point. From 1874 to 1884 Dodge City was headquarters for all cowmen from Oklahoma and Texas. During that ten years it was the toughest spot on the American continent and much history has been written of it and of the men who tamed the population and who turned the wide-open town with its Indian fighters, buffalo hunters, cowboys, dance halls, honkytonks and gambling houses, into the modern city of today, where a beautiful high school building ornaments the summit of the notorious Boot Hill, where many a mother's boy who left the East so suddenly that he forgot to take his name with him was laid away by the followers of the Chisholm Trail.

It was in the year 1881 that the writer made his first drive over the trail for Jesse Evans, one of the cattle kings of that day. He was accompanied by some twenty good-hearted, dare-devil, fear-nothing riders, and he would love to know where the remnant of that little band of good boys is and that those who have passed on were given credit for the good deeds performed in this life, and the broad mantle of charity spread over the faults that we all have, and of which (it seems to me) the writer has more than any. On this drive some of our boys quit and men were picked up to take their places, and in this way we were joined by Bill Driscoll, who had been riding the Bar L for Colonel Brooks. He was a morose, sullen man, who never spoke of his past, and as he was always practicing shooting and telling of his prowess with a "45," no one made inquiry regarding it, and in a short time all quit trying to be pleasant or sociable with him, and he was left almost entirely to himself.

Another recruit was Burt Phelps, who came from no one knows where, but he joined the drive at "Old Boot ranch." He was a mild-mannered, blue-eyed boy of 22 years, highly educated and very refined and seemingly entirely out of place on the trail, a fact of which all were sure when he was seen one day to be earnestly reading a little pocket edition of the Bible, which he hurriedly put away and blushed like a school-girl when he saw us looking at him. Though quite modest and retiring in disposition, he was soon a rank favorite with all except Driscoll, who never missed a chance to make light of "mamma's boy," as he called him. Burt was warned several times to look out for Driscoll, as he was a bad and ugly-tempered man and would probably try to draw him into a fight, and as he already had several notches on his gun, a fight with him was to be earnestly avoided. To this Burt replied that he did not fear him and, despite the notches, he was not afraid, and that if occasion required he could shoot him twice while he was pulling his gun, a statement which was soon to be borne out.

That evening in camp a fire had been built by some dry wood gathered along Red River, and Driscoll was

standing rather close to it, when Burt threw a handful
of wood on it, causing a small coal to fly up and strike
him in the face. He at once flew into a rage and grasped
his six-shooter, but before he could get it from the holster Burt had his gun in his face and smilingly took the
gun with its notches from Driscoll and, taking the shells
from it, handed it back and said: "Mr. Driscoll, you act
like you were drawing a siege gun into action and ought
to practice up some that you may defend yourself in
time of trouble. You had better go now and rest up for
a hard day's ride tomorrow." He moved sullenly away
and again Burt was warned to be careful, which only
brought a smile to his boyish face.

For some days all went smoothly, until we bedded
one night near the D H K ranch, and were asked to attend a dance at that place, and as opportunities of that
kind were few and far between, all gladly accepted, and,
leaving a few boys to watch the herd, the rest went to
the dance, where all had a fine time. At about midnight
a driver by the name of Ed Bannister, who was from
Atchison, Kansas, called to Burt through a window of
the ranch house to loan him his gun, as a man out there
wanted to kill a wolf that was scaring the horses. Knowing Bannister to be his friend, nothing was thought of
the request and the gun was handed out and soon returned with the word that the wolf had gotten away.
Shortly after all went back to camp to sleep.

The following day Driscoll and Burt met at a water
hole and Driscoll renewed the quarrel of a few days past,
and drew his gun, but before he could fire Burt had
snapped his gun twice from the hip. Driscoll fired and
poor Burt fell dead. The man who asked Bannister to
borrow the gun had removed the loads. It was Bill Driscoll. Some say Driscoll escaped and was later in the
sheep business in New Mexico. Others say that at the
foot of a dead tree on the banks of Red River could be
found a few bones and a black-barreled .45 with several

notches on the handle and four loaded shells. Who
knows? The writer does know that on a gently sloping
hill overlooking the valley of the Red River is an almost
forgotten grave that contains all that is left of the mortal
remains of poor Burt Phelps, and in the inside pocket
of his coat is a little Bible, on the fly-leaf of which was
written, "From mother to her boy." Where he came
from no one knew, but his companions on the drive believed him to be the son of a rich Eastern father with
whom he had fallen out, resulting in his leaving home
to cast his lot with the rough element to be found on the
range.

The writer could go to this forgotten grave where
poor Burt's remains are resting and where he was laid
by a bunch of cowboys, who, with hats in hand, tried to
say a prayer and, failing, their eyes dimmed with tears,
one member on his knees, with eyes raised to heaven,
said, "Oh, God, look down on this Thy child."

The writer lives now at Oklahoma City, not far from
the old trail that could tell so many stories of human
interest if it could but speak. Other men who live here
and who rode the trail from 1874 to 1884 are Frank M.
Gault. He was sent in 1880 by W. H. Davis to Laredo,
Texas, to bring 5,000 longhorns over the trail to Dodge
City, and on this drive he had as his assistant foreman
Wills McCoy, now of San Antonio; James D. Cox, who
drove through in 1874, and who, now at the age of 82,
would rather have a good cow horse and saddle than the
finest auto, has a fine ranch in Arizona and often spends
his summers there; Charley Colcord, who is now a millionaire oil man, and whom the writer recently met at
a reception attired in a full dress suit, which brought
to mind the fact that it was he who brought the first
toothbrush to Medicine Lodge, Kan., and how the punchers all wanted to borrow it till pay day, and after that
day came, for a short time, each rider had a white-
handled brush sticking out of his top vest or shirt pocket,

and thus style was introduced on the Kansas plains by Charley Colcord, the cowboy.

I could go on writing of others, such as George B. Stone, Oscar Halsell, Bill Tilghman, B. S. McGuire, F. E. Herring of Elk City, and others who were good cowboys, and are good men, who while on the range could take their own part under any and all circumstances, feared nothing, and who are now the God-fearing and peace-loving business men who have builded a modern city of 100,000 people in twenty-seven years on the site of the Chisholm Trail.

PREFERRED TO TAKE OLDER CATTLE UP THE TRAIL

By Thomas Welder, Beeville, Texas

In the early seventies we owned quite a large horse stock and, there being no market for them in this country, I decided to drive a bunch east in hopes of finding sale for them. In 1873 I gathered one hundred mules and some good horses and started with them. I first went to Wharton, on the Colorado, but, not finding a market there, I went on to Richmond, on the Brazos, then to Lake Charles, La., continuing my journey until I wound up at the mouth of Red River in Lousiana. There I remained five months, finally disposing of all the mules and horses. I continued to make drives to that region every year until 1878, when I concluded to try driving cattle up the trail to Kansas. That spring Dug Williams and I drove a herd for J. J. Welder. We gathered in February, and after branding the cattle on his San Patricio County ranch, we went to his ranch in Refugio County to finish up. We divided the cattle into two herds, having from a one-year-old up to a grown steer. I was given choice of the herds, and took the young cattle 2,000 ones and 500 twos. I soon discovered my mistake, for the young cattle, not being able to stand the hardships of the trail, soon began to give out, and I found myself with a lot of drags, as we called them. We were caught in a severe freeze on Gonzales Prairies, which made matters worse. However, I continued on my journey and reached Fort Worth, where we crossed the river there and went out to Blue Mound to spend a few days resting up. With the assistance of Jim Reed and Tom Ward, formerly citizens of South Teas, but then living at Fort Worth, I disposed of the drags, about sixty head, at six dollars per head, then resumed our journey and crossed Red River at Red River Station on the eastern trail into the Indian Territory. At the entrance of every reservation I found a sign posted up, "One Wohaw," which meant that the Indians wanted one steer to pay for grazing privileges. I always complied with the request and had no trouble, but others who failed to do so had their cattle stampeded at night and probably lost more in the end than I did. We encountered several severe hailstorms on our way, but finally reached Dodge City, where we sold part of our cattle to be delivered at Ogallala, Nebraska. The remaining ones we closed out at Dodge City. We returned home by way of Kansas City, Galveston, Indianola and Victoria.

In 1882 I put 400 head of my cattle into a herd with J. J. Welder and Wash Moss and I drove for him that year. The herd consisted of 5,000 head, which we gathered and branded at his ranch on the San Antonio River. We divided the cattle into two herds of 2,500 each, and having gained some valuable experience the year before, I chose the herd of older cattle and started on the trail with them. They stampeded every night for ten or twelve nights, and I began to think I had again made a mistake, but they soon got used to the trail and quit giving trouble. I delivered the last of these cattle about twenty miles from Denver, Colorado. We reached Dodge City some time in June, where John sold the grown steers to Major Maberry, who had a contract with the government to furnish the Indians with beef. We delivered 500 to him, I think, the remaining 2,000 of my herd were sold to a banker, Fine Eames, of Denver, to be delivered there. We started the herd from Dodge City, going up the Arkansas River some 200 or 300 miles in order to have plenty of water for the cattle. We also followed a small stream called Sandy River for some distance. We had to drive our cattle up and down this river for two or three hours at a time, then take them out to give the water time to rise, and let them go to the water in small bunches in order for the herd to get sufficient water. We reached the Kit Carson ranch on the Union Pacific or the Kansas Pacific about twenty miles from Denver, where we delivered the herd and the outfit returned home.

Before closing I want to relate one little incident of excitement that happened to me in 1878. While on the trail, after crossing the North Canadian River, I was traveling ahead of the herd to find a stopping place for the night, and after finding a good place, started back to the herd, when I was overtaken by seven Indians. They wanted to swap horses with me, but I would not swap. Then one wanted some cartridges for his gun. I had a belt full, but I pulled out my pistol, held it in my hand and kept right on traveling. One of the Indians grabbed for my hat, but I dodged and kept him from getting it. Finally I saw our lead cattle coming over the hill and pointed to them. The Indians saw the herd and at once quit me, and I felt considerably relieved.

A WOMAN TRAIL DRIVER

By Mrs. A. Burks, Cotulla, Texas

My husband, Mr. W. F. Burks, and I lived on a ranch at Banquette, Nueces County, during the days that Texas cattle could be marketed only by driving them over the old Kansas Trail.

At this time in this section of the country good steers could be bought for fifteen dollars, and were often killed for the hides and tallow. The meat was fed to the hogs.

In the early spring of 1871 Mr. Burks rounded up his cattle and topped out a thousand head of the best to take to market. Jasper Clark (better known as "Jap") was getting ready to take the Clark herd also, so they planned to keep the two herds not far apart.

They started in April with about ten cowboys each, mostly Mexicans, and the cooks. The cattle were road-branded at Pinitas and started on the familiar trail. They were only a day out when Marcus Banks, my brother-in-law, came back with a note to me from Mr. Burks asking me to get ready as soon as possible and catch up with the bunch. He also said to bring either Eliza or Nick (black girl and boy who worked for us) to look out for my comfort, and suggested that Nick would be of more help than the girl.

So Nick and I started in my little buggy drawn by two good brown ponies and overtook the herd in a day's time. Nick, being more skilled than the camp cook, prepared my meals. He also put up my tent evenings, and took it down when we broke up camp. It was intended that he should drive my horses when I was tired, but that was not necessary, for the horses often had no need of anyone driving them. They would follow the slow-moving herd unguided, and I would find a comfortable position, fasten the lines and take a little nap.

The cattle were driven only about ten miles a day, or less, so that they would have plenty of time to graze and fatten along the way. They were in good condition when they reached Kansas.

Except when I was lost, I left the bunch only once after starting. On this occasion I went to Concrete, where my sister lived, to have a tent made for the trip.

MRS. AMANDA BURKS

The night before our herd reached Beeville the Clark herd stampeded and never caught sight of us until we were 'way up-state.

All went pretty well with us till we neared Lockhart, and here we lost thirty cows in the timber. They were never recovered.

Whenever we came to timber we had to rush the cattle through, sometimes driving all day without stopping, for if they were scattered it was almost impossible to gather them again in the thick undergrowth.

Being springtime, the weather was delightful until we reached Central Texas. Some of the worst electrical and hailstorms I have ever witnessed were in this part and also in North Texas. The lightning seemed to settle on the ground and creep along like something alive.

Over in Bosque County late one evening a storm overtook us, and Mr. Burks drove me off into a more sheltered part of the timber. He unfastened the traces from the buggy and gave me the lines, but told me if the horses tried to run to let them go. Hail had begun to fall by this time and he had to hurry back to help the men hold the frightened cattle. Harder and heavier fell the hail, and rain was pouring down in torrents. The horses worked their way around to one side of the buggy, seeking protection, and it seemed that it would be only a few seconds until they pulled away from me entirely. Determined not to let the horses go, I left the shelter of my buggy top and tied the horses with a rope I always carried with me. I got back in the buggy and sat there cold and wet and hungry and all alone in the dark. Homesick! This is the only time of all the months of my trip that I wished I was back on the old ranch at Banquette.

After what seemed ages to me I could hear the rumble of wagon wheels on the trail, and later still the sound of the beat of a horse's hoofs going the same way; but no one seemed to pay me any mind.

Later I learned that it was the cook driving the wagon, not knowing which way to go after being lost in the dark woods; and that Mr. Burks rode after him to bring him back to cook supper for the hungry men who had had nothing to eat since morning.

After I heard the return of the wagon the woods rang with the sound of Mr. Burks' voice calling me, and I lost no time in answering. It was one o'clock in the morning when I reached camp.

Mr. Burks and several of the others had big blood blisters on their hands caused by the hail. One of the boys said, "The beat of the hail on my head made me crazy. I would have run, but didn't know which way to go."

There were few people living along the trail, but when going through Ellis County we saw an old woman sitting in the doorway of a small house stringing beans. We remarked to her that we saw very few women in that part of the country. She answered, "Yes, sir, I'm the first woman that made a track in Dallas County, and I would be back in Tennessee now, only I would have to go through Arkansas to get there. I guess I'll stay right here."

Once when we were camping in Johnson County I heard the bark of dogs followed by several rapid pistol shots. I ran to my tent to see what the trouble was. The Mexican who had charge of the cattle on this relay said that two dogs ran right in among the grazing herd and were about to stampede them when he shot them.

The owner of the dogs appeared soon after the shooting and seemed very downcast over his loss. He said he had "sure been having hard luck." He had first lost his two sons in the Civil War and had now lost his two dogs, which he had trained to keep cattle out of his tiny nearby field. We were sorry for the poor old man, but knew the Mexican did the right thing in preventing a stampede.

We camped a long time at Fort Worth, waiting for the Trinity River to fall low enough to cross our cattle. I counted fifteen herds here waiting to cross.

After we had crossed the Red River we seemed to have left all civilization behind. There were no more fresh fields, green meadows, and timber lands. The sun was so blistering that we hung a cloth inside the top of my buggy to break the heat that came through. Evenings and mornings were so cool that we were uncomfortable.

We had heard of the treacherous Indians and cattle rustlers of the Territory and were always on the lookout for them. The cattle and horses were kept well guarded. One day one of the Mexican cowboys who was on guard duty fell asleep. Mr. Burks could not permit such negligence and told the man that he had to go. All the Mexicans notified Mr. Burks that if this man was "fired" that all would go with him. Of course there was no one else to be employed in this uninhabited territory, so we kept the man who had to have his afternoon nap.

We had no unpleasant experiences with the Indians, although they came to camp and tried to trade with the men. We narrowly escaped having trouble with a couple of what we supposed to be rustlers. While alone in camp one afternoon two men came up and were throwing rocks in among the grazing cattle. I called to them to stop and said, "Don't you know you'll stampede those cattle," and they answered, "That's what we're trying to do." Just then some of the men rode up and the rustlers left hurriedly.

Mr. Burks always kept his horse saddled at night so that he would be ready to go at a word from the boys. As he often helped the men watch the cattle when they were restless, I was sometimes alone in my tent till late at night. On these occasions I sat up fully dressed for any emergency.

On one of these nights it was thought that Indians

were near, so a guard was left at my tent, but he was soon called to help with the cattle. A man from the other camp begged me to go over to his camp and stay until the trouble was over, but I told him I preferred my own tent. The men thought me very brave to stay alone at such a time.

Both the Clark and our herds were stampeded one day, supposedly by Indians. It was a horrible yet fascinating sight. Frantic cowboys did all in their power to stop the wild flight, but nothing but exhaustion could check it. By working almost constantly the men gathered the cattle in about a week's time. They were all thrown into one big herd, and the roar of hoof-beats of two thousand milling cattle was almost deafening. The herd was divided into two, then worked back and forth until every cow was in her rightful bunch.

After an experience of this kind the men would be almost exhausted. I felt so sorry for one of them, Branch Isbell, a young tenderfoot, that I persuaded Mr. Burks to let him rest. The boy lay down and was soon sleeping so soundly that he did not hear us breaking camp, and we forgot him when we left. I wanted someone to go back and wake him, but Mr. Burks said that it would be only a little while till he appeared again. The boy overtook us late in the evening, and said that he would not have awakened then if an approaching herd had not almost ran over him.

We seemed to be pursued by fire during our entire trip. The first night we were in the Territory Mr. Burks and I went to sleep, leaving a candle burning, and before we were awakened a box full of trinkets and small articles, including my comb, were in a blaze.

On one occasion a prairie fire ran us out of camp before breakfast. We escaped by fleeing to a part of the plain which had been burned before, called "a burn" by people of that section.

Two days later my ignorance was the cause of an

immense prairie fire. I thought I would build a fire in
a gulley while the cook had gone for water. Not later
than I had struck the match than the grass all around
was in a blaze which spread so quickly that the men
could not stop it. They succeeded in beating out the
flanks of the fire so that it did not spread out at the sides
at the beginning. The fire blazed higher than a house
and went straight ahead for fifty miles or more. Inves-
tigators came next day to find out who the culprit was,
and when they learned that it was a woman, nothing was
said, except for a remark one of the men made that he
was glad that he didn't strike that match.

Once when we were encamped on Emmet Creek a fire
crept upon us so quickly that the men barely had time to
break up camp and get the cattle to safety. There was
not time enough to harness the horses to my buggy, so
the men tied ropes to it, told me to jump in, and we
again fled to a burn. Birds and animals fled with us
before the flames.

Many of the prairie fires were started by squatters
on land who wanted to keep strangers away. They
would plough a safety boundary around their stake and
then set fire to the grass outside.

Fuel was very scarce because of these fires and the
cook often had to go miles to get enough to cook a meal.

We crossed many nice cool streams whose banks were
covered with wild plums. I noticed the ripe ones first
when crossing the Washita, and wanted to stop to gather
some. Mr. Burks wasn't ready to stop, so told me that
the Indians were very troublesome at this place, and I
needed no coaxing to start the horses on.

Later, when we came to the Canadian River, the red,
blue, and yellow plums were so tempting I had one of the
Mexicans stop with me to gather some. We wandered
farther away from the buggy than I realized, and when
we had gone back a short way I thought the horses had
run away and left us. I was panicstricken, but the Mexi-

can insisted that we go farther up stream, and we soon found the horses standing just as they were left. I forgot my scare when the cook served me with delicious plum pie made from the fruit I had gathered.

Being the only woman in camp, the men rivaled each other in attentiveness to me. They were always on the lookout for something to please me, a surprise of some delicacy of the wild fruit, or prairie chicken, or antelope tongue.

In the northern part of the Territory we left the trail a while to graze the cattle, and I drove on ahead of the bunch to a stream. "Jap" Clark motioned to me to stop, but I misunderstood him and thought he meant "go on," and plunged my horses in the swollen creek. One of the horses stumbled and fell, but was on his feet in a moment, and somehow I was jolted across to the other side. I was the subject of much chaffing because of this alleged attempt to break my neck. The crossing was so bad that the banks had to be chopped down to make it safe for crossing the cattle.

On the banks of the Arkansas River we saw two Yankees who called themselves farmers. When we asked to see their farms they showed us two plots about the size of a small garden. They said they had never farmed before, and we easily believed them. Vegetables were a great treat to us, so we bought some from the "farmers" and enjoyed them immensely.

The camp cook on this trip was a very surly negro. He was a constant source of trouble, and everybody was glad when he was "fired" and a white man took his place. I heard a commotion in the camp kitchen one day and when I looked out of the tent door I saw the cook with a raised axe and a Mexican facing him with a cocked pistol. Mr. Burks rode up in time to prevent a killing.

We were three months on the trail when we arrived at Emmet Creek, twenty-two miles from Newton, Kansas.

We summered here, as did several other Texas ranch-

men. Market had broken, and everybody that could do
so held his cattle hoping for a rise.

While going to town we would often stop at the different camps for a few minutes' chat.

On stormy and rainy nights a candle always burned
in my tent to guide the men. One very stormy night
Mr. Burks had to help the men hold the cattle, and he
saw the light in the tent flare, then all was black. He
rushed through the rain to the place where the tent was
and found it flat on the ground, me buried under it, unhurt. The rain had softened the ground and the wind
easily blew the tent down. That night all the matches
got wet and it was late next morning before we got others
with which to start a fire.

When cold weather came the market was still low and
Mr. Burks decided to winter his cattle, with others he
had bought, on Smoky River.

Mr. Burks wanted me to stay in town at Ellsmore, but
after being there a few days, and witnessing another fire
in which a hotel and several residences were burned, I
preferred camp.

A man who lived some distance from camp was paid
to feed the horses through the winter, but soon after we
heard that he was starving them. A boy was sent to
get them and as he was returning, the first severe snowstorm of the season overtook him at nightfall and he had
to take refuge for himself and horses in a wayside stable.
Next morning he was awakened by a commotion among
the horses, and found the owner of the stable trying to
punch out the horses' eyes with a pitchfork. Such was
the hatred felt for strangers in this region.

Nine horses were lost in this snowstorm. Many of the
young cattle lost their horns from the cold. Blocks of
ice had to be chopped out of the streams in order that
the cattle could drink.

The first taste of early winter in Kansas decided Mr.
Burks to sell his cattle and leave for Sunny Texas as

soon as possible, and he met with no discouragement of his plans from me, for never had I endured such cold.

So in December we left Kansas, dressed as if we were Esquimaux, and carrying a bucket of frozen buffalo tongues as a souvenir for my friends in Texas. Our homeward journey was made by rail to New Orleans via St. Louis, and by water from New Orleans to Corpus Christi via Galveston and Indianola.

I arrived home in much better health than when I left it nine months before.

Please don't think, now that I've finished telling the few stories of my trip over the Old Kansas Trail, that the journey was one of trials and hardships. These incidents served to break the monotony of sameness of such a trip.

One day Mr. Von said as we were resting along the way, "In the heat of the day, when I am riding behind my cattle, I think of you and am sorry for you," and added, as I hope you will, "but when I see your smile of happiness and contentment I know all my sympathy is wasted."

What Mr. Von said is true. For what woman, youthful and full of spirit and the love of living, needs sympathy because of availing herself of the opportunity of being with her husband while at his chosen work in the great out-of-door world?

THE EXPERIENCE OF AN OLD TRAIL DRIVER

By Richard (Dick) Withers of Boyes, Montana

I was raised on my father's ranch eight miles north of Lockhart, Caldwell County, Texas, and made my first trip up the trail in 1869. Colonel J. J. Myers, who had a ranch near my father's, had a large stock of cattle, and after the war he commenced to drive them north, and that year I gathered a hundred and ten steers and put them in one of the herds, Billie Campbell being boss. I traded a beef steer for a pair of goat-skin leggings, bought a slicker and a pair of blankets and started up the trail. I was then eighteen years old. We crossed the Colorado River below Austin, went by Georgetown, Belton and Waco, where we had to swim the Brazos, crossed Red River and struck the Chisholm Trail. Right there is where I ran my first antelope, and thought it was crippled. I was riding a bay horse I called "Buck," so I took down my rope and Buck and I lit out after the antelope, but we did not go far until we quit the chase and went back to the herd.

We had a stampede in the Territory while Noah Ellis and myself were on herd together. In the run that followed my horse fell with me, and I thought the steers would run over me. But I soon learned that steers will not run over a man when he is down under foot. They will run all around a fellow, but I have yet to hear of a man being run over by them. Ellis and I held those cattle all night. After we got rounded up the next day we moved on to the Arkansas River, where we found three herds belonging to Billie Campbell, Dan Phillips and John Bunton, who were traveling together. The river was up and no ferry to help us across, so we had to swim the stream. We made a raft to carry our wagons and supplies over, which took some time. This was at a point fifty or a hundred miles below Wichita, then consisting of a supply store, postoffice and saloon, all in dug-outs.

We went from there to Abilene, Kansas, our destination, where we sold our cattle and started for home.

M. A. Withers and J. W. Montgomery had a large number of cattle at home and I had a good bunch, so in 1870 we gathered a herd together. George Hill was also with us, and Bill Montgomery, George Hill and myself started with them to Abilene, Kansas. In those days 1,000 head was considered a large herd, but we had 3,500 head in that herd, and it was called "the big herd" all the way. We crossed the Colorado below Austin, went by Georgetown and Belton and crossed Red River below Red River Station. The river was up and we had to swim it. A few days after we crossed this stream we had a big stampede, in which we lost some cattle and had to lay over a day while George Hill and myself went to look for the missing cattle. Returning to camp that night, my horse gave out and I was compelled to roost in a thicket the remainder of the night while George went on to camp, a distance of about five miles.

We had two wagons and two cooks with us, Uncle Gov. Montgomery and Jerry Head. A few days after the stampede mentioned above, the wagons went ahead of the herds to get dinner, and when they made camp a bunch of Indians came up, and when I arrived at camp I found Uncle Gov. and Jerry were about to give them all the tobacco and coffee we had. I gave them only a portion of our coffee and tobacco and they left. All went well until we got to the North Canadian, which was also on a rise, and we had to swim our cattle across. There being three herds of us together, we all made a raft to carry our wagons over. Our herd was in the lead, and when the cattle reached the opposite bank and started out the embankment gave away and 116 head of the cattle were drowned before we could turn them back. We found another going-out place and all three herds made it across all right. When we commenced the getting of wagons over with the three outfits there was a general mixup. Somebody in the other outfit had a big lot of Confederate money, and Doom, a silly negro that was with us, found this money, $10,000 in large bills, and he hid it, and if we had not been on the north side of the river he would have left us and tried to make away with it. He showed the money to me and I told him it was worthless. I do not know what he did with it, but we would have lost Doom if the river had not been up.

We moved on and crossed the Arkansas River at Wichita, then on to Abilene, our destination. There Montgomery sold his cattle, to be delivered in Idaho, beyond the Snake River. George Hill, W. F. Montgomery, Bill Henderson and George Mohle left for Texas, while Bill Montgomery and myself started with the herd to Idaho. We went from Abilene to the Big Blue River, from there to the South Platte, below South Platte City, going up that stream to Julesburg, and crossed the river, from there to the South Platte, below South Platte City, ing oxen we had to have them shod at Cheyenne, as the gravel had worn their hoofs to the quick. After leaving Cheyenne we struck the North Platte River below Fort Fetterman. A few days before we got to Fetterman we made a long drive to water, and when we reached the water, there being no other herds there, we turned our herd loose that night. During the night a herd of five hundred big, fat steers came in, which were being driven to Fetterman, and the drivers, not knowing we were there, turned their herd loose also and mixed with our herd. The next morning we told them that as we were going to Fetterman, they could cut them out when we reached that place. When we arrived at Fetterman we rounded up our herd for them and they went to cutting out, but as they were tenderfeet, they did not succeed very well, and now and then one would come back on them. You old Texas cowboys know what it means for a wild Texas steer to come back on you. When they were through cutting there were sixteen of those big fat steers in our herd which they could not cut out, and we told them our horses were "all in," and we could not cut them, so I made a trade with them, giving sixteen head of lean cattle for their fat ones, and they sure came in mighty handy, as will be shown later on.

We went up the North Platte and struck across to Sweetwater, following the old California immigrant trail, going by the Enchanted Rock and Devil's Gate. There the cook broke one of the ox yokes and we could not get one, so we had to camp and cut down a small cottonwood tree to make a yoke with a dull axe and the king bolt of the wagon to burn the holes with. Bill assigned that job to me. It took me all evening and all night to burn the six holes in the yoke. We pulled out the next day, and all went well until we reached the Rocky Mountains. It was forty miles across these mountains and two hundred miles around, so we decided to go across them. This was in October and the weather had been good, but we were getting short of grub. The first night in the mountains it came a snowstorm and twenty-five of our horses died and our cattle scattered considerably. All we could do was to push them in the old trail from each side and let them drift along. At this time our sixteen fat steers came in might handy, for when our supply of provisions gave out we began killing them. The meat would freeze in just a little while, so we lived on nothing but beef for over a month. We had no flour, salt or coffee, and nowhere to purchase these things. Only a few trappers and miners were in the country, and they did not have enough to supply us. Our horses all gave out and we had to walk and drive our diminishing herd. We had plenty of money, but could not buy any horses because there were none to buy. However, one day a miner came along with eight big U. S. mules, and Bill purchased them. We thought those big mules would relieve our troubles, but when I saddled one of them and went after the cattle he did not last an hour, for he could not climb the mountains. We managed to secure a few more horses from miners, and after pushing on for another ten days we reached Salt Valley, where we laid over for several days while three of the men went back into the mountains to gather up cattle we had left, numbering about three hundred head. Bill Montgomery pulled on with the herd and I took a man and a pack mule and also went back into the mountains to try to gather more of

the missing cattle. I found about fifty of them and hired
a trapper to take them to Ogden, while I and my man
returned to overtake the main herd, which was about ten
days ahead of us. We camped one night near a big lake
on the trail and next morning we found the tracks of a
big grizzly bear in the snow within ten yards of where
we slept. We had our heads covered up, and I suppose
he could not smell us as he passed our camp.

We did not overtake the herd until they reached
Snake River. There Noah Ellis, who had taken one herd
on to the man we had sold to, returned to us. From there
on we had no trouble, but soon reached our destination
and delivered the cattle to Mr. Shelly. Bill Montgomery
then bought one hundred and fifty mules from Shelly,
paying $75 to $100 each for them, and started them to
Branyon to ship them to Missouri, where he expected to
sell them for good prices. I took stage for Ogden to get
the cattle I had sent there by the trapper, and when I
arrived there I sold the cattle and went on to Branyon
to meet Bill. I had to wait several days for him to
arrive, and when he got there, Noah Ellis and I pulled
out for Texas, arriving at Lockhart on Christmas Eve.

In the spring of 1871 my brother, M. A. Withers, and
I gathered a herd and started it to Kansas, but when we
reached Belton we sold the herd and I returned home.

In 1873 M. A. Withers, Bill Montgomery and myself
drove two herds to market. I was boss of one herd, and
a man named Page bossed the other. That was the wet-
test year I ever saw on the trail. It rained all the time
and we had to swim every stream from Red River on.
At Fort Worth the cook broke a wagon wheel and after
we got it fixed and went on some distance further he
broke another wheel. Red River was on a big rise, and
the stream was lined with herds, for no herd had been
able to cross for a week or more. I asked some of the
bosses of the herds there if they were going to tackle the
river, and they said they were not, so I told them to give

me room and I would tackle it, for I would rather undertake the crossing than to take chances on a mixup of the herds. They all gave room and helped me to start the cattle into the water. I strung my herd out, had them take the water several hundred yards above where I wanted them to come out. I never saw cattle swim nicer than those steers; they kept their heads and tails out of the water. I ferried my horses across. We proceeded on our way and when we reached the Washita and Canadian Rivers they were high also, but as they were small streams we had no difficulty in crossing them. Before we reached the Arkansas River I killed a buffalo cow and roped her calf. Intending to take the calf with me, I necked it to a yearling, but it was so wild and stubborn it fought until it died.

After crossing the Arkansas at Great Bend I pulled on to Ellsworth, where I found brother Mark with the front herd, and we delivered our cattle, sent our horses back to Texas and returned home by rail.

In 1874 I sold all of my cattle to Driscoll & Day of Austin, Texas.

My next drive was in 1879, when I bossed a herd for Jim Ellison, which was delivered to Millett Brothers at their ranch on the Brazos River, north of Fort Griffin. The herd was the first to cross the Colorado at Webberville. For about ten miles after crossing the river the country was brushy, but other herds followed us and soon made a good trail through there. We went by way of Georgetown, up the Gabriel and on toward Brownwood. Near Brownwood we turned north, struck the Western Trail near Albany, and on to Fort Griffin to the Millett ranch and delivered the herd. When we started back with the horses I received a telegram from Mr. Ellison instructing me to take stage for Fort Worth and hasten home, as he had another herd for me to take to Ogallala, Nebraska. When I arrived at the ranch Mr. Ellison had two herds which he had purchased from Bob

Stafford at Columbus. Bill Jackman was to take one of those herds to the Millett ranch on the Brazos, so we traveled together, and when we reached Millett's ranch he would not take the cattle, so we threw the two herds together and drove them to Ogallala. We had 5,500 head in this herd, and it was the largest herd ever seen on the trail. It was getting late in the season and water was scarce. We had nine men besides myself, the cook and the horse rustler. All went well until we reached Red River at Doan's Store. There one of my men was taken sick and two of the hands quit, leaving me with only six men to handle the herd. But we made it all right until we reached the Washita River, which was the last water until we got to the Canadian River, a distance of about thirty miles. I made a long drive after leaving the Washita, made a dry camp, expecting to reach the Canadian the next day. But we made slow progress as the weather was hot and we were short three men. About three o'clock the next day after leaving the Washita we were within five miles of the Canadian and the big herd was strung out about four miles. They were as dry as fishes. You old-timers know what that means. We were going up a long divide, the wind was from the west, and about a half mile west of us were some alkali springs. The herd smelled the water from these springs, and back about the middle of the herd they began to break away and go for that water. Right then I thought Mr. Ellison's open Y's would be scattered clear to the Red River. The old-timers know that you had just as well try to handle a bunch of mixed turkeys as to try to keep a thirsty herd away from water. We found good grass at these springs and stopped there for the night and the Indians ran off thirty head of them for us. Next morning I took the trail and went back about five miles to look for the cattle, and when I came up with them I found that the red rascals had killed one old stag. I took the others back to the herd. We reached the Canadian about noon. When I arrived at Dodge City, Kansas, I hired three men to help us take the herd on to Ogallala, about eighteen days' drive. Mr. Ellison met me at Ogallala and sold the cattle, to be delivered at Sidney Bridge on the North Platte.

After replenishing our grub supply, we pulled on and struck the North Platte, which we followed up to the Narrows. The "Narrows" is a name given to a ledge of hills which run from the divide to the North Platte River. A herd cannot be driven over these hills, but is forced to travel up the bed of the river for about a mile. The North Platte is a treacherous stream, and full of quicksand. We had to send our chuck wagon around over the hills, and it required all day for the wagon to make the trip. Just above the Narrows, in the valley, we found about one hundred graves, which I was told mark the resting place of men killed in a fight with Indians. From here we traveled up a beautiful valley all the way to Sidney Bridge, where we delivered the cattle, returned to Ogallala, paid off the men, and all hit the train for Texas.

During the fall and winter of 1880 I bought cattle in Bastrop and Lee Counties for Mr. Ellison. In the spring of that year I drove another herd of the Y cattle for him, making the start in April. This was a very dry year on the trail. While crossing the Washita we broke a wagon wheel and had to use a pole drag for one hundred and fifty miles to Wolf Creek. As there was no grass in Kansas and it began raining, I laid over on Wolf Creek and sent the wheel fifty miles down the creek to have it fixed. We rested here two weeks. After leaving the Canadian I went ahead of the herd about five miles looking for grass and water and was overtaken by about five hundred Indians. I felt a bit scared as they came up, and they wanted tobacco, and I willingly gave them all I had and moved back to my herd. As we proceeded on our journey Mr. Ellison came to meet us in a buggy. He remained all night with us, and we slept on a pallet together. Mr. Ellison undressed, but I did not, as I always slept with my entire outfit on, pants, boots and spurs, so as to be prepared for any emergency. During the night the cattle made a run, and when I started to get up one of my spurs caught in Mr. Ellison's drawers and he was rather painfully spurred. The next morning we cut out the weakest cattle in our herd and Mr. Ellison sent them back to his Panhandle ranch.

I have been around cattle during many bad nights, but the night Otis Ivey was killed by lightning was the worst one I ever experienced. Ivey and his horse and about twenty head of cattle were killed during the storm. Mr. Lytle sent out from Dodge after his body and had it sent to his mother in West Fork, Caldwell County, Texas. We often used lanterns around the herds at night, but on that night a lantern was not needed, for the lightning flashed so continuously and so bright we could see everything plainly and smell burning brimstone all the time. When we reached Dodge we had our last grass, for there was not enough on the range to feed a goose. From Fort Dodge to Stinking Water was usually fifteen days' drive, but I made it that year in twelve days. I would leave the bed ground in the morning, drive until noon, round up in the trail for two or three hours, drive on until night and round up again. For twelve days the cattle had no grazing, but had plenty of water. Cattle, if given plenty of water, can go a long while with but little to eat. But unless you give them water at least every twenty-four hours you will have trouble. After reaching Stinking Water we had plenty of grass and we grazed them on to Ogallala.

I had to wait at Ogallala for Sam Moore, for Mr. Ellison had told us to take some steers to a man near the Red Cloud Agency. Bill Jackman came up and Mr. Ellison told us the contract called for 1,000 cows, 1,000 yearling steers and not less than 700 two-year-old steers.

He found us cutting some long yearlings for twos, and said, "Dick, a Texan is going to receive those cattle, and he knows ones from twos." Anyway, we cut and got our supply, then pulled out over to the North Platte up to Sidney Bridge, then followed the Deadwood road. When near the Red Cloud Agency I saw my first Indian buried on a scaffold. I was ahead of the herd at the time, and saw something I took for a well and, being pretty dry, I decided to go to it and get a drink. But instead of being a well it was a dead Indian on a scaffold. It was the custom of the Indians to bury in that fashion, and everything the dead Indian had owned in life was left there. After that we saw a great many Indian graves like that.

Reaching the ranch where we were to deliver these cattle I found the Texan that Mr. Ellison said knew one-year-old steers from twos, and we went to work classing the cattle. We never disagreed on a single steer, and when we were through I found that out of 1,000 yearlings and 700 twos, I had delivered 800 ones and 900 twos. When we got back to Ogallala I gave Mr. Ellison the receipt, and after looking at it he said, "Dick, bring all the boys to the hotel for dinner," and he paid my fare home.

Early in January, 1881, I commenced buying cattle for Mr. Ellison. That year, when starting up the trail, I went through the mountains by way of Llano and Brady City. I had bought 500 head on the Colorado near Buffalo Gap and had to take that route to receive them. They had been gathered when I reached there, so I road-branded them and pulled out for Fort Griffin, Doan's Store on Red River, Dodge City, and Ogallala. When we reached Ogallala Mr. Ellison told me he had 6,500 cattle he wanted me to take to Belle Fourche, Wyoming, deliver them and bring the horses back to Ogallala, sell them, pay the men off, and return home. So I got my supplies, pointed the herd over to the North Platte, followed that stream up to Sidney Bridge, where we took the Deadwood road to Running Water, then turned west to Crazy Woman, thence to the Cheyenne, up that river to Lodge Pole, leaving the Black Hills and Devil's Tower to our right. Then there was nothing there but a ranch, but now there is a railroad and the town of North Craft.

I am living at Boyes, Montana, now about one hundred miles from where I delivered those cattle on the Belle Fourche River below the old ranch. I went from Lodge Pole down the canyon to the Belle Fourche River, and within a week had the cattle branded and delivered. That was in September, and as some of the boys wanted to wash up before starting back to Ogallala, several of our outfit went buffalo hunting and we killed all the buffalo we wanted. Those were the last buffalo I have seen.

In 1882 Mr. Ellison sent me to East Texas and Louisiana to buy cattle, as they were getting scarce in our country. I bought two trainloads and shipped them from Longview, Texas, to Kyle. In March we began rounding up for the spring drive. Mr. Ellison said he wanted me to drive a herd of beef cattle, and told me to pick out my remuda. Out of five hundred horses I selected ninety head of the best that ever wore the Y brand. I started on this trip with 3,520 fours and over, and delivered 3,505. Mr. Ellison asked me just before we started when I would get to Dodge City. I figured a while, and then told him June 10th. He said he didn't think I could make it by that date, "But," he added, "if you do, you can make it to Deadwood, South Dakota." He informed me that it was an Indian contract and had to be made on time. "You make it on time and I will pay your way home and give you a good suit of clothes," said Mr. Ellison. I got my clothes and my fare paid back home.

That was the most enjoyable trip I ever made. I could drive as far in a day as I wanted to. Those steers walked like horses, and we made good time all the way. Mr. Ellison went broke that year.

CORNBREAD AND CLABBER MADE A GOOD MEAL

By Joseph Cotulla of Cotulla, Texas

I was born in Grosslelitch, Germany, then Poland, March 19, 1844, and came to America with my mother and grandmother in 1856. We landed at Galveston in December of that year, from whence we journeyed to Indianola and then to San Antonio in an ox wagon, arriving in San Antonio in 1857. From San Antonio we went to Gallinas, Atascosa County, where my aunt and sisters lived. They came to America only the year before we came. I secured work with a Frenchman at four dollars per month, remaining with him a year and a half, saved my wages and bought a horse for forty dollars. I rode that horse just half a day and he died. Thus I gained my first

JOSEPH COTULLA

real experience. I was next employed by Joe Walker, the first county clerk of Atascosa County, for six dollars per month. I remained with him until 1862, when I went to work for Ben Slaughter, who lived at La Parita, and he paid me seven dollars per month Confederate money. Later Ben and John Slaughter, Lee Harris, the two Forrest boys and an Englishman named Moody, and myself, started to Mexico, and while on the way we stopped one day and took dinner with John Burleson. The dinner was fine, the menu consisting of cornbread and clabber, and we enjoyed it immensely, for we were all very hungry and could have eaten the skillet the bread was cooked in.

After bidding John good-bye we resumed our journey down the river, crossing the Presidio to our destination. After a short stay in Matamoras, John and Ben Slaughter returned to Texas, Moody went to England, and I went to New Orleans, where I enlisted in the Federal Army in 1863, remaining with the troops nearly two years. After receiving my discharge in San Antonio I went back to Gallinas and began to work for myself, branding mavericks. In March, 1868, I went to Nueces and drove a herd from the Altito to Abilene, Kansas, for L. B. Harris. We crossed these cattle below San Juan Mission, going by way of Austin, Waco and Dallas, crossing the Red River about eight miles above Fort Arkansas, passing through the Indian Territory and crossing Little Arkansas River, then on to Abilene. When we reached Abilene we found only a log cabin and three houses on Smoky River. We remained there until fall, then returned with our horses and wagon.

In November, 1868, Dick Hildebrandt, Ed Lyons, Gilbert Turner, L. P. Williams and myself came out to Nueces and located. We gathered fed beeves that year and sold them to Fred Malone, Joe Collins, Thomas and Shanghai Pierce (the man who introduced the walking stick in Kansas). In the spring of 1869 I went back to Atascosa County, where I remained until fall, then came back and we started a ranch, all working together until 1873, when we started up the trail with two herds of cattle. I drove the first herd to my place in Atascosa County, from where I put them on the trail, going by way of San Juan Mission and Austin. We never saw a house until we crossed the trail where the town of Sherman is now located. On this trip we saw a number of Indians, but they did not molest us. When we reached Wichita, Kansas, I sold my cattle to a man named Polk, who beat me out of five thousand dollars. I lost seven thousand dollars on that trip. When I came back in the fall I bought Dick Hildebrandt's interest in cattle and in

1874 drove a herd by myself, which I sold for enough to make up the money I had lost, and I never went up the trail any more.

Now, at the age of seventy-six, I am still in the cattle business and living in the same place I located in 1868.

ONE OF THE BEST KNOWN TRAIL DRIVERS

Sketch of John R. Blocker of Big Wells, Texas

The history of the old-time trail drivers would not be complete without a sketch of the above named gentleman, who is too modest to write of his experiences on the trail, and it therefore falls to the lot of the editor to perform this task.

John R. Blocker was born in South Carolina, in the Edgefield district of the Palmetto State, about sixty-seven years ago, and came to Texas with his parents in 1852, locating at Austin when that city was just a "wide place in the road." He grew to manhood there, being educated in the schools of that place, and in 1871 he engaged in the cattle business in Blanco County with his brother, W. R. Blocker. At that early date Blanco County was but sparsely settled, the ranches being many miles apart, for it was truly on the frontier and a wild, uncivilized country.

When trail driving started with the opening of the Northern markets after the Civil War, the Blocker brothers were among those to realize the opportunity afforded the cattlemen, and, starting with 500 head of stock, they soon became extensively engaged in the cattle industry. John R. Blocker, being a hardy, self-reliant young man, and a good horseman, was especially fitted for trail life. He was a good judge of live-stock and realized the possibilities that awaited the man who started out with a determination to succeed in the stock business. His first drive up the trail was to Ellsworth,

JOHN R. BLOCKER

Kansas, in 1873, and he sold his herd at such a good figure that he sent herds every year from that time on until the trail closed, driving herds to Kansas, Colorado, Nebraska, the Dakotas, Wyoming and Montana. One year, 1886, he was interested in 82,000 head of cattle on the trail at one time, and on his last drive in 1893 he delivered 9,000 head of steers to a buyer at Deadwood, South Dakota.

On one of his trips, 1885, when he had 25,000 steers on the drive, he was held up at Fort Camp Supply by Cherokee and Kansas ranchmen, who refused to allow him to proceed to his destination. After repeated appeals to the War Department, he succeeded in getting a troop of cavalry sent to pilot him through to the place where he was to deliver the cattle. George West, another prominent cattleman of Southwest Texas, was with Mr. Blocker in this fight and won out with him in reaching the market. That year the trail through Kansas was closed, and stockmen were forced to go further west through Colorado to get to the Northern markets and ranges.

In 1881 Mr. Blocker was married to Miss Annie Lane, the daughter of Dr. and Mrs. R. N. Lane of Austin, Texas. To them were born four children, William Bartlett Blocker, Laura Blocker, Susie Blocker and R. Lane Blocker.

Shortly after the organization of the Texas Cattle Raisers' Association Mr. Blocker became a member of that organization, and has given his assistance in every way possible to the improvement of the cattle industry in this state.

When George W. Saunders began to agitate the question of organizing the old-time trail drivers into an association, Mr. Blocker was among the first to lend encouragement to the plan, and when organization of the Old Time Trail Drivers was finally perfected he was unanimously chosen as its first president.

CAPTAIN JOHN T. LYTLE

Captain John T. Lytle was born at McSherry's Town, Pennsylvania, October 8, 1844, and came to Texas with his father's family in 1860. The family located in San Antonio, and the subject of this sketch, then only sixteen years old, went to work on the ranch of his uncle, William Lytle, fifteen miles southeast of San Antonio. In 1863 he enlisted in Company H, 32nd Texas Cavalry, Wood's Regiment, and served in DeBray's Brigade in the Trans-Mississippi Department until the close of the war. After the surrender Captain Lytle returned home and spent two years on his uncle's ranch, at the end of which time he decided to go into business on his own account, engaging in the ranch business in Frio County, until 1873. For more than fifteen years he directed the movement of thousands of head of cattle on the trail, handling more than 450,000 longhorns and delivering them in Kansas, Colorado, Montana and other states and territories. During this time he directed investments in livestock aggregating $9,000,000, a record never before equalled. In 1875 he disposed of his ranch holdings in Frio County and leased pastures in Frio and Maverick Counties, where he raised stock for market despite the fact that most of his time was taken up with his immense trail operations. In this business Captain Lytle had three partners, John W. Light, T. M. McDaniel and Captain Charles Schreiner. The S—L and L—M brands used by these firms were known throughout the Southwest.

In 1879 Captain Lytle moved to a ranch in Medina County, twenty-five miles south of San Antonio, where he resided until 1904, when he moved to Fort Worth, and there resided until his death, which occurred in 1907.

The thriving town of Lytle, in Atascosa County, was named in honor of this remarkable character, who was universally loved and admired by his co-workers in the livestock industry and by all who knew him.

CAPTAIN JOHN T. LYTLE

J. D. JACKSON

Joseph Daniel Jackson is another member of the Old Trail Drivers' Association who has become prominent in the cattle industry of the state, making his start during the old trail days. He was born in Bell County, Texas, in 1861. He has been identified with some of the big projects of the state and is usually found working for any movement that is for the betterment of the cattle industry.

J. D. JACKSON

Mr. Jackson's home is at Alpine, where he has extensive ranch holdings. He formerly ranched in Tom Green and Taylor Counties. At one time he owned the Monahan ranch of 60,000 acres in West Texas, but later disposed of it to Albert Sidney Webb. A few years ago he controlled three hundred sections of land in Brewster County and his cowboys could graze his cattle a straight thirty-five miles without encroaching on the land of a neighbor.

In December, 1889, Mr. Jackson was married to Miss Dorcas Ford, daughter of Mr. and Mrs. Isaac Ford of Holland, Bell County, Texas. They have two children, Miss Una Jackson and Ford Jackson.

T. A. COLEMAN

Thomas Atlee Coleman was born in Goliad County, Texas, in 1861. He spent his young manhood in trailing cattle to Montana and the Northwestern ranges. Owing to quarantine restrictions preventing the driving of cattle from South Texas to those ranges, Mr. Coleman secured ranch holdings on the line near the present location of Childress, where he wintered his cattle and then moved them north the following year. It is estimated that fully ten thousand cattle were trailed north annually on these drives.

T. A. COLEMAN

At the present time Mr. Coleman is one of the most prominent stockmen in the state, controlling ranches in Dimmit and LaSalle Counties and other parts of the country. Some years ago he purchased the famous Milmo Ranch in the Republic of Mexico, containing more than a million acres, for which he paid $3,500,000. He is also prominent in the business and commercial circles of San Antonio, being identified with a number of enterprises in this city.

TWICE ACROSS THE PLAINS IN FOURTEEN MONTHS

By Joe S. Clark, Orange Grove, Texas

Early in the spring of 1870 thirteen of the noblest men that ever crossed the plains rounded up fifteen hundred cattle at Flag Springs, near where the present town of Taylor is located, and headed them for California. Everything went along well until we reached Mustang

JOE S. CLARK

Pens, near the head of the Concho River, where two of our boys had a shooting scrape, and Ewing was killed. We continued our journey and when near Grand Falls, on the Pecos River, the Indians furnished us some excitement. They tried to stampede our horses every few nights, but we had a strong guard and they failed to get our stock. We passed on up into New Mexico, going by way of Las Cruces, and went into camp for the winter on the Mimbres River. While we were there we had a good time and lots of sport going to the fandangoes and bull fights and matching pony races.

In the spring of 1871 five of us, with our Spanish mules hitched to a covered wagon and two men on horseback started on the back trail for home. On our trip we saw many bands of Indians and every day we could see their signal smokes and their signal fires at night. They did not attempt to attack us in the daytime, so we would camp early in the evening and allow the mules to rest, then as soon as darkness enveloped us we could hitch up and drive ten or fifteen miles and camp without making a fire.

One morning we drove up within five hundred yards of a big band of Indians. We got our guns and made ready for a fight, seeing which the savages went away, leaving us unmolested. When we reached the Concho and Colorado Rivers I saw my first buffalo. There seemed to be thousands of these animals in that region at that season.

We reached Austin when the first railroad was being built to that point, and I went to working on the railroad. After a few years of that kind of work I turned my attention to farming and ranching, and thus found more good sleep and more to eat, so I stuck to the farm. I have four boys who went with the Stars and Stripes across the sea and were in some of the hottest engagements of the 36th and 90th Divisions, but they all got back home O. K.

JOHN Z. MEANS

Away out in Jeff Davis County, Texas, there resides an old trail driver and cow-man, who has achieved success in his chosen field of operations. That man is John Z. Means, known all over West Texas as "the mildest mannered gentleman that ever drove a cow."

John Means was born at old Fort McKavett, in Me-nard County, Texas, in 1854, when that town was occu-

JOHN Z. MEANS

pied by soldiers to check the raids of Indians. He grew to manhood in that part of the state, and did his full share in the work of ridding the West of the outlaw and

the cattle rustler. For many years he lived in Lampasas
County, but with the encroachment of the fence builder
and the farmer he moved further west, where he acquired
extensive holdings in Jeff Davis and other counties, and
today is rated as one of the wealthy men of that section.

In November, 1877, he was married to Miss Exie Gay
of San Saba, the daughter of Mr. and Mrs. Sam A. Gay,
and to them were born seven children, who have taken
prominent places in the social and business life of
the state.

GEORGE W. EVANS

George Wesley Evans, now a prominent ranchman
of Jeff Davis County, was born at LaGrange, Texas,
October 12, 1849, and has spent his life on the frontier

GEO. W. EVANS

of this state. He resided in
Fayette County until the
early eighties, and when that
section began to settle up he
moved to the Davis Moun-
tains in Western Texas,
where he has resided ever
since, following the stock
business successfully and becoming one of the prominent
cattlemen of that region.
As long as the range was
open he raised the old Texas
longhorns for market, but
with the coming of wire fences he began to import Durham and Hereford bulls, and his herds of whitefaces are
now among the best in the Southwest.

In 1878 Mr. Evans was married to Miss Kate Isabel
Means, daughter of Mr. and Mrs. Frank Means of Lampasas County. Their children are William F., Joe M.,

Lee S., G. W. Jr., Rube M., Ell B., Paul M., Katie Grace, and Amos Graves Means.

Mr. Evans resides at Valentiné, Texas.

COWBOY LIFE IN WEST TEXAS

A few years ago John J. Lomax, the author of several books bearing on the life of the cowboys and cattlemen of Texas, made an address before a folklore society meeting at San Marcos.

While it is true that there are many changes in the cattle country—as witness the introduction and general use of the automobile where a few years ago the big camp meetings or neighborhood gatherings saw the "ambulances," or "buggies" or "buckboards"—sufficient of the picturesque old life remains in Southwest and West Texas to give a vivid idea of how it was in the days of the trail. He drew this picture of the Texas cowboy, his speech and mode of living:

Prior to taking a herd of cattle up the trail from Texas to Montana or the Dakotas, occurred the spring roundup, which might include a range of country 100 miles in diameter. Of course, in such a stretch of land there would be a number of cattle owners. These would all join forces, and after days of hard riding would bring together in a single herd all the cattle running on this range. On this roundup ground the cattle are "worked"; that is, the calves following their mothers are branded and marked with the decorations employed by their owners, or they are cut into groups either for purposes of sale or for further identification. Those cut out are called the "cut"; the specially trained horses used for this work, so intelligent that you can remove the bridle after the animal to be cut is indicated, and the horse will separate the cow from the bunch with unerring instinct, are called "cutting horses," "carving horses" or "chopping horses.'' When fences became more common the calves were cut out through a cutting chute or ''dodged out'' so they could be counted. Some cattlemen now employ a branding chute, where an arrangement for holding the cattle while they are being branded is called a ''squeezer'' or ''snappin' turtle.'' In branding cattle, a cowboy, after the rope has dragged the animal near the fire, throws him by ''tailing'' or ''flanking.'' ''Flanking'' consists in seizing the animal by the skin of the flank opposite the cowboy, with his arm thrown over the animal's back. When the animal jumps with all four feet off the ground, the cowboy, by a jerk, throws it on its side; or he ''bulldogs'' them by twisting the neck, or ''tails'' him by giving a sudden jerk on the tail when some of the animal's feet are off the ground. I once saw a cowboy ''flank'' a calf in such a fashion that he threw him completely on his back with all four feet in the air. ''See him sun his moccasins,'' said another cowboy who stood near. When the flanker and assistants have the animals stretched on the ground they call out ''hot iron'' or ''sharp knife,'' the brander responding, ''Right here with the goods.'' Ordinarily the brand is put on by stamping with an iron stamp carrying one, two or three letters, and the different brands and marks employed, like ''Flying U'' and the ''Lazy S,'' are so various as to require a separate paper to give them adequate description. A ''running iron'' is a branding iron made of a straight piece of iron with a curve at one end. This end is heated red hot and the branding artist is thus enabled to ''run'' any letter he wishes to put on the side of the animal. Some of the terms used in marking are ''crop,'' ''under bit,'' ''over bit,'' ''half crop,'' ''split,'' ''over slope,'' ''under slope,'' etc. A ''jingle bob'' is to split the ear to the head and let the pieces flap. A jug handled ''dewlap'' is a cut in the fleshy part of the throat, also used sometimes as a mark of distinction. Roping a cow is sometimes referred to as ''putting your string on

her." If a cowboy ropes a cow without hitching the rope
to the saddle, "he takes a dolly welter," evidently a
corruption of Spanish. To "fair ground" is to rope an
animal by the head, throw the rope over the back while
still running and then throw the animal violently to the
ground, where it will usually lay until "hog tied"; tying
three feet together, "side lined," tying two feet together
on the same side, or "hoppled," both hind legs tied together. To tell the age of an animal, the cowboy
"tooths" him, meaning to make an examination of the
teeth, as is commonly done in the case of horses, which
gives fairly accurate indication of their ages.

In a cattle outfit the owner is called the "big boss,"
the leader of any particular bunch of men is called the
"boss," his first lieutenant is called the "straw boss,"
or right-hand man, sometimes called the "top screw" or
"top waddy." The chief of any group of line riders is a
"line boss," while the boss of a herd on the trail is the
"trail boss." Ordinarily, a cowboy is a "waddy" or
"screw" or "buckaroo." A green cow hand is called a
"lent," and his greenness is expressed by the word
"lenty." He is also sometimes called "Arbuckle," on
the assumption that the boss sent off Arbuckle premium
stamps to pay for the extraordinary services of the
greenhorn. The "stray man" is the cowboy's name for
one who goes to the neighboring ranches after stray
cattle. The "fence rider," also called the "line rider,"
is employed to ride fences and repair them. Before the
day of fences, line riding was following an imaginary
line between two ranches and turning the cattle back.
The "line rider" has charge of a "line camp." In addition to the "chuck wagon," a second wagon for carrying the extra beds and bringing wood and water into
camps sometimes goes along. This equipage is called the
hoodlum wagon and the man who drives it is "the hood."
The cabin where the bachelor cowboys sometimes sleep
in very bad weather is called a "hooden." A "bog

rider" is the cowboy who "tails" up the poor cows which get stuck in the mud. The "chuck wagon" is the cowboy's home! the chuck box is his store; the chuck box lid his table. After a meal, if a luckless cowboy happens to put his tin plate and cup on the chuck box lid instead of the "round pan" (a tin tub for dishes), this constitutes a "leggins case"; that is, he is laid over a barrel and treated to a dose of leggins in the hands of the most athletic cowboy. The chief man about the camp is the cook, his play usually equaling that of any of the men, and his expertness in preparing food remarkable when one considers his cook-stove, a hole in the ground, and his cooking utensils, skillets and pots. Naturally, the cook, his play usually equaling that of any of the men, "sheffi," "dough roller," "dinero," "coocy" and "biscuit shooter." His invariable cry when calling the men to a meal is "Come and git it!"

I think I may claim that these few samples of cowboy lingo are characterized by simplicity, strength and directness, and, it may be added, accuracy. I knew a saloon once in the West known as "The Wolf"; another that was aptly named with a big flaring sign on the outside, "The Road to Ruin." Out in Arizona there is a town called Tombstone, and the leading paper of that town has named itself the *Tombstone Epitaph*. Let me add a few of his miscellaneous expressions. Of a tall man he does not like, the cowboy says "He's just as long as a snake and he drags the ground when he walks." Of a fool he says, "He has no more sense than a little nigger with a big navel," or "He don't know dung from wild honey." Although a cow is one of the most stupid of animals, when a cowboy says that a man has good "cow sense" he means to pay him a high compliment. When he means a thing is easy, he says "It's just as easy as gutting a slut"; of washing his face, "bathing out your countenance" or "washing the profile"; of bathing, "washing out your canyon"; of vomiting, "airing the

paunch"; an "eye-baller" is a person who pokes himself into other people's business; going courting is "goin'
gallin'," "sitting the bag," "sittin' her"; "cutting a
rusty" means doing your best; moving fast is "faggin',"
"leffin' here" or "sailing away," "dragging his navel
in the sand"; "goin' like the heel flies are after him."
A very small town is a wide place in the road. A "two-
gun man" is a man who uses a gun in each hand, often
at the same time. A man quick to retort is said to have
a "good come-back." "Telling a windy" means telling
a boastful story; a "goosy" man is a man physically
nervous. When a man plays the deuce spot in a card
game, he is said to be "laying down his character." To
"fork a horse" is to ride him; when a man is without
information on a subject, he tells you, "I ain't got any
medicine"; "anti-godlin" means going diagonally or in
a roundabout way. The "roust-about" is a man of all
work about a camp. "Sweating a game," means doing
nothing but sitting around looking at a card game. "Tie
your hats to the saddle and let's ride" means to go on a
long hurry-up roundup. The boss' house is referred to
as the "White House." When a fellow makes a night
of it, he is said to have "stayed out with the dry cattle."
When a delicate situation arises there is said to be "hair
in the butter." The water on the plains is sometimes so
muddy that the cowboy says "he has to chew it before
he can swallow it." When he has gained a little more
experience on a proposition, he says he "has taken a
little more hair off the dog." When there is room for
doubt about his knowledge he is said to know as much
about it as " a hog does about a side saddle." A man
who is good at roping is said to "sling the catgut well."
Damp, freezing weather is characterized as cold as "a
well digger in Montana." Riding on a freight train in
place of paying regular fare on a passenger train is said
to be "saving money for the bartender." Ordinary stealing is "yamping." "Plumb locoed" is quite crazy. A

very black negro is characterized as a ''headlight to a snowstorm.''

Living in isolated groups, visiting but little except among these groups, rarely going to town, shy and timid as a result of long days of solitude, the cowboy develops his own form of speech. Cowboy words, phrases and customs therefore easily become community property— his language a dialect of his own. In closing this paper I cannot refrain from giving you one or two cowboy graces repeated indiscriminately either before or during a meal, and I shall end finally with some of his most characteristic dance calls. On some future occasion, if I am invited, and if I am provided with just the right kind of an audience, I engage myself to read a paper on cowboy profanity. There is a certain wholesome strength, cleanliness and variety in his profanity, and even his vulgarity, that I do not believe is equaled by any other race of men. The rhyme dance calls are supplementary to his spoken directions to the dancers, and add almost as much interest and loveliness of the dance as does the music. Here are two cowboy graces:

''Eat the meat and leave the skin;
Turn up your plate and let's begin.''

Yes, we'll come to the table
As long as we're able,
And eat every damn thing
That looks sorter stable.

The rhymed dance calls are chanted between the shorter calls and are supplementary to them:

Swing your partners round and round;
Pocket full of rocks to hold me down;

Ducks in the river going to ford,
Coffee in a little rag; sugar in the gourd.

Swing 'em early, swing 'em late;
Swing 'em round Mr. Meadow's gate.

Ladies to the center, how do you do;
Right hands cross, and how are you!

Two little ladies, do si do,
Two little gents you orter know.

Swing six when you all get fixed,
Do si, ladies like picking up sticks.

Chicken in the bread tray kicking up dough;
"Granny, will your dog bite?" "No, by Joe."

Swing corners all,
Now your pardners and promenade the hall.

You swing me, and I'll swing you;
All go to heaven in the same old shoe.

Same old road, same old boy,
Dance six weeks in Arkansaw.

Walk the huckleberry shuffle and Chinese cling.
Elbow twist and double L swing.

DAYS GONE BY

By Hiram G. Craig of Brenham

It was in the year of 1850 that my father and mother, John and Caroline Craig, decided to make their home in that great state of the future—Texas. Suiting the words with action, they hitched up their two bay (bald-faced) mares to the wagon, taking such belongings as were absolutely necessary, and started on the long and perilous journey from Tennessee to Texas. Their destination was Washington County, and they landed in the western part, in the neighborhood called Sandtown—so named by my uncle.

My parents must have suffered many hardships in those days of privations, raising as they did, a large family of seven boys and two girls. My father was a teamster. He hauled freight with an ox team from Houston to Austin, hauled cotton from Washington County to Brownsville, on the Rio Grande, and hauled salt, loose in the wagon bed, on his way back from the King ranch, home. He made several trips to Brownsville; also, one to Eagle Pass, Texas.

I remember one trip I made with him from our home to Alleyton, Colorado County. This was our nearest railroad station, and at that time the terminus of the Southern Pacific Railway. We were hauling cotton. In those days wagons had wooden axles with an iron skean, and lynchpins to hold the wheels on the axle.

On these trips father would take one horse along to round up the oxen. At night, or when camping, he would have a bell for each yoke of oxen, would neck them and put a hobble on one of the oxen of each yoke. I made a number of short trips with my father, as I could be of some help in rounding up the oxen and hold them while he put the yoke on them. Often he would also be breaking in a yoke or two of wild oxen. On this particular trip when we got as far as Frelsburg, where we broke an axle, and as there were few people living in the country at that time, we were in a bad way. No houses, no tools to work with, not a blacksmith within twenty miles. Here my father accomplished something that nine men out of ten of these days and times would fail in. The only tool at hand was an axe. With this axe father cut down a hickory tree, cut it the proper length, and with the axe hewed out an axle. He got on his horse and rode to the next neighbor, where he got an auger. At that time such a thing as a "brace and bit" were unheard of. With the auger he bored the holes for the hound and skean and put the wagon together. He unloaded and loaded the cotton by himself, as I was too small to do any lifting. We wound up our trip by delivering the cotton to the railway company and returned home to Washington County.

I used to plow, many, many a day with a single ox and a plow, made entirely of wood, with the exception of the point, which was of iron. Even the moldboard (the part that turns the dirt) was of timber. Father would cut a short piece of some twisted oak tree, split it open— which would almost have the shape, then hew it down to fit the point of iron and attach the handles with wooden pins—and the plow would work fine.

A word about my dear mother: During the Civil War such things as clothing, shoes, flour, salt, sugar and coffee were scarce and high—very often not to be had at any price. Flour was selling at twenty dollars per barrel. Mother, my oldest sister and my second oldest brother, carded the roll and mother spun the thread that made our clothes during the war. The work allotted to me was to hand the threads through the sleigh—at which I became quite an expert. If these threads, in any way became crossed, they would not weave. Often mother would send me to the neighbor ladies to help them with this line of work. I also peeled the blackjack bark and gathered the wild indigo to dye the cloth that made our clothes. My second oldest brother was a cripple and could not work in the field, so mother kept him in to help her with the weaving. In my mind I can still see my mother at the old spinning wheel.

The young people of today do not realize what "hard times" are. Imagine that most of the flour you were to see would be a feast of biscuits on a Sunday morning for breakfast, and then some more the next Sunday morning.

Imagine for your coffee a substitute of corn, roasted potato peeling and cornmeal bran. These were some of our luxuries. Of meats we were more bountifully blessed. Cattle were more plentiful and cheap; pork was more abundant. Hogs were running loose in the woods, and the mast was so good that hogs were generally fat in winter.

Father died at Bellville, Texas, at the age of fifty-four, and mother died in Washington County at the age of forty-four. This left the family in the hands of my oldest brother, who faithfully and conscientiously administered to our wants until we were able to take care of ourselves.

I was born at Sandtown in 1855 and lived here with my parents to the end of the Civil War, when we moved to Bellville, Austin County, Texas. Father was the proud possessor of a small bunch of cattle, and created a desire in me to be a cowboy—to have a good horse, saddle, leggings, spurs and to handle cattle. At fourteen years of age I ran away from home and went to work for Foster Dyer of Richmond, known as one of the biggest ranch owners of that time. I was proud of my job, which, however, was of short duration. My brother learned of my whereabouts and came and took me home. I remained at home with my parents for three years, when the call to the "wild" again overcame me.

This time it was T. J. Carter, who was studying to be a doctor, and I, that went on a wild goose chase in 1872. We landed at Sweet Home and hired out to George West, to help gather a herd of steers for the trail for Kansas. We gathered between 1,500 and 2,000 head of steers. There were no pens or corrals to hold such a large herd. We held and herded these steers on the prairie by day and by night. The boys would herd them in shifts, or reliefs; one shift of men would herd them from four to six hours (according to the number of shifts), when the next shift would relieve them, so that the cattle would be continually guarded. This work is hard and trying, and at our age seemed severe; however, we stayed with the herd until they were actually started on the trail, and then went home to Washington County. Carter went back to his profession, and is today a practicing physician in Fayette County, having made good.

In the fall of 1873 J. D. McClellan and I went to Oakville, Live Oak County, and worked for Andrew Nations and his son, Bob Nations, helping them gather 1,500 stocker cattle to be moved to the Wichitas. Our headquarters were at Sulphur Creek, about ten miles north of Oakville. We gathered up and down the Nueces River, as far down as Lagarto. We were short of cow hands— who were hard to get. Bob Nations decided to make a trip to San Antonio and get the necessary complement of men. The best he could do was to get a bunch of "brakemen," as he called them. These men were no good at riding or at handling cattle, being unaccustomed to the work. We were holding the herd on a prairie near the Nueces River bottom. The cattle were wild and some of them would make a break every now and then and, as sure as an animal would make a run, the trained cow pony, with his "brakeman," would take after it— and we would be minus a "brakeman."

Tom Johnson was our trail boss. He was one of the best men I ever knew, when it came to handling stock cattle on the trail. He taught me every detail in "grazing" a herd. Johnson was very fractious and hard to get along with, and Bob Nations said he doubted very much in our going through on the trip with Johnson.

The herd was started early in the spring with Johnson as foreman, everything progressing nicely. We were obliged to swim all the rivers on account of heavy spring rains, but suffered no loss of cattle. We reached Lockhart and then Onion Creek, near Austin. Here at Onion Creek we had a little stampede, for which I was blamed.

It brought on words between the foreman and I. Naturally, I was discharged and McClellan quit.

Bob took McClellan and me on to Austin, and asked us to accompany him and his family west, and assured us work as long as we cared to stay. As he started out of Austin we told him we would overtake him on the way later. But, alas, there was a drawing card back home, in Washington County, that was stronger than even a promise. McClellan had a girl there and so did I, so we went home.

That summer J. W. Nunn bought out a meat market in Brenham and McClellan went to work for him, while I did the buying and supplying of live stock for the market. McClellan lived only three months after that, leaving me without a pal. I continued working for Nunn.

In June, 1876, we gathered about 1,400 head of Nunn's cattle and started for the Plains. We left Dime Box, Lee County, June 10, 1876. We herded the cattle on the first night at Lexington, Lee County, in a wide lane. The second night we camped near Beaukiss in the woods. There were two of the Nunn boys, both much older than I, but neither they nor any of the other hands had ever "bedded" a herd. It was up to me to take charge of my first large herd. We rounded the cattle into a circle in the woods, dragging logs around the bed grounds and built fires. There were clouds rising and about 11 o'clock that night it began thundering, lightning and raining. The cattle got restless and stampeded, running all night. The third day we crossed the Brushy Creek, camping near the Olive pens on the Taylor prairie. From here on we had plenty of open country and could handle the herd more easily. We had many ups and downs, being short of horses. Our horses got very poor and were worn out from overwork; also the cattle got thin in flesh by the time we got to Buffalo Gap in July, and we were also out of provisions, no beef, no coffee, no money. Nunn borrowed a small sum from one Ben

Anderson, one of our hands, and started me off with one yoke of oxen for Coleman City, sixty miles distant, to lay in a supply of "grub."

I bought mostly breadstuffs and coffee, returning to camp a week later. This left us still shy of meat, our cattle being too poor for slaughter. We were told that fifty or sixty miles west there were lots of buffalo, so Nunn got us to rig up a wagon and to go on to the Sweetwater Creek to kill some fat buffalo. We engaged a man by the name of Jim Green at Buffalo Gap, who was a buffalo hunter, and he was to pilot us to the Sweetwater country, and incidentally give us a few pointers on buffalo hunting. Dr. John Obar, J. T. McClellan (a brother of my former pal), Jim Green and I formed the outfit. We went to Sweetwater, camping near Dan Trent's ranch, and hunted here for two days and saw only two buffalo bulls in this time. The first bull I chased until my horse gave out, shot away all my ammunition, and only drew a little blood.

It will not be amiss to state what our artillery consisted of at that time. We used a long and trusty cap and ball rifle, familiarly known as "Long Tom." Then the old cap and ball sixshooter, sometimes called "outlaws." At times they would behave and fire one shot, and again they would fire two, three or possibly all six chambers at one time. But to revert to our buffalo hunt:

On the second day we found another old, poor buffalo bull. I handed my long rifle to one of the boys and took his sixshooter, and told them I was going to get meat, in which I eventually succeeded. I was riding my own horse, one that I had bought from one of my German friends in Washington County. I had named him "Dutch," had taken good care of this horse, using him only for night herding on the trail, and so he was in good time. He was a keen runner. I took after the buffalo bull, ran him about three miles, emptying my pistol as I chased him. He was a monster and looked like an ele-

phant to me. Some of the buffalo hunters claimed that
our "outlaw" pistols would not kill a big buffalo bull,
but I demonstrated that they were wrong, for I put one
ball in the right place and stopped the bull. After a bit the
boys came up and finished the animal with their "Long
Tom" rifle. It took two horses by the horn of the saddle
to turn the carcass of the bull on his back so we could
skin him. This will give you an idea that he was some
bull. We built a fire and kiln-dried the meat. It was not
fat, nor what we wanted.

We broke camp and drifted ten miles further north,
where we came on to a herd, which we estimated at about
1,000 head. This herd of buffalo was on the move, and
going pretty rapidly. When I first got sight of them they
were traveling west; they would go down hill on the run,
while up the incline of the next hill they would be grazing. I rode around the foot of the hill to head them off
and when I reached the ridge of the hill they were coming
towards me, and about the same time I heard some shooting, which later proved to be our pilot, Jim Green, who
had already got into the herd and put them on a full run.
I had some trouble holding down old "Dutch," my horse,
when the herd of buffalo came towards us on the run.
There was one big red one leading the herd. I killed
him first. He proved to be a big red steer, instead of
a buffalo, and belonged to John Chissum. I then killed
one fat buffalo. As I came over the hill I came on to
our pilot, who had shot down five, of which one got up
on his feet and was making for Jim Green who, by the
way, was afoot. I tried to get Green to get on the horse
behind me. He declined, saying he "would get him in the
sticking place directly," deliberately shooting at the buffalo as he came on. He was holding his sixshooter with
both hands to steady his aim and downed him. This gave
us six buffalo and one fat steer, with which we struck
out for Buffalo Gap.

Another little stunt with a buffalo we pulled off while

at Buffalo Gap. Don Drewry and I were riding out among the cattle, where we came on to a two-year-old buffalo bull. Don boasted that he could and would rope him. I pleaded with him not to risk such a thing, but he declared "old Browny," his horse, could handle him, and had the loop on him in no time. He threw the bull several times, but finally wore out his horse and called to me to shoot the bull. I did so to save his horse. Don admitted that he had taken in "too much territory" that time, and said he would never rope another buffalo larger than a calf.

Old man Drewry, Don's father, and his son-in-law, Tobe Odem, had come to Buffalo Gap from Oakville with cattle and horses. Don was then quite a boy, about 17 or 18 years of age.

Along in September we gathered up the cattle and moved on out to Sandrock Springs, where Nunn located his ranch on Rough Creek, and is now living and accumulating cattle. That winter I went back home and engaged in buying and selling cattle, at which trade I worked for several years, buying quite a lot of work steers to be shipped to Havana, Cuba.

On December 15, 1881, I was married to Johanna Awalt at Burton, Texas, and lived there about one year. I went west again, locating at Snyder, Scurry County. My brother, J. M. Craig, and I carried a nice bunch of about 300 head of stock cattle with us, but one hard winter put us out of the cattle business and took us back to Washington County, where I now reside. While working our cattle at Snyder, I took a trip west to the head of the Colorado River and here witnessed the largest "roundup" that I ever saw or heard speak of. It was the C. C. Slaughter "roundup," was estimated at 10,000 head of cattle in one herd, covering a prairie one-half mile each way.

For the benefit of those readers who have never seen a large "roundup" like those on the plains in the early

days, I shall endeavor to describe this "roundup," the
wonderful system and efficient way in which such an immense number of cattle were handled, cut and assorted,
and how each rancher got his cattle. You will understand that these cattle in this roundup were not owned
by one individual, but belonged to ranches from a radius
of many, many miles, comprising possibly a number of
counties. With the exception of perhaps a small corral
for the horses at the ranch houses in those early days,
fences or pastures were unknown. The country was an
open range, and the cattle were grazing in the open
prairies, drifting to the four winds. Cattle were known
to drift as far as 150 miles north. Each stockman, or
ranch, had a line rider, who rode the line or limits of his
particular ranch in order to get his cattle "located," or
used to their grazing grounds. However vigilant, this
would not hold all of his stock. The line rider had to
sleep at night, or sometimes, or had so much territory to
cover and to guard, that cattle would drift away from
their stamping grounds at night, or when the rider may
have been engaged at other points of the line. This made
it necessary to have the "roundup," and to get the different brands of cattle to their respective owners and
ranches. The custom was to have a roundup in the
spring of the year, and one in the fall. Word was sent
to stockmen for many miles around when the roundup
was to take place at a certain ranch. Then eight or ten
neighboring stockmen would rig up a "chuck wagon"
and place a cook in charge. One of the men would
furnish the wagon one time, and the next time someone
else—turn about. These stockmen going with the "chuck
wagon" would meet at the appointed time with their
saddle horses. Each man having his bedding lashed to
a horse when they met the chuck wagon, would put all
their bedding in the wagon. This "chuck wagon" was
drawn by two and sometimes four horses. Next they
would turn all their saddle horses in a bunch, detail one

of their number as "horse wrangler" and start off for
the roundup. At the roundup there would be a number
of these chuck wagons or outfits—possibly six or eight
or ten such wagons, according to the notices sent out, or
the size of the roundup. In the Slaughter roundup there
were ten "chuck wagons," and each wagon would receive a number from the roundup boss, making ten numbers—in this case representing some ninety men, or
stock owners.

On the evening before the roundup Billy Stanefor,
the roundup boss, went to all the wagons and called for
two or three men from each wagon to go out from ten
to fifteen miles and make what is called a "dry camp."
Each man was to stake his horse so that when daylight
came every man was ready to follow out instructions to
bring all the cattle towards the grounds. The men so
sent out, all going in different directions, formed a veritable spider's web, with the roundup grounds in the
center. As soon as the boys would "whoop 'em up," the
cattle were on the run, and would make for the grounds.
There was little danger or chance for any cattle escaping,
as when they would leave the path of one man they
would drift into the path of the next man, and the nearer
they came to the grounds, the more men would come in
sight—finally forming one big herd, and then the fun
would start. We found on bringing in these cattle in this
manner that five buffalo and twenty or more antelope had
drifted in with the cattle. Several of the boys, I, for one,
were sure we were going to rope an antelope. We got
our loops ready and started for them. Our horses were
too short, and also a little too slow. We did not rope
any antelope. Some of the other boys fired into the buffalo, but did not bring in any meat either. The herd
was now ready for cutting. The roundup being on
Slaughter's ranch, the foreman, Gus O. Keith, and his
men, including old man Slaughter, cut their beef cattle,
cows and calves first, and drove them back on the range

to avoid "chousing" them. As soon as Slaughter was through with his part the herd was ready for general work.

Now Billy Stanefor calls out, "No. 1 cut and No. 2 hold," meaning that the men from wagon No. 1 were to go into the herd and cut all of their cattle, while the men of wagon No. 2 would hold the herd. No. 1 finished, the roundup boss would call, "No. 2 cut and No. 3 hold" —when No. 2 would go into the herd and cut, while the men from wagon No. 3 were holding the herd, and so on in this manner until the cutting was finished. Then, to the branding of the cattle. This was also all done on the open prairie. We made our fires to heat the branding irons, would rope the calves or cattle, as the case may be, on horseback, drag them to the fire and put the brand on them. It was also the duty of the roundup boss to see that no large calf was cut out of the roundup herd unless it was accompanied by its mother. The roundup boss had to act somewhat in the capacity of a judge. He had to see that all disputes were satisfactorily settled. If trouble arose regarding ownership of an animal the roundup boss would find out what brand each one of the disputing parties were claiming the animal under, and if they could come to no agreement, the animal was roped, the brand moistened with water to make it plainer, or he would shear the hair off where the brand was located, and in that way determine the ownership. All this was done immediately, and then the work would proceed. In those early days the ear-mark would not always be proof of ownership and an animal without brand was called a "sleeper." A sleeper was nominally everybody's property, and was so called because someone had overlooked branding this animal in a previous roundup—had slept on his rights. Naturally, all hands had a leaning towards these sleepers; and I have seen a sleeper cut out of the roundup by one man and during the day changed several times to other bunches. The man that was lucky to get away with a sleeper would put his brand on him. However, if such an animal had an ear-mark and any of the parties claimed the mark he would then hold the best title.

The roundup boss would let no one ride through the herd and "chouse," or unnecessarily disturb them; these fellows found guilty of such misconduct were called "loco'ed." Ofttimes it was known for the roundup boss to put him out of the herd and cut his cattle for him. The whole roundup was conducted in a strictly business way, and such a thing as "red tape" was unknown.

This work being finished, each wagon with its little herd would start for the next roundup. Possibly night would overtake them and pens, being unknown, it would be up to the boys to herd them and "sing" to them, as it was usually called. Each man would rope his night horse and they would herd in shifts.

This night herding is nice and novel in fair weather, and on a nice moonlit night; but when it comes to one of those dark nights of thunder, lightning and the rain pouring down on you, your life is in the hands of God and your faithful night horse. There is to my mind no nobler animal in God's creation than a faithful horse. We would always pick out the clearest-footed, best-sighted horses for this work. All horses can see in the night, and better than a man, but there are some horses that can see better than others.

Boys, in this connection, I wish to relate a little incident of what a horse can do and did at the Slaughter roundup. We were told that the Slaughter ranch possessed two horses that would cut without a bridle, and we asked Gus Keith, the foreman, to let us see the horses perform this feat. He called for two horses, "Old Pompy," a black pacing horse, and "S. B.," a slim bay horse. They rode into the herd and worked an animal towards the edge of the bunch and slipped the bridle. Each horse brought out the right cow and without a miss. This was great work for a dumb animal.

At this roundup I also saw the last wild buffalo.

It was in the year 1880 that I sold Hugh Lewis and Jim Holt, of Brenham, seven hundred steers on a contract to Mr. Runge. The steers were to be delivered at the Runge ranch near Yorktown, De Witt County. They were short of both horses and men and hired my brother and me to go through with the herd to Yorktown. On our way we came to the Colorado River at LaGrange and found the stream on a rampage. We were told of a man that had been drowned at this crossing three days before in trying to cross a herd of cattle. The man had all his clothes on besides a six-shooter. In swimming across he had taken the left point (or lead) to point the cattle across. The cattle began milling in the stream and tried to turn back. He had made the point on his horse, but got into the bunch of milling cattle and both he and his horse went under. He was found two days later some four hundred yards below the crossing. This brought up the question to us: Who would venture to point our herd across; and, what would it cost to have them pointed? Crowds of people had come from LaGrange to witness the spectacle of a large herd of cattle swimming across the river; there were men, women and children, all eager to see. I was about the poorest swimmer in the outfit, but had lots of experience in my time, no doubt more than the rest all together. Holt sauntered up to me and asked if I was afraid to point the herd, and what would I charge extra to pull off the stunt. I confessed to him that I was not a good swimmer and was afraid of water, but that I was a hired hand and would not shirk my duty. I had a first-class pony for the work, and told him that I would point the herd if allowed to strip my clothes. He told me the work had to be done, women or no women. When everything was arranged I stripped, mounted my pony bareback and took the left (or lower) point. I struck the water with the cattle and stayed near the lead until they saw the opposite bank, then I led out for the bank

and crossed the cattle without a mishap. From there on
we moved along smoothly until we got to the Guadalupe
River. Here, at night, my brother, I, and two other boys
were herding on first relief. Some old-timers had told us
that it "never rained at night in June," but we had all
doubts dispelled here. As we were short of horses, we
herded in only two reliefs. After midnight, as I rode
into camp to wake up the second relief, I noticed an approaching storm cloud in the northwest, and before the
boys could saddle their horses and get around the herd it
was thunder, lightning and a downpour of rain, all in
one. The herd started drifting south and there was no
way to hold them. They did not stampede, but kept
moving, and as it was very dark, we could only see them
by the flashes of lightning and drift with them. We
must have traveled some three or four miles when I called
to my brother to ask what had become of the other two
boys. He said they had found a tree and had climbed
up in it. We had not heard a sound from them since
leaving camp. I knew the man near me was my brother
by his voice, as he was always in the habit of singing and
talking to the cattle to quiet them. In a stampede there
are no "road laws," everything in its path must clear
out or get run over. After a few minutes' silence my
brother called out: "Everybody look out, trouble ahead;
my horse won't go any further!" A flash of lightning
revealed the banks of the Guadalupe River, the cause of
his horse refusing to go further. We worked our way
back through the cattle, as the river would hold the cattle
at this end, and waited for daylight. We found that we
had drifted seven miles during the latter part of the
night, and just the two of us in charge of the whole herd.
Our horses were "all in," for we had ridden them since
noon the day before. We figured that we would be off at
midnight, when our relief was up, and had not changed
for the night relief. This was our last obstacle to speak
of from there to the Runge ranch. Steers those days

were bought and sold "by age." When the classing and turning them over to Runge's foreman began, some trouble arose between Jim Holt and the foreman of Runge's ranch as to the age of the steers. Runge's foreman asked Holt if he did not have a man in his outfit that he would entrust with classing for him. Jim Holt had never handled many cattle, and asked me to his classing with Runge's man. We got along fine and more than pleased Holt, for when we were through Holt found himself to the "good" several hundred dollars above contract price he paid, and the amount of my classing. On our way home Holt stopped at a hotel in Yorktown. In this hotel I saw a sign that I shall never forget. It read:

PASSENGERS WITHOUT BAGGAGE

PAY IN ADVANCE

AND DON'T YOU FORGET IT.

Holt had no baggage and had to dig up the cash. He was considered a good-hearted man, but when drinking would not stand for any foolishness. He was known as a good fighter and soldier from his Civil War record. I recall one time at Burton, Texas, when Holt and Dr. Watt met, disagreed, and both pulled their "smoke-wagons" and got busy. When the smoke cleared away both men were found wounded, Dr. Watt going to Knittel's store and Holt into Hons & Bauer's establishment. Holt was wounded in the hip, the bullet lodging in the backbone. Dr. Hons, his brother-in-law, who now lives in San Marcos, probed for the bullet while I was holding Holt's leg. I could feel the forceps slipping off the leaden missile as the doctor was trying to extract it. Dr. Hons failed to remove the ball and advised Holt that it would take an operation and which would be a dangerous one. Holt sent to San Antonio for Dr. Cupples, who had been a surgeon in the army with Holt. Dr. Cupples and Dr. Hons performed the operation and Holt got well. He lived about two years when he and Joe Hoffman, also of Burton, were waylaid and shot in a saloon in Brenham.

Dr. Hons treated me during my illness with meningitis about 33 years ago. At the same time he was also attending Charles Hohmeyer's three children, who were suffering from the same malady. We all got well—but I, minus one eye. There were at the time 56 cases of meningitis in Burton and Brenham, of which 44 did not recover.

I considered myself very fortunate in securing the services of my friend, Dr. Hons, and know he is one of the finest physicians in the State of Texas.

In 1884 Sam Hale and I put up for Curtis & Cochran of California 800 head of cattle. We bought these up in Washington, Lee, Burleson and Austin Counties. Curtis & Cochran bought some 600 head more from their kinspeople and others near Bellville, and gathered them at Buckhorn, Austin County. My oldest brother, J. M. Craig, was employed by Curtis & Cochran to boss the herd through to New Mexico. He moved their 600 head from Buckhorn to Burton, where Hale and I joined him with the 800 head, making a herd of 1,400 cattle. This was entirely too large a herd to handle in the woods and among the farms.

The first day we only moved the herd some seven miles and camped at Charlie Tarno's, in Sandtown, within 300 yards of where I was born. Old man Tarno had a field of about ten acres fenced with post oak rails. Into this field we turned our herd. Cochran had made the arrangement and knew nothing about cattle. He said: "Put them in there and give the boys a good night's rest." We had some sixty miles of the worst kind of brush ahead of us before we would get to the

Taylor Prairie. I warned my brother and Cochran that the herd would break the fence and scatter in all the directions of the globe; and I, for one, would sleep with my bridle in hand. Hale and my brother followed my suggestion. Curtis & Cochran had hired every man that came to the herd, having some 14 hands, besides a cook. The firm had all their money in this herd and were down here in Texas where they did not have confidence in Texas people. They were so "darned" crooked themselves that they thought everybody was trying to beat them, so they hired all these men to be sure of their cattle, and to hold the herd. Hale, my brother and I had our horses saddled and ready. We took up our stations around the herd, one in a place. About ten o'clock that night the expected happened—the cattle stampeded. My brother was ahead of me, but could not make the lead; so he called to me: "Go to the lead of the herd and hold them up." I made the lead and on my way I passed Arthur Jones, who was in the middle of the herd, whipping for dear life to get out of the way, and caused the cattle in front to run so much faster. I did not see Jones any more that night. Later I located Sam Hale by his voice. The herd split up on us; my brother being with one part, and Sam Hale and I held the other part. At daybreak we drove our cattle towards the balance of the herd. We had the cattle counted before a single man from camp showed up—three of us holding 1,400 head of cattle in a herd through a dark night.

The cook told us that Curtis & Cochran had talked and wailed all night about their fortune being scattered in those woods, and that they would never get them back. Old man Cochran came to us in the morning, accosting my brother: "Well, John, how many of the 'band' (meaning the herd) are gone?" My brother said: "Here is the count." He handed him the envelope on which we had jotted down the numbers as we cut the cattle by in small bunches and had counted them. The figures proved we were none short. Cochran was a happy "old Yank," and declared: "You boys must have eyes like an owl, to run through these woods at night and not get killed."

With the delivery of these cattle to Curtis & Cochran my contract expired. The next day at noon I left for home. My brother carried the herd on through to New Mexico, somewhere near Las Vegas, and told me later that he had undergone many hardships. In crossing the Plains he had been without water for the cattle, at one time, for two days and nights. After all the hard and faithful work, these two old Yanks tried to beat my brother out of half of his wages. They hired him at $100.00 per month and paid him $50.00. Curtis & Cochran had lost a few cattle at Bellville while herding them and authorized me to gather and dispose of them and send them the money. I gathered these cattle, sold them, paid my brother his balance, and have never heard from them since.

One night while we were putting up cattle for the Curtis & Cochran herd we had some 150 head in my pen at Burton. After turning in for the night my brother took his money and some money that Joe, my wife, had given him for safekeeping, together with his six-shooter, stuck them under his pillow and turned in. He was sleeping on the front gallery. All of a sudden I heard a noise and found something had frightened the cattle, and they had broken fence and stampeded. They ran south, through the town of Burton. We were after them in no time and overtook them on Whitener's Prairie, rounded them together and finally succeeded in quieting them. Now, it happened that my brother began to get restless and confided to me that he came away and had left all his and my wife's money under his pillow on the front gallery. He figured that possibly my wife might have thought of it after our departure and had taken care of it, but "seeing is believing," and he was ill at ease. He rode back to assure himself while I held the herd. Luckily he found the money and six-shooter in possession of my wife, and, to say the least, he felt much relieved. There were but few banks in the country, and we were in the habit of carrying the cash with us. The German people, as a rule, would not take anybody's check, and quite often demanded payment in silver, as they did not like paper money.

Whenever I had too much money I would turn it over to my wife. This was not a "force of habit," but quite convenient. My wife would put it in what she termed the "First National Bank"—her stocking. You know that is a woman's money purse.

In 1893 Dr. Hons of San Marcos and I were buying up 1,000 head of one and two-year-old steers on contract. We sold them to H. C. Beal for Louis Runge of Menardville. We had leased the McCoy pasture, near Wetmore, on the Cibolo Creek, to hold these steers until we had the required number. We were to deliver these cattle to them at the Las Moras ranch, on Elm Creek, near Menard.

This was really the hardest trip that I ever made with cattle. The cattle ran the first four nights that we were out and gave us no end of trouble.

The first night we herded in a wide lane or pocket, some three miles this side of the Guadalupe River on the Blanco city road. The cattle stampeded. Sam Craig, Billy and Ed Eckert were holding the north end of the pocket, towards the river, while Stock Wesson, I and the other hands held to the south end. The cattle headed for the river and went onto the boys with such force that they were unable to hold them. Sam Craig was riding a little black pony named "Nigger Babe," a sure-footed and fast animal. Sam went into the lane with the cattle, taking all kinds of chances. He worked his way towards the lead, but before they got to the river he crowded them into the fence, which broke and got into a pasture. Sam was with them. He turned their lead and brought

them all back to the herd. I considered Sam the best
hand I ever had, day or night work, with cattle. Next
morning's count showed that we had not lost any of the
herd. On this trip I also had my boy, Walter A. Craig,
then 8 years old, with me. He had his own horse, leggings and spurs, and made a splendid little hand in daytime. I caught him asleep but once. He was on his horse

HIRAM G. CRAIG AND "JOHNNY"

under a tree and two other grown men were down on the
ground sound asleep. He was too young to do any night
herding.

The second night we held the cattle in another pocket
or wide lane, near Krueger's store. The fences were
good on either side, just two lanes to hold, but that night
we had a rainstorm. I took Walter, my boy, on my horse
behind me and brought him to Krueger's store. Sam

Craig and Stock Wesson held the south end of the lane. They had orders to force the cattle through the fence in case of a stampede, rather than let them go back the way they had come. The other boys, Billy and Ed Eckert, held the north end of the lane. The storm came from the north and the cattle ran south, throwing them on Craig and Wesson. They fought them with their slickers for dear life until they succeeded in turning their lead. Into the six or eight-wire fence they went. They broke through, cutting up a number of them badly, and we were obliged to kill several of them. They made another run, going north; broke through the line, and scattered all over the mountains near Blanco City. We worked for three days gathering these cattle, and Cavaness Brothers and others rendered us great assistance.

The third night we moved in above Blanco and had pretty "bed grounds." The cattle made one little run, but we did not lose any in the stampede. However, some of the boys were careless and let quite a number drift out of the herd during the night and we gathered all next day to get them back.

The fourth day we moved into an ideal "bed ground," an open prairie with mountains all around. The boys had good grounds to run on. I gave Sam Craig and Stock Wesson each two horses and told them to run the cattle down if they could do no better; also, to take their slickers and run the herd in a circle all night or hold them. I put Walter, my boy, and my little nigger boy, Bill, on the chuck box in back of the wagon, and told them to stay there till the cattle quieted down. These boys said that the cattle ran twenty-two times that night. The next morning we tried to stampede the herd with our slickers, but they refused to be stampeded. They never made another run on us. We had no more trouble of this nature, but we were quite a few short on account of so many stampedes. H. C. Beal having passed on these cattle, stayed by his classing and did not cut us any cattle on account of wire cuts. This was an exceptional trip and I was very foolish in taking my child along at his age. The trip kept him away from his mother for two months. We returned in the chuck wagon and on the way gathered what cattle we had lost and could find.

In 1914 one day I was en route from Brenham to Ledbetter with my two favorite ponies, Johnny and Charlie. I was riding Johnny and leading Charlie. Some two and a half miles north of Carmine, on the Houston and Texas Central Railroad, I met Crawford Gillespie. He was section foreman, Section 7, and was trying to push one of those motor cars down the track to where his men were at work. In some unaccountable way the motor started and the car got away from Gillespie. It went through his bunch of men, who tried to board it, but failed. He called to me to ditch it by throwing a tie across the track. The track was fenced, and I had no chance. In fact, I did not hardly have any time to "hesitate." It was all my horse could do to outrun the car, and I saw my only chance was to beat the car to Carmine and rope it. There was no way of getting close to the track on account of it being fenced. I got to Carmine in time enough to jump off my horse and throw a near-lying plank across the track, and ditched it directly in front of the depot. It was a test of horse flesh against gasoline, in which the horse won out. This little pony is now playing polo in New York.

In the early days there were in Washington County as well as in many other counties of Texas, some pretty tough people. Horse and cattle thieves were quite plentiful. The officers, knowing that my oldest brother and I were handy on horseback and ready at day or in the night to uphold law and order, would call on us to assist in running down this element. We kept this duty up more or less all of our lives, and neither of us ever held an office higher than a deputy sheriff or constable. The fact is, the court house ring were playing "safety first," and knew that some of their crooked bunch would get locked up if occasion warranted.

In those days we could not prohibit horse stealing, but nowadays you seldom hear of it in this country. The horse thieves were very bad and bold, and something had to be done. You might, for instance, go to bed at night leaving your work team in the barn or lot and awake next morning to find your team had disappeared. Every possible means were resorted to to stamp out this evil, but of no avail. Finally they experimented with "hemp" for several years. A strong dose of hemp would always tend to kind of "deaden" the desire to steal and today there is very little of it going on.

With reference to the old-time cowmen with whom I have spent all of my life, I candidly believe them to be the best people on earth today. They do not all profess to be Christians, but they are a noble and big-hearted set of men that you can rely upon when you, or your country, gets into trouble. They will divide their last dollar with you, and fight their weight in wildcats for you, their friends and their country. They are always ready to help the poor and needy. Only the other day at one of the local commission offices, a boy who had come from Arkansas with cattle told us of lending his last ten dollars to a gambler and losing it. He had a "pass" back home, but nothing to pay for meals or lodging. The boys chipped in and made up enough money for him on his way home. As he was walking out of the office, John Draper asked me to call him back, and handed him a ten-dollar bill. This is the kind of material the stockmen in general are made of, and may the good Lord favor every one of them.

Now, in conclusion, will say that my family consists of my wife and two children. The oldest child, a girl, named Willie Belle, is living in Houston, Texas, and is the wife of Judge Ewing Boyd, judge of the 35th District,

Harris County. The youngest child, a boy, Walter A., after finishing his education in Waco, worked for different banks in Fort Worth and later for Swift and Company, where he figured the value of cattle from the "scales to the vat." He also wanted more elbow room and the open air, so he engaged in the live-stock business. He dealt exclusively in Mexican cattle and had ranching interests in Mexico, but on account of the revolution, he transferred his activities to this side of the river, and is located at Laredo, Texas. He is actively engaged in the live-stock trade and considered a fine judge of stock.

As for myself, I am hale and hardy at my age, which I attribute to my life in the open air and being used to work.

May we all meet at the final roll call and accompany the chuck wagon to the last and great Roundup. Beware, if you are a "sleeper!"

CAPTAIN CHARLES SCHREINER

Of Kerrville, Texas

One of the most prominent figures in the development of the cattle industry in West and Southwest Texas is Captain Charles Schreiner, who is still living at Kerrville, where for so many years he was actively engaged in business, but is now spending his declining years amid the pleasant surroundings that his wonderful zeal and enterprising spirit has made possible.

Captain Schreiner was born in Alsace-Lorraine, France, February 22, 1838, and came to San Antonio, Texas, in September, 1852. At that time San Antonio was little more than a village, and the surrounding country a wilderness infested with wild beasts and wild men. Captain Schreiner foresaw wonderful opportunities for the man with grit and determination and, although he

CAPTAIN CHARLES SCHREINER
Banker, Merchant, Stockman and Philanthropist

was but a lad in his teens, he started out with a determination to carve out a career for himself that would place him in the ranks of the prominent financiers and business men of the state. In 1859 he entered the stock business on Turtle Creek, Kerr County, in a small way, gradually building his herds, acquiring land holdings, and thus expanding his interests as the years passed. Ten years later, in 1869, he engaged in the banking and general mercantile business at Kerrville, which business has continued to this good time, and is one of the solid institutions of West Texas.

In the establishment of a bank and store at Kerrville at that early date, Captain Schreiner placed himself in a position to assist the pioneers of that section, and thus help in the development of that favored region. He was heartily in accord with any project that was for the good of the community he had chosen for his field of operations, and with the keenest of business ability he permitted no opportunity to slip that would aid in its development. The result was that in the course of time he became identified with several industrial projects, chiefly cattle and sheep raising, was also engaged in the mercantile and banking business at Junction City and Rock Springs and was connected with banks and mercantile concerns in San Antonio, as well as possessing stock in several railroad companies, gradually building a fortune that made him several times a millionaire. Despite the burden of years, Captain Schreiner gave active attention to his banking, mercantile and live-stock interests until 1918, when he transferred the bulk of his property to his children.

At the age of sixteen years Captain Schreiner entered the Ranger Service, serving in Captain Henry's, Captain Sansom's and Captain McFadden's companies during 1854 to 1859. When the Civil War broke out he enlisted in the Confederate Army and served for four years.

For many years Captain Schreiner and Captain John

T. Lytle were in partnership in the cattle business and the firm drove more than one hundred and fifty thousand cattle up the trail to Northern markets.

Today the name of Charles Schreiner is linked with the making of West Texas, for he has been the moving, building spirit that has made many things possible for that region. The town of Kerrville stands as a monument to his genius, and the substantial business and public buildings and pretty homes in that thriving metropolis lend evidence to the fact that "he builded better than he knew."

THE EARLY CATTLE DAYS IN TEXAS

By A. W. Capt, San Antonio, Texas

My mind wanders back to the good old days of yore; back to the halcyon days of the early cattle roundups and drives up the "Chisholm Trail," when cow ponies were sure-footed s u r e enough. Cow ponies and "cowboys" were sure-to-goodness cowboys. The later term applied to them, "cow punchers," was not yet coined nor applicable, for usually the exercise was more of a race horse performance to round 'em up and hold them up before they struck the breaks.

A. W. CAPT

My cowboy experience dates back to the early sixties in Blanco, Kendall and Gillespie Counties, the then frontier of Texas. During the Civil War, when the men and boys were nearly all in the army, cattle on the range plentiful and very wild, it was mine to ride the range alone, everybody's "roustabout," to gather their scattered cattle, brand their calves and hunt their lost horses. In those days of open range and free grass, it was a custom practiced by the people to round up such cows as were easily penned, regardless of ownership in most cases, and milk them during the spring, summer and fall, branding the calves in the cow's brand. Concerning this bit of exercise, I became very proficient and much needed, for when early grass began to rise and young calves began to bawl in the spring I was called into service from "Dan to Beersheba" by war widows and other folks where there was no one on the ranch that wore a pair of pants to ride the range and run in old "Sooky" and any other cows with calves that could be penned.

Beginning in the spring of 1870, when large herds were being driven from Texas up the Chisholm Trail to Kansas and beyond, I got my best experience, joining the "roundup" for Sam and Thomas Johnson, the then largest individual trail drivers operating in Blanco, Gillespie, Llano, Burnett, Hays, Comal and Kendall Counties, with headquarter pens and branding stall at the mouth of Williamson's Creek in Blanco County and headquarters at Johnson's ranch on the Perdenales River, Johnson City, the county site of Blanco County. The roundup or range hands and range boss usually gathered, road branded and delivered a herd of from 2,500 to 3,000 head of cattle, which a trail boss and his outfit received at headquarters ranch, but sometimes we delivered them at the Seven Live Oaks on the prairie west of Austin. After a good night's rest the ranch hands, bidding their relief "So long, we'll meet you later in Kansas," with pack and ponies, hit the back trails for another herd for the next outfit.

Usually the ranch hands and ranch boss covered the retreat with the last herd in the late summer. This being

the case in the summer of 1871, when we started from
the branding pens on Williamson Creek, tired and worn,
the boss bolstered up with a pillow in his saddle, having
come in contact with the business end of a black steer
at the branding pen, was almost out of commission. We
had a herd of 3,000 head, made up mostly of beeves of
the old mossback, stampeding, bushwhacking type. The
outfit consisted of the cook, the only man in the outfit
that everybody could cuss, chuck wagon drawn by two
yoke of oxen, horse wrangler and sixty-four rode-down
mounts and sixteen typical cowboys, Dick Johnson, boss;
Col. Nat Lewis, second boss; Tom Moore (Banker Tom)
of Llano; Tom Logan, Bill Hitchbreath, Bob Collins,
Guss Butterfield, James Smith, Pete Lindweber, Henry
Lindweber Sr., Thomas Colbath, Hilliary Colbath, Fritz
Hitchfelt, Kansas Miller, Arnold Capt and Josh Nichol-
son, the cook. And today, as I pen this sketch, I feel
alone and lonely, for most of these comrades and many
other cowboy associates of that day have passed over
the river except H. C. Aten, a friend beloved and true.
No better cowboy ever graced or disgraced the hurricane
deck of a Spanish pony, and if he did usually hang his
long carcass on the left side of his mount with his hind
leg in his flank and roped with his left paw, he was always "Charley at the wheel," never found wanting, but
on the spot ready to deliver the goods.

On the trail that year water was scarce, herds plentiful and dust more so. The first few days nothing occurred to break the monotony or hush the humdrum of
the cowboys' ragtime music, until we were crossing the
Colorado River below Austin. Had a stampede there
early in the morning and after a hard day's work we
put the last bovine over just before sunset. The chuck
wagon, having been sent across the bridge into Austin
for supplies with instructions to camp on the trail north
of the city, eating was all out until 3 P.M. next day. It's
a good appetizer; try it. I am recording another stam-

pede that is written indelibly on memory's page—a stampede of men. It occurred one dreadful hot July day when the sun was at full tide and the wind refused to blow. It is said men are like monkeys—imitative creatures. One of the boys dropped back to the wagon and disrobed down to undershirt and drawers. He looked so cool that all tried the experiment, some leaving everything in the wagon but undershirt and government drawers. It was on the prairie near the head of Elm and happened to be Sunday, as we were reminded when we were met by a whole camp meeting crowd of young ladies and their beaux on horseback. The boss and the wagon had gone on ahead and the boys wished they could also vanish. The boss, who would rather have fun and go to hell in a go-cart than miss it and go to Heaven in a chariot, had instructed the young folks to pass by the herd on both sides, and they did so, hence the stampede. Some of the boys went off at a tangent east to see how the range looked, others went west in search of water to fill their canteens, a few thoughtfuls dropped to the rear to push up the drags, while others held their ground trying to hide their embarrassment by trying to put the words "I would not live alway, I ask not to stay," to music.

After crossing Red River at Red River Station and entering the Indian Nation, now Oklahoma, the things of interest or disinterest that accompanied the drive were many stampedes, sleepless nights, gyp water and poor chuck, constituted our bill of fare. Occasionally some of the boys would ride into camp weary, with a bad liver, venting their spleen on the patient cook, but as he was no hog and knew when he had enough, old Betsy (his 44 Colts), which he kept in the chuck wagon as a liver regulator, was sometimes resorted to, usually bringing order out of chaos. Buffalo, antelope and Indians were much in evidence, and an occasional buffalo was shot. Chasing them afforded great sport, but as for chasing

Indians, that was out of the question, for at that time they were under the watchful care of government agents and, as Uncle Sam was trying to tame his Indians, we quietly passed them by.

On August 1st Bluff Creek was crossed and the herd thrown off the trail to graze on the plains of Kansas. After a few more days of hard driving we stopped on Turkey Creek, a few miles south of Abilene. Some of the hands bought wagons and returned to Texas via Arkansas, where they loaded apples. Others remained with the herd, removing it later up the Platte River to winter quarters. T. J. Moore and I cut out our small interest in the Johnson herd and moved on, he going up the Solomon River and I establishing winter quarters on the Smoky Hill River above Abilene, where I wintered and suffered. Thawing out in the spring, I hit the grit for Sunny Texas, a poorer but wiser man. In closing this sketch I wish to bear joyous testimony to the fact that in all my associations with men of various vocations, I have found no friends more noble, true and generous to the limit than the cowmen of yesterday and today. Some are especially blessed with this world's goods, dear companions and many true friends, yet without the companionship of Jesus, the truest friend; the desolate winds of sorrow and loneliness will sweep over your soul and for this reason, now and then, despite all the happy experiences that may come to you through the companionship of earthly friends, there will sometimes be indescribable longing in your soul that earthly friends cannot satisfy. You need the companionship of Christ.

> "It is my joy in life to find
>   At every turn of the road,
> The strong arm of comrades kind
>   To help me on with my load.

And since I have no gold to give,
And love alone must make amends,
My only prayer is while I live,
God make me worthy of my friends."

THE COST OF MOVING A HERD TO NORTHERN MARKETS

By Col. Ike T. Pryor of San Antonio

Trail driving of cattle from Texas to Northwestern States in the old trail days was reduced to almost a science, and large numbers of cattle were moved at the minimum cost.

To illustrate, I drove fifteen herds in 1884 from South Texas to the Northwestern States. It required a minimum of 165 men and about 1,000 saddle horses to move this entire drive. In other words, these cattle were driven in droves of 3,000 to each herd, with eleven men, including the boss, and each man was furnished with six horses.

The salaries of these eleven men, including the boss, were $30.00 each for the ten men, including the cook, and $100.00 a month for the boss. This gave an outlay of $400.00 a month, and estimating $100.00 for provisions, there was an expense of $500.00 a month to move a herd of 3,000 cattle 450 to 500 miles. Briefly speaking, in those days it was possible to drive 3,000 cattle 3,000 miles for $3,000.00, or, in other words, from South Texas to Montana a herd could be driven of 3,000 head for not to exceed $3,000.00. My average expense on the fifteen herds in 1884 was about $500.00 per month. The average distance traveled by these herds was from 450 to 500 miles per month, and when I had sold and delivered all of these cattle to Montana, Dakota and Wyoming ranchmen I had lost 1,500 head, or 3 per cent.

Today it would cost $25,000 or $30,000 to move 3,000 steers from Southern Texas to Montana, and the only way they could be moved would be by rail. And I dare-say the loss would be equal to 3 per cent.

The old trail drivers had a margin of from $3.00 to $4.00 a head between Texas and the Northwest. In 1884 I paid $12.00 for my yearlings, $16.00 for my two-year-olds and $20.00 for my three-year-olds, and I had them contracted to the ranchmen of the Northwest at $4.00 a head margin; 1884 was the last heavy drive made, and in the fall of that year cattle started down and continually went down each year for nine years. In other words, stock cattle in Texas was selling at $25.00 a head in 1884 and went as low as $6.00 a head in 1893. Good Panhandle cattle were selling in 1893 for $10.00 per head and South Texas cattle were selling at about $6.00 per head. As proof of this fact, I bought the Cross S cattle, about 10,000 head, at $6.30 per head, no calves counted, a guarantee of 2,500 three and four-year-old steers out of a possible number of 10,000 head. These cattle were loaded on board the cars for me at Uvalde and Spofford at this price.

I remember one trip I made with a herd when not a man had a watch or a compass. At night when we would stop the tongue of the wagon was pointed toward the north star and the next morning when we made our start we would take the direction indicated by the wagon tongue. We maintained four guards of three hours each during each night, and although we had no timepiece, it is a fact that each man stood guard fifteen or twenty minutes over his time, and the last guard for the night had the short watch. This shows the generous disposition of those old trail boys, in that they would not throw off on their comrades.

LOST TWENTY-ONE THOUSAND DOLLARS ON ONE DRIVE

By John S. Kritzer, Taylor, Texas

I am not a member of the Old Trail Drivers' Association, having never put in my application for memberssip, but being in a reminiscent mood, I thought I would write a short sketch of what I saw and know of trail life, and to do so I will have to go back with Father Time to my earlier days.

I was born in Independence, Mo., in 1842, and raised on a farm a little while, and in Joe Shelby's Missouri Cavalry Brigade the balance of the time from 1861 to 1865. When General Robert E. Lee surrendered, General Shelby and about three hundred of us boys concluded to take a ride across the Rio Grande and help Emperor Maximilian clean up Cortina, Juarez, Diaz, and a few other brigands. We started from Corsicana, Texas, all young daredevils as ever fired a shot at the Yankees in defense of our beloved Southland, and as good marksmen with pistol or rifle as ever rode in any cavalry brigade of any country on earth. We knew the savas could not do anything toward licking us. We rode down to San Antonio, turned west and went through Uvalde and crossed the Rio Grande at Eagle Pass. At Piedras Negras we had a fight with the Mexicans, in which only fourteen of our boys were involved, but we killed fourteen Mexicans who wanted to take our horses. At Uvalde we had traded some of our American horses, which had given out, for some horses that had Spanish brands, and these Greasers thought they would dismount us. Not a man in our crowd could speak Spanish, but how we could handle our gun! They had our horses by the bridle reins and were pointing to the brands on them, while we were laughing at them, for we knew they were flirting with the graveyard. General Shelby saw that something was going wrong and came to us and asked what was the matter. We told him that from the signs they were making those devils wanted our horses. He said, "Hold your horses, and kill Mexicans." When he said that, every man pulled his gun and shot them loose from our bridles.

There was a regiment of over a thousand Mexican

soldiers in Piedras Negras, and they began to shoot from the tops of the adobe houses, so we got in line, and as their guns would not shoot more than one hundred yards, while we were shooting Sharps rifles, which would kill a man a thousand yards away. The Mexican colonel, under protection of a white flag as large as a wagon sheet, and accompanied by his staff, came out to where we had our battle line, and told General Shelby that he was the "bravest American and had the bravest men" that ever crossed the Rio Grande, and that if his people bothered our men or our horses he would have them shot. General Shelby replied through the interpreter that he had issued the same orders to us and he could find proof of that fact down the river where he had killed a few of his d—d horse thieves. After thanking the colonel very kindly for the compliment paid him and to his men, General Shelby marched us from Piedras Negras to Monterey, and we fought bandits and revolutionists all the way, killing more than twice the number of our force. Of course we lost some men, too, but whenever we ran on to the enemy they belonged to us. From Monterey, where we met the Maximilian French soldiers, and our friends who had gone there previously, we secured passports to Mexico City, where, when we arrived, Emperor Maximilian gave us land near Cordoba to start a colony. But Maximilian had to leave Mexico City and escape to Querétaro, where he was betrayed, captured and executed with two of his generals. So we abandoned the colony and returned to Missouri. After returning home I went to Wyoming and Montana and freighted for Uncle Sam.

Leaving Salt Lake City for Kansas City in the spring of 1869, I decided to come to Texas, so I came down through the Indian Territory to Llano, where I bought 1,000 steers, fours and up. Three-year-olds were not counted beeves in those days. I drove these steers to Fort Sill and sold them to an Indian contractor for the government and in the fall drove to Baxter Springs, where I made the acquaintance of Doc Day, Isom Goode and other old cowmen.

In 1871 I drove 400 yoke of work oxen to Fort Harker, in the Smoky Hills, near Ellsworth, Kansas, and was captured by the Osage Indians after I crossed the Cimarron River with my horses. They held me prisoner for about an hour, and I suppose I would have been scalped, but the Indians saw the dust of a big herd being driven by Jim Scobey and turned me loose. Each warrior had one side of his face painted red and the other side painted black. I saw the dust kicked up by that herd and called the Indians' attention to it, and they immediately left me.

The next year or two I drove to Abilene, Kansas, on the Smoky River. Bill Hickok was city marshal there, and was a desperate character. I then drove to Dodge City, taking one herd of the old Jingle Bob steers, which I had bought from Coggin Brothers and J. M. Dawson, from the Plains to Gainesville. These were the old John Chissum steers from Seven Rivers, near Roswell, New Mexico, and the most of them died with tick fever. Before I reached Chicago I lost $21,000 on them and was busted.

Major L. G. Cairness staked me in 1882, when he contracted 10,000 steers from Dan Wagoner. I received only 6,000 and drove them to Honeywell, Kansas, in four herds, which took all summer, as it was such a short drive. We made $72,000 on this drive, lost only three steers and saw lightning kill them. This was my last trail work.

I would be delighted to meet some of the old drovers again. God bless them. But lots of them have laid down their saddles, spurs and hobbles, coiled the riata and crossed the River Styx, and are resting in the shade of the trees.

Now, in conclusion, if you think this epistle of John

to the cow punchers of the old Chisholm Trail is of any consequence in the way of reminiscence, or will cast any lustre on the fame of those brave and daring men of the saddle and trail, put it in your book. If not, cast it aside, but still in friendship remember the giver, an old plainsman who has helped to skin 'em, fought Yankees, Mexicans, wild Indians and cow thieves. Farewell until we rattle our hocks on the other side.

MOSE WESLEY HAYS

1015 West Agarita Avenue, San Antonio, Texas

Mose W. Hays was a foremost cattleman and business man of the Northeastern Panhandle country, and was one of the oldest residents in that part of the state. During the quarter of a century in which he has

MOSE W. HAYS

known the Panhandle all the agricultural development and industrial changes have taken place there, for through all the ages during which Northwest Texas had been a portion of the new world continent its resources and its landscape features had never experienced such development and mutation as they have during the short time of white men's occupation and exploitation of this region. Mr. Hays has accordingly witnessed all the important history of that section of the state, and is one of the few men whose lot has been permanently cast with the Panhandle since 1877.

Born in Warren County, Kentucky, Mr. Hays at the age of two years was taken by his parents, N. M. and Sarah (Phillips) Hays, both native Kentuckians, to Jackson County, Missouri, about twenty-five miles east of Kansas City, and later the family became pioneer settlers of Colorado, in which state the parents spent the remainder of their lives. Mr. Hays became identified with the cattle industry in boyhood and it has formed his principal and most profitable pursuit throughout his active career. In 1871 he left the family home in Colorado and went West, spending five years in Nevada and California, during most of which time he was a cowboy.

From the Pacific slope he came east to Texas. With his brotherin-law, Joe Morgan, he drove a bunch of Mexican cattle from Corpus Christi, Texas, to the open range in the Panhandle country. This was in 1877, and he has lived in that part of the state ever since until the past five years, when he took up his residence in San Antonio, having retired from active business. It makes him one of the old-timers, as there are only a few now living there who were in the Panhandle as early as that. Up to 1902 his ranching operations were carried on mostly in Hemphill County, where for a number of years he had the noted old Springer ranch. His last ranch was located in the southeastern part of Lipscomb County, where he owned about thirty-five hundred acres of land, his residence and ranch headquarters being three miles south of Higgins. His ranch was known for its typical western hospitality as well as for progressive and enterprising methods of operating, which were everywhere in evidence. Mr. Hays has been uniformly successful in the cattle business and has attained a most satisfactory degree of prosperity. He was one of the three owners comprising the Higgins Hardware Company, which conducted the leading hardware store in Lipscomb County.

In numerous other affairs of public and business nature he has exerted his influence, and he is a man of recognized ability and integrity in whatever he undertakes.

Mr. Hays was married early in life to Miss Lou Turner of Mills County, Iowa, and has one child, Mrs. L. C. Kelley of Wichita, Kansas, who, as Bonnie Hays, attended the Mulholland School in San Antonio. In April, 1912, Mr. Hays married Miss Bessie Long of San Antonio (formerly of Owensboro, Kentucky) and for the past four years they have lived in their home in Agarita Avenue, Beacon Hill, building one of the first modern bungalows on that street.

THE PLATTE WAS LIKE A RIBBON IN THE SUNSHINE

By J. W. Jackson, Bartlett, Texas

My father and mother, Jacob and Jane Jackson, moved to Texas and settled on Donahoe Creek, in Bell County, in September, 1851, when I was nine years old. I have two brothers younger than myself who were cowmen, G. W. Jackson of Cleo, Oklahoma, and J. D. Jackson of Alpine, Texas.

J. W. JACKSON

When I was a lad I chased rabbits and lizards, trapped birds, fought the old ganders, rode the calves in the milk pen, and went to the country school when I could not find an excuse to stay at home. When the Civil War came on and took all of the able-bodied men, they left their cattle and horses almost at the mercy of the world, so the old men and boys tried to take care of the stock that was left.

That was when my hard work first began, for I was expected to do the work of a man.

My first long drive up the trail was in 1872, when we trailed 2,290 head of cattle from Tom Lane's old ranch in Milam County, to Cheyenne, Wyoming Territory. The old trail drivers who were out that year can tell what heavy and constant rains we had all through the spring and summer. We had to swim all the rivers and creeks, but I think we had the best herd to cross water that was ever driven up the trail. In our herd we had some three hundred old longhorn steers, from ten to fifteen years old, which had been raised in Little River and Brushy bottoms during the Civil War, and when we gathered them they were almost as wild as deer. There was a big bunch of these old steers that worked in the lead of the herd, and when we came to a river or creek that was swollen these old steers would walk right into the muddy water and pull for the other side, the balance of the herd following.

We had one little scrap with the Indians, but no one was hurt. They killed one steer during the fight.

We crossed Smoky Hill River just a short distance above the little town of Ellsworth, Kansas. The village was on the north side of the river then, and when we arrived there the river had been swollen by the heavy rains and looked to be a mile wide and was very swift. We had to wait until it ran down within its banks before we could cross. We secured a small boat to take us across and had to make two trips to get our stuff over.

We went from Ellsworth to Fort Kearney, Nebraska, and struck the Platte River, traveling up this stream on the south side for nearly four hundred miles, grazing the herd as we went. The Platte River stretched across the country like a ribbon in the sunshine. In some places it was a mile and a quarter wide, and a fertile green valley reached back to the hills on either side, no shrubbery being visible anywhere except a few big cottonwood trees. We found game here in abundance, deer, antelope and buffalo, and I roped two buffalo on that trip, as well as killing several.

We delivered the cattle near Cheyenne, Wyoming, and I took the saddle horses and chuck wagon and started back home over the same trail, reaching Bell County just before Christmas, 1872. This ended my first long drive.

PUT UP FIVE HUNDRED STEERS TO SECURE THREE HUNDRED DOLLARS

By E. L. Brounson, Sample, Texas

I was born September 14th, 1868, and have spent most of my life in the cattle business. My father was wounded in the Civil War and became an invalid, so when I was twelve years old I went to work on the range to help support our family. I helped to clean the first pasture that was fenced in our part of the country. This pasture belonged to Bob Bennett and was rented by J. D. Houston, now deceased.

We moved to Cuero in 1875, at the time when the Taylor-Sutton feud was in full sway.

In 1883 I went to Goliad County with a thousand head of cattle belonging to old man George Lord. There had been a prolonged drouth in the upper country, and we heard that there was a stretch of country comprising over fifty thousand acres in Goliad County where the range was open on Turkey Creek, so we drove these cattle there. We were the first to reach there and found grass good and water plentiful, but in a short time other cattle were moved in and by the first of November there were fully 20,000 cattle brought there to winter. It proved a hard winter, for the range was eaten off and water got so scarce the cattle died by hundreds. There is where I first met Green Davidson, who was there looking after cattle. You may not believe it now, but I skinned cattle by his side all winter, and will say he could take the hide off a cow just as quick as any man you ever saw. I also met G. A. Ray there. He and his father put 700 two-year-old heifers on that range and got back 240. In the spring of 1884 I hired to Mr. Ray for $12 per month and went home with him, where I broke horses, dug post holes and worked cattle until the spring of 1885, when I went out to Alpine and on to the Rio Grande. Here we were provided with mounts, eight horses for day work and one gentle horse for night riding. These day mounts were half-broke ponies and had been out on the range about a year. We were given thirty-six shoes to put on the nine horses and told to shoe them. I had never shod a horse in my life, but went at it and made a good job of it, for we used those horses right along and no one ever made complaint about our work. Our boss was Gid Guthrie, who died a few years ago at Alpine. We gathered our herd on the Rio Grande and drove it across the plains to Honeywell, Kansas.

In 1886 we drove a herd over the same trail for Lee Kokernot of Gonzales, with Gid Guthrie as boss. That same year we drove a herd belonging to George Miller of the 101 Ranch, then on the Arkansas River in the Indian Territory. When I got back home I had my wages in my pocket and I had two good horses, so began to buy a few cattle for myself. At that time the country was open from Cuero to Colorado, and by 1893 I had accumulated a herd of 500 or 600 head of cattle and moved them to Bee County, near Mineral City, where I rented the old Charlie Fox pasture, which I later disposed of with my cattle to Kenedy, Clair & Wood for $14 per head.

My first attempt to borrow money was at a bank in Cuero which had been in existence about a year. I wanted to borrow $300, which I needed to pay the lease on the pasture I had rented, and the president of the bank made me put up 500 two-year-old steers as security.

I went broke in 1903 at Elgin, Kansas, and have been broke so many times since that I have no record of the number. Passed through the drouth of 1917 and rented a Johnson grass patch near San Antonio and let my cattle graze the suburbs of that city.

SOME INTERESTING THINGS SEEN ON THE CATTLE TRAIL

By John B. Conner, Yoakum, Texas

I was on the trail in 1885 with the —X outfit for Lytle & Stevens, who had six herds of 3,000 head each and one herd of 2,000 head, the last mentioned herd being bossed by Al Jones, a negro. My boss was a white man named J. G. Jones of Gonzales. Other bosses from Gonzales were Arthur Johnson, W. W. Peavey, Milton Fly and the well-known Mac Stewart was our pilot through the Panhandle. I could go into details and give some interesting accounts of the drives I was in, but will confine my sketch to some of the things of interest to me that I witnessed that year.

The first bad thunderstorm I was in occurred on the Salt Fork of Red River, when I was on night herd with the saddle horses. The lightning was continuous, so was the thunder, which was most terrific. While the storm was in progress the horses bunched together around me, stuck their heads between their knees and moaned and groaned till I became frightened and decided that the end of time had come. I was only nineteen years old, and thought I was as brave as any man, but the action of the horses was too much for me, so I got down off my horse and lay flat down on the ground and tried to die, but could not. The storm passed on and I found myself unhurt, so after that fearful experience I did not mind other storms.

Another thing that interested me was the catching of mustang horses in No Man's Land. One day I ran across a party of men in camp who were making the capturing of these mustangs a business. They had several head tethered nearby which they had just captured, and showed me a large bunch standing about a mile away which they informed me they had been running for several days. These men worked in relays, or reliefs, and kept the mustangs on the go, without permitting them to rest or get to watering places. In the seven days three colts died from exhaustion. The men told me they kept just in sight of them to keep them on the run all day, and finally ran them down. The captured horses I saw there were all beauties.

About sixty miles south of the Palo Duro River I saw the first dirt fence, which had been constructed to catch drifting cattle during blizzards. This fence ran east and west across the plains and served its purpose well, but occasioned heavy losses in some instances. As I journeyed on and when within about twenty miles of the Palo Duro, I began to see dead cattle every few hundred yards, and the nearer I approached to the river the carcasses seemed to increase until I reached the river, where there were literally hundreds of dead cattle scattered around over the prairie. I was told by the roundup men these cattle had drifted down to the dirt fence, where they almost perished for water, and when they came back to the river they drank so much water it killed them.

We had 3,000 head of the —X cattle in our herd and had to make a three days' drive without water to get to the river. There were also two more herds of 2,000 each of the JA brand, bossed by Fly and Doak, following us, making 7,000 head in all, and when we reached the Palo Duro River, where the old stage line from Dodge City to New Mexico crossed the stream, we found about twenty outfits of roundup ranch hands there with a lot of gathered cattle. I thought sure we were going to have a general mixup that night, for I never saw so many cattle in my life before, but we kept separated by lots of hard work and constant riding. We did not drink the water ourselves, but dug shallow pits away from the river, let the water seep in and used that.

Sometimes the cowboys, when off herd, would have great sport chasing antelope, but could not catch them. There was a certain species of wolf in that region called a "swift," of a dark brown color, which we often tried to catch, but they were too swift for us. We often captured wild turkey gobblers which had strayed out from the rivers to the level prairie. When we jumped them they would fly a mile or two, then we would run them down.

WHEN "LOUISIANA" CAME TO TEXAS

By T. M. Turner, San Antonio, Texas

On August 9, 1869, I arrived at Goliad, from Louisiana. At Richmond I overtook Bryant Reynolds and Leander Butler, who were on their way to Goliad, and accepted their invitation to travel with them. I had come to Texas to be a cowboy. During the Civil War I had served as a scout in the Confederate Army, and had encountered some thrilling experiences while acting in that capacity, but I always wanted to be a cowboy, for it was a life that particularly appealed to me.

We traveled through the piney woods for two days, after which we came to the prairie, and here I encountered a young Englishman named Johnson, under a live oak tree unsaddling his horse. He had recently arrived from England and was on his way to Rockport, but decided to accompany us. Johnson was a pretty green tenderfoot, like myself, and when he found a jackrabbit he tried to catch him with a rope, thinking the rabbit was crippled because he ran off on three legs and had a bump on one side of his tail. The last time I saw that Englishman he was still running that rabbit. We arrived at Rance Taylor's ranch, and next day I was engaged by Mr. Taylor to build a corncrib. While at this work B. F. (Dock) Burris, a prominent stockman of Bee County, came there and wanted to know if there was a chap on the ranch who wanted work. Mr. Taylor told him he could probably employ me, so we made a trade. He was to start me at $12.50 per month and raise my wages as I made good. So I started my cowboy life August 18, 1869, on Goat Creek, Goliad County, Texas, and began rounding up on Pettus Prairie. When we threw the cattle together I thought we had all the cattle in Texas there, and would have nothing to do the following day. Dock Burris said to me, "Louisiana, you go over to those mesquite trees and hold them as we cut them out. If you need help I will send another hand to you." I did as I was told, and presently I heard Bryant Reynolds saying, "Here she is, Dock," and the reply, "All right, Bryant. Wait until I can get there, for all hell can't cut her out alone." They were talking about an old brindle cow, a typical Texas longhorn, with the bush of her tail cut off, including three inches of the bone. She was coming in my direction and Mr. Burris called to me, "Hold her up, Louisiana; hold her up." I did my best to stop her, but she had her head set and turned down within a foot of the ground, determined to go right on. One of the boys called out, "Tail her, Louisiana; tail her," and when I caught her tail with both hands my horse went one way and Old Brindle and I went another. The boys yelled with glee and shouted to me to "stay with her." Indeed I stayed, until Dock got to me and said "turn her loose," at the same time getting in between me and that maddened old brindle cow. On our way to the branding pen Mr. Burris and I were working the tail end of the cows and calves. He had a pretty little brown pony in the herd which he told me belonged to his son, Shannon, and said he did not permit the cowboys to ride it for fear they would hurt his back, but as I was not much larger than Shannon, he would let me use the pony. He staked the pony out that night so he would not be too full of grass to run after the cattle the next day. When we had everything arranged the next morning to make our start Mr. Burris caught the pony by the right ear and told Bryant to lay my saddle on him right easy. The little horse squatted right near the ground as the saddle girth was being slowly drawn tight, and when I mounted him, Mr. Burris let go of his ear and threw his hat under the pony's belly. Things became interesting about this time, and I turned the reins loose, for I had to use both hands to hold to the horn of the saddle. The boys yelled, "Stay with him, Louisiana," and I stayed until the reins became entangled in his front feet and from sheer exhaustion the little brown pony ceased pitching.

We branded about two hundred calves below the old mission at Goliad. It was my first experience in this line of work, but when I saw the boys grab the yearlings by the tail, jerk them down, run their tails between their hind legs and yell, "Come on with the branding iron," I thought it was time for me to do likewise, so I caught one of the yearlings by the tail and set back, when lo, she sent both hind feet into my stomach and I landed on my back, and then it was "twinkle, twinkle, little star— what in hell is the matter now?" This little motley-faced heifer must have been Old Brindle's calf.

I was sent to W. G. Butler's ranch in Karnes County and drove big-jawed and crippled beeves from there to Rockport, where they were killed for their hides and tallow and the meat fed to hogs.

In March, 1870, we started a herd of beeves to Abilene, Kansas. At Fort Worth, then a little cross-roads town, we met two shorthorn cowboys who were yelling and shooting, and we came near having trouble with them, because they turned our cattle back. Mr. Butler and I told them in a very emphatic manner to strike a high ball to town, and they struck it, and the last we saw of them was a streak of Fort Worth dust. We had a fine time that year, as everything was in good condition and going smooth. In those days I thought I was a "sticker" with a bunch of cattle in sunshine, rain or storm, but Pleas Butler could work all of the Karnes County starch out of any other man in Texas. No man ever drove a bunch of cattle up the trail any better than Pleas Butler.

MADE SEVERAL TRIPS UP THE TRAIL

By N. L. Word, Alice, Texas

I was born in Noonan, Georgia, June 6, 1846, and came to Texas when but a boy. Made my first trip up the trail in 1871 with my brother, Charlie, who had 500 big steers, which we placed in a herd of 500 more belonging to Emmet Rutledge and John Scott, which made a herd of 1,000, and we started from Gonzales, drove them to Abilene, Kansas, and sold the steers belonging to Rutledge and Scott, while brother Charlie drove our steers on to Omaha, Neb.

N. L. WORD

My next trip was with 1,200 head of horses belonging to D. R. Fant and myself. This was the first large bunch of horses driven up the trail. As we disposed of these horses at a good figure, I took another herd of horses the next season, 900 head.

We bought the first herd from Upshur Brookin, Mike Carrigan and Tom Welder, and I purchased the second herd from John Welder.

After that, the next year, I drove 2,000 one and two-year-old steers to Ogallala, Nebraska, and when we reached there I put in 2,000 more with the herd and drove to Sydney Bridge, Nebraska, where I delivered half of them to D. R. Fant, who owned them. The remaining 2,000 were driven to the 999 Ranch in Wyoming, where I delivered them to parties who had contracted with Mr. Fant for them.

My next trip was with 2,500 two-year-olds, which were taken to the R—S ranch on Wolf Creek, Indian Territory, and delivered to D. R. Fant, who had purchased the lease on this ranch and had also purchased 4,000 cattle with the lease. Mr. Fant also bought the 17— Ranch lease and cattle, about 1,500 head.

I made a trip from Santa Rosa Ranch with 2,500 two-year-old steers. I drove these for half the profit. The price Mr. Fant put on them was $12 per head. I took them to Runnels County and sold them to John Blocker after the trail was closed.

I have bought cattle all over the country, from the Santa Rosa Ranch to San Fernandez, Mexico, but during the past few years my activities have been limited in this respect, for I have bought and shipped only a few. I bossed the Santa Rosa Ranch for D. R. Fant for eight years and helped put up many herds for him.

PROBABLY THE OLDEST FEEDER IN TEXAS

By R. F. Sellers, Mathis, Texas

My father, Robert Sellers, came to Texas in 1835 from Tennessee, and was one of the first men to build a log house in LaGrange. He secured a head-right of a league of land in the lower part of Gonzales County, but did not think enough of it to even go to see it. He was one of the number who went from LaGrange at Sam Houston's call to hold Gonzales from the invading Mexican army, but there were not enough Texans to accomplish this task, so General Houston detailed him and a few others to keep the women and children ahead of the Mexican army.

R. F. SELLERS

I was born in Fayette County in 1849. Father bought a fine tract of land on the prairie on the east side of the Colorado River, fourteen miles above Columbus, and moved there in 1852, and when I was twenty-one years old he turned his stock and farm over to me.

In 1871 I made a trip up the trail to Newton, Kansas, with Barnes & Seymour. We had several hundred old wild steers in the herd that were from four to fifteen years old, which had been raised in the brush on the Sandies, and they stampeded frequently, giving us a world of trouble. So right there I gained a lot of experience in handling stampeded cattle that has been worth a great deal to me in working with cattle in the years that followed. We started this herd about the 10th of May and reached Newton the 12th of August. After we passed Fayette County there were but few settlements, and when we got up near Red River we found it to be a wild country. Almost every man we met carried two six-shooters and a Winchester for protection. When we passed through the Indian Territory we had no trouble with the Indians, but they attempted to stampede our herd several times. Two or three miles off the trail there were thousands of buffalo, all the way to Kansas, but they were too wild for us to get near them, and the only way to approach near enough to kill the buffalo was to take advantage of the wind and get on the wind side of them. Many men in those days made it a business to kill and skin buffaloes for their hides, which they hauled into the forts and sold. On this trip I saw seven head together that had been killed and skinned.

There were a great many wild horses to be seen, but they were also too wild for us to get very close to them. One day a man nooned at our camp who told us that he had made a great deal of money for several years capturing these mustangs. He had erected pens at convenient distances into which to run them. These pens were made of poles which had been hauled from the river bottoms twenty-five to fifty miles distant. In capturing these horses he told us that his system was to keep right after them in a walk, keeping up the same gait day and night, never allowing them to approach a water hole or take time to graze, and in due time he could drive them into his pens. He sold them to the farmers in Kansas, as that country was just settling up.

I commenced feeding cattle in 1876. In 1882 we sold our farm and I went into the cattle business, paying as high as $22.50 per head for my cattle. In 1884 the price had declined to $5 a head, and I drove them to Colorado and sold them.

In 1885 I put up a herd for Graham & Sisson of Colorado, with the understanding that I was to buy and put in with them if I wanted to do so. I gathered these cattle in Lampasas and adjoining counties, and it was a very dry spring, the worst that had been experienced in many years. There was but little water on the trail from Lampasas to the Indian Nation. We drove the herd to Baird City and shipped them by way of Fort Worth up to Pease River. After we crossed Red River we found but little water that our cattle would drink, and we traveled at one time three days and nights without water for them, but the morning of the fourth day a heavy rainstorm came upon us and filled all of the shallow holes in the ground with water and supplied our herd. I never in my life saw cattle drink as much as that herd drank. From there on we did not have difficulty in getting water and grass, and made it to the Graham & Sisson ranch in Colorado with our cattle in fine shape.

I suppose I am the oldest feeder in the state, as I commenced in 1876 and have missed only four or five winters since that time. I have bought steers in every county from Brown and Comanche to the coast, and have sold from $2.75 to $14.75.

UP THE TRAIL TO NORTHERN NEW MEXICO

By L. A. Franks of Pleasanton, Texas

I was born in Guadalupe County, Texas, on the San Geronimo Creek, February 21, 1847. Moved to Atascosa County in 1853. My father, Ben F. Franks, being a cattleman from his boyhood days, I was raised a cowboy from the cradle up and spent my boyhood days in Atascosa County. My father, having passed away in 1862, myself and brother were left to take care of our mother and sisters. I worked cattle and fought Indians for several years, and in 1867 I settled on a ranch of my own in La Salle County. Was married in 1870 to Miss Caroline Chapman of Bell County. After several years raising cattle I started up the trail with my first herd in 1872 for G. W. Chapman and myself. I left La Salle County in March for the Wichita (Kansas) market, and went by way of San Antonio, Austin and Fort Worth and straight on up the trail. We left with 1,000 head of steers and, with plenty of water and grass, we had a good trip and lost only a small number of steers on the way, arriving at the Wichita market in June. Returning to my ranch, I remained there until 1886 and started up the trail again for Presnall, Withers & Co., this time for Northern New Mexico. I left Presidio County in April and this trip was full of hardships all the way out to Roswell, New Mexico. We went by way of Alpine and Toyah and struck the Pecos River at Hash Knife Ranch, and the night we got there our herd stampeded early in the night and we did not get them checked until early morning. Again at Toyah we had a stampede that lasted all night and until sunrise the next morning, and this time we lost 22 head of steers. We went up the Pecos to Seven Rivers and on up. Striking the Pecos again, we followed it as far as Roswell, New Mexico. We had a tough time getting there, with no grass and no rain. We suffered heavy losses all the way up the Pecos, pulling and digging cattle out of bogs every day and losing some each day. We were a dilapidated looking bunch, cattle, horses and men, and when we arrived within five miles of Roswell we had a glorious rain and storm that made our trip the balance of the way very good. We left the Pecos at Roswell and went up by old Fort Sumner, crossed over to the Canadian River and by the old Bell ranch, then went on up the Goodnight Trail through the mountains and reached the market in July with 1,600 head of steers out of the 2,200 that we left Presidio County with in April. This was my last trip up the trail and I came back to Atascosa County and am still here.

THE SON OF A WELL-KNOWN TRAIL DRIVER

By Robert Farmer Jennings of San Antonio, Texas

My parents are Robert J. and Dorcas Ann Jennings. I was born September 30, 1881, in Guadalupe County, Texas, and when I was three years of age my parents moved to Frio County, where they resided near Pearsall until I was fifteen years old. The following three years

I attended school in San Antonio, after which I went to
Childress County and spent six months on the Shoe Nail
Ranch, which belonged to Swift & Co., meat packers,
where I worked as a cowboy.
My father at the time was
manager of this ranch. In
July, 1899, I returned to South
Texas and began to collect a
bunch of cattle of my own, and
ranched in Dimmitt, La Salle
and Zapata Counties for the
following five or six years,
during which time a drouth
prevailed over the country and
I lost all of my accumulation
of cattle. I went to Mexico in
1907 as manager of the Piedra
Blanca Ranch and remained
there until April, 1909, then

R. F. JENNINGS

returned to Texas and began handling cattle with my
uncle, W. H. Jennings. From here I went to Osage
County, Oklahoma, and spent two seasons, again returning to Texas to engage in buying and bringing cattle out
of Mexico. At the time of President Madero's assassi-
nation I was on General Trevion's La Bahia Ranch to
buy cattle, but we could not agree on the price. General
Trevino sold several thousand head of his cattle to other
parties and lost the remainder entirely through being at
enmity with Carranza, who confiscated the Trevino cattle
and had them driven to Piedras Negras in great herds
and killed for his soldiers. Out of 40,000 head General
Trevino lost outright probably 25,000.

I ranched in Texas until 1916, when some associates
and myself bought the majority interest in the Piedra
Blanca Cattle Company of Mexico cattle, and I went to
that ranch as manager. I stayed there one year, but on
account of having no protection from the bandits that

infested that region, we sold these cattle and brought them to this side of the Rio Grande in Texas. I returned to Atascosa County, where I was interested in cattle, and have spent the remainder of the intervening time in South Texas.

I was married to Miss Ella Alberta Lowrey in December, 1917, and am now residing in San Antonio. I have cattle interests in La Salle and Dimmitt Counties in connection with W. H. and J. D. Jennings.

In September, 1919, I was elected secretary of the Old Time Trail Drivers' Association, which position I still hold. Being the son of an old trail driver, I complied with the request of Mr. George W. Saunders, the president, to give this brief sketch of my life.

WHEN GEORGE SAUNDERS MADE A BLUFF "STICK"

By T. T. Hawkins of Charlotte, Texas

GEO. SAUNDERS
51 Years Ago

I was born in Guadalupe County, near Seguin, April 7th, 1859, and spent practically all of my life on ranches. I first went up the trail with a herd of horses, in 1879, from Corpus Christi to Cherryvale, Kansas. This was one of the hardest trips I ever made. Our chuck wagon consisted of a Mexican mule about fourteen hands high. The next trip I made was in 1879, this time with a herd of two-year-old steers owned by G. W. Littlefield, driven from the O'Connor ranch near Victoria to Yellow House Canyon.

This was a very pleasant drive, and we had good grass and plenty of water on the way.

The next year I went with a herd of 1,800 cattle bossed by Nat Jackson, going from Kyle, Texas, to Ogallala, Nebraska, where we delivered them to Col. Seth Maberry, after which we drove from there to the Red Cloud Agency to supply a government contract.

The fourth trip was made in 1881, when I went from Taylor, Texas, to Caldwell, Kansas, with a horse herd owned by Kuykendall, Sauls & Burns, with John Burns as boss.

During 1882 and 1883 I worked in the Panhandle of Texas, but in 1884 I went on the trail again with a horse herd owned by H. G. Williams and bossed by Bill Williams. On this trip, somewhere in the vicinity of Abilene, Texas, we came up with George W. Saunders' outfit as they were going up to Kansas. Here we had a stampede, our horses mixed together, so we just let them stay together and drove them from there to Dodge City.

On this trip several things took place that should be mentioned for the benefit of the readers of this book, for they give a clear idea of some of the dangers that beset the men who traveled the trail in those old days. When we reached the Comanche reservation, the Indians demanded horses and provisions from us. As George Saunders could talk Spanish fluently, and was good at making a bluff stick, our outfit and Carroll Mayfield's outfit, which had overtaken us, decided to appoint George to settle with the Indians as best he could. Accordingly he accompanied the chiefs and some of the bucks to a tepee and held a council with them. The old chief could speak Spanish, and when he learned that George was familiar with his old raiding range, he became quite friendly and told him that he knew every trail on the Rio Grande from Laredo to El Paso, knew all of the streams by name, the Nueces, Llano River, Devil's River, Guadalupe River, Pecos River, the Concho and Colorado

Rivers, besides many creeks. He became very talkative and, going to a rude willow basket he had in his wigwam, he brought forth several burrs which he said he had taken from cypress trees of the head of the Guadalupe River. He told Mr. Saunders that he had killed "heap white man" on his raids, but that he was now "heap good Indian, no kill no man."

Saunders offered to make settlement by giving them one horse and some provisions, and the Indians seemed well pleased with this offer. When we started our herd about twenty young bucks riding on beautiful horses, came and helped us swim the cattle across the Canadian River. A number of our horses bogged in the quicksand and had to be dug out, which sport the Indians enjoyed immensely. They fell right in with our boys and helped in every way they could to pull the horses out, and when this work was finished they gave us an exhibition of their riding. Some of the bucks would run by our crowd and invite us to lasso them.

Saunders finally decided to rope one of them, a tall young fellow who was mounted on a well-trained horse, so getting his lariat ready, he waited the coming of the Indian, and as he passed, laying flat on his horse, George threw the rope and it encircled both horse and rider. The Indian's horse shied around a tree and the Indian and his horse and George and his horse were all thrown heavily to the ground when the rope tightened. The Indian was painfully injured, but when we ran to their assistance we found no serious damage had resulted, although it was a narrow escape for both of the performers. The rope had been drawn so tight around the Indian that it required some time for him to get his lungs in proper action. We thought the Indians would be offended by the accident, but they laughed and guffawed over it in great fashion, and we left them in fine spirits.

As we proceeded on our way we heard the Kiowas

were in an ugly mood, and the next day the old chief,
Bacon Rind, and about 200 Kiowa bucks and squaws
came to us and they, too, demanded horses and provisions. We sent them to Saunders, of course, for he had
so successfully managed the Comanches the day before
we trusted him to handle these Indians the same way.
We told them Saunders was "heap big boss," and to talk
to him. Saunders parleyed with them for some time,
finally telling them to come
back the next day. They left
grudgingly and came back
that evening, renewing their
demands, so Saunders had all
of the wagons drawn up together, and offered the Indians a small amount of flour,
some sugar, coffee, bacon,
prunes, beans and some
canned goods out of each
wagon. All of this stuff was
placed where they could see
just what he was offering to
give them to depart in peace,
and he also told them two
horses would be given in addition to the provisions.
Some of the Indians seemed
satisfied and were willing to
accept the offer, but others

Taken in Dodge City, 1884
GEO. SAUNDERS (left seated)
VIVIAN MALDONADO
ANDALECIO MALDONADO
MATIAS IBARRA

wanted more. In the band of Indians was a pockmarked
half-breed who had been the most insistent that more
be given them, and he finally got all of the bunch demanding more. Saunders finally lost patience with them
and told the cooks to put all of the stuff back in the
wagons, and the men to straddle their horses and start
the herds. As George mounted his horse and started
off the pockmarked half-breed and a dozen bucks made

a dash at him, and before he realized what was happening they had grabbed him by the arms and caught his horse by the bridle. He had drawn his pistol, but was unable to use it because of the vise-like grip that held him. At the same time forty or fifty buffalo guns in the hands of the Indians were leveled at his head, and for an instant things looked bad. The half-breed, who spoke English fluently, was cursing and abusing Saunders, and telling him they were going to kill him right there. The squaws had all vanished, nobody knew where. Harry Hotchkiss and several of the other boys, including three of Saunders' Mexican hands, ran to his assistance, and their bravery no doubt saved his life. They leveled their pistols on the Indians, the Mexicans in a rage screaming, "Dammy you, you killee Meester George, me killee you." This was a critical moment for George Saunders, but he kept his nerve, for he realized that if there was one shot fired he would be a "goner." He talked to the Indians in every language except Chinese, telling them they were making a serious mistake, and that he would send to Fort Sill and get the soldiers to come and protect him. This talk had the desired effect, and they lowered their guns and departed without provisions, although Saunders gave them a stray horse in our herd which I think belonged to the Comanches. The Indians were in an ugly mood when they left, the pockmarked Indian swearing vengeance and saying, as he rode away, "We will come back and take all we want from you when the sun comes up."

While parleying with the Indians, Saunders offered to give them orders for provisions on men behind, who, he told them, were rich men and would gladly give them cattle, horses and money, naming Bell, Butler, Jim Blocker, Jim Dobie, Forest, Clark, King, Kennedy, Coleman, O'Connor and many other prominent trail men of that time. But the Indians said, "All no good. Pryor man give order last year; no good." Saunders was

worried and told us we had given him a h—l of a job,
but he was going to play it strong.

That night Saunders put on only two reliefs, some
of them to hold the herd and the others to reconnoiter
and give the alarm at the first sign of Indians. He told
all of the boys to get their shooting irons in good shape,
for there was likely to be trouble.

The Indians did not molest us during the night, and
early next morning Mr. Saunders told us they would
probably show up in a little while, and he gave us instructions as to what to do. He told us to congregate
behind this herd when the Indians appeared, keep in
line and not mix with the Indians, for in case of a fight
we should not run the risk of shooting some of our own
men. We were to keep cool while he was parleying with
the Indians, and if he saw that a fight could not be
avoided he would give a keen cowboy yell as a signal,
and every man was to act.

Just after sunrise we saw the Indians coming across
the plain in single file and in full war garb, headed by
two chiefs, Bacon Rind and Sundown, and the pockmarked half-breed. The Indians came right up to us,
and as they were approaching Saunders said, "Remember, boys, we must win the fight. If I give the signal
each of you must kill an Indian, so don't make a miss."
They looked hideous in the war garb, and as they rushed
up one of the chiefs said, "How, big chief bad man, no
give poor Indian horse or grub. Indian take um."
Saunders told them they would get nothing. They began to point out horses in the herd which they said they
were going to take, and George informed them that he
would shoot the first Indian that rode into the herd.
The pockmarked Indian held a short whispered conversation with the two chiefs and started towards Saunders, seeing which the boys, who were already on their
mettle and tired of waiting for the signal, began pulling
their guns, and the Indians weakened. They instantly

saw that we were determined to give them a fight, and
withdrew. Saunders had to do some lively talking then
to hold our crowd back. There were about thirty-five
men in our bunch, including the cooks and wranglers,
and the Indians numbered about two hundred warriors.
As they left the pockmarked half-breed showed the
white feather, and Saunders called him all the coward
names in the Indian, Spanish and English language that
he knew, but the rascal knew he had lost and his bluff
was called. In resentment the Indians went to Neal
Manewell's herd, which was nearby, and shot down ten
beeves. Saunders and several of our boys went over to
the herd and offered assistance to the boss, Mr. Cato,
but he said they were too late to save the beeves, and
it was best to let the Indians alone, as we could all drive
out of their reservation that day. We pointed our herd
up the trail and had no further trouble with them.

The pockmarked Indian was known to most of the
old trail drivers. He was an outlaw and thief, and was
regarded as a desperate character all around. I
learned that he was killed by a cowboy in 1886. George
Saunders had lots of experience in dealing with Indians
during those days, and he often told me that when he
made a bold bluff, if it did not stick he was always ready
to back it up with firearms or fast talking.

In 1885 and 1886 I carried herds for H. G. Williams
from Kyle, Texas, to Arkansas City, and made my last
drive in 1886, when I delivered a herd to Miles Williams
at Abilene, Texas. I have been in the cow business ever
since, the greater part of the time associated with H. G.
Williams.

How dear to my heart are the scenes of my trailhood,
When fond recollections present them to view—
The water barrel, the old chuck wagon,
And the cook who called me to chew.

PUT UP MANY HERDS FOR D. R. FANT

By Thomas M. Hodges, Junction, Texas

My father moved to Goliad County in 1838, and located fifteen miles from Goliad, where I was born August 30, 1849. I grew to manhood here and worked on the range until 1879, when I went up the trail with a herd belonging to Barton Peck. On this trip we endured hardships of all descriptions, stampedes, hail-storms, thunder and light-ning, trouble with Indians, and other things not to be mentioned. However, we reached Dodge City, Kansas, in good shape, sold the herd, and came back overland, bringing our horses and wagons.

THOS. M. HODGES

I am a brother-in-law to the late D. R. Fant, and for many years helped to put up and start many herds up the trail for him, but I made only one trip, and that was the one mentioned above.

My father moved several hundred cattle from Old Caney to Goliad in 1838 and soon had the largest herd in that section. He had a great deal of trouble with the Indians, for they came down into our settlement almost every moon for many years. They did not bother our cattle, only killing beef occasionally to eat, but they stole lots of horses and killed quite a number of settlers.

I met George W. Saunders, the president of our organization, in 1859, when his father settled near us in Goliad County. We went to school together, worked cattle together, and the ties of friendship that bind us have

endured all these years. The work that he is doing to
perpetuate the record of the men who helped to make
Texas the great state that she is today is characteristic
of the "get up and do things" manner of my good old
friend.

I am now living at Junction, Kimble County, Texas,
where I am engaged in the hotel business. I have been
a citizen of this county for many years; came here when
the population of the county was much less than it is
now, and have witnessed wonderful development since
I have been here. I have raised a large family, most of
my children having grown to manhood and womanhood
right here, and becoming useful citizens.

THE MILK OF HUMAN KINDNESS IS DRYING UP

By George F. Hindes, Pearsall, Texas

I was born in Alabama in September, 1844. My first
experience as trail driver was in the fall of 1856, at the
age of twelve years. I was put in charge of a small herd
of breeding cattle in Caldwell County, Texas, by my
father and we started west. We drove through San Antonio, down Main Street and out South Flores Street.
When the Civil War broke out in 1861, we had quite a
nice little herd of gentle breeding cattle, as well as a
good bunch of horse stock that I had caught from the
mustangs or wild horses that were plentiful on the range
on the Frio and Nueces Rivers at that time; but when
the war closed, or broke up, and I got out of the army
in the spring of 1865, our stock of cattle and horses were
all stolen or scattered to the four winds, so we were all
"broke" again. In the meantime I had met the finest
little girl in the world, and felt that the game of life
would not be worth the candle without her, and when I
mentioned the subject to her, to my surprise she told

Yours truly
Geo. F. Hindes

me that there would be no trouble about it, as I was in good standing with her papa, but when I told her I was "broke," she merely laughed and said "everybody was broke," and that she would help me, so we married and she is still helping me to this good hour—over a period of fifty-five years. After we were married in the spring of 1865, the Indians killed my father at his home on the Frio, in McMullen County, in August, 1865, so my mother, four sisters and one little brother were left for us to care for. During the reconstruction times we had all kinds of trouble on the border with the Indians, Mexicans, thieves and outlaws, too bad to write about, and would not be believed anyway (ask my friend, Ed English, if it was a Sunday School picnic), so better be it forgotten. By hard work and close economy I had got together fifteen hundred head of good mixed cattle by the spring of 1872, and started up the trail in March for my first trip.

I was herd boss, had a yoke of oxen, mess cart, one negro and eight Mexicans with me on that trip, but of the crowd only myself and the negro, Jack Hopkins, are now living to tell the tale. As a boy I had always wanted a good mount, was ambitious to ride good horses and have the best rifle, and as a married man I was anxious to have $10,000 in money in the clear. When I returned home in the fall I had $15,000 in cash and $10,000 life insurance in favor of my wife and babies, and felt that I was "some" financier, as that was the first real money I had ever had, and it was all our own. I started my herd from the San Miguel in Atascosa county, and as I traveled the well-defined trail, nothing of interest happened until I got to Red River Station on the Red River. There I found the river big swimming, and as another herd was close behind me, I could not turn back, so I asked my men if they would follow the herd across, and they said they would, so I spurred "Old Dun" into the river and swam across with my lead cattle following close behind, and all landed in safety, but I did not want

any more of it, as the river was wide, muddy and swift.
I had carried three herds across the Rio Grande before
that successfully, but this was the worst ever. We moved
along slowly through the territory trying to fatten our
stock on the fine range, but we had so many thunderstorms, hard rains and stampedes we did not make much
progress. Ask Bob Ragsdale about it. When we got
within eighty or one hundred miles of Caldwell, on the
Kansas line, we butted into the Osage tribe, who demanded a good beef out of each and every herd passing
their camp. About fifty of their ugliest bucks came to
my camp where we were making dinner and took time to
eat up everything the cook had and then made their
wants known, and I said certainly I had one for them
and asked the chief spokesman to please pick it out, as
I was in a hurry, and at the same time told my men to
"hook up" and move out, and they were ready to go. So
the chief picked out a high-grade steer, very fat, about
a fifteen hundred pounder, and was about to shoot him,
when I tried to explain that he was a favorite of mine,
but it was no use, as they thought that that would make
no difference. I think a dozen of them shot him at once
and killed him before I could say "scat." In less than
ten minutes they had him skinned, cut up and packed on
ponies and were gone to their camp. My friend, Mr.
John Redus, with whom I had been traveling and who
was camped close by, seeing what they were doing to
me, had thrown his herd on the trail and was pushing
them along pretty lively, when my men got my herd
straightened out on the trail four or five hundred yards
behind Redus' herd. By that time the Indians were coming like blackbirds. I think they were one hundred
strong, all well mounted and well armed with guns, pistols, bows and arrows. They were exceptionally friendly
with me, and uncomfortably sociable, showing a great
deal of the bulldog familiarity which I could not enjoy.
They did not ask me for anything more, only invited me

to their camp and told me all about their many squaws and babies, but I took their word for that. When they called on my friend, Redus, for a beef they disagreed with him when he offered them a crippled steer, but a good one in fair flesh, so they all bunched up between our herd for a council of war and in a few minutes I saw them load their guns, string their bows and a hundred of them ran full drive into his herd, shooting and yelling the regular war-whoop, scattering his herd of about one thousand good beeves to the winds, killing a hundred or more right there on the prairie in sight. When the smoke and dust cleared away all he had left was his men and horses and about two hundred and fifty head of beeves that ran into my herd, where the Indians did not follow them. Mr. Redus brought suit against the government for the beeves; lost it, and I was a witness for him for some twenty years. We hurried up from there until we got into Kansas and on to Wichita, on the Arkansas River. I think Redus' claim was finally paid, but not in full.

I handled cattle up the trail several years after that and delivered twenty-five hundred head to Messrs. Hackney and Dowling up at Chugwater, above Cheyenne, Wyoming. Always made a little money, but never bossed another herd through from start to finish after 1872. I know the game, and I know if a man made good at it he had two or three months of strenuous life.

The Texas pioneers and old trail drivers are fast passing away and will soon be only a memory, but that memory is dear to my heart, and when they are gone the world will never know another bunch like them, for the milk of human kindness is drying up, and the latchstring is being pulled inside.

TOOK TIME TO VISIT HIS SWEETHEART

By H. C. Williams, San Antonio, Texas

I was born on a stock ranch in Refugio County in 1856, and spent most of my life working with cattle. In those early days people lived on cornbread, beef, milk, butter and coffee, about the only store-bought articles being coffee and sugar, and not much of that. I helped to gather and drive cattle to Rockport for W. S. Hall in 1869, and for several years thereafter. In 1872 I drove a herd to that place for George W. Saunders, who is now the president of our Trail Drivers' Association. George was a good boss and a hard worker. He was also a lover of fine clothes and pretty girls, and one day while we were near William Reeves' ranch, four miles above Refugio, George had us stop the herd and make camp so he could call on his sweetheart, Miss Rachel Reeves. We had plenty of time to reach a good stock pen six miles further on, but he was so anxious to see his girl that he held us there. George later married Miss Reeves, in 1884. I have known Mr. Saunders all of my life and know he will "stand hitched" any place on earth. He never forgets a friend.

I worked stock in all the coast counties and knew all of the old-timers in that region. In 1880 I went to Kansas and drove a drag herd with pack horses from Caldwell County, Texas.

In 1871 I built seven miles of barbed wire fence for W. E. and Tom McCampbell of Rockport, it being the first barbed-wire fence in San Patricio County.

I am now living in Bexar County on a farm and ranch and can ride all day and do any kind of farm or ranch work. My father was a well-known stockman in the early days and was known as "Uncle Boiling" Williams.

REMINISCENCES OF THE TRAIL

By Jasper (Bob) Lauderdale

I was born near Belton, Bell County, Texas, August 17, 1854. My parents moved to Belton in 1849 from Neosho County, Missouri, coming in by ox wagon, then moved to Gonzales, where, after remaining a short time, they returned to Belton and maintained the stage stand until 1854, when all earthly possessions were wiped out by a flood. My parents both died when I was young, and I was raised by Uncle Alex Hodge until I came to Atascosa County in 1873. During my early boyhood in Bell County I rode the range and helped with herding and branding cattle, enjoying the experiences of the then early conditions existing in Texas, one of which caused so much amusement that I am going to recite it here.

BOB LAUDERDALE

One day a Mr. Isabell came traveling through the country trading eight-day clocks for cattle, giving one clock for four cows and calves, and as no one had a clock, it did not take Isabell long to gather a herd. One of the settlers with whom he traded, took his clock home and, after winding it, set it on the mantle, and when the family gathered round after supper, the clock struck eight. It scared the family so that they scattered, thinking it was something supernatural, and it took the old man until nearly midnight to get them together and in the house. I helped Isabell drive his cattle as far as Comanche

Springs on his way to Fort Worth and returned to the range, remaining until 1872, when, with Isaiah Mock, Hoffman and Moore, we drove a herd of cattle to Alexandria, La., with W. C. Wright, who loaded them on boats for New Orleans; then we returned home. During the fall we branded "Mavericks" and put up trail herds and in the spring of 1873 Olley Treadwell came through with a herd for Kansas belonging to Sim Holstein of Gonzales. Bob Allen and I hired to Treadwell and went to Wichita, Kansas, this being my first trip over the Chisholm Trail, with nothing unusual or exciting except we saw some buffalo.

At Wichita during the summer, Bud Chapman, Bud Hilderbrandt, Bill Bennett and I helped "Shanghai" Pierce cut and load a train of steers for the market at St. Louis. This was the first bunch of cattle I ever saw loaded on cars.

In the fall of 1873 I went to work on the range for Bill Fountain and we gathered and drove 200 head to W. B. G. Grimes' slaughter house on the coast, near Powder Horn, where they were slaughtered for their hides and tallow. On our return we gathered a herd of 250 cattle and drove them to Harrisburg, then five miles from Houston, and on this trip I led the pack horse and cooked for the outfit. I then went with Bud Chapman to Fort Ewell, where we gathered cattle and brought them back to his ranch, and in the spring of 1874 started 3,000 head up the trail, going as far as the Salado with them. Upon returning I worked for "Billy" Childress, John Slaughter and Mrs. O'Brien. In the spring of 1875 three Mexicans and I were herding 400 head of cattle near Carrizo Springs, Texas, when Lem English and Len Hay, two boys, who were playing close by, discovered a bunch of Indians. The children ran to the house and gave the alarm and Ed English came out and helped us put the cattle in his pen, and we stood guard all night, although the Indians did not attack us, as they had previously had a taste of old English's rifle. On their way out the Indians killed one of Ed's sheep herders.

In the spring of 1876 Dick Horn, Jack McCurley and I, with some Mexican hands, gathered and delivered by Billy Childress and John Slaughter, to Bill Dougherty two herds of about 5,000 head at Indian Bend Ranch. In the fall of 1876 I went to Runnels County and took charge of a herd for J. W. Murphy and George Hindes and wintered on Elm Creek, above where the city of Ballinger now stands, and the following spring drove them to Dodge City, Kansas.

On the trip I saw old Sitting Bull and about 1,200 of his bucks and squaws in charge of Government troops; these were the Cheyenne and Sioux Indians, who had massacred General Custer and his men and were being taken to Fort Reno. There were about 2,000 horses with the Indians. The troops had 100 pack mules so well-trained that you could not make them break line. They moved in single file and were taught this to enable them to travel through the mountains. The Indians were traveling in their usual way, poles tied to the necks of ponies like shafts in a buggy, but much longer, and in willow baskets lashed to these poles the old bucks and squaws rode who were too old to ride horseback—their tepees and supplies were also carried in this manner. Squaws with their papooses strapped to their backs rode bareback, and in passing through their camp I saw one old buck dressed in moccasins, breechclout, a frock-tail coat and an old-fashioned preacher's hat.

Upon my return from Kansas, in 1877, I went to a point near Oakville and received a herd of cattle for Lewis & Blunzer and drove them to Saddle Creek, near the mouth of the Concho, where it empties into the Colorado, at a point near where Paint Rock now stands. Shortly after I left the horse wrangler, Lebora Chappa, who had remained with Joe Reame, was killed near Salt Gap by the Indians.

In November, 1877, George Hindes, Volley Oden and I took an outfit to Laredo and bought and received a herd of cattle on the Gonzales and Ambrosia Rodriguez ranches and returned to the La Parita ranch, in Atascosa County, on Christmas day, 1877, then road-branded, and in the spring of 1878 started up the trail. On the trail with me was Joe Collins with his herd and a herd of Bill Dewees in charge of Joe Eggle, and when crossing the North Fork of Red River, at the foot of the Wichita Mountains, Joe Collins' cook was killed by a Mexican, who we were unable to capture. We rolled the cook in his blanket and dug his grave with an axe and a broken-handled spade, the only implements at hand. On the Mobeetie road crossing at the North Fork of the Red River, near Fort Sill, the Indians—Cheyennes and Sioux —were holding a medicine dance and afterward went on the warpath. They killed Tuttle & Chapman's cook, took 35 head of horses on Crooked Creek, near where I had camped, shot Foreman Rainey's horse and headed for the Bad Lands of the Dakotas.

We reached the H. & D. ranch on September 7th, 1878, and remained there until the cattle were ranch-branded, and returned to Cheyenne and then to Denver by train.

In the spring of 1879 I started for Dodge City with a herd for John Camp, and a little above San Antonio our oxen gave out, requiring us to use Mexican ''stags'' with Mexican yokes to Dodge City. In the fall and winter of 1879, C. F. Carroll and I made several trips down the Rio Grande below Laredo and bought cattle from the Tortilla ranch in Mexico and from Pedro Flores, Juan Benavides, Jesus Pena and others for Camp, Rosser & Carroll.

In the spring of 1880 Carroll and I started to Kansas and at Bandera we threw our herds together because several of Carroll's hands quit him, and I drove the combined herds to Ogallala and delivered them to Charles and Joe Shiner, who then sold 1,000 head of two-year-olds, steers and heifers, to Billy Campbell, and I drove this lot to Pine Bluff, Wyoming, turning them over to Campbell's men. In the spring of 1881 I took a herd of three and four-year-olds for Mitchell & Pressnall to Ogallala and turned the big steers over to Seth Maberry and then shaped up another herd of 2,500 one and two-year-old steers and 1,000 one and two-year-old heifers out of the Mitchell, Pressnall and Ellison herds and went to Crazy Woman Fork of Powder River at the foot of Big Horn Mountains, and delivered them to Stoddard, Latman & Howard.

Returning in 1881, I worked my own cattle until 1884, and that year shipped to Dryden, on the Southern Pacific. In 1885 I traded with John Camp and the Pecos Land & Cattle Company, and "hit" the trail again.

John Doak, Dan Franks and I gathered a herd and sold out to Zook & Odem and I went to Independence ranch, in Pecos County, and turned them over to Billy Alley. Returning home in 1886 with Jess Pressnall, I went to Fort Stockton and gathered a herd, drove up the Pecos to Fort Sumner and remained six weeks cutting out steers; then drove to Las Vegas and loaded them for Cheyenne, Wyo., and upon my return to Fort Sumner I took the balance of the herd, 1,000 one and two-year-old heifers, to Grant, New Mexico, and delivered to a Kansas City outfit. On this trip with me were Clem Crump, Sharp, Bob Gould, Henry Ritterman, Theo Leonard, Rainey, Jack Brown and Jim Matthews. Leaving Fort Sumner with the herd for Grant, we traveled up Yoss Creek (Isinglass), Seven Lakes, Pena Wells, Pinta de Agua, struck the Rio Grande at La Jolla, crossed the river, and came out by the Rancho Rita Coloral, struck the Indian reservation at Querrian and up the St. Jose River, and delivered the cattle, returning to Albuquerque. Pressnall, Matthews and I went to El Paso and San Antonio.

In 1887 I went to Fort Stockton and spent the year branding and tallying cattle for the Union Beef Company, returned to Pleasanton, and in the spring of 1888 went back and finished receiving between 14,000 and 15,000 head for this company, and 7,000 calves were branded during this period that were included without cost.

In 1889 I drove a herd from the McDaniel pasture at Lytle for Jess Presnall and John Lytle to Trail City, Colorado, and delivered them to John Blocker, who drove them North. This was my last trip over the old "cattle trail."

On the trail from San Antonio our watering places were at Leon Springs, Cibolo, at Boerne, the Guadalupe at Comfort, Goat Creek, Devil's River, James River, Llano, San Saba, Calf Creek, Brady, Cow Creek, Elm, Colorado, Bull Creek, Holmes Creek, Red Bank, Hord's Creek at Coleman City, Jim Ned, Pecan Bayou, Burnt Creek, Deep Creek at Callahan City, Mexia, South Hubbard, North Hubbard at Albany, Clear Fork at Brazos at Fort Griffin, Elm Creek near Throckmorton, Millett Creek and Brazos at Millett Ranch, Pony Creek, Wichita, Beaver, Paradise, Pease River and crossed Red River at Doan's Store, which, in 1877, consisted of three buffalo hides and a wagon sheet, then up the North Fork of Red River, crossed Croton Creek, crossed the North Fork at Wichita Mountains, up the North Fork of Red River to Old Indian Camp, Elk Creek, Cash Creek at its head, Washita, Canadian, Sand Creek, Wolf Creek, Otter, Beaver, Buffalo, Wild Horse and the Cimarron, where "Red" Clark conducted a road house called the "Long Horn Round Up," and on the opposite side was old Julia's "Dead Fall"; thence up Bear Creek to near its head, and crossed Bluff Creek at Mailey's road house, Mulberry Creek, within sight of Dodge City. From Dodge City to Ogallala we watered at Duck Creek, Saw Log, Buckner's, Pony Creek, Pawnee, Smokey, Saline at Buffalo, Kansas, the South and North Solomon, South and North Sappy, Beaver, Driftwood, Republican,

Frenchman, Stinking Water, to Ogallala on the South Platte, up the South Platte to Chug Water by Big Springs, Julesburg up Pole Creek to Sydney, Pine Bluff, Horse Creek and to Chug Water.

Among those who traveled with me on the trail and whom I met in Kansas were: Eli Baggett, Eli Williams, John Merritt, Tom Christian and Doc Day, Littlefield and Dilworth, Tom Mayhorn, Geo. Hodges, Jesse McCoy, Joe Murrany, Dunn and Bob Houston, Ab Denmark, Matt Patten, Sam Tate, Bill Colley, Dick Dismuke, Jim Tally, Gordon McGriffin, Uncle Jim Ellison, Alonzo Millett, Captain Millett, Hy. Millett, Bill Jackman, Mark Withers, Alex Magee, Dick Withers, Monroe Hardeman, Bob Jennings, John, Bill and Ab Blocker, Jenks Blocker, Henry Maley, Geo. Saunders, Dick Crew, John Little, Geo. Hill, Joe Crouch, Ben Gilman, Charles, Henry, Mike and Joe Shiner, Geo. Burrows, Dick Edwards, Rufe Walker, John Doak, Jim Currey, Will Peacock, Waddy Peacock, Jim Matthews, Bob Savage, Doc Rabb, Bud Chapmann, Solomon Tuttle, Bud and Tobe Driskill, Dal, Cell, Till and Jess Driskill, Hy. Patterson, Kingsbury and Holmesly, John Good, Mont Woodward, Lou O'Shea, Steve Birchfield, Bill Birchfield, Geo. Arnett, Gus Black, Billy Henson, Ace Cutcherfield, Bill Lytle, Finis Bates, Jeff Woodley, Joe Glenn, Jim and Charley Boyce, Noah Ellis, Mack Stewart, Walter Polley, Jim Dobie, Dillard Fant, Sam Glenn, Wallace Fant, Levi Anderson, Al and Dave Hughes, Henry Griffin, Jerry Ellis, "Black Bill" Montgomery, Doc Burnett, John Gamel, Billy Childress, John Slaughter, Joe Matthews, Meyer Halff, Bill Butler, Lott and Virgin Johnson, Everett and Willie Johnson, Tom Newton, Bill Waugh, Mose Stephenson, Henry Yegge, Henry Earnest, Ike, Sol and George West, Allen Harris, Jesse Evans, John Kenedy, Ira Word, John Morrow, John Frazier, Sam Willson, Ben and Bill Choate, Nat Word, George Reno, Sebe Jones, John Dolan, Bill Murchison, Jim Rowden, Bill Perryman, Jim Reel, Tom Merrill,

Uncle Henry Stephens, Jake DePoyster, Cal Mayfield, Col. Risinger, Jack Morris, Willie O'Brien, Bill and Campbell Fountain, Ike Hill, "Aus" Franks, Coleman (Uncle Coley) Lyons, Bob Ragsdale, C. H. Tardy, Nat Haynes, Bob Turner, "Eb" Stewart, Wash Mitchell, Jim Townsend, Bob Miller, Clint Lewis, Perry Thompson, "Uncle" Ed Lyons, Joe Cotulla, Sam Camp, W. S. (Bill) Hall, Lee Harris, Bill Irvin, Lee Trimble, Ben Borroum.

In 1908 I drove the last big herd to San Antonio, 1,300 head for D. & A. Oppenheimer, and delivered them to Tom Coleman at his feed pens. Dan kicked about driving so many in one herd and only a few years before he would not think of starting on a drive with only 1,300 cattle.

FROM TEXAS TO THE OREGON LINE

By W. A. Peril, Harper, Texas

I was born in Benton County, Mo., in 1845, and moved to Burnet County, Texas, with my parents in 1858, where we resided until 1861, when we moved to Gillespie County, with a small bunch of cattle which my father had bought in Milam County.

In 1862 I went with a party and bought a herd of cattle from the Toutout Beauregard ranch, forty miles below San Antonio, which we drove to Gillespie County, camping at Powder House Hill on our way up.

W. A. PERIL

In 1864 I went down into Mexico with a herd, going

by way of Fort McKavett, passing near the head of the
South Concho River, by way of Horsehead Crossing, on
the Pecos, to old Fort Stockton, on to Presidio del Norte,
on the Rio Grande in Mexico.

In 1868 I went with W. C. Lewis with a herd of beeves
for the government, to be delivered at old Fort Hudson,
on Devil's River. We went by way of Kerrville, Bandera, Uvalde, Fort Clark and San Felipe Springs (Del
Rio).

In 1869 George T. Dorris & Son of St. Louis, and
Felix Dorris of Montana, contracted with W. C. Lewis of
Fredericksburg, and Pleas Oatman of San Antonio, for
1,700 head of beeves and 150 stock cattle to be delivered
to them at Salado Springs in Bell County, and I was
employed to help make the delivery in four herds. Lewis
took one herd from Crabapple Creek, in Gillespie; I took
one herd from near Loyal Valley; Old Man Hoerster took
one from Mason, and John Oatman one from Llano.
They were all old, wild longhorns, from five to fifteen
years old, and we had to brand them on the horns and
saw off the point of the left horn when we delivered them.
The Dorris Company then hired me to go to Montana
with the herd, and we went by Belton, Waco, Cleburne,
Fort Worth, Gainesville, Fort Arbuckle, east of Wichita,
to Abilene, Kansas. We had to swim all the rivers from
the Brazos to the Republican. We had a boat on one of
our wagons to carry our camp outfit and the boys who
could not swim crossed the rivers in it. We had many
rainstorms and stampedes before we reached Kansas,
but I will not undertake to describe them. After we left
Abilene we drove north, crossing the Republican River,
the Big and Little Blue Stocking, the Platte at Fort
Kearney, thence up the Platte by Fort McPherson to
Julesburg, up Lodge Pole Creek to Cheyenne City;
through Cheyenne Pass and over the mountains to Laramie City; on around the base of the mountains by Elk
Mountain; crossing the North Platte where it flowed out

of the mountains; then through Bridger Pass on down Bitter Creek to Green River. At Green River Station we had a snowstorm, and the owners decided to winter at Brown's Hole, about seventy-five miles down Green River. Two tribes of Ute Indians came in and camped near us the following spring. They moved out before we did and took some of our horses with them. That winter we had to cut ice for the cattle to get water. We moved out from there about the first of May, 1870, when the snow was melting, and had to swim streams again. We went back to Green River Station and there the owners decided to drive the cattle to Nevada. We took the California and Oregon route west to the parting of the ways near old Fort Bridger, taking the northern route down Bear River, through Bear Lake Valley, Soda Springs, on down to Snake River to where the old routes divided, then followed the California route, crossing the Portneff, Goose Creek, Raft River, through the City of Rocks, Thousand Springs Valley to Humboldt Wells, down the Humboldt River to Lassen's Meadows. They shipped all of the cattle that were fat to San Francisco, and I took 500 head up near the Oregon line and kept them until the spring of 1871, when we rounded them up and sold them on the range, and I started for Texas via the railroad route, passing through Winnemucca, Nevada, Ogden, Utah, and Cheyenne, Wyoming, coming on through Denver, Kansas City and St. Louis; by boat down the Mississippi to New Orleans and Galveston; to Columbus by rail, to San Antonio by stage, and then went to my home in Gillespie County on horseback.

AN OLD FRONTIERSMAN TELLS HIS EXPERIENCE

By Joe Chapman, Benton, Texas

I was born in Tennessee, February 18, 1854, and came to Texas with my parents when I was about five years old. My father stopped in Parker County for a short time, then bought a tract of land in Jack County, nine miles north of Jacksboro, on Hall's Creek, and opened up a fine farm there. At that time we were on the extreme frontier, and the country was infested with hostile Indians, who made raids almost every full moon, and we had to keep our horses locked with trace chains to trees in the yard to keep the redskins from stealing them. In July, 1860, my father was waylaid and killed by the Indians, while he was out deer hunting in a little ravine near home. This tragedy happened just at sundown, and was so near home I heard his gun fire, and we all thought he was shooting a deer. But when he failed to return we became uneasy and gave the alarm, and next morning the neighbors found his body. He had been shot eighteen times with arrows, scalped, and his clothing taken. His gun had been broken off at the breech, evidently in the hand-to-hand struggle that took place when the Indians closed in upon him.

Some time previous to the killing of my father, the Indians had murdered a man named Cooley, our nearest neighbor, three miles away. Also in the same year one of the Browning boys over on the West Fork was killed and his brother shot through the breast with an arrow. Before that the Loss Valley murder took place, in which several women and children were killed, one of the women, Mrs. Cameron, being scalped and left for dead, but recovered. After father's death we went back down in Parker County and remained there until the winter of 1861–2, then moved to Cooke County, and often had to leave there on account of the Indians, sometimes going as far east as Collin County.

In 1863, on Christmas day, the Indians made a raid on the head of Elm, where the large town of Saint Jo now stands, and all of the people went to the old Spanish fort on Red River for protection. They killed many people and stole lots of stock in this raid. I knew a little boy and girl named Anderson who escaped and came to old Fort Wallace the next day. Their parents and other members of the family were murdered, and the little boy's throat was cut and gashed with lances. Another family was killed and their home burned. The Indians also killed a little boy named Guinn, cut his arms off and stuck his body on a pole. Near the same place later on the Box family were captured, the father being killed before their eyes and the mother, two grown daughters and an infant being carried away into a captivity worse than death. Up near Fort Sill one of the daughters, a beautiful girl in her teens, was treated in a most shocking manner by the savages. These tragedies occurred when I was but a child, but I remember many of them vividly.

During the four years of the Civil War the people of the Red River country, Montague, Cooke, Wise and Denton Counties, had a severe struggle to get along. Everything was of primitive style, and we had to get along the best we could. Most of our houses were built of logs, some of them roughly hewn and with the bark on, and the cracks "chinked" with sticks and mud, with dirt floors and a big, wide chimney. Sometimes a family would get "tony" and hew logs on one side and make a puncheon floor for their home and thus get into the "upper class." In the summer we would move out and live in these log houses, but in the fall and winter the Indians kept us in the forts. We had plenty to eat, although we had to take our grain fifty miles to a mill to have it ground. We had no money, but did not need much, for we could not buy such things as coffee, sugar, soap, matches, pins or anything to wear, and we were compelled to spin and weave all of the cloth that made our clothing. Rye, corn, wheat, okra seed and roasted acrons were used as a substitute for coffee.

In 1868 my brother, about eighteen years old, was waylaid and killed by Indians between Gainesville and

Fort Wallace while on a trip to the fort. Thus the savages had killed two of our family, in each instance our chief support and protector. That same year we moved to Atascosa County, where we had relatives, and as I was about fifteen years old, I was considered large enough to be of help in working with cattle, on the roundups and roping and branding on the range. In those days every waddy had two crooked irons attached to his saddle and a pocketful of matches, and the maverick that got away was sure enough a speeder. In the fall of 1870 I worked on the Redus ranch on the Hondo, working cattle with George, John and Bill Redus and Tally Burnett. Later I worked for V. A. Johnson, but mostly for Lytle & McDaniel. I learned all I know about handling cattle from V. A. Johnson and Tom McDaniel. If a boy working under them did not make a good hand in the brush or on the trail there was simply nothing to him. There is Uncle Bob Ragsdale, Will Lytle and Captain John Lytle, with whom I worked, who were all good men and true. All have reached the end of the trail and gone over the great divide, except Uncle Bob Ragsdale.

I made my first trip up the trail in 1872 with a herd for Lytle & McDaniel with 1,800 head of cattle from yearlings up to grown beeves and cows. We routed them across Mustang Prairie to the Medina, then up the Louse and over to the Lucas to the old John Adams ranch, on to San Antonio, skirting the northwestern part of the town, and passed on to the Salado. After we passed San Antonio we had quite a rainstorm and our cattle split up in small bunches and scattered everywhere. We lost about thirty head in this stampede which we did not get back. Tom McDaniel was selected as boss of the outfit, which consisted of sixteen men. Four men had interest in this herd, viz.: Tom McDaniel, Jim Speed, Uncle Ben Duncan and Newt Woofter. Gus Black, Tom Smith and myself were the only white hands with the outfit, the other hands being Mexicans, except old Jack Burckley, the cook. Jim and Dock Watts, who lived at the Man Crossing on the Medina, came to us further up the trail. Woofter went with us, but did not come back. Jim Speed was killed in Moore several years ago; Tom McDaniel died in 1887; Uncle Ben Duncan died in 1919, and the old cook also went the way we must all go sooner or later. Gus Black of Eagle Pass is the only one of my old comrades on this drive who is still living.

In 1874 I made a trip up the old Chisholm trail with 1,000 beeves which had been selected and put in the Shiner pasture below Pearsall. We went to work gathering them about the 20th of February and it took us until the 5th of March to get them out of the thickets, inspected and road-branded. These cattle were in good shape and as fine beeves as you ever saw, no she stuff, and mostly threes and up. There were a few twos, but they were all fours when we got through and ready for the market. On the morning of March 5th we pointed those old moss-headed beeves up the trail and made it to the Davis ranch that night. Uncle Bob said we could pen them there and perhaps get a little sleep, but a norther and a dry thunderstorm blew up and everybody had to get around that old pen and sing to them while they were milling around like a grindstone. We pulled out from there at sunrise the next morning and drove to the old John Adams ranch on the Castroville road, where we penned the beeves again and had another bad night. Nobody got any sleep, but we kept them in the pen. When the herd reached New Braunfels Uncle Bob, who was acting boss, turned the herd over to Bill Perryman and turned back. Our regular boss was V. A. Johnson, who had been detained in San Antonio on account of sickness in his family.

We crossed the Guadalupe River in a rain, and just after nightfall we had a severe storm with lots of thunder, lightning and cold. It was so dark most of the hands left us and went to the chuck wagon except W. T. Henson, myself and old Chief, a negro. We had to let them drift, and it took us two or three days to get them back together. We were about thirty head short when we counted and pulled out from there. When we reached the vicinity where Kyle is now located we had another big storm and a general mixup with some other herds that were near us. We had quite a time cutting our cattle out and getting them all back, especially some strays that were in the herd.

We had storms and stampedes all the way up to Red River, which we reached about the 16th of April. We never did succeed in holding all of them at any time. We had a few old trouble-makers in the herd, which, if they had been shot when we first started, would have saved us a lot of worry. They ran so much they became regular old scalawags. But, strange to say, we never had a single stampede while passing through the Indian Territory. The Indians did not give us as much trouble on this trip as they did in 1872.

Ed Chambers was killed at Pond Creek, while in charge of a herd for Tucker & Duncan. We had some exciting times getting our herd across Red River, which was on a big rise, and nearly a mile wide, with all kinds of large trees floating down on big foam-capped waves that looked larger than a wagon sheet, but we had to put our herd over to the other side. Henson and I were selected to go across and hold the cattle when they reached the opposite side. We were mounted on small paint ponies, and the one I was riding got into some quicksand just under the water and stuck there. I dismounted in water about knee deep, rolled him over and took off my saddle, bridle and leggins, then undressed myself and called some of the boys to come in and get my things, while I headed my horse for the north bank with just a rope around his neck. I figured that if my little pony could not make it across I would use one of those moss-headed steers for a ferry boat, but the little fellow took me safely over. He swam all of the way with his nose just out of the water. Three herds crossed the river that day and one man was drowned, besides several cattle. Hub Hunt of Gonzales got away from his pony in some way and we had to fish him out, and a fellow named Barkley was knocked off and pawed in the face by his horse, and we got him out too. We had one horse, which I had intended to ride, which would not attempt to swim at all, and we had to take him across on the ferry boat. We tried to get him to swim the river, but he would only turn up on his side, curl his tail, and float back to the bank. He was a fine looking red roan, was raised on the Noonan ranch near Castroville and branded circle dot on left shoulder. He fell on me one night during a stampede at Wichita, and seemed to be a Jonah all around.

It took about four weeks to move our herd across the Territory, during which time we had some fun killing and roping buffalo. Some of our outfit returned by way of the old Coffeyville trail, as the Indians were on the warpath on the Chisholm trail because some buffalo hunters had killed some of their bucks and they wanted revenge.

PARENTS WERE AMONG EARLY COLONISTS

By Henry Fest, 1708 South Flores Street, San Antonio, Texas

My father, Simon Fest, and mother, Mary Fest, were married in Alsace, France, in the fall of 1845, and immediately started for the United States, a journey which lasted three months and fifteen days, landing at Indianola, Texas. From there they came with the Castro colony, locating at Castroville the 11th day of February, 1846, where they first stopped for about two months, and then came to San Antonio, where my father took up his trade as stonemason, which yielded the handsome return of fifty cents per day, while my mother followed the occupation of seamstress at the same price, fifty cents a day, doing such work for the Bracketts, Mavericks, Nat Lewis, Dignowity and other citizens here at the time who could afford such luxury.

With such accumulations as they could make above expenses of maintenance, my father acquired a yoke of steers and an old wagon, which he used in hauling hay, cut with a scythe blade, and selling to the government for the use of the soldiers then stationed here. Meantime he bought a lot on Main Avenue, then Acequa Street, for which he paid $50, and erected a log cabin with a tullie roof, and began to live at home. As time went on he began buying cows, and trading with the Indians for hides they brought in, which he sold to Mr. Gilbeau, "the local hide dealer." After accumulating more cows than could be accommodated in the village, he acquired land at the head of the river, where Alamo Heights is now, and went back into the hay business for the government. In 1852 a colony of relations was made up with whom he went down to the Gallinas (Prairie Chicken's Paradise), where he followed the cattle business, remaining there after all the balance of the colony had dispersed except himself and his only neighbor, Simon Rieder; and at which place, the Fest ranch, I was born on the 9th day of May, 1856. He stayed there until 1859, and then moved down on the Atascosa Creek, two miles east of Pleasanton, which is called until yet "The Fest Ranch," where we lived all during the Confederate War, father having become a member of Captain Tom's company of Indian scouts, and remained with it until the war broke up, while we had to get along as best we could in his absence. The family consisted of mother, six children and two orphans father was raising. The children large enough to work, engaged in enlarging the little field father had begun to open up before entering the service, each one doing his bit. The family ran the ranch, cultivated the land, harvested the crops and cared for the livestock, in addition to doing a variety of things for use and comfort that only pioneers know how to do with skill and success. Among those other things were: Burned their own lime, dressed the hides, tanned them with live oak and mesquite bark; while the mother made the shoes for the family and for the neighborhood, made hats of coon skins, and still found time to spin the wool clipped from our own flocks, which was woven into cloth on the neighborhood loom. The cloth was dyed with a weed called "Indigo" that grew in the creek near by and my mother made into clothes for herself and children.

The important matter of food was well looked after, with plenty of meat and field produce there was no need to go hungry. But the things that go with it. Coffee? Yes, we had coffee—made out of corn, acorns and sweet potatoes, while honey was used as a substitute for sugar. With an abundance of milk, cream, butter and eggs, this home-made "Postum" went all right until we renewed acquaintance with real coffee afterwards.

While shelter, food and clothes were thus acquired, we were not lacking in matters of excitement and thrills. In addition to the usual exhilarating experiences of ranch life, there were Indians—lots of them—and they were real savages, who did not stop at stealing or murdering when it suited their purposes to do so. This constituted a real danger that had to be considered, and hence the old men past the age of going into the Civil War, were associated together as "Home Guards," and their duties were to notify all the families in the country of any reported approach of Indians, and the families were disposed of by going into a designated place, where they could be the better protected against the Indians by the guards surrounding their retreat, until all danger had passed.

With this kind of environment, boys naturally learned horseback riding, loved it, and practiced to become skillful "bronco busters" and good shots.

JOHN DOAK, Del Rio, Tex.

TOL McNEIL, Mathis, Tex.

COLEY LYONS,
Pleasanton, Tex.

C. C. LINCECUM,
Waelder, Tex.

After the war my mother became tired of life on the ranch, with its incidents, and father sold much of his stock and moved his family to San Antonio on South Flores Street, where he ran a dairy, at which I worked until I was fifteen years old. Then father made me quit bronco riding and put me in a blacksmith shop, but the repairs on Mexican carts and freight wagons which freighted between here and Mexico, was too hard a job for a boy of my nature, and my liking for the bronco-riding caused me to run away from the shop and go on the trail to Kansas. My first trip was in 1871, leaving San Antonio on the 9th day of March and returning the 8th day of September. When I got back I ran a bunch of men, doing nothing but branding "mavericks" on the Frio and Nueces for a man by the name of Goins. I continued at that until January, 1872, and in February following made a contract with a man by name of Votaw to take a herd to Kansas for him, as boss. Coming back in October of the same year, I went to work for my father again, running stock for him until 1876, in which year (the Centennial) I went North and returned the latter part of 1876. In 1877 I went into the butcher business for myself, afterwards sold out my market and engaged in the mercantile business, in which I continued until 1907, when I sold out and retired.

PHIL L. WRIGHT

Phil L. Wright, fire and police commissioner of the city of San Antonio, was born in Kentucky in 1868, the son of Mr. and Mrs. W. F. Wright, who were Tennesseeans. When only three years of age his parents brought him to Texas, where he attended the public schools until 1884, when he went to West Texas to work on the cow ranch of High Webb, near San Angelo. In the spring of 1885 he went up the trail the first time with a herd of 2,300 head of cattle belonging to Mr. Webb, William Sherman being boss of the outfit. The herd was gathered on the range covering Runnels, Tom Green, Concho and adjoining counties, and started from a point on the Colorado River where the city of Ballinger now

PHIL WRIGHT

stands, and was driven to the Rocky Mountains in the state of Colorado, fifty miles behind Pike's Peak, where the major portion of the cattle were sold to a man by the name of Frost. The remainder of the herd was ranched in the mountains and a man from the outfit by the name of Billy Irwin was left in charge of them.

The route taken by this herd was by way of Abilene, Texas, crossing the Brazos River at Seymour, Pease River at Vernon, Red River at Doan's Store, by way of Comanche Springs and out through the neutral strip known as No Man's Land, crossing the Arkansas River on the Kansas and Colorado line just above the town of Coolidge, Kansas, striking the Union Pacific Railway at Kit Carson, on to Hugo, Colorado, and from Hugo to Colorado Springs, Manitou, through Ute Pass around the foot of Pike's Peak, fifty miles up in the mountains to the Frost ranch.

The Webb ranch was in Runnels County on the Colorado River adjoining the Blocker ranch. The first year he went up the trail John Blocker was delivering herds at Hugo, Colorado, and they drove along the same trail with him and saw hundreds of dead Blocker steers along the route.

After the herd was disposed of Mr. Wright returned

to Texas with other members of the outfit and resumed work on the Webb ranch, working the range for Mr. Webb until he resigned to accept a position on the TS and SOX ranch, which was run by M. L. McAuley, where he worked for about two years, then accepted employment with the Concho Cattle Company, where he worked until the spring of 1881, when he resigned to accept a position with D. E. Simms, who was gathering a herd for the trail.

This herd started on the trail at Paint Rock, Concho County, Bob Pearce being boss of the outfit. It was driven by way of Colorado City, taking the plains at the head of the Brazos River, going by way of Plainview and Canyon, to Amarillo, where the herd was quarantined and shipped from there by rail to Colorado.

Mr. Wright then returned to San Antonio, Texas, where his people resided, and secured employment in the San Antonio fire department, his first position being that of pipeman. His promotions in the department were as follows: Assistant engineer, engineer, lieutenant, captain, first assistant chief, May 1st, 1899, and in the year 1905 was appointed chief of the department. Remained chief until 1911, when he resigned of his own accord. In 1912 he was again made chief of the department and remained chief until June, 1917, when Commissioner Lowther, for political reasons, declined to reappoint him. Mr. Wright was selected commissioner of fire and police June 4th, 1918, holding that position at the present time.

Mr. Wright was married in 1906 to Miss Pearl Morris, who died in February, 1909, leaving a son, Phil L. Wright, Jr., now twelve years of age. He was married again in 1916 to Miss Jewell Mitchell, they having a girl, Alma Ione, three years of age.

REFLECTIONS OF THE TRAIL

By George W. Saunders, San Antonio, Texas

I was born at Rancho, Gonzales County, Texas, February 12th, 1854. My father and mother settled in that county in 1850, coming with several other immigrants in ox wagons from Mississippi. In 1850 they moved to Goliad County and settled twelve miles west of Goliad, on Lost Creek, where father previously selected a place to start a cattle ranch. At that time I was only five years old, but I can remember riding a side saddle belonging to one of my sisters and helping keep up the tail end of the herd part of the time on this trip. At Helena I saw my first white house, and when we crossed the San Antonio River at Wofford I remember how excited we all were when our herd was in the swift water. Part of them floated down below the ford, and it required a great deal of time to get them out at different points for half a mile down the river. Never having seen anything like this before, my mother thought all of the cattle were lost when she saw them going down the stream. In a few days we reached our new home and camped on the site which father had selected, and father and my two oldest brothers, Mat and Bill, assisted by some hired help, began cutting and hauling timber to build houses and stock pens, while myself and brother, Jack, a third brother older than I, range herded the cattle to locate them.

Fish and game were plentiful, deer were constantly in sight of our camp; in fact, that country was in a perfectly wild state. Only a few cattle were on the range, which was as fine as could be found anywhere. In a few months we were comfortably quartered and happy in our new location. Father had taken a herd of cattle on shares from William Rupe, getting every third calf for attending to them, and we all kept busy looking after the

stock. We soon became acquainted with the settlers, with
whom we worked the ranges, and neighbored with them
in every sense of the term. The following families were
among those who lived from five to thirty-five miles from
us: Pettus, Hodges, Word, Peck, Reynolds, Meyers,
Lott, Burris, Rutledge, Best, Fant, Rupe, Choate, Borroum, Butler, McKinney, New, Rawlings, Henderson,
Paschal and others. This being before the days of the
chuck wagon, the men would set a date and place to
meet for what we called a "cow hunt." Each man would
bring bedding, coffee pot, tin cup, a wallet of biscuit, salt,
sometimes sugar, four or five horses each, and we would
work the surrounding range until all cattle belonging to
the outfit were gathered and held under herd, then we
would select a pack horse for our equipment and move
to some other part of the range, gathering cattle as we
went. When grub got scarce we would send after more
supplies to some nearby ranch. Usually it required from
ten to fifteen days to make these trips, then each man
would take his cattle home, put all the calves in a pen
in order to locate the mother cows, and range herd the
dry cattle for a few days and locate them. We were
prosperous and happy until the Civil War started, and
father and my oldest brother entered the service the first
year, and another brother enlisted the second year, which
left brother Jack and myself to take care of our stock
with the assistance of a few old men and some negroes.

We worked the range constantly during the war.
The range was full of wild mustang horses, and they
caused us a lot of trouble, for we had to keep our horse
stock from getting with them, for once they got mixed
with the mustangs they soon became as wild or wilder
than these wild horses. In order to capture or kill these
mustangs the stockmen built pens around water holes
and prepared traps to ensnare them. To these pens
wings would be constructed in the shape of a V, forming
a chute through which the mustangs would be compelled

to go to water. Once a bunch of mustangs passed through
the chute to the water hole the gate would be shut by a
watchman, who had lain in wait in concealment for the
horses, and the animals were securely snared. They
would then be forced into a small, well-built enclosure
constructed of rails to a height of eight or ten feet, where
they were roped and made gentle. These animals were
of Spanish origin and were noted for their endurance on
the range and trail. The settlers used various unique
methods of capturing them, one way being to walk them
down. Some men would take three or four days' supply
of provisions, start a bunch of mustangs, follow them as
closely as possible, and when they got out of sight of the
pursuer would pick up their trail, keep right after them,
never giving them time to eat or rest day or night.
Usually on the second day of the chase he could get
closer to them; the third or fourth day he could drive
them in home with a bunch of gentle horses and easily
pen them. They were caught in many different ways and
oftentimes shot in order to rid the range of their presence. Before long they disappeared entirely. Our cattle
increased to such proportions with new herds coming
into our country from East Texas and Louisiana that by
the time the war ended our range was overstocked. We
sold a few cattle to the government and a few to Mexican
freighters for work oxen.

I shall never forget the first stampede I experienced.
George Bell, who was exempt from military service on
account of one eye being blind, agreed to take a herd of
beeves to Mexico and exchange for supplies for the war
widows. The neighbors got together about two hundred
of these beeves, my mother putting in twenty head. We
delivered the herd to Mr. Bell at the Pettus ranch where
Pettus Station now stands. This was in 1864, when I was
ten years old. We put our cattle in the herd and brother
Jack and I agreed to help hold them. That night shortly
after dark something scared the beeves and they made a

run. I had never heard anything like the rumbling noise they made, but I put spurs to my horse and followed the noise. We ran those cattle all night and at daybreak we found we had not lost a beef, but we had five or six bunches four or five miles apart, and two or three men or boys with each bunch. We soon had them all together and Mr. Bell started them on the trip. When he returned from Mexico he brought us one sack of coffee, two sets of knives and forks, two pairs of spurs, two bridle bits, and two fancy "hackamores," or bridle headstalls, for which he had traded our twenty beeves, and we were well pleased with our deal, for in those days such things were considered luxuries, and we were glad to get them, particularly the knives and forks, for we had been drinking bran coffee and were using wooden knives and forks we had made ourselves. Those were hard times in Goliad County during the Civil War, and when the internecine strife ended the soldiers came home broke and all anxious to make up the time that had been lost during the four years that had passed. Reconstruction set in. Some outlaws and crooks drifted into our country; considerable friction and hatred existed between the boys of the blue and the gray; negro soldiers were stationed at different points to keep order, but it soon resulted in serious clashes that called for more Texas Rangers and United States marshals. As is usually the case, right and justice finally prevailed. During this time our stockmen were hunting markets for the cattle on our over-stocked ranges. We sold a few steers to Foster & Allen, Shanghai Pierce and Joel Collins, which were shipped from Powder Horn. Slaughter houses at Rockport killed considerable beeves at the time, but we needed a greater outlet for the ever-increasing herds on the ranges.

My father drove a herd from Goliad to New Orleans in 1867, swam all the streams, and bayous, and through the exposure he contracted rheumatism from which he suffered until his death, which occurred at Saunders'

Station, near San Antonio, in 1904. Mother died at the same place in 1893. Father was born at Fayetteville, North Carolina, and mother was born at Birmingham, Alabama. Besides the brothers I have mentioned elsewhere in this sketch, I have three sisters living, Mrs. F. L. Henry, wife of a prominent McMullen County stockman, and Misses Nancy and Ann Saunders, all of whom live near Christine, Texas.

In 1868 or 1869 a few stockmen drove small herds to Baxter Springs, Kansas, or other northern points, and met with such success that everybody had caught the trail fever. My two brothers, Mat and Jack, took a herd to Baxter Springs in 1870, and their reports of thrilling encounters with the Indians, stampedes, buffalo chases, and the like, filled me with a wild desire to go on the trail, too. I was barely seventeen years old, and felt that I was able to take care of myself on a long trip as well as any man. My parents finally consented for me to go, and I hired to Monroe Choate, of the firm of Choate & Bennett, to go with a herd. The firm was receiving herds in different parts of the country to send up the trail. They sent fourteen herds that year. Mr. Choate told me the name of the boss of each herd and asked me which boss I would rather go with. I told him I wanted to go with the first herd that started, and he informed me that Jim Byler would boss the first herd and would start at once. That suited me fine, so I said, "Put me with Byler." Mr. Byler was asked what he thought about taking a seventeen-year-old kid on the trip and remarked, "His age is all right, if he has staying qualities, but most kids are short on sleep, and generally sleep on watch." I told him I would not sleep during stampedes or Indian fights, and he promised to give me a trial, and that made me exceedingly happy.

We left Helena with a full chuck wagon, the necessary number of horses and men, and went to the Mays pasture on the Cibolo near Stockdale, Wilson County, and received a thousand steers. Dunk Choate counted the cattle and Mr. Byler pointed the herd north and Dunk said, "Adios, boys, I will see you in Abilene, Kansas, I must go now and start other herds."

We went by Gonzales, Lockhart, Austin and Georgetown, without any unusual happenings, but on the Gabriel we had a bad stampede during a thunderstorm, and the herd was split up into several bunches. They were all found the next day. Some of the bunches had men with them and some did not. They were all trailed and found except me and seventy-five steers. By ten o'clock the boss finally located the trail of my bunch and found it ten miles down the Gabriel. When he rode up he asked, "Are you awake? Why didn't you bring these cattle back to the herd?" I said I could not find the trail the steers made, and I did not know what direction to go to find the herd. We got back to the main herd about four o'clock in the evening, and I was so tired and sleepy I told the boss I was just bound to eat and sleep a little. He said, "Go eat and sleep all night; I will herd your relief. You deserve a rest." This sounded good to me, for up to this time I thought the boss was mad.

After a good night's rest I was on the job early the next morning, ready to do my share in keeping the herd on the move. The cattle were easily scared and for several days were very nervous and made many runs, but the boys kept strict watch on them, and they finally became reconciled. We went by Waco, Cleburne and Fort Worth. Between the last named places the country was somewhat level and untimbered, and was full of prairie chickens and deer. When we reached Fort Worth we crossed the Trinity River under the bluff, where the present street car line to the stock yards crosses the river. Fort Worth was then but a very small place, consisting of only a few stores, and there was only one house in that part of the town, where the stock yards are now located. We held our herd here two days, finally proceeding on our journey, and crossed Red River at Red River Station and took the Chisholm Trail through the Indian Territory. Here we saw lots of Indians, who came to our herd with the usual greeting, "How, John," to beg tobacco and provisions. Byler got by these Indians without any trouble, but we found all the streams in that region up and had to swim them or lose time, for Byler wanted to keep the lead, and we therefore crossed many rivers at a time when other men would have hesitated.

At Pond Creek we encountered our first buffalo. The plains were literally covered with these animals, and when we came in sight of them all of the boys quit the herd and gave chase. It was a wonderful sight to see these cowboys dashing after those big husky monsters, shooting at them from all angles. We soon learned that it did no good to shoot them in the forehead, as we were accustomed to shooting beeves with our pistols, for the bullets would not penetrate their skull. We would dash by them and shoot them between the eyes without apparent effect, so we began shooting them behind the shoulder and that brought them down. I killed two or three of the grown buffaloes and roped a yearling which I was glad to turn loose and let him get away with a good rope. I soon became satisfied with the excitement incident to killing buffalo, swimming streams, being in stampedes, and passing through thunderstorms, but I still longed to be mixed up in an Indian fight, for I had not yet had that sort of experience.

We crossed Bluff Creek into Kansas and passed Newton during the latter part of May. A blacksmith shop, a store, and about a dozen dwellings made up this town at the time, but when we came back through the place on our return home thirty days later, it had grown to be quite a large town, due to the building of a railroad. It did not seem possible that a town could make such quick growth in such short time, but Newton, Kansas, sprang up almost over night.

We stopped our herd on Holland Creek, twenty miles from Abilene, Kansas, where we were met by Pink Bennett and a buyer. Pink sold 300 fat beeves out of our herd to this man, and I went to Abilene with them to help load them on the cars. They were the first cattle I had ever seen loaded on a train, and I was anxious to see how it was done.

We held our herd there until several more herds belonging to Choate & Bennett arrived. They sold some out of each herd, and we soon had a surplus of men and horses. W. G. Butler had done likewise and he also had too many men and horses to continue on with the cattle, so it was arranged that some of us could start home, and accordingly about fifty men, with five chuck wagons, five cooks and about 150 horses, hit the back trail for Texas. We had a lively time en route home, for we had nothing to do but drive the horses, make camp, eat and sometimes sleep. When we reached the Washita River we found it out of its banks. We cut timber and made a raft by tying the logs with ropes, but could not ferry the rude craft until a rope had been stretched across the river, which was some 300 yards wide and very swift and deep. Several of the boys attempted to make it across with the end of a rope, but each one failed. Some of them got half way across, turned the rope loose and swam back. One of them got near the opposite bank, but lost the end of the rope and landed without it. I was the fifth one to try this difficult feat, and determined to succeed, so taking one end of the rope in my mouth, passing it over my shoulder, I entered the water, the boys on the bank releasing the rope gradually as I swam out, and I made it across, but grasped an overhanging willow limb and pulled myself ashore with the rope still in my mouth. The man who had preceded me across came to my assistance and helped me up the slippery bank, then there was a cowboy yell of approval from the other side as the boys realized that I had succeeded in accomplishing a dangerous feat. I felt very proud of myself, and think I added several inches to my stature right there, for I was only seventeen years old, and had succeeded in an undertaking in which four stalwart men had failed, but I am willing to confess I could not have gone ten feet further in my exhausted condition.

We soon put our outfits across with the raft, but lost the hind wheels of one of Butler's wagons. We carried the wagon beds over on the raft, but pulled the wagons across with ropes, for we had to draw the wagons and effects up a steep, slippery embankment, and this required a great deal of time, patience and profanity. When we got everything across, we rigged up our outfit and resumed our journey. I know of only three men living today who were on this trip back to Texas, they being Ben Bourroum, now of Del Rio, Texas; Louis Massengale and Jess Little, who live somewhere in South Texas.

We crossed Red River opposite Denison, rode into town and visited all of the stores and saloons. The people there were glad to see us come and glad to see us leave. Our next town was Denton, where the officers demanded our pistols. The law prohibiting the carrying of pistols had been enacted only a short time before and was then in effect, but we could not think of parting with our lifelong friends, so when a demand was made for us to surrender them we pulled our pistols and rode out of town shooting into the air. The officers did not follow us.

We stopped at Fort Worth and all the other towns on our route, as we leisurely traveled homeward, finally reaching our destination safely. I was mighty proud of this, my first trip, and reached home with a pair of shop-made boots and two good suits of clothes, one of which was a black changeable velvet affair that I had paid fifty dollars for in Kansas. I carried these clothes in a pair of saddle bags all the way home, and found after I reached there that I could have purchased them cheaper from a local merchant. But little did I care, for I was determined to "cut a shine" with the girls when I got back off that notable trip.

Referring back to some of the incidents that occurred on the trip, I can recall several amusing things that happened. The prairies near Abilene, Kansas, where we held our herds, were partly taken up by grangers, who lived in dugouts, a square hole in the ground, or on the side of a bluff, with timbers placed across and covered with dirt. Each granger had taken up about 160 acres of land, part of which was cultivated. They had no fences, so to mark the boundaries of their homesteads, they would plow a furrow around it. As there was no timber in the country, except a few cottonwoods which grew along the streams, the grangers were compelled to use buffalo chips for fuel. While we were there with our herds many other herds came in and the whole prairie was covered with cattle for many miles around. I visited lots of camps and met many old friends from Texas. Buyers were plentiful, cattle sold fast, and the grangers were active among the herds asking the cattlemen to bed cattle on their lands so they could get the chips for fuel. One evening I noticed several men and women in buggies and buckboards going to different herds and begging each boss to bed his herd on their respective lands. They soon got into a "squabble" with each other, claiming they had asked a certain boss first, and this caused the cowboys to congregate around to see the fun and encourage the row. Levi Anderson was the boss in question, and they all claimed he had promised to bed cattle on their land. Levi was puzzled, for he was not used to the customs of the country, and said the reason he had promised was because he thought they were all joking. He said those dugout people were somewhat different from the folks where he lived, remarking that "Down in Texas, if you gave a man dry dung he would fight you,

but here in Kansas they will fight you for dry dung.''
The grangers figured that 1,000 cattle would leave enough
chips on the ground in one night to give them 500 pounds
of fuel in a few days.

Ben Borroum and I were herding together one day,
and as all of the cattle were in sight, we did not notice
that they had gotten on a small patch of corn just coming
up, until they had pawed and trampled the corn, crushing
twenty little chickens to death, and ran all of the family
into the dugout. This negligence on our part cost Choate
& Bennett about $100.

Jack Potter once told me that while he was up in this
part of Kansas he got lost from his outfit one night and
rode up to one of these dugouts and asked if he could
stop with them until morning. The granger told him he
was welcome to do so, although their accommodations
were very limited. They fed his horse for him and then
invited him down into the dugout, which contained one
room about sixteen feet square, but as neat as could be.
In this room there was a nice clean bed, one table, four
chairs, a stove, cooking utensils, the man, his wife and
two small boys. The wife soon prepared a good supper
for Jack, and after he had eaten they sat up and talked
to him for quite a while, during which time the little boys
fell asleep on the bed, while the parents, who seemed
to be a very intelligent couple, told Jack about themselves and their plans. They were enthusiastic over
the prospects to make a fortune in that new country, and
talked about everything in general, but all this time Jack
was puzzling his brain over how all of them were going
to sleep on the one bed in that dugout. Finally the
mother picked up the two boys and sat them over in a
corner, leaning them against the wall still asleep, and
then she informed Jack that he could occupy the bed and
she and her husband went up the steps. Potter turned
in and was soon asleep, and slept soundly all night long,
but when he awoke the next morning he found himself

sitting in the corner with the two little boys and the man and woman were occupying the bed. Jack told me he knew that couple was just bound to prosper anywhere, even in Kansas. After breakfast he gave them five dollars, but they protested, saying that fifty cents was enough to pay for the poor accommodations he had received, but Jack informed them that what he had seen and learned right there was worth five dollars to him. Remember this was Jack Potter, not Jim Wilson.

I passed through this same old herding ground some twenty-five years later, and I was astonished to see the changes that had taken place. Pretty farms and new dwellings covered the whole region, and there were fine herds of good cattle, horses, sheep, mules and hogs everywhere, and the whole country looked prosperous.

After I reached home from my first trip I went to work on the range driving cattle to Rockport packeries in summer and winter and putting up trail herds each spring, following this occupation for several years, selling our family's cattle to the well-known trail drivers, J. D. Reed, Dillard Fant and others. Cattle accumulated fast on the ranges. Many ranches were established, each ranch owner running his own outfit and exchanging brands with stockmen in different parts of the state. The ranchmen would brand calves and sell beeves for each other, then meet and make settlement once a year. Such arrangements were made between stockmen from San Antonio to Brownsville and from Victoria to Laredo. It was nothing strange for one man to own cattle throughout the above-mentioned territory. The cattle business gradually moved westward, forcing the redskins back; many of our stockmen began buying pure-bred bulls and improving their stock. Among those who first began to grade up their cattle were King & Kenedy, Reynolds, Coleman, Matthis & Fulton, W. A. Pettus, N. G. Collins and others. The chuck wallet and pack horse disappeared and their places were taken by the chuck wagon.

Fences came and the open range passed away forever.

During those days I belonged to Uncle Henry Scott's Minute Company for two years. This company was organized at Mission Refugio in 1873 to protect the citizens of the border against Mexican bandits. During these two years a number of massacres were committed by these bandits, many of whom paid the penalty for their lawlessness. Among the families which were murdered by the Mexicans were the Swift family near Refugio, John Maden, near St. Mary's, the Nux family and others at Nux Store, twelve miles west of Corpus Christi; Lee Rabb, the Penescal family and others whose names I cannot recall. When our company was called out for duty we went at a moment's notice, regardless of what we were doing or where we were, and we rode with such vengeance that our company soon became a terror to the invading murderous Mexicans.

For one year I was a deputy under Sheriff James Burk of Goliad, during which time I had some narrow escapes and made some dangerous arrests of desperate characters.

For a few years after the war there was a woman in that region by the name of Sally Skull, who was quite a character. She traded horses through our country, and operated alone, with a band of Mexican helpers, from Texas into Mexico, and had a record of being the most fearless woman ever known. Nearly all of the old citizens of that section remember Sally Skull.

In those early days cattle buyers usually met the sellers at some appointed place to close a deal for stock, and they would bring the purchase money in gold and silver in sacks on the backs of pack horses. When they reached the meeting places the sacks of money would be carelessly dumped on the ground where sometimes it would remain for two or three days without molestation, then when the settlement was made for cattle bought the sacks were opened, the money dumped out on a blanket

in camp and counted out to each man who had participated in the trades. I fear that kind of an arrangement
would not work today, but in those days those rugged
pioneers dealt strictly on the square.

Pasture fencing commenced on the coast in 1872–3,
and in a few years each cattleman had a pasture of
from 1,000 to 50,000 acres, which stopped the exchanging of brands, for before a great while every man had
his cattle in his own pasture and ran his own cow outfit.
Space will not permit mention of the cattle stealing,
fence-cutting, trouble between cattlemen and others,
which called for the assistance of Texas Rangers and
United States Marshals, with whose aid the cattlemen
established law and order. With the organization of
the Cattle Raisers' Association a few years later the
doom of the cattle and horse thief was sealed, for the organization soon grew to such proportions, with its expert
inspectors at all markets and shipping points, that it
made it almost impossible for a thief to exist.

In 1874 I was married to Miss Rachel Reeves, who
was the daughter of W. M. Reeves, a well-known stockman of Refugio County. We began housekeeping on my
ranch, eight miles from Goliad, where the present railroad station, Clip, is now located. I later sold this ranch
to W. A. Pettus (better known as Buck Pettus), one of
the most prosperous stockmen of Goliad County, and
years later, when the railroad was built from Beeville to
Goliad, it went across my old ranch and the station was
named Clip, in honor of Mrs. Pettus, whose maiden name
was Miss Clip Lott.

In 1880 my wife's health failed and I took her to San
Antonio for treatment, and as I had to be near her, I
could not follow my work as a stockman, so decided to
get into some line of business in San Antonio to make a
living in the big city. I finally bought several hacks and
teams and ran them day and night, carrying passengers
over the city. The I. & G. N. and the S. P. Railroads were

just building into San Antonio, the city was flourishing
and full of prospectors and stockmen. As I was acquainted with many of the visitors, mostly stockmen, I
did a thriving business.

My wife died in January, 1883, and the following
March I sold out my business, carried my two little girls
to the home of my parents in Goliad, then returned to
San Antonio and bought 300 Spanish mares, which I
shipped to Vinita, Indian Territory, and drove them
through Eastern Kansas, selling a few and paying fines
for damage they did to unfenced fields along the way. I
shipped from Springfield to Hannibal, Mo., where I decided to try to dispose of all of these mares. At this
place I advertised ''Wild Texas Ponies for Sale at William L. Fry's Stables, with an Exhibition of Roping and
Riding Wild Horses.'' I put my stock in a large lot
adjoining the stable on the morning of the sale, and
everybody in the town was there to see them, all anxious
to witness the bronco busting. I mounted a dry goods
box and announced that these horses were for sale and
invited buyers to come forward and select the mares they
wanted, and in order to hold the crowd, I told them the
bronco riding would be the last act of the show, but that
they would not be disappointed. Quite a number bought
horses, and as each animal was sold two of my expert
cowboys would lasso it and hold it by the jaws and ears
until a hackamore was securely placed on its head, then
it was led through a gate and delivered to the buyer,
who in turn employed negroes to take it home for him.
We kept this up all morning, when word was passed
around that all of the horses that had been sold were running loose in the town and surrounding country with
ropes dragging. It seems that the negroes who had
undertaken to lead the horses away, in each instance did
not understand how to handle these broncos, and they
would get away. One negro said it would take a long
time to learn the nature of such horses, for they would

lay down and kick and paw all of the rope around their bodies and legs and leave him nothing to hold to, and he just had to let go the rope. The buyers were good natured and did not blame me in the least. I sold fifty head of the mares here at good prices, and when the buying slacked up, I roped an outlaw horse, saddled him Wild West fashion, and Anderson Moreland, one of my cowboys, mounted him. This horse was a professional and on that occasion he did full credit to his past reputation, to the great delight and enthusiasm of the crowd of spectators. When we drove our herd out of town several of the citizens went with us for several miles. From here we drove them to Pittsfield, Illinois, selling and trading as we went, finally disposing of all of our Texas horses, but we still had about twenty large native horses that we had taken in exchange. We shipped these by boat down the Mississippi River to St. Louis. This was our first boatride, and was greatly enjoyed by myself and my companions. We sold out at St. Louis and came home by train.

After returning to Texas I bought 150 saddle horses, or cow ponies, and shipped them to Wichita Falls, then the terminus of the Fort Worth & Denver Railroad. From this point we drove them to Atascosa, on the Canadian River above the LIT ranch, where I sold them to Will Hughes at a big profit. After the sale was made we went to the ranch house together, and there I discovered that Hughes and I were boys together at Goliad, but his Goliad name was not Hughes.

When I returned to San Antonio, Harry Fawcett and myself bought the Narcisso Leal livestock commission business, with offices and stables opposite the Southern Hotel on Dolorosa Street. We put up our sign in September, 1883, and our business thrived from the very start. We sold horses by thousands on commission for parties who drove to the San Antonio market from South Texas and Mexico. During the fall and winter we bought

considerable horse stock ourselves, which we sent to the
Bluntzer pasture near San Patricio and also to the Tobey
pasture in Atascosa County, expecting to sell them the
next spring to trail drivers. Not being able to get as
much for them as we thought they were worth, we decided to drive these horses up the trail ourselves, so we
sold our commission business back to Leal, gathered our
horses, brought them to San Antonio and for several
days held them on Prospect Hill, which is now in the city
limits. On April 5th, 1884, we loaded our chuck wagon
and hit the trail for Dodge City, Kansas. We went by
Kerrville and Junction City, following what was then
known as the Upper or Western Trail. At Seymour we
crossed the Brazos, and at Doan's Store we crossed Red
River. I will not attempt to describe the trouble we had
on this trip with Indians, stampedes and swollen streams,
as other sketches in this book have treated those subjects
with full justice. There were many herds on the trail
that year, and we wanted to keep in the lead, but to do
so required systematic work, so I kept my herd moving
forward all the time. I would go on ahead and select
herding ground for nights and grazing grounds for nooning, grazed the horses up to these grounds and grazed
or drove them off, never allowing them to graze back
at all, for in this way I gained a great deal of valuable
time, for I had learned that good time and lots of it was
lost by the old way of stopping a herd and allowing it to
graze in every direction, sometimes a mile or more on the
back trail. In such cases the stock would travel over the
same ground twice, which, in the long run, would amount
to considerable mileage when you consider that the distance from Texas to the markets was from 1,000 to 1,500
miles. Good trail bosses who made quick time with stock
in good shape were always in demand. Ab Blocker,
Gus Black, Mac Stewart, Fayette Butler, Pleas Butler,
Jim Byler, Sim Holstein, Henry Clair, Jones Glenn, Jesse
McCoy, Bob Jennings and Bob Lauterday were all

record-breakers in taking herds through in quick time
and fine shape, but Ab Blocker claims the blue ribbon.

We reached Dodge City minus a few horses which
were lost on the trail, but they were brought up by other
herds and delivered to me at this point. One night while
we were there a storm came up and caused several herds
to stampede, and there were about 15,000 horses mixed
up. Two men were killed by lightning that night. It
took several days to gather and separate the horses.
Several outfits from different parts of Texas gave the
same road brand and this caused no end of trouble. Mr.
Fawcett, my partner, had come up to Dodge City by
train, and was present during the big stampede, which
he thought was great sport. He said he would buy the
leaders if we could pick them out, as he wanted to ship
them to England to show the chaps over there what a running horse was like, and if he could ever get the blooming
rascals gentle he would run foxes on them.

Just before we started this herd up the trail Harry
Hotchkiss, who is now manager for the Houston Packing
Company, arrived in San Antonio from England and
helped us to get our herd together. Harry was an old
friend to Mr. Fawcett and was so delighted with the
prospect of getting into the horse business that he bought
100 head and put them into our herd. He made a good
hand from the very start and was of great assistance to
me on the trail. We had told him we expected to make
$15 to $20 per head profit on our horses when we sold
them up the trail, and he was looking forward to making
a neat sum on his investment. One night while we were
camped in a rough region between the Saline and the
San Saba River, west of Maberry's pasture, our herd
stampeded, during a storm. I had told the boys on first
relief not to attempt to hold the herd if they stampeded,
as the country was too broken and that I would rather
trail the horses the next day than to take any chances of
some of my men getting killed. The boys all came to

camp and at daybreak the next morning we were all ready to start cutting sign. In a few hours we rounded up most of them, while Hotchkiss was holding the herd and counting his horses as they came in in each bunch. I brought in several bunches, and each time Hotchkiss would come to me and want to know if I thought he would ever get all of his horses back. I would tell him I did not have time to talk to him, for I was in a hurry to go after other bunches. The herd was pretty badly scattered, and had left plain trails in every direction. Some were followed for ten or fifteen miles before they were overtaken and brought back. This required fast work by all of us, for we had to gather them before they could mix with other range horses and be lost entirely. I brought a bunch into the herd about two o'clock and found we were still about 200 head short. Hotchkiss rushed up and commanded me to stop and explain to him how I could figure $15 or $20 per head profit for him on his horses when half of them were gone on the first ten days out, adding that it was a ''blawsted rotten misrepresentation,'' and that Fawcett and I must make it good. I told him not to worry, that we would get them all back, and as I left him he was cussing and cavorting around in great fashion; in truth he was about the maddest man I ever saw. In a little while I met some of the boys with about twenty of Hotchkiss' horses in the bunch they were bringing in, and I told them to assure him that he would get all of them back before night, for he was in great suspense and needed consolation. By 5 o'clock that evening we had recovered all of our horses and Hotchkiss was a happy boy. Ten men riding at full speed all day, changing horses each time they brought in a bunch, accomplished a wonderful work that day.

We had another Englishman in our outfit on that trip who was also a tenderfoot and fresh from England. His name was Lambert and he had begged to be permitted to go with us, agreeing to furnish four horses and help us free of charge, as he wanted to learn to be a bronco buster. He was game and would undertake anything he was told to do. He insisted that he be allowed to do night herding, and when given the work, went to sleep, his horse drifted into the herd and he fell off, causing a stampede. After that I set him free to go and come as he pleased. He would visit other herds in front and behind us, getting all the news, so we called him our reporter. My Mexican hands were riding wild horses when in open country and during good weather. Lambert begged me constantly to let him ride a bucking horse, so one day at noon, while we were camped in a beautiful prairie country, I had the boys to rope the worst bucking horse in the herd, saddle him, tie the stirrups, and fix a roll in front of the saddle. Then I mounted a well-trained horse, took firm hold on the rope attached to the bronco's hackamore, while Lambert was assisted to get on. As soon as all was ready I gave the bucker slack enough to get his head down. Lambert was eager to show what he thought he could do, and said to the horse, "Gaddup, old Chap, I've rode worse 'orses than you." But "old Chap" did not move, just stood there all humped up. I told Lambert to hit him over the head with his hat, as the other boys did bucking horses. He took his big hat in his hand, reached forward and brought it down between the horse's ears. At that same instant the horse and the Englishman went straight up in the air with their heads toward the north, turned in the air and came down with their heads toward the south. Lambert quit the horse and hit the ground running, yelling, " 'Old the blooming rascal. 'E made such peculiar movements I lost my balance." The boys who had bet on Lambert riding the horse, raised their bets, Bill Williams betting two to one on the Englishman; so he tried it again. That horse threw Lambert five times before he gave it up, and said if the horse had a straight back he could ride him, but his back was too crooked for him to stay on.

Lambert pulled off a lot of stunts for our amusement on the trip, but decided that bronco busting was too hard to learn. One day he accidentally roped a wild mare with a rope that was tied around the neck of a little mule he was riding. The mare dashed through the herd and caused a stampede. Some of the horses ran across the rope and threw mare, mule and Englishman all to the ground. When the dust cleared Lambert was found holding the mule by the tail while the mule held the mare, until the boys roped her and removed Lambert's rope.

Lambert was the possessor of a red saddle blanket, and when we were in the Comanche country the Indians got friendly with our outfit and made signs that they wanted that red blanket. Tel Hawkins and some of the other boys told the Indians to take it, and when they began to pull it from under Lambert's saddle he pulled his pistol and I rushed up just in the nick of time to prevent bloodshed, for Lambert meant business.

While the boys were trading and hurrahing with the Indians I went to the old Comanche chief's tepee and had quite an enjoyable conversation with him. He told me he knew all of the region in South and Southwest Texas, and named many of the streams, and told of raids he had made down there. He also said he knew Creed Taylor, Captain John Sansom, John R. Baylor, Bigfoot Wallace, and other citizens of that section, who, he said, were "Heap bad mans. Killie heap Indians," and indicated that his warriors always dreaded to meet these well-known characters, for they always "shot to kill."

In July, 1884, I bought two cars of saddle horses and a chuck wagon and shipped them from San Antonio to Alpine, where I received a herd of cattle for Keeney, Wiley & Hurst, which they had bought from Millett & Lane. John Kokernot delivered this herd to me and I took them to Seven Rivers, New Mexico, via Saragosa, Pecos City and up the Pecos to Seven Rivers, where I turned them over to Mr. Keeney. It was a long, dry drive, and I was glad when through with it. After delivering this herd I went to Tat Huling's ranch in Rattlesnake Canyon, 35 miles west of Van Horn, in El Paso County, and remained there two months helping Huling do ranch work and prospecting for gold in the Delaware and Guadalupe Mountains with an old miner named Dyer, who claimed that Indians had told him where he could find a rich mine near an old Indian camp. While prospecting we camped at a spring where the Urcery boys of Oakville, Texas, later established a cattle ranch. We searched through the Delaware Mountains, going up into the Guadalupes, and came back by the salt lakes. These lakes cover a territory fifteen miles long and two or three miles wide with salt three to seven feet deep.

By appointment I met N. H. Hall at Toyah in October. He was in quarantine there with several thousand head of cattle, and was anxious to get a thousand two-year-old heifers to his ranch in Luna Valley, Arizona, for spring breeding. Mr. Hall offered me extra big wages to take them through, and as I had previously promised to make the trip for him, I consented to start as soon as the herd could be made ready. The weather was getting cold, and the route was through a dangerous region occupied by old Geronimo's band of Apaches, and I knew that I would have a hard trip, but I picked 1,000 of the best heifers in the best condition, selected the best horses and secured the best men I could find, all well armed, and pulled out with the herd, going by Cottonwood ranch, the Gran Tinnon ranch, passed the head of Delaware River, Guadalupe Peak, and stopped several days at Crow Springs, just over the line in New Mexico, to prepare for a 107-mile dry drive to the waters of the Sacramento River. When I started the herd from Crow Springs I left my horses there until the next morning, so as to have fresh mounts when they overtook us the second day, then we sent the horses on to water thirty miles up the Sacramento. From the mouth of the Sacramento the channel

of the river was a dry bed of gravel for 30 miles with
great bluffs on either side hundreds of feet high. The
herd strung out up this canyon for several miles and we
pushed forward as rapidly as possible. When we reached
the water I turned the cattle up the steep mountain side
as fast as they arrived and got their fill. It was ten hours
from the time the lead cattle reached the water until the
tail end got there. They were in very poor condition and
a pitiful sight to see, with their sunken eyes, and some
of them barely able to creep along. There was no grass
in the canyon, but we found good grass and water on
the mountains and range herded them several days, then
put them back in the canyon several miles above and
followed it up to the divide, where we crossed over to
Dog Canyon. On this divide I saw my first wild elk, and
some of the tallest pine trees I had ever seen. Dog Canyon was very steep and we had to lock all the wagon
wheels to pass many places. At the mouth of Dog Canyon our route was around White Mountain, and in this
region was where old Geronimo was depredating. We
often saw the signal fires of the Indians at night, and in
order to play safe we would bed our herd in the evening,
eat supper before dark, then take our horses and wagon
and camp a mile or more away from the herd so the
Indians would not find us if they attacked the herd. No
fire was built at those camps to guide the redskins. Next
day we would round up the herd and move on. We were
not attacked and I suppose it was because our cattle and
horses were in such poor condition the Indians did not
care for them; and, further, they were not seeking a fight
with a bunch of Texas cowboys. We went by Tularosa
and La Luz, across the Melphia at the government crossing, and crossed the Rio Grande at San Marcial, proceeding on to Magdalena, where I was taken seriously ill. Mr.
Hall met us here and took the herd on to Luna Valley, Arizona. Remarkable as it may seem, I lost only five head of
these cattle on the entire trip, which were bogged in a

marsh at La Luz. At this marsh we had considerable difficulty in pulling out about fifty herd that were bogged,
but we could not save the five head mentioned above.

The trip was made in cold weather, part of the time
freezing temperatures prevailed, and we suffered a great
deal from the cold and exposure.

This made the third herd, or trip, I had taken that
year, which was a record-breaker, and I decided to re-
cuperate, so I went to Socorro, N. M., reaching there the
20th of December, 1884, and after spending a while there
I went to El Paso, and found employment with the Newman & Davis outfit, which was working in Chihuahua,
Mexico, just across from the mouth of Van Horn Canyon.
I was over there during the Cutting trouble, and helped
to get many cattle across into Texas before the threatened confiscation occurred.

In the spring of 1886 I returned to San Antonio, and
again went into the livestock commission business under
the firm name of Smith, Oliver & Saunders, being associated with Frank Oliver, now of Victoria, and Capt.
Bill Smith, one of San Antonio's most respected citizens,
who is now deceased. I finally sold my interest in this
firm to Jace Addington and bought the cattle end of the
business, and going it alone with offices at the Sap stockyards near the Sap depot on the Hickman property, later
purchasing the Weller stockyards on Medina Street, and
was successful in building a good business. Afterward
Dr. Graves, Captain Lytle, Jess Presnall, John Price,
W. H. Jennings and myself formed a company and built
the Union Stock Yards. I sold my yards on Medina
Street and moved to the present location thirty-one years
ago, and have continued right here ever since. I am the
oldest livestock commission man in the state today who
is still actively engaged in the business. I incorporated
my business fifteen years ago, sold shares to leading
stockmen all over the country, and today I am the president and general manager of the firm, which is known as

the George W. Saunders Live Stock Commission Company, with offices at San Antonio and Fort Worth. The Fort Worth branch is managed by my son-in-law, W. E. Jary. We enjoy a liberal patronage from all parts of Texas, New Mexico, Oklahoma, Louisiana and Old Mexico, and do a gross business of between five and six million dollars annually.

Besides actively giving my attention to my commission business, I supervise the management of four small ranches and a 700-acre farm. I have always tried to follow the policies of my father and deal justly and fairly with all men, but considering the bad influences that many times engulfed me, the many temptations to deal unfairly, and the glowing prospects to greatly profit by yielding to them, it required an iron will and determination to resist, hence I feel proud that my record is not worse. I have made money in almost every undertaking, but my sympathy for suffering humanity, and my liberality in dealing has kept me from accumulating a fortune. I believe that ninety-five per cent of the people who know me are my friends, and I value them more than the millions of gold which perhaps I could have accumulated by sacrificing their friendship by unfair dealing. I have always been willing to give to charity or any laudable purpose that had for its object the uplift of my fellow man, and have always lent aid and encouragement to every undertaking that was for the upbuilding of our state and my home city, San Antonio. I served two terms as alderman of Ward 2 in San Antonio during the Clinton Brown administration, during which time we voted $3,500,000 city bonds, had them approved and sold and spent the money in municipal improvements, building sewers, widening streets and paving thoroughfares, making a modern city of the old Mexican town. During the World War I served as chairman of the Exemption Board, Division No. 1, free of charge, and did all I could to help win the war.

My two daughters by my first marriage are now Mrs. W. E. Jary of Fort Worth and Mrs. T. M. Webb of Palestine. On January 1, 1889, I was married to Miss Ida Friedrich of San Antonio. Of this union we have one daughter, Mrs. C. D. Cannon of San Antonio.

I have seen and participated in many unpleasant things during my sixty years of active life, but I think they are best forgotten. I do not think it would be amiss, however, to mention some of the hardships and examples of self-denial endured by the people of the early days. During the Civil War our family and all of our neighbors were compelled to make almost everything they used or wore; all ropes were made from hides or horse hair, all of our clothing was spun and woven at home, and I have carded and spun many nights until late bedtime. Leather was tanned by the settlers with bark from oak trees and used to rig saddles and for other purposes. Our shoes were made by country shoemakers; our saddle trees were made at home; we used water from creeks and rivers. Before the country was stocked all the streams contained pure, clear water. We carried corn in sacks on horseback fifteen to twenty-five miles to mills to be ground into meal, or ground the corn at home with small hand grist mills; wagons, ox yokes, looms and spinning wheels were made at home; hats were plaited and made from palmetto. The rich and the poor in our days were on equal footing, because these necessities could not be bought. As I look back to those times I am impressed with the marvelous changes time has wrought. The people of those good old days were brave and fearless, but if a high-powered automobile had gone speeding through the country at night with its bright headlights glaring and its horn screeching, I am sure the inhabitants would all have taken to the brush, thinking it was some supernatural monster.

The descendants of the early settlers of Texas are today identified with every industry in the country.

Their intelligence and traits of character are not surpassed by any people on earth, because they are quick to learn, quick to act, brave, honest and true to God and country. A quarter of a century of my life, from 1861 to 1886, was a continual chain of thrills, not by choice, but by the customs of those times. The dangers through which I passed during those days make me shudder when I recall them, but I attribute my preservation to the earnest prayers of my devoutly religious father and mother, who continually entreated Almighty God to protect their reckless boy. They taught me to trust in the Divine Father from infancy, and their admonitions have continued with me to this day, never dimmed but brightening as the years pass. I do not claim to have followed their teachings to the letter, but the training I received at their knees has been a guide and great support to me through life. Had I not received this early training to fortify me against the many temptations I cannot think what would have been the outcome.

I want to say a word about some of the men with whom I have been associated during my business career, for I feel that such affiliation has contributed to my success in the business world. As good fortune would have it, I fell in with the best men of our country, men of honesty and integrity, and leaders in the affairs of county and state. They helped me to attain that which I think I now possess, a good name, which is ''rather to be chosen than great riches.'' They were loyal at all times, and ever ready to advise and assist me.

And right here I want to pay a tribute to the noble women of our land, for they are more deserving of praise than all of the men combined. Consider the pioneer mothers and wives of our glorious state, and think of the hardships and privations they endured for the sake of being near and helping husband or father to make a home in the new country. Their social pleasures were few, their work heavy. Dangers lurked on every hand, but bravely and uncomplainingly these women endured their hard lot, cheering and encouraging the men who were their protectors. God bless them! I often heard it said in the days of my youth that the women were the hope of our nation. They have fulfilled that hope in every sense of the term, and I believe they will ever continue to do so.

I was the first man to introduce roping contests in this state some thirty years ago, but the practice was so badly abused and so many cattle crippled and killed, that I regretted the introduction, so accordingly in after years I was the first to petition the Legislature to pass a law prohibiting the sport.

From 1868 to 1895 it is estimated that fully 35,000 men went up the trail with herds, if the number of men computed by the number of cattle driven is correct. Of this number of men about one-third were negroes and Mexicans, another third made more than one trip. Let us conclude that one-half of the white trail drivers who made one trip have died, and we still have some 6,000 survivors of the trail scattered all over the world, all of whom ought to be members of our association. This would give us the strength to forever perpetuate our organization, for as it is now our sons are eligible to membership and they in turn can make their sons and grandsons eligible as they grow to manhood. I have urged the organization of the old trail drivers for thirty-five years. Many of my old comrades promised to participate in the organization, but it was put off from time to time, until 1915, when I called a few together and started the movement which has steadily grown until today I feel that my efforts in this matter have been in a large measure successful. If we had organized earlier, however, I am sure we would have preserved the record of many of our old comrades who have crossed over the Great Divide, and retained much of the trail slang and customs that have passed away.

I have carefully read most of the sketches that appear
in this book. They tend to show that the early settlers
and old trail drivers did more toward the development
of this state than all other things combined, and it would
be the father of all mistakes to allow the record of these
men to go down in unwritten history. Therefore, this
book was prepared to preserve that record. My greatest
wish is that the proceeds from the sale of the book will
be used for the purpose of erecting a monument, one
hundred feet high, to the drivers of the famous old trail,
somewhere on the trail near San Antonio or Fort Worth.

MRS. LOU GORE

First Landlady in Abilene, Kansas

She took charge of the Drovers' Cottage in the Spring
of '68 and conducted this Hotel for many years. In a
brief time it was learned that in the person of the new
Landlady of the Cottage Hotel the Drovers had a true
sympathetic friend and in their sickness a true guardian
and nurse, one whose kind, motherly heart was ever
ready to provide for every proper want, be they hungry,
tired, thirsty or sick, it mattered not, she was the
Florence Nightingale to relieve them. Many of the Old
Trail Drivers remember Mrs. Gore and often speak of
her as a most Noble Lady. Miss Maragret Gore, a
daughter of Mrs. Lou Gore, is living at McPherson, Kansas. She was located last year through a letter written
to Mrs. Amanda Burks of Cotulla, the Queen of The Old
Trail Drivers' Association. Geo. W. Saunders, President
of the Old Trail Drivers' Association, has been corresponding with Miss Gore. She has promised to attend
our reunion November the 6th to 8th this Fall, 1924.
President Saunders has made Miss Gore an honorary

member of the Association for life out of respect of the
memory of her most worthy Mother.

MRS. LOU GORE

BURIED A COWBOY IN A LONELY GRAVE ON
THE PRAIRIE

By Alfred Iverson (Babe) Moye, Kenedy, Texas

I was born in Georgia and reared in Texas, my father
settling in Tyler County. In December, 1870, I went to
Helena, and while I was there a young man named Silvers
was killed by the sheriff. M. J. Bean was collector for
the stockmen and I went with him on one of his trips. As
we crossed the Frio River we saw a number of people
congregating at a little house and learned from them that

the Indians had the day before murdered the Stringfield family. The oldest girl was later found by Mexicans, and she is now living in San Antonio. Two little boys, aged four and six years, respectively, were taken away by the Indians and the oldest of the two was found dead by the roadside with his head split open, but the other was never heard from.

The following spring I hired to an outfit to go to Kansas with a herd which we received in the mountains about fifty miles above Uvalde. While we were herding the cattle in the valley Indians would appear on the mountains and bow to us and make signs which we did not understand. I went out one day to hunt for a bunch of our horses and found a bunch of Indians instead. They took after me, but I outran them back to camp. I guess my eyes were out of fix, for it seemed to me that there were about a hundred redskins in the band, but investigation later proved that there were only about fifteen. Ten men of our outfit went back over the ground and found three arrows they had shot at me while in the race. About the last of March we got our herd of 1,500 beeves road-branded and, starting with them, we soon reached Red River, which we crossed at Red River Station into the Indian Territory. The Territory at that time was unsettled, nothing there except buffalo, Indians and fugitives from other states. These men would steal and rob and lay it on the Indians, so we had to guard our horses every night to prevent them from being stolen. One night a Mexican boy and myself were on guard and the Mexican struck a match to light his cigarette and as he did so somebody shot at us three times in quick succession, and when we returned the fire the boys at camp rushed out to our assistance. The scheme was to scare us away from our horses so they could get them. At Abilene, Kansas, we found a wide open town. Ben Thompson and Hill Coe were running the noted Bull Head saloon, and Wild Bill Hickok was city marshal.

There I met up with John Wesley Hardin, Buffalo Bill Thompson, Manny Clements and Gip Clements, and we went over to the gambling house. It did not take the gamblers there long to relieve me of all the money I possessed. Wild Bill Hickok told me that the best way to beat the game was to let it alone. I took his advice and have been beating the game ever since. Coe was later killed by Wild Bill and Thompson afterward closed out the Bull Head and returned to Austin.

The next year I went up the trail with the same firm, Choate & Bennett. We received the cattle on the Nueces River, with John Henry Choate in charge of the herd. When we reached Red River at Red River Station, we had to swim across. I was riding a 2×4 Spanish pony, and before I got across I had to slip off his back and grasp him by the tail to get to the other side. We had a severe storm after we left Red River and a number of our men were shocked by lightning. We drove our herd to Great Bend, Kansas, on the Arkansas River. This is now one of the finest wheat belts in the world.

The next year I went with W. G. Butler to Ogallala. My oldest brother, Andy Moye, was on this trip with us and got into trouble at Ogallala that caused us to leave in somewhat of a hurry.

I went up the trail again the next year, and it seemed that we had more storms than usual. When we reached the Cimarron River in the Territory it was bankful and we had to stay there several days before we could cross. While we were there two tramps came along who said they were going to swim the river. We tried to talk them out of the foolish undertaking, but they plunged in and when half way across they began yelling for us to come and help them out, but we could not get to them and they both drowned.

On Smoky River, in the northwestern part of Kansas, myself and several other cowboys were hunting stampeded beeves one day and found the corpse of a cowboy

who had come to his death in some manner unknown to
us. We decided to bury him there, so we dug a hole and
rolled him into it, with but little burial ceremony. One
of our crowd was a good singer, and sang the old cowboy
song that all of the old boys are familiar with, which runs
something like this:

"Oh, bury me not on the lone prairie,
    Where the coyotes may howl o'er me;
  And dig my grave just six by three—
    But bury me not on the lone prairie.

"Yes bury me under an evergreen tree,
    Where the little birds may sing o'er me;
  And dig my grave just six by three—
    But bury me not on the lone prairie."

Our hearts were sad when we left that poor unknown
boy out there under the sod of that lonely prairie, many
miles from a habitation. Some mother's boy who went
away, never to return; some husband or father, perhaps,
who went out into that wild country and lost his life there.

Nearly all of my old cowboy chums of fifty years ago
have passed over the trail to that home beyond the grave..
A few are left here, sore-footed and dragging, but still
full of life. Among those who are still in the land of the
living I will mention one, for whom I have always had
the highest regard and esteem, and that is P. B. Butler,
who lives at Kenedy, Texas. He was always found honest and square in all of his dealings, true to his friends,
and one of the best stockmen in all Southwest Texas.
P. B. Butler will leave behind him a good name as a
heritage to his posterity, and an example for oncoming
generations to follow.

A few more of the old boys are still living near me,
Munroe Hinton, Hiram Reynolds and Dick Smith being
among them. Tom Edwards passed away just a short

time ago. When I see my old comrades in town, bent
with the weight of three-score and ten, I am reminded
that my time to quit the walks of men is fast approaching, just a few years more at best, and we will all join
the silent majority.

SOME THINGS I SAW LONG AGO

By George Gerdes

Here are my credentials: "I solemnly swear and affirm" that I went the length of the trail—up to Dodge
City, Kansas, and from there to Pueblo, Colorado. "I
further solemnly swear and affirm" that I will tell "not"
all I saw and heard. Who would? It's a long time back
—to remember; and if you remember, would you care to
tell? If you cared to tell, would you dare to tell? And
if you dared to tell you'd be afraid; and if you weren't
afraid, you'd be "skeered" as Helmar Jenkins Booth.

My credentials further state that I was born when
quite young, in 1863, at a little "jumping-off-in-the-road"
place called Quihi, Medina County, Texas, on what was
then known as the old John Heven place. We moved
later to Sturm (meaning "storm") Hill, where I spent
most of my childhood days.

Father was a stock raiser, and also took cattle on
shares—attending to the handling and care of them on
the open range. My sister and I were sent to school in
an old school house near by, on the Klappenbach ranch,
to be "edjicated."

As children we were warned and taught to be on the
lookout for Indians. We were told wild and weird stories
of massacres and how Indians would steal children and
torture them; and which was not a "fairy story," but a
fact. We were on our way home one evening after school
when we saw in the distance a band of Indians coming
in our direction. It took us but a moment to hide in a

cluster of white brush. The Indians passed uncomfortably close to us on their way to some other place, as the
settlement was not molested that night. They confined
their raids mostly to stealing of stock, such as horses and
mules. However, they did not hesitate in "lifting a
scalp" if chance offered. Some time later Indians appeared at night and made a raid on our settlement, taking with them a number of horses, and happened to lose
one of their own—a little dun pony. We took up this
pony and fed him so that he was soon nice and fat. One
evening we took him out to graze near the house, and
had gone back some 300 yards when we saw a bunch of
redskins leading away our fat little pony, and we lost no
time in hiding. We found the cut hobble next morning
about ten feet from where we had left the horse, and I
guess the Indians had watched us and waited long enough
for us to leave and then took the animal. That very
night the Indians stole horses all over the settlement.
They also visited a place belonging to Nic Haby. He had
his horses and mules in a pen and was guarding them,
hiding behind a large live oak tree. Early in the night
he noticed his horses becoming restless, and directly an
Indian appeared above the fence and jumped into the
corral among the horses. Nic Haby was a good shot and
the Indian found it out. The following morning a neighbor of Haby's came over to tell Haby his trouble with
Indians and the loss of horses he had sustained, when he
espied the dead Indian. He drew his dirk and plunged it
into the redskin's body, exclaiming: "That is the son-
of-a-gun; he stole my horses." They put a rope around
the Indian's head and dragged him up on the mountain,
turning him over to the mercies of the buzzards and hogs.
They accorded him the same burial that the redskins gave
their white victims. For a long time thereafter nobody
would eat pork.

After I was large, or old enough to work out, I started
freighting, my first trip being with a two-horse wagon

from San Antonio to Fort Clark. There were generally from six to ten wagons making the trip at the same time, partly for protection and also for assistance which in the rainy season was quite imperative. After a trip or two I bought a three-and-a-half-inch Studebaker wagon and hitched up six animals. We freighted to Del Rio, to Eagle Pass and to Fort Clark from San Antonio, Texas. We would take out merchandise and bring back raw material—wool and hides, and sometimes a load of empty beer bottles, or "dead soldiers" as we called them. We had some experiences with our work teams stampeding at night, and sometimes we would catch up with them next day ten or twelve miles away, homeward bound. In those days there were no graded roads; a wagon track, or a number of them, would be called a road if it had the name of its destination tacked to it. Sometimes a road would be 100 feet wide or wider, according to where the ground was most solid and suitable for travel. When the rainy spell set in the roads were almost impassable. Sometimes we hitched as many as sixteen animals to a wagon to pull it out of the mud, and would move it 100 feet or so, then hook on to the next one, until we had them all out of the mud. I have seen the time that we were camped for weeks on this side of the Frio River on account of high water and impassable roads. We had an old mule team that we used in swimming the river when going to Uvalde for bacon and meal. We had plenty of meat, such as rabbits, venison and also fish. In 1881, with the coming of the Southern Pacific Railroad, our trade went "blooe." I became foreman of the Judge Noonan ranch southwest of Castroville, Texas, and worked there until I went up the trail in 1884.

Ed Kaufman and Louis Schorp, both of them alive to this day, gathered a herd of some 450 head of horses in Medina County, Texas. With them were J. M. Saathoff, Ehme Saathoff, a cook by the name of Ganahl Brown, and myself. We started from Castroville and drove by way of Bandera, Kerrville and over the "old trail," crossing the Red River at the old Doan Store. We herded the horses the first few nights and later let them graze or rest during the night to themselves. We had a very wet trip, it raining almost every day while we were on the way. Feed for the horses was plentiful and our crew fared on wild game, cornbread and black coffee. We came across our first Indians when we arrived in the Indian Territory. They were very friendly and would eat tobacco and sugar "out of your hand." These articles were always on their mind and after their preliminary "How" they would never fail to ask for them. When the meals we were cooking were ready there would always be some "self-invited" Indian guest or guests to fall in and help themselves and eat to their heart's content. One day an old buck rode up to me in the usual way and asked for "terback." I handed him a plug and after he gave two or three of his "compadres" each a chew he took one himself and stuck the balance in his pocket. I argued and asked him to give me back my plug, but he said: "Pony boss, he be good," and rode off.

It was customary to pay a duty on horses crossing the reservation, and our boss paid the Indians in horses, but they also stole some twenty-five head from us before we got away from them. We did not have very much trouble with the horses, and our trip took up something like four months from Castroville, Texas, to Dodge City, Kansas. We camped with our herd about six miles south of Dodge City, on Mulberry Creek. The first thing we did when we arrived there was to go to town, get a shave and haircut, and tighten our belts by a few good strong drinks. Here I also met George W. Saunders—the same George who is now the worthy president of the "Old Trail Drivers' Association."

While here our boss, Ed Kaufman, got summons that some important business demanded his immediate return to Medina County. He left the herd in our charge until such a time when he should return, in about 30 days. After he got back to the herd he sold it to Mr. Wilson, of Pueblo, Colorado, where he had to deliver the horses for him.

After delivery of the horses at Pueblo, Colo., I hired to Wilson, and worked for a couple of months, when I was sent back to Dodge City to receive and take charge of a herd of 3,500 head of two-year-old stocker steers for Wilson. I started the herd and the cattle would stampede every blooming night. Often in the morning we had to help from thirty to forty of the poorer steers on their feet by a tail-hold and lift. This was repeated for some eight or ten days, and we could only make from five to six miles per day. We tired of herding the cattle at night, so would scatter the herd over a large area of ground to give them more elbow room. This worked like a charm, for as long as the cattle were not in close formation they would not get excited so easily—and we had no more runs.

We took the herd about sixty miles below Pueblo to the Wilson ranch, branded the 3,500 head, and six more herds which had been delivered there, amounting to another 3,500—7,000 head in all; besides branding, we dewlapped every animal. We built our own pens and chutes to do this, and hard work it was. Still, we had lots of old-time pleasure to relieve the monotony. Every Saturday afternoon at two o'clock we would quit work and go to a dance, start dancing at 4 P.M. and dance till after sunrise Sunday morning. We had lots of refreshments, booze, beer and kindred "exhilarators." Sometimes a little shooting scrape would change the scenery, but was of passing interest. From the Wilson ranch I returned home by way of Kansas City. I remained at home a short time and took up some state land in 1885, fenced it—and then went west to Brewster and Presidio Counties, where I worked for Sam Harmon of Alpine, Texas. Harmon was a roundup boss and attended to the branding and gathering of stock. The first work we did was out of the ordinary—we tried to dig a well. We blasted through 65 feet of solid rock and left a "dry hole." Later I worked for F. Collins a long time.

In 1892 I left Alpine and went home to Medina County, got married to Johanna Schweers and settled down five miles north of Quihi—on Sturm Hill.

ATE STOLEN MEAT, ANYWAY

By Jim Wilson, Alpine, Texas

I was born in Bee County in 1861, so I am not as old as some of the boys who had lots of experience up the trail in the 70's. I went up the trail to Kansas in 1880, leaving Bee County with a herd for Millett & Lane, and

JIM WILSON

turned them over in the Indian Territory. Dave Clair and I went with Woodward & Oge, with Jim Newton as boss. Bill Hancock, a brother-in-law to Newton, was with the outfit, and as he was about my age, we fell in together somewhat. One night Dave Clair, Bill Hancock, myself and a boy from Kansas were on herd when a severe thunderstorm came up, and we drifted off with the cattle. The Kansas boy was pretty badly scared during the storm and kept saying that his people were all killed in a storm and he just knew we were going to be killed, too. Bill got excited, too, and asked me: "Did you ever pray?" I told him no, not in a long time. He said, "Some of us have got to pray, for the lightning is going to kill all of us." The storm increased in fury, the lightning striking near us frequently, and we got separated. When our crowd got together again we found Bill off his horse praying aloud. We found some stray cattle in our herd, cows and calves, and Bill remarked that "one of those fat calves would be good eating, if it was ours." I told him stampeded cattle in the Territory belonged to the trail and we would just take one. He said: "No. Jim Newton will fire us if we do that, and I wouldn't eat stolen meat anyway." I did not care if we were fired, for I was nearly starved for fresh meat, as we had not had any since we left home, so I cut out one of those calves, ran it over to the wagon, and the cook and I killed it. Before it quit kicking I had the sweetbread on the fire. Before it was skinned the sweetbread was hot. I went back to where Bill was with some of it in my hand and told him to go and help himself, but he said, "I'll go and get some coffee, but I won't eat any of that beef," but he came back about daylight with a chunk as big as his foot, and was eating it. When I went to camp I found that he had buried the head, hide and all. These stray cattle turned out to be Captain Lytle's, which had been lost the year before, and we turned them over to his outfit. After delivering our herd I went back to Mobeetie and then made two trips to Dodge City that fall with the Turkey Track outfit.

Times have changed since then. All of the boys of this generation are driving automobiles out to herds, and after riding around a little, back to town they go. The only way you can get them out to work is to go in an automobile after them, and if the job is within twenty miles of town you have to take them back to see the picture show. I guess we will soon have to take flying machines to get them out.

I moved to Brewster County in 1884, and have engaged in the ranch and mercantile business here for many years. I operated a large store in Alpine for a long time, and all I knew about the business was the price of horse shoes and Battle Axe tobacco. My clerks frequently accused me of selling goods too high or too cheap, and said about the best place for me was out among the cattle.

WHEN A BOY BOSSED A HERD

Sketch of J. D. Jackson, Alpine, Texas

J. D. Jackson was born January 6, 1861, on Donahoe Creek in Bell County, Texas. His parents came to Texas from Louisiana in 1852, and he and his brother, J. W. Jackson, still own the old Jackson home in Bell County.

Joe Jackson, as he is commonly called, was in charge of a herd of cattle on the trail with eight or ten men working under him, at the age of eighteen. At one time he drove a herd of stock cattle more than eighty miles across the Staked Plains of West Texas without water, driving the cattle at night and resting in the daytime.

Several older men in the outfit thought the men and cattle would all die, so they appealed to the second boss, L. B. Wells, to "Tell that d—d boy to drive day and night." But Wells told them that "that boy" knew just how to handle that herd and would get them all to water if they would stay with him. When they were about six miles from the Pecos River the cattle smelled water and made a mad rush for it. Jackson managed to stay in front of them, as he was riding a good quarter horse. As the river was up, Jackson rode in to about the center and found a sandbar and stayed there to turn the cattle out, for they drank almost half of the night; otherwise the cattle would have drifted down the stream with the steep banks on both sides holding them in and would have perished.

In 1914 Joe Jackson was elected president of the Cattle Raisers' Association of Texas; was re-elected in 1915, and many of his friends, among whom are the biggest men in Texas, plead with him to allow his name to go before the convention for the third term, but he refused. During his administration the association grew from 2,250 to 4,000 members, retaining most of the old members.

Aside from being a benefactor to the livestock interest, Joe Jackson is reported to have done more for school children than any other man in West Texas. He has been president of the school board at his home town, Alpine, for sixteen years and has been instrumental in building up a good public school system in Texas. He began work for the Sul Ross State Normal, nine years ago and has been working until his dream came true, and it is now a large school running in reality.

He and his partner, S. D. Harmon, have large holdings of land and cattle in Brewster County.

SPENT A HARD WINTER NEAR RED CLOUD

By D. S. Combs, San Antonio, Texas

My experience covers a great deal of time, as I am now just past my eighty-first birthday. You, perhaps, have lived long enough to know that a man frequently forgets many things he would like to remember and remembers many things he would like to forget, but to me the memories of the Old Trail days are very pleasant, principally on the account of my good fortune to be associated with many of the pioneer cowmen of Texas, who made the country famous by their display of nerve and grey matter.

We did not know anything about the so-called hard times; we were trained to meet conditions, overcome ob-

stacles and accomplish what we started out to do. My
first experience on the trail was in 1866, when I drove
a herd of cattle from San Marcos, in Hays County, to

D. S. COMBS

New Iberia, La. William
Earnest owned these cattle, he
put the value on them at $6.00
per head, I did the work, and
we divided profits. I had
with me young men with the
grit necessary to accomplish
this undertaking. In those
days we did not discuss hardships; it seemed to be a pleasure to accomplish our undertaking. We cooked our own
food, slept on the ground,
worked in the rain in daytime
and at night, but all this was
a pleasure. Having made a
real success of my first venture, I was determined to
tackle it again.

My next drive was in 1867. I took a herd of horses
to Kansas and on to Waterloo, Iowa. This time I had
as a financial partner L. W. Mitchell. The horses cost
us $10.00 per head. We made a profit and were pleased
with our results. In the year of 1871 I drove with Dock
Day a herd of steers from San Marcos to Red Cloud,
Nebraska, where we concluded to winter. This was my
first bad setback, for the winter was the worst I ever saw
or heard of; the country froze over early in November
and never thawed until spring. Our cattle literally
starved to death, snow covered the grass and the water
froze so they could not drink. I left in the spring, a
busted and disgusted cowman. I have never been back
to that particular country and have tried all these years
to forget it, but the memories of that dreadful experience will forever remain with me.

In 1876 I drove a herd for Ellison & Dewees. That year about 40,000 head of cattle were put on the trail, known as the Western Trail. This was real experience. We started from San Antonio over an unknown route and where no road or trail was to be followed. We were the pioneers who made the first tracks that marked the Western Trail. We reached Ogallala, Neb., after about three months' straight drive, passing through some hard country and often forced to go long distances without water. Food was an object, but we, of course, managed to get by. In all my trail driving I was fortunately never molested by bandits or thieves. I had men with me that were dependable and, with their assistance, I made what I called a success. Our meals consisted of just whatever we could find that would do to eat. In 1878 I took a herd from Bob Stafford's ranch near Columbus to Dakota, this time for Ellison & Sherrell, and my experience was about as is usually encountered on such drives. Then, in 1879, I took an interest in a herd and drove over the same ground. Was successful beyond my fondest expectations. The profits were not much, but it was in the days when a little money looked like a whole lot.

After that I bought and sold cattle in a small way in and around East Texas, often shipping to West Texas and selling cattle to stock the western range. In 1880 I went into the ranch business in Tom Green County and ranched there for about two years, being associated with W. D. Kincaid. In 1882 we moved to Haymond, in Brewster County, where we ranched until 1898. While there the firm name was Combs & Kincaid Brothers, being composed of D. S. Combs, W. D. Kincaid and J. M. Kincaid. We sold out to E. O. Louchausen and in 1900 I bought our present ranch, which is located at Marathon, Brewster County, Texas, where my son, Guy S. Combs, has managed the same for the Combs family, all being partners in the ranch.

The greatest pleasure I have is in thinking of many

of my experiences and in meeting and remembering the cowmen of Texas. My association with them has always been a real pleasure, and when I have the good fortune of attending the Annual Roundup, the pleasure it gives me to meet the familiar faces and shake hands with the boys is worth a great deal more than it costs any of us to keep the Association alive.

EXPERIENCES OF THE TRAIL AND OTHERWISE

By M. J. Ripps, San Antonio, Texas

There are "a great many ways of killing a dog without choking him with butter," as the old saying goes. In handling cattle there are also many different ways which may lead to the same result; and, again, one way, or cause, may lead to many and varied results.

No doubt many of my old-time friends and cattle punchers have here related their experiences handling cattle on the trail in a graphic and interesting way; but as there are so many "spooks and ghosts" to play Hail Columbia with cattle, I shall take the liberty of adding a few of the experiences that I was privileged, or "forced," to go through with, for the benefit of the younger set of cowboys and our dear friends, the readers.

A river changes its course in the course of time; likewise, the channels of trade are changed with the passing of the days, which the following trip will illustrate.

I think it was about February 10, 1876, that J. W. Schelcher, Dick McRae, Manuel Cuero and I, with Louis Enderle as our foreman, went into Frio County, Texas, and gathered about 1,000 head of cattle and brought them up to the True-heart ranch on the San Antonio River. Here we finished the herd by adding another 800 head. This herd was the Joe Shiner property, and right here will state how these cattle were bought. Cattle were always bought by the head, and the price per head varied

according to the age and class of the animal. There were
no cattle sold "over the scale," and platform scales for
this purpose were not even dreamed of as a medium in
the sale of cattle. Now, in gathering these cattle on different ranches we came across cattle that had strayed
from other ranches, and their owner not being present,
we would send him word that we had one steer, a cow,
or a number of his cattle, as the case may have been,
and paid him the prevailing price. This was within the
law and in use quite generally. Cattle that had no brand
or mark—well, that was not our fault. But it is remarkable the way these cattle persisted in following the herd.
Naturally, our sympathy was with them. The ranches
where we gathered the cattle had some very wild stock—
outlaws—and to get them called for strategy and cunning. These outlaw cattle would generally graze to
themselves and come to water at night, especially if they
scented danger or having seen a human being. There
was a price on their head of $2.00 for a big steer, $1.50
for a cow, and from there on down to 50 cents per head
delivered in the herd. To accomplish this we would watch
around the watering places on moonlight nights and rope
them. This netted us more money than we were able to
make "by the month." After we had roped an animal
we would lead or drag him into the herd, or otherwise
we would tie the animal down, and after we had several
of them tied we would bring a bunch of cattle and, with
the bunch, bring them into the main herd. This was
great sport, and it was very dangerous as well.

We started the 1,800 head and got as far as Goat
Creek, north of Kerrville, without any serious trouble.
We herded them at night in three reliefs, and generally
kept five horses under saddle all night in case of emergency. One night I was herding, and about midnight a
bunch of wild hogs ran into the herd and stampeded the
cattle. We were camped near a field close to a big flat,
or prairie. The cattle headed for a lane, with me in the

lead unable to hold them. The boys at camp heard the noise and came to my assistance, and were able then to control them. We lost only one steer, which was crippled in the back. At the head of the Perdernales River we killed a calf for fresh meat for the men in camp. An old bull smelled the blood and started bellowing and pawing the ground. He made a great to-do about it, and it acted as a "war whoop does to the braves." In the stampede that followed some 300 head got separated from the main herd and ran about a mile. We overtook them towards morning and brought the whole herd together without losing any. From there on to Fort Mc-Kavett we did not have any more trouble. Here I quit the herd, as I was offered a better proposition.

A second herd was started by Joe Shiner in 1878, with Louis Enderle as foreman and the same crew as on the previous trip; besides he had three or four darkies with the herd. I joined them at San Antonio, bound for Kansas City. We had a stampede on a creek near Kerrville, and it took us half of the next day to round up the 100 head that had scattered. In Coleman County Joe Shiner sold the herd to Bill Fraser and we delivered the cattle at Wichita, Kansas.

Another trip in 1898, I recall, when Manuel Lopez, Little Pete Tafolla and I, and a little boy leading the pack horse, went to Wetmore, Texas, and, with the assistance of the Classen Bros., rounded up 300 head of steers. We were to meet a bunch of 600 steers en route overland from Hondo, throw the two bunches together and take them to the feed pens at Seguin, Texas, for Short & Saunders. However, after I had my 300 head gathered I received word to take them to Austin and deliver to John Sheehan, as he had bought them. The first night we made New Braunfels, Texas, but could get no pens. An old German sold us a load of corn-fodder and some corn for our horses, so we herded all night in the open. The second night we penned them in the railroad pens at San

Marcos and took them out on the prairie next morning. Our cattle stampeded, running across a cornfield, but, being in November, did not do any damage. The herd reached Kyle, Texas, about noon and we stopped to cook a meal. A man rode up and asked if we needed any help. We were more than glad to hire him, and asked him about a pen for the night at Buda, Texas. He said there was only one pen, and it was engaged for the night. This made us feel bad, and we were thinking of sending a man ahead to arrange for some place for us to stop. Our visitor spoke up and said that he had engaged the pen he spoke of, and that he had been sent out by John Sheehan to meet us. That afternoon a passing train stampeded our herd, but we checked them in a lane. We penned at Buda that night and next day headed for Austin. When we got to the Colorado River we found it on a rise. We were not allowed to cross cattle on the bridge, so we had to swim for it. Two of my men stayed with me and the third, a "cold-footer," crossed on the bridge. The cattle swam across all right and were delivered as ordered, without being any short.

One winter George Saunders and Ripps were feeding 1,800 head of cattle in their pens at San Antonio, and these cattle had to be guarded at night. One night a Mexican named Victorian and myself were herding when the cattle broke the fence for a distance of 100 yards. The cattle ran in a southerly direction, sweeping Victorian's horse with them. The cattle ran some five miles, with me in the lead and unable to check them. They finally broke into a pasture where I was able to turn them, and stayed with them until daylight, when relief came. The other relief man, who did not stampede with the cattle, did not show up until next day. Twelve men came out to help me bring back the cattle and it was some job. There were seven head missing next morning.

In 1880 and 1881 I went on a trail of a different nature by becoming a member of a surveying outfit to blaze the right of way for the Southern Pacific Railway from San Antonio west to the Rio Grande River. Two men joined the outfit with me at San Antonio, and the crew consisted of seventeen men. We surveyed as far as Uvalde, when we got orders to arm ourselves and keep our eyes "peeled" for Indians. This was too much for the two men who had joined with me, and so they quit. We continued the survey, and were about 128 miles west of San Antonio, when the government sent twenty soldiers to us as an escort. At the Nenecatchie Mountains we had our first experience with the redskins. They came in the night and tried to steal our mules and horses by stampeding them. We had our guards, or outposts, stationed some distance from camp and they exchanged shots, but none of our men were hurt. At San Felipe, on the Rio Grande, Rangers took the place of the soldiers and acted as our protectors. While we were camped at the McKenzie Crossing on the Rio Grande, the Indians made another attempt to get our horses, but were routed by the Rangers. From there on we did not see any more Indians until we came to Eagle's Nest, on the Rio Grande. We were camped some 350 feet above the level of the river bed, and were cutting out a trail wide enough for a burro to pass with a cask, or small barrel on either side, to transport water from the river. We had stopped for the noon hour when we noticed nine Indians, seven bucks and two squaws. They had evidently descended to the river bottom some miles above and were wending their way to a point directly in front of us, where they could get to the water. They were coming in single file, some ten feet apart, and were in full war paint, the Indian in the rear being the guard. The eight went to water to satisfy their thirst, while one stood guard. Then the guard went to drink while one of the squaws stood guard, and she spied us, as we could tell from her gestures. When she gave the alarm they took to their horses and disappeared up the river. As we were not looking for trouble, we did not fire at them, but doubled our guards to protect against an attack from the rear.

Our next camp was at Paint Cave. One night we sent our mules and horses out to grass with two guards in charge. Indians crept up and tried to scare the animals. One of the guards, finding that something was not right, gave the alarm, and the fireworks started. We fired some thirty or forty shots, and one of the guards claimed he got an Indian. This Painted Cave is worth a trip to see. It is a big opening under a protruding boulder, large

MARION McBEE, Del Rio, Tex.   J. O. TAYLOR, Del Rio, Tex.

enough for ten men to ride into on horseback at one time. Its inner walls are decorated with Indian paintings of wild animals, lions, tigers, buffaloes, etc., and all the sign language on the walls—some of which we would not understand if they were played on a phonograph. Besides this it contains the autographs of some of the pioneers carved in the rock, whose carvers have long since started on the "long trail." I was told by a friend of mine the other day, who had been there lately, that he ran across my name, carved there at that time—forty years ago.

I was born December 5, 1858, in the old Ripps homestead in the western part of San Antonio on the property where Geo. W. Saunders fed cattle for many years.

The only thing that is left to remind us of the olden days is the barbecue. In preparing barbecued meats I gained some proficiency, and have been, and am, called on a number of times a year to superintend these honest-to-goodness barbecues. What is there nicer than a nice slice of barbecue and a ———— (if Volstead wasn't so bad in figuring percentage) little of 2.75 plus——?

If a bunch of stockmen get together, you can rest assured there is going to be a barbecue somewhere. A number of times at their different conventions and gatherings I have had from 1,500 to 2,000 pounds of meat roasting over the hot coals and, I believe, to their satisfaction.

SKETCH OF COL. J. F. ELLISON

By His Son, J. F. Ellison, Jr., Fort Cobb, Okla.

My father, Col. J. F. Ellison, was born in Winston County, Mississippi, November 6, 1828, and moved to Caldwell County, Texas, in 1850, settling on the San Marcos River a few miles west of Prairie Lea, where he lived until the Civil War came on, and at the beginning of the war, in 1861, he answered his country's call, leaving behind him an humble, noble Christian woman with five little children, the writer being one of them. For four long years he was engaged in the great struggle, returning home in 1865, like most of the other true Confederate soldiers, a bankrupt, with nothing left but the faithful wife and five children. With turning plow, an old-fashioned sweep and a yoke of oxen, he went to work to try and make a living for himself and those dependent upon him.

I think the first cattle that were driven from Texas

to Northern markets was in 1867. In 1869 father bought
and gathered about 750 head of mixed cattle, all kinds,
from calves to grown cows,
and started them up the trail.
He bought these cattle on
credit, to be paid for on his
return. I accompanied him
on this trip and we went to
Abilene, Kansas, crossing the
Colorado at Webberville and
going by way of Fort Worth.
We followed the old Fort Arbuckle trail through the eastern part of Indian Territory,
now the splendid state of
Oklahoma, and of which I am
t o d a y a citizen.   All the
trouble we had with the In-

COL. J. F. ELLISON

dians was their begging for something to eat. We found
that if you fed them at meal time you could count on
them being right there the next time your chuck was
set out. After disposing of our cattle and outfit we came
back through Mississippi, where father was raised, and
from there to Galveston by boat from New Orleans. This
was my first experience on a boat and it made an impression on me that I will never forget. I didn't want
any breakfast next morning.

This trip proved to be a profitable one. After paying
for the cattle as soon as he returned home, father had
$9,000 cash, which was a lot of money in those days. He
drove again in 1870, and after returning home that year
Colonel John O. Dewees, then of Atascosa County, who
was an old soldier comrade with father, wrote him that
he would sell him all the cattle on time he wanted, so
the next year he bought about 2,000 grown beef steers
from Colonel Dewees and drove them in two herds. He
contracted these steers, or a part of them, to a man named

Powers to be delivered at his ranch on Smoky River, between Ellsworth and Abilene, Kansas, at two and a half
cents per pound. They weighed about a thousand pounds
each. This was a hard year, and but for this deal he
would have lost money. Soon after this father and
Colonel Dewees became partners in driving cattle over
the trail, which partnership continued until 1877, and
was quite satisfactory all around.

Father followed trail driving for thirteen years, the
last cattle he drove being in 1882.

W. P. LOCKE, Lockhart, Texas   PRES. TOM, Runge, Tex.

In 1867 Ellison & Dewees and Millett and Maberry
drove together, and they drove from South and Southwest Texas fully 100,000 cattle to the Northern markets,
delivering some of them as far north as the Black Hills
in North Dakota.

Father died November 13, 1904, at his home in San
Marcos. He followed the cattle business until 1880 with
great success, but in that year he met with reverses which
he never fully overcame. He was known to all of the old
trail men and the hands of that time, and was held in
highest esteem by all with whom he came in contact.

SIXTY-EIGHT YEARS IN TEXAS

By Pleasant Burnell Butler, Kenedy, Texas

I was born in Scott County, Mississippi, in 1848, being the eleventh child of Burnell Butler, who was born in Kentucky in 1805, and Sarah Ann Ricks, born in North Carolina in 1811.

In 1849 my oldest brother, Woodward, then a youth of twenty years, left the home in Mississippi to seek out a new location for the family. He crossed the Mississippi River into Louisiana, where he remained long enough to make a crop and, selling out, journeyed on until he reached Karnes County, then a part of Goliad County, in 1850, where he stayed on a tract of land that is now the Pleasant Butler homestead, near the San Antonio River.

P. B. BUTLER

In September, 1852, father sold out in Scott County, Mississippi and started to join my brother in Texas. I was at that time four years old, but remember distinctly the start for Texas, father and mother, twelve children, and seven negro slaves, traveling in covered wagons, each drawn by two yoke of oxen, mother driving a hack with a team of big horses and father riding a fine saddle horse. I recall clearly a stop made near Jackson, Miss., to bid good-bye to my aunt, Mrs. Porter, and how my aunt drove down the road with us in a great carriage with a negro driver on a high seat in front—a barouche of the real old South.

We crossed the Mississippi River at Natchez, where the high red banks, down which they drove to the ferry boats that carried us across the great river, made an impression on my childish mind that has never been effaced.

When the family reached the spot on the wild prairie lands where the town of Nordheim now stands, we camped under a great liveoak tree, the only tree in miles to break the prairie lands about us. Father and mother drove ahead in the hack to find Woodward in his camp on the San Antonio River and to send him back to meet us as we came on with the wagons. He met us the next evening, December 24, 1852, on the banks of the Eclato.

The new country, with its wide prairies, its wonderful grasses and abundance of game, became the home of the Butler family. I recall that my brother could go out in the evening when the sun was a quarter of an hour high and bring in a deer by nightfall. Turkeys also were plentiful.

In the spring of 1853 father cleared fourteen acres of brush land, pushing the brush back to make a fence, and planted corn. He harvested 700 bushels of corn, or fifty bushels per acre. Also that spring he leased a part of the Stafford & Selmer tract of land and bought cattle. He gave a small heifer to me, from which, up to the year 1862, I raised eighteen head. But in 1863 came a great drouth and my cattle diminished to one small steer.

In November, 1863, Woodward, who had led the family into the new home and blazed the trail for their future prosperity, drove to Port Lavaca to bring the winter's supply of groceries. While there he contracted yellow fever and died.

The years wore on and the great war between the North and the South shook even this remote corner of the country. I remember seeing great wagons, drawn by twelve steers, hauling cotton to Mexico, where it brought fifty cents a pound. Flour was not available at

$26.00 per barrel, and corn in various ways became the staple diet. In 1862 my brother, W. G. Butler, who had joined the army, was sent home to gather a bunch of cattle for the Arkansas post. I was then a youth of fourteen and went along to the Hickok pens, near Oakville, where the cattlemen had assembled 500 head, which were headed at once for Arkansas. I helped to drive them as far as Pecan Springs, near the present town of San Marcos, where I bade my brother good-bye and returned home.

In 1863 came the great drouth. The Nueces and San Antonio Rivers became mere trickling threads of water with here and there a small pool. The grass was soon gone and no cattle survived except those that had previously drifted across the Nueces River on to a range that was not so severely affected by the drouth. In 1864 came rains and plentiful grass, and a search for drifted cattle was organized. All the young, able-bodied men were in the army, so a party of forty-five young boys and old men, headed by Uncle Billy Ricks, of Oakville, went to San Diego to the ranch of Benito Lopez, from which point they worked for a month rounding up cattle and cutting out those of their own brands. Every week a herd was taken across the river and headed for home, and in this way 500 head were put back on the ranges of Karnes County, where thousands had grazed before the drouth. My steer was luckily among the five hundred.

In 1868 W. G. Butler, home from the war, dròve a herd to Abilene, Kansas, to market, and I went along as far as Gonzales. This fired in me an ambition to ride the whole trail, and in 1870 I made my first trip through to Abilene in the outfit of my brother. The trail then followed lay along the line from Austin to Belton, Valley Mills, Cleburne to Fort Worth, which at that time boasted of a livery stable, a court house and a store operated by Daggett & Hatcher, supply merchants, on the public square, through which we swung our great herd of cattle.

At Fort Worth it was necessary to take on supplies for a month, there being no big stores between Fort Worth and Abilene, Kansas, so at Daggett & Hatcher's we purchased flour, coffee, bacon, beans and dried fruit, three-quarter pound of bacon and the same of flour being allotted to each man for each day.

From Fort Worth the trail ran on to Gainesville, crossed the Red River and from there our outfit went up Mud Creek to the house of Bob Love, a Choctaw Indian, from whom we had to obtain passports through the Indian Territory. I remember that Love demanded 10 cents a head for the 500 head in the herd, and that after considerable business talk we compromised, Love accepting a $20.00 gold piece, and in return gave the necessary papers. From Love's we traveled the Chisholm Trail, crossed the South Fork of the Arkansas, through the Osage country into Kansas.

Along the trail the Indians showed great interest in our party, particularly the chuck wagon. Hospitality had to be limited, and little grass grew under our feet through this part of the country.

Buffalo were very plentiful, so numerous in fact that it was necessary to ride ahead of the cattle to prevent them from cutting into the herd. I killed four buffalo on this trip, using only my six-shooter. I had little use for the sights on a gun and shot just as true when on horseback and on the dead run as when on foot.

In 1871 I started for Abilene in charge of an outfit of my own and was joined at Gainesville by several other herds, one belonging to Columbus Carroll, of Gonzales, in charge of Jim Cox; one of Murphy of Victoria, in charge of Captain Lynn; and one of Clark & Woodward, in charge of Judge Clark. This time we were to travel a new trail, through a more open country, but where there had been no previous travel.

We crossed the river at Red River Station, seventy-five miles above Gainesville, where an Indian named Red

Blanket waited to pilot us through the new country. The herds traveled ahead in turn, a day at the time, the first herd breaking the trail for those following. For some time the trail ran along Line Creek, which lay between the Osage and Comanche nations. Red Blanket warned us that if we got above the creek the Comanches would surely kill us. After this there was little discussion of which side of the creek made the best trail. Reaching Kansas in May, our outfit made camp on the Smoky River, twenty miles from Abilene, where the cattle grazed until September, when they were ready for market.

I made four trips over the trail to market my steers, and saw many miles of splendid country, but nowhere could I see the prosperity and the future that lay in my own part of Texas. So in 1874, when Capt. Tom Dennis bought the 7,000-acre Jim King ranch, now known as the Wilson ranch, I bought from him the north half of the ranch and paid 10% interest on the debt until it was paid. The next year I bought one-half interest in the Burris cattle and worked them on the range.

During the years 1874, 1875 and 1876 W. G. Butler and I operated on the range together. During this time we sold 600 head to John Belcher, and delivered them at Fort Worth.

In the fall of 1876 I sold my interest in the Wilson ranch to Coleman and Stokely, also all my cattle I had on the range at that time, range delivery.

In the year 1877 Coleman and Stokely delivered to me 2,200 head of steers, yearlings and two's, for payment of the cattle I sold them on the range. These cattle I rounded up and started up the trail, but on my arrival at Fort Worth I found a buyer and sold out to him.

In 1878 I finished receiving cattle from Coleman & Stokely and bought more from Sullivan & Skidmore to make out a herd of 3,500 head, and again started up the trail to Dodge City, Kansas, going through several storms and enduring lots of hardships, and then, last, but not least, could not find a market for the cattle at Dodge City, so I was compelled to make the drive to Ogallala, Nebraska, where I sold out.

Arriving home in September, 1878, I began laying my plans for another drive up the trail. In February the following year (1879) I began receiving 3,500 from Jim Upton and others, getting everything in readiness for the drive. I started back to the prairies of Nebraska in March, and it took me three months to make the drive. I kept my cattle under herd, between the North and South Platte Rivers, until some time in August, when I sold out.

I then started my camp outfit towards good old Karnes County, Texas, arriving home in September.

I was married to Miss Sarah Elizabeth Ammons on the 14th day of February, 1871. She was the eldest daughter of H. R. Ammons, who immigrated from Northern Mississippi to Karnes County during the dark days of 1850, settling on the beautiful San Antonio River, near the town of Helena. To this happy union one son and four daughters were born, all of whom are living except my son, Burnell Butler, who died in 1895. My daughters all reside in Kenedy and are: Mrs. J. W. Russell, Mrs. Van S. Ingram, Mrs. George H. Tips and Mrs. G. G. Ruhmann. I also have twelve grandchildren.

MY FIRST FIVE-DOLLAR BILL

By J. L. McCaleb, Carrizo Springs, Texas

I went up the trail in 1868 with a herd for Mitchell & Dixon of Hays County. We were holding our herd alongside of an old rail fence at the Red River Station crossing, waiting for a herd to cross. I was in front (by the way, my place was always in front) on the left, and a good place compared to the boys further back, where they had to ride back and forth, as there was always a muley or a one-eyed steer leaving the herd, and further back, especially the rear, you had the lazy and sore-footed cattle to keep moving. The best place around a herd while on the move—that is, if you want to keep well posted in cuss words—is the tail. At times the boys will not only cuss the cattle, but cuss each other and everything else in sight or hearing.

Now about my first $5.00 bill. I saw a small piece of paper in a fence corner, and as the cattle seemed quiet, I got down and picked it up, simply because I was hungry for something to read, if not more than one or two words. We did not have papers forwarded to us while on the trail. Well, I read that it was good for $5.00. I had never seen one before, so after crossing our herd, and when we struck camp for dinner, showed it to the boss. He said that it was sure enough good money, so I rolled it up stuck it away down in the pocket of my leather leggins. Money was of no value on the trail, as there was no place to spend it, but I valued that $5.00 more than any $5.00 I have ever had since. One day while at dinner the negro cook offered to bet me a two-year-old heifer he had in the herd against my five dollars that he could beat me shooting, only one shot each. I was good with a pistol, but I knew the cook was hard to beat. But I did not get nervous, as the two-year-old was about six to one if I won. One of the boys got a little piece of a board, took a coal out of the campfire, made a black spot about the size of a twenty-five-cent piece, stepped off fifteen steps (about 45 feet) and yelled, "All ready, shoot." I was to shoot first. I jerked my old cap and ball Navy out and just about one second before I pulled the trigger I saw the heads of six Indians just over a little rise in the ground coming toward the camp. This excited me so that I did not hit the spot, only about one-half of my bullet touched the board just to the right of the target. I yelled to the negro, "Shoot quick! Look at the Indians!'' By that time we could see them plainly on top of the rise. He fired, but never touched the board. So six big Osage Indians saved me my valuable find—the five-dollar bill.

We bedded our cattle for the last time near Abilene, Kansas. The boss let myself and another boy go to the city one day. As it had been a long time since we had seen a house or a woman, they were good to look at. I wore a black plush hat which had a row of small stars around the rim, with buck-skin strings to tie and hold on my head. We went into town, tied our ponies, and the first place we visited was a saloon and dance hall. We ordered toddies like we had seen older men do, and drank them down, for we were dry, very dry, as it had been a long ways between drinks. I quit my partner, as he had a girl to talk to, so I went out and in a very short time I went into another store and saloon. I got another toddy, my hat began to stiffen up, but I pushed it up in front, moved my pistol to where it would be handy, then sat down on a box in the saloon and picked up a newspaper and thought I would read a few lines, but my two toddies were at war, so I could not very well understand what I read. I got up and left for more sights—you have seen them in Abilene, Dodge City and any other place those days. I walked around for perhaps an hour. The two toddies were making me feel different to what I had felt for months, and I thought it was about time for another, so I headed for a place across the street, where I could hear a fiddle. It was a saloon, gambling and dance hall. Here I saw an old long-haired fellow dealing monte. I went to the bar and called for a toddy, and as I was drinking it a girl came up and put her little hand under my chin, and looked me square in the face and said, ''Oh, you pretty Texas boy, give me a drink.'' I asked her what she wanted and she said anything I took, so I called for two toddies. My, I was getting rich fast—a pretty girl and plenty of whiskey. My old hat was now away back on my head. My boss had given me four dollars spending money and I had my five-dollar bill, so I told the girl that she could make herself easy; that I was going to break the monte game, buy out the saloon, and keep her to run it for me when I went back to Texas for my other herd of cattle. Well, I went to the old long-haired dealer, and as he was making a new layout I put my five on the first card (a king) and about the third pull I won. I now had ten dollars and I thought I had better go and get another toddy before I played again. As I was getting rich so fast, I put the two bills on the tray and won. Had now twenty dollars, so I moved my hat back as far as it would go and went to get a drink—another toddy, but my girl was gone. I wanted to show her that I was not joking about buying out the saloon after I broke the bank. After this drink things did not look so good. I went back and it seemed to me that I did not care whether I broke him or not. I soon lost all I had won and my old original five. When I quit him my hat was becoming more settled, getting down in front, and I went out, found my partner and left for camp. The next morning, in place of owning a saloon and going back to Texas after my other herds, I felt—oh! what's the use? You old fellows know how I felt.

The winter of 1868 was spent having a good cowboy time. Wherever my horse, saddle and hat were I was there, spending my trail money. When spring came on I helped to get together one herd, branded a lot of mavericks and sleepers. But there was a little freckled face girl that I had danced a lot with in the winter months, so I made up my mind that I would stay in Texas that year, 1869. I fiddled, danced and worked cattle over a territory as big as the state of Maine. A ranch fifty years ago was not measured by acres or miles—they were boundless. Schools and churches back in the wild days were not handy and most of the ranchmen and cowboys did not care. No mails, no papers, neighbors miles apart, what could one expect from such a wild life? We would civilize up a bit when we went to a dance; that is, we would take off our spurs and tie a clean red handkerchief around our neck.

I drove beeves from the W. B. G. Grimes pens on the Leona to Matagorda Bay in the winter of 1869, then hired to John Redus on the Hondo, where I finished the winter. In the early spring of 1870 I helped him get together 2,000 of the wildest longhorns that was ever started up the trail. They were travelers when strung out, but were inclined to stampede in front, the middle or rear. It did not take us long to mill them if in an open country, but in timber that was different. I took sick this side of Waco and left the herd horseback for the Redus ranch on the Hondo. I punched cattle, fiddled and danced some years after, getting wilder all the time, until I met a curly-headed girl from Atascosa County, fell in love and married. It took her a long time to tame me. But she did, and for the last fifteen or twenty years I do not have to be tied. Just drop the reins on the ground, I'll stay there.

SLAKED THEIR THIRST IN A DRY TOWN

By A. D. McGehee, San Marcos, Texas

I was born in Hays County, four miles below San Marcos, October 17, 1857, and have never lived out of this county. I was raised on a farm, and on December 17, 1876, I was married to Miss Fannie Johnson. We raised six children to be grown, three girls and three boys, and we think they are all pretty good cattle, but do not know if they are much improvement over the old stock.

I first went up the trail in 1868, when I was just eleven years old, with my brother, George T. McGehee. We drove from Belton to Abilene, Kansas. The trail then went by the village of Dallas, crossed the Red River at Colbert's Ferry, near where Denison is now located. At Abilene I met several of the old Texas drivers, among them being Colonel Meyers of Lockhart, Captain E. and Lonnie Millett of Seguin, Doc Day, and others. After holding the cattle at Abilene for about thirty days we shipped them over the M. P. Railroad to Springfield, Illinois, and put them in pastures belonging to W. K. and Joe McCoy, who were commission merchants, and sold them to farmers for feeders. I returned home by way of New Orleans that fall, taking about two weeks to make the trip.

After this for about ten years I went to school a little and stayed on the farm until 1879, when I went into the cattle business altogether, buying, selling and ranching. Started a ranch in 1883 in Pecos County, which I later consolidated with the Toyah Land & Cattle Co., of which M. Locker of Galveston was president. Associated with me in this company was J. M. Nance, H. Hillman, W. T. Jackman and W. C. Johnson. Sold out in 1886 and I, with Sam Head and Bill Jackman, delivered to Ike T. Pryor 3,200 cattle at Brady City to be driven to Wyoming.

In 1885, in connection with Bill Good, H. G. Williams, Bunton & Jackman, I drove 9,000 cattle from the Stafford ranch in Colorado County to Trail City, Colorado.

In 1886 I again drove to Trail City, Colorado, and sold out at Pueblo. From that time up to 1906 I was engaged in feeding and handling with M. A. Withers of Lockhart and H. C. Storey of San Marcos.

From 1906 I was tax collector of Hays County for twelve years. Since that time I have been handling a few cattle, and for a while engaged in shipping horses north.

I remember a little incident that happened on one trip. I fell in with D. S. Combs and about daylight one morning we loaded at Burlington, Iowa, and started up the street to get breakfast, and a toddy was suggested. After going up the street some distance, not knowing that Iowa was a dry state at that time, we stopped on the corner of a street and looked about as strangers would do, when a man standing on the opposite side, without asking a word, but, I think, from Comb's drouthy look, sized us up and said: "Go back two doors and go in a back room and you will find what you are looking for." We followed instructions and located.

LIVED IN SAN ANTONIO AT TIME OF WOLL'S INVASION

By George W. West, Jourdanton, Texas

I was born in Jefferson County, Texas, March 5, 1835. My father, Claiborn West, was one of the signers of the Declaration of Texas Independence. I entered the stock business in 1854 in Atascosa County, and afterward went up the trail twice, each time with my own cattle; endured the usual hardships, but was not molested by Indians except when passing through the Territory, where the Osage tribe demanded toll, and I gave them a few steers. I wintered one of my herds in Nebraska and fattened them on corn which I bought at fifteen cents a bushel. I sold those steers for $5.00 per hundred pounds, which was considered a good price.

I lived on the San Miguel when the Indians were very bad. One night we had our saddle horses tied in the yard to keep the Indians from stealing them and when I went out at daylight to stake them out they were gone, but moccasin tracks showed plainly who had taken them. Notwithstanding the fact that I had two dogs in the yard which would have torn a man to pieces, those Indians got those horses without arousing the dogs.

In one Indian fight in which I was engaged I killed

one redskin and got his bows, arrows and shield, which I gave to Frank Hall, a brother of Bill Hall. Frank took them to Maine and gave them to his relatives.

The old-timers living on the San Miguel at that time were L. B. Harris, Alex, Steve and Nat Walker, Jim Lowe and old man Pierce.

I went to school in San Antonio in 1845, when Woll's Mexican army came and occupied the town.

Seven years ago I had one of my legs amputated just above the knee and since that time I have had to occupy an invalid's chair. My wife and I are living with our daughter, Mrs. Lula West Ray, near Jourdanton, in Atascosa County.

GOT THEIR NAMES IN THE POT FOR SUPPER AND BREAKFAST

By E. M. (Mac) Storey, Lockhart, Texas

I was born in Lockhart, Caldwell County, Texas, December 12, 1857, was raised here and served as mayor of the town for sixteen years. My first experience in handling cattle began when I was nineteen years old. My father was not a stockman and therefore I did not grow up from babyhood handling cattle. After my school days were over I, with others, drove a mule team, hauling freight from Lockhart to Austin and down to the coast. In 1887 I started on the cattle trail, first going to the Erskin pasture in Guadalupe County, to get the cattle for Dewees & Ellison, and gathered them out of the brush so thick, as Green (Pap) Mills said, you could hardly stick a knife in it. Our boss was N. P. (Uncle Nat.) Ellison. The hands with us, as well as I remember, were W. M. Ellison, Green Mills, W. F. Fielder, E. F. Hilliard, John Patterson, Albert McQueen and Asa Jackson.

We had no serious mishap until we reached Onion Creek, where we had a storm and stampede. We counted next morning and were out over 300 cattle in the mountains and the mud, but we soon gathered them all in and moved on, getting out of the brush at Burnett, where we rested a half day. When we reached Red River at Red River Station we had a stampede one night which was caused by a panther coming into camp to get some fresh beef we had on a line.

In 1871 I went with William Green for Bishop & Head. We gathered our herd that spring at Joe Cotulla's ranch in La Salle County, and delivered them to Millett & Erwin on their ranch in the Panhandle, after which R. G. Head sent J. R. Saunders, H. F. Mohle, Billie Gray, Jim Foster and myself to Dodge City, Kansas, to cut all herds that came that way. We had two pack mules and seventeen horses, and when we reached Pease River one of the pack mules laid down and wallowed with his pack, turning it under his belly, so when he got up he stampeded and scattered clothes and blankets everywhere. We finally caught him, gathered up our plunder and went on and camped on a little creek three miles south of the Washita River. That night we had an awful rain and had to move to higher ground. We devoured all of our grub here, expecting to overtake one of Ellison & Dewees' herd before this, but they had crossed the Washita the day before. We started to cross while the stream was on a big rise, and as soon as our loose horses and pack mules struck the swimming water they turned down stream. Being nearer to them, I jumped my horse into it and he did not try to swim a lick, so I floated him out to a sandbar on the other side and lost my saddlebags and all of my clothes except those I had on. When we reached the Washita it was also on a rampage and we decided to wait until the next morning to see if the stream would run down, but the next day it was higher than ever, so we roped logs that were floating down the stream with which to construct a raft. While doing so Billie Gray roped a large tree top and it pulled him into the river. As he could not swim, I threw him the end of my lariat and, thinking he had failed to catch it, I plunged into the water to go to him, still holding my rope. Before I came up I felt him pulling on it, and when I again saw him he was overhanding the rope about ten or fifteen feet from me, so I caught a willow limb. By that time he reached me, caught me around the neck and ducked both of us. I held onto the limb, and he to my neck, and we got out all right, and I lost my lariat. Our craft got water-soaked and we had to make several trips with it to get our bedding across. I swam that river seventeen times that day without a bite to eat, and had had nothing the day before.

The third day we rode all day without food and camped at night in the mud. The fourth day we rode as fast as we could and decided that if we did not get something to eat within a very short time we would kill a horse and eat him, but about one o'clock we struck fresh herd signs and then we shoved our horses and pack mules to the limit. I was about 200 yards behind the other boys when they reached the camp of one of D. R. Fant's herds, and when I got there the boys were still on their horses. They informed me that the boss said he had no grub to spare, as he did not have enough to last him until he reached Dodge City. I remarked that I would just as soon die there as further up the creek, and that I was going to eat or get blood, and I meant every word of it, for I did not intend to perish from starvation when I could smell grub. The other boys were in the same fix, so I felt sure they would stand by me. I got off my horse, walked to the chuck box, where I found some cold corn-bread and fat bacon, and ate some of it, went out to one side and vomited it up. We tried that performance several times before we could get the grub to stay with us. The cook put our names in the pot for supper and breakfast, and the boss apologized for the manner in which he had refused to give us anything to eat, saying he thought perhaps we were a bunch of horse thieves, as we had so many good looking horses, and was afraid to encourage us to remain near for fear we would steal his horses that night. We took our dinners with us the next day and caught the Ellison herd at Wolf Creek. Joe Ague had charge of it. We stayed with him two days, then went on to Dodge City, where I remained and cut cattle three and a half months. Then we threw all of the cattle we had cut, about 600 head, in with one of Dewees & Ellison's herds, and went from there to Ogallala, Nebraska, where the most of the herd was sold to Bosler & Lawrence on the North Platte, near the mouth of Blue Creek. There I was employed to do line riding until October. We gathered a shipment of beef cattle, crossed the river at Sidney Bridge and went to Ogallala, and from there with them to Chicago, when I came home to Texas.

In 1879 I went up with L. T. Pierce for Bishop & Head. In 1880 I went with Giles Fenner for the same firm as far as Cheyenne, Wyoming. There I received a wire from Mr. Head instructing me to go by train to Ogallala to take charge of a range herd of 3,700 cattle. In about two months he sold them back and I took 125 head of horses to Buffalo Bill Cody's ranch near Platte City, then took the train back to Ogallala and from there back to my place of birth and residence.

SETTLED ON THE FRONTIER OF TEXAS

Sketch of Ed B. English of Carrizo Springs, Texas

Ed English, son of Captain Levi English, was born in DeWitt County, Texas, near Yorktown, April 7, 1852. His mother was Matilda Burleson, a cousin to General Edward Burleson, and also a cousin to Joe Hornsby, who lived on the Colorado and figured in the frontier history of the state. She was a member of the well-known English family and was likewise a cousin to the father of our present Postmaster General, Albert Sidney Burleson.

From DeWitt County the English family moved to Bexar County, remaining a short while, then went to Atascosa County and settled just above the present town of Pleasanton, being the first white settlers, along with Uncle Sam Lytle's family, to locate on the Medina River near Von Ormy. From Atascosa they moved to Frio County in 1860 and settled on the Leona River. While they were living there a band of 300 Indians made a raid in that section and killed several white men, among those murdered being Len Eastwood and Jim Saunders. The families got together, gathered up their horses, cattle and household goods and started back to Atascosa. On the road close to a place known as the Brand Rock about fifty Indians threatened to attack them, but when the white people showed fight the savages made haste to depart. The people remained in Atascosa about a year and then moved back to their homes in Frio County.

At a later time the Indians made another raid in that section and Captain English, with ten men, overtook them near where Dilley now stands. There a desperate engagement took place in which three of the white men were killed and six wounded. Those killed were Dan Williams, John English and Dean Oden. The only man living today who was in this fight is Aulsie Franks, now residing at Pleasanton. John English was the oldest brother to the subject of this sketch. He also had another brother accidentally killed near Derby, Texas.

In 1865 Captain English moved his family to Carrizo Springs. There was only one house in Dimmit County at that time, and he settled three miles below this house and was the founder of Carrizo Springs in 1869.

One day in July, 1866, Ed English, with his little brother, was out on the range horse hunting. The two

boys were attacked by seven Indians, who had come upon
them unawares. Ed shot one of their horses and the
Indians closed in upon him, shot him in the arm and
knocked his gun out of his hands. An Indian made a
lunge at him with a lance, which pierced his pistol scabbard. He managed to pull his pistol and killed the foremost Indian with it, then the other Indians ran to the
fallen brave and Ed and his little brother made a dash
for the ranch, with three Indians following, and in the
chase one of the Indians shot Ed in the back with an
arrow. The boys outdistanced their pursuers and
reached home, where Captain English pulled the arrow
out, and found that it had a long steel spike on the end
of it. Ed was laid up with his wounds for nearly two
months.

The next raid the Indians made was in 1870. A band
of about 200 swooped down on the ranch of Charles
Vivian, killed a Mexican and captured a Mexican boy.
Before they reached the Dave Adams ranch the Indians
met a party of five cowboys, Will Bell, Joe Tumlinson,
Si Hay, John Smith and a Mexican. As they were greatly
outnumbered, the boys had to retreat. Adams was at a
pen near his house when the Indians came up and, having
no gun with him, he tried to gain the brush, but was cut
off and killed by the savages. The alarm was spread and
when some of the Indians were within a half mile of
Carrizo Springs several men went out and engaged them
in battle, but were driven back. Other men had come in
from the upper region and got around the Indians to
the Adams ranch and engaged the main body in a desperate fight. While the Indians were killing Adams a
wagonload of people who were going to Carrizo Springs
drove upon the scene. They were Jack McCurdy, Jake
Burleson, Pat McCurdy, Pleas English and Mrs. Levi
English. They turned the wagon and ran from the Indians with only two following them, the others being
engaged in the fight with the cowboys.

Mr. English drove his first cattle up the trail in 1872 to Wichita, Kansas. In 1873 he drove another herd to Dodge City, Kansas. During those days the stockmen formed an association and all worked together on the cow hunts. They sold all of the unbranded yearlings, then known as mavericks, and used the money to buy provisions for the cow hunts.

When Mr. English was quite a small boy he had a great desire to make money, so he took a contract to herd and shear some sheep, for which he received five dollars. He put that money aside to use it to go into the cattle business. One day a cow hunt was stopped at his home, and they had some mavericks which they were going to auction. So Ed decided that was his chance to get into the business. Among the number to be auctioned were two brown heifer yearlings, and Ed went to the man in charge and asked if he would be permitted to bid. The old man told him he could do so and asked how much money he had. The lad proudly replied, "five dollars," and told him how he had obtained it. About thirty men were there, but none of them would bid against the ambitious boy, so he got the two yearlings for four dollars.

Mr. English is one of the most prominent pioneer characters in the southwestern part of the state. He grew up on the frontier and was raised to the cattle business, which he has followed throughout his life, making his home in Dimmit County ever since those early days. He has business interests in San Antonio also, and has spent a great deal of his time during the past few years in the Alamo City. He has a fine ranch of 15,000 acres, beautifully situated on the divide between the Nueces and Rio Grande Rivers, and stocked with high-grade Hereford, Durham and Red Polled cattle.

During his career he has had more power of authority to handle cattle than any other man in his part of the state, that power extending from Brownsville to the Conchos. The last settlements he made were with Jim Lowe,

Billie Slaughter, Mont and Cal Woodward, Bill Ward and Lease Harris. In his cow business he never learned how to block a brand or run one over. He never handled a wet horse because he didn't need him in his business. He still buys and trades in cattle, and when he wants to buy a bunch he generally goes to see George W. Saunders at the Union Stock Yards in San Antonio, for he is a personal friend and deals on the square.

Mr. English has been married twice. His first wife was Mrs. Margaret English, and to them were born five children. In 1886 he married Mrs. Elizabeth Brock. They have one daughter, Celestyne, born July 4, 1900.

SOME THRILLING EXPERIENCES OF AN OLD TRAILER

By L. D. Taylor, 429 Pruitt Avenue, San Antonio, Texas

In the spring of 1869 my two brothers, Dan and George Taylor, with Monte Harrell, rounded up a thou-

L. D. TAYLOR

sand longhorn beeves, four to twelve years old, and started them to Kansas. I had never been out of our home neighborhood before, so I went along to get some experience on the trail. The herd was rounded up in Gonzales County, about where the town of Waelder is now located.

We swam the Trinity at Dallas, where our herd stampeded and ran through the streets of the town, creating quite a commotion. The damage they did cost us about two hundred dollars.

When we reached Waco the Brazos River was level

with its banks, and we had to swim the herd across. It is a wonderful sight to see a thousand steers swimming all at one time. All you could see was the tips of their horns and the ends of their noses as they went through the water.

Near Waco I learned some law, by taking two rails off a fence for firewood with which to cook supper. Was glad to get off by paying two dollars for those rails. We proceeded on to the Red River, which we crossed and traveled several days in the friendly Indian Nation. The first night there we rounded up the herd, but next morning they were gone, for they had been stampeded by Indians shooting arrows into them, and it required several days to get them all together again. The Indians resorted to that kind of a trick to get pay for helping to get the cattle back again. When we left this section of the Indian Territory we turned our backs to civilization, for the remainder of the trip was to be made through a wild, unsettled, hostile country. After a few days' travel we struck the Chisholm Trail, the only thoroughfare from Texas through the Indian Territory to Kansas, and about this time two other herds fell in with us, and, not knowing the country we were going through, the three outfits agreed to stick together, stay and die with each other if necessary. Ours was the third herd that had ever traveled that trail. We had plenty of stampedes, and one day we had a run just after crossing a swollen stream. I was with the chuck wagon, and was left alone, so I just kept right on traveling. Late that evening, after I had turned out and struck camp for the night, my brother George came up and told me the herds and other wagons were ten miles behind. He gave me his pistol and went back to the herd, and I stayed there alone that night. The next day the herd overtook me, and I felt somewhat relieved.

One night the herd was rounded up about a half mile from camp, and during the night I was awakened by the shaking of the earth and an awful noise, and found the whole herd coming down upon us in a furious run. I was bunking with Monte Harrell, and when I jumped up Harrell tried to hold me, but I jerked loose and ran around to the other side of the wagon. I soon had Mr. Harrell for company. I think every beef must have jumped over the wagon tongue, at least it seemed to me that every steer was jumping it.

From here on we had considerable trouble crossing the creeks and rivers, having to float our wagons across. When we reached one of these streams that was on a rise three or four men would swing on behind each wagon to hold it down until we got into the water, then the men would swim alongside the oxen and guide them across.

After going about three hundred miles without seeing anyone or knowing our exact location, we came to the old military road running north. That day about noon two negro soldiers came to our camp mounted on two big fine government horses. They asked me for grub and I told them I had none cooked, and as brother George spoke rather harsh to them, they rode away, going by one of the other herds. After they had passed on, two young men with one of the other outfits decided to follow these negroes and take their horses away from them, suspecting that they were not in rightful possession of the animals. When they overtook the negroes a fight ensued in which one of the boys was killed. The other boy returned to us one of the government horses and told us of the affair. We went out and found the body and buried it there on the trail, using axes and knives to dig the grave with. I have forgotten the murdered boy's name, but he was from Texas. The negroes, we learned afterwards, were deserters from the army. We found the other government horse grazing near where the fight took place, the negroes having secured the horses belonging to these two boys and made their escape on them.

The next day I was about a mile behind the herd with

the chuck wagon and four Indians came up. They grunted
and asked for "tarbucket," so I grabbed the tar bucket
and gave it to them, but they shook their heads and put
their hands in my pockets, took all of my tobacco, gave
another grunt, and went off with the tar bucket. In camp
that night my brother asked why I permitted them to
take our tar, but I replied that I was glad they did not
take my scalp.

A few days later as we were traveling along we saw
ahead of us something that looked like a ridge of timber,
but which proved to be about four hundred Comanches
who were coming our way. They were on the warpath
and going to battle with another tribe. When they came
up to our herd they began killing our beeves without
asking permission or paying any attention to us. Some
of the boys of our herd went out to meet them, but the
boys of the other herds hid out in the grass, and only
one man from the other outfit came to us. They killed
twenty-five of our beeves and skinned them right there,
eating the flesh raw and with blood running down their
faces, reminding me of a lot of hungry dogs. Here I
witnessed some of the finest horsemanship I ever saw.
The young warriors on bareback ponies would ride all
over the horses' backs, off on one side, standing up, laying down, going at full speed and shooting arrows clear
through the beeves. We were powerless to help ourselves, for we were greatly outnumbered. Every time
we would try to start the herd the Indians would surround the herd and hold it. Finally they permitted us to
move on, and we were not slow in moving, either. I felt
greatly relieved, and they could have left us sooner without my permission. These Indians had "talked peace"
with Uncle Sam, that is all that saved us. We heard a
few days afterwards that they had engaged in battle
with their foes after leaving us, and had been severely
whipped, losing about half of their warriors.

In 1869 Colonel John D. Miles was appointed Indian

agent by President Grant and served in this capacity in
Kansas and the Indian Territory, for the Cheyennes,
Arapahoes, Kiowas and Comanches, which tribes frequently went on the warpath in those days, making it
very dangerous for the trail drivers. We met Colonel
Miles the next day after the Indians had attacked our
herd, and he made a note of the number of beeves they
had killed belonging to us, and said he would report it
to Washington, and we would receive pay for all we had
lost. He was traveling alone in a hack on his way to
some fort, and to me he looked very lonely in that wild
and woolly country.

When we reached the Canadian River we found it on
a big rise, so we decided to stop there a few days and
allow our herd to graze while waiting for the river to
go down. While we were there a man came along one
day and warned us to be on the lookout for Indians, saying they were liable to attack us at any time. He passed
on, and the next day we crossed the river and after
traveling about ten miles we came to a pool of water
where we found this man's clothes on the bank. Investigation revealed that he had been stripped and dumped
into the pool.

We reached the Arkansas River, where we had a little
trouble getting across. There were a few houses on the
Kansas side, and we began to rejoice that we were once
more getting within the boundaries of civilization. Here
we found a store and plenty of "booze," and some of the
boys got "full." After leaving that wayside oasis we
did not see another house until we were within ten miles
of Abilene. We had several stampedes in that region.

One evening Monte Harrell said the prospects were
good for a storm that night, and sure enough we had a
regular Kansas twister. We had prepared for it by driving a long stake pin into the ground, to which I chained
the wagon, and making everything as safe as possible.
At midnight the storm was on, and within a moment

everything was gone except the wagon and myself. The cattle stampeded, horses got loose, and oxen and all went with the herd. The storm soon spent its fury and our men managed to hold the cattle until daylight and got them all back the next morning and we resumed our drive to Abilene, reaching there in a few days. Abilene at this time was just a small town on a railroad, consisting of three saloons, one store and two hotels. Here we tarried to graze and fatten our cattle for market, and as several of the hands were not needed, they were paid off and allowed to return home, I being among the number.

While we were in Abilene, we found the town was full of all sorts of desperate characters, and I remember one day one of these bad men rode his horse into a saloon, pulled his gun on the bartender, and all quit business. When he came out several others began to shoot up the town. I was not feeling well, so I went over to the hotel to rest, and in a short time the boys of our outfit missed me and instituted a search, finding me at the hotel under a bed.

The next day we made preparations to start back to Texas, and went on the train to Junction City, Kansas, to get our outfit. It was the first train I ever rode on, and I thought the thing was running too fast, but a brakeman told me it was behind time and was trying to make up the schedule. We secured our outfit, took in several men wanting to come to Texas, elected a boss and started for home. The second night out we camped in a little grove of timber and during the night a storm struck us, another one of those Kansas zephyrs that was calculated to blow hell off the range. I located a stump and anchored myself to it, while the boss, a long-legged fellow, had secured a death grip on a sapling near me. During the progress of the storm his feet were constantly in my way, flying around and striking my shins and knocking the bark off the stump I was hanging to for dear life. I could hear him trying to pray, but I was so busy at that particular time that I did not pay much attention to what he was saying. The wind would pick us up and flop our bodies against the ground with great force, but I hung to that stump and got through all right.

We reached Fort Gibson, on the Arkansas, and here we were compelled to stay a week on account of high water. The boys chipped in and bought a lot of whiskey at this place, paying twelve dollars a gallon for it. I opposed buying the whiskey because it was a serious offense to convey it into the Indian Territory, but they bought it anyway, and after we had started on our way again some trouble arose among the outfit. One day an old Indian brought a horse and outfit to our camp and I bought this outfit, paying the Indian seventy-five dollars for it, so I left the bunch and pulled out alone through the Indian country. I reached Red River safely and made it through to my home without mishap, reaching there with only seventy-five cents in my pocket.

In conclusion I will say that I have seen cowboys who had been in the saddle for twenty-four hours without sleep or anything to eat, come into camp, lay down on a log and go to sleep almost instantly, and sleep sound with the rain pouring down and water four inches all around them. All of the boys who were with me on this trip mentioned above are dead except one, William McBride. I was twenty years old when I made that trip; I am now seventy years old.

THE MAN WHO HAD HELL IN HIS NECK

By Ab. Blocker of San Antonio, Texas

I was born three miles south of Austin, Texas, January 30, 1856, and spent my boyhood days in farm and ranch work. In 1876 I went to Blanco County to work for my brother, John R. Blocker, on his ranch, roping

wild steers out of the brush and mountains, and moved
them to the Lockhart Prairie, fifteen miles south of Austin.   In 1877 we drove these steers—3,000 head—to
Wyoming Territory and delivered them to John Sparks,
forty miles this side of Cheyenne.   There were sixteen

AB. BLOCKER

men with this herd, but brother John, myself, and an
old negro named Joe Tasby, are the only ones living now.
We carried the herd through from Austin to Cheyenne
in eighty-two days. John and Bill Blocker owned them,
and John was the boss, Bill remaining at home. Frank
Smith was the cook, the best that ever went on the trail.
    In the spring of 1878 we again started up the trail

with 3,000 head of wild steers for John and Bill Blocker, with John Golden as boss. At Ogallala, Nebraska, John Blocker overtook us and put me in charge of his herd and, I delivered them near Cheyenne to Swenson Bros. Golden took the other herd to the Red Cloud Agency, and had one man killed by lightning. Forty miles this side of Cheyenne, while we were in camp, I had my horse caught for the night relief. It began raining and the cook went to the wagon and began handing out slickers to the boys. A bolt of lightning knocked five of the men down and killed seven horses in camp. I had just left camp for the herd when this occurred.

When we crossed Red River, Golden told me one evening to look out for the herd, as he and Bill Biles were going back to the other side of the river. I thought they were going back for whiskey, but the next morning just at daylight they drove up with forty head of fine four-year-old steers. He had given the old inspector some drag yearlings to cross our herd. That was a pretty hard set of people there at that time. Every man you saw had a pistol and Winchester and the children at the houses we passed were cutting teeth on cartridge shells.

In 1881 I drove 3,000 cattle from Williamson County to the Cross S ranch, twelve miles from Carrizo Springs, for Seeright & Carruthers.

In 1882 I drove some 3,000 head from Austin to Crazy Woman and Powder Rivers, Wyoming, for Stoddard, Howard & Blocker, and delivered them at the Stoddard & Howard ranch. After I returned from that trip I worked some, but not much, spending most of the time driving six yoke of steers for Bill Blocker, working twenty hours out of every twenty-four, hauling everything that was to feed to cattle; the balance of the time I spent in "acting the dude" in Austin and blowing in my easy-made money.

In 1884 I drove a herd of 2,500 cows and heifers from Tom Green County to Buffalo Springs, in Dalham

County, for John Blocker and delivered them at the XIT ranch. Old Barbecue Campbell was in charge of this ranch, which was owned by a syndicate that had bought a lot of cattle down in South and Southwest Texas with which to stock it. At Mobeetie I was turned back and had to go down across the plains. My herd was the first to reach the ranch, and I got there first by driving at night around Joe Collins, who was in charge of a herd belonging to George West. Old Barbecue Campbell was undecided as to selecting a brand to be used by the ranch syndicate, and when I suggested XIT it pleased him so well he decided to use that brand, and it became known all over Texas, Oklahoma and New Mexico as the XIT ranch. I branded the first cow to carry the XIT brand, and after delivering this herd Alex Caspares and myself went to Los Animas, Colorado, where we sold our saddle horses and went by train to Dodge City, Kansas, where I received a message from brother John, who was at San Antonio, instructing me to go to Camp Supply, get a horse, go back the trail and stop two or three herds of his cattle, as he had sold part of them and wanted me to deliver them and take the balance to Deer Trail, Colorado. I went by stage to Camp Supply and there met the bosses of John's herds. They had been stopped by the ranchmen on No Man's Land, who would not permit herds to pass. Several herds belonging to George West and others were also there. As soon as John Blocker and George West received news that their herds had been held up they immediately came up there and began to plan to get their cattle across that strip of country. Fourteen armed men were riding fence to keep all herds from passing, and refused to meet any reasonable demands. Blocker and West went to Camp Supply and began wiring the authorities at Washington, sending several messages, one message alone costing them about $60.00, nearly all of the messages passing through the hands of Colonel Carr, who was very courteous and ex-

tended every facility at his command to assist them.
Things were looking pretty "squally," and I began to
feel creepy. A ranchman friend of John told him that
if he would give the word he would take his men and kill
all of the fellows who had stopped the herds, but John
told him that he thought he could beat them by law.
After several days' parleying, Blocker and West got a
telegram from Washington telling them to cut the fence
and pass through with their herds, and if there was
further trouble troops would be ordered there. When
this telegram came I had a herd ready to move. A lot of
the boys with axes cut the fence for a quarter of a mile,
I took the lead and was the first to cross the line. In just
a short time all the herds were on the move, and as far
back as you could see the cattle, men, chuck wagons, horse
rustlers and all were coming, all eager to get across No
Man's Land. I took my herd to Deer Trail, Colorado,
this side of Denver, and delivered them to a Mr. Robinson, who had bought them. Bill Blocker came up and
helped me count them out to Robinson, then Bill went to
Denver and left me to rope and pull down those cattle
with a wornout trail pony. I borrowed a good horse
from Mr. Robinson to rope on, and got him killed by a
cow hooking him through the head. Robinson said to me,
"Now you have played h—l with my horse, and I can't
loan you another." He then suggested that I turn the
cattle out to graze and let them rest, and start with them
for the ranch, twenty miles away, the next day, but I told
him my wagon and cook had already gone and I had instructed the cook to drive until I caught up with him,
therefore the cattle would sleep just behind that wagon
that night. He and his boss walked through the pen and
I heard Robinson say, "I thought Blocker had hell in his
neck all the time," and I spoke out and said, "You are
right; I have hell in my head four stories high, and I don't
want you to forget it." The next day between 11 and
12 o'clock I met him at his pasture gate, drove the cattle

Ab. Blocker and Outfit Starting on Trail to Deadwood, South Dakota, in 1893

and horses through, delivered the wagon to him, as he had bought everything but the men, and asked him where his ranch house was. He told me it was about a mile away at a cottonwood mot on the creek. I called the boys and struck a gallop, and when we got there I unsaddled my horse, pulled off my leggins and six-shooter, laid my head on my saddle on the shady side of the house, and said, "Now, boys, I am going to sleep, and the first d—d man that wakes me I'll kill him." I slept until dark, and when I awoke Mr. Robinson had a fine supper prepared for us boys. Bill Blocker had sent me sufficient money to pay my men, and the next day Robinson took us all to the railroad. The men all went back to Texas, while Robinson and I went to Denver, where we found Bill Blocker at a hotel. I was wearing an old tattered Mexican hat, my clothes were showing the effects of the trail work, and I had a mashed foot. Bill said to me, "You can't eat at this hotel dressed like that." I remarked, "I'll come d—n near eating if anyone else does," and walked into the dining room with the well-dressed guests. After dinner Bill asked me how much money I wanted and I told him about $200. He gave it to me, and I went out and got a shave and bath, and dressed up in great style, then went back to the hotel and Mr. Robinson did not know me. I remained there several days, had my picture taken and gave one to Robinson and told him to hang it in his ranch house so that he would never forget the man that had hell in his neck at Deer Trail. He thanked me and assured me that he would never forget Ab. Blocker.

In 1886 I went to San Antonio, got a wagon, horses and hands and went below Pearsall to receive a herd of 1,500 steers. Drove them for Blocker, Driscoll & Davis to Hugo, Colorado, and turned them over to old Fine Earnest. Blocker, Driscoll & Davis had 57,000 cattle and 1,800 saddle horses on the trail that year. After I turned over the herd at Hugo, I came back with a few men and

W. B. BLOCKER, Austin, Tex.

wagon to Tom Green County and gathered a herd of
cattle and drove them to the mouth of Devil's River,
where I delivered them to George Berry and he wintered
them there for John Blocker, then put them into Mexico
the next spring, and I went to Austin, where I went to
work on the farm for my father and mother. Here I
worked like h——l for two years and never made a cent
because of the drouth. I got four cents for my cotton the
first year and five cents the next year, and I swore if I
ever planted cotton any more I would boil the seed before
I planted it. Mother sold the farm and I went back to the
saddle on the hurricane deck of a little pony.

In 1889 I drove 3,700 cattle from Tom Green County
to Wyoming for John Blocker. He met me at Fort
Laramie, where he sold 1,000 out of this herd and I went
to the Belle Fourche River with the balance. When I
got back to Austin I had a fine time while my money
lasted.

In 1890 I went to the Chupadero ranch near Eagle
Pass and worked for my brother, John, for a while, then
went back to Austin, got a wagon and four mules from
Bill Blocker and tanked for brother John and Tom Cole-

man. Got so d—d tired of that job Johnnie put me on
that Chupadero ranch as boss. In 1891 John put me to
feeding 1,500 steers eight miles from Eagle Pass, and I
spent the winter there.

In 1892 I ran an outfit all over the lower country for
Blocker & Coleman, working cattle day and night.

In 1893 brother John sent me with wagon and eighty-
two horses from Spofford to a ranch about seventy-five
miles from Colorado City, Texas, to drive a herd from
there for Harris Franklin to South Dakota. Mr. Franklin and his boss were there and had received the cattle,
but brother John had told me that I had the right to cut
out all I thought would not stand the trip, so I cut out
some and left here with 2,997 cattle and delivered all
but fourteen head near Deadwood, South Dakota. John
drove these cattle for $2.75 per head and paid the bosses.
He had never seen the herd until I reached the ranch
with them and when he looked them over he said, "Well,
Ab, that is the best herd I ever saw come over the trail."
I told him the cattle were all O. K., but I had lost thirty-
seven of his d—d old horses, and he remarked, "I did not
expect you to get here with more than one horse to the
man." So I felt pretty good. He sold all of the horses
but two to one of the hands, and I sent Link Norwood,
the cook, with the wagon and four mules back to Eagle
Pass. He drove from near Deadwood, South Dakota, to
Eagle Pass, Texas, in fifty-nine days. The accompanying photograph was taken just before my outfit started
on this trip, and the mules shown therein made the entire
trip, going and coming, with the chuck wagon.

In 1896 I married Miss Florence Baldwin, on the Rio
Grande River, and lived at the Chuparedo ranch until
1897, when I moved to a ranch fifteen miles southeast
of Cotulla, and went broke there during the drouth. In
1902 I went to Oklahoma and in 1903 came back to Eagle
Pass, where I worked for Blocker & Ford, later going
back to the Chupadero ranch, where I remained until

1912, then commenced working for the Cattle Raisers' Association, and have been engaged in this work ever since.

MY THIRD AND LAST TRIP UP THE TRAIL IN 1886

By R. J. Jennings of San Antonio, Texas

I left Frio County on the 20th of March, 1886, in company with eleven Pearsall boys, headed for the Pena ranch to take charge of a herd of 1,100 one and two-year-old Mexican cattle belonging to Blocker, Driscoll & Davis, which were to be driven to Deer Trail, Colorado. We went by rail to Laredo and on to Hebbronville, and from there out to the ranch, where we found Mr. Blocker waiting for us, and when we had the herd ready to start he told us to go to the Catarina ranch in Dimmit County, where I would be given 1,400 more. Some of the first herd were very poor, and those we received at the Catarina ranch were big, fat, strong fellows, and I remarked to Mr. Blocker when I saw them that I would either have to drive the poor ones to death or starve the fat ones, to which he replied that I could graze them. We pulled out with the herd and passed near Carriza Springs, on to Eagle Pass, and out by Spofford Junction, where we came into the Western Trail and went up the Nueces River by Kickapoo Springs. There the hard road began to get harder, and we found no grass and but little water, therefore I did not "graze them through," as Mr. Blocker had suggested. The first rain that fell on us was at Vernon, on the Pease River.

This herd belonged to Driscoll, Blocker & Davis, who at the time had about 20,000 cattle on the trail in different herds. On account of the exceedingly dry weather that had prevailed for a good while it was a very hard year for trail men, and many of them sustained heavy losses.

When we got over the divide into Llano County, where cattle rustlers were thick, I picked up a red and white hided beef which had the road brand, a big D, on him. Some rustler had tried to efface this D, but made a failure and left the brand showing very plainly. A day or two later a mountain gent came to my herd, saw this steer and claimed him for another party. I refused to give the steer up, and that is where I made a grave mistake, for, in consequence, I lost about twenty-five head of cattle and seven horses, and besides sustained serious injury. The actions of the fellow made me suspicious, and I warned my hands to look out for trouble, for we were in a region infested with rustlers, and there was no knowing just what they would resort to. I always held the herd while the first watch was getting up their night horses and at their supper. That evening I rode into camp after being relieved, and was eating my supper when the herd started to run. It was just after dusk, and as the moon had not yet risen, we had no light to see what caused the stampede, but I straddled my horse and went down the hill in front of the frightened cattle. That was the last I remembered until about midnight. The boys missed me, and supposed I was somewhere with a bunch of the cattle, but finally they discovered me sitting on my horse in the middle of the herd. Sam Oden said he called to me but I did not answer, and he came to me and found me in a dazed and speechless condition. He led my horse to camp and tried to get me to lay down, but I could get no rest in that manner. I had in some manner been painfully injured and for two weeks afterward I could sleep only when I was leaning against the end gate of the wagon. How it all happened is a mystery and will probably never be known. Even to this day that injury is still felt and I suffer from it. I do not know how I came to be on my horse when they found me. When we reached old Runnels City I was still spitting blood, and Mr. Blocker insisted that I go back home, but I refused and stayed with the herd. Instead of going to Deer Trail, I delivered the herd on the north side of the Arkansas River at Coolidge, Kansas, or rather at Trail City, Colorado, there being only the state line between the two towns. My outfit went to a point about twenty miles north of Trail City, where the firm had 3,400 two-year-old steers which they had sold to a man whose name I have forgotten. We cut them out and took them back to the south side of the Arkansas River and then up that stream for some distance where we delivered them. This man had a certified check to give me in payment for these cattle. He was in a buckboard with a driver, and getting out to ride with us on the herd he told his driver to go on ahead for some distance. The driver pulled out, traveled at a lively gait and got lost from us, being found two weeks later down at Dodge City with the buckboard and everything all right.

I left a part of my crew, some went on, while others came back home. George Mudd and Frank Blair had a fist fight on this trip which helped to liven up things in camp.

COLONEL DILLARD R. FANT

Sketch of One of the Most Prominent of All Trail Drivers

Colonel Dillard R. Fant, who died in 1918, was born in the Anderson district of South Carolina, July 27, 1841, his parents being W. N. and Mary Fant, who were also natives of that district. They moved to Texas in 1852, locating near Goliad. At the age of fourteen, the boy Dillard began freighting with ox teams between San Antonio and Goliad, and at the outbreak of the Civil War he joined the Confederate forces, enlisting in Captain Kinney's company of the Twenty-first Texas Cavalry and Carter's Brigade, serving in the Trans-Mississippi department in Texas, Louisiana, and Arkansas.

COLONEL DILLARD R. FANT

After the Civil War ended Colonel Fant engaged in farming for a short time in Goliad county, but in 1886 he went into the cattle business and rapidly rose to prominence because of the extent and importance of his operations. He drove cattle to Kansas, Nebraska, Wyoming, and other markets, and for a number of years he had large contracts with the government to supply beef cattle to various military posts and agencies, including Yankton and Standing Rock agencies in Dakota, and Fort Reno and Fort Sill in the Indian Territory. These contracts extended over a period of about fourteen years, during which time Colonel Fant delivered many thousands of cattle to the government. During a period of about four years he wintered vast herds of cattle on the Loup and Platte Rivers in Nebraska, but his operations extended to Wyoming, where he sold a great many cattle, and even as far as Idaho where he spent two winters. Colonel Fant drove one of the largest bunches of cattle ever taken over the trail in 1884, numbering 42,000, going in several herds to Wyoming. The magnitude of this undertaking may be imagined from the fact that these cattle cost him from $12 to $20 per head, requiring 1,200 saddle horses in making the drive, and fully two hundred men were used to handle the herds and supplies on the trail.

After the quarantine laws against Texas became effective, Colonel Fant ceased taking his cattle to the north and confined his operations to trips to the Indian Territory, where he secured pasturage and grazing privileges for his herds. It is estimated that he took fully two hundred thousand head of cattle over the trail to the north during the fifteen years he was engaged in the business. During all these years Colonel Fant had continued in the cattle business at his home in Goliad county, and it is claimed that he was the second man to fence a pasture in Texas, enclosing his first range in 1874, when he began to improve his stock by the introduction of Durhams and

Herefords. He gradually extended his land holdings, placed more pastures under fence, and located ranches in Frio, Live Oak, Hidalgo and other counties, some as far north as Tarrant county. He owned and operated the Santa Rosa ranch in Hidalgo county, which comprised 225,000 acres, a pasture of sixty thousand acres in Live Oak county, and altogether had holdings amounting to 700,000 acres of grazing land in various parts of the state.

Colonel Fant was married at Goliad, Texas, October 15, 1865, to Miss Lucy A. Hodges, daughter of Colonel Jack Hodges, a prominent Texan who won distinction in the Mexican war. Eight children were born to Colonel and Mrs. Fant, and some of them are today prominent in the business and social life of the state.

A few years ago Colonel Fant disposed of his ranch holdings, retired from the cattle business, and established his home in San Antonio, where he resided until his death.

RELATES OF A TRIP MADE IN 1872

By M. L. Bolding, of Bartlett, Texas

I was born in Mississippi and there I spent my childhood and early manhood, coming to Texas in 1867 and settling in Williamson county.

My first experience on the trail was in the year 1871, which was followed by another trip in 1872, and concerning the latter I shall relate.

I was a member of the crew of W. T. Avery of Hutto, Texas, and after rounding up two thousand steers and with all the necessary paraphernalia consisting of chuck wagon, extra saddle horses and other things, we left Brushy Creek for Kansas on April 15, 1872. We crossed Little River west of Temple, Texas, which at that time

was a prairie; the Brazos at Waco, which was then a
small town; the Trinity at Forth Worth, which consisted
of a blacksmith shop, and Red
River west of Sherman, which
was at that time a large country town. Upon entering the
Indian Nation, now the state
of Oklahoma, we encountered
Indians, buffaloes and wild
horses. We followed a trail
known as the main western
trail and, due to heavy rains
and the cattle stampeding, together with trouble with the
Indians, we experienced many
hardships. We crossed the
Arkansas River into Kansas
and stopped at Baxter

M. L. BOLDING

Springs, spending one month resting and fattening the
cattle. From there we moved to Ellsworth, located on
Smoky River, the extreme frontier of Kansas, from
which point we shipped the cattle by rail to Kansas City
and sold them. On the return trip I had charge of a
wagon and some extra saddle horses and after spending
six weeks on the journey I arrived home in November.

I am now seventy years of age and live at Bartlett,
Texas.

PAID THREE DOLLARS FOR FIVE GALLONS OF WATER

By Sam Garner of Lockhart, Texas

I was born in Tennessee in June, 1847, and have lived
in Caldwell county over sixty-three years, witnessing all
of the wonderful changes that have occurred in that great
space of time. When I was sixteen years old I went into
the Confederate Army and "fit, bled and died" for the

great cause that was lost, returning from the war to engage in cattle raising and farming.

In 1869 I made my first trip up the trail with a herd belonging to Colonel J. J. Myers of this county, and we went through without mishap to Abilene, Kansas, where the herd was delivered. While we were camped near Abilene, I witnessed one of the most terrific cloudbursts and water spouts that I ever saw. It washed away wagons and every movable thing, drowning several people and many head of stock.

When I left Abilene I went with a lot of fat cattle that were shipped by rail to St. Louis, coming down through Kentucky, Tennessee, Indiana, and Louisiana. On my route home I took the Morgan line from New Orleans to Galveston, and there took the stage coach for Gonzales, which put me within twenty miles of home.

In 1870 I gathered a herd for Peck & Evans, which I drove to Nebraska, and held them and other cattle until winter to fatten for market. When they were fat they were shipped to Chicago. While going up the trail with this herd, just as we struck the Kansas-Nebraska line, two men came to us one day and told us it was too late to cross the line into Nebraska and we would have to remain right there and consider our herd under quarantine. One of the men claimed to be a sheriff and the other was his deputy. As grass and water were plentiful I told Mr. Sheriff that it made no difference to me whether I stayed there or not, as the cattle could not be shipped until they fattened, and that they would fatten there as quick as any place I ever saw. He stayed all night with us, and after he was sound asleep I had the boys to quietly move the herd across the line, getting beyond his authority to molest us. When he awoke and found we had out-generaled him, he took the trick good naturedly, and left our vicinity.

In 1871 I gathered a herd for Colonel J. J. Myers, but did not drive this herd as Wash Murray and myself gath-

SAM GARNER

ered enough of our own cattle to make a herd and we went along with them. We sold this herd to Colonel Myers and delivered them on the Solomon River in Kansas, from where I took them to Salt Lake City for him. On this trip we had a great many hardships. Snow fell so deep that it covered the grass and our cattle and horses froze to death right in camp, and many of our cattle died. The old wild beeves became as gentle as work oxen, and we could handle them easily enough, but the extreme cold caused us much suffering. Our oxen would bog down in the snow just the same as if it was mud, and we frequently were compelled to ram snow into their nostrils to make them get up and move. We had to walk about three hundred miles through the snow, for we could make no headway on horseback. We could not night herd because we were afoot, and it took us six weeks to make the trip, and when we arrived at the place of delivery the parties who had contracted for the cattle refused to receive them until the weather moderated, because they wanted to wait and see how many would die from the effects of the weather. It may have been good business on their part, but it gave us boys the devil to hold the herd still longer after all we had gone through to get them there.

On one of the trips I made I recall what a "dry" time we had when we got up in a region where the water was full of alkali. We were all very thirsty, and came to a beautiful stream of clear water. A spring was flowing out of the side of a mountain, and inviting us to partake freely, but all things that look good do not prove to be good. That was the saltiest water I ever tasted—we could not drink it at all. We had passed a spring a few miles back on the trail, and it was good water, so an Irishman said if we would give him three dollars he would go back and bring us five gallons of water from that good spring. Well, he got the money and we got the water, and while I have drank some good liquor in

times gone by and thought it was the best stuff that ever
went down a cowboy's neck, that five gallons of water on
that occasion beat any liquor I had ever swallowed.

In 1872 I gathered 600 or 700 head of my cattle and
put them in with Colonel Myers' herd and Mack Stewart
and myself drove the herd to Salt Lake again. This trip
was much more pleasant than the previous one. We
started earlier than the year before, consequently we had
no trouble in delivering them. Just before reaching the
point of delivery, however, we passed through a very
brushy section, and lost some of the cattle. Fanny Hart
and myself went back about forty miles and found a lot
of them which I sold to a fellow and got his check for
them. We had to hire the horses we rode on this hunt,
and paid three dollars per day for each of them besides
a dollar and a half a day for boarding our own horses
while we were away. While I believe in honesty under
reasonable conditions, I did steal some oats for my horse
on this trip. We had had a very hard day's drive
through a region where there was no grass and when we
came to a place where oats were stacked I just couldn't
keep from swiping a few bundles for Old Doc.

I am now seventy-three years of age, and while I have
had some very hard times in life, especially while on the
trail, still, as old as I am, I think I would have the nerve
to undertake to go through it all again if I knew where
there was a country like this was in those good old days.

LISTENED TO THE CHANT OF THE NIGHT SONGS

By I. H. Elder, Sanderson, Texas

My first trail work was under the direction of Tom
Lane, in the spring of 1877, around my home at Clarksville, Texas. We put up a herd that was driven to Cheyenne, Wyoming. In the spring of 1878 I put up a herd
which later was thrown in with the famous Northup

herd of 3,000 head, which were driven through to Parsons, Kansas, by Northup and his Kansas jay-hawkers. This was the largest herd ever moved from that part of the state.

In the spring of 1879 I worked with Bass Baker from Red River county to Kechi Valley in Jack county, near old Fort Hog Eye. About this time, boys, we were handling them pretty lively. It is good to remember how all the boys gathered round the camp fire and told of their experiences. Many is the time I have listened to the chant of the night songs as the boys went around the herd.

I followed the trail work until 1882, when I retired from the trail and drove a herd for myself from Red River county to the western part of Brown county, and from that date to the present time I have been after the cow. I am now on the Rio Grande in Terrell county.

SKETCH OF L. B. ALLEN

L. B. ALLEN

L. B. Allen, better known among his friends as Lew Allen, was born in Mississippi on February 14th, 1848, and came with his father, W. W. Allen to Texas and settled at Sweet Home, in Lavaca county, when he was about four years of age. His father was engaged in farming and stock raising. At an early age he became interested in the stock business, and is rightly classified as a pioneer of the cattle business in Texas.

He entered the Civil War on the side of the Confederacy at a very early age and in about 1866 returned to

Lavaca county and from that time up to the time of his·
death, which occurred December 2nd, 1911, he was continuously in the cattle business.

In about 1873 L. B. Allen, W. J. Moore and Sam
Moore formed a partnership which continued until the
death of Sam Moore, and was continued with W. J.
Moore up to the time of the death of L. B. Allen. They
first had their ranch in Lavaca county and later moved
their ranch to Uvalde and Kinney counties. Mr. Allen
made many trips up the trail, driving cattle to Dakota and
Nebraska. At one time Moore & Allen opened up a ranch
in the Black Hills. L. B. Allen, W. J. Moore, Sam Moore,
J. M. Bennett, Sol West, Ike West, George West and Mr.
McCutcheon were all stockmen in the early days in
Lavaca county at Sweet Home, all of them became large
cattle owners and were successful in business.

One of the best evidences of the integrity of Mr.
Allen and his associates and neighbors is that they all,
since their early settlement at Sweet Home, have remained intimate friends.

L. B. Allen was the brother of W. W. Allen, who was
also engaged in the stock business, also of R. B. Allen,
who was an attorney and also engaged in the stock business.

The above early settlers of Sweet Home, Texas, were
all large men of stature, and also large in character, and
in their dealings with each other no other obligation was
required in any contract except their word.

HAD LESS TROUBLE WITH INDIANS THAN WITH THE GRANGERS ON THE TRAIL

By J. E. Pettus, of Goliad, Texas

My father, John Freeman Pettus, came to Texas with
Austin's Colony in 1822. He fought with old Ben
Milam in San Antonio, and was also in the Battle of San

Jacinto. I was born in DeWitt county, when but few settlers lived there and spent my boyhood on the frontier. When I first started on the trail it was with my own

J. E. PETTUS

cattle, my brother W. A. Pettus loaning me the money to buy these cattle and I drove them to Dodge City, Kansas. I drove one year to Ogallala, Nebraska.

In making trips up the trail I was always happy when we crossed Red River for we had less trouble with the Indians than with the grangers. The Indians would sometimes come into camp and beg from us, demanding fat beeves, but we always managed to pacify them. But the grangers displayed a degree of animosity toward the trail drivers that was almost unbearable.

My father settled in Bee county in 1857, and lived there for many years, moving to Goliad county in 1877. When we first resided in these counties the population was small and the country almost a wilderness. Today shows quite a contrast, and as I look back over the intervening years I can see the remarkable changes that have taken place. But foremost and above all the cowman has had his full share in the making of this glorious country, for he was the pioneer, the advance guard of the high state of civilization that is enjoyed by the present generation.

I had three brothers, W. A. Pettus, J. M. Pettus and T. G. Pettus. The two first named died several years ago, and T. G. now lives at Charco, in Goliad county.

MY TRIP UP THE TRAIL

By W. F. Thompson, Pearsall, Texas

It was in the clay hills of Mississippi, February 5th, 1863, where I first sprung to light. My father, being an officer in the Confederate Army, soon saw the cause was lost and in 1865 ran the blockade and came to Texas. Hence, Texas got another missionary. In 1870 we landed in Medina county, where I grew up among the hardships of a frontier life, as there were no churches or schools to go to. In 1863 I left the Lytle ranch on the Chicon creek with a herd of horses and went to Kerrville where we began receiving cattle to go up the trail. We bought the cattle between Fredericksburg and Blanco City, and in a few days we had two thousand cattle under herd. The first night we herded out we had the worst stampede I ever saw. At twelve o'clock at night when I went to call first relief, the cattle came right into camp where the boys had the horses tied to a fence. Several broke loose, dragging rails and coming into the herd. I tried to cut them off from where the horses were grazing, all being hobbled, but they beat me to them, soon got mixed up and turned down a lane with a mad rush, cattle, myself and horses. We went for some time before I could get around to one side, and then held them until daylight, when I got help from the camp. We remained there several days getting the cattle together, at last hitting the trail with some three thousand steers and had but little trouble until we reached the Red River at Doan's Store. Zack Stucker, our boss, had gone ahead to look for a crossing on the river, as it was up very high from spring rains, and when he came back he ordered me to get ready to cross at two o'clock in the evening. I informed him that all the boys were drunk as old man Doan had some wagon-yard whiskey, and that we had better not cross as the men would have to swim, and a drunken man cannot swim. I told him to move camp up the river and wait until the next day, which we did, and crossed all right. We had some trouble in the Indian Territory, but got through by giving the Indians some steer yearlings. We came to Camp Supply where we saw a signboard, reading "The Way to Camp Supply is closed—go to right." Gus Black, Til Driscoll and J. A. Kercheville were waiting for some one else to go there. My boss, Zack Stucker, being a fighting man of some reputation, said that a "bunch of shorthorns could not turn him back," and we went straight ahead, ignoring the signboard instructions. The next day we came to the finest country I ever saw. Here we struck the first range cattle that we had seen in the Territory. My boss came to me and told me to get another boy and go out and butcher one of these fine calves. They were sure fat and good. I told him that Mr. Lytle did not hire me to steal cattle, and I would not do it. He had no trouble in getting some one else, so the calf was butchered. He told me to go ahead and camp the wagon and have the calf ribs barbecued for dinner, which I did; but before we had gotten the ribs on the fire, I saw him coming to camp and he said "Hide the meat," as there were some ten or twelve "shorthorns" coming and all had double-barrel shotguns, and said that we would have to turn back and that they would see that we did so as they had plenty of soldiers to help them. My boss lost all of his fighting spirit and promised to turn back, and here he certainly showed his "gall." He said to the gang of men that had just come up and ordered him to turn back that "I would ask you to eat dinner with me but we have nothing but bacon, as you watched us so close that we haven't had a chance to steal anything."

They told him (the boss) to come to their camp and they would give him a quarter of a beef, which they did, and the boss of course accepted their hospitality. The stolen calf was the best meat, however.

I landed at Fort Dodge, Kansas, and I had a date to take a young lady to a Fourth of July barbecue and dance. I resigned my position and came home. The same lady I took to the barbecue and dance, is the same one I am taking around with me to the Old Trail Drivers' reunions.

We have six children, one girl and five boys, and all the boys are engaged in the stock business. I am living quietly on my ranch in Frio county, where I expect to pass my remaining days.

RICHARD KING

One of the most useful men in South Texas was Captain Richard King, who died in the eighties, aged sixty years. Mr. King was born in Orange county, New York, July 10, 1825, and came to Texas when he was twenty-two years old. He first became engaged in steamboat traffic, and built up quite an extensive business, becoming associated with Captain M. Kennedy, Charles Stillman and James O'Donnell in the operation of twenty-six steamers on the Rio Grande, the firm being known as King, Kennedy & Company which continued until Captain King began to devote his entire time to cattle raising. He began purchasing grazing land and imported domesticated stock from Mexico in the later fifties. He was the pioneer importer of graded stock, purchasing Durhams from Kentucky and rams from the North. His livestock holdings at one time were 100,000 cattle, 20,000 sheep and 10,000 horses. Thou-

RICHARD KING

sands of longhorns owned by him were driven over the trail to Kansas and the territories to market and the ranges. Before the Northern markets had opened to any extent Captain King erected rendering establishments on his ranch and shipped tallow and hides to market via water.

Captain King interested himself in every enterprise that was for the good of the Southwest. He was a builder in every sense, and was interested in the construction of the San Diego, Corpus Christi & Rio Grande Railroad.

At the time of his death Captain King owned outright more than 500,000 acres of land. He made his wife his sole legatee and executrix without bond. His son-in-law, R. J. Kleburg, was placed in charge of the estate and under his management the King ranch has increased to more than 950,000 acres, on which today graze thousands of head of high-grade cattle. As many as 30,000 calves have been branded on this ranch in a single year.

In December, 1854, Captain King was married to Miss Henrietta M. Chamberlain, daughter of Rev. Hiram Chamberlain of Brownsville, Texas. Of this union the following children were born: Robert Lee, deceased; Nettie M., who became the wife of Brigadier General E. B. Atwood; Mrs. Ellen M. Atwood, Richard King and Mrs. R. J. Kleburg.

DROVE CATTLE FOR DOC BURNETT

By L. Beasley, Junction, Texas

I was raised on a ranch in Gonzales county, Texas, and moved to Kimble county and located a ranch in 1897, and am still here, raising high-grade cattle, goats, sheep and hogs. Have been in the cattle business all of my life. I drove cattle up the trail in the early eighties for Doc Burnett, and could relate many thrilling experiences of those good old times, but I guess they have been pretty well covered by the sketches of other old-time cowboys.

I was a member of the local exemption board during the war just closed and served as county commissioner of Kimble county for four years. My ranch is located nine miles south of Junction, in one of the best sections of this part of the state.

WORKED WITH CATTLE FOR OVER SIXTY YEARS

By E. M. (Bud) Daggett, Fort Worth, Texas

I was born in Shelby county, Texas, in 1850, and have resided in this state ever since, following the cattle business all of my life. If there is one class of people I love better than another it is the class that dates back to my childhood days, for I went into the saddle at ten years old. The first night I can remember of camping out on a cow hunt was in the spring of the year. We camped on the banks of a creek called Deer Creek, south of Fort Worth about fifteen miles. At that time the boys carried their biscuits and dried beef and a little coffee in sacks tied behind their saddles, and their blankets generally piled on

E. M. (Bud) DAGGETT

their saddle blankets and their saddles on top of that making pack horses out of the boys' saddle ponies. From that time on I have worked with cattle a part

of every year without missing a single year for over
sixty years and am still handling cattle as a commission man and salesman on the stockyards, Daggett-
Keen Commission Co., at Fort Worth. I could give so
many different statements concerning trailing and cattle
driving that it would take too much space. Have been
with scouting parties many times, day and night, in this
section of the country doing such scout work against
Indians and Indian raiders. Forty-nine years ago in
this month was the last raid the Apaches and Comanches
made in the vicinity about the stockyards, Fort Worth,
Texas, at which time they killed hundreds of horses
within a mile to ten miles of this location. At that time
I pulled twenty-seven arrows out of horses that they had
shot. As to myself I used to be a bronco buster and an
expert roper, not as a wild west show man but roping
and riding at that day and time was part of the business.
It was like going into battle to make charges on wild
bunches and capturing the whole band of wild outlaw
cattle if possible or else capturing a part of them without
ropes. The same would apply with either horses or cattle, sometimes deer, antelope or wolves for a change. I
have played checkers across parts of our country by
driving cattle in different directions with herds.

The hardest trip I believe I ever made with cattle
was in July, 1865, when I helped move a herd of steers,
ages four to eight years to Shreveport, Louisiana. Seems
to me they stampeded pretty nearly every night from the
time we left the prairies directly north of Fort Worth,
until we got them loaded on boats for shipment to New
Orleans, and will say here that the net price of those
cattle after the freight, feed bills, commission and yard-
age was paid was $6.00 per head. Our work taking the
cattle through on that drive was just added in the steer
and made a part of the steer, to say nothing of the expense for driving. From the time we arrived at Marshall, Texas, the road from that point was lined with

negro soldiers dressed in blue, called Yankee negro soldiers. They kept us in the brush from there on to Shreveport, most every prominent corner in that city had a
negro soldier on it with a gun and a bayonet who would
slightly touch the people with the bayonet and tell them
to move on. Of course this was generally people that
were not singing gospel Sam to them; those they would
prod with the bayonet; I often wondered why this great
American Government patrolled this beautiful American
country with negroes instead of white men, when it had
more than sufficient numbers of white men who could take
the place of negroes. But I want it understood I am not
especially a negro hater, as we owned a few negroes; we
raised some of those negroes and those negroes helped
to raise us. Mr. Negro is all right in his place.

I loaded out the first train of cattle that was loaded
out of the Fort Worth stockyards in the fall of 1870, and
had the first consignment of cattle on the North Side
twenty-seven years ago.

MADE FIRST TRIP IN 1877

By B. D. Sherrill, Rocksprings, Texas

In 1877 I went up the trail with Dave Combs, who
was then driving for Ellison & Sherrill. We left the
coast country with 3,000 big steers and stags and delivered
to Millett & Ervin in the Indian Territory. This was my
first trip as a cow-puncher, and when we reached Red
River a lot of Indians came and stayed with us all day.
To me, a beardless boy, those Indians in the war paint
was a wonderful sight. After delivering the cattle I
went on to Wolf Creek, near Camp Supply, remained
there two months and picked up sore-footed cattle and
carried them to Ellison & Sherrill's Ranch on North
Fork of Red River near old Fort Elliott. That was the

finest country I ever saw, and it was full of Indians, buffalo, antelope, deer, turkey and prairie chickens by the
thousands. I remained in that region several years and
finally drifted back to Staples on the San Marcos River.

I drove a herd from Staples to the San Miguel in
Frio county, where we ranched a number of years, afterward going back to my old stamping ground, Staples.

In 1886 I drove a herd from San Marcos to Mobettie,
sold out in the late fall and came home.

It is a great pleasure to attend the old trail drivers'
meetings and meet my old time friends, especially my old
comrade Dave Combs, a cowman and gentleman in every
respect.

COWBOYS DRESSED UP AT END OF THE TRAIL

By R. J. Jennings, San Antonio, Texas

On April 10th, 1870, in company with George Lyons
as trail boss for Ellison & Co., with 1,500 cattle, and I as
boss for Crunk, Jennings & Co., with 1,600 cattle, we
pulled out for Dodge City, Kansas. That was a good
year, grass and water plentiful and a good open range.
We had good horses and good men on that trip, our boys
getting along like one large family. Went by way of
Austin, crossed the Trinity River at Fort Worth and
passed near where the union depot in that city now
stands. There were but a few houses in Fort Worth
then. We crossed Red River at Doan's Store and went
up North Fork, which we crossed, and pulled on to
Dodge City, crossing the Cimarron and Washita Rivers
on the way. Indians, deer, antelope, and prairie hens
were plentiful; there were a few buffaloes, too, but not
many, but the prairies were covered with the skeletons
of these animals which had been killed for their hides.

When we reached Dodge City we crossed to the north
side and remained there six weeks. These cattle were

sold on contract to J. F. Ellison, Sr. We delivered 500 cows and had to take them to Fort Sill, Indian Territory. Mr. Lyons delivered them and left me with the big herd. I was two or three days getting away from where we cut the cows from their yearlings; we moved like a snail climbing a slick log, so far up in daytime, slipping back at night. Gus Staples, one of our boys, was a fiddler and we had music all the way. Gus saw his first antelope on this trip, thought it was crippled and tried to catch it, but the longer he ran it the faster it got. Monkey John, the negro cook, spent a half a day trying to drown a prairie dog out of a hole, but nothing doing.

Captain Ellison finally sent us word to cut all cows above three years old and take them on towards Powder River, catch up with the herd and turn them over to his boss, who he said was waiting for us two days ahead. With five men I pulled out, ate up all of our grub the second day at noon, and were four days catching up with that herd. For two days we had nothing to eat but boiled Irish potatoes without salt. We delivered the remainder of the herd as soon as I got back and checked up. I found we had about the number we started with and a few over which we picked up along the trail, which of course, if no one claimed, we did not point out.

In 1881 I left Martindale, Caldwell county, with a herd of 1,500 cattle and went to Travis county, where John R. Blocker gave me 1,500 more, making 3,000 cattle belonging to Jennings, Blocker & Co. This herd was sold to Ike T. Pryor and delivered to him on the north side of the Washita River in the Indian Territory. Rufus Fuller then took the herd to Fort Sill, while Mr. Blocker and I went to Dodge City on horseback. I left Mr. Blocker there and came home.

In those days I received $30 a month, furnished three horses and had money at the end of the trip. Our way back home was paid by those who employed us. We came back as immigrants, all dressed up in new suit, boots and hat, the rig-out costing about $30, and when we reached home we were "somebody come" sure enough, as we were usually absent about four months.

A TENDERFOOT FROM KENTUCKY

By J. D. Jackson

In the summer of 1887, D. G. Knight was working as manager for the Durants, and was also selected as round-up boss of Presidio county. He had about 60 men and over 400 horses in the outfit.

Friends of the Durants in Kentucky had a son who was very brave and anxious for some real excitement, so they sent him out to Mr. Knight. He was a very talkative young man, and often told us of the good times people in high society had in Kentucky and of their great dinners, costing from $1.00 to $10.00 per plate. He was quite free to state that he did not think we would know how to act in such high society, and while we knew that this was perhaps true, we did not care to have him tell us that.

The boys immediately started in to show him how they did things in high cow-camp society. The first thing we did was to slip the cinches off his saddle, so that when he tried to head a steer, his horse stopped quickly, and he went off with the saddle, landing on his head. He thought it was purely an accident.

He wore a blue shirt. Every man in the outfit started telling Indian stories, and told him that the Indians thought that those who wore blue shirts were soldiers, and they would hide behind rocks and pick them out from among the cowboys. This scared him so that he pulled off his blue shirt and wore his white, short-sleeved undershirt on top until his arms were blistered by the sun. The boys then started in telling him about the narrow escapes they had had from "gwinders," a very vicious animal with one short leg in front and one behind, so they could circle around a mountain and catch a man and tear him all to pieces. That made him afraid to get out of camp after dark.

One night we camped about sixty miles south of Marfa, and the boys decided it was time to put on an "Indian fight." We took it turn about telling of narrow escapes from Indian raids, until bed time, and warned him to be prepared for an attack any time during the night. After we had bedded down for the night, ten or twelve of the boys slipped off, and tied bunches of grass on their heads and got sotol stalks for lances. About 12:30 Den Knight woke him up and told him to saddle his horse and go with him to unhobble a bunch of their horses and move them closer to camp so the Indians wouldn't get them. Just as they got off their horses and got busy with their work, the other boys came charging up on their horses, yelling, shooting and making all kinds of wild noises. Knight fell over and yelled to the boy that he was killed and for him to make his escape if possible. The boys thought they could catch him before he could get to his horse, but they failed and he got away and rode sixty miles to Marfa before 10 o'clock the next morning. He arrived there almost exhausted and told the citizens that Indians had attacked the party and he was the only one to escape. When he found out that was all a joke on him, he decided the West was a little too strenuous and went back to swell society in Kentucky.

A TRUE STORY OF TRAIL DAYS

In the late '70s, when herd after herd of Texas cattle were driven north over the old Chisholm Trail, Ike Pryor's herd was a few weeks ahead of the herd driven by Bill Jackman.

It was the custom for the man following to pick up lost cattle and drive them on until the herd they were lost from was reached. Bill Jackman's herd picked up a steer lost by Ike Pryor and was taking him along for Ike, with good intentions. Red River was crossed and Bill's herd had now gone a few days' drive into the Indian Nation. One afternoon a band of about forty Indian warriors including their squaws, rode up to Bill Jackman's herd and the chief handed him a letter, which read as follows:

"To the trail bosses:
"This man is a good Indian; I know him personally. Treat him well, give him a beef and you will have no trouble in driving through his country."
(Signed)   IKE T. PRYOR.

After reading the letter, Bill rode into the herd, and cut out Ike's steer for the chief. They killed the steer then and there and had a big feast. Then Bill went on North with his herd, in peace, thanking Ike for his good advice.

TRAVELING THE TRAIL WITH GOOD MEN WAS A PLEASURE

By J. F. (Little Jim) Ellison, Jr., Fort Cobb, Oklahoma

My first trip over the trail was in 1868 with my father, Col. J. F. Ellison, with about 100 cattle, which at that time, was considered a large herd. We left the old McGhee Crossing on the San Marcos River in Caldwell county, about seven miles from the town of San Marcos, and went over the old Fort Arbuckle trail to Abilene, Kansas, crossing the Trinity River at Fort Worth, which at that early date was just a small frontier town. Our mess wagon was drawn by two yoke of oxen, and as it was our last chance to lay in supplies we stocked up at Fort Worth with enough to last us to Abilene.

My second trip was in 1871, over the old Chisholm trail. I went over the same trail again in 1874, and in 1876 I drove a herd for Ellison & Dewees, and Mac Stewart having charge of a herd for Millett & Maberry, we traveled together, receiving our cattle southwest of San Antonio. We went as far, if not farther west than any cattle had ever gone, crossing the Washita about eight miles west of where Chickasha is now located. This was a hard trip. We passed through the Wichita Mountains at the foot of Mt. Scott, and saw lots of buffalo and antelope. Our first stop was at Dodge City, Kansas. We delivered part of these cattle north of Cheyenne, Wyoming Territory. This year Ellison & Dewees and Millett & Maberry drove together and drove about 100,000 cattle to the northern markets. Their cattle were strung out from San Antonio almost to Dodge City. Ogallala, Nebraska, was their distributing point. For some time that year I held 7,000 head just south of Ogallala, across the Platte River, my camp being near a cold spring that boiled out of the ground. The water from this spring was the coldest I ever drank, so cold in fact that it would make your teeth ache. They cut cattle from my herd to deliver in every direction.

In 1877 I did not drive a herd but worked on the train for Ellison & Dewees wherever I was needed, and Monroe Hardeman did the same. R. G. Head was our general foreman. On Washita River, near where Chickasha is now, I cut from the herds of Giles Fenner, N. P. Ellison and Bill Green about 2,000 one and two-year-old steers and delivered them to Miller & Green of Paul's Valley. Their foreman was Tom Grant of Fort Arbuckle and he took charge of the cattle. As well as I remember they paid $9.00 for the yearling steers and $12.00 for the two-year-olds. These were good cattle for those days, and good colors because they were all colors. From there I went to Dodge City on horseback. Had good company, for I struck up with Charley Shiner who was headed for the same point. I think I can truthfully say we were never out of sight of a herd of cattle from there to Dodge City. Arriving at Dodge City I delivered the proceeds of the cattle to Miller & Green and after resting up I was sent back down the trail by Col. John Dewees on some business that carried me almost to the Washita. As I started back to Dodge City I was again fortunate in having good company and more of it, this time coming up with Green Mills and Zeke Hilliard of Lockhart, and A. B. McQueen of Winston county, Miss. It was a pleasure to travel with such good men.

In 1880 I made my last trip over the trail, this time for myself, but in 1884 my two younger brothers, T. H. Ellison and R. R. Ellison, J. T. Block and myself sent a herd from Presidio county in the Big bend country in charge of the late Nat Jackman, who was a brother to W. T. Jackman. I met these cattle up there and delivered them to the Durbin Land & Cattle Co. on Sweetwater, about 150 miles north of Cheyenne, and had to throw them all down and brand them, some four or five thousand head.

I believe this winds up my trail experience. There is a warm place in my heart for all of the old cowmen and trail boys. The men who bought the cattle and paid me to drive them are nearly all gone now; many of my comrades who worked with me on the trail have also passed on, and the balance of us are on the shady side of life. Like the cowboy who, when asked why he had cut a certain cow back, reared in his stirrups and said "She is too ancient," we, too, are getting "ancient." Trail driving is but a memory now, and will never return. When the summons comes for our last trip let us be ready to go. My postoffice address is Fort Cobb, Oklahoma, and I would be pleased to hear from any of the old boys who would care to write to me.

HAD PLENTY OF FUN

By Gus Black, Eagle Pass, Texas

I have no time to write books. If I gave all of my experience on the trail it would fill this book and then some. From 1875 to 1882 I suppose I had more experience, good and bad, than any one man on the trail, with Indians, buffalo, horse rustlers, and cutthroats, and during that time I worked eighteen hours out of every twenty-four. Wound up in 1882 without a dollar in hand, but in possession of several thousand dollars worth of fun. I am now seventy-one years old and can ride a horse just the same as of old. I have been right here in Texas ever since the morning star first "riz," and when you publish your next book I hope to be a retired stockman, for my time will then be my own, and I will give you something good. However, since you insist, I will relate a few incidents and you can arrange them to suit yourself.

I went up the trail the first time with Ben Duncan and Jim Speed of Frio county, and the second time with Woodward & Oge of the same county. For many years I was boss for Lytle & McDaniel and Lytle & Schreiner.

One year while on the trail we found Red River out of banks at Red River Station, with fifteen or twenty herds there waiting to cross. I was in charge of a herd of 3500 cattle and was anxious to get across. The toll man was demanding $1.25 per head for crossing cattle at that point, but I was determined not to pay it, for the total amount seemed too high, so of two high things I decided to choose the river. While my herd was stopped on the Texas side of the river, and the toll collector was absent, I swam across to the other side and made arrangements with a man over there to come and ferry my wagons over. Then I swam back and got from two to five men from each outfit there to help me. This gave

GUS BLACK

me a bunch of some forty or fifty men and we pushed my cattle right into the raging river and rushed them across. Just as we emerged on the other side the toll man appeared on the bank we had left and I yelled back to him: "You are too slow to collect from Gus Black."

I delivered many cattle for Lytle & Schreiner in Wyoming and Nebraska. One year this firm sold several herds to Governor Bush of Wyoming. One trip Governor Bush came out to meet the herd in company with Captain Lytle, and we entertained him in camp. That morning I had found a couple of long horns which had slipped off the head of a dead cow on the trail, and in a spirit of fun I fitted them onto the just-sprouting horns of a dogie yearling with our drags. That little old yearling was a comic sight with those great long horns on its head, and caused lots of fun for the boys. When Governor Bush was looking over the herd he espied this "long-horned" yearling, and began to hurrah Captain Lytle about the animal. I told the Governor that it was just a yearling, but he said it was a four-year-old, and would bet any amount of money on its age. I told him I would bet $200 it was a yearling. He promptly covered the bet, saying he knew I was a hard-working man, and he hated to take my money, but he wanted to prove my ignorance and teach me a lesson. At the same time he said he would just as soon bet me $1000, but knew I could not afford to lose that much money. I told him to put it up, that I always "blowed in" my money anyhow and would just as soon let him win it as anybody else. So the bet was made, and then I roped the dogie and took those horns off. Governor Bush was dumbfounded, and the laugh was on him. When settlement came around I told him to keep his money, as he was so d—d ignorant I just wanted to teach him a lesson. Then he set up the whiskey and cigars to the outfit.

On another trip, after we crossed Smoky River we

encountered a colony of grangers who made it a rule to charge every herd fifty dollars for permitting passage through their community. I rode into the village and consulted with their chief leader who informed me that the charge was made to pay for inspecting herds for contagious diseases, etc. I told him I had no money but would give him a draft on Captain Lytle, which he said would be satisfactory as Captain Lytle's check was good anywhere in the world. He asked me to kindly add another ten dollars to the amount for tobacco for the villagers, which I did, and then put my herd through. The first telegraph station I reached I wired Captain Lytle that I had been buncoed out of sixty dollars and to refuse to pay the draft. Those fellows were skinning us and I figured that turn about was fair play.

I am glad George Saunders took the lead in the organization of the trail drivers of the early days, for such an association has long been needed to preserve the history of the rugged noble men who made the cattle industry. I hope to live to see the day when that monument suggested by Mr. Saunders is placed on the old trail as a tribute to those who have gone their way and a reminder to oncoming generations that we "blazed the trail" and vouchsafed unto them peace, happiness and prosperity.

SLUMBERED THROUGH THE SHOOTING

By H. H. Peel, Jourdanton, Texas

I went up the trail the first time in the spring of 1881 with a Crouch Brothers' herd from Frio county, in charge of George Wilcox. We had the usual experiences of driving and stampeding, and at Doan's Store on Red River a near-shooting. Fortunately the bad man's pistol hung in the scabbard and as he was well covered by several guns he had to accept orders and leave. In the Territory we had, I suppose, the usual tense moments when the short-barreled hairtrigger boys wanted to cut our herd for strays, and Wilcox would not stand for it. We did not have trouble with this outfit who wanted to cut our herd because the leader recognized Wilcox as a friend who had once given him a horse, saddle and gun to leave a section of country where he was "wanted," so he was very anxious to do something in return for the favor. He offered to stop the fellow we had turned off at Doan's Store, and who had threatened to follow us up and "get" one of our men, our new friend saying he would not have any trouble, just tell some Indians he knew that a bad man and a good horse were coming and he would never get by. George refused to give him a description of the man.

We arrived at Dodge City, took in the lively town, then put two Crouch herds together and drove them to Ogallala with Dick Crewes as boss. There I left them and went East and to England.

Went again in 1885, I think, to Caldwell, Kansas, and from there to Camp Supply and delivered to D. R. Fant at his ranch, then took the mail hack to Kiowa, and the trip and gypsum water wore me out, so I went to the hotel in Kiowa, a board affair, to rest. Some Texas boys who had had a difference with the town marshal were in the adjoining room, and I slept through all the shooting, though some twenty shots were fired by the posse from the street and the boys from the windows, the marshal being wounded. The boys were still in their room when I left the next morning.

Those old days may have been a little rough at times, but there was always such kindness and good feeling among the boys it is a pleasure worth remembering to have been one of them.

ANOTHER SUCCESSFUL COWMAN

By J. B. Murrah, San Antonio, Texas

My parents were James M. and Malinda A. Murrah. I was born in Goliad county, Texas, August 24, 1856, and lived there with my parents until the fall of 1865, when father moved to DeWitt county and gathered a remnant of about twenty-five head of cattle, all we had left out of about two hundred head after the close of the four years of Civil War. Father subsequently sold these few cattle for the low price of three dollars per head.

J. B. MURRAH

In 1866 we moved to Bell county, and myself and a negro helped my uncle drive two hundred head of horses through on the trip. This was my first trail work. We settled on a little farm in Bell county, where I plowed and worked the farm, but all the time longing to get old enough to go "up the trail" with the cowboys. When I was twenty years of age I made my first trip to Austin, passing through San Antonio. I heard of a ranger company up on the Sabinal River and went there to get a job, but did not succeed in getting it, so I went on and secured employment with an uncle where I taught Mexicans how to use an American plow. After three months of this work I was offered a job on the trail and lost no time in accepting it. I drove on the trail from 1882 to 1887 and knew many of the old cowmen of that time. I knew D. H. and J. W. Snider quite well; worked a great deal for Capt. Dud Snider, and think he is one of the best men living. A short time ago I read a sketch of his life, and while reading it I felt that the half had not been told of his honesty and goodness.

I have been in the cow business ever since leaving the trail, and it seems to me that I have known the "dogies" almost from the beginning of time. I have ranches in Val Verde and Webb counties, but my home is now in San Antonio. I am proud to be the vice president of the Old Time Trail Drivers' Association, for it is an organization of men who made history.

THE REAL COWBOY

By Bulah Rust Kirkland, Phoenix, Arizona

I wish I knew as much about cowboy life of today, as my father knows of the early cowboy days in Texas. I firmly believe that my love for the open range and a good cow pony is inherited. Good cow punching is just as much an art and just as appreciated, as it was when he was a boy. Of course there is not the range, or the wild cattle. Just the same, a ranch in New Mexico or Arizona could hardly be managed without good men who thoroughly understood their business. So, the real live cowboy still exists; here and over in Old Mexico, especially, and of course in South America.

BULAH RUST KIRKLAND

I am sure that nothing would please our little world better than to see the old cowboys make a proposed trip to California. Also to re-establish the old trail. I am especially interested in that noted old trail; and would like to make the trip from start to finish. For the old cowboys to make the trip to California would be one of the grandest things of this century, it would be history.

While I am not a man, I love to work with cattle; and have spent a good deal of my time on the range in Southern Arizona. There is something about the way startled cattle raise their heads and look toward a horseback rider, that I enjoy. For me there is real pleasure in noting their earmarks at a glance; and studying out their brands. Ranch life is not so exciting as it was in the early days. For one thing, when pay day comes the boys do not shoot up the town, as of old. Though the rustler is still with us, we handle him strictly within the law, but we do not love him any better than they used to thirty years ago.

I believe I could walk along the streets of any town or city and pick out the real cowboy, not by his clothes especially, but because one can nearly always notice that he has a very open countenance and almost innocent eyes and mouth. He is not innocent of course; but living in the open, next to nature, the cleaner life is stamped on his face. His vices leave no scars, or few, because old mother nature has him with her most of the time.

The cowboys in this part even, are rapidly passing out, for the wire fences and short horns are coming in. While in Texas last summer I noticed that very few kept up the old custom of good saddles, ropes, etc. Here, a good saddle, rope, boots, chaps and a good "cutting" horse are still the pride of any cowboy, for they are still very much needed.

In Old Mexico and along the line in Arizona, cow punching goes on in earnest. We still have the big round-up; the chuck wagons, the "remuda." Camped out for nights, the boys still tell old-time yarns and sing good old songs and play pranks on the tenderfoot they find in their midst.

Long live the cowboy, young and old. He is the American in my opinion.

(EDITOR'S NOTE. The above sketch was written in 1914, since which time Mrs. Kirkland has died. She was the daughter of C. H. Rust, of San Angelo, Texas, one of the active members of the Old Trail Drivers' Association.)

COWBOY FROM THE PLAINS OF NEBRASKA

By V. F. Carvajal, in Floresville *Chronicle-Journal*

In March, 1872, I was engaged by Colin Campbell to take a herd of cattle to Nebraska for him. I went to Lodi (recent suburb of Floresville, Texas) and hired the hands to go with me; being among them Miguel Cantu, ex-police of San Antonio, Masedonia Gortari, Aurelio Carvajal, my brother, Francisco Longoria, Melchor Ximenez, and others, whom I do not remember. We started in the same month, March, 1872. Mr. Campbell gave me $1,500 for general expenses, and went with us as far as Lockhart. I had close to 1,800 head of cattle, so we went on; we crossed the Colorado river close to Austin and went on through Round Rock, Georgetown, Belton, Lampasas, and Fort Worth, which was a small place then. At Fort Worth we bought sufficient provisions to take us across the Indian Nation, which was nothing but wilderness. We crossed Red River at Red River Station in Montague County, and went into the Indian Nation. We met some Indians and gave them three or four lame cattle in payment of custom's duties which they claimed for us going through their territory, and on to Ellsworth, Kansas, where all the cowboys were taking their cattle. My boss, Colin Campbell, was there waiting for me, and he ordered me to go to North Platte, Nebraska, and he would meet me there. He bought me a compass and a map of the state of Nebraska. In those days the western part of Nebraska was nothing but wilderness. So we started for Ellsworth without any roads; just following the North Star by the compass and examining the map to find out where we could get water for the cattle. In going to North Platte I got too close to a settlement of "short horns," where there was a big river called Solomon River. My cattle were suffering for water for three days. Before I got to the river, there came about twenty "short horns" armed with double-barreled shot guns; they stopped me from watering the cattle—finally leaving. All at once there came a "short horn" on a big horse to where I was. I asked him if he had a section of land on this side of the river where we were watering the cattle. He said yes, about half a mile below here. I told him that I would give him $100 gold or two cows and calves if he would let us water on his land; he told me all right, but you must not cross the river here, that we would have to go about twenty miles west and cross it on the government lands. So I watered the cattle and went west and crossed the Solomon River. Then we kept traveling due north for many days; camping one day for dinner on the divide between the Republican and Platte Rivers. Four of us having been out from camp, went back to camp and staked our horses, and started to eat our dinner. All of a sudden there came a cloud of buffaloes running toward our wagon, and three of our horses broke their ropes and started to run ahead of the buffaloes. There was one horse left in camp, so I got on him and started in pursuit of my horses that were ahead of the buffaloes. From the camp to where I overtook the buffaloes and horses there was a large city of prairie dogs and I had considerable trouble keeping my horse away from the holes. When I overtook the horses I tried to catch them but my horse was almost exhausted; so I continued to run even with the horses until my horse could get sufficient breath to maintain his gait. I kept about one hundred yards from the horses and buffaloes, both still running. Finally I came to a nice level valley and I said to myself, if I do not catch the horses now, right here, I am going to let them go. So I put spurs to my horse and it seemed to me that he was flying. The leading horse had a piece of rope around his neck and I gained on him and caught him, holding to the rope on his neck. The other horses following as soon as I caught him. After having put my rope on him I started back in the direction of the camp. I had gone about a mile when I met one of my hands, coming to my rescue. So it made me feel happy, because I was afraid I never would find my way back, as it was getting late in the day, almost dark, and we were some fifteen miles from camp. As we were going back we met about 1,000 buffaloes coming over a ridge toward us. I asked my companion if he wanted to see my horse get on top of those buffaloes, and he answered, yes. So I turned my horse after the buffaloes and I scattered them in all directions. Finally we got into camp all right without getting lost in the wilderness. Next day we continued our journey toward North Platte, Nebraska, our destination, where we found our boss, Colin Campbell, waiting for us, after being on the trail for six months.

There we delivered the cattle to the parties to whom he had sold them.

This story is not eloquent; but it is genuine, and perhaps will never be repeated again.

ECHOES OF THE 1916 CONVENTION

The following was published in a Houston paper at the time of the convention of the Old Time Trail Drivers in that City in 1916:

"Y' know," observed the little old man with the thin, brown fingers, "y' know, when the boys went into Mexico befo', I drove one of the wagons. That was 'way back in '46.

"Back in '48 and '49 I used to know 'bout every one along the Colorado and Brazos rivers."

C. P. Vance, who admits to 89 years and who is "down from Williamson County" to attend the Stock Raisers' Convention, was the speaker. Mr. Vance glanced over the gray-haired youngsters assembled and remarked:

"These boys took their herds no'th. When I was a young fellow we used to drive our herds out to New O'leans."

The old man smiled. It was a smile of good will toward children whose memories only go back to these latter 50 years of trail driving. Mr. Vance sat in the front row at the meeting of the Old Trail Drivers yesterday afternoon at the banquet hall of the City Auditorium.

"Hello, there, boy."

"Well, well. I ain't seen you since that day you swum them four herds across Red River."

"Back in '77, wasn't it?"

"Where you been all this time?"

"Thirty-one years up in Wyoming. Livin' at Sundance, no'theast corner. Wintered at Abilene. Back in Texas for good."

It was the greeting of W. D. Driscoll, late of Sundance, as aforestated and G. W. Mills of Lockhart, Texas.

Then came a series of rapid-fire questions about Ab and Tobe and Tennessee and Red and Eli.

"Remember the fellow that tried to swim the Red River that day to get away from the sheriff? He was under arrest."

"Yes, I pulled him out."

"And wasn't that sheriff some mad when he got safe on the Oklahoma side?"

"Wonder what happened to him?"

"Oh, he died some years ago."

"Know whar any of the Day boys are? They lived up Hash Knife way."

"Tony's the only one left. He's out in California somewhere."

"Know what year the Chisholm trail was blazed?"

"Must a been about in '68 or '69. I went up with a herd in '70 and the blazes were still bright on the trees then all through the Oklahoma timber country."

"Now this Chisholm trail, where it started and where it ended and when it was blazed, we're not plum sure of it an' I'd like to find someone that is," said George W. Saunders, presiding.

"Put it up to Eli Baggett, over in San Angelo, he'll know."

So, by vote of the house it was decided that Mr. Baggett of San Angelo should be asked to fix the Chisholm trail.

"I tell you John Blocker was the outdrivin'est man with a herd I ever did see," observed one with a gray moustache.

"Up in the territory an Irishman told me sumthin' one day that pictured him just right."

"What was it?"

"Said the only kick he had driving with a Blocker outfit was that he had to eat two suppers every night!"

"Two suppers?"

"Yes, one after dark at night and the second befo' sunup next mo'nin'."

And two old trail drivers' sides shook with laughter.

"I've been figgerin' on writin' some recollections of my trail drivin' days," confided an old man to his friend,

C. P. Vance, who drove a wagon when the soldiers went into Mexico "the first time, way back in '46."

"But these modern maps ain't right. I can't find Brown's Hole, an' I can't find Bridger Pass, nor Spear Fish, nor Bear River. Why, these new maps ain't got the old streams. They've got railroads an' railroads all over 'em—but the rivers we used to cross ain't there.

"It just mixes me all up an' I can't tell where I am. If I could only get one of these old maps."

"Write to the headquarters of the United States. They'll send you an old map."

"Sure, I will, I never thought of that."

W. H. ADAMS, New Braunfels, Tex.

EARLY DAYS IN TEXAS

J. T. Hazelwood, San Angelo, Texas

Something like seventy years ago, in 1852 to be exact, my father, George W. Hazelwood, emigrated with his family from Mississippi to the plains of Western Texas. There being no railroads or other means of transportation at that time, he came by the mule team mode of convey-ance. The country was sparsely settled after reach-ing the Texas line, and the trip was a long tedious one. The family would travel for days without meeting a hu-man being, only coming in contact with vast herds of wild buffalo and numerous tribes of still wilder Indians.

J. T. HAZELWOOD

The journey occupied several months, and my father with his family eventually located in Panola county, Texas. The country being wholly an open range, and the pioneers who blazed the way into this new western civilization being extremely few and far between, the early settlers apparently did not remain very long in any one place, but moved about from location to location, seeking a better range, more ample water and greater safety from marauding Indians. Fort Worth, in Tarrant county, was the nearest trading point, and all provisions and supplies of every character and description was brought into the Western country by freighters, some-times accompanied by United States troops, but more fre-quently they traveled in little bands for better protection against Indian raids.

From Panola county my father moved into Palo Pinto county, settling on Eagle Creek, west of Palo Pinto, at that time a small trading point. Here he went into the ranching business, driving his cattle from one location to another, but due to Indian raids he remained in Palo Pinto county about four years and then was compelled to move to a location of greater security. The Indians, who were very numerous at this period, were making raids over the entire country on all "light nights," stealing horses and mules, driving off cattle and murdering the settlers; the soldiers stationed at the various points in Texas were few in number and insufficient to offer adequate protection to the scattering settlements of white people; and while I was yet quite a small boy during these periods of stress, I can remember very distinctly the conditions and circumstances under which the early settlers were compelled to live and fight for their lives, for the preservation of their herds and for the protection of their families. It was no uncommon thing for the Indians on their raids to steal the entire working outfit of the early settlers, including their horses and mules, and driving away their live stock; in fact, it was almost impossible to keep horses or mules, and it was for that reason the settlers abandoned using them for farming purposes and adopted the ox team instead. It would be impossible to enumerate the number of Indian encounters which took place during the early years of the settling of West Texas between these settlers and these roving tribes. I remember on one occasion when a German by the name of Fred Cola, an employee of my father, was out after cattle on the open range when the Indians made an attack upon him and after running him for several miles finally killed him with an arrow from an Indian bow.

It was in 1860 when my father moved with his family to Stephens county, near the line of Shackelford, settling on Sandy Creek, but the Indian depredations continuing,

he again moved to a safer place, as he thought, over on
Battle Creek. The ranges were covered with countless
herds of buffalo, deer, antelope, bear and other wild
game. We lived in picket houses, covered with sod and
dirt, and the flooring with buffalo hides—nothing to compare with the comfortable homes which the people of this
country enjoy at the present time, but, nevertheless, the
conditions for that day and age were ideal, and we lived
in comfort, except that we lived in continual fear of
Indian raids.

My father killed many deer and dressed their hides,
and my mother made clothing of these for the boys and
I remember very distinctly the "coon-skin" caps and the
"home-made" shoes which were made for the children
of our family, and which we were glad to get and took
great pride in wearing regardless of the fact that they
would not be considered up to date by the present young
man about town or the present young society lady preparing for a modern ball. I do not remember very much
about fashions in those days, but I am quite sure if I
should dress today in the garb which I wore sixty years
ago, or if my sisters should dress in the garb which they
wore some sixty years ago, and walk down the streets of
San Angelo they would cause no little comment and, perhaps, some of the modern up-to-date fashions would be
cast into the shade by the old-time apparel worn by the
early pioneers. I also remember that we did not regard
clothes so much in those days as they are regarded now,
and such a thing as ribbons and bows, and lace and silk
hose, silk hats and canes for the young men, and a poodle
dog with a string around his neck for the young women,
would have been considered as much out of place in the
early days as, perhaps, our "coon-skin" caps and "home-
made" shoes, and our "deerskin britches," our "buffalo
coats" and "buffalo shirts" would appear at the present
day. Times change, customs change, fashions change,
conditions change, but human nature changes but very

little, and even when I compare the boys and girls of the present day, in the last analysis of their human make-up, with the girls and boys of seventy years ago, I find that they have the same warm hearts, the same happy, cheerful smile, the same creative youthful ambition, and the same desire to succeed, regardless that we are living in a day and age of automobiles, that we are free from Indian depredations and raids, that we no longer see the buffalo roam the plains, and that where the buffalo once roamed and where the Indians perpetrated their raids, beautiful homes and every modern convenience now can be found, and agricultural conditions are changed likewise with modern improvements, yet the heart and mind of the pioneers of the Western range still are found to permeate the posterity of these early pioneers to a very large extent.

Having neither railroads nor street car lines, nor electric lines, nor electric lights, nor automobiles, nor auto trucks, nor paved streets, nor hard surfaced roads, nor good bridges across the streams, traveling in those days was indeed very slow, and the method of communication was even slower. As we had no telegraph office, nor telephone office, nor radio stations for wireless communication, the only method of communication and carrying the news was what one neighbor could take to another—and when these neighbors lived some fifty to one hundred miles apart, they did not see each other very frequently and they did not have the opportunity to gossip. The truth of the matter is, as I remember it now, the conditions sixty years ago, while very primitive, were at the same time, from the standpoint of rearing a good and happy family, very substantial, and though we lived far apart, the very fact of this great distance between neighbors only added to the interest which we took in each other, and it was a great pleasure indeed when one family would have the opportunity to spend the night and day with a neighbor fifty or one hundred miles off, and it was a greater pleasure for a traveler from some of the more thickly populated settlements to wander through our neighborhood and sit up the entire night and repeat the news to those most interested, in his purely personal way. The latchstring always hung on the outside of the door to everyone but Indians, and a neighbor or a stranger always met with a hearty welcome. We were always glad to see them and sorry to see them go. Our fare may have been homely, and the menu which we set before them might not have consisted of twelve or fifteen courses, but such as it was, it was very wholesome and appetizing, and it was a pleasure to sit around the table in those days.

My father did a great deal of trading from Ft. Worth, in the first instance, and afterwards from Weatherford, with ox teams, for the reasons I have heretofore stated —that horses and mules could not be kept on account of Indian raids.

In the spring of 1868 my father, with a number of other ranchmen, went out on a roundup, gathering and branding a large number of calves which they had failed to find during the fall roundup. One day they gathered a bunch of these calves and put them in a corral on the Jim Walker ranch, located on Sandy Creek. They always had to camp out because there were no pastures for these roundups. The horses were hobbled at night. The next morning, on this occasion, my father told the men to continue with the branding of the calves, and he would go out and bring in the horses. Finding only a few of them, he returned to camp, then went back to locate the others. During his absence a man coming from another ranch observed a bunch of Indians and he hurried to the camp and gave the alarm, while the men in camp saddled their horses and went to the point where the Indians were last seen. They rode up on a high elevation, looking down into a canyon, where they discovered the Indians, and the Indians at the same time discovered the men. There being a large party of these Indians and only a few white men, a running fight took place as the men started back to camp, the Indians shooting with bows and arrows, while the men used their guns and pistols. After the Indians had retreated search was made for my father and he was found about a mile and a half from the camp, lying in a branch, where he had been killed by the Indians. He had fought them single-handed for some time, and several pools of blood were found near the battle ground. The Indians were in the canyon preparing to carry off their wounded when the settlers came upon them. After killing my father they did not disturb him except to take his gun, pistol, horse, saddle and bridle. The men went back to the camp, procured a wagon and brought father's body to the ranch the next day. The soldiers came and took the trail of the retreating Indians to the westward, and followed them for several days. The Indians attacked the Ledbetter salt works and then continued their flight westward until overtaken by the cattlemen out near the plains. They were still carrying their wounded, some three or four Indians and a negro. Seeing that they could not retreat further with their wounded they abandoned them in order to make their own escape, and the pursuing settlers coming upon them, killed the wounded themselves. Among these wounded was the Indian who slew my father. A careful examination being made of him, it was found that two of his fingers on the left hand, where he had held the bow, were injured by a bullet wound corresponding to the hole in the bow; the bullet passed on through the bow into the Indian's breast, ranging around his side and coming out at his back. This was conclusive evidence, after the finding of the bow and the blood stains thereon and comparing the wounds found upon the Indian, that he was the same one who slew my father. This bow was afterwards turned over to the government, and is now in the museum of the Smithsonian Institute at Washington, D. C.

The description of the death of my father on this Indian raid is almost identical in manner and form with hundreds of others who were killed in the early days while West Texas was being settled, and while the account may differ in some few respects, their method was always the same, their character of fighting was always the same, and what has been said of the death of my father would only be a repetition if I should describe the death of a number of other pioneers who were killed during Indian raids, and I am merely giving these facts to show the uncertainties under which the early pioneers lived, the great danger which they constantly faced, and the trials through which they had to pass in order that they might build up the ground work of a greater civilization in this Western country.

My father was a pioneer trail driver, and participated in a number of the drives of cattle from the plains of West Texas to the Kansas markets.

WORKED FOR GEORGE W. SAUNDERS IN 1875

L. T. Clark, Quanah, Texas

In 1869 I hired to Randolph Paine of Denton county to help drive 3,000 four and five year old steers to Abilene, Kansas. We left Denton some time in May and crossed the Red River above Gainsville, crossed the Washita at Fort Arbuckle, crossed the Canadian and Arkansas rivers and went on to the Smoky River. It was a good year and the steers fattened all the way. Paine bought these cattle at $12 per head on time and sold them for $30. He brought the money back to Denton county in a wagon and paid for the steers. Although Mr. Paine was owner and boss of the herd he stood guard at night with the rest of us.

In 1870 I hired to Hopkins of Denton county to help
drive 2,500 big steers to Bax-
ter Springs, Kansas. But
Hopkins sold the steers before we reached there, and we
came back to Texas.

L. T. CLARK

In 1871 Randolph Paine
drove 3,200 steers to the end
of the M. K. & T. railroad,
where a town of tents and
shipping pens had sprung up.
On this trip we encountered
many electrical storms and
had several stampedes.

In 1872 Mr. Paine drove
three herds to Denison, which was a short drive from
Denton county.

Mr. Paine died in 1873 and Alec Belcher bought the
Paine stock of cattle. I helped to gather and move them
to Cook county.

In 1874 J. H. Paine, a nephew to Randolph Paine, and
I bought 125 saddle horses and drove them to Brown
county, where we traded them for 540 grown cattle which
we drove to Denison and shipped them to Saint Louis.

In 1875 I decided to drift south where they worked
cattle the year round. My first stop was south of Goliad,
where I hired to George W. Saunders to help gather a
herd of cattle he had sold to Dillard Fant of Goliad.
When the cattle were counted out to Fant my job was
finished. I then went to Atascosa county and hired to
Jerry Ellis, who was taking three herds to Dodge City,
Kansas. I went up with the last herd of 3,100 head.
Moore was boss, and he was a good trail man. When
we reached Denton county I went to see my father. J. H.
Paine was going to drive a herd of stock cattle to Young
county to ranch them, and I made a trade with him to
run those cattle four years for one-fourth of the entire

herd, I to pay all expenses. At the end of the four years
Mr. Paine sold the cattle to Ikard of Henrietta, Texas,
for $60,000, range delivery. Paine paid me $15,000. I
then bought an interest in J. W. Medlin's cattle, range
delivery, ranching in Archer county, and in 1885 moved
them to Greer county. Then in 1886 I bought an interest
in S. F. Reynold's cattle, located in Greer county, and
we claimed a range twenty miles wide and thirty miles
long, but we did not own any of the land. In 1888 I gathered 1,200 steers and drove them to the Cherokee Strip
to pasture. After we crossed the Cimarron River I went
on ahead of the herd to secure grazing, and when I
reached the next stream it seemed to be bank full and
about 400 yards wide, so I decided to swim it. I pulled
off my clothes and tied them securely to my saddle and
as I started to take the water a man and a woman galloped down on the other side to see me cross. I surmised
that I could stand the ordeal if she could, and in I went.
The water was not so deep as it seemed to be, and did
not swim my horse at all. As I approached the opposite
bank where the man and woman were, they turned and
galloped away. The woman was from Chicago and her
father was one of the stockholders of the Rock Island
railroad. They evidently did not like the cut of my
"birthday" suit, for they did not remain to see me
"come out" in it.

In 1890 the settlers moved inside of our range and
Medlin and Reynolds thought it best to sell, as the nesters were going to take the country. We sold the cattle
to Clark & Plumb of Fort Worth for $9 per head, calves
not counted. I drove the cattle to Archer county and
turned over 9,030 to them, then sold them the remnant
of 300 head on the range. Dayton Moses, now the attorney for the Cattle Raisers' Association, went with the
first herd, and made an excellent hand.

In 1891 I engaged in buying yearlings for myself,
holding them until they were three or four years old and

shipping to market. I was ranching in the northwest corner of Greer county, and fattened my steers in the Kiowa country, which joined me on the north. I never had any trouble with the Indians. In 1898 a lot of Kansas farmers came into my pasture, so it was my move again. I drove my steers north of Woodward, Oklahoma, fattened them there and put them on the market, sold my claim in Greer county and moved back to Texas, and have been in the cow business ever since. I now own a ranch in Tom Green county, which is in charge of my son, who is twenty-four years old. We have about 2,000 cattle on the ranch.

I have been in partnership with J. H. Paine, J. W. Medlin, and S. F. Reynolds, all first-class gentlemen, and all lived in Denton county. They have all passed away. No better men ever lived. I sold steers to E. H. East for four years. He never put up a forfeit, and we never counted a bunch twice. East lived at that time in Archer City, and owned a ranch in Archer county. He now lives at Kingsville.

WAS A FREIGHTER AND TRAIL DRIVER

J. M. Cowley, Fentress, Texas

My father was born in Tennessee, and he and my mother, whose maiden name was Miss N. G. More, were married in Alabama. They came to Texas in 1853 and located in Milam county, on Little River, where they remained until 1855, then moved to Guadalupe county, where they bought cattle and after a time took them to Caldwell county and located on the San Marcos River. Six children were born to my parents, three of whom are dead. Father bought some mares near the King ranch and drove them to Caldwell county, where he raised horses and mules. The year 1857 was very dry and we had to go to the Brazos River region to buy corn for bread. Cornbread, beef, sorghum molasses and coffee was the principal diet in those days, and it was a wholesome diet.

I was born in Alabama May 29, 1847, and have lived in Texas sixty-nine years. In 1858 Father, Warner Polk and Matthew Clarke began to plan to get their stock back on the home range, as they were pretty badly scattered over the country. T. F. Clark, Frank Polk, W. B. Cowley, my brother, and myself worked together until the Civil War broke out, when Father sent me with Joe Eustace, Fred Houston and Bobbie Dorn to Brownsville with a lot of cotton for Mr. Huff, who lived two miles

J. M. COWLEY
Fentress, Texas

below the present site of Luling. We brought back dry goods and groceries for him. In 1862 we went below Corpus Christi after salt, and used ox teams to freight with. My team was composed of six yoke of oxen that were pretty hard to manage. In 1865, in company with P. G. Holmes and T. F. Clark, I went to Mississippi with a drove of horses and mules which we had to sell on time, returning home in January, 1867, and the balance of that year I hauled cotton to San Antonio, freighting with mule teams.

In the spring of 1869 I went up the trail to Abilene, Kansas, with J. H. Smith, George Eustace, Will Hardeman, S. M. Eeds and Cout Rountree in the outfit. We had 1,500 cattle in the herd, 160 of which belonged to me, 175 belonged to George Eustace, and the remainder belonged to J. H. Smith, who bossed the herd. We went by Waco and Fort Worth, where we purchased supplies to carry us through to Abilene. It was cold and raining most of the time, and the creeks and rivers were all

overflowed. When we came to the Smoky River, Jack
Kyle pointing the herd, I was riding a little mule, and
when I started in to swim the driver, a man whom we did
not know, who was riding a bob-tailed horse, said if my
little mule could swim the river "old Bob" could swim
it. His horse sank with him and the man was drowned.
I threw a rope to him but he failed to catch it. His
body was recovered three days later. From Abilene myself and S. M. Eeds shipped our horses and mules to
Junction City where we bought wagons, loaded up and
started back to Texas, reaching home in November.

In 1870, 1871 and 1872 I and my brother, W. B. Con-
ley, freighted to Port Lavaca, and in 1873 we built a
home for our parents where Fentress is now located.
On November 19, 1874, I was married to Miss Amanda
Eastwood, and the following year we moved to the place
where my wife was born, two miles above Fentress,
where we have lived all these years. We had three
children, one of whom died five years ago. The other
two, boys, live at Fentress. I served as county commissioner from 1909 until 1916.

SOLD CATTLE IN NATCHEZ FOR $4.50 A HEAD

A. E. Scheske, Gonzales, Texas

I came to Texas with my father and his family in 1855
when I was a small boy. We settled about two miles
north of Gonzales, which at that time was a very small
place, with just a few stores and a handful of people.
The country was all open, mostly prairie, with an
abundance of cattle, horses and hogs. And we used to
go hog hunting like people hunt deer today, and kill
wagonloads of them, some of the finest you ever saw.

I believe the cattle business to be the greatest enterprise the world has ever seen, even greater than the
manufacture of automobiles is today, considering the
time and the conditions. In the early days the cattle

business was not only the greatest thing to Texans and to the people of the South, but people from everywhere flocked to Kansas to see the vast herds that came from Texas, and the herds that were on the plains there, as well as the buffalo that were so numerous in the early seventies, and which men killed by thousands for their hides from which to make leather and robes. In 1876, when we passed Doan's Store on Red River, we were told that 400,000 cattle had passed there that year for the markets. Lots of them were left unsold and thousands of them froze there that winter. The herd I was with was among those which had to remain through the winter. I do not know of very many of the boys who went up with me that trip. John Henry Lewis, who lives a few miles north of Harwood, a fellow named Van Dyke of Marfa, and my brother, J. A. Scheske, of Terrell, are the only ones that I know of just now, except some negroes.

My experiences of the trail dates back to the early sixties, when I was a mere boy. The first trip I ever made was with a bunch of horses for the Confederates under Captain H. S. Parker. We drove to Harrisburg. I made three trips there with horses, two under Parker and one under Captain Kelley. The news of Lee's surrender reached us at Harrisburg, but Captain Kelley went on nevertheless. After the war we drove cattle there in small herds to be shipped. I remember one trip I made with Sam Moore. We had about 400 steers and it was in December, 1868, a very cold winter, Eugene Johnson and I were on herd the first part of the night, a high norther was blowing and it was so cold we couldn't keep our cattle from drifting, and we stayed with them all night. When the boys found us the next morning we could not stand up, our feet and legs were so chilled.

In 1869 the first herd went to Kansas and one to Shreveport, La. Bill Greathouse was the first man to leave Gonzales county for Kansas with a herd of cattle.

He lived about a mile west of the present town of Dilworth, on Peach Creek. They had about 1,000 head. Greathouse himself acted as boss. C. A. Mitchell and Lump Mooney were two that left here with him. In Kansas they all had the cholera and were nursed by the Indians. Mooney and Greathouse died there and Mitchell got well and came back to Gonzales. Andy Moore, who I was with, left Gonzales county for Shreveport, La., in 1869 under the N7 connected brand. We went to Natchez, where the cattle were sold for four dollars and fifty cents a head, steers and stock cattle mixed.

In 1870 I left Lavaca county for Sam Moore, who at that time lived at Moulton. A fellow named Burnett of Lavaca county owned an interest in the herd. They turned over to me a thousand head of cattle on the Lavaca Prairie under the Figure 2 brand. Lee Goss, Will Thornton and John Walker (negro) were some of the boys with the herd. We made the trip to Abilene, Kans., in sixty-four days. When we crossed the Red River it was on a rise and we had to make a raft of willow logs. John Walker, and I put the cattle across. We had a fearful electrical storm that night and the other fellows got cut off from us and the negro and myself were left with the herd all night in the Territory. These cattle were sold to a man named True of Missouri, for whom I herded until fall. On this trip, in Kansas, after the cattle had been sold, we lost part of the horses and I went after them, and rode across the plains for three days trailing them by a drag chain. I came across Big Foot Wallace coming from Columbus on his way out to California, and he told me that our horses had taken up with another herd about five miles south of the Little Arkansas. He insisted on me staying all night with him and his crowd.

In 1871 I went up the trail for J. H. Paramore, who at that time lived at Gonzales. We had a thousand head of the 3P cattle which we also sold to Mr. True, and we crossed the cattle into Iowa where we turned them loose in the cornfields. Those farmers had made lots of corn that year, which was sold for ten cents per bushel where they could sell it. Corn was so plentiful the farmers were using it for fuel instead of wood. We crossed the cattle where St. Louis is today. That place was then about the size of Gonzales today. An election was being held there and Mr. True tried to get the ferry to take our cattle, but the boatman would not do it, said he was too busy getting people across to vote, so we started them across ourselves and the ferryman ran his boat right into the middle of our herd and turned them so we had to clear the way in the usual manner Texans cleared the way in those days. We were in St. Louis when Chicago was burned.

In 1872 I started up with a herd of horses for myself, but decided to turn to Louisiana, and we got into the worst money panic the South has ever experienced, and we couldn't sell any of them. We almost starved for lack of food, and when we got down to our last fifty cents we bought a bushel of apples which we lived on for about three days, without anything else.

In 1873 I went up with 1,800 head of cattle for Bob Houston and G. W. Littlefield with the Mallet herd. We reached Selina in fifty-five days. The late Ship Parks of the Cross ranch near Fort Stockton, was along, as was also the late D. B. Hodges, J. H. Lewis, a man named Robertson and my brother, J. A. Scheske. That year we passed everything on the road. We made one trip in fifty-four days. A man came to us in Kansas and said that he had heard of us all along the trail and tried to catch us but couldn't. After our herd had been delivered we were started to Fort Sill with 2,200 beeves for the Indians. On our way we had lots of trouble with the Cheyenne tribe. We started with a guide, but he got off with some other herd and the Cheyennes got into our cattle. We had several mix-ups with them, and when the old chief got them to milling around he laughed and seemed to be in the height of his glory. After awhile our guide came back to us and advised us to give them two calves and get them stopped, which we did. This guide's name was Porter, and he had a cork leg. I will never forget him, nor how glad I was to see him. He could speak seven Indian dialects.

In 1878 I went up the trail with the F— herd for G. W. Littlefield. These cattle were gathered near where Oak Forest is today, and delivered to me on the Lockhart Prairie by W. P. Littlefield, now of New Mexico. We had about 2,000 head. Hess Parks, Jim Cochran, Marcus Dilworth and a fellow named Gay were among those who went with this herd. We delivered on the Platte River in Nebraska.

The last trip I made up the trail was in 1882, when I went for the late J. D. Houston of San Antonio, then of Gonzales, and John Rutledge of Yorktown, with the Figure 2 herd. We had 4,500 head and we reached Dodge City, Kansas, in fifty-five days. When we reached the South Canadian it was up and all herds were blocked for seven or eight days. When I rode up the boys asked me if I was going to cross, and after studying the matter over, I decided that I had better cross, so we crossed our cattle and one other herd. We went up the river and the other herd went down it and that night we had another storm and our cattle almost got back into the river, in fact they got into flank water and I told the boys to take their slickers and stampede them. They ran to the Wichita Mountains where we stopped them without losing a steer. The other herd got all mixed up and drifted south that night and we never saw them any more for we went on without any further trouble.

DAYS THAT WERE FULL OF THRILLS

Branch Isbell, Odessa, Texas

My desire to become a cowboy had its inception on the old plantation in Sumter county, Alabama, when I was born November 5, 1851.

During the fall of 1863 a squad of Confederate soldiers was driving a herd of about 300 big Texas steers through our country and pastured them over night in my mother's fields from which the corn had been harvested. The next day when the herd was started to cross the Tombigbee River at Gainesville, four miles distant, I persuaded mother to let me accompany the outfit that far on my pony. On the way the soldiers sang over and over a song which one of their number had composed. The song had many stanzas, but two of them so impressed my boyish fancy that I recall them still:

"Driving cattle's our promotion,
  Which just exactly suits my notion,
  And we perform with great devotion,
  There's work enough for all.

"I'd like to be a Virginia picket,
  But I'd rather be in the cattle thicket
  Where the hooting owl and screaming cricket
  Make noise enough for all."

That night when I returned to my home—a happy home indeed, in spite of the Civil War then raging—I told my dear, now sainted mother, that as soon as I reached manhood I intended to go to Texas and become a cow-puncher.

In 1870 Mr. Frank Byler, now gone to his reward, as good a friend as I or any man ever had, brought a drove of Texas ponies to our neighborhood. When he had disposed of them he invited me to accompany him home and assured me that I would get rid of malaria from which I suffered if I would remain in West or Southwest Texas.

That assurance added to my predilection for an out-door life, decided me to accept his invitation, and we landed at Corpus Christi, January 16, 1871.

I remained at Mr. Byler's home at old Nuecestown two or three weeks, during which time I formed a deathless friendship for his wife, which grew stronger every year during the last ten years of her life. When I left them to seek my fortune among strangers, Mr. Byler loaned me a gentle steed, named Old Heart Seven, telling me that when I found employment I could turn the horse foot-loose anywhere within one hundred miles of home and he would return to his remuda — the saddle bunch with which he ran. I headed for Banquette, but before I had gone five miles the beast showed signs of laziness and seeing some mesquites a short distance, as I thought, from the road, I turned off to procure a switch (old-state substitute for quirt) with which to urge him on. I rode fully a mile and seemed no nearer the switches(?) than when I started, when I discovered that I was lost on the apparently boundless prairie. I dismounted and took the bridle from the horse that he might graze while I reflected what to do. After a few moments—being more than ever bewildered—in sheer desperation I engaged in a game of solitaire mumble-peg. After a little while I looked up and observed an object approaching me through the distant mirage that appeared like a very tall old woman in a long black robe. Then and there, believe me, I saw visions of witchcraft and witches galore. However, on arrival it proved to be a lone horse-hunter in the person of John Burks, long since deceased, of

BRANCH ISBELL

Banquette, the Mecca which I sought. After self-introductions and mutual explanations, he invited me to go home with him. That invitation was accepted with less hesitation and more alacrity than any I can recall either before or since that time. John was living with his brother, William Burks, husband of Mrs. Amanda Burks, now of Cotulla, and one of the few lady members of our organization. Mr. Burks engaged me to make a trail trip to Kansas, and Mrs. Burks, in a buggy, made one of our outfit. That trip was an experience I can never forget. Being a "tenderfoot," I was started in at the rear end of the herd and Mrs. Burks took me under her protecting wing. I verily believe that her business success since her widowhood began, has been given her as a reward for her unfailing kindness to myself and others. I met her at the Cattle Convention in San Antonio in March, 1915, for the first time since the early seventies of the last century, and could have picked her from a thousand. My prayer for her is that her shadow may never grow less, and may she "live to eat the hen that scratches above her grave." Returning to the incidents of that trip I will state that the herd we drove was half and half grown cows and steers, and that season it was customary to kill the young calves found on the bed-ground. I had a pistol and it was my duty to murder the innocents each morning while their pitiful mothers were ruthlessly driven on. It looked hard, but circumstances demanded the sacrifice, and being the executioner so disgusted me with six-shooters that I have never owned—much less used one from that time to this. It is likely, too, that not being a gun-man during the following five or six years kept me from becoming involved in several shooting tragedies that I saw enacted. Unpreparedness has kept me peacefully inclined. My bedding on the trip consisted of a saddle blanket, a black rubber coat and an old-fashioned man's shawl. Luxury played no part in our surroundings then.

June, I think it was, we passed by the then infant towns of Wichita and Newton and gained the vicinity of Abilene, Kansas. Then I decided I wanted to return to Texas, over the trail we had gone by. Mr. Burks paid me an extra month's wages and furnished me a saddle horse and pack animal and bade me Godspeed on my journey. I got back to Newton on the morning after the famous night gunfight among cowmen, officers and gamblers, in which seven or eight men were killed. That tragedy clinched my aversion to habitual pistol toting. At Newton I met a Mr. Duke, who had charge of a big herd of steers for the John Rabb outfit. He persuaded me to return the horses to Mr. Burks and take employment with him. He sent me to his camp on Cowskin Creek where Sam Glenn was in charge. From Sam I got my first real lesson in grazing and watering a herd of big steers, an art which is now almost lost, but in which I became an expert. I remained with Duke until December, when three Mexicans he had became dissatisfied with the weather, and he induced me with little difficulty to pilot them back to Corpus Christi by rail and water. To those Mexicans that experience was a revelation, and what they saw convinced them that Mexico might require more than they thought it would in whipping Uncle Sam. Thus ended my first trail trip.

In 1872 I hired to Scott & Byler to work on the range for the modest stipend of $20 per month by the year, work or play. I had the privilege of trading horses, and at the end of a year I had $150 in cash and five good ponies— more clear profit than I ever afterwards saved at wages varying from $50 to $125 per month. Jim Miller of Banquette, Nueces county, was boss over myself and from twelve to fourteen Mexicans, and our range was from the Nueces to the Rio Grande Rivers. Miller was paid $700 a year and the Mexicans $10 or $12 per month when at work. Those receiving $12 were called "henetes" and were supposed to ride any horse they might be given.

We worked eight months out of the twelve, during which time we gathered many steers, skinned 4,000 dead cattle —1872 being the year of the "die-up"—and branded several thousand calves, among them a big per cent of "dogies," defined by an old Texas cowman to a garrulous and inquisitive lady from up North as "unfortunate calves whose mothers were dead and whose fathers had eloped with other cows." Selah!

During the year we had some comic and some tragic experiences. One of the comic episodes, in which I played the "goat," I recall as follows: One Saturday night, when we were camped near Banquette, Miller asked if I would like to go with him to a dance at a home near San Patricio, about twelve miles away. We went, and there I was handed the sourest lemon I had ever tasted. During the evening I approached a young miss of "sweet sixteen," Lizzie Hinnant, whom I had met a few times before, and asked her for a dance. Without even the stereotyped excuse of a previous engagement she answered simply and curtly "No." Feeling somewhat melted I thought I would embarrass her in turn, so I thanked her and told her that since there remained in the sea as good fish as had ever been caught, I'd cast my line in another place. Instead of "wilting," as I thought she would, she came back with this: "Certainly there are, but unfortunately for you they have quit biting at toads." I retired to the "shade of an old apple tree" and butted my head against it in sheer desperation. Since then I have known that the "Yellow Rose of Texas" grows on a thorny bush. After dancing until almost daylight we returned to camp about sun-up Sunday morning. I being somewhat weary, had laid the flattering unction to my soul that Miller certainly would observe that beautiful and blessed spring Sabbath, and he did—but in a manner altogether unexpected to me. He awakened the sleeping Aztecs, and after a little coffee, he led us all forth to labor. That day we gathered and branded more than 300 calves. We branded for everybody then exchanging tallies, later with other outfits working in different parts of our extensive range—and when nightfall came again I was completely petered out. I uttered no word of protest, but when, on another similar occasion Jim asked me if I deserved to go dancing, like Poe's immortal Raven, I answered "Nevermore!" Miller was a great fellow in many ways. I once heard his father try to persuade him to forsake cattle work and take up farming. He listened patiently to the old man's arguments and when he had finished his laconic answer was: "Father, I didn't make this world, nor shall I undertake to tear it up." He enjoyed riding and dancing better than anyone I ever knew, and over-indulgence in the two exercises caused an abscess to form on his liver which called him hence in 1876.

"So struck the eagle, stretched upon the plain,
  No more through rolling clouds to soar again,
  Views his own feather upon the fatal dart
  That winged the shaft that quivered to his heart."

Too oft, alas, the capable die young.

In 1873 Mr. Byler sold me 104 head of big steers, not even requiring a note as security, which I threw in a herd driven by J. P. Cox and A. B. (Arch) Lockhart. They allowed me wages and made me no charge against my cattle. Not one of mine was lost on the way, and in September I sold them to J. B. Hunter & Company for $20 per head. They paid me $580 and were to pay $1,500 in a few days. Before the time expired the memorable "Black Friday" fell on Wall Street and Hunter & Company's failure lost me my $1,500. I returned to Texas owing Mr. Byler the original cost of the steers, $1,248. I worked for him and others, paying a little at a time on my debt, until it was finally paid in full. That circumstance gave me a credit that is good to this day, and which I have been careful never again to strain.

In 1884 and 1885 I worked with Dave Mangum who drove for Scott & Byler on the profit-sharing plan. I remember that Jack Mangum, Wiley Thorton, Jim Buckley and myself were the only white punchers on one or both these trips, the rest being Mexicans. Nothing out of the ordinary—barring two or three stampedes—occurred on either drive.

In 1876 I had full charge of a herd for Mr. R. R. Savage, who still resides at Corpus Christi, and is yet my friend. On that journey we had a big stampede one stormy night near Monument Rocks, in Oklahoma, then Indian Territory, about forty miles north of Red River Station. The next evening we found the lead cattle standing on a bluff and looking south across Red River. When we rounded up and counted we were thirty head short. Leaving all the hands except one old Mexican to hold the herd, I took him, and both of us being unarmed, started out to hunt those thirty steers. We found where they had been penned on Beaver Creek the night before and one of them killed for beef the hide being left on the fence. We followed them across the big herd trail to Mud Creek, where we found them in another pen. I saw that, besides our twenty-nine steers there were twelve other steers in one road brand, and ten cows in another. I first forged a power of attorney to handle the twelve steers, before I asked a woman, who was sweeping a log cabin near by, who claimed the cattle. She said her husband and some other men were gathering stampeded cattle and holding them for the trail men. I told her that I claimed about half there were in the pen, and that I intended to start them towards the trail and would settle with the men if I saw them. She warned me that I would best wait until they returned or there might be trouble.

We did not heed her, however, and started driving the bunch towards the trail. Before we had gone half a mile about ten heavily armed men, very tough looking customers, suddenly emerged from the brush and rounded us up. To borrow his favorite salutation from Ex-Senator Bailey when he speaks, I thought "My fellow countrymen' my time had come. But, by being unarmed and looking innocent—while feeling scared—we got them down to a parley. After about thirty minutes of bluff on their part and diplomatic language on mine they decided they would accept the ten cows in payment of their philanthropic (?) labor. They cut the cows from the steers, and pointing towards the trail, said, "Now you git" and we "got." From 10 A.M. until nightfall we drove those steers about thirty miles and landed them safely among their lowing fellows. Without further adventure we reached the head of Thompson's Creek, a tributary of the Medicine River about thirty or forty miles Southeast of Dodge City, Kansas; where we grazed the herd until some time in July, when it was sold at a good profit. We returned to Texas by rail and the Kansas pasture lands have not known me since.

I could fill a volume with yarns about the clash of wits between settlers and drovers, but let just one, in which I was compelled to play the part of Ananias, suffice:

In 1874 the country north of Great Bend, Kansas, was being settled by farmers from more Eastern States, who when they had secured a land claim, would plow a furrow around it and the Kansas law declared such furrow to be a fence and woe to the drover whose stock dared cross it. Unreasonable damages were invariably claimed and usually collected either by law or reprisals of some kind. Animosity was thus engendered between the herdsmen and husbandmen. Late in October I was hunting a bunch of steers that had escaped my herd, when, late one afternoon I realized that both myself and my horse, being tired and hungry, had to find a refuge or suffer greatly from cold. I discovered a settler's shack in the distance and decided if possible to buy or beg a night's entertainment. So disguising myself and my mount to appear as much as might be like a "hayseed," I approached the place with many misgivings. The proprietors proved to be a young married couple from Southeast Illinois. After some parleying they asked where I came from to Kansas, and on what mission I was bent. I told them that I was from the northwest corner of the same good old commonwealth from which they came; that I also had a claim about thirty miles from them and that I was following some Texas cattle that had run through my corn and destroyed several rows of it. At this (mis) information they bade me welcome and my steed, "Old Bowlegs," and I fared sumptuously that night! Until late bed-time I entertained them as best I could by exchanging my fictitious yarns for their true stories of "our childhoods' happy days down on the farm" in dear old Illinois. Before I left them the next morning repentance came to me like a clap of thunder from a clear sky, and I made known my identity. They admitted that if I had spoken truly the night before I would have been turned away. I invited them to visit my camp and share my frugal fare as long as they could relish it. Under protest from them I threw them $2 and galloped away to find my cattle in a herd a few miles distant. That couple (I hope they ride in their auto now), like many of their kind, were good people at heart, but they and we drovers misunderstood each other badly, each side in selfishness failing to grasp the other's viewpoint. I surely hope the time has mellowed their feelings towards us, and my fellow oldtimers' dispositions towards them, as much as it has my own.

In 1877 I drove a herd of heifers from Nueces county to the head of Pecan Bayou in Callahan county for Mr. Byler, where I threw them in with a herd of stock cattle which G. W. Waddell had carried to that locality the year before. Together, Waddell being the boss, we moved the whole lot to Mitchell county and in July established the first ranch there at Pecan Grove on Champliers—now called Champion Creek—about nine miles southeast of where the town of Colorado was laid out after the Texas & Pacific railroad reached there early in 1881. However, A. W. Dunn had built a store there in the fall of 1880 and enjoyed a big ranch trade. The four years on that ranch, before the coming of the railway, were as happy as any bunch of punchers ever knew. The creek was alive with fine fish, and game of all kinds, from cotton-tail rabbits to mammoth buffaloes abounded. I killed one of the latter near where the Baptist church in Colorado City now stands. I could write indefinitely about occurrences while on that ranch, but shall relate just one, which always seemed funny to others, though in those days it grew irksome, to say the least, to me, the joke being on "yours truly," with a big Y and T. Once when I was returning from a trip to Belle Plain, a hundred miles away, where we sent almost monthly for our mail, I was harbored for a night by a gentleman named Altman, who had a few cattle, and as bright and handsome a daughter as one might encounter in any country. Their house was a one-room shack, but no palace ever covered two warmer hearts. They gave me a hearty welcome and entertained me royally in every way. When it came time to retire for the night, a wagon sheet was stretched across the room behind which I was assigned to a pallet on which a real feather bed had been placed. Before my departure next morning, Miss Emma (I hope she is alive and happy yet, and that God has ever blessed her), inquired if I had enjoyed my bed. Thinking to give her a cute reply, I answered that my rest had been unbroken except for one brief interval during which my "goosehair" surroundings had caused me to dream that I was a goose. Like a flash her retort came: "The truth will prevail even in a dream." Once again the protecting thorn of a Texas rose had gaffed me to the quick, and my ill-timed and would-be wit received its just rebuke. "O Tempora, O Mores," how you both have changed!

That was in 1878, and I rejoice that I am so constituted that I can chuckle yet when memory recalls that ridiculous episode from forty-four retrospective years.

In 1881, after the town had come to us, Mr. Byler sold his ranch, lock, stock and barrel and we woke with a start, to find ourselves in a new day, with all our former lives cut off from us and become as a dream. From the day the town was christened up to 1884 Colorado, Texas, was the livest village I have ever known. Cattle and sheep more than doubled in value, and money flowed in streams. It was a Mecca for gamblers and their associates. Three combination dance halls and variety shows flourished side by side for eighteen months, and the largest cattle and sheep deals were consummated in the gilded back rooms of the most prominent saloons. There were three such, besides several lesser lights whose average daily sales, Sundays included, must have exceeded $100 for at least two years. During 1884 the tide began to ebb, and within two or three years, it seemed to me Colorado was as staid a community as Puritanic heart might wish to see. Why in 1887 when the State at large voted anti by a majority of more than 92,000 the Prohibitionists of Mitchell county led us antis by thirty votes. Then it was that sadly the roisterers exclaimed, "How have the mighty fallen."

When the boom was over I found myself bankrupt, but free from debt. I read law long enough to procure a license, and, in 1888 was elected county attorney of Scurry county and located at Snyder. I served two terms as attorney and one as county judge, during such service, when I was in my fortieth year, I married Mrs. S. M. Gourley. She was a teacher, a childless widow, having lost one little girl. She was ten years my junior, and a daughter of Rev. J. S. Abbott, a Baptist minister, well known in Gonzales and adjoining counties for many years. She blessed my life more than seven years, and died at her sister's home near Lockhart in May, 1898, where she "sleeps 'neath the old arbor trees" of that town's beautiful and, to me at least, most sacred cemetery. She was the only woman I ever met whom I felt inclined to wed, and since she was called away her memory has been my bride. I visit her relatives in South Texas from time to time and they treat me as a brother yet. Some natures blame the Almighty for their bereavements, but, sinner as I am, I believe He who marks the sparrow's fall doeth all things well, and, with Ella Wheeler Wilcox, I can believing exclaim:

"I know there is no error in the great Eternal plan,
    And that all things work together for the final good
        of man;
And I know as my soul speeds onward, in its grand
        eternal flight,
I shall cry as I look earthward—whatever is, is right."

In the summer of 1898 I came to Odessa, Ector county, Texas, my present home, where I have been engaged in merchandising in a small way ever since. I have never "hustled" much or been "up-to-date"—I abhor both expressions—but, by close economy and a few lucky deals in local real estate, I have accumulated a sufficiency for my frugal wants, but not enough to worry over. If work kills half the people and worry the other half, my chance should be good to survive indefinitely—for I've quit them both.

For the last seven years I have been a regular attendant on the annual conventions of the Texas Cattle Raisers' Association, where I go for the sole purpose of meeting my associates of "days lang syne." At these meetings I have met many of their sons whom I have found to be worthy scions from the parent stock. As in all flocks there may be a few "black sheep" in each generation, but, taken as a whole, they will bear favorable comparison, in physique and native intelligence, with any earthly body of men. They may be boisterous and uncouth in some respects, yet, at heart they are "diamonds in the rough," while for charity, manhood and chivalry they stand erect—the peers of any ancient bearer of shield and lance "when knighthood was in flower."

The saddest feature of each recurring convention is the fact that we miss some faces that were with us the year before. Old Father Time has laid his hand upon them, let us hope "not smitingly, but gently, as the harper lays his hand upon his harp to deaden its vibrations." Let us also hope and believe that when the last of the original founders of the Old Trail Drivers' Association shall have laid his burden down, their sons will perpetuate the organization, and, as each succeeding generation shall struggle, one by one, across life's great divide, the spirits of those who have gone before may meet and greet and welcome them to the fresh and verdant grazing grounds beyond, to dwell forever there "where the wicked cease troubling and the weary are at rest." Adios, Amigos Viejos. Let each of us maintain a stiff upper lip and a heart for every fate as we drift adown life's stream saying to each other as the "cheerful cherub" of the *Dallas News* remarked while pointing a fat, rosy finger at his disconsolate pup:

> Don't whine now because we've no money;
> It's really a good thing, I think—
> The longer you wait when you're thirsty
> The better it tastes when you drink.

Explanation: The foregoing manuscript was prepared and sent to the secretary as my contribution to a volume "The Trail Drivers of Texas" brought out one or two years ago. After its receipt by the Secretary all records were burned accidentally and through a misunderstanding a copy was never sent in. Hence it was not included in the book.

Since it was written many changes have been wrought

in my life. Chief among them was my second marriage in April, 1920, to Mrs. Nettie S. Nicks, widow of Dr. J. M. Nicks, who practiced several years at Ranger, Texas, and died in that city in February, 1916.

I was a childless widower in my sixty-ninth year and my wife, a childless widow, is several years younger. I was then and am now in robust health, neither bald nor gray, and wife is very active, with but few gray hairs, but her health has to be zealously guarded—so far I have made it my special business to be its guardian, and I expect to do so to the end.

We both feel that we are making each other's declining years more pleasant than they would have been had we never met.

The best wish I can make for the friends of my cowboy days is that each survivor among them may face the future as calmly and fearlessly as I do as life's evening's shadows appear.

Odessa, Texas, August 25th, 1921.

SOME TRIPS UP THE TRAIL

James Marion Garner, Texarkana, Arkansas

Among the army of veteran cowboys of the Texas plains yet living to recall events and environments of the early days is James Marion Garner, of Texarkana, Arkansas, the author of this sketch. Mr. Garner, though fairly advanced in years, continues in the cattle business and is a familiar figure as he rides a sturdy horse over the streets of the Gateway City from Arkansas into Texas. He bears the rugged appearance of one inured to the elements and heroic living, and one can well imagine him in his early days as a free rover of the plains. Mr. Garner writes:

I first saw the light of day in Jackson Parish, Louisiana, but when I was two years of age my father moved his family to Texas to a point near the present town of

Cuero. We lived there, and my father assisted in laying the town off. In 1869 he moved to San Patricio county, where we were principally reared, and early in my manhood I was honored one term with the office of county sheriff. Messrs. D. C., E. R. and A. P. Rachel were our neighbors, and real cattlemen they were. I worked for them more than a year.

In the spring of 1872 when I was eighteen years of age, I went with Dillard Fant's cattle to Wichita, Kansas. My boss was Bud Hodges. We branded out near Goliad and started with about 2,000 steers and reached our destination with about that number, having picked up as many crippled trail cattle as we lost. We experienced no bad luck until we crossed the Red River but when near the

JAMES MARION GARNER

Monument Stones in Indian Territory, in a difficulty one of our crowd shot and killed one man of our outfit.

We killed and ate plenty of buffalo and antelope, mixed with, and fed lots of red men, but had no trouble with them.

The next spring, in 1873, with a letter of recommendation from Bud Hodges I got to be boss of a herd of 2,000 cattle for Mr. John Wade, of Nueces county. Nearly all of my hands appeared to like me, and they reached their journey's end with me and the cattle, and with very small loss of the latter.

I did have a little trouble with the Marlow boys, on Wild Horse Creek, in the Indian Territory. These fellows were a lot of bandits and stampeded our cattle and ran twenty head of them off. We followed them twenty miles and got our cattle back.

Another time, about seven years later, I drove up 440 head of my own horses and mares. Had a fine set of boys and the trip was a good one, there being only two little incidents out of the ordinary. Eight to ten Indians frequently would come up just about time for dinner, and I would always have our cook, a white boy, to prepare lots of food and we would fill the Indians up. Then the Indians would always want to shoot our guns. The cook became angry one day at this habit, and he filled his old Enfield rifle half full of powder and a tight wad. About this time he saw nine Indians riding up. He placed the gun against the wagon and said he would bet one Indian would not eat much dinner that day. The Indians came riding up, dismounted, and proceeded to wait for dinner. One of the number set up a can, took up the overloaded Enfield, squatted down and fired at the can. I think that gun flew about twenty feet in one direction and the Indian an equal distance in the opposite direction. Then there was a profound silence. The Indians got on their ponies and rode off, one behind the other, thinking no doubt, the accident was the work of a ghost.

We did not herd our horses at night. Just scattered them out north of us and let them go, so one morning about daylight we had just saddled our mounts and saw our drove grazing peacefully when all at once we heard the stampede. We hastily got on our mounts and ran toward them, only to see a large, wild bay horse among them. There was a pair of red blankets tied across his back and hanging nearly to the ground on either side. Stampeded buffalo could not run at all in comparison with our drove of horses. I rode into the moving mass of equines and soon cut out the wild horse and when near the edge of the drove shot and killed him. The animal fell into a creek full of high bullrushes. It then required until 10 o'clock that morning to get our drove of horses together, and when we counted them we found we were two horses short.

It was in 1883 that I dropped $40,000 in the Dimmit County Pasture Company, between Cotulla and the Rio Grande, and after I realized I was broke I came to Texarkana and settled, and have handled stock here on a small scale ever since. For the past ten years I have conducted a wholesale butcher business under the name of the Texarkana Dressed Beef Company. I married Miss Anna Rogers in Corpus Christi. My wife was the daughter of Col. C. M. Rogers, and her stepmother, before marrying Mr. Rogers, was the Widow Rabb, and was one time called the cattle queen of Texas. We have raised five boys and three girls, the latter being married and living in Texarkana. We have one son married and living here, one in Atlanta, Texas; one unmarried, living in New Mexico; and have two younger sons living at home with us.

I must say that the trail drives appear now more like a dream to me than a reality. Every man should possess at least one good quality, so if there is one creditable man who can say he ever heard me swear an oath I will send a check for $50.

There are two more trails that lead to new countries, and I think our parents have blazed out and traveled the straightest trail. I hope we will all travel that trail and meet again to talk about the buffaloes and hostile

Indians with whom we did not come in contact on our journey.

THRILLING EXPERIENCES

Levi J. Harkey, Sinton, Texas

I was born April 6th, 1860, at Richland Springs, San Saba county, Texas. My parents came from Yell county, Arkansas, (now laugh, you darn fools) in the year of 1853, and first stopped on Wallace Creek, about ten miles southwest of the town of San Saba. In 1856 they moved

LEVI J. HARKEY

to Richland Springs, fifteen miles west of San Saba and there settled permanently. My parents died in 1866, their deaths being about three weeks apart, leaving thirteen children, eight boys and five girls, the eldest being only eighteen years old, to fight it out with Comanche Indians, and believe me we had a time. I have seen as many as seventy-five Indians in a bunch, and have been

chased by them several times, but was too fleet on foot for them. You may talk about the Indian troubles experienced while going up the trail, but it was nothing to compare with the dangers we had to contend with. They came into our immediate section every light moon and on one occasion they came down upon us seventy-five in number, all giving the Comanche yell. Five of us little brats were about two hundred yards from the house fishing. My sister Sarah thought it was cowboys, and she ran up a live oak tree to watch them, while we ran to the house. When I reached the house, the other children were inside and closed the door, and I never got inside until after the danger was over. My two oldest brothers were in the field plowing at the time and when they came and got the old flintlock rifles the Indians fled. The Indians passed under the tree where my sister was but never discovered her. Another sister, Julia, now Mrs. C. T. Harmon, hid in the cornfield. That Indian raid caused all the people on Richland Creek to fort up near the town of San Saba. The Indians and the United States soldiers stayed around there until the following spring, and left with all the cattle and horses in that section. A short time after the Indians left, the soldiers left, but not until they had destroyed all the log cabins in the neighborhood.

In 1876 I left Richland Springs with C. T. Harmon and wife, and landed at the Rocky Ammons Ranch, on the Atascosa River, eighteen miles west of the old town of Oakville, on October 21st, 1876. Ammons and Bill Harmon were partners in the cattle business at that time.

In 1877 I left the Ammons Ranch with a herd of 2,000 mixed cattle, cows and steers, belonging to C. C. Lewis and Nick Bluntzer, for Dodge City, Arkansas, Bill Harmon as road boss. I returned to the Ammons Ranch the same year and did general ranch work for Mr. Ammons until 1883. From 1883 till 1890 I speculated in Spanish horses in and out of San Antonio.

Many times have I ridden with our genial president, Geo. W. Saunders, who in those days was a live wire.

In 1891 the horse business took a tumble downward, and I went to Beeville, Texas, and ran a wet goods shop until 1906, when I sold that business, and went into a dry goods business. While retailing wet goods, I accumulated about $100,000.00 worth of property, but while I was in the dry goods business I signed notes at the various banks for a friend who speculated in cattle, and he broke me flatter than a pancake.

In 1911 I sold my business and moved to the Panhandle, to a place called Dickens, Texas. While up there

I sold my land in Live Oak county and all of my Beeville property, and paid everything I owed. In 1912 I moved from Dickens to San Patricio county, and went to work in the Tax Assessor's office for Chris Rachal, who was assessor at that time. In 1916 I was elected Tax Assessor for San Patricio county, and am still holding it down, and hope I will be able to hold it down a few years longer.

November 27th, 1921, I took C. T. Harmon to San Antonio in my old reliable Ford, to attend the Old Time Trail Drivers' Convention with no intention whatever to attend myself, but Charlie persuaded me to go over to the hall with him, and I met so many of the old timers it made me feel good, so I walked right up and joined and paid my dues, received a badge, and was as happy as a lark, and am very proud I belong to the Association. I shall always take off my hat to the old timers of Texas. Too many people never give them credit for anything, much less for blazing the way for the development of the greatest state in the Union, Texas. May God bless them is my prayer.

NOTED QUANTRELL WAS WITH HERD ON TRAIL

Dr. J. Hargus, of Dimmit County

I was born in Washington county, Mo. My parents were T. J. and M. A. Hargus.

In 1854 we moved to Texas and settled in Caldwell county, near Lockhart, when I was just a small boy. Then my father went into the cow business. He died in 1858 and was buried near Lockhart, Texas.

My mother married Rev. W. H. Farmer in 1860, who was the grandfather of "Farmer" Jennings, the present secretary of the Old Time Trail Drivers' Association.

In 1860 we moved to the present site of Martindale. Here my stepfather traded his holdings for beef cattle and we started up the trail in March, 1866. We traveled the lower trail, passing through Austin, Waco, Dallas

and Sherman and crossed at Talbot's Ferry, which, I
believe, is the present site of Denison.

Our cart drivers consisted of myself, two step-
brothers, R. C. and M. K. Farmer, and a nephew, Cyrus
Robinson. The hired hands were Neal Barefield, Dave
Hall and Watkins, also a Confederate soldier, C. C. Gibbs,
and a man who called himself Porter. When we reached
Waco, we camped on a little creek, at which time we had
a fight with a negro band in which my stepfather was
badly cut. After this nothing of particular importance
happened until we crossed the Red River; it was very
much swollen on account of recent rains. The herd ahead
of us belonged to Millett, Lane and Colonel Meyers.
Their cattle would not take to the water under any circumstances, but when we came up with our cattle they
crossed the river as if it were a little brook. The cattle
of Millett and Lane were placed right at the heels of our
herd, as well as Colonel Meyers', then they passed over
without any trouble. Since the negro would not ferry
the people across, they were left stranded on the banks
of the Red River. Several of us cowboys tried to swim
across, the stream being about three hundred yards wide,
with very high waves, but none were successful except
R. C. Farmer and myself and I only upon second trial, as
my first horse drowned and I was forced to another. We
two had our hands full, as we had to sing to about six
thousand head of cattle in order to keep them together.
It was midnight before any of the others could cross over.
This was a pretty cold job, as it was in the early part of
April and was rather cool, and we had on only our shirts.
After spending two or three days there we had no trouble
until we reached the Kansas and Missouri line, where
we found Mr. Daugherty tied to a tree after being
whipped by some people of Kansas and Missouri. They
claimed our cattle would give their cattle the Texas fever;
this was the first time we had ever heard of this. My
stepfather was well acquainted in Newton and Jasper

counties, Mo., where he had lived several years and obtained permission to enter Missouri, providing he would pay for all cattle that died within ten miles of his camp. We located in Jasper county, Mo., the present site of Joplin, Mo., where we herded cattle all summer. When we reached the Missouri line, Porter left us, claiming that ·he had to go back to Kentucky. He afterwards proved to be Quantrell, the noted guerrilla.

I wish to say that W. H. Farmer, our worthy secretary's grandfather, drove cattle across the plains in the early fifties, long before this, so you see that our secretary is more than worthy to be an old trailer's son.

I returned to Texas in 1876 and since that time have been water bound by the Nueces River and the Rio Grande. I am at present residing in the county of Dimmit. This is God's country.

LOST MANY THOUSANDS OF DOLLARS

C. S. Brodbent, 110 East Craig Place, San Antonio, Texas

In the early days of the trail drivers I lived in Summer county, Kansas. Caldwell, in that county, was one of the chief herd rendezvous after running the gauntlet of the Indian Territory. From Caldwell the trail led north through Summer county to Wichita, Newton and Abilene, Kansas. There was no Wellington or Newton at the beginning and Wichita was but a frontier hamlet.

We bought trail cattle and drove them to our farms and made good money, as we put up large quantities of hay and raised some corn. As winter came on, the trail cattle on the open range starved and froze by the thousands, and many owners met disastrous losses. The prevalent idea that the trail days were halcyon days of easy money making is erroneous. Many a man in comfortable circumstances in Texas became impoverished, and many a Kansas farmer who thought he was getting cattle dirt cheap from the trail, found himself a loser before spring by not having prepared enough feed.

Living so near the trail I was near the center of this great industry and became acquainted with Texas cattle owners and cowboys and, I suppose, became somewhat fascinated with the life, and in 1875 I located in the Rio Grande valley, in the Nueces and Devil's River country and about the last year of the Overland Drive, put up two herds and drove from Val Verde county to Indian Territory. Our cattle were dying from drouth and the drive was our only recourse. The venture was not a success. There was almost no demand in the Territory and the constant expense and Indian tax made sad inroads. I got out of this mess with a loss of over $10,000; not all, however was legitimate loss, for I heard of my brands being sold on the Kansas market, for which I never received any pay.

There was some dishonesty in this trail driving. A trail boss who did not reach his destination with an equal or greater number than he started with was considered incompetent. Hence ranchers along the trail made bitter complaints of moving herders "incorporating" their stock. On the other hand many of the cattle lost from the herds were picked up by these ranchers, which partially recouped their losses thereby. We had no Cattle Raisers' Association as we have now, and the business of the cattle trail was, in its nature, not such as encouraged a high standard of honesty, though many of the drivers and owners were of the strictest and loftiest moral character.

It is perhaps a surprising feature of the cattle drive that the owners of many herds that illegitimately increased the most on what they made a piratical journey north, went broke, and some of the most noted "cattle kings" became herdsmen or dropped into oblivion. A considerable number of Texas home ranchers got pay for the cattle they had sold to drivers. In some cases losses were unavoidable—in other cases dishonesty.

The most fortunate ranchers in the increase of herds in those open range days, were, I think, those bordering on the Gulf coast. Cattle drifting from the north before winter storms, could drift no further, and I have often been told that some of the greatest fortunes there were based on drift cattle. The Texas fence law and railroads obliterated the Texas cattle trail, and in its passing there should be no cause for regret. The old-time cowboy had heroic attributes, was generous, brave and ever ready to alleviate personal suffering, share his last crust, his blanket and often more important, his canteen. He spent his wages freely and not always wisely, and many became an easy prey to gambling and other low resorts. Some among them became leading men in law, art and science—even in theology, proving again that it is not in the vocation but in the man, that causes him to blossom and bring a fruitage of goodness, honor and godly living.

This screed is not much of a story of the trail, but you will have enough recitals of hairbreadth escapes from Indians, floods, lightning and accidents, enough of suffering from cold, heat, hunger, thirst and dust, and this variety may be one of the species of your book. You will also hear many amusing incidents for fun and frolic formed a part of the cowboys' life—many pathetic stories, too, for sickness and death followed the trail. But I had seen such before trail days when wearing a soldier's uniform, and I do not care to dwell thereon. Paraphrasing a favorite stanza:

> Cowboy rest, thy labor o'er.
> Sleep the sleep that knows no breaking;
> Dream of cattle drives no more,
> Days of toil and nights of waking.

WERE HAPPIER IN GOOD OLD DAYS

Oscar Thompson, Hebronville, Texas

My father would never consent for me to go up the trail, but I helped put up several herds. Helped Charlie and Jim Boyce put up two herds of horses. Jim Gibson had charge of one of the herds. I helped Jack Walton put up a herd near the old Consado Ranch on the Chiltipin, and helped J. I. Clare put up a herd at the old Mulas Hills pen for Capt. John T. Lytle. Later I worked for J. M. Chillin for nearly three years, and handled more than 40,000 cattle. Was moving cattle all the time. Never could find a pen large enough to hold our herd, so always had to herd out. I became thoroughly familiar with trail work and was foreman and boss of a cow crowd, mostly Mexicans, for fifteen years, most of the time in camp, and seldom in a house. We worked in those days. Now we go out in our "Tin Lizzie," meet the roundup, get out of the car and onto a good horse, cut cattle for a couple of hours, then get back into the car, have someone lead the horse back to the ranch, then spin for the ranch, take a bath and wait for the boys to come in with the herd. When they arrive I stand in the shade and watch them brand the calves or dip the cattle, as the case may be. But we were happier in those good old days than we are now.

THE LATCH STRING IS ON THE OUTSIDE

R. T. Mellard, Eddy County, New Mexico

I was born in Mississippi in Lawrence county, July 10th, 1849. My father and mother were slave holders and wanted to enlarge their holdings, so my father, in 1855, visited Texas, and was so impressed with the vast possibilities that he sold his farm on Pearl River, loaded his family and slaves in buggies and wagons and started to Texas. He arrived in Walker county in the latter part of 1856, and bought 880 acres of rich bottom land on the Trinity River and immediately began to improve the same, until December, 1860, when he was assassinated. My mother's brother in Mississippi heard of the tragedy and came to Texas in March, 1861, and persuaded my mother to let me go back to Mississippi with him. We took the little steamboat, *Mary Leonard,* went down the Trinity River to Galveston, thence by steamer to New Orleans, La., and went up to his plantation on Pearl River. In April, 1861, when war broke out he put me in school in Brook and immediately went to Virginia where he was engaged in some of the bloodiest battles of the Civil War, and I never saw him until the latter part of 1865, and I only heard from my mother once during the entire war. I remained with Mr. and Mrs. Larkin, who were both father and mother to me, and I attended school until the Yankees burned our school building in 1864, and practically wrecked the town. In October, 1865, my uncle furnished me funds and I started for home, not knowing whether my mother and two sisters were alive or not.

I went to New Orleans, stopped there for a few days with relatives, then took a steamer for Galveston, from there by rail to Navasota, where I bought a horse and went to Huntsville, a distance of fifty miles, and thence fifteen miles to where I found my mother and two sisters. The great war had practically broken her up, since the property consisted mostly of slaves. With a little money that was left to us children, I took my share (a few hundred dollars) and entered Austin Male College at Huntsville, in 1866, where I remained until the fall of 1867. I rented a small farm on the Trinity River in 1868 and worked that until the spring of 1870. Not being impressed with farming very much I saddled my horse and in company with a young friend left there and rode to

Wrightsboro in Gonzales county where I arrived in May, 1870, and began my career as a cowboy. Fortunately for me I met and worked for A. B. Johnson, one of the finest men I ever knew. I also got acquainted with Mr. Crawford Burnett, a better man Texas never produced, and to him I owe my success in life. In the spring of 1871 he made a contract with P. D. Armour & Co. of Chicago, to road-brand and put on the trail ten thousand big steers, four years old and up. The price of these steers was $12.00 in gold. They were to go one thousand in a herd. I made a deal with Mr. Burnett to go up the trail for fifty dollars per month, to be paid in gold. I think the ratio between gold and greenback at that time was $1.25.

On April 10th, 1871, I bade my sweetheart, Miss Sallie Wilson, the charming stepdaughter of A. B. Johnson, farewell and together with T. V. DeWoodey, Jack Harris, John and Bill Fullerton, and other boys whose names I can't recall, went over to Sandies Creek, where we met our boss, Ischam Finche. The next morning with a little pair of dun oxen we left for San Antonio, where we met Mr. Burnett. We fitted up our outfit and left for Mason county on the Llano River, where we were to receive the steers. There had already been constructed huge corrals made of big logs, so we at once began putting the famous "Flower de luce" road-brand behind the left shoulder. When we had branded about eight hundred steers the Germans began pouring the cattle in so rapidly we had to give up the pens. I think at that time we had about fifty men in camp, it being the intention to put ten men with each herd, besides the boss and cook. The first night out, Mr. Burnett selected about twenty men who had had some experience in cow driving, but none of whom were ever around a herd of big steers on a dark night. I was one of the twenty selected and I shall never forget the first night. Any old driver can tell how hard it is to hold a bunch of big steers on the range where

raised, and among timber on the banks of the Llano.
About midnight there was an old cow that kept bawling
around and trying to get in the herd. One of the boys
chased her off, and thinking he had her a half a mile
away pulled his pistol and fired it to scare her. It being
very dark he did not know he was in the edge of the
herd, and at the report of the pistol business began to
pick up. Those steers got up "some speed." A part
of them broke away and ran into our remuda and business also picked up with them. Some of the ponies are
going yet. And it is said that one of our bosses and
some of the boys were up in liveoak trees, trying to pull
their horses up too. However, we succeeded in holding
the largest part of our herd and in a day or two we had
the one thousand steers ready for the trail. Mr. Burnett
asked me to go with the first herd. First I want to mention the fact that there were no banks in that part of the
country and the gold to pay for the steers was brought
from San Antonio in a hack in a very heavy sack and was
kicked out into camp and lay there like a sack of oats,
twenty thousand dollars to the sack, until it was paid out.
Mr. Burnett informed me years later that if he ever lost
a dollar he never knew it. Any of the boys that were
with me could vouch for this statement. We crossed the
Colorado River and got on the prairie near Lampasas
where we waited a few days for the next herd. Riley
Finch was our boss. It was Mr. Burnett's plan to have
two herds travel in close proximity and when it arrived
we started north up the old Chisholm trail. The grass
was fine and we moved along without mishap until we
were crossing the Bosque River at Clifton, where a
drunken Mexican, who was cooking for another outfit,
let his oxen run into the tail end of our herd and two of
the boys engaged in a little cussing scrape. Late that
afternoon when they met the Mexican alone, his boss having turned him off, they shot him and threw his body
into a clump of prickly pear, where it was discovered by

the civil authorities a few days later. While we were
between the Bosque and Brazos it began raining and we
were delayed quite awhile and had several stampedes. In
the meantime all of the men of both herds were arrested,
and taken to Meridian by the sheriff, not all at once, however; there were enough left to take care of the herds.
When the sheriff became satisfied that the two men who
had done the killing had left he permitted us to go on.
I have never heard of those two men since. I knew them
quite well. This was the only killing that ever occurred
in our outfit.

When we arrived at the Brazos it was running bank
full. Jack Harris and myself, being expert swimmers,
plunged into the river and pointed the steers to the other
side. When we would become a little tired we would
swim up and catch a big steer by the tail and you ought
to have seen him move. We finally got both herds across
and swam the ponies, then crossed the chuck wagon on a
little ferry boat and resumed our journey. The rains had
been abundant and the grass was never better. We arrived in Fort Worth, then just a very small fort, where
we purchased supplies and moved across the Trinity
River; thence to Doan's Store on the Red River, where
we got supplies enough to cross the Indian Territory.
We then proceeded across the North Fork of the Red
River, and on to Wichita, Kansas, and crossed a number
of streams between the North Fork and the Arkansas
River, including the North and South Canadian. When
we arrived at Wichita, Kansas, there was no railroad
there, just a small village springing up in anticipation of
the Santa Fé railroad coming. We proceeded from there
to Abilene, Kansas, then north across at Solomon River
and on about seventy-five miles to the northern line of
Kansas, where P. D. Armour & Co. had erected a large
plank corral, on a beautiful creek, with large cottonwood
trees and rolling hills where no cow had ever been. A
few buffalo were still there. This was about the first of

August and we had been on the trail since April. The first night after our arrival at the corral, the boss had us to pen those steers, the first pen they had seen since they left the Llano River. The boss told us to go to the camp and informed us that we were through night herding, which was music to our ears, but while we were sitting around the camp fire that night spinning yarns, those steers stampeded and tore down about one-half of the plank corral. A few of us ran and with our coats succeeded in cutting a part of them off, and held the gap until daylight. Those steers which got out of the pen were at a loss to know where to go, and were nearby the next morning, minus a lot of broken horns. I remained there about a week and as I had an engagement in Texas I left with one companion for home. We took the Union Pacific train to St. Louis; from thence to New Orleans; across the Gulf of Mexico to Galveston; to Columbus on the Colorado River; then the Southern Pacific railway; by stage to Gonzales; on horseback to Wrightsboro, where I had bidden my sweetheart good-bye. On the 17th day of August, 1871, Miss Sallie L. Wilson and I were married.

In the spring of 1872, my wife's half-brother bought a mixed herd of cattle, and I went into the Indian Territory with them, over the same trail, and I think J. B. Wells, of Gonzales, is the only one living at present who went with us. I returned home and began to accumulate some cattle of my own, until 1876, I moved my herd to San Saba county on account of range. Later, in 1877, I moved them back to Gonzales county, and in 1879, together with John Putman, Della Shepard and Desmuke we pooled our cattle and started the herd to Albany in Shackleford county where I cut my cattle, the range not being good, and drove them west of Oak Creek, in Tom Green county. In the fall of 1880 I turned them over to my wife's half-brother, W. A. Johnson, on shares for a period of five years. In the latter part of 1880 I returned to Gonzales county and in 1881 began driving cattle again for Crawford Burnett, driving to Colorado and Wyoming and continued until the railroads took them away from us, driving in 1887, the last herd that left Gonzales county and delivering on the Platte River in Wyoming.

I have been engaged in the cattle business all of these years, having ranched in the Panhandle and Western Texas. I sold my ranch and cattle in El Paso county because the youngest of my five sons, being interested with me, had to go into the army. I sold this ranch and cattle in 1917, except the registered part of the herd, and bought an irrigated farm and small ranch in Eddy county, New Mexico, where I am now engaged in raising Hereford cattle, alfalfa hay and red apples.

On the 17th day of August my loving wife and I celebrated our golden wedding, surrounded by eight living children, one grandson, and a host of relatives and friends. On the grassy lawn there was an old-fashioned barbecue prepared by the children. We were recipients of many nice presents.

My advice to all young people is to marry early and live an active outdoor life. I am now seventy-two years old, hale and hearty, and can rope and tie down, single handed any steer in Texas or New Mexico. I am a Baptist, a Democrat, a 32nd degree honorary member of the Amarillo Lodge No. 731 and past master of same lodge. I have two sons who are 32nd degree Masons. The youngest became Scottish Rite and Shriner before reaching the age of 22 years, and one among the youngest Scottish Rite who faced the German firing line.

My wife and I would be glad to hear from any of the boys, and should any of them pass this way the latch string is always on the outside of my door.

DEDICATED TO THE MEMORY OF W. J. EDWARDS

E. M. Edwards, San Antonio, Texas

My father, William J. Edwards, was born in Choctaw county, Mississippi, May 12, 1840. His parents moved to Texas, when he was quite small, settling near Austin, where his father died. After living a widow three years, his mother married Captain Thomas W.

W. J. EDWARDS

Grayson, who owned the "Yellowstone Kit," afterwards named the "Tom Tobey," a vessel that sailed in Texas waters. My father attended school in San Antonio until he was about fourteen years old and then took up the occupation of cow-hunting.

When he was seven years old the family lived at New Braunfels, and he was an eye-witness while living there to the shooting of Prince von Solms. At Selma he saw the Indians that made the last raid in this part of Texas.

When he was engaged in the cow-hunting he worked the JMC the SIS and 2R stocks of cattle until the Civil War broke out and then enlisted in Company D, Duff's Regiment of cavalry and served throughout the war. The first engagement he was in was at Noris Bridge, Texas, where the Confederates met with defeat. Father was leading a pack-mule in the retreat, and although urged to abandon it he would not do so. He said all of his belongings were on that mule and he was determined to keep them. The Yankees threw bombs all around them but most of the Confederates escaped unhurt.

He was afterwards an express messenger between

Brownsville and Matamoras, and once, while returning from one of his trips, he had thirty shots fired at him, but they all missed their mark. Next day D. Daschiel, a brother to Tom Daschiel of the Salado, and a Mr. Littrell volunteered to take my father's place as messengers. D. Daschiel was captured and hung and his body riddled with bullets. Mr. Littrell had his tongue shot off, but escaped and made his way back to camp. He was able to write and let his company know what had happened.

In marching to Louisiana the soldiers had to swim a bayou while a freezing norther was blowing. Father contracted inflammatory rheumatism from the exposure and had to be left with a family there to be taken care of. His mother hearing of his illness immediately set out in a private conveyance, accompanied by her daughter and a neighbor to bring him home, but before she arrived there he had sufficiently recovered to take the stage for home, and missed her on the way. So much for a mother's devotion. After reaching home father was treated by Dr. Herff, Sr., who soon effected a cure, and father went back to his company.

When the war was over he resumed his work with cattle. Later he married my mother, Josephine Walters, bought a place in Bexar county on time, and suffered the privations of a pioneer's life. To my parents there were born eleven children, nine boys and two girls. Our home was virtually "the cowman's home." Frequently there would be several cowhunters taking meals at our house for a week or more.

John W. Pirie, my father's brother-in-law, and his half brother, Thomas Grayson, gathered a herd in the spring of 1873 and started for Kansas, but after crossing the Red River both Pirie and Grayson were knocked in the head while asleep one night. A man named Utz and a Polander named Tom Adams, were also beaten up at the time. Grayson died within a few hours, Pirie lived two days, without regaining consciousness, and the other

two men recovered, but Adams' face was awfully dis-
figured. As soon as father heard of the affair he went to
Kansas City to attend to the sale of the herd, and was
absent two months, during which time our neighbors
were very kind in rendering all assistance possible to my
mother. The Mexican who murdered these men in their
camp was a much trusted work hand in our neighborhood, and had gone along with the outfit. The motive
for the deed was never known. The Mexican escaped to
Mexico and was never apprehended.

In those days people felt more interested in each
other's welfare than they do now, and when there was
distress or trouble in the neighborhood, everybody was
willing to lend help and sympathy.

Father was devoted to the cow business and followed
it many years. He prided himself upon being a cowboy,
and up to the time of his death he often talked of those
good old days.

I am his fourth son and was named after his childhood playmate and cowboy friend, Eugene Millett.

LIVED IN LIVE OAK COUNTY MANY YEARS

W. M. Shannon, Lytle, Texas

My father came from Missouri to Texas in 1847, and
settled in Live Oak county. Assisted by my eldest brother,
father cut logs in the river bottoms and hauled them up
to Oakville where he built his home. He engaged in
blacksmithing and my brothers, John and Joe, worked
for the cattlemen in that region. Before the war they
worked for the two Jameses. One was called Red Tom
James and the other was Black Tom James, so called to
distinguish them. Our neighbors were three to four
miles apart. On the west side of the river lived Ray
Williams, and other neighbors were the Dobeys, Shipps,
and Bill Rix.

At that time there were Indians prowling through the country and the settlers often lost their horses. The

W. M. SHANNON

horses had to be herded in the day time and placed in strong pens at night, and then they were sometimes stolen by the redskins.

I was five years old when the Civil War commenced. For safety and protection father moved his family further East, but in 1869 we moved back to Oakville. I remember those days quite well, for we had a hard time making a living. Brother Joe, my two sisters and myself farmed with oxen. We had two heavy wagons and worked four yoke of oxen to each wagon. We also had two oxen that worked in single harness, with a short yoke and one bow in it. This yoke had a hook in each end to which the traces were fastened. Father would hook up the oxen in the morning and plow the corn and those fellows would follow furrows just like a horse. We lived on milk and butter, and wild game which was plentiful. Prairie chickens, wild turkeys and deer could easily be obtained, but breadstuff was scarce. Sometimes we had biscuits on Sunday morning. For coffee we often used parched okra or parched corn. Our clothing was made by hand. My mother and sisters spun and wove the cloth for our clothing. Father made a spinning wheel and loom when I was a small boy. I climbed to the top of the loom while mother was out of the room and fell off and broke my hip. So I guess I will never forget that old loom.

My father made my first pair of shoes. My grandfather, Joe Bartlett, taught me how to ride and how to handle a gun, when I was quite small. He was a good shot and did a great deal of hunting. He gave me one of the old-time cap and ball five-shooter pistols and often took me with him when he went out hunting. I became quite expert in using that old pistol and could shoot a hog's eye out with ease. In those days there were lots of wild hogs in the woods as well as deer, panther, lobo wolves, and javelina hogs.

After we moved back to Oakville, Father bought a piece of land east of Oakville on the Beeville road, and when we moved there Grandfather Bartlett lived with us a great deal as he had no family of his own. He owned a good house in Oakville, but would come out to our place in winter time, and he and I would kill wild hogs. That is the way we secured our winter meat and lard. We would hook up a pair of ponies and go off down the creek to a water hole with a pot in which to scald the hogs. We would take along a wallet of bread, coffee pot, skillet and lid, a small sack of corn meal, his old cap and ball rifle, a roll of bedding, my five-shooter pistol, our saddles and three good dogs. When the dogs would find the hogs we would ride up and shoot them down, and grandfather would fasten a rope around the hog's tusks and we would drag it to camp.

My father built large pens for the cattlemen to pen their herds, and as a result there was lots of camping done at our place. Sometimes the stockmen camped there for as long as two weeks, and in consequence there was plenty of rawhide left laying around the place. A Mexican who worked for us, used his idle time in making quirts, whips, hobbles, and lariats from this rawhide. He taught me how to do this kind of work, and I became somewhat of an expert too, because of which I was often called "Rawhide Bill."

My first trip up the trail was in 1878 with Bob Martin from Refugio county with 1,100 two-year olds and upwards. Our chuck wagon was drawn by two yoke of steers, and Adam Johnson, a negro, was our cook. We started our herd about the 15th of March, crossed the Colorado below Austin, went by Round Rock and George-town. On the North Gabriel we had a heavy rain and hail and our cattle stampeded, drifted back and mixed up with one of the Kokernot herds. Next morning I was five miles from camp with a hundred steers. It took us two days to separate the cattle and get started on our way. We went by Waco, Cleburne and Fort Worth and crossed the Trinity River. We crossed the Red River at Red River Station and took the Chisholm trail through the Indian Territory. We got by the Indians without any trouble. At Pond Creek we saw our first buffalo, and it seemed as if the plains were literally covered with them. I joined in the sport and killed my first buffalo by shooting him behind the shoulder.

I had my share of swimming swollen streams, passing through thunder storms and being mixed up in stampedes but did not get into an Indian fight.

We crossed Bluff Creek into Kansas and passed New-ton about the last of May. There was a blacksmith shop, a store and a few dwellings there at that time, but the railroad soon came and Newton quickly grew to be a large town. We crossed Holland Creek and went to Abilene and there the cattle were sold, and we all hit the back trail for Texas with our saddle horses and chuck wagon. Joe Shannon, Tom Williams, John Harrison, Buck Wright and myself were in the crowd. On my way back I met my old friend, D. S. Combs.

(EDITOR'S NOTE. Since the above sketch was written Mr. Shannon has departed this life and gone to that bourne from which no traveler returns. He died November 2, 1921. Peace to his soul.)

WILLIAM JAMES SLAUGHTER

William James Slaughter, a very remarkable man, without whose enviable record the history of Southwest

Texas and the story of the cattle and sheep industries and the trail would be incomplete, was born on the outskirts of civilization in the state of Mississippi, November 9, 1835; died near Friotown, Frio county, Texas, August 31, 1906.

His parents, in the fullest sense, always frontier people, fearless at all times, were Benjamin and Minerva Slaughter.

In January, 1836, the father, attracted by the wonderful and exciting news of Texas, with an intrepid band of

followers, set out to join the forces in the field, maneuvering for the Independence of Texas, but on account of one obstacle and another having arisen, made slow progress, and only reached within one hundred miles of the glorious battlefield of San Jacinto, when they learned of the complete rout of the Mexican army under Santa Anna, and thus he was denied the cherished hope of participation in the conflict made historic by heroes for all time.

WILLIAM J. SLAUGHTER

He served the Republic for ninety days as a ranger, and when his enlistment had expired, with a few survivors of his original command, he hastened back to his home in Mississippi, soon to return to Texas, for as he expressed in his determination, "Uncle Ben has got a taste of Texas and he can't get rid of it." Four years from the date of his first taste, he and family, already inured to hardships and privations, knowing that worse were probably in store for them, dared the future and soon found themselves identified with Texas, settling in the part known as East Texas where the subject of this sketch acquired amid varying vicissitudes under adverse conditions a liberal education, which he measurably expanded by contact with stern realities in life, that equipped him for achievements and success that came to him in his after public and private career.

In 1855 Mr. Slaughter came to Southwest Texas, locating a ranch in Atascosa county on La Parita Creek, near Pleasanton. On July 25, 1858, Mr. Slaughter and Caroline M. Vickers were most happily married at Georgetown. This good woman, ever undaunted and courageous at all times in the upbuilding of home, survives, esteemed and loved most endearingly by five living daughters, grandchildren, relatives and a host of friends uncircumscribed in numbers; all these rejoice to enjoy the privilege of calling her Grandma Slaughter.

Mr. Slaughter served most valiantly in the Civil War, and his excellent and soldierly conduct was attested specially by Capt. John W. Stayton, who was in 1888 made Chief Justice of the Supreme Court of Texas, of which Mr. Slaughter was justly proud that he held commendation from such a pure and noble man, ever conscious that as a Confederate soldier without regret he had made great sacrifice. Mr. Slaughter held tenaciously to the principles for which he fought, to the day of his death.

Sore and tired of war, he sought a new field hopeful of peacefully bettering his conditions when in 1865, with his family he located in the unorganized county of La Salle. For eight years for them it was worse than war. During the entire time the worst type of outlaws and hostile Indians murdered and plundered to such an extent as to render life and property insecure, and especially was life endangered. It is not known that any part of Texas during this time suffered from marauders like La Salle and surrounding counties. Here they pillaged boldly and without let. The situation was deplorable, to cope with which required men of iron nerve and doughty spirit to the limit—elements of Mr. Slaughter ingrown and in him firmly fixed for the worse, which enabled him to endure the distresses, finally to become victorious over all disadvantages in achievement of success, arduously won.

In 1873 he moved to Frio county, locating near the then prosperous and busy little Friotown, where he died as noted, surrounded by as fine a family as is contained in the Southwest, and as many friends as were the individuals that knew him. Things for several years were like those of the adjoining county, from which Mr. Slaughter had come; the Indian raids continued unabated, more frequent and worse than formerly, discouraging to many indeed. Mr. Slaughter always was wont to say, "When troubles multiply sooner or later they get their worst—then they mend." Things did mend, times got better, and in Frio county the greatest agent and factor in the accomplishment of such result was Mr. Slaughter, and it was spared to him to live three score years and ten, man's allotment, to witness his fond hopes of good government reign supreme, with plenty and prosperity abounding, and happy homes building where once existed chaos, confusion and desolation.

From poverty to wealth of immense proportion Mr. Slaughter by indomitable exertion, helpfully stimulated by the encouragement of his faithful companion, his venerable relict, provided well, and the extended possession originally known as the Slaughter Ranch was one of the largest in West Texas.

He was a qualified man of business, had a thorough insight of cattle, horse and sheep raising, and no detail of importance escaped his attention. As a cattleman, driver of herds to Kansas and other markets, sheepman, and promoter of other enterprising matters, he was safe, conservative and eminent—signally successful.

The heart, the head, and the hand of this man throughout his busy life joined in right doing, and his efforts were not confined to his advancement solely, but he labored for others as well. He was the purest type of citizenship, a just, honest and upright man; he belonged to the class that worked for the happiness of the people among whom he lived; and if the almost unremembered kindnesses bestowed upon the rich and poor alike were recounted, they would fill a large book. His money and his name saved many from insolvency; his word was his bond, never violated. It recurs to the writer in this connection that Mr. Slaughter, with others, was once on a contractor's bond, and default of compliance was made and payment of damages demanded on the obligation, when it was suggested that payment could be averted. This suggestion Mr. Slaughter resented, and to his honor be it said that he paid without murmur the full liability of all, running into thousands of dollars.

JAMES ALFRED McFADDIN

James Alfred McFaddin of Victoria, Texas, was as closely identified with Texas and its development as any man in the state. His grandparents, James McFaddin and wife, came to Texas from Tennessee in 1817, stayed about a year, moved to Louisiana and returned to Texas in 1821, when J. A. McFaddin's father, William McFaddin, was about two years of age. They settled in Liberty county and after a few years moved to Jefferson county. His grandfather and father were soldiers in the Texas army in the War of Independence between Texas and Mexico.

William McFaddin was married to Miss Rachel Williams, and the subject of this sketch was their oldest child, born May 5, 1840, at Beaumont, Texas. He received his schooling at Beaumont, finishing his education at a private school in Galveston, Texas.

When J. A. McFaddin was fifteen years of age he was doing a man's work. In 1855 he helped drive a herd of cattle from Jefferson county to Refugio county, about 400 head owned by his father and Mr. Herbert. In 1858 they brought out a second herd of 600 head, and J. A. McFaddin was placed in charge of these cattle. At that time he owned about fifty head of cattle and twenty-five head of horses, and from this start he increased his property to his present splendid possessions.

In 1861 he married Miss Margaret V. Coward, daugh-

J. A. McFADDIN

ter of Richard Coward and Harriet Coward, in Galveston county. From the old Coward homestead on Clear Creek the young couple took their wedding journey on horseback, going to Louisiana, and returning from there to Beaumont. From there they rode to the home built by J. A. McFaddin on Melone Creek, about three miles from Refugio, bringing their household goods in a wagon.

In 1863 he joined the army of the Confederacy as first lieutenant in Capt. Dan Doughty's company. From that time to the close of the war he was with this company in active service. Their operations extended from Refugio to the Rio Grande, and from Corpus Christi north to the frontier. His story of the privations these men endured equals in fortitude, courage and endurance that of any band of men who ever fought for a just cause. Large portions of the territory they covered were deserts. Frequently they lived for days with nothing to eat excepting meat and coffee, sometimes not coffee, sometimes neither. They never went into winter quarters, and in fact did not have quarters at all. They fought the Federals, the Mexicans and the bandits. They were peace officers, rangers and soldiers, and J. A. McFaddin did his part.

His oldest child, A. M. McFaddin, one of the ex-presidents of the Texas Cattle Raisers' Association, and member of the Texas Live Stock Sanitary Commission, was born during his father's absence in the army. Notwithstanding J. A. McFaddin's anxious desire to be with his wife and child, and to look after his worldly goods, he stayed with his command until Lee and Grant met at Appomattox, and the news came down to Texas that the cause for which he was fighting was a lost cause. It was not until then that J. A. McFaddin turned his horse's head toward the Coward home in Galveston county, where his wife and son were. He brought them to his home on the Melone, and again took up his life's work.

He was by that time regarded as one of the foremost citizens of his section of the state, and not only attended to his own business affairs but managed the properties of many others. Even in those days the business of others handled by him brought in thousands and thousands of dollars. During the years from 1867 to 1874 he had many thousands of dollars in his charge. He filled every safe in the town of Refugio with silver, had several boxes full of it in Mr. McCampbell's store, had his own safe so full that not another fifty-cent piece could be put in it, and had two nail kegs full of silver in his room. Frequently during this time he was away from home, and often his wife was alone at home with the servants. This was a condition of the times. But the people of that section had such a love for J. A. McFaddin and his good wife that not even the Mexicans or negroes ever attempted to steal as much as fifty cents of this money. His possessions and the possessions of others in his charge were regarded as sacred, for the people loved the McFaddins.

In the years from 1873 to 1878, times changed and the cattle rustler made his appearance. It was then again that J. A. McFaddin came to the front. The mandate went forth that stock stealing must stop, and it stopped in that section. Of a kindly disposition, easily approached, and never heedless of the cry of distress, nevertheless Mr. McFaddin was stern and uncompromising when it came to a matter of right and wrong. The wrongdoers knew that if they depredated on the property of McFaddin or McFaddin's people, that a grim and relentless pursuer would be on their trail, and they, too, grew to respect this just and courageous man.

In 1876 he sold out in Refugio county, and took his family to the southern part of Victoria county, where he had purchased large bodies of land, and all of which he owned up to his death. This land is now located at the station of Marianna. For three years they lived on this ranch. It became necessary that he should be in position to observe the financial affairs of this section of the state, and get more in touch with its stockmen. They moved to Victoria, buying Col. Rogers' old home, where Mr. McFaddin still lives.

J. A. McFaddin's father was a stockman, and he was brought up a stockman. He had followed the stock raising business his entire life. He kept abreast of the times, however, and even ahead of them. Thirty years ago he commenced his work of solving a most serious problem of the Texas cattle raiser, the tick on cattle. He observed that the Brahma breed did not have ticks on them; that they were more prolific, hardy and matured better than the other breeds of cattle. He bought a herd of Brahma cattle. There were not many of these in proportion to the cattle owned by him, but it was a start. At the World's Fair in St. Louis he saw in Hagenbeck's menagerie a magnificent Brahma bull and cow. This was his opportunity. He made a number of visits to the menagerie. The manager was attracted by the genial disposition of Mr. McFaddin, and they became fast friends. Very soon they agreed that Mr. McFaddin ought to have these Brahma cattle, and the tick problem was finally solved. The Hagenbeck bull, "Prince," became the head of his herd. Today the thousands of cattle owned by J. A. McFaddin are graded Brahmin cattle, immune from ticks, and he has several hundred head of practically purebred Brahma cattle, the offspring of "Prince" and two other bulls imported from India by the estate of H. A. Pierce and Thomas O'Connor. He had at the time of his death a breed of cattle second to none for the combination of the qualities of prolific breeding, early maturing, beef producing, hardiness and immunity from ticks.

About fifteen years ago this far-sighted man saw that the old range cattle business would in time cease to be profitable, and he prepared himself accordingly. He had seen land in this section of the state go from ten cents an acre to seventy-five dollars an acre. Cattle raising on high priced land does not pay. The time was coming for a change from the old range style of cattle raising to the stock farming proposition. He had always done some farming. He had several thousand acres of land that had been swamp, and which had been thrown in with his purchase at from $1.00 to $1.50 per acre. It was not suitable for grazing. He reclaimed this land by leveeing it and cleared it, all at a large expense. It is now fully protected from overflow, and is a magnificent field. On this land, in 1912, his corn crop averaged seventy bushels per acre, his cotton about three-fourths of a bale to the acre—most of the tracts growing a bale to the acre; some more. He constructed a levee along the Guadalupe River and across to the high lands, over twelve miles in length. This has reclaimed more than five thousand acres of overflow land. He estimated that the cost of building the levee, clearing and putting the land in shape for cultivation, building tenant houses, barns and other improvements would be about $100,000. But there has been over five thousand acres reclaimed of alluvial soil as a farming proposition. The cattle raiser is fast becoming a stock farmer.

This ranch, which is being converted into a vast farm, aggregates about forty-two thousand acres. In addition he had about twelve thousand acres of land eight miles north of the city of Victoria. Besides these, he had other lands which made him a comfortable living.

Mr. McFaddin did not ask aid from the county or the state. He built his own levees and roads, digging ditches, and building school houses. He did not ask for issuance of road bonds, drainage bonds, school bonds nor levee bonds. In other words, no other man's lands were taxed to put improvements on the McFaddin lands.

In his home life, Mr. McFaddin was as successful as in his business career. For nearly fifty years, he and his wife lived happily and contentedly together. Mrs. McFaddin assisted him greatly in achieving success. One of the most charitable women ever in that section of the state, she was loved by all who knew her. No strangers passed by their ranch house without being invited to partake of their hospitality.

Mr. McFaddin has indelibly impressed upon that section of the state his mark as a genius in executive and business ability. Mrs. McFaddin died in June, 1911, but she left the impress of her character upon the social life of the community, and she will be remembered with love and affection for generations. These two sturdy Texas pioneers have helped the people of this state to change from a wilderness to a great commonwealth, and they will go down in the history of this state as promoters of law and order, of peace and happiness. On June 25, 1916, Colonel McFaddin died very suddenly at his home in Victoria, aged seventy-six years.

AN OLD COW HAND

By John Pat Ryan, Skidmore, Texas

I was born near Sweet Home, in Lavaca county, Texas, October 10, 1850. I came to what is now Bee county in 1856 with my parents, Henry and Regena Ryan. My mother died in 1862, and father died in 1902. Working horses and cattle has been my occupation the most of my life. I farmed about twelve years.

My first trip to Kansas was in 1871, with H. T. Clare as boss. He drove beef steers for Jim Reed and Tom O'Connor. I remember well our first night in Indian Territory, for we did not sleep much. Five herds crossed Red River that day, in charge of H. T. Clare, D. Rachal, Buck Gravis, John Henry Choate, John Booth and Rutledge and Bill Gentry. I think every herd stampeded. I know when our herd was stopped several miles from the starting point. I was the only man that stayed with them and when the sun came up it rose in the west for two mornings before it rose in the east with me. Fortunately I never got turned around any more. Bud May of Yoakum, John Holland, John Stewart, Monroe Stewart, Bud Clare and myself brought the horses and wagon back to Texas. That fall and winter I drove cattle to the Rockport packery, and later worked in a cow outfit for Pat Burke. Made two trips to Colorado with horses for myself.

In 1873 H. T. Clare, Tom Marsden, Gus and Hillary
Clare and myself drove horses and mules to Red River,
Lamar county, and there we held them in camp for seven
weeks on account of yellow fever. We made no sales.

In 1875 I worked in a cow crowd with Hugh O'Riley,

JOHN PAT RYAN

Jack Hughs, and John M. Corrigan. In 1876 and 1877
J. I. Clare and myself ran a cow outfit. In 1878 I took
charge of a herd for J. I. Clare, J. E. Little and P. S.
Clare and went to Fort Worth. There I sold some fine
springer cows for them. I got hurt in a stampede and
had to quit and come home. Bill Raglan came up with a
herd for Jim Scott and they put both herds together and

he and Hillary Clare took them on to Dodge City,
Kansas.

In 1879 I took a herd to Northwest Texas, and in 1880
I drove a herd for D. C. Jordan of Montague county to
Indian Territory. Buck Pettus, Jim Reed and Jim Ray
put up the cattle on the range.

I am still running and working cattle and never feel
tired or wearied.

WILLIAM C. IRVIN

The following sketch was taken from the "History of
Southwest Texas," published in 1907: William C. Irvin
was born at Seguin, Texas, in 1846, a son of J. A. and
Sarah (Tom) Irvin. The father was a native of Alabama
and located in Texas in 1838.
His death occurred in 1865.
The mother represented an
old family of Tennessee, some
of its members having be-
come distinguished in the
early history of Texas, particularly in Indian fighting.
Her brother, Captain J. F.
Tom, was numbered among
the early pioneers of this
state and had command of a
company of rangers during
the Civil War and took active

W. C. IRVIN

part in subduing the redman both prior and subsequent
to the war.

William C. Irvin has two sisters, Mrs. Ann Elizabeth
Dewees and Miss Tommie Irvin, who make their home
in San Antonio. Mr. Irvin was reared in Guadalupe
county. He was quite young at the time of his father's
death, and later lost his elder brother so that the responsibility of caring for his mother and sisters was thrown

upon him at a very early age. He took his place at herding cattle when quite young and has been engaged in the stock business throughout his entire life. He made trips over the old Chisholm trail soon after it was first opened, and became thoroughly familiar with all the cattle country from the Rio Grande to the Canadian border, and has passed through all the hardships of the cattleman's life of the early days although owing to his conservative business qualities and careful management he has escaped the difficulties which usually confronted the stockman's career. He made altogether seven trips over the trail to the north, and on his return trip in 1875, he located a ranch at Seymour, in Baylor county, where he placed 7,000 head of cattle during the winter. He remained in that district about five years, and then returned to the southwestern part of the state, establishing what is known as the Irvin ranch in La Salle county, this ranch embracing 60,000 acres of land, lying east of Cotulla and almost bordering the limits of the town, although the house stands twenty miles from that place. During the last few years there has been a great influx of settlers to this region so that the land has become very valuable and perhaps in due time the ranch will be divided into farms for it is becoming too valuable to retain as pasture land. Mr. Irvin has sold 10,000 acres for cultivation.

Mr. Irvin has become one of the wealthiest stockmen of this state. He has spent a busy, active and useful life and through his careful business management and sound judgment and has now acquired a competence that enables him to leave the more arduous duties of a business career to others, while he spends a portion of his time in his home in San Antonio, while his ranch is managed by his two sons.

Mr. Irvin was married in Seguin to Miss Medina Dewees, a representative of a prominent pioneer family of this state. Their family numbers two sons and four daughters: Jourdan J. and Eugene, who conduct the ranch; Mrs. Mabel Wilson; Grace; Mrs. S. T. Lowry, and Clara Irvin.

LEE L. RUSSELL

The subject of this sketch is one of the successful cattlemen, commission merchants, and bankers of Texas. He was born in Dawson, Ga., December 6, 1867, and came to Texas with his parents when he was four years old, settling at Menardville. Mr. Russell started in the cattle business when he was fifteen years old, his first venture being in connection with the driving of a herd into New Mexico. Later he became an employee of the Nathan Hall Cattle Company o f N e w Mexico, at a salary of $35.00

LEE L. RUSSELL

per month, which was shortly afterward increased to $65.00 per month upon his promotion to the foremanship of the Western Ranch. He remained in that position one year, when a second promotion installed him as beef manager, his duties including a safe delivery of the company's cattle in Oklahoma, Colorado and Montana. In 1889 he became affiliated with the Russell-Bevans Co. as their beef manager, in which position he had the opportunity and right to operate on his own account, and in three years his personal business had grown to such proportions that he then started in business for himself. He later admitted his brother, W. W. Russell, and T. P. Kyger into business as his partners, and the firm continued until 1910, when he purchased the interest of

his brother for $125,000 and continued with Mr. Kyger.
Mr. Russell has many other interest, among them being

BUFFALO IN THE PIEGAN COUNTRY
Courtesy ''Book of Cowboys.''

the Stock Yards Loan Co. of Kansas City of which he
is vice-president, the Cassidy-Southwestern Commission
Co. of which he is vice-president, director and assistant

BUFFALO IN THE PIEGAN COUNTRY
Courtesy ''Book of Cowboys.''

general manager. He is also vice-president of the Fort Worth State Bank, president, Bank of Hardy, Okla., and vice-president of the Citizens National Bank of Pawhuska, Okla. He is a stockholder in the Farmers & Merchants Bank of Ballinger, Texas; a stockholder in the Co-operative Realty Co. of Fort Worth. He is interested in several large cattle companies, and controls large ranch holdings in Texas and Oklahoma, as well as being interested in mining properties. He is vice-president of the Metropolitan Hotel Co., and other investments.

On October 14, 1895, Mr. Russell was married to Miss Mary Callan, a member of a prominent Texas family. He is a member of several fraternal organizations, among them the Shriners, Elks, Woodmen of the World, Eagles and Odd Fellows.

THOMAS B. SAUNDERS

Thomas B. Saunders, senior member of the firm of T. B. Saunders & Co., noted live stock brokers of Fort Worth, Texas, was born in Goliad county, Texas, September 23, 1872. He is the son of W. D. H. and Ann (New) Saunders. Mr. Saunders attended school in this locality until he was seventeen years old, when, in common with other youths of that era, he assumed the sterner activities that called for attention. In 1889 he began working in the cattle business in which he acquired considerable valuable knowledge that equipped him for his chosen line of business. For a time he worked for his father, then his uncle, George W. Saunders, employed him in the commission business in San Antonio for three years. In 1893 he went to Houston where he worked in the commission business for several months, and when he attained the age of 21 years he determined to engage in business on his own account, and under the name of Saunders & Hotchkiss the firm that he established became a potent factor in the commission live stock trade for seven years of its existence.

THOS. B. SAUNDERS

When the packing houses located plants in Fort Worth in 1900, Mr. Saunders immediately perceived the field for wider operations that he had constantly sought, and he moved to Fort Worth where he remains today. He was the first trader to do business on that market, and soon became a familiar figure until now he is acknowledged one of the heaviest buyers and strongest traders frequenting that market. His business has prospered steadily and his transactions on the market alone aggregate an average of 100,000 head of cattle handled annually. Mr. Saunders is also an extensive operator in ranches. He, together with C. L. Brown and Lee Russell, control large ranch interests near Avant, Okla., where they pasture more than 7,000 cattle. He also has ranch interests in Texas. Mr. Saunders married Miss Hattie Straw in San Antonio in 1899. They have two children, Thomas B. Jr., and Miss Venita Saunders. No man enjoys higher esteem among his contemporaries, or is more universally respected.

ATE TERRAPIN AND DOG MEAT, AND WAS GLAD TO GET IT

Ben Drake, South San Antonio, Texas

On the 3rd day of January, 1855, I first saw the light of day, on Wilbarger Creek, twenty miles below Austin, in Travis county, Texas. Lived there until I was twelve years old, then mother sold the place and moved to Bastrop, where she and my stepfather taught school. When I was sixteen years old one of the Murchison boys asked me to go up the trail with him. Of course I was willing but my mother objected, and it took a great deal of persuading on the part of Pete Murchison and myself to get her to consent for me to go. She gave in to our entreaties, however, and I accompanied Pete to a shoe shop where he ordered a pair of boots made for me. Those boots cost $14.00. He also gave me a pair of bell spurs, a Colt's cap and ball six-shooter, and a rim-fire Winchester, as well as a pair of leather leggins which cost

A TEXAS LONGHORN

$12.00. This was the first time in my life that I had been rigged out, and you bet I was proud. He sold me two horses and agreed to pay me a good salary. We started with the herd about the middle of March, 1871, with 2,500 head of stock cattle. Among the boys in our bunch were Glabe Young, Pinkey Stull, Peter Sneed, Johnnie White and several others whose names I cannot recall.

We crossed the Colorado about a mile below Austin, and drove out below Manor and camped on Cottonwood Creek that night. As I was only two miles from where my grandmother lived, Pete and I went there to stay all night. Leaving there early the next morning we went back to the herd and were soon on the trail again. When we reached Brushy Creek it was up and we camped on this side crossing over the next day. This was the first stream I ever helped to swim a herd across. The next creek we crossed was called Boggy, and it lived up to its name, for it would bog a snake. Before we reached Alligator Creek we had a heavy rain and hail storm. When we got to the Gabriel it was bank full but we swam it, and on the other side we counted our cattle and found thirty short.

The first lot of Indians I saw was when we reached the Territory, and then I wished I was home with my mother. We reached our destination, Kansas City all right, where Pete sold out, and we came back home together, coming back by Austin where we were paid off. When I reached home I gave all of my wages to my mother, stayed there three days and went back to the ranch to work for Murchison.

In 1872 I again went up the trail but before going I bought my second pair of boots from the same man who made my first pair. On this drive we followed the same route we had taken the year before. It rained and stormed almost all of the way, and we had to swim all of the streams we crossed. This was a sad trip for us. While we were in the territory, near where Oklahoma City now stands, our herd stampeded and mixed with another herd there and we had a hard time getting them separated. Several of the men in the other outfit had some trouble and a regular battle took place, in which nine men were killed. None of our hands were mixed up in it. I understand the row started between two boys over a stake pin. We buried the dead men as best we could right there on the prairie.

Pete sold out in Dodge City, Kansas, horses and all, but I kept my horses and came back with a man who was bringing a bunch of horses.

In 1874 I went with one of Snyder's herds, and also in

1875 and 1876 Snyder sent herds to Wyoming. While
there I was in a party that went to join Custer, but when
we reached Fort Reno he was gone. But we had several
fights with Indians anyhow. Then I went to Kansas
City, sold my horse and came back to good old Texas.

In 1877 I again hit the trail, this time with a herd of
the Blocker cattle which we drove through to Wyoming.
Went again in 1878.

I started in 1879, but got done up just about the time
we reached the Territory. I was carried to an Indian
camp and there I had to remain three months. While
there I ate dry land terrapin and dog meat cooked together and was glad to get it. Finally the old chief went
to Texarkana and got some one to come after me. A
United States marshal brought me to Austin in a buggy.

GIVES SOME EARLY TEXAS HISTORY

W. F. Cude, Pearsall, Texas

I was born on the banks of the San Jacinto River, in
Montgomery county, Texas, April 4, 1844, while Texas
was still a Republic with a president and cabinet of
officers. In 1845 we were annexed to the United States
which gladdened the hearts of the few people in Texas at
that time. I will relate a few things which I heard from
the lips of some of General Sam Houston's soldiers about
the battle of San Jacinto. My mother had three brothers
who were in that battle, Billie Winters, John Winters
and J. W. Winters. "Uncle Jim" as we called him, died
in Frio county some twenty years ago. He often told
me about that fight, and said it did not last longer than
thirty minutes. They killed six hundred Mexicans and
captured about six hundred, among the prisoners being
General Santa Anna. Three Americans were killed and
four wounded; General Houston and Billie Winters were
among those who received wounds. My mother was

camped within hearing distance of the battle. The first news she had from the battlefield was to the effect that Gen. Houston's forces were all killed, but in a little while word came that the Mexican army had been defeated and utterly routed. My stepfather, Charles A. Edwards, was a cavalry officer under Captain Lamar, but was on scout duty with Lieutenant Karnes when the battle occurred.

W. F. CUDE

During the early days in Texas there were no farming implements. Horse collars were made from shucks, plow lines from rawhide, wagon wheels were sawed from a sweet-gum log, which served to good advantage. In the winter of 1849 we sold our home, bought two large wagons at Huntsville, and moved to Lavaca Creek, twelve miles from Halletsville, the county seat. In 1861 I joined a Texas Ranger Company. John Donaldson was my captain under Col. J. S. Ford at Brownsville. When we arrived at Brownsville we camped in the fort there. There were twenty recruits in our bunch; my brother, A. J. Cude, recruited for the company. There I heard my first bugle call, and when I asked brother Jack what it was he told me it was the rations call. He went to get the rations and returned with some sacks of grub. He informed me that some soap was in one of the sacks, and as I wanted to wash out some of my clothes I took out what I supposed to be a cake of soap, went down to the river and used it. When I got back I complained to him that the soap was no good. When he looked at it he gave a hearty laugh and informed me that I had not used soap. The stuff was peloncia (Mexican sugar).

We remained on the border about a year, guarding
the Rio Grande from its mouth to Rio Grande City.
In June, 1862, we left the border service and went to San
Antonio and joined the Second Texas Cavalry under Col.
Charley Pryon.   James Walker was lieutenant colonel.
He was placed in Sibley's Brigade and Bankhead Magruder was our general.   In October we were ordered to
the coast near the mouth of the Brazos, where it was
said Union forces were landing.   Later we were ordered

A STRIKER ON THE TRAIL

to Houston, and about the middle of December the Yankees captured Galveston.   A call was made for volunteers to go on the steamboats to go to Galveston.   As
most of the volunteers were cavalrymen and as they had
to fight on water they took the name of horse marines.
General Magruder recaptured Galveston after a fight
lasting less than an hour.   This battle was fought on the
first day of January, 1863.   We captured one warship
and two transports, sunk one warship and captured about

five hundred prisoners. We had two steamboats with about two hundred men on each boat. One of our boats was sunk, but it was in shallow water and no one was drowned. Captain Pryon remained on the Island until June and was sent to Lousiana. General Tom Green was now our commander and our brigade soon joined the Confederate army under General Taylor. General Banks' Union army was on its way to Texas, 35,000 strong. Our army numbered about 17,000 men, and was composed of Arkansas, Texas and Louisiana troops.

INDIANS ON THE MOVE

The two armies met about the 15th of June and fought a three days' battle in which Banks was defeated. We captured several thousand prisoners and many wagon loads of supplies.

After this I was in a number of desperate engagements and was captured and taken to City Point, Virginia. Later we were taken to Jackson, Miss., on parole. After we reached Jackson, Miss., four of us left there one night and walked from there to Beaumont, Texas, in sixteen days. My shoes had worn out and when I got to Houston I went to a store and bought a new pair and told the clerk to charge them to Jeff Davis.

My experience was hard on me and I endured many hardships and privations, sleeping on the bare ground nearly three months after I was captured. In 1864 our regiment was stationed on Galveston Island and remained there until the end of the war, and we had an easy time there. Our duty was to ride the beach five miles and back every two hours and watch on a signal station day and night. The enemy's warships would come around and shell us occasionally, but never any of us got covered up with sand except one time when one of the big shells weighing 164 pounds hit near us.

In the summer of 1864 yellow fever broke out in Galveston and fourteen members of our company were stricken. Captain C. D. McRae and James Cowley died. Our company was camped on the west end of the Island during the last year of the war.

In the fall of 1865 I went to school at Moulton, Lavaca county, and in 1866 I went to Live Oak county where I secured a wagon and ox team and hauled freight from Indianola to San Antonio. That fall I hired to a man named H. Williams who lived on Lagorta Creek, thirty miles from Oakville. Only a very few settlements were there at that time. One family named Weaver lived about a mile from the Williams place, and there were two grown girls in the Weaver family. These girls would assist their father in hunting cattle, and carried their pistols with them wherever they went. They had a pack of hounds and hunted with them. One day they found where a panther had killed a colt belonging to their father, ten miles from their home, so they came to the Williams ranch and got two of Mr. Williams' daughters to go with them to hunt the panther. About one o'clock in the morning two of the girls came back to get help to kill the panther as they had found it. Mr. Williams sent me to help them, giving me an old Enfield rifle to use. We reached the place where the other two girls were about daylight, and found they had the panther treed.

I dismounted and took a shot at him, the ball passing through his foot, and causing him to jump out and make for me. I could not run, for those four girls were all looking at me, and expecting me to do something. Luckily one of the dogs laid hold of the panther about that time and things got interesting. The other dogs took a hand in the fight and the panther whipped them all, fearfully mangling some of them. I rushed in and killed

DANCING IN THE COW CAMP
Copyrighted by Frank Reeves, Stamford, Texas.

it by beating it over the head with my gun. I have been a friend to dogs ever since.

In 1867 I made a crop in Gonzales county, and in the fall of the year I drove my first cattle, going to Houston for a man named Tumlinson with about fifty head. I made ten bales of cotton that year and collected $15 per bale for war taxes.

I made my first trip up the trail to Kansas in 1868, and other trips followed, accounts of which are given in Volume I of this book.

On January 2, 1872, I married Miss Mary Harrell. Her hair was black then, but it is not now, for time has changed it to a silvery grey. I often think of the many changes that have occurred during the last forty-nine years. My wife's father was Milvern Harrell and he deserves worthy mention in the history of the Old Trail Drivers of Texas. He went to Kansas several times with cattle. During the Civil War he drove cattle to Louisiana for the Confederate army. Previous to the Civil War in 1846, he joined a company under Dawson, about fifty men in all and when they reached the Salado near San Antonio they were surrounded by a large force of Mexican cavalry and captured, only three Americans making their escape. Mr. Harrell was wounded with sabre cuts and was taken to Mexico City and imprisoned for twelve months. He told me the Mexicans were very kind to him while he was in the hospital there. When he was released he went to Vera Cruz and sailed to New Orleans. Students of Texas History are familiar with the account of the massacre of Dawson's men.

DROVE HORSES TO MISSISSIPPI

F. G. Crawford, Oakville, Texas

I was born May 1, 1843, in the town of Gonzales, in the Republic of Texas. My mother died when I was an infant, and I was one of those who had to suck a bottle. My father bought a small tract of land near the Guadalupe River, two miles north of New Braunfels, and we moved there when I was four years old. Among other things we raised a great many watermelons on this place which were taken to San Antonio and sold to soldiers stationed there. Father owned a trusty negro slave who would take the melons there, and I often went with him in a wagon drawn by oxen. We would usually be away from home two nights, and of course I had to sleep on a pallet on the ground with the old negro man, but I was always glad to make the trip and see the sights in San Antonio, which at that early date was considered a large town. If the government buildings would have been removed it would only have been a small town after all. That was seventy-one years ago. Many changes have been wrought since then.

When I was seven years old father bought and settled on a larger tract of land seven miles north of New Braunfels, on what was called the Springtown Road, leading to San Marcos. I grew up here, and when the Civil War came on I enlisted in the Confederate army. I have papers to show that I served four years in the Confederate ranks. I also have my amnesty certificate, which restored my citizenship.

In May, 1868, Joe Burleson and myself formed a partnership and bought 250 head of horses, suitable to work on farms and drove them to Water Valley, Mississippi. As there were but few boats and bridges we had to swim many streams on account of high water. One time while we were camped in Arkansas a hurricane passed near us. The thunder and lightning was terrifying and we had to keep riding around our horses to prevent them from stampeding and running off.

Soon after I returned from this trip to Mississippi, Capt. E. B. Millett came to me and asked me to take charge of 1,000 beeves and drive them to California, and he would take another 1,000 to Dakota. But I had not fully recovered from a serious illness and had to decline his offer.

There are four counties, that corner with each other near York's Creek, about four miles from my father's old home, Comal, Guadalupe, Caldwell and Hays, and in my boyhood days I hunted cattle in all of those counties. Often we had some rough times, being exposed to hot and dry weather in the summer and cold and wet in the winter. There were no pastures then—strictly a free range country.

Joe Burleson, mentioned above, was a son of General Edward Burleson, who was with General Sam Houston at the battle of San Jacinto.

WHEN JIM DOBIE LOST HIS PANTS

E. S. Boatright, Falfurrias, Texas

I was born in Pike county, Alabama, August 2, 1855, and came to Texas in 1876, landing at Houston, but there I decided to go west in search of adventure. I boarded the *Sunset,* which had not then been completed to San Antonio, and stopped at Luling, and from there I went by wagon to Gonzales where I secured work on a farm owned by G. W. Newberry. Five months later I went to Live Oak county, where Robert Dobie and I bought a bunch of horses which we drove to East Texas and

E. S. BOATRIGHT

peddled out. In 1876 I gathered horses with Dave Johnson for my brother-in-law, H. B. Newberry. Our camp was near where George West is now located. We drove these horses to East Texas, and while passing through Williamson county we stopped at Old Man Olive's ranch and were treated royally. After disposing of this herd I went to work for J. M. Dobie. After I had been working there almost a year Mr. Dobie bought 500 or 600 horses from Isam Railey and put in some of his own to send up the trail. I do not remember just how many there were in the herd, but I do recollect that they could run, especially on a dark stormy night. After we got the herd trimmed to Jim's liking, and his four horse chuck wagon loaded with lots to eat, we started for Dodge City, Kansas. We intended to drive to the McKenzie ranch the first night where we expected to pen the stock and get a good night's rest. We reached the pens about dark and just as the lead horses started into the pen an old peacock, perched in an oak tree, gave one of his hideous squalls and those horses stampeded, and there was no sleep for us that night. Afterward every time I saw one of those fowls I felt like killing it. We traveled on until we reached the San Saba River, where the worst hail storm I ever experienced suddenly descended upon us. Our slickers were in the chuck wagon, so I got a wetting as well as a hard beating. When the storm was over the boys picked up hail and filled the water barrel, and when I came in to camp they asked me if I wanted a drink of ice water. I told them I would like to have a drink but it was not ice water I needed. When we reached Albany the boss loaded the chuck wagon with everything good to eat, including all kinds of dried fruits. We had a good cook named Juan Gomez, but he had never cooked dried apples, and the first time he attempted it the outcome was rather amusing. He filled the kettle full of the dried fruit and it soon began swelling and in just a little while he had all of the vessels in camp full, including the wash basin. When we reached the Cimarron we saw our first Indians. One of them asked me for tobacco, and when I handed him my plug of Star navy he kept it. I was fighting mad but I let him go. After we crossed into the Indian Territory we encountered a severe thunderstorm in which lightning played around us all night long while we stayed with the herd. The next day on old chief came to camp and was very friendly with us. He invited me to his camp and said he had two pretty girls, but I was afraid they would want some more tobacco and I did not have enough to do me until we reached the next place where I could buy some. When we reached the Washita River it was very high and we had some difficulty in crossing. One day we saw a bunch of Indians coming in a run and Jim Dobie rode around to where I was and said, "Boatright, I want you to stay with me." I told him I did not know whether I could stay with him or not, as he had the best horse, but I would do my best. The Indians wanted to trade horses, but as they could not get a trade they rode away. I must tell a little joke on the boss: He left home with but one pair of pants, and by the time we reached the Territory they were showing considerable wear. He mounted a bronco one morning that was some pitcher, but that made no difference for Jim was some stayer. I don't know just how it happened, but his pants got hung on the pommel of the saddle, and when the horse got through pitching there was not much left of Jim's pants. I was the only one in the outfit that had breeches that would fit him, and I gave him a pair to relieve his distress. We reached Dodge City in due time, and notwithstanding some hardships and dangers we encountered on the trip we all had a good time. There was never a better man to work for than J. M. Dobie. I know of only one of the boys now living and that is Dick Dobie, who lives at Mathis, Texas.

SKETCH OF COLONEL J. J. MYERS

One of the best known trail drivers of the early days was Col. J. J. Meyers, who died in December, 1874, from chloroform poisoning by robbers in Omaha, Nebraska. He had just delivered a large herd in Utah, and was returning home. His death occurred from the effects of the poison after he reached home. Col. Meyers had four sons, all of whom were trail drivers, taking herds to northern markets. These sons were George Meyers of Batesville, Texas; John G. Meyers of New York City, A. E. Meyers of San Antonio, and R. E. L. Meyers of Austin, Texas. His daughter, Mrs. John I. Pool, now resides at Lockhart, Texas. Col. Meyers was a Mexican War veteran, was first lieutenant under John C. Fremont, and in the war between the states was colonel of DeBray's 26th Texas Cavalry.

The following sketch taken from "Historic Sketches

of the Cattle Trade of the West and Southwest," published in 1874 by Joseph G. McCoy, gives full account of the prominent part Colonel Meyers played in the development of the cattle industry:

COL. J. J. MEYERS

"The demand for cattle to supply the territories was great in 1866, and the turning of attention of territorial operators to Abilene as a place to buy, greatly aided that point in becoming a complete market, one in which any kind, sort or sized cattle could either be bought or sold, and the driving of herds purchased at Abilene to the territories became as common as driving from Texas to Abilene.

"There were certain Texan drovers who looked almost exclusively to the territorial operators for buyers for their stock. In case they succeeded in meeting a purchaser, the drovers would often deliver their herds at some agreed point, in which territory the buyer might desire. In such cases the same outfit and the same cowboys that came from Texas with the stock, would go on to its territorial destination. Perhaps the most prominent drover engaged in supplying the territorial demand is Col. J. J. Meyers of Lockhart, Texas. In June, 1867, during the first visit of the Illinoisan to the West, and whilst his project of a cattle shipping depot was not yet fully determined upon, and whilst stopping temporarily at the Hale House in Junction City, he, Joseph G. McCoy, author of, "Sketches of the Cattle Trade of the West and Southwest," was introduced to a small sized, quiet gentleman, who was evidently entering that class upon whose head Time had begun to sprinkle her silver frosts. The gentleman was introduced as being late from Texas, and here thought the Illinoisan, was just the man before whom to lay the plan of the contemplated project and thus secure the Texan's judgment upon it, whether or not it was plausible or advisable, and if such a shipping depot was created, would the Texas drovers bring cattle to it. So inviting the venerable gentleman to take a walk, they strolled to a lumber pile on a vacant lot and there sat down for two hours or more, in which time the Illinoisan explained the contemplated project fully, and noted closely the comment and opinions of the Texas drover, for such he proved to be. He there told that young Illinoisan that a depot for cattle and shipment was the greatest need of Texas stockmen, and that who-ever would establish and conduct such an enterprise, upon legitimate business principles, would be a bene-factor to the entire Texas livestock interest, and would undoubtedly have all the patronage reasonably desired. From the hour of that formal interview between the Texas drover and the Illinoisan, the project, such as was soon developed at Abilene, became a fixed fact or purpose in the mind of its projector. There are moments in one's existence when decision, or a purpose arrived at, shapes future actions and events—even the whole tenor of one's life and labor.

"Such was the effect of the two brief hours spent in conversation by the Texas drover and the Illinoisan. When they shook hands and parted there existed in the breast of the Illinoisan an impression that he had been talking to a sincere, honest man, who spoke his convic-tions without deceit or without any desire whatever to mislead anyone, but with a firmly fixed determination to give credit only correct information. The decisions and determinations formed at that interview fixed the life and labor of the Illinoisan. That Texas drover was Col. J. J. Meyers, a man of peculiar build and stature that can endure untold physical hardships without fatigue. There are few men in the West or Northwest who have so thorough a knowledge, gathered from actual travel and observation, of all the territories of the Union, as Col. Meyers. One of his early tours over the west was made across the continent with John C. Fremont on his famous exploring expedition. This occurred almost forty years ago when the Colonel was but a youth just entering into vigorous manhood. Such a strong desire to roam became implanted in his bosom that he did not rest until he had traversed almost every foot of territory between the Mississippi River and the Pacific Ocean. And when he had seen all that Dame Nature had to show, he turned his attention to stock raising in Texas, making his home in Lockhart. He too, was a drover in 1866, and endured all kind of outrages before he was able to sell his herd. But in 1867 he decided to drive in Western Kansas, and so flank all settlements, and take his chances to find a purchaser somewhere on the frontier, but just where he did not know. The Colonel was among Abilene's first patrons and warmest friends, and so long as it was a market he annually made his appearance with from four to sixteen thousand head of cattle, which of course were driven in several herds, never more than three thousand in one herd.

"The class of cattle the Colonel usually drove was just suited for the territorial demand, therefore he never shipped but a few carloads. For four years he sold his herds to parties living in Salt Lake, genuine Mormons of the true polygamist faith, and delivered his stock to them in Utah. The Mormons, as all well know, are very clannish people, especially the lay members and are little disposed to trade with or buy anything of a Gentile. Therefore, to avoid this religious prejudice, and in order to get into and through the Utah Territory without any trouble, or having to pay exorbitant damage bills to the Latter Day Saints, it was his practice to instruct his men to tell every resident of Utah they met that the cattle belonged to Elder Kimball, one of the elders or high priests in Mormondom. No matter whose farm the cattle run over, nor how much damage was done to the crops, it was all settled amicably by telling the residents that the cattle belonged to Elder Kimball. No charge or complaint was ever made after that statement was heard, and it did appear that if Heber Kimball's cattle should run over the saints bodily and tread them into the earth it would have been all right, and not a murmur would have been heard to escape their lips. When the cattle reached their destination the Colonel never went near them, but allowed Elder Kimball to dispose of them always as if they were his own, which he could do at a rapid rate. The Mormons appeared to consider it a great privilege to buy of this sainted elder, although they were paying from one to three dollars in gold more per head than they would have to pay to the Gentile drover. Indeed, they would not have bought the same stock of the Gentile at any price. When it is known that this people are such complete dupes of cunning smart men is it any wonder that they submit to be plucked like a goose for the benefit of their quondam keepers? Or is it anything strange that their leaders manage to get immensely rich? But Utah, notwithstanding her great city, and her immense mining operations, has now more than a supply of cattle for her own consumption, and is beginning to export cattle to Chicago and the East. Several thousand head of fat beeves were driven from Utah over the mountains to Cheyenne and there shipped to Chicago during the year 1873. So there is no longer a demand for stock cattle in that territory.

"There are few Texas drovers who handle or drive more cattle from Texas than Col. Meyers; few are more widely or favorably known than he. He is a man that has few enemies, but wherever he is known his name is spoken with respect, akin to love and admiration. He is a man true to his pledges, and one who would not reap advantage from or oppress a fellowman, simply because he had the power or legal right to do so. When he is given the title, 'a father in Israel' among the drovers there will be found a few, if any, who will dispute his right or worthiness of the appellation.''

CAME OVER FROM GERMANY IN 1870
F. Cornelius, Midfield, Texas

I was born in Rothensee, County Hersfeld, Germany, on the 2nd day of December, 1850, and came to the United

F. CORNELIUS AND HIS HORSE, ''DICK''

States in December, 1870, landing at New Orleans, from whence I sailed to Indianola on a Morgan steamer. At

Indianola I secured a position with H. Runge & Company, then one of the largest firms there. I soon learned to speak English and with the assistance of Mr. Rudolph Kleberg (afterwards congressman), who taught me after business hours, I got along pretty well. Later I went to work for Ed Clary, who owned a schooner making regular trips from Carancahua to Indianola.

In the spring of 1873 I went with Ged Cothrey, who was in charge of a herd of beeves belonging to Mr. Bennett, to Kansas, and after I reached there I spent most of the year in that section, close to the Platte River, working cattle for Dilworth & Littlefield, later returning to Texas.

In the spring of 1875 I went to work for W. B. Grimes in a packery, canning beef for northern markets. We killed as many as 125 beeves a day. I worked for Mr. Grimes for quite a while. On the 24th of June, 1875, I was married to Miss Annie Downer, who lived near the mouth of Trespalacios. That fall Mr. Grimes persuaded me to take a couple of hands and sufficient horses and overtake his herd which had gone nearly a month before, and go with Mr. A. Dowdy, who was in charge of the cattle, to Kansas. Overtaking the herd above Austin on the San Gabriel River about ten days after we left home, everything went smoothly, only at Valley Mills we had a lot of rain and were not able to move for several days. Soon afterward we heard of the terrible storm which swept Indianola and the entire coast country, drowning many people. We reached Wichita, Kansas, about the middle of December, and never lost much time in starting back to where the weather was not so cold.

After I reached home I purchased a small tract of land from John Moore on Casher's Creek, and moved on it. We were the only family living on the east side of Casher's Creek, but there were four families living on the west side, John Pybus, Jacob Selzieger, Horace Yeamans, Sr. and Alexandria Morris. While naming the old set-

tlers on Casher's Creek I will also pretty nearly name
all of the settlers who lived on Trespalacios at that time.
Beginning at the mouth of the west side were Mr. Dow-
ner, John Moore, Joe Pybus, W. B. Grimes, Godfrey
Selzieger, August Duffey, John Rowles, Mrs. McSparren,
Joe McIntyre and Uncle Tom Kuykendall; on the east
side were J. F. Garnet, J. B. Smith, T. E. Partain, Mrs.
E. P. Pybus, R. A. Partain, W. M. Kuykendall, J. E.
Pierce, Jack Wheeler, Daniel Wheeler and Uncle Tom
Williams. In the fork of Trespalacios and Wilson Creek
lived Fred Sparks, Alex Gyle, David Dunbar and John
Hicks. Jack Elliott lived up on Wilson Creek.

Times have changed a whole lot. Where we used to
see herds of deer and large numbers of turkey, and
nothing but cattle on the prairie, there are now thousands
of acres of rice growing, and new towns and settlements
growing up—where we old fellows, N. Keller, Jim Keller,
W. E. McSparren and others spent some of the happiest
times of our lives camping out.

In establishing a home on Casher's Creek, we had to
deny ourselves many things. I went to Indianola and
bought at a sale enough lumber to build a small house.
My only means of conveyance was a yoke of oxen and
a bedstead made out of a head and footboard found in
the "slide." Our furniture consisted of a home-made
table from old lumber I had bought in Indianola and sides
I made myself, a bench and a few boxes to sit on. My
stock consisted of three horses, a few cattle and a yoke
of oxen with a slide that I had made myself, but my wife
and I felt as rich as Jay Gould, and were as happy as
could be in our little home. We used the oxen in making
my crop, and when we wanted to go anywhere we yoked
them to our family carriage, the slide, and were off.
Wagons were scarce in those days and buggies were not
to be seen there. The only hack in the neighborhood
belonged to Mr. Grimes.

In 1885 we moved to Juanita, my present place, where

Mrs. Downer and I bought the W. C. Clapp quarter league in 1882 from Shanghai and John Pierce. Later Mrs. Downer and I bought a three-fourths interest in the L. P. Scott Survey, joining the W. C. Clapp Survey on the north. I later bought Mrs. Downer's interest and the interests of the heirs of the Scott Survey, giving me about 2,100 acres.

My wife died in April, 1894, leaving me with seven children to care for. I met with many reverses during the next few years. Hailstorms and floods destroyed my crops and killed my stock and I had a pretty hard struggle, but I kept digging along and overcame most of the difficulties.

On October 24, 1899, I was married to Miss L. E. Gainer, and to us were born three boys and one girl.

A FAITHFUL NEGRO SERVANT

By J. E. Folts, Columbus, Texas

In the spring of 1870 my uncle, R. B. (Bob) Johnson, drove a herd of cattle up the trail to Abilene, Kansas.

GEORGE GLENN

He took with him as one of the cow-hands a young negro whom he raised on his ranch, and whose picture accompanies this sketch. The herd was started from Colorado county, crossing the Colorado River at La Grange and intersecting the Chisholm Trail near the Red River, and passing across the Indian Territory. Soon after reaching Abilene my uncle became ill and died. His body was embalmed, put in a metallic casket, and temporarily buried at or near Abilene about the last of July of that year, and the following September the body was disinterred and placed in a Studebaker wagon and the negro cow-hand, George Glenn, as driver, started on the long trip back to Texas. It was impossible at that early date to get a dead body shipped back by rail, as there were no railroads, at least none leading from Abilene, Kansas, to Texas. This faithful negro brought his old master's body back, being forty-two days and nights on the road, sleeping every night in the wagon alongside the casket. He carried the body to the cemetery at Columbus where it was laid to rest by the side of the wife who had died some years before. Of such stuff were the old trail drivers, white and black, made of.

The badge on the negro's coat is the road brand of the trail herd and is called "scissors."

GRAZED ON MANY RANGES

T. J. Garner, Loveland, Colorado

I was born in Tennessee in October, 1853. My parents died when I was a small boy, and I lived in Caldwell county until I was large enough to ride a horse into the brush after those wild cattle which were not looked after during the Civil War.

In 1850 I made my first trip up the trail for Peck & Evans. We left Gonzales about the first of March and got along fine until we reached Fort Worth. There we had four inches of snow and very cold weather. Went to Gainesville, crossed Red River and went out by Fort Arbuckle, on to Wichita and Abilene, Kansas. We saw a great many buffalo and lots of Indians, but had no trouble with them. We delivered our herd and went home.

In the fall of 1870 I joined the Texas Rangers at Gonzales, and was mustered in at San Antonio. Went to Montague county and fought Indians that winter and also the following spring and summer. Had some close calls but came out without a scratch.

In 1872 I went with a herd of cattle from Lockhart, Texas, to Salt Lake City, Utah, with Mack Stewart as boss. We had a very good trip and only a few stampedes. Reached Salt Lake about the first of October. When we left this place we took a stage for Ogden and boarded cars for Kansas City, and from there came to Austin.

In 1873 I went with a herd for Jack Meyers from Lockhart to Ellsworth, Kansas. Coleman James was boss. We had a fine trip. Went back to Texas with the horses, and there worked on the range for a number of years.

T. J. GARNER

In 1877 I again hit the trail, this time with a herd for Hood & Hughes, from Uvalde to Caldwell, Kansas. They sold out there and I took 640 of those old mossheads down to the Kaw Nation for Smith & Leedy. We held them there until the 10th of October and then started for the feeding pens. Swam them across the Arkansas River a few miles below Arkansas City, and went along the flint hills to the head of Elk River, near Eureka, Kansas. When we reached a point within about a mile of the pens ten French ranchers came out of a gulch and were going to give Hank Leedy a grass necktie. Hank was scared almost to death, and his face went as white as my hair is today when they caught his horse by the bridle and began to curse and abuse him. I said: "Don't get scared, Hank, I am Johnny on the spot," and I lit off old Gray Eagle alongside of a rock that stood about four feet high and prepared for action. Bringing my Winchester into position I started in to make those fellows a speech, but they did not wait to hear it, and went back into the gulch faster than they had come out of it. Hank said: "Jack, you must have lots of gall to talk that way to those fellows." I told him it was not what I said that turned the trick, it must have been my looks or my Winchester that caused them to scamper away. While I was at Uvalde, Texas, a Mexican gave me his hat and what money he had because I was better at monte than he was. I was still wearing the hat and I had not been in a barber shop for several months, so I did not look like a band-box boy, and my looks may have had a great deal to do with their sudden departure. We were three days too early with our cattle, and that was the reason those ranchmen got so "riled" up. We put the steers in a pen about fifteen acres in size. It was located in a canyon which had been walled up at both ends, except a space of about twelve feet for the entrance. This space was closed by pole bars. We went to Hank Leedy's house and he introduced me to his good wife and told her to prepare a good supper for us. And when it was ready I promptly got on the outside of six or seven hot biscuits and boiled eggs. It was the best meal I had had for six months. Hank's house was on a bluff overlooking the pens where we had put the cattle, and that night a great hail and rain storm came up. When the lightning flashed I could see those old steers run from one end of the corral to the other, but they could not get out. That was the only stampede I ever enjoyed. Hank insisted on us staying with him a few days to rest up, telling us our pay would continue as long as we remained there, and we stayed there several days. I don't think Hank cared so much for our "rest" as he did about something else. One day one of the boys and myself were out in the hills a few days later and met four men driving a bunch of cattle. We rode up to them and talked awhile and learned that they were among the crowd that had stopped our cattle and threatened to lynch Hank. I told them there was no danger of Texas fever affecting their cattle as

there had been so much weather and frost, and they
seemed satisfied, and we parted friendly and wished each
other good luck and good-bye. I remained with old Hank
a few days longer, then told him I thought he was safe
and I would go to Eureka, and sell my horses and go
back to Texas. He wanted me to give him my Winchester
and pistol, but I could not part with both of them so I
gave him the Winchester only, and bade him and his excellent wife good-bye. I went to town, sold out and then
hired a farmer to haul me to Humbolt, a distance of
sixty miles, where I hit the cars for Texas. Went by way
of Sherman, Dallas, Houston and San Antonio. Remained in San Antonio a few days and then went to Bell
county and wintered.

In 1878 I went from Round Rock to Allen's ranch on
the Colorado River below Columbus, for Dudley and John
Snyder, and got 2,700 one, two and three year old steers,
and drove them by way of Gonzales to Lockhart, through
Austin, Round Rock, Fort Worth, Red River Station,
on to Dodge City, Ogallala and Julesburg, where they
were branded and turned loose on the range. All of the
hands were tenderfeet except two. The cattle would get
to drifting in the fog and stampede and run all night
long. For three weeks I did not unroll my bedding, and
did not get more than an hour's sleep each night. Finally
they got settled down and we made it through with but
little loss.

I worked on the L L range at Julesburg until November, shipping out beeves, then went back to Ogallala, and
from there to the Spotted Agency in South Dakota.
Stopped at Bill Shope's ranch a few days and he wanted
me to go back to Ogallala with him and help ship out
beeves from his North Platte ranch. When I finished
this job I went to Denver and wintered there.

In 1879 I went to work on the range at Hugo, Colorado, for Frank Cochrane. Worked for him four years.
While on this job I went to the Blue Mountains near

Durango and gathered a herd of mixed cattle, drove them to Rocky Ford, shipped the beeves to Kansas City, drove the stock cattle to Brush Station on the South Platte, cut out the dry stock and put 4,000 cows with their calves and 2,500 yearlings in one herd and drove them down the river twenty-four miles to Bush's Ranch and delivered them, then returned to the station and drove dry stock to Cheyenne and sold then to Richie Brothers. I delivered them on Powder River near the Montana line and came back and spent the winter in Denver.

In 1883 I went to the Black Hills in South Dakota and worked on the range there and in Northern Wyoming and Montana for a few years, and then started a cow ranch of my own. I got married in 1891 to one of the finest little seventeen-year-old girls in that country, and we held down the ranch for a few years, but you know the old saying about the big fish eating up the little fish, so I sold out what I had left and came to Loveland, Colorado, and have been running a shoe shop here ever since. I have a few cattle up on the Thompson River near Loveland, and am at present raising milk goats here. Also I have a ranch in Texas, with my nephew as partner and manager.

I see in the first volume of the Trail Drivers' book a sketch wherein one of the old boys stated that he would like to make the drives again. I would not care to do so, for I would not again take some of the chances I took then for all the money in these United States. I had enough of three to seven months' work, night and day, in hailstorms, stampedes, blizzards, and the like. And then when the cattle were delivered and we would go to town to find lead whizzing around too close to be comfortable, and see poor fellows falling to rise no more. I do not want any more of the old life.

I see some of the old trail drivers are living on Rough Row, and my sympathies go out to them. My little wife and I are living on Easy Street, and would be pleased to have any of the old trail boys call on us if they should ever come to Loveland, Colorado.

JOHN H. ROSS WAS A BRONCO BUSTER

John H. Ross was born in old Bandera county 60 years ago, grew up on the frontier and worked with stock all his life. In the early days he was the champion bronco bustler of Bandera county, and rode everything that came his way. He made several trips up the trail to Kansas and had some thrilling adventures which he delights to tell about, but could not be induced to write a sketch for this book. He has a nice ranch near **Bandera**, and extends a welcome to all trail drivers.

JOHN H. ROSS

HAS HAD AN EVENTFUL CAREER

William B. Krempkau, San Antonio, Texas

William B. Krempkau, the subject of this sketch, was born in a house on Salinas Street, three blocks from the San Fernando Cathedral, San Antonio, Texas, March 9, 1863. His parents came from Ransbach, St. Arnin, Alsace, with the Castro Colonists in 1844, and located in San Antonio. At that time the principal trading done by the early settlers was with Indians and Mexicans, very few white people living in San Antonio. Money was very scarce and trading was done by exchanging goods for buffalo robes, furs, gold and silver ore which the Indians and Mexicans brought in. Wood and prairie hay was transported on burros. Water was hauled on skids, or rolled in barrels from the river, creeks and ditches; there were only a few wells in the town. In relating his experiences Mr. Krempkau said:

BILLIE KREMPKAU
Ready for Action

"My grandfather joined Napoleon's army in 1808 and served until 1815, and was promoted to be a captain. He was wounded three times, and decorated several times for bravery. One of my uncles was killed at the Battle of Manassas the same day General Albert Sidney Johnson fell. At the time of his death my uncle was carrying a sword that was carried by my grandfather in France. The weapon is now in possession of one of my cousins who lives in Medina county.

"I entered school in San Antonio in 1868 in the old building on Military Plaza used by the Spaniards as a government headquarters. I always liked cow work, and while I was attending school I frequently went out on the open range and brought in cows with young calves for the dairymen, usually receiving $1.50 to $2.50 per head. In this way I managed to make a little spending money. The call of the wild became so strong, however, that I left school and divided my time between the cow camp and the freighter's camp. Mr. Monier was a neighbor to our family and was one of the most extensive freighters out of San Antonio to government posts in Texas and to different points in Mexico. I often lounged around his corral, which was always full of wagons, teams and teamsters, and made myself useful in assisting the freighters in every way possible with the result that I soon became a favorite with those old grizzly teamsters, and they encouraged me to take up their line of work. Mr. Monier took contracts to break wild mules for the government to use as pack mules. He often received fifty or a hundred mules at a time, and had a novel way of breaking them in. His hands would rope each animal in the corral, and securely tie bags of sand on their backs, and then lead or drive them around for quite awhile, repeating the performance every day, until the mules were gentle. At first they would buck and cavort around pretty lively, but a mule is quick to learn, and after two or three days they would be easily handled. In this kind of work I soon became an expert, and learned to throw the lasso as good as any of the men. I could throw the rope and catch a wild mule by the foot or head with perfect ease.

"Mr. Monier needed hands that were quick with rope or gun, and soon employed me to accompany him on his perilous journeys to Mexico. I remained with him several years, often going to Chihuahua, San Luis Potosi, Saltillo and other points, and I experienced all the thrills and excitement incident to those early days, with Indians, high water, Mexicans, dry weather, and crossing deserts. For protection against attack by Indians we always corraled the wagons at night, and in making a corral I could swing the wagons around as quick as any one.

"I was with Mr. Monier on the last trip he made to

Mexico, in 1880. This was a cotton train, twenty bales
to the wagon, and it was delivered at San Luis Potosi.

"In 1882 I went up the trail to Dodge City, Kansas,
for Smith & Elliott of Sringfield, Illinois. The herd was
bought in Mason, Gillespie and San Saba counties, and
delivered to my boss, Charlie Baldo of Uvalde county.
Baldo was one of the best trail bosses I ever knew. He
treated us all fine, and was liked by every man in the
outfit. We went the western trail and had all sorts of
exciting experiences on the trip, thunderstorms, swollen
streams, stampedes, Indians, long dry drives, wild animals, loss of sleep, and a frequent hankering for the

CALDERON'S TRAIN STARTING FOR MEXICO IN 1870

chuck wagon when kept in the saddle for twenty-four
hours or longer. We delivered the cattle at Dodge City,
and there I met many of my old friends from Texas. As
soon as I could get loose from the herd I took a bath in
the river, went to a barber shop and got my face beauti-
fied, put on some new clothes, and went forth to see the
sights in the toughest town on the map—and I saw 'em.

"I came back home on the train, my first railroad
experience, and was surprised to find when I reached San
Antonio that my baggage had arrived also. Pat Mc-
Cluskey and Jim Hogan of San Antonio were with me on
this trip."

The interest Mr. Krempkau has taken in procuring

and preserving pictures of early-day freighting, and in posing for pictures depicting early cowboy incidents, is commendable and shows he recognizes the importance of rescuing this kind of history from oblivion. His liberal contributions to this volume are deeply appreciated.

Mr. Krempkau has owned a farm and ranch, sixteen miles west of San Antonio, on the Krempkau Divide, for over twenty-five years. He lives in San Antonio, and is sergeant-at-arms for the Old Time Trail Drivers' Association.

Captain T. P. McCall, who carried the first mail from San Antonio to Franklin, now known as El Paso, was a brother-in-law to Mr. Krempkau. His guards were Bigfoot Wallace and Louis Oge. This route passed through Castroville, the first colony west of San Antonio.

In 1855 the United States government established a post at Camp Verde, just two miles north of Bandera Pass, and for a number of years kept about eighty head of camels there, to try the experiment of carrying messengers and freight across the desert to El Paso and to the border. The experiment proved a failure. Mr. Krempkau remembers seeing many of those camels that had escaped and gone wild.

Mr. Krempkau's father was one of the early day rangers and Indian scouts, and as such was the bunkmate and messmate of the late Maxene of Leon Springs. The elder Krempkau died in San Antonio November 29, 1871.

NO ROOM IN THE TENT FOR POLECATS

By W. B. Foster, San Antonio, Texas

I was born January 6, 1849, one mile from Foster Cross Road, Sequado Valley, East Tennessee. I lost my mother when I was seven years old. One year later my father married Mrs. Julia Morris and moved to Hickory Hill, Gallatin county, Illinois. I stayed there until I was eighteen years old, then I went to East Tennessee, staying there three years and then drifted over to Trotters Landing, Mississippi, and from there came to Texas. I landed in San Antonio April 6, 1871. Killed my first

W. B. FOSTER

wolf on Dignowity Hill, now being in the city limits. I was there only a short time until I hired to W. M. Todd to go north with cattle. Wade Hampton of Seguin had charge of the herd. Todd bought horses for himself. Major George of Seguin and Monoy & Wilbert of Nevada also hired men for Todd's three outfits. We camped for several days under a big hackberry tree that now stands on Roosevelt Avenue in San Antonio. From there we went to Guadalupe River. Major George took one outfit to Seguin. We camped in a little pasture belonging to Mr. Braners just north of Youngford. While there Col. Todd bought a fine pair of steers from Edwards & Ervin. He wanted them broke to work so we drove them out on the prairie, roped and tied them down, yoked them and tied their tails together, tied the bed to the wagon, put a rope around their horns, put a half hitch in their mouths and then hitched them to the wagon. Al Meyers and myself got into the wagon to drive, the boys untied their legs and other men rode on each side to keep them straight, and if you don't think we had a ride over those hogwallows, you have another thought coming. We could handle them when we went to receiving cattle.

We next moved to Cordova Pens, four and a half miles northwest of Seguin, where we road-branded the cattle TOD that we had received from J. Plumer at the May pasture, two miles from the Sutherland Springs, the ranch brand being AT. We received 1,300 head in four herds. In coming from the May pasture to the branding pens, we came by Sutherland Springs, crossed the Guadalupe River at Sheffield Ford below Seguin, and passed north of Seguin.

Just as we started on the trail, W. M. Pusey came from Denver, Colorado. Todd let him have Wade Hampton to help him gather a herd. Pusey was Todd's son-in-law. Todd then hired Col. G. W. Nail of Hunter to boss his herd. We crossed the San Geronimo Creek at the Austin Crossing, the San Marcos at the McGee crossing by the Manchaca Springs; here I witnessed the densest fog I ever saw. We crossed the Colorado River west of Austin, left Round Rock to the left, and crossed the Gabriel River some distance east of town. Little River was up, as it had been raining and everything crossed but one steer. I roped him and got him in the water and he swam across.

Todd had a very fine mare which he had bought from Nick Crenshaw at Seguin. A man by the name of Thompson, who was riding her, went around a bend of the river here and we never heard or saw anything of him or the mare after that.

We crossed just above the suspension bridge at Waco. At Hillsboro the cattle stampeded around a school house. The young lady teacher was quick to close the door, but the kiddies were scared just the same. I rode a big horse that I called "Jack Moore" and he was some horse. We had just left Hillsboro, when the cattle spied a little girl going to school with a red shawl on her head. Each corner of the shawl was blown by the wind and this was more than the cattle could stand. I was behind the herd and saw what was exciting the cattle so I got all there was in "Jack Moore" and picked her up just in time.

At Cleburne a bad man beat up Tony Wilder, a seven-

teen year-old boy that belonged to our outfit. Al Meyers
tried his hand on the bad man, using his quirt. Wilder
never carried arms of any kind; he was more like a girl
than a boy and everyone in the outfit loved him. He and
myself were the only ones out of an outfit of twenty-two
men that had not killed a man.

At Fort Worth the river was up. We went up about
ten miles west of town and cut brush to build a chute to
the river in order to force the cattle into the water, the
bank being about eight or ten feet higher than the water.
I always led the cattle across all streams and on this
occasion I went down that chute in front of a stampeded
herd. On the north bank my horse bogged, I jumped off
him and as I did so I discovered several Indians sitting
on a log nearby. I shouted back to the men on the other
side that there were Indians there. It was some time before the other men crossed on a ferry just below the
mouth of the Clear Fork of the Trinity River, and when
they got there the Indians were gone.

At the Trinity River we wound up a wild drive of 100
miles in four days with stock cattle. Col. Todd was
drinking all the time and was very disagreeable, which
caused Colonel Nail to leave us. Every one in the outfit
was sorry to see him leave as he was a fine man and one
of the best cowmen I ever saw.

As we neared the Red River Cañon, we were strung
out on the trail, a small herd to our right tried to rush
to the mouth of the cañon. When they got close, and were
about to pass us Al Meyers commenced to shoot in front
of them. They had business the other way, and like they
were in a hurry to get there. Red River Cañon is about
twenty-five miles through and only one place where a
herd could be bedded. When we camped near the Red
River Station, I quit and went to town ahead of the herd.
The river was very high. People tried to get Todd to
wait until the water went down. None of the men would
lead the herd. The cattle got about the middle of the

stream and then went to swimming in a circle. Todd began calling for me. He had long white hair and was wild for short time. He turned to Al Meyers and said: "You know where my son Foster is? Tell him I will give him anything in the world if he will save my cattle for me."

I stripped to my underclothes, mounted "Jack Moore" and went to them. I got off the horse and right on to the cattle. They were so jammed together that it was like walking on a raft of logs. When I finally got to the only real big steer in the bunch I mounted him and he pulled for the other side. When he got near the bank I drifted down the stream to the horse. It must have been about 9 o'clock in the morning, on the 8th day of June, 1871, so I kept the herd together all day until nearly sundown; no hat, no saddle—just my underclothes.

At Monument Rock some of the boys put the Colonel's tent over a bed of polecats and when he went to bed they tied the front of the tent. In trying to get out a little later the Colonel tore down the tent.

The next morning the Colonel sent me to Fort Sill after the mail. It was thirty-five miles to Fort Sill and the Indians were on the warpath, but I did not see any. I caught the herd again at the old stage stand. I had a letter for Al Meyers, and in thirty minutes he was on his way to Philadelphia, Pa., to get married. Jimmie Billings also got a letter telling him that he could return to New York City, his old home. He had been a bounty jumper during the war.

The next day Colonel Nelson and I were near the trail when the stage came along. The driver told Nelson that the officers had learned where he was and that they would be after him soon; he then rode around the herd and was gone. Nelson was the right-hand man to John Morgan, the raider, during the war between the states. He had been boot-legging in Indian Territory.

We crossed the Washita River where the McDonald

ranch is now and crossed the Canadian River at Billie Williams' store. That night Colonel Todd and I fell out and I quit. He talked a long time to me before I would agree to stay with the outfit until he got out of the Indian country.

The next morning when I went out to try to get a wild turkey, I rode into a bunch of Indians. "Jack Moore" carried me from them and when I got to the herd, I had been struck with several arrows, so was "Jack Moore." Jimmie Billings cut the arrows out of both of us with a pocket knife. I lost quite a lot of blood. While they were at work on me, William Packer rode up and had me put in his wagon and in a few days I was in the saddle again. But "Jack Moore" and I parted forever. I finished my trip with Harrow & Packer, who had three hundred head of butcher cattle which they were taking to Bloomington, Ill.

We passed Caldwell, Kansas, and were in Wichita Falls on the 4th day of July, 1871, just two years after the first peg was driven into the ground to lay out the town. The cattle were shipped from Florence, Kansas.

William Slaughter and I went across the country to Abilene. Wild Bill, or I should say William Hickok, was city marshal. He was very kind to me and I thought a great deal of him.

I shipped cattle from Abilene to St. Louis for Jim Reed, a one-armed man. One day while I was asleep at the Belle Hotel in St. Louis, Zack Mulhall called and asked what I was dreaming. I told him of "home." He then asked me why I did not go home. I told him to go to the ticket office with me and the first train that went out I would go on it. The train went east just one hour before the one went west. I found things changed from what they were when they left.

GARLAND G. ODOM

Among the foremost men in the cattle industry of Texas was G. G. Odom, of Ballinger, Texas. He was born in Baldwin county, Alabama, December 16, 1852, and was brought to Texas by his parents a year later. The family settled at San Antonio where his father, Thomas L. Odom, engaged in ranching. Garland Odom was a cowboy on his father's ranch until 1872, when he embarked in the cattle business f o r himself, becoming a trailer and driving his herds to Kansas markets. In 1876 he and his father drove 4,000 head of cattle to Runnells county and established the O. D. Ranch, with Fort Chadbourne as headquarters. While engaged in trail driving, Mr. Odom met and enjoyed the friendship of such old timers as Dewees, Maberry, Dawson, Fountain Hemsley, Nunn, Burnett, Deedis, Lowe, Slaughter, Collins, Cood Adams, and others whose names are familiar to the cowboys of those days.

G. G. ODOM

In 1879 he organized the Odom-Luckett Land & Livestock Company, of which he was general manager, and proceeded to buy and acquire title to a large body of land. In 1883 his company fenced in about 100,000 acres, the first pasture of any great importance in that section of the state. This met with a great deal of opposition from a certain element, and "wire cutting" gave the company no end of trouble, the "cutters" clipping about forty miles in one night. In 1886 Mr. Odom drove a large herd to Arizona and established a ranch at White Mountain, in Apache county, and again took up trailing, driving several herds to Montana and the Dakotas.

Mr. Odom became connected with leading business interests of Ballinger, Texas, and in all of his ventures he attained remarkable success. He was married at San Antonio, January 28, 1875, to Miss Sallie M. Crigler, and to them were born two daughters.

REMINISCENCES OF AN OLD TRAIL DRIVER

John C. Jacobs, San Antonio, Texas

Any one who would like to make a trip over the old cattle trail, from Texas to Montana with a herd of cattle, should meet President George Saunders, with his organization of old trail drivers, at their annual meet at the Gunter Hotel, San Antonio, Texas, in October of each

JOHN C. JACOBS

year, where they proceed to tear down every wire fence in the State, load up their chuck wagon with its raw hide stretched under the hind axle, get their cow ponies together, round up vast herds of long-horned cattle, throw them on the trail for a three to seven months' drive to northern markets, and after they have sold out and got their big roll of the long green, they stage a two-nights' ball at the Gunter. It would do your heart good to see the old timer swing the modern girl a-goin' and a-comin'. "In his mind" he owns more cattle than Job of Uz ever saw. His grand-daughter has to step some to keep time with him in an old-fashioned square dance. He has gone back on the range, turned his wolf loose, and forgotten the years that have flown. The most of his life has been spent out under Mother Nature's great blue, and the sixty-five to seventy-five years rest lightly upon his shoulders.

The rattle of horns and hoof (in the lobby) is to him as the fountain of youth. He has mounted his cuttin' horse and "lit a shuck." Herds of cattle going over the trail run in numbers from one to five thousand. After a herd is thrown on the trail, cattle of different temperament take their different places in the herd while traveling—they, like men, have their individuality. A few take the lead and keep the lead during the entire drive, others follow and keep their places. Then comes the middle and principal part of the herd, and last what is called the drags, and they are drags from the day they leave the ranch to the end of the drive. When watering and grazing they mix and mingle but when thrown back on the trail each division finds its respective place.

To handle a herd of all steer cattle on the trail requires the very best cowboy skill, and a herd boss who can speak the bovine language. If they ever stampede one time, there is danger of trouble the entire drive. A cowboy might carelessly get off his horse while the cattle were resting on the bedding ground, and if the horse should shake himself the rattle of the saddle would likely start a stampede, and only a cow puncher knows what that means. When the cattle are restless on the bedding ground the boys on night herd hum a low, soft lullaby (like a mother to her child). It has a quieting effect and often saves trouble.

A frontier cow range develops many peculiar characters, and many incidents that are stranger than fiction. I haven't the space to touch on more than one of them.

Judge Roy Bean was justice of the peace in a suburb of San Antonio, which is now in the city limits, but still known as "Beanville." Civilization was closing in on the Judge, so he bundled up and went West, and located on the Mexican border, west of the Pecos river. Lily Langtry, while filling an engagement here, met the old

Judge, and was very much taken with his personality. The Judge named the station he founded west of the Pecos, "Langtry," and in after years Miss Langtry, while crossing to the Pacific coast, would stop over and spend a day with her friend and admirer. None of the counties were organized in that part of the country, so the Judge got an appointment as Justice of the Peace at Langtry. He was running a saloon there, and he built a house near by and painted on it in large letters: "Judge Roy Bean's City Hall and Seat of Justice. He is the Law West of the Pecos."

It is said of the old Judge that a man was found dead on his range, and he had $50 and a pistol on his person. The Judge held an inquest over the body and fined the corpse $50 for carrying a pistol!

It is said that a friend of the Judge's killed a Mexican and when the constable brought the man in for a preliminary trial, the Judge said he could find no law in his books against killing a Mexican, and instructed the officer to release the prisoner. The Judge never adjourned his court and was always ready for action.

Stations were far between on the Southern Pacific railroad and Langtry was a water station. Passengers had time while the engine was taking water to rush over to the Judge's saloon and take something stronger. On one occasion a passenger took a bottle of beer—price one dollar—and handed the Judge a twenty. The customer thought the Judge a little slow in making the change, and indulged in a few cuss words and fears of getting left. The Judge fined him nineteen dollars for contempt of court, and informed the gentleman that if he had anything further to say derogatory to the dignity of the court he would lock him up for thirty days. The old Judge was a fine man and a most interesting character. At his death he willed Miss Langtry his brace of pistols.

I would be pleased to go on and write of the splendid character among the cowboys. They have a side to their character that the outside world knows nothing of. They were to a man defenders of women and children. Drop a woman down in an isolated cow camp and she was a queen and her will and wishes are absolute. They are to a man Chesterfields in the rough, and in my fifty years of life on the cow range I have never known a cowboy to insult nor heard of one attempting the unpardonable crime against the sex.

From the Rio Grande, which is the border between Texas and Mexico, to Red River, which is the north line of Texas, going over the cattle trail, is a distance of about 600 miles, so it took cattle leaving the southern part of the state from six weeks to two months to cross the northern border of Texas. Some of these herds were headed for Montana and often snow would be flying by the time they reached their destination.

All of the old trail drivers will remember Fort Griffin in Shackelford county, which was the last organized county on the trail, and all herds had to be inspected at the crossing of the Clear Fork of the Brazos, near the mouth of Tecumpsee. The writer at one time had the honor of being inspector there, and the memory of many pleasant events come back over the fleeting years as I sit here and write.

It seems now as though it was all in some other world and under fairer skies. The cowboy as he was then is gone from the earth. The railroads and wire fences have got his job. His old sore-backed cow pony is aged and wobbly. The automobile has got his job and his old three-quarter rigged saddle, with its busted raw-hide cover, hangs out in the old rickety shed—a relic of former days—and soon the last of his tribe will sack his saddle, roll and light his last shuck as he bares his breast to the winding trail out over the Great Divide, where, we trust, vast herds of long-horned cattle roam over fertile plains and slake their thirst from crystal streams.

"CHAWED" THE EARMARKS

J. C. Thompson, Devine, Texas

On the first day of March, 1878, I left my humble home on the Chicon Creek in Medina county, Texas, in company with Reas and Boon Moore, for the Leas Harris ranch on the La Gonias in Atascosa county. Lewis & Bluntzer had leased the ranch for the preceding year, and were then rounding up stock cattle to be driven to Kansas. Before leaving with the herd I witnessed a deal between Lewis & Bluntzer and Billie Childers, a son-in-law of Harris' for the ranch, receiving five hundred cows and calves for the ranch. We turned the herd out of the pasture on the 16th day of March and the drive for Kansas began. I was seventeen years old but was not a novice in the business by any means as I had been gathering, roping and branding mavericks all of my life. I remember on one occasion W. F. Thompson, my brother, and I caught a fine maverick one day and we had no knife to mark him with. Our mark was crop off one ear and underbit the other. Brother said if I would bite out the underbit he would bite off the crop. It took some "chewing" but we did a fairly good job of it.

But back to the trail: Mr. Bluntzer was along in person. He was a fat, jolly good fellow and we all loved him. We told him that he had the advantage of us when it rained, as he could lay on his back and spread a blanket on his belly and have a good roof over him. If you have never driven a herd consisting of two thousand cows in the spring you just can't imagine the time we had. We would leave from five to ten calves on the bedground every morning, and the cows would have to be roped and hobbled to keep them from going back the next night to their calves, and this thing lasted until we reached the Indian Territory.

I shall never forget that it was on this trip that I saw

a railroad train in motion. We were approaching Dodge City when I looked across Arkansas River and saw a real locomotive pulling a train of cars. I can shut my eyes now and see that picture far across the plains. There might have been railroads somewhere in Texas at that time but they had not rambled around my way.

I can remember some of the cowboys on that trip but some have faded away from my memory. One of the jolly good ones, the wit of the gang, was Clinch Bright. I thought more of him than I did of anyone in the bunch and he was the only one I had a fight with, but we were both to blame, ma'de it up in a few days,and were better friends than ever. Others were Arch, Larimore, Rufe and Frank James of Fort Worth, and old Lem Pegrum, who never spent a cent from the time he would leave here until he reached Fort Dodge, and then spent every dollar he had the first night.

I was contented to work on the ranch until 1883 when I went to Old Mexico after a herd of cattle for Lot Johnson. The boys composing this outfit were J. A. Kercheville, Everett Johnson, Ben Ridgus, Lem Kercheville, Wiley Mangrum, Bill Walker and Charlie Mulligan. We left the Salado River in Old Mexico with these cattle and made a sixty-mile drive to the Rio Grande, crossing just above Laredo without a drop of water. About forty miles north of Laredo about 12 o'clock in the night a regular blizzard swept down upon us which had just been preceded by a very hard, drenching rain. That cold wind whistled all night and the next day but calmed down about 6 o'clock the next evening, and the next morning we counted 180 head of cattle dead on the bedground. At this stage of the game I left this outfit and came back to the settlement, but on or about the first day of April of the same year, 1883, I went up the trail with a herd of cattle for Lytle & McDaniel, with Walter Trimble as foreman. When this herd was delivered at Fort Dodge, Kansas, I got in with another herd for Lytle with Gus

Black as foreman. This herd of steers was delivered by
Gus Black to Conners & Weir in South Dakota. B. L.
Crouch delivered a herd brought by Dick Head to the
same parties at the same time. I got a job with Conners
& Weir and took these cattle on the Montana, put their
ranch brand on them and turned them loose on Powder
River, Montana.

I intended to stay in Montana that winter but after
finding out you could not get outside the house for seven
months without snowshoes ten feet long, it was TEXAS
for me.

JAMES MADISON CHITTIM

James Madison Chittim was born on a farm in Gentry
county, Missouri, May 1, 1858, and died in San Antonio,
Texas, April 1, 1911. Mr. Chittim located at Victoria,

JAMES M. CHITTIM

Texas, in 1888, and within a
few years he became one of
the largest handlers of cattle in the Southwest. In
1889 he removed to San Antonio and made that city his
home until his death. For
many years the cattle owned
by him were numbered by the
tens of thousands, and he
controlled hundreds of thousands of acres of land, either
through actual ownership or
under lease. At the time of
his death he owned the largest ranch west of San Antonio.

In 1888 Mr. Chittim was married to Miss Annie Elizabeth Oberle of Memphis, Tennessee. To them were born
two daughters.

A BIG MIXUP

W. M. Nagiller, Williams, Arizona

I am one of the old timers that went up the old Chisholm Trail. I was born June 18, 1864, in Burnet county, Texas.

I started from Burnet in May, 1882, with 3,000 head of

W. M. NAGILLER

steers, owned by Hudson & Watson. Our trail boss was John Christian, also of Burnet. We went north and crossed the Red River at Doan's Store. There we laid over two weeks for two more trail herds to overtake us which belonged to the same men, Hudson & Watson. When the two herds arrived we threw all three herds together, which made about 9,000 head of cattle. There were to be 4,000 head of picked cattle to be cut out of this herd. We started cutting out this number in the afternoon. By evening we had 500 head cut out, and my boss and his men took these cattle to hold that night. The other two bosses and their men took the remaining 8,500 cattle to stand guard around. At sundown when we bedded the cattle down for the night there were eleven trail herds in sight. Along in the night a terrible storm came up. It was the worst that I ever experienced. The thunder, lightning and rain was awful. All the cattle were turned loose except small cuts we were holding. The following morning cattle were dotting the plains in every direction as far as the eye could see. All the trail herds were mixed up. After we had finished our breakfast we started to make the big roundup. There were about 120 cowboys. When we had the roundup made we had about 33,000 head in one bunch. We worked about ten days before we got the cattle shaped up to start on our way. One of the herds went to Caldwell, Kansas, and one to Cheyenne, Wyoming. The herd I was with went north of Cheyenne.

From Doan's Store we went on through the Indian Nation to Dodge City, Kansas, and then on to Ogallala, Nebraska, where we crossed to the South Platte River. We passed through Fort Fetimon and Fort Laramie and went northwest into Wyoming. We were on the trail four and one-half months, and had to stand guard every night.

I now own a cow ranch near Williams, Arizona, and I have been here twenty-eight years.

GEORGE T. REYNOLDS

George T. Reynolds was born in Montgomery, Alabama, February 14, 1844, and came to Texas with his parents, Mr. and Mrs. B. W. Reynolds, in 1847, locating in Shelby county. After residing there thirteen years the family moved to Palo Pinto county where he sojourned only a few months, finally lo-

cating on Clear Fork of the Brazos in Stephens county, where he engaged in the cattle business. A large herd of cattle was purchased from J. R. Baylor, Mr. Reynolds paying in part with a negro girl, valued at $1,000, and giving the difference in gold. Young Reynolds was then about sixteen years old, and materially assisted his father in looking after the cattle.

GEO. T. REYNOLDS

George T. Reynolds secured his first start in business by conveying mails for the government from Palo Pinto to Weatherford. Thirty or forty miles was covered on each trip, and he usually rode his pony at night to avoid meeting hostile Indians. When eighteen years of age he enlisted in the Confederate army and served until 1863, when he was severely wounded and received an honorable discharge to return home. In 1865 he made his first venture as a cattle speculator, purchasing 100 steers which he drove to Mexico and sold at a good profit. In 1866 he rented the Stone Ranch in Throckmorton county and started in the cattle business on a larger scale. In an Indian fight near the south of Double Mountain Fork in 1867 Mr. Reynolds received a serious arrow wound. The shaft was removed but the arrow remained imbedded in the muscles of his back for sixteen years.

Mr. Reynolds was extensively interested in cattle and land in Throckmorton and Shackelford counties, and owned a large ranch in North Dakota, near the mouth of the Yellowstone River. He assisted in the upbuilding of Albany, Texas, organized the First National Bank of

Albany, of which he became president, and was also connected with banks in Oklahoma.

COLONEL ALBERT G. BOYCE

The subject of this sketch was born in Travis county, Texas, May 8, 1842, and his life was one of thrilling events in which courage, perseverance and fair dealing were manifested to a marked degree. His parents moved to Texas from Missouri in 1839, and located in Travis county. In 1853 the family moved to Round Rock, Williamson county, and thence to Burnet county, where the elder Boyce and his four sons established a ranch and farm, and were among the first to turn the sod and plant the Golden corn. Indian raids were frequent in those days and the Boyces could be depended upon at all times when courage and endurance were in demand. At the age of nineteen Albert G. Boyce enlisted in the Confederate army and spent four years of hard soldier life. He first saw service under Captain Nick Darnell, serving in the Mississippi department. He took part in several engagements, was captured at the fall of Arkansas Post, and was imprisoned several months at Fort Douglas, Chicago. He was afterwards exchanged, and was in General Bragg's Division, where he was wounded at Chickamauga in 1863. When able to travel, he was given a parole and walked the long distance back to his home in Texas. He afterwards was in General Ford's command on the Rio Grande, under D. M. Wilson, and was

ALBERT G. BOYCE

in the last battle of the Civil War, which was fought between Banks' soldiers and the Confederates on the old battlefield of Palo Alto, April 13, 1865, four days after the surrender of General Robert E. Lee.

After the war Colonel Boyce embarked in the cattle business. He was one of the few men who drove a herd of Texas cattle to the California coast in 1867. The trip required two years, and the entire route was fraught with great danger from hostile Indians and bands of outlaws. In 1887 he took up his residence on the Staked Plains of Texas, as manager of the XIT Ranch, the largest in the world, composed of 3,000,000 acres. He was in active management of this ranch for eighteen years.

On December 20, 1870, he was happily married to Miss Annie E. Harris of Round Rock, Texas. Six children were born to this union. Mr. Boyce died at Fort Worth, January 13, 1912.

BORN IN A LOG CABIN

G. O. Burrow, Del Rio, Texas

I was born in Marshall county, Mississippi, near Holly Springs, in a double log house (it was not a disgrace to be born in a log cabin in those days) in 1853. I lived in Mississippi until 1867. My father came home out of the war, sold what few things the Yankees had left us and moved to Texas.

My first recollections were of war times, as there were two or three battles fought right around where I lived. When we came out to Texas to Ellis county where Farris now stands, I heard so much of the West that I lit out for the West. I went to Fort Griffin where I went to work for Jim Browning, who afterwards became Lieutenant-Governor of the state, but at that time neither he nor I knew that Texas had a capital.

I had my share of hardships running from Indians and being about as scared as a fellow could be, and I had my times running out of saloons and gambling houses when some fool would start to shooting.

I left the Northwest and came to the Leona, in Zavalla county and went to work for Mont Woodward. I went up the trail eighteen different times. My first trip was in 1878 or 1879, I forget which. In 1875 I brought cattle to this county, Val Verde (Kinney then), for Mont Woodward.

I married here in 1877, and raised three children, one boy and two girls. My wife and boy are both dead, and I am just waiting for the Master to call me. The only real enjoyment I have is our reunions of the Old Trail Drivers.

SIXTY YEARS IN TEXAS, AROUND GOOD OLD SAN ANTONIO

Jesse M. Kilgore, San Antonio, Texas

My father, J. J. Kilgore, came from Mississippi to Texas in 1850, bringing with him slaves and coming through in ox-wagons. He bought land and settled on the Cibolo in Wilson county, five miles above the old Carvajal Crossing. Jose Luis Carvajal was living there then, having settled there in 1830. Afterward other settlers moved in, among them being Isaac Butler, Joe Gouger, Geo. Hutchins, Bill Canfield, Sam Edmontson, and a few other people.

My father went into the stock business and was very successful. His brand, the old JK, was known far and near. When the Civil War broke out he joined Captain Duncan's company in San Antonio and served throughout the war, part of the time as flag-bearer. When he returned home there were not many cattle left.

In 1873 or 1874 a party of us followed a bunch of

cattle rustlers from Gonzales county, in the West Hardin community. In our crowd were Jim Sutton, Fred House, Tom Patton, Belger Baylor, J. J. Kilgore, Emil Neil and myself. We overtook the rustlers at Leon Springs, now Camp Stanley, with 350 head of cattle belonging to cattlemen throughout our section of the country, and we captured the whole outfit about sundown. After guarding them all night we took them to San Antonio and turned them over to the sheriff. The following day

JESSE M. KILGORE

we drove the cattle back below Floresville and turned them loose. The leader of the gang was convicted and sent to the penitentiary for six years, but was pardoned shortly afterwards.

In 1871 my father went up the trail with a herd, his straight mark and brand. He came back with his outfit, horses and wagon. With him came Dick Crew, whose native state was Ohio. Dick lived with us quite awhile and we thought it strange that a man from the north could ride and rope so well. I would like to know what became of him. We all thought a great deal of Dick Crew.

In 1875 we left the Cibolo, in Wilson county, with 2,100 head of mixed cattle going West. We followed the Cibolo as far as Selma in order to have water. From Selma we crossed the Salado at the old Austin Crossing, then to the head of the San Antonio River where Brackenridge Park is now located, where we watered. Then went on to Leon Springs. The next water at San Geronimo, then Pipe Creek, and from there to Bandera, following the Medina River up to the present site of Medina

City. Here we held the cattle and rested for a month. The cattle were sore-footed from traveling over the rocks, and the horses were skinned and poor; in fact some of them died afoot, and during the time we rested we sent back to the ranch for fresh horses. After breaking camp we followed the West Prong of the Medina River to its head, where we made another stop to rest. We were then on the divide. Leaving there we went out by the Frio Water Hole, and on to the Frio River where we again stopped, men and horses all in. Charles L. Kilgore, Joe Crossley and myself intended to start a ranch, but did not fancy the rocks.

The Indians came frequently with the moon, but so far had given us no trouble. No doubt they had sized up our horses, concluded they could not use them and passed them up as too poor.

The following winter we gathered up and went to Frio county, about one hundred miles south of where we were. After two days' travel down the Hondo, fifteen redskins came by our old camp in behind us. A man named Phillips ate dinner with us and started back to Bandera and was killed and scalped by those Indians. No doubt they saw our herd and passed us somewhere near Frio City. We had eight men in our crowd, John J. Strait, John Muhr, Price Preston, Charles L. Kilgore and myself, and others whose names I cannot recall. It is believed that the Indians thought our party too large to attack. Brother Charles and myself are the only members of that party that I know of who are still living. Reaching Frio county we bought land and fenced it with timber, like all the pastures were fenced in those days. Wire fences were then unknown.

About the last raid made by the Indians near Frio City was in 1877, when a band of redskins passed through the Oge and Woodward pasture five miles from Frio City. Louis Oge, Cav. Woodward, Bill Henson and two Mexicans took their trail, sending one Mexican to town to notify the citizens, and requesting help to meet them at the Votaw pens on Elm Creek. Some thought it was done to break up a dance that was coming off, so we did not go. During the afternoon another Mexican brought word that Oge and the others were fighting the Indians, so we rushed out there but arrived too late as they had fled, leaving forty-six head of stolen horses. There were ten Indians in the band. Some of the horses belonged as far up as Bandera. After the fight was over we had our dance.

Afterwards Billie Parks and the boys on the Leona killed an Indian. This was about the winding up of the Indian raids in this section.

Shortly after this Joe Crossley was killed at Uvalde by Sam Griner, and later Griner was killed.

In 1893 Chas. Kilgore and myself bought and drove 330 ewes to the Pecos River, and located a ranch fifty miles west of Fort Lancaster. Jack Sheppard was a third partner. We were three months on this trip. We had a hard time crossing the Pecos River. It sure tries a man's patience to make such an undertaking as we attempted. You can't belong to the church and swim sheep across a stream. Only by the help of Halff's cowboys were we able to get those sheep across, otherwise we would have stay on this side. They were like the old timer—can't make him "take water over the bar." Finally we sold out and quit the Pecos, going as far as Fort Worth, later selling out there and came back home. Fort Worth was quite a small place then. In Volume I of this book our president, George W. Saunders, in his write-up of the settling of this country, and the hardships the people endured during those times, did not exaggerate in the least. His memory is wonderful, and the only thing he forgot to mention was about our living on "jerked" beef, and how old he was when he first saw any flour. I know I was a good sized boy before we had any flour. My father owned the first cooking stove and buggy on the Cibolo. Our few neighbors came over to see our stove and, of course, pronounced it a fake, but it was not long until the old skillet was cast aside and stoves were plentiful.

I first saw the light in Texas in 1854. I have two brothers living, Chas. L. and J. K. Kilgore. Have three sisters dead. Ella, the oldest, married L. H. Browne. They had two sons, J. L. and N. H. Browne, both of whom are now living in San Antonio. My next sister, Mattie, married J. J. Strait. Both are dead, but are survived by six children: J. B., J. S. and Y. C. Strait, Mrs. Viola Ward, Mrs. Dell Ward, and Mrs. Alma Parr. W. Y. Kilgore, now dead, married Miss Mary Little and has one child living, Mrs. Artie Barnhardt.

In 1879 I married Miss Flora A. Matthews of Palestine, Texas. In 1887 she died at the age of 26 years, leaving two children, both girls, Elna and Callie. Elna married George W. McDaniel, they have three children living; Flora V., Robert G. and Maggie. Callie married first Geo. T. Crusins; they had two children, Geraldine K. and Alton B. Crusins. In 1918 she married Thomas N. Scroggins, a World War veteran and a member of the 36th Division.

I have five grandchildren and one great-grandchild living. We are passing away fast. In a few years we will meet here no more. If it had not been for the president of our association, George W. Saunders, there would have been nothing left for the younger generation to know who opened good old Texas for them to live in.

HARDSHIPS OF A WINTER DRIVE

Alf. Beadle, North Pleasanton, Texas

In January, 1894, Mr. Pruitt, whose ranch is situated twenty-five miles north of Alpine in the Davis Mountains, put up a herd of cattle to be driven up into the

Panhandle country. He hired Tip Franklin, Jesse Parker, Will Heard, myself, George Owens, Jim McMahon,
Jess Pruitt and Will Pruitt;
also a negro cook and negro
horse-wrangler. Jess Pruitt
was boss.

On the second day of February we started out with the
herd in good shape. The first
night out the cattle stampeded several times and kept
all hands up most of the night
as well as the second night.
One day about twelve o'clock
a low cloud was seen in the
north. Some of the boys said

ALF. BEADLE

it was only the sand blowing on the plains, while others
said it was a blizzard coming. We were then going over
the long prairie near the Leon Holes and about 4 o'clock
it struck us. It was a sandstorm and turned to sleeting. We were compelled to stand a midnight guard
with the horses as well as the cattle. The cattle milled
and ran most of the night. Could not bed them at all
and we made slow progress owing to the cold. We got
to the Horse Head Crossing on the Pecos River in the
middle of the afternoon. The river was up and as we
had good protection on that side of the river Jess
stopped there for the night, but on account of the salt
grass he had to double the guards again. Bob the horse-
wrangler was put on guard again. The next morning we
had no horses nor horse wrangler, all were gone. We
found where Bob had burned a rat den and after it had
burned out he raked the ashes away and lay down and
went to sleep. Upon waking up, Bob discovered the
horses were gone and he began hunting for them and got
lost himself. We found him that day about one o'clock
twelve miles up the river with two of the horses. We

were there all the balance of the day getting across the river. Everything went well for several days. The day we went into the TX pasture at the foot of the plains, it began snowing again and we had to water the herd at troughs at some squatters in the TX pasture, and we worked most all day at that. When this was finished our boss ordered us to start on while he would help the cook fill up the water barrel on the wagon. On going upon the plains that night we tried to set a rat den on fire so we could warm, but were so cold we could not strike a match. It was then agreed to go back and tell our boss we could not hold them that night on the plains. Jess quickly agreed with us and we turned the herd loose and struck camp there in the sand hills at the foot of the plains. Every day we would wrap our feet in old gunny sacks and ride the string of fence and keep the cattle turned back as much as possible. One of the hands that worked on the TX Ranch was lost and stayed out all night and had both his feet frozen. We were several days late and as Mr. Pruitt had gone on the train to Midland and could not hear anything of us, he hired a horse at a livery stable and started out to find us. We were out of grub and started the wagon on to Midland after more provisions when they met Mr. Pruitt. He came on and stayed several days with us. When we started to gathering the cattle again, we found most of them and went on with them. Things went smoothly for some time. Our next blizzard was not so bad, as it only rained and drizzled for some time. This was an unusually bad time for moving cattle.

MONT WOODWARD WAS A FRIEND

G. O. Burrow, Del Rio, Texas

Mont Woodward was born in San Antonio about seventy-five or seventy-six years ago; was raised out on the frontier; and was a Confederate soldier. After the war he married Miss Helen Thomas of Austin, moved out on the Leona and lived there for years in ranch business. He drove lots of cattle on the trail, and in 1876, he and Slaughter drove 7,000.

Mont Woodward was an honest cowman. If he promised to brand your calves for you, you could rest assured that he would do it.

His ranch was on the Leona about twenty miles west

MONT WOODWARD   MRS. MONT WOODWARD

of Frio Town, where everyone passing was welcome to stop and rest, sleep and eat.

This little sketch of Mont's life would not be complete without saying something of his wife. When she married Mont Woodward she had never cooked a meal of victuals in her life; she was raised in the city, and came right out on the Leona with him and no man had a better wife than Mont Woodward. She stayed on that ranch as long as eighteen months without seeing any other woman. She sat in her door of the ranch several times and saw Indians rounding up the saddle horses.

Mr. Woodward's ranch was a great stopping place for people going to Carrizo and Eagle Pass, and it made no difference what time of day or night you got there,

Mrs. Woodward would get up and get you something to eat and do it with pleasure.

To show you what our old Texas women were made of, I will say that in 1873, when we were all gone to Kansas the Indians came into the country acting awfully bad. This was the same bunch of redskins that killed old man Massey. Mr. Woodward's father, who lived in Frio Town, went out to the ranch to bring Mrs. Woodward and the children into Frio Town. On the way back they came over a brushy hill out on a prairie and saw five or six Indians coming towards them. Mr. Woodward wheeled the hack around back into the brush and unhitched the horses and told Mrs. Woodward to hide the children. He got his gun and walked out in front and looked around, and there stood Mrs. Woodward with her gun. He said: "Helena, what do you mean out here? Go back to those children." And she answered, "No, I will not. I will stay here with you and fight for those children."

The Indians squabbled around awhile and went off. This only shows what the old frontier women had to go through with. Mrs. Woodward lives at Pearsall now.

Mont Woodward went to Arizona and was brutally murdered for twenty-eight dollars, while giving two tramps a supper.

The world is better off that Mont Woodward lived in it.

DREAM WAS REALIZED

Charlie Bargsley, San Antonio, Texas

I was born near Austin, in Travis county, Texas, July 25, 1867. My father was a native Texan, and was born in 1829. He fought during the Mexican War, and also fought Indians during the Civil War. He was a farmer and stock-raiser, not exactly what you would call a stockman, but he had enough cattle to make a cowboy out of me, and like most young boys of that day and time, the dream of my life was to go "up the Trail" with a big herd of cattle, and the dream of my life was realized in 1883 when I went with John and Bill Blocker. Louis Deets was foreman. Then in 1884 I went with Mayberry

CHARLIE BARGSLEY

Photo Taken at San Antonio Old Trail Drivers' Rodeo in November, 1922, When He Caught His Steer in 7½ Seconds

& Houston. Tom Buntin was foreman as far as Brady City, then he turned back and Andrew Duff, of Santa Anna, went as foreman for the rest of the trip. I will not relate any of my experiences on these trips, but will leave that for the older fellows to do, as I am sure their trips were more exciting than mine.

WHEN HE GOT BIG ENOUGH TO FIGHT, THE INDIANS WERE GONE

W. T. (Bill) Brite, Leming, Texas

I was born in this, Atascosa county, July 24, 1856, and I am now the oldest native-born white man in the county. My father moved from Caldwell county in 1854 and settled seven miles above Pleasanton. This county was then a part of Bexar county, and was organized in 1856.

BILL BRITE

I think he was the first treasurer the county ever had. In the campaign he and Captain Peter Tumlinson were candidates for the position and father was elected. He died in 1859. There were only three children in our family; Charles, four years older than myself; he died in 1911; Dan, two years older than I, died in infancy. My mother moved to Bee county in 1860, and we lived in Beeville for a time during the Civil War. Coffee was then a dollar a pound and lots of people parched meal bran and sweet potato peelings for coffee. Flour bread was unknown to me until about 1867, and the first biscuits I ever saw I thought were about the prettiest things in the world. The only biscuit we had was the little fellow that was always cooked in the middle of three pones of corn-bread baked in a skillet with a lid on it.

Indians were very bad in this country during the Civil War, but when I got big enough to fight them they were all gone. I saw lots of them, but the folks always put me under the bed when the Indians came, so I have never fought any Indians. They would make raids down

into this country every light moon and take out a great
many horses. At that time the country was very thinly
settled and every man that was able was fighting the
Yankees in Arkansas, Mississippi, Tennessee and Virginia. When the war closed there were lots of cattle
here, but no market for them until the drives to Kansas
started in about 1870. Old Man Leroy Pope was about
the first man to drive a herd from Atascosa. He started
from his ranch on the La Partia, where Christine is now
located, with 2,200 big steers, none of them under seven
years old and I think some of them were twelve or fifteen
years old. People in those days called them "scalawags." He got them as far as Positas in Bexar county
when they stampeded and he lost the whole herd. It took
him about thirty days to get those steers rounded up.
I helped in the roundup and we found most of them
twenty-five miles away. Among those who drove herds
from this section in those days were Bennett, Musgrave,
Hines & Murphy, Drake, Gilliland, Jerry Ellis, John
Dewees, Charlie Hines, Mitchell & Presnall, John Camp
and many others. I helped to gather several herds, but
never went up the trail very far. They paid only $30
or $35 per month for hands and I figured that I could
do better on the range, so I stayed here. Some of the
boys who went along never came back. I never liked to
get up and herd cattle at night, so never had any desire
to go to Kansas.

I married in 1879, just forty-one years ago this day,
December 24, 1921, when I am writing this, and there are
fifteen children in our family, nine boys and six girls, all
living, and my wife and I are still hale and hearty. Including grandchildren there are about forty-five members
of our family, and there has been only one death. None
of my boys have ever been sent to the penitentiary or
elected to the legislature, and I think that is a pretty good
showing. I have had a good time all of my life, have had
but few scrapes and what few I did have I always came

out second best. I believe I have had pretty smooth
sailing generally. When broke I could always strike a
friend that would help me up, and most of them were old
trail drivers. May the Good Lord look after them as He
has looked after me, for they are the best people on
earth.

FIFTY CENTS A DAY WAS CONSIDERED GOOD PAY

Louis and Joseph Schorp, Rio Medina, Texas

Louis Schorp and Joseph Schorp were born and
raised at Castroville, in Medina county, Texas. They

JOSEPH AND LOUIS SCHORP, Rio Medina, Texas

went to school there until they were sixteen years of age,
then were sent to St. Mary's College in San Antonio
where they received the finishing touches to their education. After they returned home from College they
went to work on their father's farm and looking after
his cattle. The plowing was done with oxen, which were
also used for freighting and hauling of the farm products
to San Antonio. The last hauling these brothers did
with ox teams was in 1878 when they hauled rock and
sand to build the Medina county court house and jail at

Castroville. In 1893 the county seat was moved to Hondo. When these brothers had no work on the farm and on the range they would hire out at whatever they could get for their work. Fifty cents a day was considered good pay. During the seventies they helped to round up steers for the trail drivers. Their father had about 500 head of cattle and they always had some of their own to sell. In the late eighties they purchased land on the line of Frio and La Salle counties and located a ranch, which they still own.

WHEN THE ELEMENTS WEPT AND SHED TEARS

W. F. Fielder

I was born in Neshoba county, Mississippi, November 9, 1857, and landed on Seal's Creek, near Prairie Lea in Caldwell county, Texas, in the spring of 1867, coming with my parents overland in a wagon drawn by oxen. My first experience with cattle was rounding up a bunch of milk cows with my uncle, Matthew Clark, Bill Butler and Frank Polk. In those days the cows were not heavy milkers, and it required from thirty to fifty cows to give sufficient milk for a good sized family; and they raised families then, although they seem to have gotten away from the habit now. On those roundups my hardest job was to keep up with the crowd. My uncle promised me a nice two-year-old heifer on one condition, that I keep up with the bunch and not make so much noise when I got out of sight.

My first real job was herding sheep for Lee Holms near Prairie Lea. There were about 500 head in the herd, and I stayed on the job five months, or until he sold them in the spring of 1872. I formed a partnership with Tully Roebuck and we went into the cattle business. I soon got tired of mavericking and sold my interest to Tully in the spring of 1876, and went to work for my

uncle, J. K. Blount, in Kendall county. He was buying
cattle for Ellison & Dewees. I helped him for awhile,
then went to work for A. J. Potter, the "fighting parson," who had a contract to gather a lot of cattle for
Louis Heath which had been turned loose to winter on
the Cibolo. We were about a month on that job and delivered them to Jim Bandy and he drove them up the
trail. I next worked with Jake Tally, who was buying
cattle for Jim Ellison, and was with him until the spring
of 1877, when I agreed to go up the trail with Uncle
Nat Ellison. We met at his home the first of March of
that year, and went to the Guadalupe Pasture below
Seguin to receive our herd. The winter had been dry
and cold, the cattle were poor and were dying in such
numbers that the three men in charge of the pasture were
considerably behind on skinning, so we went to skinning
too and it wasn't long before it looked like our herd
would all be hanging on the fence. There were about 300
acres fenced with rails and we had that fence pretty well
covered with hides. However, about the first of April
we began to round up the cattle that looked like they
could pull through, getting about 2,600 out of the 4,600
that had been put in there in the winter. We moved out
and stopped on the prairie near Lockhart for about ten
days, and while we were there the hostler quit and Mr.
Ellison asked me if I would look after the horses until
he could get another hostler. I accepted the job and
after a few days I told him if it was satisfactory with
him I would just stay with the horses. They were so
poor and sore-backed I thought the hostler had a better
chance to ride than the boys with the cattle on the trail,
and I had caught up with my walking while herding
sheep. When we left Lockhart the outfit consisted of
N. P. Ellison, boss; W. E. Ellison, E. F. Hilliard, E. M.
Storey, Albert McQueen, Ace Jackson, John Patterson,
G. W. Mills, myself, a negro named Luther Merriweather
and a negro cook named McStewart. Our first trouble

was at Maze Prairie where we had our first stampede. The cattle got scared on the opposite side of the wagon from where we were sleeping and came directly toward us. The awful noise of their tramping feet and the rattling of their horns naturally stampeded the sleeping boys and they all broke for the wagon seeking safety. The excitement was only momentary for in a little while all hands were mounted and after the cattle. We soon had them circling and in a few hours they had quieted down on the bedground. Hilliard was complaining awfully with his head, claiming that I had ran over him in the excitement and stamped him over the eye with my boot heel. The boys got a lantern to see how badly hurt he was. They found a circle over his eye, showing that in his fright he ran against the spindle of the axle of the wagon instead of being run over by me. Hilliard claimed he was not frightened, and the verdict was that the wagon became frightened and ran over him. Everything went well for a few days, and then it began raining, and more trouble was in store for us. The elements seemingly selected the night time to do the weeping and tear-shedding act, and just at the time when the tired cowboy was sleeping and dreaming of home and sweetheart, the cattle would become restless and all hands would have to get up and get around them to prevent stampedes.

When we reached the Colorado River it was up and we had to swim it. We went on to Lampasas, Buffalo Gap and Fort Worth, which place was then just a small town. The grass was fine there and we grazed them right up to the depot and down the Trinity River. When we reached Red River it looked like a young ocean, so we camped on Panther Creek, which was rightly named for the screaming of panthers at night sounded as though there must have been several hundred of them. It was on this creek that our worst stampede occurred. They started about 1 o'clock at night and the next morning at daylight we were short 2,200; we had only 400 head. In a few days we had about all of them under herd again, so we put them into the Red River and they went right across. We crossed at Red River Station, and when we got into the Indian Territory we found the grass fine and the cattle and horses began to fatten. You could see their hides moving away from the bones, but the elements didn't let up their tear-shedding job, and in those "diggin's" it thundered and lightninged so it was hard to tell whether it was thundering at the lightning or lightning at the thunder. It did both to a chilly finish, and these storms had a tendency to make a fellow feel homesick.

The saddest sight I saw on the trail was at a place where we had stopped to camp. We spied a little mound of fresh earth and a pair of new-made boots sitting by it. It showed the last resting place of some poor cowboy.

A few days after crossing the Washita River our boss received instructions to turn the herd over to Giles Fenner, and to bring his outfit to Dodge City. Four days later we met Little Jim Ellison, son of the owner of the herd, who advised the boss that they would not need his outfit any longer, and wanted him to take the outfit back to Texas. Green Mills, Zeke Hilliard and Albert McQueen each bought a horse from the boss and went on, taking a chance on getting a job after reaching Dodge City. The rest of us turned our noses southward and landed back at Lockhart about the middle of August.

SKETCH OF CAPT. JAMES D. REED

Lou Best Porter, Mountainair, New Mexico

Capt. J. D. Reed, better known in the old days as "One Armed Reed," was born in Alabama in 1830. His parents moved to Mississippi when he was a small child, and remained there until he was about fifteen years old, then came to Texas with George W. Saunders' father, and settled in Goliad county. When the Civil War

started he enlisted in Capt. Scott's Company, Curtis'
Regiment, and was commissioned first lieutenant. At
Arkansas Post in 1863 he was wounded and taken prisoner. The wound caused him
to lose his arm. After he was
exchanged he returned to
Goliad county and organized
an independent company and
served his country until the
close of the war.

In 1867 he married Miss
Georgia Best, and for several
years worked for wages, buying cattle for other parties,
finally deciding if he could
buy successfully for others he
could buy successfully for

CAPT. J. D. REED

himself. He was one of the first to commence driving
after the war, and drove to Powder Horn, and Louisiana,
and later to the Kansas markets.

In 1877 Captain Reed moved his family to Fort
Worth, and bought a ranch in Stonewall county, placing
Jack Best in charge of it. In 1883 he sold this ranch and
his cattle and went to New Mexico and stocked it with
cattle. He placed Jack Best in charge of this ranch also.
In most of his ventures he was successful and was often
called the Cattle King of the West. He died in New
Mexico in 1891. His wife died in Los Angeles, California, in 1919.

A TRIBUTE TO THE CHARACTER OF WILLIAM BUCKNER HOUSTON

By Thomas H. Lewis

William Buckner Houston was born in DeWitt
county, Texas, May 6, 1852, son of James A. and Julia
Harris Houston. He departed this life at his residence
in Gonzales, on the 22nd day of December, 1916.

James A. Houston was born in Mecklenburg, North Carolina, and in the early settling of Mississippi his father, Robert B. Houston, immigrated to that state with

WM. B. HOUSTON

James and four other children. There he became an extensive planter and slave owner. James A. Houston was educated in Oxford University, Mississippi, and just after completing his course became impressed with the idea and determination to seek his fortune in the southwest, at that time considered the land of promise, of adventure and romance, and so he came to Texas. In his new home he turned his attention to farming and stock-raising, and in 1848 married Miss Julia A. Harris, daughter of Hon. Buckner and Nina Steel Harris. Judge Harris was prominent in the early days of Mississippi in law and statecraft, and was closely related to that eminent lawyer and judge, Hon. Wiley P. Harris, Chief Justice of the Supreme Court of that state. James A. Houston bought a home in Gonzales county in 1863, but died before he came into possession. Of Southern blood, of Southern thought, sentiment and feeling, he had enlisted in the armies of the Confederacy, but was prevented by ill health from participating in active service. Shortly thereafter he died, leaving a wife and six children. William Buckner Houston was the third child and is the subject of this sketch.

On January 20, 1884, the subject of this tribute was married to Miss Ada Lewis, daughter of Judge Everett and Alice J. Lewis of Gonzales, Texas. One child, Ada Lewis Houston, was born to this union. Mrs. Houston died January 5, 1889. Mr. Houston was again married and selected as his second wife, Miss Sue Jones, daughter of Captain August H. Jones, a gallant soldier of the Mexican War, and Minerva Lewis Jones. Of a Southern ancestry, his lines were cast upon a stage of action harking back as a connecting link between the days of the old South and the more recent of the pioneer days which have made Texas the most prosperous and most progressive of states constituting the old Southland. Born in Texas, and bred in the wholesome, manly, broadening and liberalizing atmosphere of the Southwest, he developed a love for Texas, and things indigenous to her soil, as tenaciously patriotic as that of a Scotchman for his favorite meadows and moorland, his forests and fens and highland crags.

Mr. Houston was a man of large stature and commanding presence, remarkable for his clear logical thinking, a leader among his business associates and friends, so much relied upon by them that they fondly called him "General."

In politics he was a Democrat, in religious affiliation a Baptist, fond of a practical joke, possessing a large fund of humor, a mimic beyond compare in portraying the eccentricities of human nature, generous to the needy and distressed, without show or demonstration, and in his daily walk of life and in his dealing with his fellows, an upright man.

While proud of his birth and lineage, and prizing most highly the inheritance of blood, breeding and a good name, he himself was a man of action and impatient of those who in their own life could only borrow and not reflect as much light as they received from a noble past. "Be an ancestor, not forever boasting one," seemed to be his motto.

Educated in the schools of Gonzales county, he received his broader culture in the open and under the star-lit canopy of the ethereal blue, where heavens declare the glory of God, and the firmament showeth His handi-

work in the rugged and the rough experiences of daily
life. If the poet was right in saying the chiefest study
of man is man, then, where others became technical in
colleges that teach the stress and strain of steel, to weigh
with chemistry the material atoms, and to measure the
heat of the sun and the distance of the stars, he became
technical with rare exactment in his appraisement and
estimates of men, for man was his study. He studied the
elements and the character that go to make up a man, as
measured by the yard stick of those who have achieved
the most, thought the noblest, and governed themselves
the most perfectly.

Thrown on his own resources, without means, at the
early age of nineteen, he branched out for himself in
the cattle business, living chiefly on the range, breathing
the fresh air of the open and communing with nature at
first hand, developed a self-reliance which with native
endowments of mind, keen perceptions and decisive judg-
ments of things, of affairs, of human nature and of men,
made him the master of his fate, with the result that
wealth with honor was easily acquired and accumulated
to comfort those dependent upon him.

Could from the tomb the lips of him in whose honor
this tribute is written make answer to this inquiry, What
did you in this life most value, and by what chart did
you steer your course of action over life's sea? I am of
the unalterable conviction he would quickly answer:
Loyalty. Loyalty in all its ramifications and in all that
trust and confidence, loyalty to the highest conception of
honor's code, loyalty to the principles of justice and right
and fair play, loyalty to one's dignity, manhood and self-
respect, loyalty as a son, as a father, as a husband, and
brother, loyalty as a friend.

Fidelity has been defined by one as the conformity
of our actions to our engagements whether express or
implied, if in such case love is added to fidelity it becomes
loyalty.

This dominant trait of his character has been the wonder and admiration of his friends as they beheld his tender solicitous care for the gray-haired mother, his devotion to those he honored with the name of wife, his tender watchful care for his only child and the regardful concern and sympathetic interest in those whom he classed as friends. This trait made him to be recognized as a man in whom the fullest confidence could be reposed in whose bosom friendship could not be betrayed. This commendable trait bound to him, naturally, numerous

A MULE PACK TRAIN IN THE MOUNTAINS

friends, staunch and true. No deaf ear was turned to any appeal made in the name of friendship; nothing he could do was left undone at the behest of a friend; his time, his energy, his effort, influence, his credit, all were at the disposal of him who in his thought was worthy to be called a friend.

Let the drum sound a muffled note, the evening of life has come, his day is done, his sun is set. His spirit has taken its flight to its God. But his memory triumphant like the streamers and afterglow of an Italian sunset on a golden day, remains to remind those of us who look up and higher that a right life may be rightly lived.

SERVED WITH LEE AND JACKSON

J. C. B. Harkness, Pearsall, Texas

I was born in Green county, Alabama, July 23, 1842. Enlisted in the Confederate army in March, 1861, in Company "C," 11th Alabama Regiment. Was assigned to the army of Northern Virginia, commanded by Generals Robert E. Lee and Stonewall Jackson. Engaged in

J. C. B. HARKNESS

more than twenty battles. Was appointed captain of my company to date from the great Battle of the Crater at Petersburg, Va. Recommended by Generals Mahone and Sanders. I remained in the service until the close of the war. Came to Texas in 1874, and went up the trail to Ogallala for Slaughter & Woodard in 1876, with Allen Harris in charge. Owing to the mode of handling cattle like an army it was no new job to me. Returned to Frio county in 1877, and was elected sheriff of Frio county in 1878 and served in that capacity for ten years. Waiting in Pearsall for Gabriel to "toot his horn" but not by invitation from me.

HARROWING EXPERIENCE WITH JAYHAWKERS

The following account is by J. M. Daugherty, of Daugherty, Texas, a charter member of the the Old Trail Drivers. He is better known to all cattlemen as Uncle Jim Daugherty, and is one of the best known Texas cattlemen still in the business. At present he is sole owner of the Figure 2 Ranch, located in Culberson and Hudspeth counties, Texas, estimated to be the largest and best equipped ranch in Texas. He maintains his head-quarters at Daugherty, Texas. Uncle Jim has made many trail drives, starting as a boy in his teens in 1886 and continuing until 1887, during which time he has driven many trails and deliv-ered many herds to all parts of Kansas, Nebraska, the Dakotas, Montana, Wyoming, Utah and Colorado:

"In the spring of 1866 I made my first trail drive. Starting from Denton county, Texas, with a herd of about 500 steers and five cow hands and myself, I crossed Red Riv-er at a crossing known at that time as Preston. From there I drove to Fort Gibson, In-

J. M. DAUGHERTY

dian Territory, and from Fort Gibson I drove to Baxter Springs, Kansas, close to the Kansas and Indian Terri-tory line. I had started to Sedalia, Missouri, where I intended shipping the cattle by rail to St. Louis. On arriving at Baxter Springs I found that there had been several herds ahead of me that had been disturbed by what we called at that time Kansas Jayhawkers, and in one instance the Jayhawkers had killed the owner, taken the herd, and ran the rest of the cowboys off. This herd belonged to Kaynaird and was gathered in the southern part of the Choctaw Nation in the Indian Territory.

After hearing this news I decided to stop and lay up for awhile, and stopped with the herd on what was then known as the Neutral Strip, a strip of land about twenty miles wide that ran across the northern part of the Indian Territory, next to the Kansas line. Here I left the herd and my cowboys and I started to ride alone up the trail to investigate conditions.

I rode as far as Fort Scott, Kansas, and there I met a man by the name of Ben Keys, whom I told I had a herd on the Neutral Strip I would like to sell. He agreed to buy them if I would make deliverance at Fort Scott, Kansas. I returned to the Neutral Strip and we started driving the herd north along the Kansas-Missouri line, sometimes in the state of Kansas and sometimes in Missouri. From the information that I had received regarding the big risk we were taking by trying to drive through, we were always on the lookout for trouble.

Some twenty miles south of Fort Scott, Kansas, and about four o'clock one afternoon a bunch of fifteen or twenty Jayhawkers came upon us. One of my cowboys, John Dobbins by name, was leading the herd and I was riding close to the leader. Upon approach of the Jayhawkers John attempted to draw his gun and the Jayhawkers shot him dead in his saddle. This caused the cattle to stampede and at the same time they covered me with their guns and I was forced to surrender. The rest of the cowboys stayed with the herd, losing part of them in the stampede. The Jayhawkers took me to Cow Creek which was near by, and there tried me for driving cattle into their country, which they claimed were infested with ticks which would kill their cattle. I was found guilty without any evidence, they not even having one of my cattle for evidence. Then they began to argue among themselves what to do with me. Some wanted to hang me while others wanted to whip me to death. I, being a young man in my teens and my sympathetic talk about being ignorant of ticky cattle of the south diseasing any of the cattle in their country caused one of the big Jayhawkers to take my part. The balance were strong for hanging me on the spot, but through his arguments they finally let me go.

After I was freed and had joined the herd, two of my cowboys and I slipped back and buried John Dobbins where he fell. After we had buried him we cut down a small tree and hewed out a head and footboard and marked his grave. Then we slipped back to the herd. This being soon after the close of the Civil War, the Jayhawkers were said to be soldiers mustered out of the Yankee army. They were nothing more than a bunch of cattle rustlers and were not interested about fever ticks coming into their country but used this just as a pretense to kill the men with the herds and steal the cattle or stampede the herds. After rejoining the herd I found that during the stampede I had lost about one hundred and fifty head of cattle, which was a total loss to me. I drove the balance of the herd back to the Neutral Strip, and after resting a day or two, went back to Fort Scott, and reported to Mr. Keys what had happened. Mr. Keys sent a man back to the herd with me to guide us to Fort Scott. On my return to the herd with the guide we started the drive to Fort Scott the second time. The guide knew the country well, which was very thinly settled. We would drive the herd at night and would lay up at some secluded spot during the day. After driving in this manner for five days and five nights we reached Fort Scott about daybreak of the fifth night and penned the cattle in a high board corral adjoining a livery stable, which completely hid them from the public view. We put our horses in the livery stable, and went to a place Mr. Keys had provided for us to sleep and get something to eat, as we had left our chuck wagon a day behind us on the trail. As soon as the cattle were penned Mr. Keys paid me for them. Then we ate our breakfast and slept all day. When darkness fell we saddled our horses and started back over the trail to Texas. I returned to Texas without any further incident worth noting, and continued to drive the trail, rarely missing a year that I did not make a drive.

MAJOR GEORGE W. LITTLEFIELD

The passing of Major Geo. W. Littlefield in November of 1920 took from the cattle industry of Texas one of its most spectacular figures for Major Littlefield's life was really a section of Texas history. A connecting of

the hardships and chivalry of the days of the trail to the wonderful development and progress. In each section he acted well his part. He was not lucky in the shirkers' idea of the word. From boyhood he worked with unremitting diligence and saved part of what he made.

His early life was spent largely on the free and open

GEORGE W. LITTLEFIELD

range—a life that is conducive to fairness in a deal, loyalty to comrades. Both of these attributes Major George W. Littlefield had to a great extent.

Major Littlefield was born in Mississippi, June 23, 1842, but came with his parents to Texas when only eight years old. True to his ideals he enlisted in the Confederate Army when only eighteen as second lieutenant. On May 1, 1862, he was made first lieutenant, and within a few days rose to the rank of captain of his company which was a part of the famous Terry's Texas Rangers. He was promoted to Major on the battlefield for exceptional bravery in action. A severe shrapnel wound disabled him and he was sent home to Gonzales.

It was here he embarked in the cattle industry that proved the golden trail for him. His first money was invested in land which became the nucleus for the famous Yellow House Ranch in Lamb county. Later he bought other land and established other ranches in Texas and New Mexico. From the longhorn of the range he bred up to the very best type of Hereford. In the good old days from five to six thousand calves were branded on his ranch every year.

Major Littlefield moved to Austin in 1883, and from that time he conducted his enormous business interests from Austin. In 1890 he opened The American National Bank in Austin with a capital less than $100,000. It has grown and expanded until now its resources are over $10,000,000. With the expansion a bank home commensurate with the dignity of the business became necessary and the Littlefield Building on Sixth and Congress became a monument of his business success and enterprise. The splendid nine-story building of steel and brick with trimmings of gray Texas granite and terra cotta is fireproof throughout. It is equipped with two 16-passenger elevators. The wainscoting of the main corridor is of Pavonazzi marble in frames of verde antique. The corridors and floors including the bank are of tile. But the bank was his pride. In it he builded the memories of a life time. The huge bronze doors of the main entrance are of bronze representing actual scenes on Major Littlefield's ranch and the door handles are steers' heads. *The Financier* of New York featured these doors as a frontispiece saying they "were the most famous bronze doors in America. That other doors featured carnage and destruction but these doors represented a great industry." On the exquisitely tinted walls the mural paintings depict scenes from Yellow House Ranch and an apple orchard from his ranch near Roswell. A huge American Eagle sent from one of the ranches stands guard with outstretched wings over the main entrance exemplifying one of Major Littlefield's strongest characteristics, Loyalty. During the late war Major Littlefield gave his money without stint to the Red Cross, and bought Liberty Bonds in sums that made the uninitiated gasp. They were only outward expressions of this brave old soldier who chafed that he could not join the fray in person.

Major Littlefield's palatial home adjoins the University of Texas campus—nay, is now a part of it and he learned to love this institution of learning as if it was a favored child. Specially was he interested in the Department of Southern history, that future generations might look with pride on the deeds of the Southland. His bequests from time to time grew into the goodly sum of nearly three millions, the Wrenn Library, his personal gift, makes the name of Littlefield known on two continents as a philanthropist of a high order.

His gentle little wife, Mrs. Alice Littlefield, lives in his palatial home and her devotion to "George" is as loyal today as when she was a real helpmate to him in days when with other splendid Texans, the Old Time Trail Drivers, builded better than they knew.

Major Geo. W. Littlefield left as trustees for his large estate, men who have been by his side a lifetime—kinsmen tried and true: J. P. White of Roswell, New Mexico, Whitfield Harral of Dallas and H. A. Wroe, president of the American National Bank of Austin, Texas.

KIDNAPPED THE INSPECTORS

Leo Tucker, Yoakum, Texas

I was born October 16, 1851, at St. Mary's, Perry county, Missouri, and came to Texas when a very small child with my parents, Mr. and Mrs. Hilary Tucker. When I was twelve years old I was seized with the desire to travel, and made my first trip from Bovine to San Antonio with a load of government bacon which was to be sent to Fort Smith, Arkansas. This trip required four weeks and the one thing that stands out most vividly in my recollection is the trouble I encountered with Mexicans, when I awoke to find they had stolen my best pair of oxen. This was in 1863.

I began my work with the cattlemen in 1869, going up the trail and serving as cook at a salary of $10 per month, which was later raised to $35. Sitting around the camp-fires and listening to the men tell of their trips caused me to decide that the life of a cowboy was the route I wanted to follow. Fortunately I was associated with a few of the grand old stockmen of Lavaca county, namely, Jim Hickey, John May, Joel Bennett, J. X. May, Bill Gentry, Dick May and A. May, to whose fine charac-

LEO TUCKER

ters I am indebted for that training which carried me through many trying times.

In 1871 I left Bovine, Lavaca county, going out by the Kokernot Ranch, by Peach Creek, passing Gonzales, and Lockhart, and on by Onion Creek; then passing Donohue, the old stage stand, following the trail on by Austin, Round Rock, Georgetown, Waco, Belton, to the left of Dallas, by Sherman, then Gainesville, and crossing Red River out by Carriage Point, by way of Fort Arbuckle into Indian Territory, out by Oswego, Kansas. Here we met a bunch of friendly Comanche Indians who had been out on the banks of the Arkansas River making a treaty with another tribe. Our next place was Ellsworth, Kansas. Here we met George West and a bunch of boys on the trail. As Abilene was the end of our trip I returned home.

In 1872 I made a trip with A. May. This trip nothing unusual occurred, except we met a lot of Osage Indians who had their faces painted. They were great warriors but were afraid to attack a bunch of white men if they were outnumbered.

In 1873 I again started up the trail with my old comrade, D. May. When we reached Red River Station two inspectors came up and looked over our herd and found two unbranded beeves. They told us we would have to pay $50 each for having cattle without a brand. There were thirteen herds belonging to a man named Butler. Mr. Butler instructed the boys to capture the two inspectors and put them in a wagon. They were taken into the Indian Territory, across Pond Creek, where they were turned loose, and they had to swim the creek to get back home. This was the last trouble we had with inspectors.

In 1874 with John May and Joel Bennett, I made one of my hardest and most eventful trips. We left Bovine in February with 3,000 head of cattle and had a splendid drive, with a few mishaps, until we reached Rush Creek. From here we proceeded to Hell Roaring Creek, about fifteen miles north, with a blizzard raging. That night was the coldest I ever experienced. Snow, sleet and ice were one and a half feet deep, and our stock suffered. Our loss was not as heavy as some of our neighbors, under Sol West, whose horses froze under their riders. West, Boyce McCrab and Al Fields lost many of their horses. We went on to Ellsworth, and from there to Norfolk, Nebraska, on the Missouri River. Millett & Mayberry were to receive the beeves here, but made us an offer of $1,000 extra if we would deliver them across the Missouri river to Yankton in Dakota. We would not take the risk of the loss of the cattle as we knew a blizzard might overtake us while the 3,000 beeves were being crossed over. However, we swam them across 75 at a time, the boys using three canoes and kept fighting them in the face with water to keep them from angling across. It was there I first saw a steamboat. It was the *Mary Mag-*

dalen. The next morning a thousand Indians passed us going from Niobrara and going southward. We talked and traded with them through their agent. The squaws had their children strapped to their backs.

At Brookville, Kansas, in 1874, I took charge of 3,000 beeves for Dick May and Bill Gentry, and took them to Shenandoah, Iowa, where I delivered them on Christmas Eve to Mr. Rankin on his large ranch. I experienced many hardships in Iowa on account of the blizzards. In order to secure water for the cattle I had to break ice for over a month. Dick May was taken very sick and I started back with him. When we reached Kansas City we put up at the Lindell Hotel, and were assigned a room on the highest floor, but for some reason or other I objected to it, and we were given a room on the lower floor. We left next morning for Brooksville and when we reached there we learned that the Lindell Hotel had burned down.

The year 1875 marks the end of my going over the famous old trail, with its excitements of killing buffalo and elk, meeting Indians, and swimming streams. I have swam the Red River, often half a mile wide, as many as thirteen times in one day, always going ahead of the herds, and right here will say that after all of my good swimming I was finally nearly drowned in a small creek named Elm near St. Joe. I was asleep when the noise of the rush of water brought about by a cloudburst caused the cattle to stampede. Jumping on my horse I made a dash to cross the stream to get to the cattle when the water swept my horse from under me. Jim Skipworth saw my peril and threw a rope around me and dragged me to shore. After hard work they succeeded in resuscitating me, but I was unconscious all day. My faithful pony was drowned. I made the last trip with May & Hickey, to Ellsworth, Kansas. While we were returning home, and when east of Fort Sill, the Indians got on the warpath on the night of July 24, 1875, and burned all the stage stands from Caldwell, Kansas, to Red River Station in Texas. They rounded up three government wagons, killed the drivers, shot the oxen, burned the wagons, and stole the horses. We crossed the river just in time to miss them and saved our lives.

On October 5, 1875, I was married to Miss Jane Hogan in Yoakum, Lavaca county, and to us were born seven children, all yet living. They are John H. Tucker, Alfred Tucker, San Antonio; Lorena Dullye, San Antonio; Mary Kuenstler, Yoakum; Rosa Dullye, Yoakum; Vira Sheffield, Yoakum; Minnie Buenger, Edna, Texas.

DAVID C. PRYOR

David Christopher Pryor was born on a plantation near Alexandria, Louisiana, March 27, 1850, of Scotch-Irish descent. His parents were David C. and Emily A.

DAVID C. PRYOR

McKissack Pryor. His father died when he was four years of age and his mother four years later. Mr. Pryor was reared by a maternal aunt and uncle jointly in Alabama and Tennessee. In 1870 his eldest brother, A. M. Pryor, then living in Texas, visited relatives in Alabama and Tennessee and advised his brothers, David C. and Ike T. Pryor, to return with him to Texas and seek their fortunes. Immediately on their arrival in Texas, David C. was employed as a cowboy to help drive a herd of cattle up the trail. This occupation appealed to him, so he drove to Western markets for several years. Then came the railroads with rapid transit, and trail driving ceased to be the popular route for marketing cattle, after which time he made his home in Austin, Texas, and in the state of Colorado, following various occupations. Finally in 1889, when Oklahoma was opened for white settlement, he was "on the ground," secured a claim, and has lived there ever since, save a few years in which he managed a West Texas ranch for his brother, Ike T. Pryor. For some years he has been engaged in oil development in Oklahoma. By nature Mr. Pryor is a gentleman of the "Old South"; is well informed on historical and current events, fond of literature, of a literary mind and has written some clever verses. In politics he is a Democrat, takes a lively interest in both State and National politics. While not actively engaged in the cattle business, nothing delights him more than to meet the "boys" of the early seventies and live over the good old days of trail driving, "chuck-wagon eats," night watch and when the Indian and buffalo roamed the plains.

HELPED DRIVE THE INDIANS OUT OF BROWN COUNTY

By J. W. Driskill, Sabinal, Texas

I was born in Missouri on January 15, 1854, and moved to Texas with my father's family in 1858 and settled four miles south of the town of San Marcos.

I made my first trip to Kansas in 1871 with William Hewitt and my father's cattle; in 1872 with West & Musgrove's cattle; in 1873 with Sam Johnston's cattle and my uncle, J. L. Driskill's cattle in 1874 and 1875. Then I quit the trail until 1880.

In the fall of 1875, I moved to Brown county with about three hundred and fifty head of cattle and helped to drive the Indians out of that country. I settled on the Pecan Bayou seventeen miles below Brownwood.

Stayed on the Pecan Bayou forty-two years. That was a good stock country when I moved there. Then I drove mine and my brother's, S. L. Driskill's, cattle. That was a dry year and when I got to the Indian Territory,

J. W. DRISKILL

I had to make a drive of ninety-six hours without water. I thought my time had come, but on the fourth day, just about sundown, I struck water and all the old trail drivers can guess how those cattle looked. I had about fourteen hundred and fifty head, drove them to Dodge City, Kansas, with four men and myself and only lost one cow.

I now live in Uvalde county, at Sabinal. The latch string hangs on the outside of the door and if any old "trail driver" should chance to come this way, stop and see me. I have had many ups and downs in this life but I am proud of one thing: I have plenty to keep me and my wife the rest of our days.

ROBERT E. STAFFORD

Robert Earl Stafford was born March 27, 1834, in Glynn county, Georgia, of English-Welsh descent. His parents were Robert and Martha A. Stafford. He received an academic education at Waynesville, Georgia. His nature was highly unselfish, his mind broad, generous and enterprising, and his spirit courageous. His purse was ever open to the calls of charity and his ear attentive to the appeals of the unfortunate. Having, unaided fought his way, encountering many of the vicissitudes of life, his heart instead of becoming hard and cold was capable of a warmer and wider humanity. December 27, 1854, he was united in marriage to Miss Sarah E. Zouks of Liberty county, Georgia; to this union seven children were born, of which only one survives them. Ambitious and progressive, his attention was attracted to Texas as offering a fine field for financial advancement, so in 1858 he came to this state and located in Colorado county and engaged in stockraising and farming on a small scale. When war was declared between the states in 1861, he joined the Confederate Army as a volunteer in Company B, commanded by Captain Upton, Fifth Texas Infantry, John B. Hood's Brigade. He was as faithful

R. E. (Bob) STAFFORD

a soldier as any who shared the fortunes of that band of veterans. At the close of the war, he like many others, came home penniless, but resumed the conduct of his affairs with an energy that knew no diminution and an ability capable of accomplishing any undertaking.

In the spring of 1869 he drove a herd of cattle to Kansas. This venture proved successful and he enlarged his business by purchasing all the brands in his section that were for sale. In 1872 he entered into a contract with Allen Poole & Co. to supply beef for the Havana, Cuba, market. The returns of his enterprise not being satisfactory he abandoned it and engaged in selling cattle to Western men for Indian contracts. In 1878, when the firm of Allen Poole & Co. failed he bought their cattle, ranches, etc. His fortune increased rapidly and finding it profitable to manage his own exchange in 1882 he organized a private bank, R. E. Stafford & Co., of which he was president and sole owner.

In 1883 the idea occurred to him that it would be profitable to the stockmen of his community to sell dressed beef in Western and foreign markets, so he therefore organized a stock company known as the Columbus Meat and Ice Company. He was unanimously elected president and put in a plant at the cost of $250,000, with capacity of 250 head of cattle and forty tons of ice per day. The company filled an order with an English syndicate and for some time shipped dressed beef to Chicago, New Orleans, Galveston and other points. But the business was not as successful as he desired so he closed the factory, and again confined himself to selling to Western buyers, and shipping from his ranches to New Orleans, Galveston and Houston.

July 7, 1890, about seven o'clock in the afternoon, Robert E. Stafford and his brother John, a partner in many enterprises, although unarmed and unable to defend themselves were slain upon the streets of Columbus, by men, one of whom Robert E. Stafford had befriended. He was a member of the Masonic fraternity and of the Knights of Honor. In politics he was a Democrat and took a deep interest in public affairs. He was many times a delegate to state conventions.

Robert E. Stafford was a devoted husband, kind and loving father, true friend and a citizen above reproach. He did much to develop the section in which he lived.

LAFAYETTE WARD

Lafayette Ward was the son of Lafayette Ward, Sr., a Kentuckian by birth, and Agnes Ward, who were married in Missouri and moved to Texas in 1840 and settled on Carancahua Bay, in Jackson county, where the elder Ward helped make a part of early Texas history. It was here that Lafayette Ward was born in the year 1854. He grew to young manhood under his mother's guidance having lost his father when he was only seven years old. His mother operated a cattle ranch and young Ward grew up in the business, looking after his mother's interests and then began operations for himself when still a young man. His education was received at Concrete and at Salado in Bell county, to which place he rode horseback from the Gulf. In the latter seventies he carried large herds of cattle up the trail, wintering near Dodge City, Kansas. In his later years he was a member of the Old Trail Drivers' Association.

LAFAYETTE WARD

He was married to Miss Lottie B. Compton of Galveston in 1880, and is survived by his wife and two sons, A. P. Ward, and Lafayette Ward, Jr., and one grandson, A. P. Ward, Jr., all of San Antonio, Texas.

Mr. Ward began buying the rich Jackson county lands very early in his career and stocked them with cattle until he owned at one time 76,000 acres in a solid body and at the time of his death still owned 40,000 acres of the choicest lands in the county, in the center of which is located the town of La Ward on the St. Louis, Brownsville and Mexico railroad. In keeping with his naturally progressive nature he was a pioneer in the Gulf Coast country in the breeding up of cattle until today his herds of Herefords and Brahmas are classed among the best in the state.

In addition to his holdings in Jackson county Mr. Ward owned large holdings of city property in San Antonio and a ranch of 18,000 acres in Kimble county and 23,000 acres in Hardeman and Foard counties.

THOMAS JEFFERSON MOORE

Possessed of rare virtues of heart and mind, a personal magnetism rarely met with in life, a personality that stamped him as a man of prominence and a leader in every gathering, the late Thomas Jefferson Moore, of Llano, Llano county, Texas, at the time of his death,

Wednesday, May 31, 1911, was recognized by all as a pre-eminent leader in the livestock world, and one of Texas' great men. Born in Tuscaloosa county, Alabama, March 31, 1847, of good old Irish stock, he came to Texas with his parents, Jefferson Moore and Susan Jeffreys Moore, in 1855. Guadalupe county, near Seguin, was the location selected for the new home, where the elder Moore engaged in farming and stock raising on a small scale.

T. J. MOORE

Endowed at his birth with a splendid constitution and a magnificent brain, young Moore was given the sturdy training of the frontier. Industry and work came to him as a matter of course, and throughout his long and eventful life, he was an indefatigable worker. His business acumen was recognized in every section of the Southwest and many of his associates in the livestock industry came to him for advice which when followed out, almost universally led to success.

At the age of sixteen young Moore joined the Confederate army, enlisting in Captain Nixon's Company, Wood's Regiment, and with this splendid fighting organization he saw service until the close of the war. He never shirked a duty, his bravery was tempered with kindness and generosity and he had many warm friends among the members of his regiment. Seeing the proverbial Irish sense of humor and optimism, he set an inspiring example of cheerfulness under every hardship.

When the war closed, young Moore returned to Guadalupe county, where he worked on his father's farm and engaged in the freighting business with ox teams. This was the only means of distributing merchandise in those days, and the work, while very arduous at times was highly remunerative. His first venture in the cattle business was in the early 70's, when he bought cattle in Blanco county and drove them up the trail to Kansas, where he wintered his stock and sold in the spring. He continued in this work for several years, and his buying and selling of stock reached a point where he handled thousands of head each year. He used the trail for marketing cattle as long as it remained open to the North. In the latter 70's he went into stock raising on a large scale and this was his life occupation. He was a pioneer in stock improvement and early began improving registered bulls, although he made a specialty of prize-winning stock.

His various land and cattle investments were not confined to Texas, where he had extensive possessions in Llano and Webb counties, but in 1889, with John T. Lytle, J. R. Blocker and W. H. Jennings, he purchased more than 500,000 acres of land in Coahuila, Mexico. This tract of land is known as the Piedra Blanco Ranch, and is stocked with thousands of head of high-grade cattle. Captain Lytle died in 1906, when the remaining members bought out his heirs. The Piedra Blanco Ranch is still owned by the T. J. Moore estate, W. H. Jennings and J. R. Blocker. The Piedra Blanco Ranch was a source of much satisfaction to Mr. Moore, and many hours of his last years on earth were spent in mental direction and advisement of procedures on his property.

Mr. Moore became a member of the Texas Cattle Raisers' Association early in its organization and was alive to its interest and progress. Through personal influence and acquaintance he secured a large number of members for the Association among the stock raisers of North and South Texas. As an active worker in the Association he contributed toward the upbuilding of the cattle industry in the Southwest. For many years he was president of the Llano County Bank, of Llano, Texas, which later became the Home National Bank, and in which Mr. Moore was the largest individual stockholder.

Mr. Moore was married to Miss Carrie Roberts, a daughter of Captain and Mrs. Alexandria Roberts, of Blanco county, August 10, 1875. Of this union there was born one child, Edna Jeffreys, who now resides with her mother in the Moore home at Llano. Mr. Moore was reared in the Primitive Baptist faith, and his early Christian training shaped his entire life. His life-long friend, John C. Oatman, pays this tribute to his memory:

"As a husband and father, he was ever loving and tender. To supply their wants and make his wife and daughter happy was the greatest joy. As a friend, he was as true as the magnetic needle to the north star. In the darkest hour of their adversity he stood closest to his friends, and with his money and his counsel he assisted many. We are told in Holy Writ that pure and undefiled religion consisted in visiting the widows and fatherless in their afflictions, and it was in this Godlike and Godgiven trait of character that Tom Moore shined brightest. How many unfortunate, helpless persons he assisted during his life only the Great Father knows. True it is that he never turned any away empty. All this he did for sweet charity's sake, for no one ever heard him boast of what he had done."

WILLIAM G. BUTLER

When the trains began to haul their first long strings of clacking freight cars loaded with cattle, many ranchmen were happy that for their sons the getting of cattle to market in the future would be so simplified. Weeks on the trail, driving their slow moving herds, through days of sun and days of rain, with always nights on the great outside, were now over. But life has a way of compensating, and from these men who had been called on to use the best that was in them of courage and of resourcefulness through those years, there grew a line of sturdy, hardy men who could not have just happened to be as they were. They had been developed.

W. G. BUTLER

Among these Knights of the Cattle Trail—the old trail drivers—was William G. Butler, of Karnes county, known all the way up and down the trail as Bill Butler.

When Texas was young and raw and the bad man seemed ever ready to get the better of the good man, because there were more of them, Bill Butler came with his father and mother, Burnell and Sallie Butler, in 1852 to Texas from Scott county, Mississippi, he being eighteen years old at that time. The trip was made, as were all others in the days before the railroads had come, overland in wagons; there were three ox-drawn wagons, the family and seven negro slaves. At the end of three months they reached the San Antonio River on December 24, 1852. Home was there made, they then began the raising of cattle and the taking up of wild and—then thought to be—almost worthless land.

In 1858 Mr. Butler was married to Miss Adline Burris and they made their home always in the same old county of Karnes, near Kenedy. Their family consisted of Newton G., who died March 12, 1895; Mrs. Helen Nicholes, Mrs. Lou M. Adams, Emmett, who died December 26, 1884; S. C., T. G., Cora, and William G., Jr., who died November 20, 1913. Mrs. Butler, who as a wife and mother was never found lacking in the courage and comfort these early days demanded, died April 7, 1908, and Mr. Butler four years later, June 14, 1912.

When the Civil War broke out, he enlisted and fought through its long years of struggles. Coming home at the close of war he found his cattle had scattered and were suffering from thieving bands who were accustomed to go through the country and drive along all the cattle they could find. One such band he located to the Northwest of San Antonio; gathering a number of men to go with him, they set out to overtake these thieves, the leader of whom was known to him to be as bold as he was evil (bad). Mr. Butler came on them with their big herd of cattle forty-five miles above San Antonio, they being in plain sight in a valley below, and when the thieves saw the pursuing party, they gathered in a group and stopped; the Butler party kept advancing and when not far away the leader boldly spurred his horse forward to meet Mr. Butler who had done the same and they thus came face to face, both being ready for what we of late days would call "an eventuality." The man recognized Mr. Butler and because he was known everywhere as having the courage of a lion and nerve of steel and the most unswerving honesty and justice, the meeting proved to go after this manner: "What do you want, Mr. Butler?" And the answer, "To cut my cattle from that herd," and "It is all right with me, sir," which was done. When some miles from San Antonio on the trip back, they met Buck Pettus and Tom O'Conner going to hunt for the thieves, Mr. Butler had just visited. Mr. Butler was asked to go back with them and, although he was homeward bound with his own cattle and the going back was hazardous, these men were his friends and he turned and went with them, sending his own herd on with his men. This is but an illustration of what it meant to be Bill Butler's friend, and if we were called on to name the dominating trait of this man, we should say "loyalty to a friend." If you were poor or if you were rich; if you were right or if you were wrong, and you were in trouble, he was with you and for you, and there were many men who were better men for having had this trust placed in them. In the early days when life was more often demanded and taken than now, he was ready always to help his friend, even risking his own life; in later years his resources and counsel were as freely given out to a needy friend, and there are many, who becoming stranded through the ceaseless buffetings of an unkind fate or maybe from a sudden stroke of ill fortune, found a new chance given them through Bill Butler's generosity, "for auld times' sake."

His first string of cattle were driven to Abilene, Kansas, from Karnes county in March, 1868, with the following hands: Robert and Wash Butler, his brothers; L. C. Tobin, Buck and Jess Little, John Sullivan, Jim Berry Nelson, Boxie White, John Brady, M. Benavides, Juan Concholer, Juan Mendez, and Levi and William Perryman, the latter two negroes. Only Tobin, Jess Little and the Perrymans survive today. From one to three herds were driven by him every year afterward up to 1886, in some of these he was his own boss and some were in charge of Pleas and Fayette Butler, A. J. (Bud) Jourdon and Alfonso Coy. Some of the herds were driven to Ogallala, Nebraska and Dodge City, Kansas.

For many years he and Major Seth Mabry of Austin, were partners and sent up many herds of cattle. During these years I should estimate that he sent 100,000 cattle up the trails. In Karnes county he owned nearly 75,000 acres of land, had leased 25,000 acres, fenced and stocked with 10,000 head of cattle.

After sixty-five years, there are left of the family who moved to Texas from Mississippi, Pleas Butler of Karnes county, Albert of Bee county, and Mrs. Ruth Burris of Karnes county.

SETH MABRY

SETH MABRY

Major Seth Mabry, who was a major in the Confederate Army during the Civil War, was one of the pioneer drivers of cattle from Texas to Northern markets beginning immediately after the Civil War and success crowned his efforts in this direction. He bought a large ranch in Mason and Kimble counties and built one of the most beautiful homes in Austin, Texas, in the seventies. From Austin he moved to Kansas City at which place he died, leaving a wife and one daughter.

J. B. MURRAH CAUGHT THE MEASLES

Dan Murrah, Del Rio, Texas

In the spring of 1885 I went over the trail from the Williams Ranch in Brown county to Dodge City, Kansas. We had plenty of rain on this trip, and the creeks and rivers were all full and we had to swim. My brother, J. B. Murrah, was boss, and in our bunch were J. R. Murr, John Goode, Lavigor Goode, myself, and a negro

boy named Buck Johnson. When we reached Fort Griffin, J. B. Murrah broke out with the measles, and had to
return home. J. R. Murr took charge. Grass was fine
and our horses fattened every day. As we neared Bear
Creek, we came to where hunters had been in camp and
had just killed a bear. One
foot was lying in the main
trail, and when the horses
smelled the blood they seemed
to telephone to the rear that
they were coming, and they
went. Goode and I were
pointing, and I was riding a
race mare bought from Judge
Vardeman at Gatesville, and
we succeeded in getting to the
top of a hill where we threw
them into a mill and the other
boys brought up the drags.

DAN MURRAH

We reached Dodge City in good shape, and met several
Texas men there, among them Jim Dobie, Bonner, Hawkins, Lemons and others.

MEDINA COUNTY PIONEER

Xavier Wanz, Castroville, Texas

I came to Medina county with my parents from Alsace, France, in the year 1845, with other Castro Colonists, and first settled in Castroville. About a year
afterwards we moved about fifteen miles northwest of
Castroville to what was then known as "Vanderburg,"
and settled down, as I may say, in the midst of a tribe
of tame Indians who had their camps about two miles
from our location. When I was quite a young boy I
remember seeing these Indians coming to our little burg

with venison and bear meat and honey to trade to us for
bread, whiskey and tobacco. In the little settlement of
Quihi, about six miles from Vanderburg, there was a
small saloon, and an Indian went there and got on a
spree. He stayed around for about a week, drunk, but
did not molest anyone. A man named Allen came along
and found this Indian there and killed him without cause,
and from that time on the Indians became hostile and
killed many of the settlers.

My father died while I was quite young, but before

XAVIER WANZ AND ED TSCHIRHARDT

his death he bought two cows, and from this start we
raised a nice stock of cattle. When the Civil War broke
out I joined as a private and remained in the army until
the close of that great struggle. When I returned from
the war I found that our nice stock of cattle had dwindled
down to only a few head. But, not discouraged, I made
another start in that line and after several years of trading, buying and raising I accumulated several hundred
head of cattle and fine horses.

A long time before the Civil War we had to plant and

hoe our corn in the open land, as there were no fences. We had no teams or implements to prepare our land. It was a hard matter in those days to make a living, but we had to pull together—and pull we did. We had no school or church in our neighborhood, none nearer than Castroville, fifteen miles away, and through such misfortune I received no education. I am now 77 years of age. In conclusion I wish to say that I farmed and raised cattle and good horses from the time I was a boy until a few years ago, when I retired and sold my entire stock of cattle, horses and my brands, and divided my ranch lands among my children.

EDITOR'S NOTE. Since the above sketch was written, Mr. Wanz had been "gathered unto his fathers," his death occurring in the fall of 1922.

EXPERIENCES OF A TEXAS PIONEER

By John M. Sharpe

No résumé, writeup or talk on the development of the cattle industry in Texas, or the Northwest for that matter, would be complete without giving considerable space to the achievements of the Snyder Brothers, D. H. and J. W., who have been residents of the state for more than sixty-five years, their operations extending from the Gulf of Mexico to the Pacific slope. While it is almost impossible to speak of the experiences and achievements of the one without the other, for they were not only brothers but steadfast friends and business associates, it is our privilege at this time to speak of a few of the vast

D. H. SNYDER

and ever-changing experiences of Col. Dudley H. Snyder, the oldest brother and senior member of the firm, who was known for more than fifty years in all the great cattle marts of the country as the one man who could, and did, fill his contracts promptly, it mattered not the number of the thousands of head he had agreed to furnish nor the distance it was necessary to traverse in order to make the delivery. There was never any doubt in the minds of the contractors who had purchased cattle from him; they knew that delivery would be made on the day appointed and at the place agreed upon.

Col. D. H. Snyder was born in the grand old state of Mississippi in 1833, the year the stars fell. His father died in 1840, leaving a widow and four children, three sons and one daughter. The father, a prudent business man, had prepared for the eventuality of death, and left the dependent wife and mother in reasonably good circumstances, her property being composed of interest-bearing securities, loans, etc. In 1841, the year following the death of the father, the great panic came upon the Republic and the studied investments of the widow were carried away on the swelling tide of misfortune, leaving the family in circumstances, from a financial standpoint, that were more meager than they had ever known before. Col. Snyder, being the eldest son, assisted in caring for his mother and the younger children, during the years that intervened, and in 1854 he came to Texas by way of Ozark, Ark., and Mansfield, La., having secured a position with a horse dealer who furnished him a horse to ride and the food he ate in consideration of his services with the herd. From this trader, Col. Snyder says he learned one of the most important lessons of his life, "a man never makes money in selling a horse—the money is made in buying it."

Arriving in Texas, his first stop was at Round Rock, in Williamson county, where he visited his grandfather, Dr. Thos. Hade, who also was a pioneer merchant. The good man gave the young grandson a job collecting accounts at ten per cent on the total amount collected. This work carried him on horseback all over Central West Texas, and from the employment he realized a net earning of fifteen dollars per month. Finding this a very slow process toward fortune the young Mississippian concluded he would try farming the next year. Renting some land from one of the settlers in the community where his grandfather resided, he set to work getting things in order to make a crop. He had no team, but succeeded in borrowing one work-ox from a neighbor with which to do his plowing. One not being enough, the resourceful pioneer caught up a wild steer from the range and with the team set to work breaking land and planting his crop. After gathering the crop he secured a team of five yoke of oxen, a heavy wagon and hauled cedar from mills in Bastrop county to Williamson and Travis counties. After that he made several trips to Missouri, returning at intervals with teams and new wagons, and these were loaded with apples and other delicacies unobtainable in Texas, which were sold at a good profit.

Deciding to go into the horse business, Col. Snyder walked to San Antonio where he put all of his earnings into a small herd of Spanish ponies, which he drove to Missouri and exchanged for Missouri horses. These he brought back to Texas, and on account of their size and adaptability as draft horses he sold at good prices and a substantial gain over their purchase price, taking advantage of the valuable lesson he had learned from his first employer, i.e., that the money made in handling horses is to be made on the purchase and not the selling price.

In 1862 Col. Snyder received a proposition from Terrel Jackson, a wealthy planter and land owner of Chappell Hill, Washington county, proposing to put him in charge of a contract to deliver beef cattle to the Commissary Department of the Confederate Army, he having made a contract with Major Ward, of that department, to furnish the Confederate government with thousands of head for the purpose of providing meat for the soldiers. These cattle were driven to a point of delivery under the personal supervision of Col. Snyder through sparsely settled and dangerous country, and in order to reach their destination it was necessary to swim the herd across some of the greatest rivers of the South, one of these being the Mississippi. In order to expedite the work of crossing these rivers Col. Snyder secured two "lead steers" which were trained swimmers, and upon arriving at a stream these water steers would plunge right in and the herd would follow without trouble.

After the close of the war, in which Col. Snyder did valiant service, both as a citizen furnishing beef and as a soldier, he turned his face to the great Northwest, and his herds year after year, in ever-increasing numbers, for more than a quarter of a century, wended their way toward the setting sun, followed by the sturdy cowboys of that day who placed their faith in God, their trusty six-shooter and the "chuck wagon."

In the spring of 1868 Col. Snyder employed Col. W. C. Dalrymple, of Georgetown, a noted scout and Indian fighter, to command his outfit, and with a large crew of cowboys, every one veteran, well provisioned and armed, started Northwest with a herd of fourteen hundred head of cattle. These were secured in Burnet, Llano, and Mason counties and were paid for in gold at the rate of $1.50 per head for yearlings and $2.50 for two-year-olds; $3.50 for three-year-olds and cows and $7.00 for beef steers. On this drive Col. Snyder learned another important and remunerative lesson. It had been the custom of cattlemen when driving large herds of cattle across the unwatered plains to stop and kill all the calves in the herd on the theory that they impeded the progress of the herd and were unable to stand the tortures of thirst. After putting in a day at this gruesome business

Col. Snyder ordered the men to proceed, and the calves reached their destination in as good condition as any of the balance of the cattle, and there were never any more calf-killing days with the Snyder men. The herd was driven through New Mexico and part of them into Colorado, the beef steers being sold at Fort Union, N. M., for $35.00 around, and the balance were finally sold to Goodnight & Curtis at $7.00 per head. This was in many respects, perhaps, the most notable, though not the longest, drive made by this famous stockman, in that the entire herd reached their destination, although the course of the drive led through an Indian infested region and the entire herd of the Chisholm outfit was captured by the redskins just after crossing the Texas-New Mexico border. Col. Snyder attributes this to the presence of Col. Dalrymple, who was a terror to the Indians, and the constant readiness of the entire personnel of the outfit to fight at the very first sign of trouble. So constant were they on the lookout that the drivers of the supply wagons were instructed to throw out any side-arms left in the wagons. This caused the men to always keep their guns in their scabbards, and consequently they were ever ready for any emergency that might arise. At this time there were no ranches from the Concho River to Las Vegas, N. M. The payment for these cattle when sold was made in greenbacks, which at that time was not worth its face value in Texas, and upon arriving home Col. Snyder was compelled to exchange same at seventy-one cents on the dollar, but in spite of all handicaps he cleared five thousand dollars on the trip.

In 1869 the drive to Abilene, Kansas, from Texas through the Indian Territory was made. There were fourteen hundred head in the herd when the drive began, but 140 head were captured by the Indians while passing through the Territory. A neat profit, however, was realized in spite of this misfortune. A claim was placed with the U. S. government for pay for the cattle lost to the Indians, and after the unwinding of much red tape and several years' time, the amount was finally paid. In 1871 and 1872 the drive was made to Wyoming. Cheyenne was then a great and popular trading point. These were uneventful years; the trading was good and all went well with Col. Snyder and his men, but the following year 1873, was to see reverses.

Again in 1873 the Snyder outfit was headed for Wyoming with a splendid herd that it seemed might prove the most profitable of his career up to that time, but alas, upon arriving at his destination he found the greatest panic that the country had ever known in full blast. Friends that were worth millions the week before were almost paupers now—everything had been swept away and bankrupts were on every side. It was a time for cool heads and deliberate action. Col. Snyder made arrangements for money to winter his herd at three per cent per month, thirty-six per cent, per annum. This was dear interest to pay, but the money thus obtained saved himself and his associates. The next year he sold the cattle for $38.00 per head, thus being well paid for the trying experience that he had undergone during the winter previous.

In 1877 Col. Snyder made what proved to be the greatest deal of his experience and began huge operations that led to the making and losing of hundreds of thousands of dollars. A contract was made with J. W. Iliff, then noted banker and ranchman of Denver, who proposed to furnish ninety per cent of the money for the operation, Snyder Bros. to furnish ten per cent and handle all the details of the transaction. Iliff was to receive forty-five per cent of the profits and Snyder Bros. the remaining fifty-five per cent. The contract called for the delivery in Colorado of 17,500 head of two and three-year-old steers, and not only was this contract fulfilled, but a total of 28,000 head were handled by these wizards of the cattle industry before the season closed.

Before the contract was completed Mr. Iliff died and upon request of Mrs. Iliff, Col. Snyder closed up the business of his deceased friend and business associate. The estate owned one of the greatest ranches in the Northwest, and Captain J. W. Snyder was placed in charge of this vast property and handled same in a most successful manner for nine years, the business growing into a great syndicate with thousands of head of the finest cattle and horses in the world within its confines.

HEAT AND THIRST

From "Book of Cowboys."

In 1885 Col. Snyder made his last great drive to the Northwest, and as a boy, this writer saw the splendid herd of five thousand beef cattle in its seemingly endless column pass, as he sat on a gate-post and gazed in childish wonder and admiration at the stately herd and the gallant cowboys charged with their delivery in a distant state. Little they dreamed of the disappointment that awaited them; little they suspected that even then events were shaping themselves that would not only preclude the vast returns from the years' work that were expected, but would wipe out accumulations studious men had spent years in gathering. From the broad plains of Texas the vast herds were picking their way across the trackless miles of terrain that separated them from the markets that promised such a rich return for labor expended. In Wyoming the junior member had handled the vast holdings successfully. An offer of one million dollars cash was received at headquarters for the property. Snyder Bros., who knew a good deal when they saw it, favored closing the trade; others interested in the holdings objected and their desires were respected by the big-hearted men who were responsible for the success of the undertaking.

Against their better judgment Snyder Bros. refused the proffered million for holdings in Wyoming, and in a few months the panic of 1886 began. Like a clap of thunder from the clear sky it came, and there were but few who were able to withstand its fury—huge fortunes that it had taken years to accumulate were swept away in a day and wealthy men were made penniless overnight. Everything was sacrificed by these giants of business acumen and honesty to protect those with whom they were associated and save them from absolute ruin.

Returning to Texas, Col. Snyder began anew to retrieve the great losses sustained in the terrible crash of the panic. Ranches were conducted in Cook, Mitchell, Stonewall, Lamb, and Hartley counties. the one in the last two counties named comprising 128,000 acres of land. All were well improved, having comfortable ranch houses, and numerous wells for the furnishing of water for the stock. The business was continued until 1894, when it was closed out and one of the men knew as much about the cattle business as anyone who had ever followed in the wake of the lowing herd, retired to a quiet life.

This closes a brief review of the experiences of Col. Dudley H. Snyder in the cattle business, but there are other activities in which he has been engaged that gives a larger vision of the real heart that beats within this man of big affairs than any that have gone before; a few of these we will mention here. Throughout the years now far gone he has been a friend of the friendless and many a successful business man owes his success to the kindly spirit of Col. Snyder and his good and faithful wife. A staunch Methodist, he has given unstintedly and repeatedly of his means to her institutions and Southwestern University has been particularly an object of his benefactions. Many who have received their training within those walls owe their privilege of doing so to Colonel and Mrs. Snyder, whose home has been a mecca for those who come to teach or to learn throughout the years of its splendid history.

September 20, 1905, Col. Snyder suffered the total loss of his vision and now after a well-spent life, although he sits with, "the door shut in the street," the "silvery chord" of his life of happiness and activity is just as sweet as in the days gone by. The companionship of the devoted wife of his youth, his children, and friends makes the remaining days of this grand old cattleman, scholar, and friend of man, a pleasant one, and they, in turn, know that his pilgrimage here has been a benediction to them. May his fourscore years ripen into the fifth and his good deeds continue to bring their reward.

———

Since the above sketch was written Col. Snyder has crossed the Great Divide to roam on fairer ranges. He died at his home in Georgetown, Texas, in August, 1921.

W. A. (BUCK) PETTUS

W. A. (Buck) PETTUS

There are thousands of people in Texas today to whom the name at the head of this page would seem unfamiliar, but would recognize our subject at once under the familiar designation, "Buck" Pettus, by which he was known all over the state. In the Southern counties he was particularly well known, for it is there that his entire life was spent.

His father, John F. Pettus, was a Virginian of Scotch-English ancestry, born in 1808, and was brought to Texas in his fourteenth year by his parents. The family settled at San Felipe, in Austin county, where they were granted a league of land and engaged in farming and stock raising. John F. Pettus was a man of great daring and enterprise, and took an active part in the early struggles of the Texan colonists for their liberty. He was one of Milam's 216 men who were in the storming of San Antonio in 1835, and was also at the battle of Conception, where ninety-two men, under Captain Fannin, met and repulsed Morales' battalion, the flower of the Mexican army; was at the battle of San Jacinto, in which the power of Mexico was broken and her warrior president was captured. He took part in many of the minor engagements of the war, and after its close had but little opportunity to lay aside his arms, for, for many years the settlements were constantly harassed by Indian and Mexicans bands, and the fighting men of the "colony" found ample use for their nerve and skill in border warfare. John Pettus married Miss Sarah York, born in Alabama, but a resident of Texas since her early infancy. They were married in 1836 and became the parents of six children, of whom our subject was the eldest.

W. A. Pettus was born in Austin county, near the town of Industry, November 17, 1838. He attended schools in Austin county for a few months, and was several sessions in attendance on those of DeWitt county, where his parents moved when he was in his ninth year. After his seventeenth year his education received no further attention, for he had tired of schooling and his help was needed in handling and caring for his father's cattle. To this work his attention was exclusively given until the beginning of the war. He enlisted in the 21st Cavalry under Captain Martin M. Kinney, and leaving the cattle, which he personally owned, with those of his father, marched forth with his brave companions to meet enemies of the Confederacy. He was with Gen. Marmaduke in his unsuccessful assault upon the Federal forces at Cape Girardeau, Missouri, and after this engagement was sent south with his command to contend with Banks, who was then pressing through the Red River country on his memorable "expedition." Skirmishes were of daily occurrence, with occasionally a fight worthy of being termed a battle; the most important of all being that of Yellow Bayou.

When the war ended Mr. Pettus returned to his home and began the work of gathering his scattered cattle and getting his herd, though sadly reduced in size, in shape for a satisfactory resumption of business. This was a task of no small difficulty, for the range was open in every direction, and had to be thoroughly worked over to discover the numerous strays that had wandered into other herds. He was married February 4, 1866, choosing for his mate Miss Myra A. Lott, one of the fairest flowers of Southern Texas. She was the daughter of Thomas P. C. Lott, one of the pioneer settlers of Goliad county, and about the first of its citizens to engage extensively in cattle raising. Mrs. Pettus was born in Harrison county, Texas, April 24, 1842, and shortly after her birth her parents moved to Jackson county, continuing westward a year later to Goliad county, where they established the ranch which is now the Pettus' home.

After his marriage Mr. Pettus continued to reside with his father, who was too feeble to attend to his own business interests—a task which devolved upon the son. Mr. Pettus built and occupied a home of his own in 1870, in Bee county.

Mr. Pettus, when he moved to his Bee county ranch, was the owner of about 800 head of cattle; but he continued to manage his father's herd until 1873, receiving for his trouble a one-third interest in the cattle. His first beginning in the business had been secured, as we have seen, through his personal efforts, and in his subsequent transactions he had never any great amount of capital to operate upon. Therefore, he had no opportunity to engineer any extensive deals; but by close attention to his business he prospered and the extent and value of his property gradually increased. He had, all his life, been a ranchman, a cattle grower of the oldest and best type; but never a speculator. He followed in the footsteps of his father, who certainly can be accepted as the true type of a cattleman, since his history as such antedates the history of the state, and even of the republic which preceded it. The colonists at San Felipe had no cattle except a few which were purchased along the Louisiana line, and John F. Pettus got his first cattle in exchange for horses driven by himself and Captain John York to Louisiana. There were no "cowboys" in those days, and the first to be given that name were a number of reckless young fellows who would make trips into the Rio Grande country, gather cattle among the Mexicans and drive them East in search of a market.

W. A. Pettus always conducted his business in an honest and honorable manner, believing that ill-gotten gains can never prove of actual benefit to their possessor. His father never branded a "maverick" in his life, and neither would he permit his son to do so, and the Pettus family—father and sons—have always stood in readiness to assist in putting down cattle stealing or any other lawlessness. The reputation earned by W. A., or "Buck" Pettus, in this work of necessity and general importance is universally known throughout the Southwest. He was for years a terror to the cow thief, the "rustler" and evil-doers of other descriptions, and aided very materially in making the sinister efforts of such characters unsafe and consequently unpopular.

The banner years of our subject's life, so far as his record as cattle grower goes, were 1877–88. His herd then numbered about 10,000 head; but the depression in price led Mr. Pettus to reduce his holdings considerably. He possessed a large number of cattle, mules and horses, and about 60,000 acres of land altogether. His home farm embraced about 325 acres of good bottom land, all in cultivation. He had also another farm of about the same size, and some smaller ones, which bring the total area of his farming lands up to nearly 900 acres. He was interested to some extent, in property of other descriptions, and with Messrs. Levi, and Maetze, owned the Bank of Goliad.

Mr. Pettus died at his ranch home in Goliad county, February 20, 1922. He is survived by his wife and seven children, three daughters and four sons, all married, as follows: Mesdames Al McFaddin of Victoria, G. B. Reed and John Dial, and W. F. Pettus, R. L. Pettus, T. W. Pettus and J. M. Pettus.

R. G. (DICK) HEAD

The subject of this sketch, generally known as Dick Head, was born in Saline county, Missouri, April 6, 1847. When six years old his father moved to Caldwell county, Texas. When he was thirteen years of age young Head

entered the employ of Bullard & McPhetridge, who were preparing to move a herd of cattle to Missouri, but the breaking out of the Civil War prevented the drive and the herd was sold to the Confederate government. At the age of sixteen he entered the Confederate army and served until the close of the war, and after farming for about a year Mr. Head entered the service of Col. John J. Meyers, the pioneer drover of Texas, who took the first herds to Abilene, Kansas, which place was then a mere post containing but half a dozen habitations. Mr. Head camped a herd of cattle on the spot where the city of Wichita, Kansas, now stands, when not a white man

R. G. (Dick) HEAD

resided there, but as many Indians as there are now white inhabitants. He began working for Col. Meyers at a salary of $30 per month, which was steadily advanced until the third year, when he took entire control of his employer's trail business at a salary of $1,800 per year and expenses. He continued in this position for seven years, during which time he drove herds to Abilene, Wichita, Great Bend, Ellsworth and Dodge City, Kansas, and also to Cheyenne, Wyoming, Salt Lake City, Utah, and the Humbolt River in Nevada, across to California, and to the various Indian agencies on the Upper Missouri River and the Black Hills country. His business relations with Colonel Meyers were terminated in 1873 by the death of the latter gentleman. In 1875 he assumed the general management of the extensive cattle business of Ellison, Dewees & Bishop of San Antonio, handling from 30,000 to 50,000 cattle annually. In the spring of 1878 the firm dissolved, and Mr. Head formed a partnership with Mr. Bishop for the handling of the cattle on the ranch and on the trail. The firm of Bishop & Head existed until 1883, when the prevailing high prices induced Mr. Head to insist upon a sale of the partnership property, which was accomplished over the friendly protest of Mr. Bishop. In May, 1883, Mr. Head accepted the management of the Prairie Cattle Company, the largest concern of the kind in the world. He filled this position for three years, during which time he marketed from the ranches of the company 54,000 head of cattle, netting $1,300,000, and branded for the company from its herds more than 83,000 calves, and after paying all expenses, interest on debenture bonds, and also paying dividends to its stockholders amounting in three years to 42 per cent of the capital invested, the company had about 5,000 more cattle than when he assumed the management of its business, and an undivided surplus of about $80,000. His salary for his service with the company was $20,000 per annum. When he severed connection with the Prairie Cattle Co., its employees presented him with a solid silver service costing $1,500.

In 1886 Mr. Head was elected president of the International Range Association, representing the live stock industry of the plains, from the Gulf of Mexico to British Columbia, and west to the Pacific coast. He was one of the original promoters of the American Cattle Trust, and maintained his headquarters in Denver, Colorado, while acting as general manager of that association. He was principal owner of the Phoenix Farm and Ranch Co., of Mora county, New Mexico, which was one of the most systematically conducted properties in the entire West. Mr. Head was also a large stockholder in the Fort Stockton Livestock & Land Company of Texas, which owned 50,000 acres of land, 20,000 of which was under irrigation. He also owned a farm of above 700 acres at his old home in Caldwell county, Texas.

In 1892 Mr. Head moved from Denver, Colorado, to his famous Phoenix Ranch near Watrous, New Mexico, and from there to Las Vegas in the fall of 1901. He died April 8, 1906, leaving his wife, two daughters, and a son, R. G. Head, Jr.

SKETCH OF J. M. CHOATE

The subject of this sketch, known to all the old cowmen as "Monroe" Choate, was born in Tennessee, April 28, 1822. He was married to Miss Mary Elizabeth Adkinson, June 2, 1844, and they had ten children, eight boys and two girls. Only one of these children is living today, S. P. Choate of Kennedy, Texas, who was next to the youngest child.

Mr. Choate moved to Karnes county in 1855 and settled on Hondo Creek, where he lived until his death, which occurred August 9, 1899. He was buried in the Runge cemetery.

Monroe Choate was one of the largest cattle operators in that section of the state, and often drove cattle to Louisiana before the trail opened to northern markets. When the driving of stock to Kansas started he was among the first to send cattle up the trail. He was a man of many sterling qualities, generous, whole-souled, thoughtful of his men, full of wit and humor, and the life of his outfit on the trail and in camp. He was highly esteemed by all who knew him, and after the trail driving days were over he settled down to a quiet and active life on his place in Karnes county.

Several of his sons were trail drivers, among them we mention, J. H. Choate, born in Mississippi, August 29, 1847, died at Helena, Karnes county, Texas, and is buried there; D. C. Choate, born February 17, 1851, in Leon county, Texas, died in Dodge City, Kansas, in 1878, and is buried there; K. B. Choate, born February 1, 1858, in Karnes county, Texas, died in Dodge City, Kansas, July 4, 1884 and is buried at Goliad, Texas.

W. M. CHOATE

W. M. Choate was born in Leon county, Texas, May 14, 1854, moved to Karnes county with his parents in 1856 and lived there continuously until 1889, then moved to Del Rio, and worked cattle in Mexico for three years. He was for two years a deputy United States marshal at Del Rio. In 1895 he returned to Karnes county, and was appointed inspector for the Cattle Raisers' Association, which position he held for fifteen years, living at Karnes City and Cuero during the time. Later he made his home in San Antonio for three years, and then moved to Beeville where he died in June, 1915.

Mr. Choate made his first trip up the trail when he was fifteen years old with his father's herd. Later he drove horses for himself to Kansas. The greater portion of his life was spent in stock business. On January 9, 1884, he was happily married to Miss Pollie Porter, who still survives him and resides at Pettus, Texas.

CROSSED THE ARKANSAS RIVER IN A SKIFF

James Henry Saul, known among the old timers as Little Jim Saul, was born six miles from Huntsville in Walker county, Texas, June 26, 1849. While he was quite small his parents moved to Williamson county, and located on the San Gabriel, twelve miles above George-town, where they lived for two years, then moved to Brushy Creek, about twelve miles below Round Rock.

Mr. Saul grew up in the cattle business. When he was 23 years old, in 1872, he took a herd of 1,000 head of his own cattle from Williamson county to Baxter Springs, Kansas. Among his hands were Buck and

JIM SAUL

Jack Blanton, the Crum brothers, the Summers brothers, and his brother, Charlie Saul.

His next drive was made in 1879 to Ogallala, Nebraska, with 2,800 head, and in 1879 he drove 2,900 head to Caldwell, Kansas. On one of these trips, when Mr. Saul reached the Arkansas River he found it on a rampage and about five hundred yards wide. The ferry had washed away, so he employed some Indians to make a skiff out of a cottonwood log, and the men and supplies were taken across in this skiff, while the wagon was taken down and floated across. The herd took the water and made it by swimming.

ON THE TRAIL TO KANSAS

A Painting by Warren Hunter, from a Description Furnished by George W. Saunders

In his trail driving Mr. Saul had no trouble with the inspectors, and very little with the Indians. When the redskins asked him for a beef they got it.

Mr. Saul now resides on his ranch near Bandera, Texas, and delights to meet up with comrades of those good old days when "going up the trail" was in order.

WHEN THE TEMPERATURE WAS 72 DEGREES BELOW ZERO

C. C. French, Fort Worth, Texas

My father, Joseph H. French, and family left Philadelphia in the late fifties and came west to the Ohio river, then down the Ohio to the Mississippi to New Orleans, then to Galveston by steamer, from Galveston to Columbus by rail, thence to San Antonio by four-mule ambulance. During the Civil War father had a contract for delivering beef cattle to the Confederate army. He was paid in Confederate money and it broke him. After my father's death, my mother took my brother, sister and myself back to Philadelphia.

My brother Horace G. French, was one of the bosses who drove many herds of cattle over the trail. In 1874 he had delivered a herd in

C. C. FRENCH

Wyoming and while on his way back to Texas, he came to his old home in Philadelphia to visit us. I was then a boy in school, but my brother's narratives about trail driving interested me so that I determined to come to Texas the first opportunity that presented itself. In the spring of 1876 I landed in Austin, and the first sight

I had of the trail was that wonderful herd of wild steers Ab Blocker tells about, in the first volume of this book, that were roped on the Perdinales by John and Bill Blocker. It was a sight and it is a great pity that a picture of that herd was not made and kept.

In 1878 a small outfit left Austin in charge of my brother and we received a herd of steers and a herd of cows and calves on the head of Camp Creek in Coleman county. We had a trail wagon in which to carry the calves that were born on the trail. The herd was owned by Col. Wm. Day. We reached Dodge City, Kansas, in good shape, but it was a wretched trip as the calves gave us a lot of trouble. The next year we started a herd of steers from Kimble county for Major Seth Mabry, going to Ogallala, Nebraska. There the herd was re-arranged and we started with 4,000 steers for the Cheyenne Agency in Dakota. Half of the herd went to Bismarck, Dakota. The herd we drove to the Cheyenne Agency was for the United States government and were fed to the Sioux Indians. One day early in December an Indian courier came to our camp with a message from the commander of the post saying that if the mercury went 28 degrees below zero he wanted 250 steers that day, to commence killing for the Indians' winter beef. We delivered the steers and the Indians killed them all in one day. The meat was exposed to the cold for a few days and then stored in an immense warehouse to be issued out to the Indians every week. During the killing period about 800 steers were slaughtered. About 7,000 Indians were present at the killing. It was no uncommon sight to see a squaw at one end of an entrail and a dog at the other end, both eating ravenously. When the killing was completed we had about 600 steers that had to be crossed over the Missouri River on the ice, which was then about 28 inches thick across the channel. After this was done we had to deliver the horses at Fort Thompson. At this time the government thermometer at Peeve recorded 72 degrees below zero. On our way home we were in that fearful blizzard which froze the bay at Galveston and ruined the orange trees in Florida. I have never liked cold weather since that time.

HISTORY OF AN OLD COWMAN

Robert Samuel Dalton, a wealthy stockman of Palo Pinto, controlling extensive and important business interests, wherein he displays excellent business ability,

MR. AND MRS. ROBERT S. DALTON

marked enterprise, and keen, discernment, was born March 8, 1859, on his father's ranch on the Brazos River, eighteen miles north of Palo Pinto county, Texas. His parents were Marcus Lafayette and Lucinda Gamble Dalton. The Dalton family, together with the family of Rev. Slaughter, father-in-law of Robert Dalton, were among the oldest and most noted in Northwestern Texas. Marcus L. Dalton was born in Tennessee and came to Texas in 1838, locating first in Red River county, whence he removed to Palo Pinto county in 1855, settling at the mouth of Rock Creek on the Brazos River. It was a wild and unsettled country, infested by hostile Indians, who

made raids into this locality from their reservations in
Indian Territory. Mr. Dalton was an excellent business
man and prospered in the cattle business notwithstanding the fact that frequently his cattle were stolen by the
Indians. As the years passed his lands and cattle increased in value. He made many trips over the trail
with his cattle to Kansas and on returning from one of
these trips he was killed by the Indians, November 4,
1870, in Loving's Valley, six miles north of the present
town of Mineral Wells and twenty miles east of his
home on the Brazos. He had left Weatherford, Texas,
and from that town he was accompanied by James Redfield and James McCaster. The latter was driving a
bunch of horses, while Mr. Redfield and Mr. Dalton each
had a wagon and team. They were attacked by the
Indians at the point mentioned and all three men were
killed, the Indians taking everything they could carry
but leaving an iron-bound leather trunk in which there
was $11,000. In Mr. Dalton's shoes were $11,000 in bills
of large denomination, which was not taken by the
Indians.

Mr. Dalton of this review still has one of the bows
from which was shot the arrow that killed his father.
The three men were scalped and their bodies mutilated
in an inhuman manner.

Robert S. Dalton was reared upon the home ranch to
the life of the cattle trade, his boyhood days being
fraught with exciting incidents and dangers characteristic to that period in the development of Palo Pinto
county, when it was a largely unsettled district and the
Indians were on the war-path. In the course of time he
embarked in the cattle business on his own account and
his entire career as dealer in the stock has been successful and free from financial embarrassment of any kind
even in times of widespread financial depression. He
is today one of the largest taxpayers and one of the
wealthy citizens of that part of the state. His first in-

dependent venture in the business was when he was fifteen years of age. His mother gave him twenty-five calves and it was at this time that he started the brand L. A. D.; which has ever since been the brand he has used.

On the 8th of October, 1879, in Palo Pinto county, Mr. Dalton was married to Miss Millie Slaughter, the fifth daughter of Rev. Geo. W. Slaughter, a historical character of Western Texas. She was educated at Emporia, Kansas, and at Staunton, Virginia, and is a lady of superior culture and refinement. Her father, Rev. Slaughter, was trusted lieutenant of Houston during the early days of Texas and afterwards a Missionary Baptist minister for more than half a century and a devoted exponent of the Gospel. He was also a physician and practiced medicine, thus carrying healing to the body as well as to the souls of men.

At the time of his marriage, Mr. Dalton started with his bride for Western Texas, where at the foot of the great plains on the Salt Fork of the Brazos he established himself in the cattle business. He took over 800 head of his own cattle in addition to several thousand belonging to his mother and brothers, all of which he herded on a free ranch, such as was common in those days. He lived there for five years. In 1884 he sold his cattle on the ranch for fifty-one thousand dollars and returned to Palo Pinto county, where he purchased the Kyle ranch. Later he sold this place and for some time engaged in the business of buying and selling cattle. His next transaction of note was the purchase of his present ranch six miles north of the town, for which he paid eleven thousand dollars, but which has gradually increased in value through the addition of other tracts of land and the improvements he has placed upon it. His ranch now comprises over nine thousand acres all in one body. This is a beautiful ranch located in the rich Brazos Valley and is stocked with immense herds of fine cattle. In 1909 Mr. Dalton removed from his residence on the ranch to Mineral Wells, where he has since made his home.

Unto Mr. and Mrs. Dalton have been born eleven children, namely, Otto D., George Webb, Marcus, Lafayette, Millie Robert, Sarah Jane, Georgia Lee, William Carroll Slaughter, Columbus Charles (deceased), John Bell, Vivian Ruth, and Mary Allie Leta. Mr. Dalton is a member of the Knights of Pythias fraternity, prominent in the organization, and enjoys the unqualified esteem of his brethren of the fraternity and of the general public as well. His life history, especially concerning his boyhood days, if written in detail, would furnish a most thrilling story. He has lived to see great changes while in Western Texas as the comforts and conveniences of a civilization have been introduced, while the business methods of a settled district have given place to those of pioneer times. In all his business transactions he has displayed marked ability, strong purposes and unfaltering diligence and his investments have been carefully made so that he has gathered therefrom a rich financial return.

In the past year oil has been discovered on Mr. Dalton's Palo Pinto county ranch and he has today from his lease royalties an income of $800 per day.

The old ranch is not what it used to be before these wells were discovered, so far as his cattle interests are concerned. He will not be permitted to raise any more herds of cattle on this ranch as it is now a great oil field.

INDIANS GOT THEIR HORSES

W. H. Crain, Pipe Creek, Texas

I was born in Leon county, Texas, November 25, 1849, in a log house which my father and neighbors built. In those days when a new family moved into a community everybody attended the "log rolling" and helped to put up a comfortable log cabin for the newcomers to live in. Our farm was just in the edge of the timber and the Leon prairie spread out in front of our cabin and we had a fine view for miles. There were no fences then, everything ran loose. People depended on bells and hobbles to keep their work animals near home. My father sold this place and bought land in Burleson county, and we lived there until some time in 1864, when we moved out to McCulloch county, on the Colorado River. Our nearest postoffice was Camp San Saba, about twenty-five miles distant. My father's brother-in-law, Judge John Beasley, had moved out there from Missouri, and father decided to make his home there too, but after a time the Indians became so troublesome he concluded to move again, and we went to Kendall county in 1865. Marion Hodges, well known in Bandera county for many years, came along with us. His wife, Nancy A. Hodges, was my father's niece. We rented a log house from Charlie Sughart on the east side of the Cibolo, and the next year we raised a fine crop of corn right in the heart of the present town of Boerne. We often went out and caught wild cattle and made good steers of them after they became gentle.

In 1869 I went back to McCulloch county with Jim Dophlemier and Billie Beasley to help Newt Beasley gather a herd of cattle to drive to Kansas. I had to ride a mule. Her name was not Maud, but she proved herself to be Maud's equal. When we reached Newt Beasley's we found George Chamberlain, Tom Keese, Jim Parker, Dick Hudson, Charlie Ellington, Jeff Singleton helping to gather the cattle. Jeff Singleton, Newt Beasley and myself went out to gather some cattle one day and rode up on three Indians. One of them had a very pretty striped blanket and before Newt could prevent him, Jeff made a dash for the Indian, saying that he was going to have that blanket. He ran right up to the Indian,

with his pistol in his hand, but when he saw two of them
armed, with guns he turned his horse quickly and started
back toward us. The Indian with the blanket shot him
in the back with an arrow. The other Indians then began
shooting at Jeff, and Newt went to his assistance, having
only an old cap and ball pistol with three loads in it.
The Indians beat a retreat and got away. I was only
a boy in my teens, and riding that mule I thought my
time had come, but I kept up with the other boys. We

THE CHUCK OUTFIT IN THE EARLY DAYS

took Jeff to Mrs. Lindley's house and with a pair of
dentist's forceps pulled the arrow out of his back.

Newt Beasley and a man named Gotcher had just
bought twenty fresh cow ponies in Coryell county, and
had them out grazing. When we went out to bring them
in to camp about fifteen Indians dashed in between the
boys and the herd of horses, and they had to run for hiding as they had no arms to fight the redskins with. The
Indians got every horse they had for the drive, and left
Beasley and Gotcher with a thousand cattle rounded up
and only about twelve head of tired, worn-out horses to

take the trail with. They had to go on to Kansas with what we had.

When I got back to Boerne in Kendall county, William and Henry Deaters were preparing to go down to Powder Horn after a steam engine for their mill, and I

THE CHUCK WAGON CAME LATER

went with them. It took us twenty-one days to make the trip.

I have a small ranch at Pipe Creek, in Bandera county, where I am raising a few cows, horses and goats. If any of the old trail drivers ever get lost up on the Bandera road I want them to hunt me up.

GEORGE WEBB SLAUGHTER

George Webb Slaughter was a native of Lawrence county, Mississippi, his birth occurring May 10, 1811, William Slaughter, his father, was a Virginian, born in 1781, his death occurring in Sabine county, Texas in 1851. The elder Mr. Slaughter was a farmer and had seen service in the war of 1812, fighting with Jackson at New Orleans. He married Miss Nancy Moore, of South Carolina, and was the father of eight children, four of them boys. In 1821 the family moved to Copiah county,

Mississippi, and four years later started to Texas, but stopped for a time in Louisiana, and it was while living in the latter state that George Webb Slaughter received the only schooling (three weeks in all) which he ever had an opportunity to obtain. In 1830 the Slaughter family crossed the Sabine River and settled in what was then the Mexican state of Coahuila and Texas. At that time the country east of Austin was divided into municipalities governed principally by military laws. Petty officers were in charge at the different points and alcaldes, or mag-

GEORGE WEBB SLAUGHTER   MRS. GEO. W. SLAUGHTER

istrates, were appointed by them, while all matters of importance were referred to the District Commandant. Col. Piedras was in charge of the country along the Sabine, with headquarters at Nacogdoches. He was a man of narrow and decided views and but poorly qualified to exercise authority over a people reared in the enjoyment of American liberty. There was no tolerance of religious belief beyond a blind adherence to the Catholic church and an arrest by Col. Piedras of several Protestant clergymen, who had attempted to hold services in the colony, precipitated one of the first conflicts between the colonists and the Mexican government. G. W.

Slaughter, then a boy of nineteen or twenty, took an active part in the armed resistance to this act of tyranny, and his relation of the events which followed is vivid and interesting. A commissioner, sent to Col. Piedras to intercede for the prisoners' release, was treated with contempt, and Col. Bean Andrews, who repaired to the City of Mexico on the same errand, was thrown into prison. Despairing of obtaining recognition and relief through pacific methods, the colonists held a mass meeting at San Augustine about June 1, 1832, and resolved to take matters into their own hands and release the prisoners, if need be, through force of arms. Preparations for this decisive step went quietly on, and in a short time 500 armed men met within two miles of Nacogdoches and sent Col. Piedras under a flag of truce, a demand for the prisoners' liberation. In reply a company of cavalry came out with a counter demand for the surrender of the whole party. Immediate hostilities followed. The Mexicans were driven back to town after one or two ineffectual stands, and eventually forced to evacuate the fort and seek safety in flight. Quite a number of Mexicans were killed, but only three Americans, one of whom was G. P. Smith, an uncle of G. W. Slaughter. At that time the Angelina River was swollen with recent rains, its bottom lands flooded and impassable except at one point, some eighteen miles from the fort, where a bridge had been built. Here all the men who were provided with horses, were directed to hasten and stop the retreat of the panic-striken Mexicans, while the remainder of the force followed on thus bringing the enemy between two fires and compelling the entire command to surrender. Col. Piedras was allowed to return to Mexico under promise of excusing the colonists' acts and interceding for their pardon, but he proved false to his trust and his report of the affair at Nacogdoches only still further incensed the government. Mr. Slaughter was under fire for the first time in this skirmish or battle. During the

temporary lull which followed previous to the general
outbreak of war, he was occupied in freighting between
Louisiana and Texas points, and one of his loads—perhaps the most valuable of them all, consisted of the legal
library of Sam Houston, which he hauled to Nacogdoches
in 1833. He had previously met Houston while attending court at Natchitoches, La., and he mentions the fact
that upon this occasion the future president of the Texas
Republic was dressed in Indian garments and decked out
in all the glory of scalp-lock, feathers and silver ornaments. Mr. Slaughter was an earnest admirer of Houston and was more than pleased when the latter assumed
control of the Texan forces. The company in which he
enlisted reported to Houston for duty at San Antonio,
and was in several engagements which immediately followed, among others the famous "Grass Fight," one of
the hottest of the war. Houston then advanced toward
Mexico, but halted near Goliad upon intelligence that
Santa Anna was approaching with an army of 15,000
men. Col. Fannin with the forces under his command
was encamped in a strong position in a bend of the river
below Goliad. Travis was in the Alamo with those gallant spirits who were to remain with him faithful and
uncomplaining until death. Houston, safe in the consciousness that on the open prairie lay perfect safety
from beleaguerment, watched the approach of the Mexican army and pleaded with Fannin and Travis to abandon the fortifications and join him. Mr. Slaughter served
as a courier, making several trips to Fannin and Travis
in the Alamo. On one of the latter, in obedience to instructions from Gen. Houston, he delivered into the
hands of Col. Travis an order to retreat. After reading
it, Travis consulted his brother officers, acquainted his
men with the contents of the message, and drew a line
with his sword and called upon all who were willing to
remain with him and fight, if need be, to the death, to
cross it. The decision was practically unanimous to

defend the fort to the last extremity. Only one of the
little band chose to make his way to the main army; he
was let down from the walls and made his escape.
Travis hoped for reinforcements that would enable him
to inflict upon Santa Anna a bloody and decisive repulse
that would check him on the outskirts of the settlements,
or, failing in this, detain his army a sufficient length of
time to enable the colonists to mass an adequate force
to meet him successfully in the open field. He fully realized the peril of his situation and concealed nothing from
his comrades. They determined to stake their lives upon

Houston's trusted Lieutenant, George Webb Slaughter, delivering a
message from Houston to Travis, Bowie and Crockett advising the
Evacuation of the Alamo

the hazard and were immolated upon the altar of their
country.

Mr. Slaughter returned to headquarters and reported
the result of his mission. Later while on a hazardous
trip to the Alamo, then known to be invested with Santa
Anna's army, he encountered Mrs. Dickinson and her
negro slave, survivors of the massacre, who had been
released by the Mexican commandant and instructed to
proceed to General Houston with tidings of Travis' fate.

The butchery of Fannin and his men followed shortly after, and Santa Anna pressed on after General Houston, who had retreated to the east side of the Brazos. Meantime Mr. Slaughter was employed in carrying messages and in procuring subsistence for the army, accepting many dangerous missions and performing them all to the satisfaction of his commanding officer. History relates how Houston retreated and how the Mexican army followed until they were led into the trap at San Jacinto, where the tables were turned and Santa Anna defeated and captured, his troops slaughtered, and his invasion brought to an ignominious end. The victory at San Jacinto was not the end of hostilities; but, following it, there came a breathing spell, of which Mr. Slaughter hastened to take advantage. Gaining a leave of absence, under promise of returning at once in case he was needed, he hastened to his home, and on the 12th day of the following October he was married to Miss Sarah Mason, to whom he had been engaged for some time. The ceremony was only deferred to this date because under the disorganized state of the country there was no officer with legal authority to perform it. The marriage of Mr. Slaughter was the first ceremony of the kind under the sanction of the Republic which he had been instrumental in establishing. The newly wedded couple settled in Sabine county, and Mr. Slaughter resumed freighting for a livelihood, engaging in the employ of the new government.

At the time of the Cherokee troubles, in 1839, the eastern counties organized companies in pursuance of President Houston's orders, and Mr. Slaughter was elected captain of the company organized in Sabine. The newly recruited forces assembled at Nacogdoches, and in a body marched to reinforce General Rusk, who was stationed with a small force on the Neches River, near where Chief Bowles was encamped with 1,600 Cherokees. Two days were spent in an ineffectual attempt to arrange a treaty and the Indians dropped back from their position, but were followed and a fight ensued in which the Cherokees lost eleven killed and the whites only three, though fourteen of their number were wounded. The Indians again retreated and the following day there was a general battle; Chief Bowles was killed, with several hundred of his followers, while the remainder of the Cherokees fled westward, being followed to the Bois d'Arc fork of the Trinity, three or four days' march, by companies of Captains Slaughter and Todd.

The need which had prompted the organization of an armed force now no longer existing, the men disbanded, and Mr. Slaughter returned to the labors and attendant comforts of home life. In 1852 he moved to Freestone county, intending to turn his attention to stock-raising. He brought with him ninety-two head of cattle and established a ranch near the old town of Butler, and in five years he resided there his herd increased to 600 head. Mr. Slaughter believed there were better opportunities to be gained by removal further west, and in 1857 drove his herds to Palo Pinto county, locating five miles north of the town of that name, at that time known as Golconda. He bought 2,000 acres of land and located by certificate 960 acres more, and the ranch located at that time was thereafter his home, though his residence at this point was not continuous. In 1858–59 Mr. Slaughter was occupied in raising stock and running a small farm, but the following year moved his stock to Young county, at a point near the Ross Indian Reservation. He had then 1,200 head of cattle and a small bunch of horses, but lost forty head of the latter through theft by Indians in 1860, and for these and other property stolen, he later filed claims against the government aggregating $6,500.

Mr. Slaughter's holdings of cattle had increased in 1867–68 to such an extent that he decided to sell the greater portion of them, and he accordingly disposed of 12,000 to James Loving and Charles Rivers at a uniform price of $6.00. Rivers was afterwards killed by the Indians while in camp in Jackson, in June, 1871. Following the sale of his cattle Mr. Slaughter formed a partnership with his son, C. C. Slaughter, and began driving cattle through to Kansas. The first drove only consisted of 800 head, but they brought the neat little sum of $32,000. For the seven years up to and including 1875, the herds of Slaughter & Son were driven to Kansas points and thence shipped to St. Louis and Chicago. The drove in 1870 was probably the largest, numbering 3,000 head, and the returns from this herd footed up $105,000. In 1870 Mr. Slaughter moved his family to Emporia, Kansas, in order that his children might have the advantage of the superior facilities at that point, but in 1875 he returned to Texas and resumed operations on his old ranch in Palo Pinto county. The number of cattle handled and the money received from their sale can be expressed in round figures as follows:

1868, 800 head, $32,000.00; 1869, 2,000 head $90,000.00; 1870, 3,000 head, $105,000.00; 1871, 2,000, $66,000.00; 1873, 2,000 head $66,000.00; 1874, 2,000 head, $60,000.00; 1865, 1,000, $45,000.00. Such figures as these go a long way toward impressing the reader with the importance of the cattle business twenty years ago. In 1876 Mr. Slaughter dissolved partnership with his son, C. C. Slaughter, taking into business with him another son, Peter, and in 1878 they sold and shipped 4,000 cattle. Six years later on account of declining health, Mr. Slaughter disposed of his cattle interests and afterwards devoted his time to the care of his ranch and other property. He had at his Palo Pinto ranch 1,280 acres of land, and owned 1,300 acres in other portions of the state, besides town property in Mineral Wells. Securing his land when nearly the entire country was open for selection, Mr. Slaughter had one of the most desirable locations in the country, and prized it more highly in remembrance of the hardships and dangers attendant upon

THE TRAIL DRIVERS OF TEXAS

its settlement. During the first few years of his residence
of Palo Pinto county the Indians were very troublesome,
and Mr. Slaughter could relate many incidents of border
warfare from the standpoint of an eye-witness and participant. In 1864 he had a skirmish with seven Indians
on Cedar Creek, in Palo Pinto county, several shots were
fired, but the Indians were finally frightened away. Three
years later the Indians made a raid on his ranch and
stole all the horses, and John Slaughter, a son, received
a bullet wound in the breast. Skirmishes with the redskins were then of too common occurrence to attract
much attention beyond the immediate neighborhood. The
entire Texas border was a battlefield, and those who lived
on the upper Brazos had to guard themselves the best
they could. In 1866 Mr. Slaughter was driving a small
bunch of cattle on Dry Creek, near Graham, when he
was attacked by thirteen Indians, but his carbine and
revolver proved too much for their courage and they
retreated after he had wounded one of their number. In
the month of April, 1869, a bunch of Indians surrounded
and massacred thirteen government teamsters near Flat
Top Mountain, in Young county. Mr. Slaughter was
within two miles of his place, camped with fourteen men,
holding 800 head of cattle which he had gathered. The
Indians attacked them, and they only escaped through
strategy. Six of the men were sent with the cattle in
the direction of Sand Creek, and the remainder of them,
including Mr. Slaughter and his son, C. C. Slaughter,
made a breastwork of the horses and awaited an attack.
Profiting by a deep ravine at hand, some of the men crept
cautiously away, and suddenly appearing at another
point, made a charge upon the Indians, who supposed
there were more re-inforcements coming, and beat a retreat.

Mr. Slaughter was an earnest worker all his life, and
few men proved themselves so useful in so many and
varied capacities. He was for many years a minister

of the Baptist church. During his ministry he baptized over 3,000 persons and ordained more preachers and organized more churches than any other person in the state of Texas. When Rev. Mr. Slaughter first came to Palo Pinto county, in starting out to fill his appointments as minister, he would saddle his horse, fill his saddle bags with provisions, take along his picket rope and arm himself with two six-shooters and his trusty carbine. The distance between the places where he preached being sometimes as great as sixty miles, it was often necessary for him to camp overnight by himself. Twice he was attacked by Indians but escaped uninjured. On one occasion, while he was preaching in the village of Palo Pinto, the county was so filled with hostile Indians and wrought up to such a pitch that Mr. Slaughter kept his six-shooter and his carbine at his side during the sermon, and every member of his congregation was likewise armed. He never permitted business or fear of the Indians to interfere with his pastoral work, and always made it a point to keep his engagements.

He first united with the Methodist church in 1831, but in 1842 joined the Baptist church and in 1844 was ordained to preach. He studied and practiced medicine, and was for a number of years the only physician in Palo Pinto county. It would be impossible to overrate his usefulness during those long years when the citizens of the northwestern counties were practically isolated from the world and dependent upon each other for comfort and aid in times of extremity. Ever thoughtful and kind, Mr. Slaughter gave freely of his time and money to the poor of his community.

Eleven children were born to Mr. and Mrs. Slaughter, six boys and five girls. Seven of them are still living, as follows: C. C., Peter E., W. B., Fannie, Sarah, Jane and Millie. Mrs. Slaughter died on the 6th of January, 1894.

He died at his home, six miles north of Palo Pinto,

Texas, at 11 P. M., March 19, 1895. During his last illness he had the consolation of having with him his three
sons, C. C., J. B., and W. B. Slaughter; his three daughters, Mrs. Jennie Harris, Mrs. Millie Dalton, and Miss
Fannie Slaughter, and also his long cherished friend,
Rev. Rufus C. Burleson, of Waco, and a number of neighbors and other friends. His end was peaceful and in
keeping with his Christian life. Just before he died, he
expressed his willingness to obey the summons, his trust
in God, and his belief in a happy immortality.

THOMAS M. PEELER

Thomas M. Peeler was born November 15, 1848, in
Kosciusko, Mississippi. He came to Texas when about
eighteen years of age, and from Texas went to Idaho and

MR. AND MRS. THOMAS M. PEELER

Wyoming and spent eight years on ranches there, then
came back to Texas and lived on the Irvin & Millet ranch
in Baylor county until that ranch was sold to Simpson.
Then Mr. Peeler settled in Atascosa county in 1882 and
lived there until his death May 18, 1897. He was married
January 21, 1880, to Miss Alice Jane Irvin, and to this
union were born seven children, five boys and two girls.

HARDSHIPS OF A COWBOY'S LIFE IN THE EARLY DAYS IN TEXAS

James T. Johnson, Charco, Texas

I was born in Jackson county, Mississippi, April 15th, 1852, and came to Texas with my parents at the age of six months, landing at Corpus Christi in October. My father was county clerk there for one term. Mother took sick on the ship coming to Texas, and lived only six weeks after landing at Corpus Christi. My grandfather came to Texas with the Irish colony, and served a few years in the Confederate army, was wounded and came home on a short furlough, but took blood poisoning and lived but a few hours.

At the tender age of nine years, I was left an orphan, and was sent to live with the Bookman family, where I was treated as one of their own children. For two years I enjoyed myself in the home of these good people, but an uncle in Falls county sent for me to come and live with him, but I was abused so much that I left and went to live with another uncle who was just as bad, so I drifted out into the wide world for myself at the age of thirteen.

JAMES T. JOHNSON

I worked for Kade Lewis, in the town of Bremond, hauling water, and freighted to the town of Kosse. I stayed two years with this job earning $400 in wages, but when I tried to collect, I had to be satisfied by exchanging my saddle, worth about $9.00 for his, which was not worth over $15.00. Soon afterwards, I began to work for widow Thomas, gathering and herding range horses, where I learned my first work on a ranch.

I hired to Wash Grey to bring a herd of cattle to Goliad county, delivering them to his brother, Bob Grey. I remained in Goliad county and worked as a freighter again, hauling supplies from Old Indianola to Goliad and Sutherland Springs. The ox teams we had to drive were too slow for a boy of my age, and I longed to get back on a ranch chasing mavericks. For the next four years, I worked for H. A. Lane, near my present home, twelve miles west of Goliad. Here I received $20.00 per month, breaking broncos, gathering and branding cattle, etc.

At the age of twenty-one years I left Goliad with a herd of mixed cattle for H. A. Lane and J. Gus Patton, and drove these cattle over the Old Chisholm Trail to Dodge City, Kansas, with only two stampedes on the entire trip.

One year later I again went up the trail with a herd of mixed cattle of over 3,000 head for J. Gus Patton, who is now our county attorney, and one of the truest friends I have ever known. On this trip we had Patton for boss, and Sidney Chivers, Uncle Billie Menafee and Will Peck as cowboys. Returning from this trip, I gathered wild horses in Goliad, Victoria, Refugio, Bee, Live Oak and Karnes counties, gathering several thousand head for the various ranches.

In 1876 I again went up the trail with 4,500 head of aged steers for Dillard Fant, with Charley Boyce as herd boss. On this trip we had the worst weather I ever experienced, losing cattle in blizzards with the most vivid electrical displays imaginable. We had seven stampedes on this trip.

In the winter of 1871 and 1872, I helped skin dead cattle on the prairies in Goliad, Victoria and Refugio counties, as the cattle were starving to death by the thousands, and very few grown cattle lived through this terrible winter. I have seen as many as a thousand head of dead cattle in one day's ride on the prairie near Lamar. Horses, cattle, deer and sheep suffered awfully during these times.   Wild game in those days was almost a nuisance.   I have seen deer a few miles southeast of Goliad in droves of fifty or more at a time, and all the settlers had hogs running wild on the range, fat in the fall of the year on post oak and live oak acorns, pecans, etc.

In 1876 I returned to Limestone county, near Pottersville, where I was married to Miss Martha Thomas, who has been the most faithful helpmate and partner a man could be blessed with, and still doing her part in every way to assist me in the ups and downs of this life's uncertainties.   Returning to Goliad, we settled near the Minneauhuila Creek six miles north of Goliad, where we tried farming, while I worked at odd jobs for the late John Taylor for fifteen years.   In the early seventies I experienced quite a lot of difficulty trying to play neutral in the Taylor, Sutton and Tumlinson feuds, as my sole desire was to work for wages and not get mixed up with either side.

All the schooling I ever got was about two weeks a year for three years.   I did not have a chance to attend school as other boys did in those days.   I realize now more than ever what I have missed by not having an education, and it has been one of my greatest desires in life to give my children a good education.   I live on my farm near the town of Charco, on some of the same land I roamed over as a cowboy, when land could be bought at thirty cents per acre, and which is now worth $75 per acre, and considered as good as the state has. I am now seventy years of age, can do a hard day's work yet, and as old as I am, I feel like I could go through all these hardships again if necessary.   If any of my old friends happen to see this article I would be glad to hear from them.

ASSOCIATED WITH FRANK JAMES

Sam H. Nunneley, San Antonio, Texas

I was born in Hickman county, Middle Tennessee, April 3, 1851, and in 1869 I started to Texas. I arrived at Memphis on a train, then the terminus of all roads going west. There I took the steamer, *Bismarck*, down the Mississippi to the mouth of Red River, and up Red River, to Soda and Caddo Lakes to Jefferson, Texas. I had lots of sport shooting alligators on the trip. From Jefferson I traveled in a freight wagon drawn by eight yoke of oxen to Bowie county. The next year I saddled my horse and pulled out for West Texas, landing at McKinney, Collin county, where I met Townsend Megeath, and we traveled together, slept together and that winter we stayed with Sam Hilderbran, which was an assumed name I learned in after years. Mr. Megeath turned out to be Frank James. Both were good, unassuming gentlemen in every way. It was from this county I made my first trip over the trail with Sneed, Clonch and Gatling. I made one trip with horses to Mississippi and after selling them I went down into Florida, where I remained all winter, then went to New Orleans and Shreveport, and on to San Antonio, and then out to Uvalde, where I went to work helping drive over the trail for Hughes, Nunn, Hood and Birchfield. We had four-teen thousand cattle cut into four herds, and we drove them to Wichita, Kansas. This was in 1875. After all were sold I came back to Texas

SAM H. NUNNELEY

on the train to Seguin, and there took the stage to San Antonio, and stayed all night at the well-known Menger

Hotel. Next morning I purchased a saddle for $40 and a horse for $16 and rode to Uvalde. There I fell in with a bunch of fellows, eleven in all, and we started horseback to Silver City, New Mexico, a distance of 900 miles. We went there to live but nobody lived there outside of government forts except wild Indians, so we started back to Texas, coming to Fort Stanton, down the Pecos River to Horsehead Crossing, then across the plains ninety-five miles without water to the head waters of the Concho River. There I killed my last buffalo. I spent two weeks with a buffalo hunter there who had killed that season upwards of 5,000 buffaloes for their hides and tongues. He sold the hides to Fort Worth people at six bits to a dollar each.

From Johnson county I drove 125 horses to Arkansas for a Mr. Sparks. I bought beef cattle in the Indian Territory from the Indians for four years, and drove them to the Hot Springs market, then bought cattle in Arkansas to drive to Kansas, but sold them to the chief of the Choctaw Nation, after which I went back to Arkansas and engaged in the mercantile business for awhile. I was in the "run" in Oklahoma, and helped to make a state out of the Territory of Oklahoma. I now live in San Antonio.

THE TANKERSLEY FAMILY

By Mary Tankersley Lewis, San Angelo, Texas

Richard Franklin Tankersley was born February 19, 1828, in Mississippi. Moved to Texas in 1853, stopping for awhile at Round Rock, Williamson county, afterward living in Cherokee county, then in San Saba, then in Brown county, and from there moved to the head of the South Concho River, in Tom Green county, which was not organized until many years later. He served in the Texas Rangers from 1863 to 1865.

About January 1st, we were visited by a band of Kickapoo Indians who were going to Mexico and had stopped at Dove Creek spring to spend a few days. We had at first thought they were hostile Indians and my father had drawn his gun on the leader, who waved a white cloth and called out, "me no fight." There were about fifty men and two women in the party. They were very friendly and in scouting some days later, found some of our horses which had strayed off and brought them home. On January 8, they were overtaken by a company of Texas Rangers under Captain Gillentine, and a fight

R. F. TANKERSLEY

was forced on the Indians. A number of white men were killed and my father helped bury them. While living at the head of the Concho, he gathered a herd of cattle with the intention of trailing them to New Mexico, but he sold them to John Chisum, and the Indians took them from him on the plains. In June, 1869, my father trailed a herd of twenty-five hundred cattle to Los Angeles, California, being on the trail about eight months. On the way home, two men who camped with him for the night, cut open a saddle bag and stole five hundred dollars. In the pair of saddle bags there was twenty-five thousand dollars in gold, and why they did not take it all is a mystery. At that time and for many years afterwards there were no banks in this part of the state, so all the money we had was buried under the house.

Increasing depredations by the Indians caused us to move to Fort Concho in 1869. Many times every horse and mule on the ranch was taken. All the salt we used was hauled by wagon from Pecos. On one of these trips

my father and a hired man were run into by Indians near
the head of the main Concho. They got into the river
under bushes and fought the Indians off. My father
was shot in the ankle and the bullet was never extracted.
In February, 1870, we were living in San Angelo, about
where the American Legion opera house now stands, and
Indians came trying to get horses out of the corral back

G. W. TANKERSLEY   FAYETTE TANKERSLEY

of the house. About 10 o'clock that night the late Judge
Preusser came to our door and said he had dreamed of
seeing Indians and looking out saw them in fact. About
that time they began yelling and shooting. They did not
get the horses and it was thought that an Indian was
wounded as a bloody war bonnet was found the next day.
In this fight a Mexican was shot through one ear.

A kind and all-wise Providence guarded us through
all the dangers and hardships of pioneer life and will
be with us to the end. Father passed away December
11th, 1912, leaving three sons, G. W., Fayette, and H. M.
Tankersley, and four daughters, Mrs. Elizabeth Emerick,
Mrs. Clarissa Frary, Mrs. Sallie Phelan and Mrs. Mary
Lewis. Since his death, the oldest son and youngest
daughter have "crossed over the river," and are resting
with him " 'neath the shade of the trees."

TRAIL DRIVING WAS FASCINATING

W. A. Roberts, Frio Town, Texas

My parents were J. E. Roberts and Elizabeth Stahl Roberts. I was born in Montgomery county, Texas, January 16, 1863, and came to Frio county with my father and mother in 1869, where I lived ever since. We made the trip to this county in an ox wagon, and about the only thing I remember about the trip was crossing the Brazos River on a ferry boat. When I was about thirteen years old I went to work for Capt. B. L. Crouch on his Frio county ranch, and worked there for several years. I made three trips up the trail. In 1883 I went to Benkelman, Nebraska, and re-mained over for the fall round-up on George Benkelman's ranch on the South Prong of the Republican River, then returning to my old job on the Crouch ranch.

W. A. ROBERTS

In 1884 I went to Seven Rivers, New Mexico, and re-mained there to help gather and deliver the D. J. Crouch cattle to the Holt Cattle Company in November of that year, then drove a bunch of horses from Seven Rivers to Marfa, shipping them from Marfa to Uvalde and drove them from Uvalde to the Crouch ranch in Frio county.

In 1885 I went with a herd of steers for Crouch & Crawford to the Chickasaw Nation in the Indian Territory. Bert Brown was our boss on this trip.

Barring stampedes, and storms when balls of lightning played on the tips of our horses' ears and great balls of electricity came rolling along the ground, trail

driving was a fascinating life. We have forgotten the
hardships and remember only the pleasant things.

FOLLOWED CATTLE FROM THE RANCH TO THE SHIPPING PEN

Mrs. A. P. Belcher, Del Rio, Texas

Alvis Powell Belcher was born September 7th, 1854,
in Jackson county, Missouri. His parents came to Sherman, Grayson county, Texas, when he was six weeks old.
He commenced going up the trail with herds of cattle at
the age of fourteen. From 1870 to 1878 he made many

trips trailing cattle to Kansas
and Missouri. In 1878, together with C. W. Easley he
established an R2 ranch on
Wander's Creek in Harde-
man county where the town of
Chillicothe now stands. A
short while afterwards the Indians made a raid down
through that portion of the
country and killed two cowboys working on the ranch.
Because of the danger from
Indians he sold the R2 stock

A. P. BELCHER

of cattle, consisting at that time of 10,000 head, and
located on the Wichita near Henrietta, Texas, where he
lived and ranched until he moved to Southwest Texas in
1897.

He went through all the hardships of the ranchman,
wirecutters, droughts and many panics, but he always
came back believing he could win out. He started up
the long, long trail the 3rd of March, 1919, and it is certain that he and T. B. Jones and a host of other trail
drivers will greet the drags as they cross the river with

the same cheery smiles and handclasps that they gave them while here.

Surely I am eligible to a membership in the Old Trail Drivers' Association, for my Grandfather Emberson trailed his little herd of steers from Lamar county to Arkansas and sold them to the United States Government. A few years prior to 1830 my father, Calvin Copenhaver, trailed cattle to Shreveport and other places in the fifties and sixties, and my husband, Alvin Belcher, in the seventies to eighties. My sons have driven herds throughout Western Texas. I have trailed behind the old chuck wagon, have eaten son-of-a-gun from a tin plate off the chuck box and followed cattle from the ranch to the shipping pen.

TELLS OF AN INDIAN FIGHT

W. A. Franks, Pearsall, Texas

I first saw the light in Montgomery county, January 24th, 1853. The family came to Frio county in 1869, in the month of June. I worked for B. L. Crouch and his brother, Joe Crouch, for twelve years and want to state right here that the Crouches were two as fine men as I ever knew. Captain B. L. Crouch came from Michigan just after the Civil war, and was a captain in the Union army. He first engaged in the sheep business in Williamson county, from there he came to Frio county, where he became one of the big cow-men of Texas, becoming the owner of a ranch between Old Frio Town and Pearsall, containing some sixty thousand acres. My mother had charge of the boarding or dining hall, at the head ranch, where the cowboys and anyone visiting the ranch got their meals. I recall one incident, to show the true gentleman the captain was. Some three or four of his rich friends from the north were at the ranch on a visit, and a cowboy of the one-horse kind came to the ranch looking for a cow that had been lost out of a small herd when passing through

the ranch. When the bell rang at the dining hall for supper, twenty-five or thirty men marched into the hall, took
their respective places, and there they stood while Captain Crouch took the one-horse cowboy by the arm and
escorted him to a seat at the table. After he had been
seated, he said, "Gentlemen, be seated." I don't think

WM. A. FRANKS

he had a superior for being a refined, cultured, polished,
intelligent gentleman, and those who transacted business
with him held him in the highest esteem. The cowboys
who worked for him loved him like a father. He, like
his "Pisano," Henry Ford, believed in a fair wage for
the working man. Though he had lost his fortune, in
his later years he never quit working for the flock master,

by advocating the scalp law against the predatory animals.

My first trip on the trail was made in the spring of 1874, with J. W. Allen as boss. The herd was owned by Lytle McDaniel, and was delivered at Dodge City, Kansas.

In 1874 we went from the Crouch ranch and shipped to Wichita Falls, Texas, then drove to Bingham, Nebraska, on the Republican River. A bad storm struck us on Smoky River, five herds being in sight, and we were the only boys that held our herd. George Wilcox, the boss, said it was the worst storm that he had ever seen and he had been on the trail thirteen years. Will King from Lockhart, Texas, came near being drowned that night, as the face of the earth was covered with water, and one could not distinguish ravines from level ground.

In June, 1873, during the light of the moon, while working on the Crouch ranch one of the sheep herders failed to show up. Some two weeks after he disappeared I found his remains about one mile and a half from the ranch, his body stripped and mutilated, hands tied behind and seven arrows sticking in his back.

In 1875 Indians made a raid on the Crouch ranch during the night and the next morning when we discovered their trail and missed the horses, seven of us followed them. Nelse Brice, Jap Brice, Jim Crawson, T. W. Everete, L. L. Everete, Ben Steadman, M. W. Franke and myself. We overtok them at Loma Vista in Zavala county. The country being open, they discovered us when we were a half a mile behind them, so we had a running fight for a mile, until they took the brush. We captured sixty head of horses, twenty of them belonging to Rothe on the Hondo. There were nine Indians in this bunch. The horses they were mounted on were all they got off with. Quite a number of shots were exchanged, but I don't think any damage was done on either side.

REMINISCENCES OF THE OLD TRAILS

C. F. Doan of Doan's

I am now 74 years old and looking back over my life I find the main part of it has been spent near the Old Chisholm Trail, or on the Dodge City, Kansas trail.

My first introduction to the Old Chisholm Trail was in 1874 when in company with Robert E. Doan, a cousin, and both of us from Wilmington, Ohio, we set out for Ft. Sill, Indian Territory, from Wichita, Kansas. We

ORIGINAL SETTLEMENT AT DOAN'S

made this little jaunt by stage coach of 250 miles over the famous trail in good time.

In 1875, very sick, I returned to my home in Ohio from Fort Sill, but the lure of the West urged me to try my luck again and October 10, 1878, found me back in the wilds and ever since I have lived at Doan's, the trail crossing on Red River known far and wide by the old trail drivers as the jumping off place into the great unknown the last of civilization until they hit the Kansas line.

While sojourning in the Indian Territory in 1874 and 1875 with Tim Pete, Dave Lours and J. Doan, I engaged in trading with the Indians and buying hides at a little store on Cache Creek, two miles from Fort Sill. Our life at this place was a constant thrill on account of Indians. During the month of July, 1874, the Indians killed thirteen hay cutters and wood choppers. Well do I remember, one day after a hay cutter had been killed, a tenderfoot from the East with an eye to local color decided to

DOAN'S CROSSING ON RED RIVER

explore the little meadow where the man had been killed expecting to collect a few arrows so that he might be able to tell the loved ones at home of his daring. But the Indians discovered the sightseer and with yells and his collection of arrows whistling about his ears, chased him back to the stockade. Terror lent wings to his feet and he managed to reach safety but departed the next day for the East, having lost all taste for the danger of the West.

January 8, 1875, found me caught in a blizzard and I narrowly escaped freezing to death at the time. Indians around Fort Sill demanding buckskin, as their supply had run low, I was sent by the firm on horseback to the Shaw-

nee tribe to buy a supply. This was my second trip.
Soon after my departure the blizzard set in and I was
warned by the mail carrier, the only man I met on the
trip, to turn back or I would be frozen. But the thoughts
of the buckskin at $4.00 per pound caused me to press
on. I managed to reach Conover ranch badly frozen,
I was taken from my horse and given first-aid treatment.
I was so cold that ice had frozen in my mouth. The mail
carrier, who had advised me to turn back, never reached

DOAN'S STORE IN THE SEVENTIES

the fort, and his frozen body was found some days after
the storm.

For two weeks I remained in this home before I found
strength to continue the journey. I was held up another
week by the cold near Paul's Valley, but I got the buckskin, sending it back by express-mail carrier and returned
on horseback.

Indians during this time were held in concentration
camps near the fort, both Comanches and Kiowas, and
beeves were issued twice a week. A man by name of
Conover and myself did the killing and about seventy-
five or eighty head were killed at one time. The hides
were bought from the Indians and shipped to St. Louis.

After the bi-weekly killings, the Indians would feast

and sing all night long and eat up their rations and nearly starve until the next issue day came.

It was at this time that I met Quanah, chief of the Comanches, who was not head chief at that time, and Satanta, chief of the Kiowas. I was warned during that time by Satanta that the Indians liked me and they wanted me to leave the country because they intended to kill every white man in the nation. I rather think that the friendly warning was given me because I often gave crackers and candy to the hungry squaws and papooses and of course Satanta's family received their share.

Satanta escaped soon after that and near where El Reno now stands, at the head of his warriors, captured a wagon train and burned men to their wagon wheels. He was captured again and taken to the penitentiary where he committed suicide by opening a vein in his arm.

After moving to Doan's of course I saw a great deal of Quanah, who at that time had become head chief. He told me that he had often been invited to return to his white relations near Weatherford but he had refused. "Corwin," he said, "as far as you see here I am chief and the people look up to me, down at Weatherford I would be a poor half breed Indian." Perhaps he was right.

Big Bow, another Kiowa chief, often followed by his warriors, rode up to the little store on Cache Creek one day and arrogantly asked, would we hand over the goods or should they take them? We told them we would hand over the goods as he designated them. Later when Big Bow and I became good friends, he said, "Us Indians are big fools, not smart like white men. 'Cause you handed over the goods that day, but Washington (Uncle Sam) took it out of our pay." It was quite true for as soon as the wards of the government had departed, the bill was turned into their guardian, Uncle Sam.

We had but one bad scare from the Indians at Doan's, and that date April, 1879, is indelibly fixed on my memory.

The Indians came close enough to the house to be recognized by the women and they ran our horses off. I was up in the woods hunting at that time and reached home at dusk to find three terror stricken women, a baby and a dog for me to defend. All the other men had gone to Denison for supplies and our nearest neighbor was fifty

ADOBE HOME OF CAPT. C. DOAN

Captain Doan and his daughter, Mrs. Bertha Ross, in the foreground. Mrs. Ross was the first white child born in Wilbarger county. The adobe house shown in this picture was destroyed by fire December 26, 1922, since this sketch was written.

miles away; so thinking discretion the better part of valor, we retreated to a little grove about half a mile from our picket house and spent the night, expecting every moment to have a "hair-raising" experience. The Indians proved to be a band of Kiowas returning from near where Quanah now stands where they killed and scalped a man by name of Earle. Three days later the soldiers came through on the trail of the Indians expecting to find our home in ashes and the family exterminated. The Indians had returned to the reservation. The Kiowas told me afterward quite coolly that they would have attacked us that night but believed us to be heavily garrisoned with buffalo hunters—a lucky thing for us. This was the last raid through the country. The Indians after that became very friendly with us and told me to go ahead and build a big store, that we would not be molested. They had decided this in council.

The spring and summer of 1879, I saw the first herds come up the trail, though the movement had started two years before. My uncle, J. Doan, who had been with me the two years in Fort Sill, had established this post at Doan's, April, 1878, and we had arrived, that is, myself, wife and baby and the Judge's daughters, that fall. So we had come too late to see the herds of 1878. One hundred thousand cattle passed over the trail by the little store in 1879. In 1881, the trail reached the peak of production and three hundred and one thousand were driven by to the Kansas shipping point.

In 1882 on account of the drouth, the cattle found slim picking on their northern trek and if it had not been for the "butter weed" many would have starved to death as grass was all dead that year. Names of John Lytle, Noah Ellis, Ab and John Blocker, Harrold and Ikard, Worsham, the Belchers, Ligon and Clark, Wiley Blair, the Eddlemans and others come into my memory as I write this, owners and bosses of the mighty herds of decades ago. One man, Dubose, with whom we would go a piece, like school kids, up the trail, complained plaintively that he never in all those summers had a mess of roasting ears, of which he was very fond, as the corn would be about knee high when he left Corpus Christi and as he came slowly up the trail he would watch the fields in their various stages but by the time he left Doan's and civilization it was still too early for even a cob.

Captain John Lytle spent as high as a month at a time in Doan's preparing for his onward march. Accompanied by his secretary he would fit out his men and everything would be shipshape when he crossed the Red River. He was a great man and his visits were enjoyed.

Wichita Falls failing to provide suitable branding pens for the accommodation of the trail drivers, pens were provided at Doan's. Furnaces and corrals were built and here Charley Word and others fitted with cartridges, Winchesters by the case, sow bosom and flour, and even to Stetson hats, etc. This store did a thriving business and thought nothing of selling bacon and flour in car-load lots, though getting our supplies from Denison, Sherman, Gainesville, and later, Wichita Falls.

The postoffice was established here in 1879 and I was the first postmaster. It was at this office all mail for the trail herds was directed as, like canned goods and other commodities, this was the last chance. One night while a crowd sat around the little adobe store someone struck up a lively air on a French harp and the door opened and in sailed a hat followed closely by a big black fellow who commenced to dance. It was one of Ab Blocker's niggers who had been sent up for the mail, giving first notice of the herd's arrival. Many a sweetheart down the trail received her letter bearing the postmark of Doan's and many a cowboy asked self-consciously if there was any mail for him while his face turned a beet red when a dainty missive was handed him.

The old trail played a part in the establishment of the Doan's picnic. For in 1884 when grass had risen and the cowmen had gone up the trail or out to the spring roundups; the women of course were playing the rôle of "the girl I left behind me," so a picnic of five women and one lone man was inaugurated. I have never missed a picnic from that day. Now the crowd is swelled to thousands, the dinner is a sumptuous affair and every two or three years the state and county candidates for offices plead with the people to give them the other fellow's job or one or more chance as the case may be.

The first house at Doan's was made of pickets with a dirt roof and floor of the same material. The first winter we had no door but a buffalo robe did service against the northers. The store which had consisted mainly of ammunition and a few groceries occupied one end and the family lived in the other. A huge fireplace around which Indians, buffalo hunters and the family sat, proved very comforting. The warmest seat was reserved for the one who held the baby and this proved to be a very much coveted job. Furniture made with an ax and a saw adorned the humble dwelling.

Later the store and dwelling were divorced. An adobe store which gave way to a frame building was built. Two log cabins for the families were erected. In 1881 our present home was built, the year the county was organized. This dwelling I still occupy. Governors, English Lords, bankers, lawyers, tramps and people from every walk in life have found sanctuary within its walls. And if these walls could speak many a tale of border warfare would echo from its gray shadows.

Here, my old adobe house and I sit beside the old trail and dream away the days thinking of the stirring scenes enacted when it seemed an endless procession of horses and cattle passed, followed by men of grim visage but of cheerful mien, who sang the "Dying Cowboy" and "Bury Me Not on the Lone Prairie" and other cheerful tunes as they bedded the cattle or when in a lighter mood danced with the belles of Doan's or took it straight over the bar of the old Cow Boy saloon.

MADE MANY TRIPS UP THE OLD COW TRAIL

E. P. Byler, Wadsworth, Texas

I made my first trip up the trail in 1868. In May of that year Brother Jim Byler and myself hired to Steve Rogers, who was boss for Dave Puckett, to take a herd of 1,000 longhorn steers through to Abilene, Kansas. Wages were low then and we drew only $30 per month and expenses. We were allowed a month's pay returning home. This was all an inexperienced hand could get, while experienced men drew $40 per month. We had to stand guard from one-third to one-fourth of every night except when it rained, and then we stood guard all night. We were supposed to travel fifteen miles per day. When we left Helena, in Karnes county, with cattle in living order, if they didn't stampede at night and run too much, they would be in good shape when we reached our destination. Each man had four horses, and we never fed them grain for the grass was good and sufficient to sustain them on the trip. There were no fences—the range was open from the Gulf of Mexico to North Dakota as far as I went.

Fortunately on this trip we did not have to swim any swollen rivers, and made good progress.

Each evening when we prepared for the night we would catch up our night horses and stake them so each man would be ready to go on guard when he was called. In catching our horses we took lariats, tied one end to the wheel of the chuck wagon, a man holding the other end, and form a sort of a corral into which the horses were driven. The horses soon became accustomed to this and would not try to get over the rope pen.

On this trip we left Helena, Karnes county, and went by way of Gonzales. When the herd strung out it was over a half a mile long. The chuck wagon, drawn by a yoke of oxen driven by the cook, brought up the rear. While we were passing a settler's cabin an old setting hen flew cackling across the herd, and there was a stampede. The cattle in the lead kept going right on but the cattle in the middle of the herd doubled back and ran pell mell in the opposite direction. The men held them for awhile but they ran over the cook's steers and partly turned the wagon over. We had to run them for awhile before they became quiet again, but we had to take them around the place where they found the old setting hen.

We left Gonzales and camped on "Mule Prairie," and here they stampeded again and next morning we did not have a hoof left. We hired a number of men to help us get them together again. We went by way of Lockhart, crossed the Colorado at Austin, on to Georgetown, Salado, Belton, Valley Mills, Fort Worth and Denison, and crossed the Red River at Gainesville, and from here we went to Boggy Depot near the Arkansas line, and on to Abilene, where the cattle were put on the market.

We started back home and were on the return trip a month. These cattle were fullgrown steers, and were good walkers. I hugely enjoyed this trip, as well as coming back and was ready to go again when the opportunity offered.

In 1870, by which time I had become an expert cow hand, I was hired by Choate & Bennett at a salary of $75 per month, to go through with a herd in charge of Don Pace. Brother Jim was also with me on this trip. I worked in the lead, and we went the Chisholm Trail as before, crossed the Red River and went on up through the Indian Territory, where there were but few settlements. When we reached Wild Horse, that stream was up, and we had to take our wagon bed, put a wagon sheet around it and make a ferry boat which carried our things over. On the banks of the North Canadian we found a newly made grave with a head-board bearing the inscription, "Killed by Indians." I do not know who the unfortunate victim could have been, but these graves were not uncommon. We went on and delivered the cattle at Wichita, Kansas, and then took the trail for home.

On March 15, 1871, Brother Jim, as boss, started with a herd for Choate & Bennett. I went through the same route as before. On this trip we saw plenty of buffalo and antelopes, and the country was full of wolves. At Wichita, Kansas, we threw the two herds together, Brother Jim and hands came back home, and I went north with the cattle a thousand miles, passing through Nebraska, crossed the Platte River and struck the Missouri River which was a mile wide, and steamboats were on it. The stream was so wide the cattle could not see the landing on the other side, and we worked nine days trying to get them across. We hired some civilized Indians to assist us, but they were of very little use. Three hundred head of the cattle refused to swim the river and we sold them on this side to the government. We hired a man with a small boat to ferry our bedding and provisions across, and we took our wagon apart and floated it over. We had forty head of horses, and only four of them succeeded in swimming the full distance, the others would swim a part of the way and then turn over on their side and float. We had to hold their heads up to keep them from drowning. They were taken over two at a time alongside the little boat. So you can imagine what a time we had had getting across that river, and how much time was lost. We gave the man with the boat the best horse we had for his service.

From here we went right up the north side of the Missouri River to deliver them at a place three hundred miles distant. That country was full of savage Indians, but we did not encounter any of them. There were several government forts along the way, and these cattle were being taken there to feed the civilized Indians, who came to the forts at regular intervals for "rations" which the government issued to them.

On our way up we had the exciting experience of being almost swept away by a cyclone. This was in Dakota. It was without rain, but the noise was awful. None of us had ever seen a cyclone, and did not know what it was until it struck the ground, milling and twisting the sage grass. Right there we let the cattle take care of themselves, and every man made a run to get out of the path of the twister. It soon passed, going north, and missed the herd and men but a very short distance. We all felt that we had a very narrow escape from death.

We went on up through North Dakota to a point near the line of Canada where we delivered the cattle, and then started back home. On our way back we camped at the home of a white man who had married an Indian squaw. That night three of our horses disappeared. We hunted for them a couple of days and not finding them we were satisfied they were stolen. Lew Allen, owner of the cattle, reported our loss at the nearest fort and soldiers came down and arrested the squawman, burnt his shack, and made him tell where the horses were. He had the Indians steal them and take them across the Missouri river. They were found where he said they were.

We moved on back towards home, and one night something stampeded our horses, all getting away except one little Spanish pony. We hunted for them two days and located them where somebody had penned them, and we had to give a horse for trouble and damages claimed.

Lew Allen persuaded me to bring an Indian boy back with me. He was about fifteen years old, and lived with Allen in Lavaca county until grown. This Indian killed a man there and in trying to escape was killed himself.

I stopped at Wichita, Kansas, and hired to Read & O'Connor as boss, and took charge of their cattle until the following November. When the cattle were disposed of I came back through Indian Territory and reached home all right. For nine months I had not slept in a house.

On my fourth trip up the trail I took 1,000 beeves for Read & O'Connor, and was paid $100 per month and all expenses. This was in March, 1872. We left Goliad and went up the same route as before. We held these cattle at Wichita, Kansas, out of the settlements, and herded them on one bed ground for five and a half months. As I was boss I didn't have to herd. I looked after three herds until December when they were fat and we put them on the market. I didn't sleep in a house for nine months and kept well all the time. After the cattle were sold I took a bunch of ten men and the chuck wagon and struck out over the back trail for home, and got back in time to be married to Miss Fannie M. Crossley, on Christmas Day, 1872.

In March, 1873, I was again employed by Read &
O'Connor, this time at $125 per month. Mr. O'Connor
and I gathered cattle around Matagorda Bay. There
were a thousand head of beeves, and seven hundred of
them had O'Connor's brand on them. We took them to
J. D. Read's near Goliad, and put the road brand on them.
The road brand was made in the shape of a horse shoe.
We headed toward Yorktown, where we struck the old
trail and followed it all the way. Not a stampede
occurred on the trip of over a thousand miles. We delivered these cattle to Shanghai Pearce at Wichita, Kansas.
I had formerly worked for Pearce, and he induced me to
deliver these same cattle down in Missouri. Now there
was a law in that state against taking cattle through
which had not wintered over, but we took the chance.
When we got to Missouri with our old beef hide still hanging under the wagon it looked suspicious to a fellow who
came out to our camp one evening. He asked me my
name and a few fool questions, and then departed. Pretty
soon this fellow came back to camp accompanied by several men riding longtailed horses, and carrying muskets.
They served a writ on me and said, ''E. P. Byler and
crew, consider yourselves under arrest.'' And I did not
resist. When we got to a little town I wired to Shanghai
Pearce at Wichita about the mess I was in. They put a
man to watch us and see that we didn't move the cattle,
and we awaited Pearce's coming. He soon got there with
a bunch of men, and we decided on a course of action.
Pearce got very intimate with the guard and took him
for a buggy ride. The hands he brought took charge of
the cattle and told us to rattle our hocks and strike for
an Indian reserve about ten miles away where we would
be safe. When Pearce got back with the guard we were
gone—''E. P. Byler and crew'' could not be found. The
guard was put in jail. Pearce got into a wrangle with
the authorities about the cattle, but a compromise was
effected and we returned and took them to where he

wanted them delivered. I then took the train for my home in Helena, Karnes county, Texas, and this wound up my trail driving.

FIFTY YEARS AGO

J. J. (Joe) Roberts, Del Rio, Texas

I was born in Caldwell county, Texas, in the year of 1851, and made that county my home for twenty years. It was in the spring of 1871 that I took my first trip up the trail. I drove for Joe Bunton and our destination was Abilene, Kansas, but owing to the rapid settlement of that surrounding country, there was but little room to hold a herd of cattle so we stopped this side near Newton, Kansas, which was the terminus of the Santa Fé Railroad. I drove the next year for Col. Jack Meyers who will be remembered by many old-time drivers. Those were in the days of Dick Head, Billy Campbell and Noah Ellis.

J. J. (Joe) ROBERTS

My later drives were for Billie and Charley Slaughter of Frio county, who sent cattle as far north as Wyoming and Montana and I continued with them up to 1876, when I went into the ranch business for myself. I settled in Kinney county and remained there for about five years, but now I am in Val Verde county, a part of old Kinney county, where I lived for forty-five years. The hardships and privations of the trail life have been duly set forth by those who have preceded me and in a passing way I will say that we all fared about the same.

It has been my pleasure of late years to visit some of

the towns and stations in Oklahoma, Kansas and Colorado where the old Trail passed through in those early days, and the change that meets your eyes is but little short of marvelous. Where saloons and dance halls stood are now substantial school buildings and magnificent churches and the merry prattle of happy children is heard on every corner. And it was a deep feeling of pride that came to me, to know that I had had an humble part in bringing about this wonderful change, which in a measure helped to settle the great Northwest, which has proven so valuable an asset to our country. Memory fails me in recalling the names of the old boys who were associated with me in those early days. Milton Taylor and Joe Loxton of Frio county were with me on my last trip and I have been in touch with them ever since. Doubtless many of them have passed away and those who still remain are, like myself, aged and gray. And it will not be long before we will have taken our last drink out of the old canteen of life that has refreshed us so often in days gone by.

May the blessings of our Heavenly Father attend us in our last days and when we come into His presence may we hear that welcome plaudit—"Well done, my good and faithful servants, enter into thy rest."

P. E. SLAUGHTER

Peter Eldridge Slaughter was born September 11, 1846, in Sabine county, Texas, the third son of George Webb and Sallie Slaughter. His father moved from Sabine county to Palo Pinto county in 1857, when he was eleven years of age. He joined the Confederate Army in 1864, belonging to Capt. Jack Cureton's Rangers, Cureton being under Col. Sull Ross, who afterwards was governor of Texas. He would not attend school at the little school in Palo Pinto county. His father gathered twenty head of cattle and sent him to McKenzie College, conducted by a leading Methodist preacher, who had established a boarding school for young men eight miles southwest of Clarksville, Texas.

A younger brother, W. B. Slaughter, assisted him in driving these cattle to this school from Palo Pinto a distance of 250 miles. The younger brother returning with the saddle ponies and pack horse, as soon as he arrived and delivered the cattle to the school. He remained eight months in the school and came home. In 1868 he went to Abilene, and two years later to Coffeyville, Kansas.

P. E. SLAUGHTER

The representative of the Fort Worth Live Stock Stockyards, W. J., (Billie) Carter went with him up the trail in 1871. That year he was married to Miss Mollie Chick, of Palo Pinto, and from this union six children were born —five sons and one daughter, namely: Monte, Arthur, Paschall, Joel, and John, and Callie. His youngest son went to France as a soldier and now sleeps on Flanders' Field. He drove two herds of cattle to Cypress Hills on the line of Canada and Northern Montana, and three herds to California. He and his father under the style name of G. W. and P. E. Slaughter, were extensive cattle traders in North Texas, during the years 1876, 1877 and 1878.

W. E. Crowley, former secretary of the Texas Cattle Raisers' Association, and at present a leading Attorney of Fort Worth, says that in 1877 P. E. Slaughter delivered a small herd of steers to him, and he had no check book nor blank paper, and it was at one of the old ranches whose roof was made of cypress shingles. He pulled out a shingle from the roof and wrote a check for the amount due him on it. He was doing business at this time with J. R. Couts & Co., of Weatherford, Texas, and Crowley presented the shingle check and it was paid. He and his father dissolved partnership in 1878, and he moved his herd of stock cattle to Crosby county, West Texas, and the town of Dockum now stands on his ranch ground.

In 1882, he moved his cattle from Crosby county, to the head of Black River, the main tributary of the Gila River, in Arizona, and he ranched there until he died. He was buried at St. Johns, Arizona, Nov. 6th, 1911. He left a large herd of cattle to his children, now valued at $500,000.00. His death was caused by a cancer at the root of his tongue, claimed by physicians as caused by the amount of tobacco he used.

SKETCH OF THE LIFE OF CAPTAIN J. J. (JACK) CURETON

W. E. Cureton, Meridian, Texas

My father, Capt. Jack Cureton, enlisted in Company H of Col. Yell's regiment of Arkansas as a volunteer soldier under General Taylor, bound for the war in Mexico. Col. Yell was killed in the battle of Buena Vista. Father's company was commanded by Capt. William Preston, afterwards a famous frontier captain in the Indian wars of Texas. He was discharged at San Antonio, Texas, in 1846, in his nineteenth year. He went back to Arkansas, married, and four boys were born in that State as the fruit of this marriage. In 1852 he joined the gold rush for California, and carried a bunch of cattle to the gold fields of that state from Ozark, Arkansas. On return he shipped from San Francisco "around the Horn" to New Orleans, and thence by boat up the Mississippi and Arkansas Rivers home. In the winter of 1854 he moved to Texas, crossing the Red River at Old Preston, famous in the history of the settlement of northern Texas, and began raising cattle on the wide prairies he had traversed while chasing the Mexicans during the Mexican War and on his strip to California in the wake of the forty-niners. He had settled first on Keechi Creek, near the Brazos River, in the territory afterwards, in 1857, organized into what is Palo Pinto county. At that time the Comanches, Caddos, and other tribes of Indians were partly on two reservations, one under Captain Shaply Ross, father of General Sul Ross, one of the most knightly and famous soldiers ever produced by Texas, who afterwards became its Governor; the other under Capt. John R. Baylor, afterwards General Baylor. Captain Ross and Captain Baylor were agents for the Indians under the government on the reservations in Young county territory, one being stationed near where the town of Graham is now located. These reservations, though designed by the public authorities for a good purpose, in effect only furnished supply stations for others of the Indian tribes who claimed to be wild Indians, and depredated on the few settlers all along the border from the Red River on the north to the Rio Grande. They came regularly to the reservations to replenish their supplies of arms, ammunition, beads, etc., trading the horses and mules and other plunder they had looted the whites of to the friendly "buds" on the reservation.

Matters grew from bad to worse until the settlers arose in their wrath about 1858. On Salt Creek, below Belknap, quite a battle was fought, all Indians looking alike to the Texans. Several were killed on both sides, Captain Cureton being in command of his neighbors. It may be said that these old frontiersmen sometimes had more courage than discretion in these conflicts, and in this instance Captain Cureton had to be on guard to keep William McAdams and others of the company from exposing themselves by climbing on the tops of some log cabins which afforded them shelter. In order to appease the outraged citizens, the United States Government in a few days moved the Indians from the Brazos, in Texas, to Fort Sill, Indian Territory. After this open warfare by all of these tribes, augmented by the assistance of the Kiowas and Navajos of New Mexico, became general and more relentless all along the Texas border. Captain Cureton and his neighbors were in the saddle almost constantly every light moon, without any pay or equipment from the government. Many Texans who became noted in after years were of these noble patriots who suffered through these perilous days. Among them I might mention: Col. Charles Goodnight, of Goodnight, Texas, who produced the cross between the cow and buffalo, known as the catalo; Col. C. C. Slaughter and his brother, Pete; one of the Sangers, of Sanger Brothers, the famous merchants; the Hittsons; the Bells; and many others.

Of the numerous battles these volunteer pioneers had with the Indians, I will mention one on Yellow Wolf Creek, a tributary of the Colorado, near old Fort Chadborne, in which several Indians were killed and Jimmie Lane, one of the whites, was mortally wounded. In the last days of November, 1860, the Comanches murdered several people, including women and children, near where Mineral Wells, Texas, is now situated; and on the 5th day of December, 1860, Captain Cureton assembled his citizen soldiers, and the noble merchants of Weatherford, Texas, Carson, Lewis, and others, freely gave supplies for their packs, and they took the trail. At or near Belknap, Captain Cureton sent a messenger to Captain Sul Ross, who had a small company of state troops nearby, and Capt. Ross applied to the United States commander at Fort Camp Cooper, and the latter sent a lieutenant with forty men with the expedition. When the forces arrived on a tributary of Pease River, they encountered the Comanches under Chief Peta Nocona, father of Quanah Parker, and pretty well slaughtered the entire band, Captain Ross wounding the chief in a hand-to-hand encounter in the battle. Upon refusal of the chief to surrender he was killed by Captain Ross' interpreter. In this battle was captured Cynthia Ann Parker and baby girl, who were brought back to her relatives, who had not seen or heard of her since her capture by the Comanches at the massacre at Parker's Fort in the '30's.

In March, 1861, Captain Cureton and his old frontier volunteers joined the Confederate Army, and served in the territory assigned them during the entire period of the Civil War.

In the meantime, the Indians were a great menace, and there were many adventures and battles too numerous to mention in this brief sketch of my father's life.

A band of Lipans, Kickapoos, and Potawatamies left Fort Sill to emigrate to Old Mexico, purporting to keep out of the war, in which they had nothing in common with the combatants. They routed themselves just beyond the Texas ranchers; but, unfortunately perhaps, Captain Gillentine, of Erath county, was buffalo hunting near old Fort Phantom Hill, located in what is now Jones county, in 1864, and discovered the trail of these Indians going southwest. Captain Gillentine at once gave the alarm, and some 500 Texans rushed to the scene, Captain Cureton in the thick of the swim. They took the trail of the Indians near the place of discovery, and on the 8th day of January, 1865, came upon them on Dove Creek, a tributary of the Concho, and the fight was on. In the encounter the Texans lost some 30 or 40 men, and had to outrun the Indians to save the others. In fact, it may be said that the Texans were routed "boots and spurs."

Many times the Indians sacked the town of Palo Pinto, robbed the stables of horses and mules, and on one occasion shot John B. Slaughter when he stepped out of his house at night.

We early Texans of the upper Brazos had to go to Dallas or McLennan county, Texas, for our breadstuff in those early times. Near the beginning of the Civil War, Cravens and Darnell built an inclined wheel cornmill in Golconda, the first name given to Palo Pinto, run by the tread of oxen on the wheel, and we fared well, as we were able to grow corn along the Brazos where the Indians had set the example before us. But the Red Man, always, bent on some mischief, came along and killed the big mulatto negro who was the miller while he was out hunting his oxen, and we had to fall back on the old hand steel mill, which was demonstrative evidence that man should eat his bread by the sweat of his face.

In 1870 Captain Cureton took an immigrant train of 70 people overland from Texas to California, and owned most of the herd of cattle carried by his boys to the Pacific coast at the same time. Captain Cureton returned from California, and was sheriff of Bosque county from 1876 to 1880, the period of time immediately succeeding the reconstruction days, when the country was infested by the worst of criminals, and when the sheriff and his deputies literally stood between the inhabitants of the community and assassins and thieves. He died and was buried in Bosque county in May, 1881, survived by all of his children and by his wife, who survived him until May, 1906, when she died at the home of her daughter, the wife of Judge O. L. Lockett, of Cleburne, Texas.

TRAIL RECOLLECTIONS OF GEO. W. ELAM

I was one of the earliest settlers in Bandera county, when that section was wild and unsettled. The country was full of game. I established my ranch on the West Prong of the Medina River. As with most of the pioneers of those days, I erected a log house, and left the opening for the fireplace, and was waiting for a chimney builder to come and put up my chimney. To keep the rain out,

I covered the opening with a wagon sheet. One night, after we had gone to bed, a negro boy whom I had brought with me from Dallas county, and who slept on a pallet on the floor near the fireplace, suddenly cried out, "O, mas Elam! Fo God! Ole Satan hisself is here, an' done come for us!" I raised up and looking towards the frightened "coon," whose eyes were bulged out so that you could have roped them with a grape vine, I saw, to my surprise, a great big, black mountain bear making himself at home in the room. There he sat on his haunches, by the fireplace, looking as unconcerned as you please. Before I could get my gun, Mr. Bruin suddenly jumped out of one of the window openings and disappeared in the darkness.

Stock raising was the principal and virtually the only industry in the country, and the range was open and free for all. I did not go up the Trail until 1875. In the spring of that year we left Bandera with a herd of one thousand head for Ogallala, Nebraska. Lige Childs was boss, but as he was not as well acquainted with the country as I was, I was virtually made boss of the herd. Our outfit in addition to Childs, was composed of Sammy Schladaer, John McKenzie, John Brock, Sylvester Bethreum, and myself, with one or two others whose names I have forgotten. When we got to the Colorado River, it looked to me like it was five miles wide. This, however, didn't "faze" us in the least, and we swam the herd across without any material loss. As the weather continued bad, with rains and storms, we had to swim the main Brazos and the Clear Fork. When we got to Denison, on Red River, Childs sold out, and we came back over the trail.

Some funny things happened on our way up, but one of the most serious episodes occurred when we got near Fredericksburg. One of the sturdy farmers of that section (there were but few farming settlements in the country) near whose farm we had passed, came to the

herd and to his surprise saw his old family milk cow, as
he honestly thought, marching slowly and peacefully
away from home, in the midst of our cattle. The news
spread through the settlement like wildfire, and in a
short while there must have been a hundred or more
indignant neighbors of his around our herd. They had
the effrontery to insinuate that Childs was trying to steal
old Betsy. The result was that Childs was arrested by
the Sheriff and taken to jail at Fredericksburg. It did
look like he was a "goner." However, just as they got
him to the jail door, one of the boys who had gotten there
and had shaken hands with Childs, suddenly reminded
him that he had a bill of sale to that cow in his coat
pocket. Whereupon Childs reached into his pocket and
produced the paper which showed that he had bought
old Betsy down in Atascosa county. There was a consultation among the irate farmers and the Sheriff. It
didn't hardly look right to put a man in jail for stealing
an animal when he had a bill of sale to it. So they told
Childs he could go, but that the farmer would keep the
cow. Childs grew indignant, and told them that just as
soon as he had delivered his herd he was coming back
and file suit for his property and would have that cow if
he had to take the case to the Supreme Court of the
United States. For some reason or other, Childs never
did file that suit. This unjust and unfortunate suspicion
on the part of that farmer caused us to hold up for three
days on the Perdinales. After proving his innocence,
Childs went back to Bandera for five hundred head more
cattle, and I went on in charge of the herd and waited
at the Colorado for him to come up.

Those old times, with their frontier ways and customs,
have long since been superseded by the modern conveniences and developments of civilization. But the men
who blazed the way for the material greatness which is
ours today, were grand and noble spirits and are entitled
to the grateful remembrance of their fellow-countrymen.

TELLS ABOUT BOB ROBERTSON

W. B. Hardeman of Devine, Texas

R. W. Robertson was a soldier under General Shelby of Missouri. On receiving his discharge here in Texas, he and a number of others went to Mexico expecting to join General Maximilian's army. On reaching Mexico they discovered Maximilian's cause was a hopeless case. They then tendered their services to the Mexican government and were offered only a dollar a day and they bear their own expenses. Being disgusted, he sold his gun and pistol for $43.00, mounted his weary cavalry horse and came back to San Antonio, after having purchased some pretty fair clothing in Mexico. He then went to the Menger Hotel and asked for a bed, where he understood many Confederate soldiers had been given free beds. The clerk remarked, "You are dressed very well and we are not giving away free beds any more." General Tarver, a brother-in-law of the late General Ham P. Bee, having overheard part of the conversation stepped up and said, "What's the trouble?" Bob Robertson stated his case and Tarver said, "Give the man a bed; I'll pay for it." The next morning he went to Sapplington's Livery Stable, mounted his horse and pulled out for San Marcos, where he knew a comrade by the name of Breeding resided. On reaching San Marcos neither he nor Breeding could find any work for him. There was to be a picnic the next day and a dance that night which he attended, and the next morning he went down the San Marcos River and landed at Prairie Lea. Shack Jones coming out of a groggery hailed him saying: "Where are you going?" his reply was "I am hunting work." Shack, being a big-hearted fellow and an ex-Confederate soldier replied, "Well let's go in and get a drink, then you come on home with me to my mother's," which he did. The next morning at the breakfast table Mrs. Jones said, "Johnnie," (speaking to Shack) "I don't want you to leave, I need you here to help run the farm," so he gave his job of cow punching, down near Gonzales, to Bob Robertson.

Bob Robertson settled in Guadalupe county and married Miss Mary Lancaster, daughter of a pioneer Methodist preacher. He became deputy sheriff in that county and did efficient service. He afterwards drove cattle to Kansas with Will Jennings and Jake Ellison as partners. His wife died many years ago. Sid Robertson, a prominent business man of San Antonio, owning the White Star Laundry, was his son and died during the war with flu. There were five brothers, Bob Robertson being the oldest, who had not been together in twenty years. They all met in Pearsall in 1883 and five finer looking specimens of manhood I don't think I ever beheld.

"DOC" BURNETT

DOC BURNETT

Mr. C. Burnett, better known as Doc Burnett, was born in Harris county, Texas, April 19th, 1835, and died in Gonzales county, January 12th, 1915. He was one of the first to drive herds to Kansas in the late '60's and has the credit of driving the last herd out of Gonzales county to the northern markets. No man was better or more favorably known in Texas, on the trail, and on Northern markets than Doc Burnett. His many good deeds and the part he played in developing Texas was surpassed by very few men.

BEN C. DRAGOO

Herewith is presented a likeness of Veteran Ben C. Dragoo, who lives at Eden, Texas. Mr. Dragoo is now nearly ninety years old, but is still active. He was a scout and trailer for Sul Ross' Rangers, and was at the Battle of Pease River when Cynthia Ann Parker was taken from the Indians after a captivity of twenty-eight years. When a little boy, Ben Dragoo was a playmate of Cynthia Ann Parker, his father living near Parker's fort, and by strange chance the young ranger was present and assisted in the identification of the unfortunate girl when she was recaptured. Mr. Dragoo relates many thrilling incidents of early days, and did his full share in making

UNCLE BEN DRAGOO

the frontier safe for the present generation. His son, A. J. Dragoo, lives at Whiteland, in McCulloch county, where he is manager of a large ranch.

AN OLD TRAIL DRIVER

Captain William Carroll McAdams was a native of Tennessee, being born April 3, 1825, a son of Douglas and Sarah McAdams who emigrated to the United States from Scotland on account of religious differences existing in Scotland at that time. They were related to Queen Mary of Scotland by blood. Douglas McAdams, his father, constructed the first macadamized road in the United States.

Captain McAdams, at the age of seventeen, ran away from home and joined General Taylor's command on the

CAPTAIN McADAMS

Rio Grande. Before annexation he had become famous along the Rio Grande as "Mustang Bill." He was employed by the president of the Texas Republic and afterwards by the commander of the United States troops as a scout. It was a time of bold outlawry. Incidents of thrilling character were frequent on the border. Captain McAdams was concerned in several raids on robber strong-

holds, and when war with Mexico began his services were needed, for he knew all about the region General Taylor had mapped out for his campaign. He was in the battle of Palo Alto and Resaca de la Palma. He crossed the Rio Grande and fought and scouted for the American army. At Buena Vista he saw the brigade of Mexican lancers repulsed by Col. Jefferson Davis and next witnessed the rout of Santa Anna's army. By order of General Taylor he reported for duty to General Scott and was sent by the latter commander to rescue three prisoners of war under death sentence. The men, natives of Mexico, joined the American army and were captured by General Santa Anna's cavalry near Cerro Gordo. A kinsman of one of the doomed men deserted and informed the Americans, offering to assist a rescue party. Time was precious. It was past midnight and the men were to be shot at sunrise. Captain McAdams, with fourteen Texans and the Mexican deserter, entered the lines of the enemy, captured all the sentinels, killing the soldier who was on guard over the doomed men, and before daybreak he was back within General Scott's lines with the rescued men, having accomplished the task given him without loss to his own party. For this service he was honored by General Scott with special mention, and from that time to the close of the war he was the trusted scout of the commander-in-chief of the American army in Mexico. After an honorable discharge by General Scott, he returned to North Texas and married Miss Ann Alexander of Parker county, who was also from Tennessee, and settled in Palo Pinto county and commenced raising cattle.

He immediately joined Jack Hays' Rangers and served with them until the Independence of Texas was acknowledged, and in a battle with the Comanche Indians he was wounded with an arrow and the scar went with him to the end as a decoration on the breast of the old veteran of three wars.

He was one of the original organizers of the Masonic Lodge of Palo Pinto, and was a great Mason. Later on in life two of his daughters, Mrs. D. C. Kyle, now of Saco, Montana; formerly Molly McAdams and Mrs. W. B. Slaughter of San Antonio, formerly Anna McAdams, joined the Eastern Star. Mrs. Kyle being eighteen and Mrs. Slaughter sixteen at the time of joining. Mrs. Slaughter is now a past worthy matron.

Captain McAdams had a disposition to make everybody his friend. His wife, during his absence, dressed in the garb of a man always went with her six-shooter belted around her and a gun on her shoulder for the purpose of making the Indians think her husband was at home. He reared a family of eight children, two boys and six girls, namely: David McAdams, Molly McAdams, Anna McAdams, Lizzie McAdams, Louie McAdams, Quinne McAdams, Webb McAdams and Collie McAdams. Only four of them are now living namely: Mrs. D. C. Kyle, of Saco, Montana; Mrs. W. B. Slaughter of San Antonio; Mrs. Louie Harrison, of Hansford, Texas.

In 1863 he drove a herd of cattle to old Mexico and

traded for sugar and many other articles the early settlers were compelled to have at that time. His second
drive in 1865 was to Shreveport, Louisiana, and he sold
his herd to a Mr. Spencer. In 1867 his third drive was
started to Baxter Springs, Kansas, and at Fort Gibson
in the Indian Territory he sold his herd and returned
home. After that he only made one short drive in Texas
and remained with his ranch and raised cattle. His last
severe fight with the Indians was in 1870, on Salt Creek,
in Young county, Texas; at the time Shapely Carter and
many others were killed. Shapely was the oldest son of
Colonel Kit Carter, who was the first president of the
Cattle Raisers' Association for many years.

Captain McAdams during the Indian wars of Texas
was called a "minute man"; he kept his horse especially
for long and hard rides and it was said of him by his
associates he could ride further with less food and sleep
than any man of his day.

Captain McAdams and his good wife were both ad-
herents of the Methodist church and believed in the good
old-fashioned camp meetings and Mrs. McAdams would
go to any length possible to arrange for some good Methodist pastor to hold annual camp meetings on their ranch
near Sand Valley Peak, Palo Pinto county, and it was
nothing uncommon to see thirty or forty women shouting
and praising the Almighty for the great things He was
accomplishing.

RICHARD ROBERTSON RUSSELL

One of the active builders of West Texas was Richard
R. Russell, who died in San Antonio in 1922. Mr. Russell
was born in Georgia in 1858, and with his parents, Mr.
and Mrs. J. O. Russell, came to Texas when he was twelve
years old, locating in Menard county, where Dick Russell
grew to manhood. For many years he was in the employ
of his uncle, Peter Robertson. During the seventies

Menard county was the scene of numerous Indian raids and young Russell, catching the spirit of the times, enlisted in Captain D. W. Roberts' Rangers and remained with that company for two years, resigning to embark in the cattle business. In 1886 he was elected sheriff of Menard county, and held that office for ten consecutive years. He refused to be a candidate for re-election at the end of that time, as his personal affairs needed his attention. He was

R. R. RUSSELL

interested with William Bevans and James Callan in various cattle deals and ranch operations. In 1909 he organized the Farmers & Merchants Bank of Ballinger, Texas. He headed the organization of the Bank of Menard, of which William Bevans was active manager. He was a stockholder in the Citizens National Bank of Pawhuska, Oklahoma, a stockholder in the Central Trust Company of San Antonio, and was organizer of the Del Rio Live Stock Loan Company, and identified with Del Rio banking interests. He was also identified with the Ballinger Cotton Oil Company, the Winters Oil Company of Runnels county, the Russell-Coleman Oil Company of San Antonio; he was interested in extensive ranch holdings in Runnels and Menard counties, as well as ranch interests in Oklahoma. His largest individual Texas holding in one tract of land was as a stockholder in the Big Canyon Ranch in Terrell and Pecos counties, which consists of 245,000 acres of land and thousands of cattle and sheep. For the past several years and until his death he has been connected with leading banking firms in San Antonio.

Mr. Russell came from a pioneer family. His father

J. O. Russell, and two uncles settled and built the first houses on the site of Denver, Colorado. This settlement was made in 1857, and the city was duly platted and named Auroria. W. A. McFaddin was president of the company, and Dr. L. J. Russell was secretary. Another uncle, Green Russell, mined the first gold in that section of Colorado.

In 1892 Mr. Russell was married to Miss Mattie E. Strickland of Tom Green county. Two daughters were born to them.

FROM THE NUECES TO THE NORTH PLATTE

J. R. Humphries, Yoakum, Texas

In my earliest boyhood days the great ruling ambition was to become a cowboy, and the information that my brother was to take up a bunch of cattle in Live Oak county my ambition was about to be realized, as I was to be a member. In March, 1883, we left Yoakum and went to George W. West's ranch in Live Oak county and took charge of 2,500 old cows and brought them to Lavaca county, where grass was plentiful. This was my first drive and no happier boy lived in the great state of Texas. These cows were ranged on the prairies now where the little thrifty city of Shiner is located. After this we were sent to the Bennett & West ranch in Jackson county to get 3,000 yearlings and brought them back with us. A few days after this we started on the trail with the herd, for the North Platte in what was then regarded as the very life itself of the cattle movements. The trip might well be called "The River Route," as we crossed practically every river of any importance in this country. The San Antonio, the Guadalupe near Gonzales, the San Marcos, the Colorado at Austin, the Brazos and Lampasas, the Pease at Vernon, the Red River South Fork at Donner, Okla., the Cimarron, the Wichita and the Arkansas, all rivers of more or less importance and as there were no bridges in those days, fording was the means of crossing.

On this trip we made good headway and crossed into what was then the beautiful Indian Territory. A few Indians were seen and some very fine ranches and thoroughbred cattle. We were now nearing the junction of the eastern and western trail and the wonderful city of Dodge was our destination. Dodge City enjoyed a reputation of being the fastest cowboy town on this side of the globe and it was our joy and delight to know that ere long we would see that famous place. It is told that a drunken cowboy got aboard a Santa Fé train at Newton one day and when the conductor asked for the fare, the boy handed him a handful of money. The conductor said, "Where do you want to go?" and when the boy replied: "To Hell!" the conductor said, "Well give me $2.50 and get off at Dodge."

Numerous stories of this sort permeated the lower section of the cattle country about Dodge and everybody wanted to see that "tuff guy."

The first trouble of any consequence that we had with our herd was the night we crossed the Arkansas River. The cattle stampeded and in the excitement my horse fell with me and my first thought was that the joy and pleasure of the continuance of the trip was gone. A fearful storm was raging, and everything seemed to have turned to thunder, lightning and rain, and all was confusion. After the storm abated, the sun shone brightly, and we had rounded up the last yearling, we made an excellent entrance into the town of Dodge. We spent one or two wild and joyful days there and on the 17th of July we left for Ogallala, Nebraska. The trip had taken us nearly three months, and now one can go to the same place by train in two days.

On our way to Ogallala we were met by Mr. West, the owner of the cattle that we were driving, and he told us that he had sold 1,600 of the yearlings to a ranch owner in Colorado. We turned back and delivered this sale, and we returned to the outfit which was in charge of Arthur Burnes. My brother, Charley Humphreys, was main boss of the herd from Texas to the North Platte, and to my young imagination no finer cowboy ever rode a saddle.

Burnes had then about 3,500 head of cattle of all sorts and sizes and soon after this he quit and I was given his herd. Bill North, an old Texan, was there with 2,000 steers also owned by Mr. West and the two outfits were put together, making a herd of something like 6,000 head and with this immense herd of cattle we started to the Shandley ranch where they were rebranded and then we headed towards Wyoming in the woolly west. We arrived on the North Platte on September 1, and after a few days' of milling around there we were paid off and began making our plans to hike back to South Texas, the land of flowers and warm sunshine.

In March the next year I was again at the George W. West ranch, rearing to start on the trail again. Again under Charley Humphreys, my brother, we gathered up about 3,000 head of yearlings and on April 1st, 1884, we began the journey which took us to an entirely different section of the world, to the Rio Grande.

In this outfit there were ten men with the herd, one cook, one with horses and the boss, making thirteen men in the outfit. We passed Pearsall, Uvalde, Devil's River, Del Rio, the Painted Caves, and up the Devil's River to Beaver Lake, then to Howard Wells, and Live Oak Creek to the Pecos River. From Del Rio to the Pecos one of those many-year droughts had prevailed and there was no water or grass, and some suffering was done by both men and cattle, but no complaints. We left Del Rio May 1st, and reached Pecos City June 1st, a distance of 300 miles. There our bunch was increased about 4,000 head that had been brought there by Jeff Bailor and Bill Calloway. We now had about 8,000 head and with this we started to Old Fort Sumner on the Pecos River.

We delivered to the Dorsey ranch at Sumner 4,500 heifer yearlings and 500 to another ranchman in that section. The balance were taken to the Read & Broaden ranch on the other side of the Rio Grande. Our business was then done and another hike was in order for Texas where we landed in October after one of the hardest trips in the way of real hardships that we ever had. This was owing to dry weather conditions and the lack of grass, and navigating the mountains that abound in that section with a herd of 5,000 yearlings. The next year in March found me again in the saddle and with Steve Bennett, Phil Ryan, John Humphries, better known as "General Twiggs," Will Griffin, Mose Morris, Dan Mc-Carty, three negroes and the boss, Chas. Humphreys. We left for the West ranch again in Live Oak county. On this trip we were to go to Colorado and in the early part of March we got a good get-away with 2,500 yearlings. We selected the old western cattle trail which went through Coleman, Ft. Griffin, and up the Panhandle country, to Dalhart, where the outfit was delivered to the XIT Ranch.

From this time on I worked in several capacities on various ranches, and in the service of D. R. Fant on his Santa Rosa ranch where I was employed as a cowboy until some weeks afterwards, when I joined Charley Humphreys and his outfit which was ready to hit the trail. We left early in March with 2,500 head of mixed cattle and believe me, we had some hard trip. There was no grass in the Spofford section and when we reached Spofford the cattle and horses both had fallen off so that it was impossible to make the passage through the Nueces Canyon. Mr. Fant was sent for and he decided to take the best and strongest from the two herds that were of about equal number and push on to where there was grass. So we left Spofford some days later with 2,600 tolerably fat and hit the Canyon and made its passage without difficulty. When we reached old Ft. McKavitt

in Menard county we were afoot and both horses and
cattle were as poor as Job's turkey. Good grass and
plenty of fine water was found after this. We kept at
the job and in about a week wonderful changes had taken
place and we were able to ride our horses and the cattle
were able to take up their journey to Colorado. This
trip carried us through the Panhandle of Texas and the
western part of Kansas and we enjoyed it very much. The
herd was delivered to the Holly Ranch at Colorado
Springs. We rode the horses back and landed in old
Lavaca county none the worse for wear and tear to our
systems.

Soon after this I went to work at my old job of riding
the range for George W. West in Live Oak county. In
the following spring I went to Alice to get a bunch of
3,000 young cows and shipped them by rail to Purcell,
Oklahoma, and from that place we drove them to El Reno
and turned them over to John Johnson and then went
to Quanah and took up 2,000 beef cattle and drove them
to the North Canadian and left them with Mack Stewart,
who afterwards created quite a lot of excitement in this
section by being thrown in a Mexican prison for an
alleged shooting that occurred on the other side of the
Rio Grande. From El Reno we drove the cattle to Kingfisher where we took on 1,000 beef cattle and with the
bunch of about 4,000 beef cattle we went to Anadarko
where we delivered the herd in good shape to the Indian
agent, and then back to Live Oak county where I worked
until the fall of 1893. I went to work for Ed Lassiter
on the San Diego ranch and was in his employ until the
latter part of the fall, when I went back to Oakville. In
May the following year I was married and quit cow-
punching and took up railroad work and have been in
that line of work for many years with the S. A. & P. Ry.
and reside in Yoakum.

The cowboy life that I have led is one of the pleasant
memories of my career, and money could not buy the

delightful recollections of it. No boy can really get a thrill from any other sport than to be member of a bunch of real cowboys on the trail and in charge of thousands of head of cattle. The cowboy was one of the gay and festive characters of the early day history of Texas and he has not been overdrawn. He worked hard and played hard and to him there was no task too difficult or dangerous and the life of one head of stock in his charge was as precious as the entire herd.

A LONG, HARD TRIP

E. R. (Nute) Rachal, Falfurrias, Texas

My first trip over the trail to Kansas was in 1871, when we drove 1,200 steers, from six to sixteen years old, which we gathered and branded at the old Coleman ranch, known as the Chiltipin ranch. John R. Pulliam bought them from T. M. Coleman, Sr., for $10 per head. My brother, D. C. Rachal, was in charge of the herd, and I was second boss. Our hands were A. P. Rachal, William Allen, William Lewis, Ebb Douglas, Dick Bean, Bill Unit, one Mexican called "Big Dirty," and a German cook. We started from the Chiltipin about March 20, 1871, and the second night out, near Sand Mounds on the Arkansas Creek, it rained all night, and our herd became scattered. When he reached Fort Worth we laid in supplies, and went on, and the next night had a stampede and our herd got mixed up with a herd Buck Gravis was driving. From there we just drove the two herds together to a point near Abilene. When we reached Bluff Creek at the Kansas line the first house of Caldwell was being put up. It was a log house. Here we found an old friend, Milam Fitzgerald, with a tent full of trail supplies, so we stocked up. We stopped at Cottonwood Creek, about twenty miles from Abilene, and separated our cattle from the Gravis herd, and drove them across to Ellsworth and from there on to the Smoky River, near Wilson

Station, where Dick Bean, myself and two other Texas boys stayed all summer. All went well until October, when the buffaloes began to come in vast herds, stampeding our horses and causing much annoyance. Cap-

E. R. (Nute) RACHAL

D. C. RACHAL

A. P. RACHAL

FRANK RACHAL

tain Pulliam could not find a sale for the cattle, so he had us to move them up near Ellsworth and shipped to Chicago to be slaughtered. He sold his horses to a rancher about 75 miles up on the Saline River, and sent Tom Pulliam and myself to deliver them. A severe snow storm came up shortly after we started and when we reached Wilson Station we turned the horses loose and took refuge in a box car which had a stove and some coal in it. We spent two days there, and when the storm was over we found all of the loose horses and took them on for delivery. The ranch owner started us back to the railroad station in a one-horse wagon driven by one of his ranch hands. The distance was twenty-five miles, over a hilly country, and the road was wet and sloppy from melting snow. About three miles from the ranch the old horse gave out, and Tom and I had to walk to the station, reaching there about dark. We went to Ellsworth, settled up, and started for home November 20, traveling by rail and stopping off at Kansas City, St. Louis and New Orleans. From New Orleans I came home by water. I helped to gather those cattle, was with them eight months, and during that time was away from the herd only two nights. It was a long, hard trip, but on the whole we enjoyed it. We went from the mouth of the Nueces River to Ellsworth, Kansas, without going through a gate. I am now (1921) seventy-two years old, and still able to ride horseback and work with cattle.

A. P. RACHAL

A. P. Rachal made his first trip up the trail to Kansas in 1871, going as a hand. Thereafter he drove for several years, but in the herds driven after this one he was partner. He was well known to many of the trail drivers, and was highly esteemed by all as by many other friends and acquaintances. In later years he handled cattle extensively in the Indian Territory. One year he, in partnership with J. M. Chittim, grazed thirty thousand cattle in Creek Nation. Of these twenty thousand head were cows, all of which were shipped into the Creek Nation in the spring, and all of them with all of their

calf crop shipped out to market during the summer and
fall of the same year. That meant "some stirrin' about"
for the cowboys. Mr. Rachal had a reputation of working his cattle fast and furiously. This was to such an
extent that among the Territory boys often when cattle
were to be rushed or crowded you would hear, "Rachal
'em boys, Rachal 'em."

A. P. Rachal died in Chicago, and was buried at San
Antonio, his home town.

D. C. RACHAL

Darius C. Rachal was born January 23, 1841, at
Cloutierville, Natchitoches Parish, Louisiana. His parents were Ciriaque, and Anais Rachal, both lineal descendants of the Acadians who sought asylum in Louisiana
and who have been the subjects of song and story for two
centuries. At the outbreak of the Civil War Mr. Rachal
enlisted in the 5th Texas Infantry, a part of Hood's
Brigade. He took part in the "Seven Days' Battle in the
Wilderness," was at the "Second Manassas" at "Sharps-
burg" in "Lee's Invasion of Pennsylvania" the immortal
three days at "Gettysburg," was foremost in the defense
of Fredericksburg and was with Hood during the terrific
hand-to-hand struggle at "Chickamauga." When the
battle flag had been furled and the last musket had been
stacked, Mr. Rachal returned to Texas and engaged in
the cattle business, living two years in Calhoun county,
subsequently he removed to San Patricio county where
he resided until his death, August 27, 1918.

From 1875 to 1890 Mr. Rachal was one of the largest
cattle-raisers in the State and sent large herds up the
trail during this time. He was married to Miss Julia
Bryan at Liberty, Texas, and lived at White Point, seven
miles across the bay from Corpus Christi the last fifty-two
years of his life.

FRANK S. RACHAL

Frank S. Rachal was born at White Point, San Patricio county, Texas, November 29, 1868. He spent his boyhood on the ranch of his father, D. C. Rachal, going as far as Red River with one of his father's herds. He married Miss Anna C. Webster in April, 1891, living in San Patricio county for nine years thereafter. Mr. Rachal now resides at Falfurrias, Texas, where he is engaged in the cattle business.

JOHN REDUS

Mrs. Sallie McLamore Redus

John Redus was born in Athens, Alabama, December 25, 1833, and moved to Mississippi when a boy. He lived there until he was about twenty-two years old, when his

MRS. SALLIE REDUS   JOHN REDUS

health failed and he got in with a party coming to Texas. His father furnished him with a buggy and negro driver, and on the way he was so sick he had to be helped in and out of the buggy. When they reached Austin, there

was a big crowd from San Antonio to hear General Sam
Houston speak, and he met up with some people from his
home town, Aberdeen, Mississippi. My father and some
others from Mississippi had bought land and settled on
Hondo Creek, ten miles west of Castroville, then the
county seat of Medina county. I don't know how he ever
found us, but he did, and came right out and joined us.
This being a stock country, he soon got in with the stock
men, and his health improved so rapidly that he decided
to stay and go into the stock business. His father sent
money with which to buy land and cattle, and he purchased land from the Adams brothers, who had a big
ranch on the Hondo, thirteen miles south of us. John
Redus was soon joined in his undertaking by his brothers,
William and George Redus, and they started business
on a small scale. I was the first girl Mr. Redus got
acquainted with in Medina county and naturally we had
to be sweethearts, and on December 11, 1859, my twen-
tieth birthday, we were married, and the next day we
went to our new home as happy as any couple could
be, although I knew I did not have a neighbor nearer
than four miles. The Indians came in every light moon
and stole horses, killed a man occasionally, and were
very troublesome, but all went well with us. We were
prosperous until the Civil War came on, and all the white
men joined the army, and the negroes and I had to go
back to my father's place near the German settlements.
When the war was over the men came home and we went
back to our ranch and began anew. The men had to be
out on the range for weeks at a time to round up the
stock, which had had but little attention during the period
of the war, only our nephew, Tallie Burnett, and the
negro boys would go once a week to put out salt and
look around. But all hands had to hustle. The Indians
were bad for a long time, and we always had to keep
guns handy, although luckily we never had to use them.
Notwithstanding these troublous times, we prospered.

Mr. Redus would buy more cattle every year and locate more land, and finally he bought the Adams brothers' land when they went west to get larger holdings. About this time the drives to Kansas started. Mr. Redus was one of the first to engage in trail driving and one of the last to stop. He was successful for awhile, but got to speculating, buying remnants of herds wintered in Kansas, and when the great panic of 1873 came on, and so many banks failed, he had to sell for less than he gave, and we went broke. I made one trip with Mr. Redus to Kansas, taking along my baby boy, Robert. I have always regretted that I did not go every year, for I could have gone if I had known it. At that time the railroad came only as far as Luling, and we had to go there by stage from San Antonio. In looking back it seems a long time, and many changes are noticeable, but really I believe we had better times and were happier then than now. Everybody was your friend, and were glad to entertain you. In reading the first volume of the Old Trail Drivers' book I find many familiar names, people I knew personally, and many who did business with my husband, but most of them have passed on, and some, like us, had lost everything they had accumulated. Mr. Redus died July 25, 1895, of the same disease he had left Mississippi to escape—lung trouble. I am now eighty-two years old, am in good health, keep house and do all my work. I have written this by request of my friend, Mr. W. B. Hardeman.

JAMES DAVID FARMER

The subject of this sketch was born in 1858, and received his education at Mansfield College, Mansfield, Texas. He is today one of the interesting characters engaged in commercial activities in Fort Worth, and widely known stockman, politician and promoter of civic progress. His operations in the cattle trade cover a period of over forty years, during which time he has striven manfully in aiding the cattle industry in a growth from struggling infancy to its present mature prosperity. He engaged in the commission business when he removed to Fort Worth, and organized the Fort Worth Live Stock

Commission Co., later organized the Rhome-Farmer Live Stock Commission Co., one of the best known of all the numerous commission companies operating in the great Southwest. He was elected the first Mayor of Fort Worth, serving satisfactorily in that capacity for two full terms. A live wire in all things, he believes in Texas first, last and all the time; is one of those hustlers who believes

JAMES DAVID FARMER

that nothing is too good for his native state; is a solid, substantial man of affairs and has a host of friends throughout the Lone Star State and adjacent states.

A WELL-KNOWN FRONTIER CHARACTER

The accompanying photo is a true likeness of the well-known frontiersman and ranger, William (Big Foot) Wallace, whose remarkable career reads like a romance. He was born in Rockbridge county, Virginia, and came to Texas, in 1836, just a short time after the battle of San Jacinto was fought. He was at the battle of the Salado in 1842, and was also in the Mier Expedition, being one of the lucky ones to a draw a white bean. After returning to Texas he joined Captain Jack Hayes' rangers, and was in many exciting Indian campaigns. He later commanded a ranger company which was organized to protect the settlers on the frontier, and subsequently

had charge of the overland mail line from San Antonio to
El Paso. The town of Big Foot in Frio county is named

"BIG FOOT" WALLACE

in his honor. He died January 7, 1899, and his remains
rest in the State Cemetery at Austin.

ALONZO MILLETT

Alonzo Millett was born in Bastrop county in 1845,
and spent his boyhood days in that county and at Seguin,
where he attended school. He had two brothers in school
with him, and when the Civil War broke out the three
Millett brothers were the first to volunteer. Alonzo
Millett, at the time only 16 years old, entered the Confederate army and with General Wood he went through

all of us got covered with body lice and had to boil our clothes to get rid of them. When we reached Dodge City we stayed over a couple of days, and while there we sold some saddle horses to a man named Eddy, who ranched on Seven Rivers, New Mexico. Finnessey and the two

C. E. JOHNSON, Charco, Texas

Williams boys went with him to his ranch, and I have never seen them since. From Dodge City on to Ogallala we had bad weather, with plenty of lightning and thunder. One young man was killed by lightning. We disposed of the horses at Ogallala and I came back on the train.

In 1882 I went up with a herd for O'Connor & Lam-

bert to Caldwell, Kansas. We had a little trouble with
the Indians and had to give them several horses to get
them to behave. O'Connor met me at Caldwell and took
the saddle horses to Dodge City, leaving me to sell the
others. On this trip I passed Jap Clark, Charlie Boyce,
the Rachal boys and number of others. I sold the horses
to a man named McClain and had to take them back to
the Indian Territory and hold them for a month. When
I got back to Texas I married the sweetest girl on earth,
and of course could not go up the trail the next year,
but in 1884, in March, I left my wife and five-months' old
baby with her mother and went up with a herd driven out
of Goliad county for D. R. Fant, road-branded F and ID.
Mr. Fant had 40,000 head of cattle on the trail that year
which he drove to Dodge City, Kansas. That was the
year Bing Choate was killed. When I got to Dodge City
I stayed and cut the Fant cattle out of herds as they
came in. I stayed with George Stokes who was in charge
of the Choate & Bennett cattle.

I moved to Goliad county in October, 1884, and have
raised a family of eight children, seven of whom are
living in the largest city of Texas, except one married
daughter, who lives in Saginaw, Michigan. I own a little
farm of 320 acres, on which my wife and I are living in
contentment, and I don't owe any man a cent. I am now
sixty years old, and my wife is the same age. We are
both as spry as ever, and I feel like I could easily ride
one hundred miles in a day just like I did years ago,
when I took the long, long trail to northern markets.

RANSOM CAPPS

All of the early settlers of Mason county, Texas, knew
the subject of this sketch, for he lived in their midst
many years. He died at San Antonio, October 15, 1921,

and the *San Antonio Express* published the following account of his career:

Survived by 121 descendants, Ransom Capps, Confederate Veteran, who died Saturday at the home of his daughter, Mrs. R. F. Pipes, 251 Diaz Street, was among the last of the living pioneers of Texas whose deeds have been immortalized in history and song.

He was 91 years 9 months and 2 days old. A native of Missouri, he came to Texas when a young man and settled near the head of the San Antonio River, about five miles north of town, which then consisted of an army garrison and a few stores. That was 72 years ago.

To his children, six of whom survive him, Mr. Capps has often related the stories of Indian attacks on the settlements near San Antonio.

At the beginning of the Civil War he enlisted in Company I, 3rd Texas Infantry, and served under the late Captain J. M. Trainer in Col. Lucket's brigade of Walker's Division in Louisiana and Arkansas through the entire period of the war.

His wife and children moved from their ranch north of town into San Antonio during his absence for protection against Indian attacks. The Apaches and Comanches were on a rampage, the former being especially treacherous at that time.

After the war Capps, with his family moved to a point near the head of the Salado, about twelve miles from town, where he lived until the death of his wife about 20 years ago. Fifteen children were born of their union. Following the death of his wife, Capps lived at the homes of his children in San Antonio and in Mason and McCulloch counties.

Besides his six children, he is survived by 36 grandchildren and nine great-grandchildren, most of whom live in Mason county.

Three daughters, Mrs. Pipes, Mrs. C. E. Jones and Mrs. E. H. Neal, live in San Antonio. Two of his sons,

S. B. Capps and John Capps, live in Mason county, while the other one, J. P. Capps, lives in McCulloch county.

Interment was made Sunday at Coker Cemetery. The Rev. John W. Smith officiated. Funeral services were held from the residence of Mrs. Pipes.

WHY I AM A PROHIBITIONIST

George F. Hindes, Pearsall and Hindes, Texas

I was born in Alabama, September, 1844, and graduated in a little home-made school house in the piney woods of Lauderdal county, Mississippi, near where the city of Meridian now stands. I graduated at the age of eleven years, and moved with my parents in wagons from there to Caldwell county, near Lockhart, Texas, that fall. I visited Lockhart on Christmas day for the first time, and in those days Lockhart was wild and woolly, a wide-open town, where whiskey and every other kind of "blue ruin" flowed freely. That day I saw a Mr. Perry kill a Mr. Cabaniss with a knife. To me it was a frightful experience. My curiosity caused me to ask what caused the trouble, and I was told it was whiskey. Then I went strong for prohibition, and was never intoxicated in my life. We lived in Caldwell county until the fall of 1856, when my father sold a likely negro woman to Major Fields for stock cattle, and we started west with the cattle to grow up with the country, as per Horace Greeley's advice. I was "herd boss" on the trip. We drove our herd through San Antonio, from Alamo Plaza to Commerce Street, and down Commerce Street to South Flores Street, and on to Atascosa county. This was before the county was organized, and my father served on the first jury empaneled in the county. We settled on the San Miguel Creek, where the town of Hindes is now located, and where we had a world of free range, with great abundance of wild game of every kind, even wild mus-

tang cattle and mustang horses. I soon got to be an
expert shot with rifle and pistol, a good roper, and a fast
and fearless rider, and soon made friends with all the
mustangers and hunters. We killed the native wild cattle
for their hides and tallow, and the meat we could save.
I caught and tamed lots of mustang horses, mostly young
stock.

In the pioneer days of danger and adventure, and with
no other or better job, I learned to be so fond of hunting
and the chase, that I have never gotten over it, and can
still ride a horse and shoot a rifle as good as anyone. On
two occasions, the Indians rounded me up. Once, with
a Mr. Seals on the San Miguel, when we stood them off
half of one night, and another time with a Mr. Atkins,
when they kept us surrounded half of one afternoon at
Charco Largo. A good run always suited me better than
a doubtful stand, but either one is lonesome and frightful.
In August, 1865, twenty-eight redskins gave me a hard
race, but I beat them to the river bottom and got away.
Another time fifteen of them gave me a close chase and
would have caught me, but in their trying to cut me
off from the river, they ran on to a steep bluff bank and
could not get down. On one occasion three friends and
myself went on a hunting trip south of the Nueces River
for a week's hunt. Had a good time, but in a short time
thereafter all of the three were killed and all dying with
"their boots on." At another time, my father, a Mr.
Wheat, and myself had a good and successful hunt on
the San Miguel; and in a short time the Indians killed
Mr. Wheat in Medina county, and my father was killed
by the Indians at his home in McMullen county.

The pioneers that were on the frontier before and
during reconstruction days suffered many privations
and hardships, and half of them did not live to tell the
story. But during these times, as dreary and dull as
they were, there was a man whose life was as brilliant
as a ray of sunshine following the dark and tempestuous

clouds. That man was Jim Lowe, who was one of the first settlers in McMullen county, and who was the best fixed man in that section. He was truly one of God's noblemen—a philanthropist of the first order. He made it possible for many poor families to have bread in their homes, who, otherwise, would have had to live on meat alone. I was truly benefited by his wise counsel and good backing.

In March, 1865, about the close of the Civil War, I married the best little girl in the world, and she lived to bless my life for fifty-six years to a day, and passed on to her reward in March, 1921.

"When musing on companions gone,
We doubly feel ourselves alone."

The year 1865 was an eventful one in my life. Married in March (I was promptly notified that I must "quit my meanness"), the war closed in May, and the Indians killed my father in August. However, with all the energy and determination I possessed I went to work on the "wreck," for we lost practically everything we possessed during the war. I proceeded under difficulties too numerous to mention, but by the spring of 1872, had gotten together a pretty good little herd of mixed cattle, and drove them to Kansas that spring. I had about the usual amount of trouble that a man has on his first drive over the "trail." Was compelled to swim swollen streams, had storms at night, and several stampedes. Finally I bumped into the Osage tribe of Indians, and they gave us an exhibition of what they could do to a Texas herd, shooting and yelling the regular Indian war-hoop. They killed about one hundred beeves right there on the prairie, in sight, and scattered the others to the four winds, causing Mr. Redus great loss and trouble. I drove my herd to Wichita, Kansas, and held them there on fine grass until fall, and sold out at good prices. When I got home that fall, I had more than $15,000 cash, in gold,

$10,000 life insurance policy, a remnant of cattle and a good bunch of horses that I had left in Texas. I did not owe a dollar, and felt chesty as Croesus, in his palmiest days, ever dared to feel. I handled several herds after that in Kansas and Wyoming, and always made a little money. I never bossed another herd all the way from start to finish, but I knew the game, and if a man made good, it was indeed a hard trip. At another time I delivered 2,500 head of cattle in Wyoming, on the tenth day of September, in an all-day snowstorm; and while it was indeed something different to what I had been accustomed to, I could not enjoy it at all. I kept buying, selling and trading cattle until 1882, when I made the best money in my life by buying about forty thousand acres of San Miguel land where the town of Hindes is now located on the San Antonio, Uvalde and Gulf Railroad, at a very low price. I have watched it go up in value in these forty years while I was using it for pasture until I have sold some of it for $100 an acre; some at $75 an acre, and have never sold any for less than $20 an acre. I allotted my children sufficient land that if used and managed with prudence and care, will provide them liberally with life's needs, still have a good block of it left, and expect to develop an oil field in the near future.

In the fall of 1903 I helped organize the Pearsall National Bank at Pearsall, Texas, and have served continuously on its board of directors. For the past ten years I have been its president, resigning just recently in order to enable me to give my personal business the attention it deserves. In 1909 I also helped to organize the Atascosa County State Bank at Jourdanton, Texas, and served as its president for six years, relinquishing my post of duty only after the bank was thoroughly established and was doing a nice business. However, I am still one of the largest stockholders in the Atascosa County Bank, and a large stockholder and director in the Pearsall National Bank.

Looking back now it seems that Providential guidance has been instrumental in my living through the many harrowing experiences of the early days, when Indians roamed the country, and later, especially after the war, when outlaws gave so much trouble to the pioneers of the Southwest. It gives me much pleasure and consolation in having been spared to see the great Southwest transformed from pioneer to the modern stage; where folks mingle with one another in security and all friendliness, and where now exists a spirit of democracy and helpfulness that makes the country a desirable place to live, grow and prosper. I do not say boastingly, but there is a great deal of personal satisfaction in knowing that I was permitted to have a part in the upbuilding of this section of our wonderful state.

FIFTY YEARS A POLICEMAN

After pacing his "beat" for fifty years, faithfully and true, John Fitzhenry, the oldest policeman in San Antonio, has retired.

JOHN FITZHENRY
1870

The veteran lawkeeper has served under 11 Mayors. He has made so many arrests that he has long since lost count, and he has been instrumental in bringing to justice some of the worst criminals the Southwest has ever known. He removed the uniform of his country, which he served from '64 to '71, to don the uniform of an officer of the law, and this he has worn continuously for half a century.

His retirement brings to a close one of the most

interesting and thrilling official careers in San Antonio's past history.

John Fitzhenry has lived the life of the great Wild West. In his book of life have been written hundreds of chapters of range and pioneer life as intensely thrilling and exciting as the boldest adventures of "Diamond Dick" or any of the other great Wild West heroes.

"It was a border town, rough and woolly." With these words the veteran officer begins his narrative of early San Antonio history. "It was the jumping off place for all the desperadoes in the country, when I came down here in '64. San Antonio, 50 years ago, was a cow town of 8,000 souls. The only railroads in Texas were one from Bryan Station to the coast and another from Victoria to Port Lavaca. No one dared live farther west than Fort Clark, about 150 miles west of San Antonio. Beyond there the Indians and such scouts and soldiers as the government saw fit to station on the frontier lived. San Antonio in those days was a rendezvous for Mexican bandits as well as frontier outlaws. The bandits used to hold up a town just as they have done in the past few years, and come up to San Antonio to spend their money. It was so wild in those days we couldn't wear uniforms. The six day policeman wore the clothes of a civilian. If we had worn uniforms of the law there would have been a shooting as soon as we came in sight. A policeman didn't make an arrest, either, as he does today. None of the boys in those days would have stood while a warrant was being read to him. We had to throw them down and tie them, and then read the warrants for their arrest."

Mr. Fitzhenry holds this remarkable record of serving for 50 years as law enforcement officer without having shot a man, or having been shot. Desperadoes and Wild West bandits, famous in early American history, were often seen about San Antonio. The Yeager boys, Pitts, one of Jesse James' former lieutenants, the Suttons and Taylors, of the famous Sutton-Taylor feud, Sam Bass and others used to disguise themselves, dash into town, frequent the various drinking and dancing places and dash out before the law could touch them.

"Those fellows used to have lots of friends," he said. "It was mighty easy for a fellow to get out of a killing scrape here if he had some friends. Pitts and the Yeager boys lived for a time between San Antonio and Boerne, up in the hills." Mr. Fitzhenry was a pal of Marshal Gosling, who was shot while escorting Pitts and one of the Yeager boys to the penitentiary.

"Marshal Gosling was warned," he said, "that the boys were desperadoes. He permitted, however, the sister of one of the boys and another woman to come aboard the train with a basket of provisions. Yeager reached into the basket, apparently for a piece of fruit, drew out a six-shooter and shot Gosling dead. A guard on the train and the woman were killed during the fight."

Billy Taylor was in jail at Indianola, awaiting trial, when a great storm came up and the lives of hundreds along the coast were in peril. Taylor was released from jail, and, with courage characteristic of these men, he dashed to the rescue of the drowning and saved dozens of lives. When he was tried before a jury some time later for his crime, he was found "not guilty."

Mr. Fitzhenry was born in Ireland in 1844. He removed with his parents to Quebec, Canada, when he was seven years old, and later the family came down into the states, locating in Massachusetts.

He attended school in Stetson Hall, Randolph, Mass. and was 20 years of age when he enlisted in 1864 on the side of the North. He was sent to New Orleans as a train master and later to San Antonio. He was in charge of mule trains which bore provisions to the frontier posts. San Antonio was then but a supply and distributing post. The government reservation was a 10-acre plot fenced in between the Austin road and the Post proper, and was used as a mule corral. The famous Alamo was used as a store house for grain, and feed for the mules, oxen and horses was piled to the ceiling.

"When General Merritt and General Custer came to San Antonio in 1865, they were accompanied by 10,000 cavalrymen, the largest number of soldiers ever stationed here prior to this date," Mr. Fitzhenry said. They were en route to Mexico to drive out the French, who, in defiance of the Monroe Doctrine, had established an empire and enthroned Maximilian. The scheme, however, history relates, was abandoned and Maximilian was shot some time after that.

Mr. Fitzhenry loved the early days, but he says that the people of today have a better sense of fair dealing as well as a greater respect for the law. "I do not believe the world is growing worse," was his optimistic assertion. "Just because we have all the crimes that are committed in the country, and all the wrongdoing dished up to us in the newspapers, makes us think the world is pretty bad. But in years gone by, a life wasn't worth a farthing in this part of the country, and news traveled so slowly that it was forgotten before it got in or out of the State."

Mr. Fitzhenry has seen the wild pigeons and the buffalo disappear from wild life in Texas. And he has seen the building of railroads and the steady advance of civilization that has made San Antonio today a law-abiding town. He has seen outlawry disappear and culture take its place. He has witnessed the passing of the "bandit," and watched wild days fade into the background of Texas history.

"San Antonio has been my home for over 50 years," said Mr. Fitzhenry, whose appearance defies time and who might pass as a middle-aged man. "And I'll stay on here till the end."

He has never married and has not a relative living. He makes his home at 239 Garden Street.—*San Antonio Evening News,* January 24, 1921.

TAILED 'EM ACROSS RED RIVER

Gus Staples, Skidmore, Texas

One beautiful spring morning in 1876 our bunch pulled out for Dodge City, Kansas, with a herd of cattle. Bob Jennings and George Lyons were the bosses. After we had been on the trail about three weeks we encountered a severe cold spell during which my saddle horse froze to death. The blizzard was accompanied by rain which froze as it hit our slickers, and we suffered from the extreme cold. We stayed with the cattle as long as we could and finally the boss said, "Let 'em go to hell, boys, and we'll go to the campfire." We rustled all of the wood out of the creek bottom and kept busy roasting first one side and then the other. When we reached Fort Worth the weather had moderated considerably. That is where I saw the first railroad. We renewed our supply of grub here and went on our way. When we got to Red River it looked to me to be more than a mile wide, and I did not fancy going across, but I was six hundred miles from home, and it was either turn back or grab an old cow by the tail and let her pull me across, so I tailed her and reached the other side safely. When we were in Indian Territory we experienced many thunder storms and heavy rains. Saw many Indians, too. While we were passing through Valley Mills George Lyons and I traded our pistols off for horses, and as we were in the Indian Territory where Indians were numerous I often wished for my pistol, and was ready to swap jobs with the cook.

WAS IN A RAILROAD WRECK

John B. Conner, Yoakum, Texas

When I was three years old my parents came from Mississippi to Texas in an ox-drawn schooner, arriving on Five Mile Creek, in Gonzales county in 1869. In Five Mile vicinity the settlers were Carson, Sedberry, Atkinson, Killough, Gill Womack, O'Neal, Gibson, Boathe, Price, Floyd, Ward, Jeffries, Casey and others. Some of those pioneers built their houses out of oak logs, while

JOHN B. CONNER

others hauled pine lumber from Indianola and Port Lavaca with ox teams. My father, Jim Conner, built a pine lumber house in 1872, and it is still standing in good shape. Father died in 1873, and we lost the place, later moving into a log house over on the West Prong of Five Mile Creek to the old Gibson place, near which was a cattle trail. We lived on this place several years and saw thousands of cattle and horses pass up the trail. There was another trail which ran from Victoria to Cuero by Concrete on to Town Prairie two miles above Gonzales, where the two trails came together.

I remember the summer of 1877 was so dry the creeks dried up and hundreds of cattle perished for water, and that winter hundreds of others died in piles, many of them being skinned for their hides. The first pasture fence in that section was built by John Jeffries on the head of East Five Mile Creek in 1878. It was constructed of two elm planks at the top and black wire at the bottom.

In 1878 or 1879 Bob Floyd built a large pasture south of West Five Mile Creek, and made it of large split rails and finished it with two strings of elm plank and one strand of black wire. Rail and brush fences around fields were the rule in those days.

When I was 18 years old, in 1885, I had my first chance to go up the trail. On the 18th of April of that year we left Gonzales, seven outfits going at the same time. We went to Kyle with 160 wild Spanish ponies and there another bunch of 400 was thrown in with ours and shipped for Wichita Falls, both horses and men. At Ft. Worth we laid overnight and day, then took the Fort Worth & Denver Railroad, struck a washed out bridge between Bellevue and Bowie, and had to take a freight train for Henrietta, leaving there at sundown, and backing up for Wichita Falls. We were all in and all over those box cars. I was outside on top when the engine turned over, killed the engineer and two negro trail hands, and I was thrown into a slough of water several feet deep. About 3 o'clock that night we reached Wichita Falls and slept in the depot. Next day we got our chuck wagon fixed up, and went to housekeeping. For two or three days we made preparations to take the trail, picking up our horses. Each man was allowed one night horse and five day horses, changing three times a day. We went to Doan's store on Red River, and crossed and went up the Salt Fork to the Goodnight ranch where we received 3,000 head of two and three-year old heifers, steers and bulls of the —X brand. The horses on this ranch were branded Diamond F on the left hip. My boss was J. G. Jones. The cattle were bought by Lytle & Stevens and were bound for Colorado. As I was a young chap I was made horse-wrangler, but I had to do everything from punching drags to night-herding on the bed ground. We had some terrible storms, and stampedes, and several head of cattle were killed by lightning while we were on the west side of Red River in Greer county, Texas. We went from there to Wheeler county and crossed the North Fork of Red River, then crossed Sweetwater creek east of Mobeetie, went on to Hemphill and crossed the Wichita east of Cataline, then into Roberts county, crossed the Canadian, and on to the Staked Plains, struck near the head of Wolf Creek and on to Palo Duro Canyon. We saw where hundreds of buffalo had died on the plains, many of them killed by hunters just for their hides. In Ochiltree county we saw three buffalo and some of the boys killed one, but the outfit with next herd got the meat. At Palo Duro we struck the old trail and the stage line from Dodge City, to Tascosa, Texas. The cattle quarantine turned us from going to Colorado, and we went into Kansas, where as soon as we struck the railroad I decided to pull for home as I was not well. I went to Dodge City, the honkatonk town, cleaned up and bought a suit of clothes, and left for San Antonio, reaching home July 1, 1885.

THE RUTLEDGE BROTHERS

The four Rutledge brothers, Jim, John, Ed and Emmett, were well known among the early cattlemen of the state. They moved to Texas from Alabama, with their parents in the early fifties, and settled on the Hondo in Karnes county. All of these brothers, except Emmett, who was too young at the time, enlisted in the Confederate army and served throughout the war. John and Ed Rutledge each received wounds in battle. After the war the Rutledges began driving cattle up the trail to Kansas, and continued their drives until 1879. Jim Rutledge made trips with cattle to New Orleans and to Powder Horn. He was considered an expert in the art of catching mustangs, sometimes catching a whole herd at one time. Emmett Rutledge was for many years an inspector for the Cattle Raisers' Association, with headquarters at San Antonio, and was considered one of the best on the force.

JIM RUTLEDGE

ED RUTLEDGE

JOHN RUTLEDGE

EMMETT RUTLEDGE

JESSE PRESNALL

The subject of this sketch was born in Bozier Parish, Louisiana, October 31, 1849, and died at his home in San Antonio April 5th, 1916. He came to Texas with his parents in the early fifties, settling in Bexar county. While quite a young man he engaged in the cattle business

which he followed until his death. He was one of the early trail drivers to the northern markets, continuing right up to the closing of the trail. No man in the cattle business in Texas was better or more favorably known than Jesse Presnall. He drove many herds individually and was interested at different times with Capt. John T. Lytle, John Blocker, Hart Mussey and others. Mr.

JESSE PRESNALL

Presnall was a strong believer in the strict enforcement of the laws of our country, and many times he rendered valuable assistance in bringing to justice cattle rustlers and outlaws. His noble traits of character will never be forgotten by his many surviving friends. At the time of his death he was operating a farm and ranch in Atascosa county, which his widow still maintains.

GEORGE W. WEST

Among the prominent figures in the cattle industry of Southwest Texas is to be found George W. West, cattleman, capitalist, town builder and philanthropist. George W. West was born in Tennessee, and came to Texas with his parents some time in the fifties, settling in Lavaca county. It was here the subject of our sketch entered the stock business. He was one of the first to drive cattle from Texas to Kansas, and he continued driving until the trail closed. He sold and delivered cattle to Indian agencies, and to ranches in Montana, South Dakota, Wyoming, Colorado, and Kansas, making drives to Abilene, Wichita, Ellsworth, and Dodge City. It was in 1886 that he, with John Blocker and others had their herds held up at Camp Supply by ranchmen who tried to keep them from crossing their ranches. The number of cattle held up amounted to more than 100,000 head, and Mr. West and John Blocker spent more than $100 sending telegrams to the authorities at Washington to get the government to take action in the matter. Finally orders came from Washington for them to cut fences and pass through and with a rush the cow outfits started their herds on the move. Within just a few moments after orders came from Washington a thunder storm came up, lightning struck the telegraph instruments, demolished the office and put the line out of commission. Captain Carr, of the U. S. Army, who was in San Antonio a few months ago, was telegraph operator who took the message. Messrs. West and Blocker narrowly escaped being killed by the lightning.

GEORGE W. WEST

Mr. West has maintained large ranches in different parts of South Texas since the early seventies. No man in that region has matured, fattened and shipped to market more fat steers than George W. West. He owns at present 60,000 acres of choice land in Live Oak county, the best equipped cattle ranch in South Texas, fenced and crossed-fenced, with dipping vats, stock pens, and everything it takes to make a model ranch. This ranch surrounds the town of George West, the thriving county seat of Live Oak county. Mr. West has retired from business, and now lives quietly in his modern home in San Antonio, but he keeps in close touch with state and national affairs, and watches closely the livestock industry. If his views and advice could be carried out, conditions in Texas would be much better. He claims less laws and strict enforcement of them is the best remedy to save our country. His neighbors and business associates in the early days were his brothers, Sol and Ike West, Willis McCutcheon, Sam and Bill Moore, Lew Allen and John Bennett.

PLAYED THE FIDDLE ON HERD AT NIGHT

Lake Porter, Falfurrias, Texas

I was born January 5th, 1854, in Chickasaw, Mississippi, and came to Texas with my parents before my

LAKE PORTER

eyes were open, landing at Seguin, Guadalupe county, where we lived three years, then moved to Goliad county and settled on the Maha Rayo Creek, where we were living when the Civil War broke out. Among those living on the Maha Rayo at that time were Peter Smith's family, Pate Allen, the Batemans, McKinneys, Nat Burkett, Mayas Catherin, T. B. Saunders, J. B. Hawk, Jim Ronean, Jim and Gip Dowty. We moved to the town of Goliad while the Civil War was going on, living there until its close, at which time my father, S. P. Porter, was

killed in the town of Gonzales. My mother was left with
eight small children, one pair of twins in the bunch. I
was about the middle of the bunch, being at that time
about nine years old. As father was taken from us
suddenly, leaving mother without means, it was "root,
hog, or die" with us little fellows, so your humble servant
went to work for R. T. Davis for my grub and clothes,
and, bless your life, the clothes did not consist of any
broadcloth suits either. I worked for Davis one year
and was then employed by A. C. Jones, Sr., of Bee
county, who had a small horse ranch on the extreme
head of Blanco Creek, then known as the Coleman ranch
and now owned, I think, by the McKinneys of Bee county.
I spent some lonesome days on this ranch, but I was
getting well paid, as I was drawing the enormous salary
of five dollars per month and my feed. I worked two
years at this price and while the wages look small, I had
more ready cash when the job ended than I had many
times since, working for much larger wages. When I
left the Jones ranch I went back to my dear mother,
who still lived at Goliad. At that time she was in poor
health and confined to her bed a great deal of the time, so
I did the cooking and sometimes the washing for the
family, while my two older brothers, Dave and Billie
Porter, made a crop on land rented from R. T. Davis,
my first employer. In the fall my mother traded her
place at Goliad for what is known as the old Reed place
on Goat Creek in Goliad county, where I grew to manhood, and where the happiest days of my life were spent.
I was barely in my teens when the big Kansas cattle
drives started, and, like other boys of that time, I wanted
some of the experience of outdoor life, so in the spring
of 1871, with a herd belonging to One-armed Jim Read,
I bade adieu to the southern climate for a season and
headed northward, finally winding up at Abilene, Kansas. After remaining there for a short time we got rid
of our incumbrance, the long-horned steers, and turned

our faces southward and in due time arrived safely at our starting point in Goliad county. Nothing apart from the usual happenings of the trail life took place on this trip. Abilene was a wild and woolly town in those days, at least it seemed to be to a country boy out on his first jaunt. There was plenty of game on the trail, Indians, buffalo, deer and antelope. The principal hotel in Abilene was the Drovers' Cottage, Mrs. Lou Gore, proprietress, which was general headquarters for all cattlemen. After a five months' trip I arrived at home pretty well hooked up, my earthly possessions being a suit of clothes, a pair of star-topped boots and two dollars and fifty cents in cash for my trip. Well done, good and faithful servant!

I went up the trail three years for Jim Read and one year for W. G. Butler of Karnes county. When I was growing up I learned to play the fiddle, but there were only two tunes that I could play to perfection, one of which was "Seesaw," and the other was "Sawsee." Often I have taken my old fiddle on herd at night when on the trail, and while some of my companions would lead my horse around the herd I agitated the catguts, reeling off such old time selections as "Black Jack Grove," "Dinah Had a Wooden Leg," "Shake That Wooden Leg, Dolly Oh," "Give the Fiddler a Dram," "Arkansaw Traveler," and "The Unfortunate Pup." And say, brothers, those old long-horned Texas steers actually enjoyed that old time music. I still have the old music box which I used to play in those care-free, happy days.

My last drive up the trail was in 1875, after which I quit the trail, but never quit the cow-punching job until many years later. Sweet is the memory of the old by-gone days. Many of the old trail boys have passed over the Divide, and it will not be long until we, too, will pass out, to give our places to those coming on. My associates on the trail, as I recall them now, were Emory Hall,

Babe Moyer, Young Collins, Bud Jordan, Bill White, Hiram Reynolds, John Reynolds, John Naylor, Dave Porter, Bud Lansford, Ysidro Morris, John Young, Jack Best, and others.

I was married December 10, 1878, to Miss Nelia Williams of Refugio county, daughter of Judge J. Williams, who for many years was sheriff of Refugio county. Three children were born to us, two boys and one girl, all of whom are still living. In 1882 I moved my family to Atascosa county, settling one mile south of Pleasanton, near the Tilden road, where we remained fourteen months, then moved to McMullen county, where we resided until 1912, then we moved to Brooks county, our present home. While a resident of McMullen county I served as sheriff there for eight years, and I am now serving my second term as sheriff of Brooks county.

REMINISCENCES OF THE TRAIL

A. F. Carvajal, 231 Simpson Street, San Antonio, Texas

In the early part of March, 1882, Mr. Collin Campbell employed my brother to get hands and carry a herd of cattle to Kansas and Nebraska, and he employed the following: A. F. Carvajal, Miguel Cantu, Brijido, Don Hilario, Francisco Longoria, Melchor Ximenz, Juan Bueno, Anastacio Sanches, and a man by the name of Luna, and old Betancur, the cook. The cattle were gathered by Jake Dees and Jim Sutton, and we started from the Ecleto Creek, Campbell's ranch. We penned the cattle the first night in Fred House's pens, and the next day we drove

A. F. CARVAJAL

them in the direction of Gonzales. We crossed the Guadalupe at or near Gonzales and traveled through a very thick brushy region to Lockhart, from where we went on to the Colorado, crossing it below Austin. At this place we fired the cook for getting drunk. We went from there to Georgetown, through Rockdale, Salado and Belton, making about fifteen miles a day. Our route carried us on to Lampasas, where there was a roaring spring and four or five houses. We proceeded due north and crossed the Brazos and passed through Valley Mills, Thence on the west side of Nolan River, west of the Chisholm Trail. Here we learned that the Comanche Indians had killed two persons just above where we were, then we traveled eastward and went by a small place called Cleburne, and on to Fort Worth, where we purchased supplies enough to enable us to cross the Indian Territory. From Fort Worth we drove to Montague, thence to Red River Station, where we crossed Red River and went due north about thirty miles east of Fort Sill. When we had crossed Red River all of us buckled on our six-shooters, for we expected to have to use them. We were on the Chisholm Trail in the Indian Nation, and on the Wichita River some Indians came to us and wanted us to give them some cattle for allowing us to pass through their country. We gave them a few lame cows, and they never bothered us any more. When we reached the Canadian River it was on a rise and swimming, but we made our cattle go across and about twenty of them were drowned. We followed the old trail and crossed the Cimarron River at a place where there was a grove of wild plums. Some men lived in a little house at this point who made it their business to trade with the Indians for furs and buffalo robes. We crossed the Arkansas River about forty or fifty miles west of Wichita and went on towards Ellsworth, Kansas. When we got to Ellsworth the owner of the herd, Collin Campbell, was there waiting for us.

We had been on the road four months. While traveling through the wilderness some of the boys roped and killed a few young buffaloes, and we found it very exciting sport.

At Ellsworth, Kansas, Mr. Campbell gave my brother a compass and a map of Nebraska and told him to take the herd to the North Platte, so we started on our way. Just before we left Ellsworth a man by the name of Crump, who was searching all of the herds for road cattle belonging to Captain King, found a few steers in our herd, and through the advice of our friend, Kilgore, who was there with a herd, we turned back. After leaving Ellsworth we had difficulty in getting enough water for the cattle until we reached the Solomon River. Here we were met by a crowd of about twenty armed men who told us we had crossed the deadline, and could not water the cattle there, and that we would have to go up the river some twenty miles where we could cross on the public lands. They permitted us to water our horses, and gave us orders to move on. Our cattle had not had any water for three days and some were almost perishing. The twenty men left us before dark, and a little while after they were gone there appeared a lonely "short horn," riding a big horse, barefooted and with a small cap on his head. We hailed him and asked if he owned land near there. He said he owned a section about half a mile away, where he lived, but said his neighbors did not want anybody to take cattle across the river for fear of the Texas fever. We told him if he would allow us to water our cattle on his property we would give him two cows and calves or $100 in money, and remove our cattle as soon as they had been watered. When they had slaked their thirst we gave him two cows and calves and got him to accompany us twenty miles up the river, where we crossed to the other side. This was near a place called Republican City. We traveled due north for several days and saw many buffaloes. One day about noon they began going by and at six o'clock that evening they were still passing. Our horses stampeded at the sight of them and my brother had to follow them about eight miles before they could be overtaken and brought back. We proceeded on in the direction of the Platte River, and when we reached that stream we turned westward, following the Northern Pacific Railroad which ran in the direction of Salt Lake City. From Fort McPherson we went to North Platte and at a ranch near there we delivered the cattle to the purchasers, and started back home. We were on the trail six and a half months from the time we left Karnes county. Of the crowd of boys who went with us on this trip only three are now living, myself, my brother, V. P. Carvajal and Francisco Longoria.

JAMES DOBIE

James Dobie was born in Harris county, Texas, in 1856, and entered the stock business in Live Oak county

JIM DOBIE
in the late seventies. He drove cattle and horses to Kansas for several years, endured all the hardships incident to trail life, had lots of trouble with Indians, which he says his comrades can tell about. He shipped many thousands of cattle to the Indian Territory to fatten on the ranges there for many years, and operated large ranches in Bee, Live Oak, Duval, McMullen, La Salle and Webb counties, and at the present time has a large ranch and land holdings. In 1911 he shipped 12,000 fat

steers from his Texas ranches, and is one of the biggest operators of Southwest Texas at the present time.

MADE SEVERAL TRIPS UP THE TRAIL

R. J. Jennings, San Antonio, Texas

I am a native of Texas, arriving in the Lone Star State on March 23, 1856. I made three trips "up the trail," the first being in 1876, the second in 1881, and the third trip was in 1886. I have ranched more or less all of my life in various parts of the state, and have kept in touch with cattle conditions all of the time, witnessing the passing of the old longhorn steer and welcoming the introduction of the shorthorn breed. I have experienced the thrills of trail driving, standing guard, swimming rivers, being pelted with hail, seen streaked lightning played promiscuously around, been in the middle of stampedes, and all those other things mentioned by others in this book.

R. J. JENNINGS

CHARLES DE MONTEL, JR.

Charles de Montel, Jr., was born at Castroville, Texas, February 3, 1848, and grew to manhood there. He was the eldest son of Charles de Montel, one of the founders of Bandera. In 1888 he was married to Miss Annie Steinle, and now lives on his ranch a few miles above old Camp Verde in Kerr county. He is in his 74th year and still quite active, being able to frequently ride horse-back to Bandera, a distance of about sixteen miles.

Mr. Montel remembers many thrilling incidents of frontier days in Medina county, where he was raised. He knew John T. Lytle, John Redus, and many other of the prominent trail drivers of those days, and was well acquainted with Mrs. Sallie Redus, who has a sketch in this volume. Her parents, Mr. and Mrs. McLamore, lived on his father's ranch near Castroville for some time.

Charles de Montel, Jr. early in life became an expert rider, and could handle the lariat and rifle with precision, and despite his advanced age, he still maintains his skill. In 1869 he made a trip to California with a herd of cattle belonging to Jack Tilley and Gideon Thompson, wintering them on the Colorado River in that state and selling them to buyers in Los Angeles.

WAS IN PACKSADDLE MOUNTAIN FIGHT

From a Sketch by N. G. Ozment, in "San Antonio Express"

James R. Moss was born in Fayette county, Texas, January 24, 1843.

When he was a small boy, his parents moved to Travis county, settling near Lake Brushy, some 12 miles northwest of Austin. In 1857 he moved with his parents to Llano county. It was this year that the town of Llano was laid off. John Oatman erected the first store ever built in the town. His father donated 50 acres of land on which to build the town. In an election held to locate the county seat, Llano was selected. When but a youth, young Moss took his place as one of the defenders against the incursion of the Indians.

In February, 1862, a volunteer company of 700 men, including young Moss, was formed in the town of Llano to fight for the defense of the Confederacy. From Llano the company went to Camp Terry, southeast of Austin. Mr. Moss was in Company E, 17th Infantry, McCulloch's brigade, Walker's division. He was in the battle of Milliken's Bend. The day before the capture of his company he was transferred from the Infantry to the Third Battalion, Texas Cavalry, on account of a crippled ankle. He remained with the cavalry through the succeeding period of the war.

When young Moss returned from the war he was broken in health and without as much as a full suit of wearing apparel. With that indefatigable energy and purpose, characteristic of the man, he at once began to lay a foundation for the future. In the absence of the young men during the war the Indians had driven away many horses and driven their owners back further east. The elder Moss had taken the precaution to have his sons move the horses down on Barton's Creek, near Austin, before young Moss joined the army. A year after his return, James and his brother, Charles, took charge of their father's cattle on shares. Week after week, after working all day, they, with some hands working for them, would take the horses to some favorable grazing place and take shifts in guarding them through the night. The moonlight nights increased the vigilance of these young cattlemen, for they well knew these were the nights the Indians were most likely to swoop down after the ponies.

Besides the cattle, the two young men raised many hogs. As there was no local market for these, they killed and baconed about two hundred head one winter and the next summer loaded the meat into ox wagons and took it to Austin, Bastrop, LaGrange and as far as Old Washington to secure markets for same. The weather became so hot that the boys drove at night and rested through the day.

Watching every chance to turn time into money, after the spring work with the cattle, young Moss took the contract to harvest the wheat crops of Cadwell and Saeter. He hired a negro man to help him. The wheat was cradled and handbound. The shocking was done at night. In the later '60's he, with others drove cattle through to Louisiana and sold them to a United States contractor, delivering on board a steamboat on the Mississippi River at Hogs' Point, below the mouth of Red River.

In April, 1869, Mr. Moss threw in with Damon Slater and started to California with about fourteen hundred head of cattle. The year before Mr. Slater found the market good out there, hence this trip. James had his brother Charles with him on this trip. The entire outfit was composed of nine cow hands, two horse herders, two wagoners and the cook. Here is, in brief, the route taken: From Llano to Concho, thence up the Pecos River, and Rio Hondo, up San Benito, a branch of the Hondo, thence across the Divide to Tula Rosa, N. M.; thence to Rio Memphis. Here they saw the first white woman they had seen since leaving Llano. She seemed perfectly happy with her husband in those wilds. From there they drove to Apache Pass, Arizona, through Tucson, and on to Gila River, crossing the Colorado below the mouth of the Gila, at Fort Yuma. They drove into old Mexico and traveled ten or fifteen miles in this country, thence across what is now the Imperial Valley in California. From here they turned southwest toward the mountains. Entering these, they drove up to the old Warner Ranch. Here they struck the Immigrants' Trail, finally arriving at Williamson Port, on the Pacific, where they wintered. The following spring the cattle were delivered some 25 or 30 miles from Los Angeles.

On August 4, 1873, a band of redskins were depredating in Llano county. A company of eight men, consisting of S. B. Harrington, Arch Martin, Robt. Brown, Pink Ayers, Eli P. Lloyd, W. B., S. B., and J. R. Moss, struck their trail in the early morning and followed it for 35 or 40 miles, locating the Indians on Packsaddle Mountain about noon.

The redmen had gone up the mountain from the south side and when discovered by the settlers most of them were sitting around eating some of the beef which had just been roasted. One or two were lying on the ground, either asleep or resting. There were 17 bucks, two squaws and a boy.

Before giving an account of the battle it will be noted that the Indian who was supposed to be on guard was guilty of negligence that proved fatal to some of his comrades, if not himself. Had he been watching he could have seen the approaching Texans a mile away, which possibly would have changed the result of the conflict. When the settlers rode up the mountain they observed 20 or more horses stolen by the Indians but a short distance away. Beyond the horses the Indians were seen eating and resting. The white men by a quick dash ran in between the enemy and the horses. By this time the redmen were up and armed. Their weapons were Winchesters, breech loaders, muskets, pistols, and bows and arrows, though the latter was not used.

The Texans all used Winchesters save W. B. Moss, who used a Colt-Ranger pistol. W. B. Moss began firing at the Indians before dismounting. Firing two shots, he dismounted and joined his comrades, all of whom save Pink Ayers had dismounted. Ayers was shot in the hip. The mule he rode was also shot, and the rider did not reenter the fight. So it was 17 to 7 against the whites. The Indians retreated to a ledge of rocks behind some black jack timber, where they quickly formed a line of battle and rushed at the Texans with a vengeful determination to make quick work of them, but they found the settlers ready for them. W. B. Moss emptied his pistol at them and was bending over to knock the shells from it when a bullet crashed into his body near the right shoulder, and passing through his lungs, lodged in his left side dangerously near the heart. The battle was now on in earnest. James Moss saw his brother fall and thought at first that he had down to reload, but noticed later he was struggling. He ran to him and asked him if he was hurt badly. The brother spit out a mouthful of blood before he could speak, then said:

"Yes, I think they have killed me. I wouldn't hate it so bad if I could have fought till the battle is over."

James gently turned the wounded brother over, then renewed the battle with the foe, some of whom had now rushed within six feet of the white men. Arch Martin threw his gun into position to fire. At the same instant a bullet from an Indian's gun struck the guard of his Winchester, glancing downward and went into his groin. The Indians were putting up a hard fight. Mr. Moss says that some of them were game and seemed to fear nothing. Though they were game, they soon found they were having no walkover in this fight.

One fellow rushed towards James Moss, shooting over his shield at him. The Indian covered his chest with precision while he was firing. The Texan aimed just below the shield and fired and a bullet crashed into the redman's bowels. Moss then turned on another Indian who was getting too close for it to be comfortable. The savages now retreated once more to the ledge, reformed line and came at their foemen again, but showed more precaution this time, for they kept at a greater distance. When Mr. Moss had a chance to take his eye for a moment off the foe he glanced toward where the Indian he had shot fell, but he was gone. One buck who seemed determined to make his way to the horses advanced alone some distance to the right of the others. With gun raised he came within a few feet of the Texans, some of whom fired at him, then he suddenly retreated to the edge of the timber and fell forward, dead. When found he still grasped his gun. The Indians were now retreating. Some four or five of them started up a chant as they retreated, leaving three of their number dead on the ground.

One of the three had moved some distance away from the fight when found. He had a bullet hole in the bowels and one in the chest. This was likely the Indian Mr. Moss shot below the shield. Eli Lloyd was shot in each arm and also had a bullet to cut the skin between his fingers.

W. B. Moss' wound proved to be a serious one, as he lay for weeks before he was able to get around. The bullet was never extracted from his body. The Texans recovered the stolen horses by the Indians.

In September, 1877, Mr. Moss was married to Miss Delia Johnson, daughter of Capt. A. J. and Martha Johnson. The following sons and daughters were reared in this home: Zella, bookkeeper and cashier of the Moss Mercantile Company of Llano; Matthew, president of the Llano National Bank; Edgar, a well known and prosperous stockman of Llano county; J. Ray, manager of the Moss Mercantile Company, Llano; Mrs. J. B. Gage, Austin; Inez, teacher in Dallas; W. R., engaged in oil business at Rockdale; A. J., deceased; Mary, a student in the School of Arts in Chicago; Otilla, an ex-teacher, now with her father in Llano; Richard Olney, assistant cashier of the Llano National Bank.

Mr. Moss by habits of industry and thrift rose from cowboy to cattle king. He bought ranch property in Legion Valley, Llano county, amounting to 8,000 acres of land. He was one of the pioneers of this section in raising Durham cattle. Some years ago he moved from the ranch to Llano. His faithful companion, who shared with him the hardships and privations incident to an earlier day in Texas, passed peacefully to rest December 3, 1918.

THE COWBOY'S PRAYER

O Lord, I've never lived where churches grow;
    I love creation better as it stood
That day You finished it so long ago
    And looked upon Your work and called it good.

I know that others find You in the light
    That's sifted down through tinted window-panes,
And yet, I seem to feel You near tonight
    In this dim, quiet starlight, on the plains.

I thank You, Lord, that I am placed so well;
    That You have made my freedom so complete;
That I'm no slave of whistle, clock or bell,
    Or weak-eyed prisoner of wall and street.
Just let me live my life as I've begun,
    And give me work that's open to the sky;
Make me a pardner of the wind and sun
    And I won't ask for a life that's soft or high.

Let me be easy on the man that's down,
    And make me square and generous with all;
I'm careless sometimes, Lord, when I'm in town,
    But never let them say I'm mean or small,
Make me as wide and open as the plains,
    As honest as the horse between my knees,
Clean as the wind that blows behind the rains,
    Free as the hawk that circles down the breeze.

Forgive me, Lord, when sometimes I forget;
    You know about the reasons that are hid,
You know about the things that gall and fret,
    You know me better than my mother did.
Just keep an eye on all that's done and said,
    Just right me sometimes when I turn aside,
And guide me on the long, dim trail ahead,
    That stretches upwards toward the Great Divide.

                        —Chas. Badger Clark, Jr.

The above was recited by Mike H. Thomas, Grand
Master F. & A. M., at the funeral of Thomas A. Coleman, who died in San Antonio in March, 1923.

WHERE THEY PUT A TRAIL BOSS IN JAIL

W. T. (Bill) Jackman, San Marcos, Texas

I was born in Howard county, Missouri, on the 19th day of April, 1851, and remained there until the year 1859, when my father removed to Bates county, near the Kansas State line. We were here until the Civil War be-gan, when the depredations, murders and all kinds of law-lessness became so numerous by organized bands of out-laws that we were compelled to go north of the Missouri River where better protection could be had. The atrocious deeds of these marauders be-came so rife that this section of the country became almost depopulated, the men all hav-

BILL JACKMAN
1883

ing gone to the army and the families fleeing for protection. Afterward, these outlaws came into our section, burning residences and property of all kinds, taking with them stock or other valuables found. After endur-ing all kinds of hardships for about two years, my mother and the family of children were banished by the Federal authorities and sent to the Confederate lines in the state of Louisiana.

Our trip was first to St. Louis, Missouri, thence down the Mississippi River to Natchez, Mississippi, then across the country to Alexandria, Louisiana, under guard of twenty-five soldiers. From this place we went across the country by stage line to Shreveport, La. We re-mained one year, our father then being in the army of Missouri and Arkansas with General Sterling Price. At this time, by some means unknown to me, my mother received instruction from my father to remove to Red River county, Texas, near Clarksville. We arrived there late in the fall of 1864 and immediately afterwards rented a small piece of farm land.

After Lee's surrender father came and we started south with the intention of going into old Mexico. About 200 officers and soldiers of the army, father being among this number, anticipated going into Mexico or other foreign countries to avoid the oath of allegiance to the Federal government.

On our arrival at San Marcos my father talked with some of the old settlers and was advised not to go into Mexico with his family. This advice was accepted and father proceeded on the trip alone, leaving the family in a tent on the Blanco River.

We were in destitute circumstances, having but a few dollars on which to subsist. I rented land again and started a crop the following spring. Being among strangers and almost penniless I and my little brothers began the struggle for a living. The citizens were kind in assisting us in many ways, besides advising us how to cultivate the land. Such advice was very helpful, I being perfectly ignorant of the mode of cultivating cotton, never having seen any raised in my native state. The friends found here have all passed away without an exception, and the younger generation have taken their places. I will mention a few of the old friends as I think their names should be perpetuated. Among them were: Maj. E. Nance, Capt. G. Story, Shady Dixon, Dr. P. C. Woods, Felix Kyle, Jas. L. Malone, John and Joe Brown, Nestor Boon, C. R. Johns, Ed Burleson, Ferg and Curran Kyle and many others.

Father returned from Mexico, not being satisfied with the country. He surrendered to Federal authorities in San Antonio and was taken to New Orleans and delivered into the hands of Phil Sheridan, who was in charge.

After a few months he was discharged; he came home to the family and found us trudging along with our little farm project. We continued to live on the Blanco until we made the fourth crop, when father bought the property on Blanco River and there spent the balance of his life, passing away at the age of 60 years. I remained with the family until I was 20 years of age. I then tried to farm one year in my own interest. I did not succeed financially, being overcome by drouth and other misfortunes. Dissatisfied with farming I decided to change occupation, so I saddled my horse and drifted to the West. After three or four days' travel I found myself in Uvalde, Texas, ninety miles from San Antonio. Here I met Cood Adams, a member. of the firm of Adams Bros. in the ranch business on the Leona and Frio Rivers, some fifteen miles from Uvalde. Cood and Mart Adams composed the firm of Adams Brothers, though John Adams who lived 15 miles west of San Antonio on the Castroville road, James Adams who lived at San Marcos and Bill Adams of San Antonio, worked some on this ranch while I was there. Cood Adams agreed to give me employment; I asked the amount of wages to expect and he replied, "I am getting Mexicans for $12.00 and board," and with this understanding I commenced to work. I had worked about four months when I decided to go home and spend the Christmas holidays. When ready to start Mr. Adams gave me a check for $80.00 and asked if I intending returning. I replied that I would if the price would justify. He made me an offer of $100.00 per month and in one minute he had my reply, "I will be here." On my return he stated that he intended making a drive to the Northern markets in the spring of that year and must commence gathering cattle on the range and placing them in pastures until ready for the drive. I started preparations with seven Mexicans, about 30 horses, and a pack horse. The Mexicans could not speak English and I could not speak

Spanish. I did not know any of the range and thought I was up against a hard proposition but, believe me, we brought home the goods. When I asked the particular brands to gather, he said, "Bring everything you find, regardless of brand." There was a custom among the ranchmen to use each others' cattle and the other fellow got the credit on the book. A thoroughly educated gentleman by the name of Captain Cooper was the bookkeeper and lived on the Frio ranch at that time. I never saw him again and do not know what became of him afterward.

When the cattle were gathered from the range we commenced branding and putting them in shape for the trail. Afterwards I was assigned the task of driving one of the herds. This was in 1870 and my first experience in handling cattle. I walked into the harness without flinching, though my experience on this trip was in many respects very trying, there being so many new lessons for me to learn. The country through which we traveled was rough and brushy, making the work heavy on the men and very trying on the horses and cattle. We passed from Uvalde county through Bandera, Mason, Llano and Coleman counties, keeping our general course to the north. About four miles before reaching the town of Bandera, one day about noon, while dinner was being prepared I had the herd rounded up to brand a few head which had been overlooked at the ranch. After finishing the work and eating dinner we were drifting slowly along when a young cowman rode up beside me. He was very talkative and seemed to be a nice fellow. After conversing some time in a general manner he asked: "Where did you get that yearling?" referring to the one I had just branded. "At the ranch," I replied. He said, "I would be sorry to see you get in trouble, but that yearling belongs to an old Dutchman who lives down the creek and he is as mean as h—ll. There is one trail boss in jail at Bandera now for driving one of his yearlings." The young fellow rode away and I felt that he was telling facts so I commenced thinking fast. I could almost feel the cold bars of the jail in company with the other boss, but the yearling disappeared right now and so did Bill. I caught a good horse and just kept on high places near the herd for several days. At our next reunion I would be pleased if the trail boss who was in jail would speak out and give his experience; I would be glad to meet him.

We moved on slowly to a point near where we crossed the Llano River. Here a young fellow applied to me for work. He was probably 30 years of age, rather small in stature, roughly dressed, wearing long yellow hair which hung gracefully down over his shoulders, giving him the appearance of a very tough character. Needing help I looked the gentleman over while I talked; he finally said, "Hire me, I know all about cattle and will make you a d—d good hand." I decided to hire him and asked his name to record the date. He said, "Just put me down as Rusty," which I thought very appropriate and used it all the time when addressing him. He gave fine satisfaction in his duties. When we had reached a point 20 miles west of Ft. Griffin on what is known as Elm Creek, we made camp for the night. Next morning on looking over the herd, I found a cow was gone and I knew she would return to our last bed ground some 15 miles back on the trail, and I went back and found the cow and returned to camp with her. On my arrival at camp I found that "Rusty" had shot John Rice, one of my hands. The weapon used was an old model brass mounted 44 calibre Winchester rifle which he carried on his saddle at all times. The bullet had passed entirely through the body on the opposite side of the spine from the heart and blood was flowing from both front and back. I sent at once to Ft. Griffin for a doctor, also giving instructions that a hack be brought for the purpose of conveying the wounded man to the hospital. The doctor came and pronounced the case almost hopeless, though we rushed for the hospital as speedily as possible. I arranged with those in charge to keep me posted as to his condition and on my arrival at Dodge City, Kansas, received a letter stating that he had recovered sufficiently to return home, and that he would entirely recover in a short time. I never heard of him again and I hope to find some one who can give me information regarding his whereabouts. Rusty took one of my best horses and I have not seen him since. Should he be a member of this Association under another name, I would like to hear from him, as all offenses are now barred by statute of limitations.

I never saw Cood or Mart Adams after the drive. One of the brothers, Bill, received the herd at the point of destination and I returned home, thinking my aspirations in this line of work were satisfied in the extreme, though in 1877 Col. Jas. F. Ellison, who then lived at Martindale, Caldwell county, prevailed on me to drive a herd for him, which I delivered at Ogallala, Nebraska. During 1878 I drove for Ellison & Sherill. This firm was composed of Jas. F. Ellison and Jas. H. Sherill, who had formed a co-partnership for the purpose of conveying one herd to the northern markets over the trail.

During one of these drives Givens Lane and I were driving a herd each, and were traveling near each other. The country was dry, grass scarce and watering places for two herds at one time was hard to find. We were then near Buffalo, Kansas, and were having hard times. Givens and I had gone to the front hunting grass and water. A creek, some distance north of Buffalo, had nice running water, but the nesters of that section had plowed a furrow on each side of the trail and posted signs reading about as follows: "Keep your cattle inside these furrows or be prosecuted." The creek north of the trail had the finest water sufficient to swim a good sized steamboat and the grass was excellent. We had

become enraged on reading these warning signs and
Givens said, "Bill, suppose we put our herds into that
fine grass and water and take the chances," to which
I agreed. The cattle were now in sight and looked as
though the two herds were strung out for a distance of
three miles. My herd came first and Givens and I rode
in front of the cattle until the water was scented and the
cattle began running. The nearer the water, the faster
they got, but now came the nesters, who were living in
dugouts and could not be seen until they all mounted
their old mares, bare-backed. They were bare-footed,
bare-headed and all carrying double barrel shotguns,
yelling and demanding that we turn the cattle back to
the trail. We said, "We cannot stop them—you boys
stop them if you can." You never saw such maneuvers
in your life, but the cattle went to the water just the
same. The nesters went for the officers and we had to
keep on the dodge for several days by riding on the high
grounds and keeping a close lookout over the country
for officers.

On another occasion I did not get out so well. I
made camp about 4 P. M. There was not a house or
farm to be seen near us and we supposed we were not
trespassing. A Dutchman suddenly rode into camp and
said, "You must move these cattle. This is my land and
you can not camp here tonight." I reasoned with him,
saying that it was late and danger of stampeding the
cattle and I thought I made him a first class argument,
but it didn't work. He still said, "You must move this
tam cattle right now and do it quick, you shall not stay
here." Then I said, "You move right now and do it
quick," and he did so. But the next morning the constable came with a warrant of arrest and said I must
go to justice court with him. When we arrived the High
Court was on his rostrum and the Dutchman was on hand
also. As the constable and I walked into the court, the
judge looked as knowing as any man I ever met and the

constable acted as if he had arrested one of the worst criminals on earth. I shall never forget this deal. As I walked into the room the Dutchman said, "Judge, there is the fellow vot told me to go to hell mit a pistol." After parleying a little, his majesty said, "This seems to be a very aggravated case, I fine you $100.00 and costs." The fine and costs totaled $130.00, which I paid.

You will notice that the pleasures on the trail were mingled with troubles and hardships. During the spring of 1878 Mr. Ellison engaged me to take a herd to Ogallala, Nebraska. I did not know either the men, the horses or the cattle. All the stock were poor but this was an exceptionally good year, there being plenty of grass and water, I made the trip in good time with all horses and cattle looking fine. When I delivered this herd and was ready to start home Mr. Ellison made me a proposition to take charge of his ranch, to buy cattle through the fall and winter and make preparations for another drive the following spring. This class of work continued with me in the same manner for several years, buying each fall and winter and making the drive afterward. My early spring work was to get all the cattle properly branded and start the first herd with the earliest grass and continue to send them each ten or twelve days until the last herd, which I would take myself. The first herds were generally over one-half of their journey before I got started from the ranch.

Many of my readers will remember Mr. Ellison perfectly well, his acquaintance extending entirely over Texas and many other states. I would like to say that he was one of the best men I ever knew, honorable and upright in all his dealings and greatly loved by those who knew him best. Well do I remember his admonition to me when I commenced work; "Bill, do all you can to save my cattle under any and all circumstances and I will protect you with my money to the last, but do not handle cattle belonging to others, I want nothing but my own.'' I remained with him until he discontinued the cow business. I made nine of these trips over the trail, beginning in 1870 and ending in 1890. I learned to love the work, though many hardships attended each trip. Finally barbed wire came into use, agricultural pursuits became of great interest to the people, and the trail country was closed by farms and pastures.

The successful trail boss or cowboy was happy when he found plenty of grass and water, and prouder still when he would reach the market with his horses and cattle in nice condition. The number of men necessary in handling a herd of 3,000 head of cattle was the boss, eight men with the cattle, a cook, and one man with the horses called the ''remuda man,'' making eleven in the outfit. About 60 horses were furnished to each herd, or six to each man, excepting the cook. The best horse of each mount was selected for his night horse and was used for no other purpose. This horse was supposed to be perfectly gentle, easily handled, clear footed, of good sight and to have all qualities of a first-class cow horse. His other five horses were used each one-half day until all had been used, then he commenced over again with the same process. A first-class new wagon was furnished each outfit and the same was generally drawn by four mules or two yoke of oxen, mules being preferable. Thirty days' provisions or more could be handled in addition to the bedding, slickers, clothing, etc. belonging to the men. A barrel was placed inside the wagon bed, generally between the wheels, fastened securely and with a faucet running through the bed outside, where water could easily be drawn. One barrel of water could be made to last for two days or more. A box was made into the front part of the bed on the outside and fastened securely for the purpose of carrying different trinkets, which could be used in case of trouble. The chuck box was made into compartments for holding the cooking utensils, a lid was fastened by hinges to the back to the box which could be lowered to make a table for the cook. The most important addition to the wagon was the "cooney" which consisted of a cowhide placed under the wagon loosely and fastened to each side of the wagon securely, making a place to hold the wood for cooking purposes. The cook was furnished all necessary utensils to make his part of the work easy, and better still, was supplied with provisions which would enable him at all times to furnish a good and wholesome meal. Plenty of good chuck brought plenty of good work, and satisfaction among the men. The best cook was paid the best price for his services.

The trail men all dressed in about the same manner, their costume consisting of a substantial suit of clothing, fine Stetson hat, the best shop-made boots with high heels, spurs of the best make, red bandana handkerchief for the neck, a good pair of leather leggings, and quirt and a good fishbrand slicker. All used splendid saddles and bridles, the bridle bit generally shop or home-made. When diked out in this garb a man was supposed to be ready for all kinds of weather and all kinds of emergencies. The outfit was then worth about $100.00 but would now easily cost $250.00.

In Kansas and Nebraska were many nesters and farmers who had taken up claims of land under the laws of those states were scattered over the whole country, and these people often came to the herd and asked if they might have the calves which were born on the bed grounds, as the drovers generally killed them. On one occasion, one of these fellows came in a two-horse wagon just about dusk. One of the boys met him and claiming to be the boss made a trade with him to the effect that he should stand guard, for which he was to receive any calves that might be found next morning. This fellow was put on first relief and the boys let him remain on guard all night. To the shorthorn's astonishment when daylight came the herd contained nothing but steers.

The boys gave him the "horse laugh" and he pulled out for home.

At Ogallala in 1879, I met a man by the name of George Knight. I do not know from what part of Texas he came, but I think he was owner of a herd and drove them in person over the trail. He was a great talker and had much to say about the hardships endured on his trip. Said he was almost killed by hail on one occasion and was only saved by turning his horse loose and putting the saddle over his head. Another time the rain fell in such torrents that he had to swim two miles in making his escape from high waters; again during a severe rain and hail storm accompanied by the most terrific thunder and lightning he decided to turn his herd loose, go to camp and get under the wagon. The storm still raged and he took from his pocket a memorandum book and by the light of his lantern wrote, "George Knight, struck and killed by lightning 20 miles south of Ogallala on July 20, 1879." I would like to hear from Mr. Knight or any of his people at our next reunion should any of them be members of our association.

After my trail work was over I embarked into the ranch business and was quite successful for several years, but drouths came, low prices of cattle and other misfortunes and so this adventure was a financial failure.

During 1892 I became a candidate for sheriff of Hays county; was elected by a fine majority and held this position for twenty years. Afterwards was marshal of San Marcos and now I find myself postmaster of this place, a position I have held for eight years.

My father was Col. S. D. Jackman of fame in the Confederate army with General Sterling Price and Joe Shelby. He did much recruiting in the state of Missouri, was severely wounded on one of these trips and never entirely recovered. He was born in Kentucky and removed with his father and family at the age of four years to the state of Missouri. He served two terms in the Texas Legislature and was United States Marshal of the Western district of Texas at the time of his death in 1886, at the age of 60 years. He was married in 1848 to Martha R. Slaven of Boon county, Missouri. To this union was given five sons and three daughters. Of this number three sons have passed into the Great Beyond, leaving Thomas J. and myself, who were the eldest and youngest of that number. Tom is now with our State Ranger force. My mother passed into the Great Beyond in 1869, and afterwards my father was married to Mrs. Cass Gaines of Hays county. To this union four children were born, two of whom are now living and two have passed away. I was married in 1883 to Miss Lou Green of San Marcos, Texas. To us two sons were given, S. D. and Edwin G., now 32 and 34 years respectively. S. D. Jackman was married to Miss Cecil Muller of Laredo, Texas, and Edwin G. Jackman to Miss Etta Olds of San Marcos. The former couple have a son 12 years of age called S. D., Junior, and the latter a daughter of three years named Margaret. These children and grandchildren are the pride of our lives and give us much pleasure in our declining years.

MADE SEVERAL TRIPS

Joe P. Smith, Click, Texas

I was born in Blanco county, August 10, 1855, nine miles west of Round Mountain. My first trip up the trail to Kansas was in 1872, when I went with a herd from Cedar Creek, belonging to Monkson. I brought the horses and wagon back to Cedar Creek. Next trip I went with J. R. Blocker to Pine Bluffs, Wyoming, in 1877. We turned this herd over to Jim Taylor. The third trip I made with Col. Ike T. Pryor's herd to Dodge City, Kansas, in 1882. In 1886 I took a herd for Crosby & Gallagher from Mason, Texas, to the western part of Colorado. In 1887 M. B. McKnight, myself and others took a herd to Vernon, Texas, and sold them. I have worked with cattle since I reached the age of nine years, up to 1911, when I purchased a store at Click, 18 miles southeast of Llano, and besides being engaged in the mercantile business I am also the village postmaster.

RELATES INCIDENTS OF MANY DRIVES

William Baxter Slaughter, San Antonio, Texas

WILLIAM B. SLAUGHTER

My parents, Sarah Jane and Rev. George Webb Slaughter, a Baptist minster, came from Alabama in 1830, crossed the Sabine River, settling in what was then

Mexican Territory, Coahuila, now Texas. The Mexican government at that time was enforcing in such tyrannous manner the regulations of adherence to the Catholic church that armed resistance was made by the settlers and my father, then a young man, joined in the resistance. He was closely connected, with the Independence of Texas from that time on, a full account of which is recorded in John Henry Brown's "History of Texas."

My parents moved from Sabine county to Freestone county in 1850 and settled near the old town of Butler, at which place I was born in 1852. In 1857 my father moved to Palo Pinto county and engaged in the cattle business. In 1861 he moved part of his cattle into Young county, Texas, and during the Civil War furnished the Tonkaway Indians with beef under a contract with the Confederate government. An older brother, J. B. Slaughter, now of Post, Texas, and I with our father gathered the steers each week and delivered them at the Agency. This was continued until the close of the Civil War and two of my older brothers, Colonel C. C. Slaughter and P. E. Slaughter, were rangers under Captain Jack Cureton, grandfather of the now Chief Justice of the Supreme Court of Texas.

Upon return of my oldest brother, Colonel C. C. Slaughter, we found the Confederate money received in payment for the cattle furnished to the government for the Indians during the Civil War had no value. It was turned over to the children attending the school to use as thumb paper for the old Blue Back Spellers of those days. Hence we had no money, but plenty of cattle and Colonel Slaughter suggested to my father that we gather a herd of steers and drive to Shreveport, Louisiana, and ship to New Orleans in order to get ready cash. In the fall of 1867, my father, my oldest brother, and myself, with three other hands, left Palo Pinto with 900 steers, our destination being Shreveport, Louisiana. When we reached Rockwall county, we met Colonel T. H. John-

son, who had made a contract to deliver 1,500 steers at
a small packing plant just east of Jefferson, Texas, situated on a little bayou. With the 600 head of steers
he had gathered and the 900 we had, it was possible
to complete the contract. The time for delivery was
short and a trade was made with him. My brother, Colonel C. C. Slaughter, and Mr. Johnson left in a buggy
for Jefferson immediately after closing the trade, being
followed up with a herd of 1,500 steers in charge of my
father. As soon as we struck the piney woods we would
place the herds in the fields over night in order to get
crop grass for them and the rainy season being on we
were continually having to pull them out of the quicksand in the mornings. When we arrived at the packery
we held the cattle there about two weeks until they were
all killed. My father received $24,300 gold, or $27 per
head, for the steers and we immediately went back to
Jefferson and loaded the wagon with merchandise, including some oranges, the first I ever saw. He bought a
pair of oldfashioned saddle bags and packed $20,000
in gold and put it across the rear of my saddle. I rode
the pony with the gold back to Palo Pinto. This was
the first drive I ever made.

In 1869 I went with a herd of cattle to Abilene, Kansas, my brother, P. E. Slaughter, being in charge. We
crossed the Red River at the old Gaines crossing about
15 miles north of Gainesville, Texas, and went on by
what is known as the Old Love Ranch, in the Indian
Territory and then turned northwest, keeping on the
south side of Paul's Valley, on the Washita River, crossing at Washita Springs and on through Indian Territory, entering Kansas on Bluff Creek where Caldwell,
Kansas, is now situated. Then we went on north across
the Arkansas River where Wichita is now located. I
remember an old fat merchant by the name of McClain
who had a store made of cottonwood logs on the south
side of the river with the sign to the south reading,

"The First Chance" and the one to the north, "The Last Chance" to get supplies. We crossed the broad prairies from there to Abilene. This herd of cattle was sold to Lem Hunter of Illinois, by my brother, Colonel C. C. Slaughter.

The third drive was in 1870. I went this time as foreman, with a herd of 1,800 head of steers which was turned over to me on the head of Bear Creek, now known as the Corn Ranch in Parker county. I went over the same route as we had gone the year before, everything moving nicely until I came to the Red Fork of the Arkansas River, where I came in contact with the Little Osage Indians, who were out under a permit from the agent of the Little Osage Agency, telling what a fine civilized tribe they were and saying that they would harm no one. Their only object was to kill some buffalo and deer. They played havoc with W. B. Grimes' herd which was just ahead of me. Two of Grimes' cowboys, who had quit, were returning to Texas gave me the information that if I went on I would lose my herd, and advising me to change my routing. This herd had been contracted to Lem Hunter of Illinois, Jack Gillespie, and Billy Rogers of Kansas City, and I knew that I could not turn back and get them to Abilene in time to comply with the contract, as there was a forfeit with the Chick Bank at Kansas City of $10,000 by Hunter and his associates and a like amount by my brother, that the herd would reach Abilene on time specified by the contract. As the cattle had been sold for $35.00 per head, a fancy price in those days, I made up my mind to follow the instructions I had always received from my father to never turn back or to think of the bridge that I was to cross until I came to it—and then go over.

Being familiar with the habits of the Tonkaway Indians, to whom my father had supplied beef during the Civil War, I knew what they admired. I had one cowboy who had what we call a "desperado" or "Mexican sash.'' It was made of silk, about six feet long, three to four feet wide, very gaudy, each end having silk tassels, I also had three bandana handkerchiefs, two red and one blue. I made up my mind this was the bridge that would get me by, if I came in contact with the Indians, as stated by Grimes' two cowboys. The next day when we reached the south side of Red Fork,

INDIANS MEETING COWMEN ON THE TRAIL
Courtesy ''Book of Cowboys.''

and where the city of Kingfisher is now located, I found the statements made by these cowboys were true. I discovered the village made by the Indians; it was a city of tepees made out of buffalo hides which had been thoroughly dressed and smoked. As soon as we discovered them, we halted and had our dinner. The herd had not been watered and could not get to the river as the high bluffs on the south side were impassable and extended up to where we were to cross the river. I instructed the cook to separate some flour, coffee and bacon, enough for three meals, and cache it in the cowhide stretched under the wagon, where we used to carry the old Dutch oven, camp kettle and the wood, picked up along the trail. I told the cook if the Indians came up

and asked for flour, bacon and coffee, to throw out all
the bedding and let them have it. We looked and saw
about thirty Indians coming. The chuck wagon was in
the rear of the herd and the horses in front, leading
the herd. The chief asked for the foreman and I told
him I had charge of the herd. He had three squaws
with him. He had his Indian war paint on, and had a
shield fastened to the back of his hair, ornamented with
all kinds of feathers which extended about ten feet back,
and two of the squaws were riding in the rear of the
chief holding his head gear to keep it from dragging on
the ground. The chief called for flour, bacon, sugar and
coffee and the cook threw it out on the ground and it
was put on a pony and two of the Indians returned to
the village with it. The Indians immediately commenced
whipping the cowboys' horses but I had told the cowboys to pay no attention to this. About this time the
wind commenced blowing from the south and my herd
could smell the Indians and I saw they were getting very
restless, I said to myself, "Now is the time to cross the
bridge." I pulled the desperado sash and the three handkerchiefs which I had hid in the bosom of my cowboy
shirt, spread the sash over the chief, handed each one
of the three squaws the handkerchiefs and you would
have thought I was a little god for a little while, for
they had a great talk in their own language, making
much of me. This gave a chance for the herd to get
to the crossing and as the front cattle were following
the horses across, we rushed up behind the rear cattle
and the scent of the 'Indians made them cross quickly.
They demanded beef so I cut out three large steers that
had sore feet, caused by wet weather. They had these
steers killed in less time than I can say it and took the
hide off and went into the little manifold or maw, scraped
the grass back off of it and ate it raw while it was warm.
But I could not understand why they wanted beef while
there were thousands of buffalo in sight. When the herd

was across the river, they bantered us for horse races. I had eight of the horses brought back to the south side of the river, myself and two of my cowboys ran races with them all that afternoon. I had about $30 in silver and they had some very handsome dressed buffalo hides, I would put up about $2.00 or $3.00 against those beautiful hides, and allowed them to use their warriors as judges—and they were honest. When I won they gave hides up and when they won I gave them the money. I had about five hides when the sun was about down. I sent all the horses except the one I was riding and the cowboys were riding across the river and put up the $20.00 I had on the last race and instructed the boy that was going to run it, as he was riding the best horse I had, to jockey with them about fifteen minutes after I left, before running and turning the horse loose and he would be across the river before they knew it, directing him that when he crossed the river to turn to the left and follow the big hollow up to the high hills and I would wait there, which he did. The Indians shot at him several times but I think only to scare him. I had "crossed the bridge" with the Mexican sash. It saved my herd I feel sure.

We turned west at the point of the Blackjacks, ten miles north of Red Fork, and camped between two deep bluff hollows that night and did not unstop the bells on the oxen. Early next morning we pulled the herd across to the west side of Turkey Creek and kept up Turkey Creek on the west side which runs due north until we came to Sewall Branch Supply Station where we secured enough supplies to carry us to Bluff Creek where Capt. Stone had a large store. All of the old trail men knew Capt. Stone, who in the later years was one of the great buyers for our Texas cattle, when they reached Kansas. We had no more trouble and reached Holland Creek, near Abilene, three days before the expiration of the contract for the delivery of the cattle.

As soon as we reached Holland Creek my cowboys all wanted to go to Abilene. I divided them into squads and picked up two straws, one long and one short, and informed them that the ones that got the long straw would be allowed twenty-four hours in Abilene, when they would return and let the others go. The young man, Wash Wolf, who furnished me the sash that saved my herd, was in the first squad and never returned. He immediately got on a spree on arriving in Abilene and was killed in a dance hall there and I saw him no more. The herd was delivered and I received instructions from my brother to return to the Young county ranch with the outfit.

My fourth drive was in 1871. I had charge of the herd as in the previous year. I went from Young county where Graham is now situated, through Lost Valley, known as the old J. C. Loving ranch, on due north by Buffalo Springs, out by Victoria Peak, where Stephens & Worshan had a cattle ranch, about 20 miles north to the upper sand timbers. It commenced raining, about the time to bed the herd. We noticed northeast of us in another grove of timber a fire which later proved to be a band of Indians. Our herd stampeded that night. Next morning we counted the herd and found we were short 200 cattle. We soon found the trail which went southwest about two miles and split into two parts, part of them going south and part going west. Myself and another man followed the trail south about ten miles and found part of the cattle and brought them back to the main herd. We waited on the other two men to return until the next morning and as they did not return we went to where the cattle had separated and took the trail of the two horses, following the ones that went west about eight miles and found the two men had been murdered by the Indians, scalped and their bodies badly mutilated. We buried them there and returned to our herd and moved rapidly until we reached Red River Station, getting on the old Chisholm Trail.

In 1872 I went the same route but stopped the herd twenty-five miles south of Wichita and held them there until they were sold, which was in August. I had instructions to return to the Jack county ranch, on what is now known as Dillingham Prairies, and receive a herd of cattle from J. C. Loving and Charlie Rivers, a brother-in-law, Charles Rivers, a son-in-law of Oliver C. Loving, learned the business under his father-in-law, who had made two or three trips with Loving by the way of Ft. Sumner in New Mexico. The day I commenced receiving the cattle from Loving and Rivers on Dillingham Prairie we tallied out part of the herd and Mr. Loving waited for the arrival of Mr. Rivers for enough cattle to fill this contract. Mr. Rivers was on his way from Lost Valley to Dillingham Prairie. He arrived that evening and the cattle were penned and he made his camp nearby and guarded his horses. The Indians made a raid on the horses and in trying to protect them Charlie Rivers was shot, from which wound he later died at Weatherford, Texas.

In 1873 I drove a herd for my father to the head of Fall River. That spring in February I stopped at Ft. Worth several days and made a trade with E. M. (Bud) Dagget and Jake Farmer for a herd of young steers on my own account, as I had saved considerable money and my father endorsed for me at the First National Bank at Emporia, Kansas, for an additional amount to pay for the herd. As soon as the herd I went up with in the spring was turned over I immediately returned to Fort Worth and received this herd from Dagget and Farmer and drove them on the same route as I went before until I reached Chiloche Creek, south of the Arkansas River, and went due east to the mouth of Grouse Creek on the Arkansas River and wintered this herd there. Next spring they were carried to Verdigris River, Greenwood county, where Mr. Martindale had a large ranch. I sold this herd to him and returned to Texas.

In 1874 I drove a herd from Elm Creek, Young county to Dodge City, Kansas, and sold them to a Mr. Rob who represented one of the packing houses at Kansas City. I returned to Texas in 1875, bought a herd of cattle from John Gamel and Christy Crosby of Mason, Texas. I had a letter of credit from the City National Bank of Dallas, but they would not take checks, which forced me to go to San Antonio and get $15,000 in currency from Mr. Brackenridge, which I carried back to Mason to pay for this herd of cattle, traveling only at night until I got the money in Mr. Ranck's bank at Mason. I drove this herd to Jack county and returned and bought another herd from Charlie Lemburg of Llano county. Colonel I. T. Pryor, now of San Antonio, was his foreman at that time. I carried them to Jack county and wintered them there. In the spring of 1876 I drove one part of these cattle to Dodge City, Kansas, and sold to J. L. Driskill & Sons who had a ranch; but his home was at Austin, Texas.

In 1877 I drove a herd to Dodge City again and also my brother, Colonel C. C. Slaughter, drove two herds there and we sold the three herds to Hunter, Evans & Newman, who had secured the contract to furnish beef to the Indians in the Territory. I delivered this herd at Fort Reno, to Jesse Evans, who had charge of the outfit.

In 1879 I drove a herd of steers from Blanco Canyon, Crosby county, to Hunnewell, Kansas, and sold to Hewens & Titus, who were heavy buyers for good Texas steers. That year I got my first experience on the Texas fever proposition. Striking the trail at Rush Creek, east of Ft. Sill, following it for five days I saw that something was the matter with some of my steers, and I threw them east of the trail. I had been skeptical up to this time on Texas fever but the loss of steers sustained on this drive fully convinced me that there was such a thing as Texas fever.

In 1881 I drove two herds of steers from Palo Pinto

county, to Caldwell, Kansas, sold one herd to A. Golson,
a hotel man at Caldwell and the other to Barbecue Campbell.

In 1882 I drove a herd to Trail City, Colorado, on the
Arkansas River and sold to Jones Bros. of Los Animas,
Colorado. In 1883 I moved two herds of stock cattle
from Crosby county, Texas, to American Valley, Socorro
county, in the western part of New Mexico. In 1885 I
drove a herd of steers from Socorro county, New Mexico,
to Laramie Plains on the Laramie River, just west of
Laramie City, Wyoming. This was the hardest drive I
think I ever made.

In 1886 I drove a herd from Blanco Canyon, Crosby
county, Texas to Chino Valley, near Prescott, Arizona.
In 1887 I drove a herd from Socorro to Laramie Plains,
Wyoming, onto Crow Creek and sold them in small lots.
They were shipped out over the Rock Island Railroad
to Nebraska. In 1889 I moved two herds, one from New
Mexico and one from Panhandle of Texas, to Malta,
Valley county, Montana, situated on Milk River. In 1890
I drove a herd from Clayton, New Mexico, to the Cypress
Hills on the south line of Canada.

In 1901 I carried a herd from Clifton, Arizona, to
Liberal, Kansas. My wife was with me on the trail this
time.

During all this time I had moved many herds in Texas
from one part of the state to the other and also in New
Mexico. My last drive and the only one of its kind so
far as I know by anyone, was when I moved 104 buffalo
from Dalhart, Dallam county, Texas, to Fort Garland,
Colorado. I had no trouble with this herd of buffalo—as
I had with herds of cattle. They had become domesticated by feeding them cottonseed cake and each night
I would move them about one-fourth of a mile north
of where I located my camp and about dark gave them
about 50 pounds of cake. They would consume the cake
and lay down until about midnight and get up to graze

on the buffalo grass and lick up what waste cake was left and bed down until daylight next morning, at which time I would be up, (for I had an alarm clock) and head them on north. One of the large buffalo bulls became vicious when we reached Fort Garland. We killed him and sent him by express back to Pueblo, Colorado, where he was held in cold storage twenty-one days. The State Bankers of Colorado met with the Bankers of Pueblo that year and he was barbecued and served to them.

A PIONEER MOTHER'S EXPERIENCE

Mrs. Mary Kate Cruze, R. F. D. Box 178, San Antonio, Texas

I was born October 21, 1849 in Baton Rouge, Louisiana, daughter of Peyton and Mary Cox. My father died in 1850 and in 1851 mother married Mr. Albert Heaton from Washington, Maine. He was a kind and just step-father. He took mother and her two children to Pattersonville, La., where he had a good home.

Then we moved to Franklin, La., mother and father going overland in the buggy, while the old negro nurse and we children, with the household goods and my old cat went on steamboat. We settled near the bayou and father established a cooper shop and wharf where boats came and loaded with his product of barrels, casks, etc. He had nine men working in his shop, when a terrific scourge of yellow fever swept over Louisiana and when the fever abated there was only one man left out of the nine. Whole families died. Mother and father both had the fever, though somehow we children escaped. My father never went into his shop again because he imagined he could see and hear his men working as he had seen them last. He sold the cooperage and engaged in the hotel business, though at one time he was judge of St. Mary parish. He had heard so much about the "great state of Texas" that he finally decided to cast his lot in this land of promise, so in 1856, in com-

pany with two friends, Messrs. Cooper and Smith, he
set out on horseback for the Lone Star State. Cooper
and Smith located at Austin, but father went on to Hays
county, where he bought land in the new town of Cannonville, owned and sponsored by Mr. Rufus Cannon
and later run against San Marcos for the county seat.
Father wrote glowing letters to Mother, telling of the
wonderland he had found, of the trees, flowers, knee
high grass and abundance of crystal clear water. There
was a gushing spring at the corner of the lot he planned
to build our house on and he urged Mother to pack up
and come as soon as possible. On June 27, 1856, Mother's twenty-seventh birthday, she started to Texas, via
New Orleans with her four children, Charles, the eldest
aged nine years, myself seven, and two half brothers,
Albert and William Heaton, aged four and two years
respectively. I will never forget the sea voyage on the
"Charles Morgan" from New Orleans to Galveston with
its sea-sickness and seemingly never-ending smell of tar
and rope. The overland journey to Austin was made by
stage coach and there we stopped with Mr. and Mrs.
Smith, who lived in a double loghouse on Congress Ave.

Father came to Austin a day or two after we arrived
and we were overjoyed to see him. The next day Father
hitched up the oxen, "Lion" and "Berry," to a big
covered wagon and we left our kind Louisiana friends
for a wilderness and strangers. We children enjoyed
each step of the journey, as we would get .out of the
wagon, gather flowers, shells and all kinds of pretty rocks,
wondering the while if we would ever reach "Cannonville." If I remember rightly there was only one house
that could be seen from the road in the two days that it
took to make the twenty-five miles, as the oxen never went
faster than a walk. Cannonvile was situated about three
miles south of where the village of Dripping Springs
now stands. We lived three months with the Cannon
family before our house was finished. We carried water

from Onion Creek, a mile distant. We had many hardships. The crops were almost failures and to make our troubles worse, our good friend, Mr. Cannon, died.

There were only three houses ever built in Cannonville. Mr. Newton Jackson of Austin, built one, a Mr. Schropshire one, and Father the other one. Then Mrs. Cannon refused to give deeds to the land her husband sold. The election for county seat was held and "Cannonville" lost and "Cannonville" died a natural death. Mrs. Cannon, her children and an old negro "Mammy" moved to Bastrop and we moved into their home on account of its having a good well of water. A post office was established and Father was appointed postmaster of "Cannonville." The mail, which was carried on horseback, came from Austin and it was a great day when it arrived, as people came for miles for the occasion. Meantime Father tried farming but a late frost came, followed by grasshoppers and a disastrous drouth which it seemed would put an end to everything. But the people were undaunted. The men hitched their oxen to the great lumbering ox-wagons and set out for Port Lavaca or Indianola to purchase supplies. People are grumbling about today's high prices, but who among them has seen flour sell for $25.00 a barrel, corn meal at $3.00 a bushel and everything else in proportion? I never knew flour being cheaper than $16 or $18 a barrel until after I was grown.

We had no church or school and the mothers taught their children. The most popular school books of those days were the "Blue Back Speller" "McGuffey's Reader," "Ray's Arithmetic" and "Webster's School Dictionary." A popular punishment for misconduct during our lesson hours was to have us memorize an entire page of the dictionary. Father read a chapter from the New Testament each night and Mother heard our prayers. Mother had a beautiful voice and often sang hymns to us. We were a happy family indeed.

Reverend Johnson of Blanco City was circuit-rider for our district. He came each fourth Sunday to preach to our neighborhood and held meetings in some neighbor's house. Everyone within a radius of ten miles attended and if too far to walk, Father hitched "Lion" and "Berry" to the ox-wagon and took us in style. Occasionally Rev. Johnson would bring with him his wife and little daughter, Mary Kate, whose name was the same as my own. We were great friends as long as she lived.

Our nearest neighbors were families named Wallace, Moss, Perry, and Dr. J. M. Pound, who was our family physician for thirty years. Mother belonged to the Good Samaritans and the Episcopal church, though later she united with the Christian church. Father was a Royal Arch Mason and, though he did not belong to any church, he was a just man. The Ten Commandments were his creed.

In 1860 we moved from Cannonville to Jacob's Well, on Cypress Creek, where Father contracted to take care of a herd of cattle owned by John Meeks and sons of Webberville, but knowing nothing about handling stock he gave it up and moved to the Blanco River, about twelve miles from San Marcos, where he farmed, made shingles and shoes. A neighbor, Mr. W. A. Leath, had a tanyard and made very good leather. We still had no schools so Father built a cypress-slab school house, where Mother taught her own and the neighbors' children. In 1861 and 1862, I attended a boarding school in San Marcos, which was then only a small village. My teacher was Prof. T. L. Lyons.

When the war between the states broke out, Mother had a hand loom and spinning wheel made, on which she spun and wove most of our clothing. I felt dressed up in my homespun dress and Father's home-made shoes. We knitted our stockings and gloves and braided our hats of wheat-straw or corn husks.

There was a little settlement below us on the Blanco

River called "Arkansaw" and three or four men from there were forced to go to war. One morning we were startled to see a detachment of soldiers drawn up before our house. The commander explained that they were hunting three men from "Arkansaw" who had deserted the army and asked Father to be on the lookout for them, naming a place where he might report in case they were seen in that locality. He asked if he might have some bread baked. Mother and I went to work in a hurry and soon had 100 biscuits done, to which we added all the butter we had on hand. The commander was delighted and insisted that we accept pay, but we refused. The soldiers marched away after repeating their request for Father to be on the lookout for "Jap" Brown, "Little John" Pierce and Harris, the deserters. These men were never found, though they were hunted from time to time throughout the war and we learned later that they had lived in caves a short distance from their homes. After the war they came out of hiding, though no one outside the little colony knew where they had been. A sister-in-law of Jap Brown told me of the many narrow escapes he had while in hiding. Apparently Mrs. Brown was a very industrious woman and the neighbors wondered how she wove more cloth, raised better crops and more hogs than anyone. When a soldier left for the front, Mrs. Brown invariably donated socks and gloves, did sewing or any other useful favor that she could do.

Father and Brother Charlie went to war, as did my "best friend and schoolmate," and I had an anxious time thinking of my loved ones, though they all came home safe and sound. Great was the rejoicing from then on and balls, picnics and many kinds of amusements took the place of our sad lonely hours. Many were the weddings that followed, for few indeed were the boys who had not left their girls behind them.

On July 24, 1865, I was married to Joseph S. Cruze

at my father's place on the Blanco River. Though I was not yet sixteen and my husband lacked three days of being twenty, we felt full grown and far from children. We had lived through many trials and tribulations, we felt that we had missed our childhood.

Father was a magistrate in our precinct for several years before and after the war, also was elected assessor several terms. Then he moved to San Marcos and was appointed postmaster, his health failed and he moved to Pearsall. In 1888 he came to visit us on our ranch where he took sick and died. We laid him to rest in the Leath graveyard on the Blanco River, beside his little daughter who died in infancy. Mother died in Dallas, January, 1897.

In the first years of our married life we had hard times. We moved to Bastrop county where Mr. Thomas McKinney had a saw-mill on the Colorado River and my husband contracted to haul the lumber to Austin. McKinney agreed to furnish ten wagons and teams, but he let him have only two. It was well, for the mill broke down, Mr. George Maverick, the mill foreman took sick, likewise my husband and I, with chills and fever, so we moved back to the mountains in Hays county. We had no home so we moved into a little vacant shanty that some one had built near a small spring that my husband had found when he was a little boy. The house had neither floor nor chimney and was chinked with mud which fell in on us when it rained. Mr. Cruze soon built a chimney and floored the house and we lived there for four years and were happy as larks.

He made several trips to Port Lavaca; likewise he had all the pleasure and hardships of cow hunts. I know I have baked a thousand biscuits for his trips. The time he spent on the trail seemed very long to me, as I stayed at home, took care of the babies and the place. He had the same experiences that most trail drivers had, swimming swollen streams, thunder and lightning, stampedes, etc., but came out uninjured. He used a pack horse to carry his bedding and provisions and sometimes he would pack the old horse so heavily that he would sit down and had to be helped up. Once when he had gone about two miles from home the pack turned under the old horse and he ran away, kicked the pack to pieces and scattered biscuits for a mile. Later he made a big "KYAX" as he called it, somewhat on the order of the old saddle bags, but very commodious, then he bought a real pack-saddle and had no more mishaps with his kitchen outfit.

In 1868, two cattlemen hired him to help round up a herd of cattle near the Perdinales River. He worked a month at two dollars a day and when the work was done, neither man would pay him. Mr. Cruze also made two trips to Kansas over the Chisholm Trail and of all the men he associated with on these trips and cow hunts, my half brother, Albert Heaton, of Del Rio, is the only man now living that we know of. On his last trip to Kansas his main helper was Adam Rector, a negro boy, who could ride and rope with the best. One morning he and Adam were leading the herd when suddenly he saw the negro wheel and come tearing by him shouting, "Indians! Indians!" and in spite of his yells, Adam kept going to the rear of the herd. He knew that it was poor time to run so he stood his ground. Soon the Indians came up to him looking very savage, and one of them made a grab for his quirt. Instantly he grabbed the Indian's, the strings slipped off each wrist and they had traded quirts. Then they began a guttural demand for beef. He motioned to the rear of the herd and they went on until they found the boss, who gave them a yearling.

Mr. Cruze drove his own cattle and made wages besides which was more money than we ever had before and wisely did not waste any of it. He bought two "Kansas" wagons, as they were called, complete with sheets, bows, etc., a Wheeler & Wilson sewing machine, a set of moss agate jewelry, a side saddle, bridle, blanket, riding skirt and a fine pacing pony, which would go only as far as he liked, then turn around and go home in spite of me. He bought and established the "Cruze Ranch" where we lived for fifty years. In 1917 we sold it to our son, Joe S. Cruze, Jr., who has made it his home.

Our eldest son, Albert, lives in Houston, Will in Travis county and John in California, while two daughters, Margaret and Mrs. Addie Harlan and her son, Forrest live with us. Our youngest daughter, Mrs. Nell Curry, lives in Floresville. We have eight grandchildren, including twin baby girls, slightly more than a month old. We are well satisfied in our new home, Los Angeles Heights, San Antonio, and we are never so happy as when our children or some old friend comes to see us, for as ever the latch string hangs on the outside.

A COWBOY UNDERTAKER

W. K. Shipman, San Antonio, Texas

I was born in Caldwell county in 1864. My father was one of the first settlers of that county. In 1882, with my younger brother, Joe Shipman, I began work for John Davidson, who then ranched on the Jim Ned, near Coleman City. About May 1st of that year we received 1,400 yearlings at Brady, a n d started them up the trail. On the way two of our hands, one called "Short" from Oak Grove, and the other we called "Stumpy," got into a fight and "Stumpy" was badly wounded. We hauled him to Fort Griffin and left him there. I do not know if he ever recovered. We went

W. K. SHIPMAN

up the Western Trail, by way of Vernon on Pease River, Doan's Store on Red River. We got along with the Indians pretty well by giving them a yearling now and then. As we neared Dodge City Mr. Davidson came out to meet us, and told us we would have to hold them for a few days. Later we moved on to Ogallala, Nebraska, where the cattle were sold. I started on the trip as a hand, but got to be boss before we reached Dodge City, and drew $100 per month for wages.

In the fall of the same year we took another herd up into the Indian Territory and delivered them to a ranch just south of Camp Supply. Brother Joe and I came back home to Coryell county and got a job building rock fences. I went to all of the dances and neck lickings in the country while I tarried there, but in the spring I went west again and took another trip up the trail for John Davidson. Sold out at Dodge City, Kansas. In July, 1883, my brother, Joe, was killed by a horse falling on him. In the spring of 1884 Mr. Davidson employed me to take charge of his ranch near Fort Stockton. Everything was dry that year and many cattle died. Later I went to New Mexico and worked in the V-V ranch near Fort Stanton until 1887, when wages were cut and I drifted back to Texas, going up to McKinney, in Collin county, where I took a position in a marble yard, and kept it until July, 1889, then went to Brownwood and opened a marble yard of my own, which I managed until 1900, when I sold out and went to San Angelo and started another marble yard, later putting in a branch business at Sweetwater. I was successful in this line of work, and in course of time I added undertaking as a side line to my business, taking up the study of embalming and in 1905 I went before the board of examiners, and successfully passed the examination and became a licensed embalmer. In 1910 I moved to Del Rio and bought an undertaking business, added real estate business as a side line, and remained there until 1919, when I sold out and moved to San Antonio and purchased 500 acres of land on the Blanco road, ten miles north of the city, where I am now living.

CAPTURED THREE THOUSAND QUARTS

Captain W. L. Wright is one of the present efficient ranger captains stationed along the border. The illustration herewith shows a pack train loaded with tequila which Captain Wright and his men captured on the Jim Gibson ranch, fifteen miles northwest of Realitos, Duval county, November 22, 1921. Captain Wright says:

Top Row—PACK ANIMALS AND 3,000 QUARTS OF TEQUILA
Bottom Row—CAPT. W. L. WRIGHT'S RANGERS

"We captured thirty-seven head of horses and mules with 3,000 quarts of tequila, and had a fight with the Mexicans, wounding several, and some got away. We had trailed them seventy-five miles, and overtook them about two miles from Jim Gibson's ranch house. Old man Jim took this picture himself. When the rucas started Jim was out hunting and was about 150 yards from us sitting down, and when the shooting began he went in high, and when we reached the ranch he had his remuda in the pen and was catching a horse to come to us. There were sixteen smugglers, while I had eight men in my command."

WOULD LIKE TO GO AGAIN

Webster Witter, Beeville, Texas

In 1884 I went on the trail for M. A. Withers of Lockhart. We left the Teague ranch in LaSalle county about the first of April with 4,300 aged steers for Ogallala, Nebraska. Gus Withers, a real man, was our trail boss. That spring was a wet one, and besides having to swim swollen streams and contend with stampedes and thunder storms, we experienced a siege of Spanish itch and pink-eye. In the quicksands of the North Canadian River we lost two horses, and the Indians were very troublesome. I remember when we went out the Nueces

WEBSTER WITTER

Canyon we crossed the Nueces River twenty-eight times in forty miles, and our cattle became tender-footed from rocks and crossing water so much. But despite the hardships and trouble on the trail I would like to go again. I believe S. B. Brite of Taylorsville, M. A. Withers of Lockhart and myself are the only ones left who made this drive. I am now fifty-three years old, and as strong as any man in the state for my age. I have traveled in every state in the Union with a Wild West show as an expert roper.

I am always pleased to meet up with the old boys of those good old days, to swap yarns with them and recount experiences of the time when a forty-dollar saddle and a ten-dollar hoss was a combination that was hard to beat. In the language of Rip Van Winkle, "Here's to your good health, and your family's good health, and may you all live long and prosper."

MY EXPERIENCE ON THE TRAIL

Mrs. W. B. Slaughter, San Antonio, Texas

My experience on the cattle trail was with a herd of 1,500 cattle in charge of my husband. We left Fort Sumner, New Mexico, May 25, 1896, and arrived at Liberal, Kansas, on the Rock Island railroad, July 25th, following. We crossed the Canadian River at old Fort Bascom, New Mexico, and had to swim it. My duty on this trip was to hunt the watering places, and also the camp grounds for the herd at night, and to assist the young man (George Longan, who is now assistant editor of the *Kansas City Star*) to catch the change of horses for morning, noon and night. I also had to see that the man who drove the trail wagon had plenty of wood with which to cook the meals and have them ready at a certain time. When

MRS. W. B. SLAUGHTER

we arrived near Clayton, New Mexico, my husband, Mr. Longan, and myself, went across to Springer, New Mexico, and received 250 cattle which we drove back to the main herd at Clayton. I had a large Hines buggy which I used on this trip. When we left Clayton we traveled along the north line of Texas, as the Capitol Freehold

Land & Cattle had all of Texas fenced for about fifty miles north and east. We went across to where the city of Guyman is now located, as the Rock Island railroad was built only as far as Liberal, Kansas, at that time. I really enjoyed every minute of the drive, for the weather was fine, and everything moved along nicely. When we reached Liberal a few cars of the cattle were shipped to the Kansas City market. I took the passenger train and went to Kansas City. All of the country we came over was unsettled at that time.

ED C. LASATER

Ed C. Lasater, well known throughout the United States as owner of the largest Jersey-cattle farm in the world, is a native Texan, and owns a ranch of three hundred thousand acres. The following sketch was taken from the National Magazine, issue of February, 1920:

ED. C. LASATER

Ed. C. Lasater was born near the little town of Goliad, Texas, just a little more than fifty years ago. His father was a ranchman who moved to Texas before the Civil War, when Texas was an open range. Losing his cattle interests during the re-adjustment period the senior Lasater engaged in the mercantile business at Goliad, immediately across the San Antonio River where the battle of La Bahia was fought and where the subsequent massacre of Fannin's men took place. Young Lasater grew up in an atmosphere of independence and with love for freedom. The wide open range of the prairies afforded him time to think, so he decided to become a lawyer. A suggestion of future ill-health caused him to abandon his studies and he engaged in the sheep business with his father. A little later, he was called to assume charge of his father's herd; and with Mexican sheep-herders for his assistants and companions he began his career as a sheep raiser which continued up until the passage of the Wilson bill and wool was put on the free list, killing the industry for many years.

We next find Ed Lasater operating on a large scale as a cattle buyer, though still a very young man but with fine personal credit. He would buy cattle from the Texas ranchmen and ship to Chicago markets, but all the time he was making a close study of grazing lands which had, at one time, been so valuable for sheep raising. During the panic of 1893, Mr. Lasater had bought heavily of Texas cattle; in fact he had nearly 30,000 head on hand. A drouth hit Texas and the cattle could not winter on the range. It was necessary to feed them through the winter; then the bottom dropped out of the cattle business and fat steers sold for $2.70 a hundred on the Chicago market, and Ed Lasater was $130,000 loser on his cattle—he lost everything he had except his credit, and says himself that all he has accumulated since his failure has been done as a result of his financial disaster. He kept his contracts, paid for all the cattle that he bought, and accepted his loss. About this time, something happened in Lasater's favor. Practically all the land was owned by Mexicans through grants from the Spanish and Mexican governments. In 1893, the great drouth year, the ranchmen lost all their cattle, and the cry for water went up everywhere. The Mexicans depended upon shallow wells which were no more than trenches; and while they were no worse off than Lasater who had lost all his cattle, he had one thing they did not have—credit, and confidence in his ability to provide an adequate water supply. He investigated the situation, and found that the English companies which had been lending money to the Mexican grantees desired to have the land worked or otherwise utilized. He knew the lands, and what they would produce, provided the water supply was assured, and was enough of an engineer to ascertain that by making the wells deeper and installing pumps he could have an unlimited supply. He put up his proposition to some bankers who knew his ability and honesty. With this assistance, he contracted for 30,000 head of cattle to be delivered the following spring. At the same time, he began buying up all the land he could get from the descendants of the Mexican grantees, making small cash payments, the balance on long time which was handled through loan companies. He had faith in the country. The water was there, all the time, and its lack was due to the inefficient methods of the Mexicans. In time, Mr. Lasater became owner of 360,000 acres in Duval, Brooks and Willacy counties, comprising now the Lasater ranch, known as "La Mota," at Falfurrias. "Falfurrias" (the name given by the Lipan Indians to a tree-crested motte or knoll and translated means "Heart's Desire") is a prosperous and thriving little town of 2,500 people, many of them Mexicans. Before the coming of the railroad in 1906 it was a cattle ranch less than 200 people occupying the adjacent 400,000 acres. Now it has modern schools, churches, city conveniences, an empty jail, the finest creamery in the South and many modern homes. The palm trees and orange groves and balmy atmosphere strongly suggest California. But this was far from the condition of the country a few years ago when Ed Lasater first dreamed of establishing a great dairy industry and the largest and finest herd of pure bred Jerseys in the world.

Since 1906 Mr. Lasater has sold to actual settlers and farmers 60,000 acres of his original ranch tract of 360,000 acres. This would probably represent five hundred families, or 2,500 people—thrifty and industrious farmers from Iowa, Kansas, Texas, Nebraska, Indiana and other states. Practically all of the ranch land adjoining or near the town of Falfurrias is suitable and capable of maintaining a large population.

THE PLUCK OF A POOR GERMAN BOY

B. Vesper, Big Wells, Texas

I was born in Germany in 1845, on a farm. My father died when I was seven years old, and I was reared by a good mother. I served as an apprentice in the blacksmith trade for three years, working for my board, and would walk home, a distance of six miles, every Sunday.

B. VESPER AND GRANDDAUGHTER

In 1868, when I was 23 years old, I left Germany and came to America, landing in New York, where I took an immigrant train for Leavenworth, Kansas. There I found some former friends, and I secured a job hauling brick in a wheelbarrow at one dollar per day. I soon gave that up and went to work in a sawmill, but that didn't suit me either, so I accepted a position in a livery stable, washing buggies and caring for 14 horses and 14 sets of harness. During this time I made the acquaintance of Herbert Peck, a coachman for H. L. Newman of Leavenworth, and he secured me a position with Mr. Newman's brother-in-law, a Mr. Moorehead. I served Mr. Moorehead from 1868 until 1870, receiving $30 per month and board, and was treated well by the family. While working there I met George Lang, who had a butcher shop in Leavenworth, and he invited me to go with him to Texas after a bunch of cattle, so on March 1, 1870, we left Kansas for Texas, when the ground was covered with snow and the weather was as cold as blue blazes. We were on the road one week when we reached Red River in a storm. Next morning we crossed the river into Texas and went to a ranch on Beaver Creek, owned by a man named Terell, of Fort Worth. Mr. Lang and I left the outfit at the ranch and rode over to Fort Worth, which was then only a very small town with one bank, a blacksmith shop and a store. We made a trade with Mr. Terrell for 700 beeves, to be gathered as soon as possible, and by the fifteenth of April we were ready to start back to Kansas with them. That was the largest herd of cattle I had ever seen, and it was all new to me. I shall never forget our first night out, when we had a stampede. I flew right in and tried to keep up with the herd, but my horse fell with me and when we got up and together again the cattle were out of sight. I could hear a big bell on something that was running so I decided to follow it, but soon lost the direction of the bell, and concluded to go back to camp. The old horse I was riding kept trying to go in the opposite direction from the way I thought the camp was. I rode and rode and got so tired I climbed up in a tree to take a nap out of reach of the coyotes that were howling all around, and when I dozed off to sleep I tumbled out of the tree, waking up in time to catch onto a lower limb. Then I again decided to try and go to camp, and told the old horse if he knew more about its location than I did to go ahead. And right there I learned that a good cow horse knew more than a green Dutchman, for in just a little while he took me right into camp. I told the boys if they had stayed with me we would have held the herd. We had no other trouble for several days, but just after crossing Red River we caught up with two herds, one of them belonging to a man named Hunter, and the other to man named Eikel of Fort Worth. Hunter had an escort of soldiers with his herd.

In passing through Fort Sill on this trip we saw the Navajo tribe of Indians, consisting of 700, which the government was feeding at that time. There was a motherless calf which followed our herd out of Texas, and after we had been on the trail a short time four Indians overtook us and made signs that they wanted the calf. Mr. Lang gave it to them. They roped and killed and had all the meat packed to take back with them in less than ten minutes. This just gave them a good appetite, for in a short while sixteen young warriors overtook us, caught Mr. Lang's horse and yelling like the devil, demanded more beef. They stampeded our herd, but we managed to keep the cattle in line and let them run. They soon rode up with Mr. Lang and he cut out four big steers for them and they let us go. That night we were only seven miles from their camp and deemed it expedient to stand guard. We got through without mishap, except being in a storm or two, and reached Wichita, which was then a very small place, where Mr. Lang located a place for us to herd, while he went to Leavenworth to find a buyer for the cattle. He returned in about a month and we moved on to Abilene, where Mr. Lang had sold the cattle and we shipped out from there, and then we all went to Leavenworth, where Mr. Lang settled with us and told us he was going back to Texas in the fall after another herd. All of the hands quit the outfit except myself and Jim White. We got the outfit ready and shipped everything to Baxter Springs, and from there we went down by Sherman,

Whitesboro and Gainesville, where we struck camp and stayed several months to let our horses fatten while Mr. Lang made a trip to Kansas. When he returned in March he contracted a bunch of cattle from Yarborough and Bob Sparks, and we received them at Old Fort Jackson on the range. Mr. Lang went out with them to help them round up, leaving me in charge of the camp with instructions to make each of our men take so many horses a mile or so from camp before nightfall, hopple them and sleep there, but for one of us to keep watch each night, as the Indians were stealing everything in that country. They made a raid on the Yarborough & Sparks outfit, getting about 30 horses, including one of mine that had strayed off. We took their trail, but soon turned back and went to Fort Jackson and reported the raid to the scouts there and joined in the pursuit again. We had quite a little excitement when we overtook the redskins. One Indian was killed and a Mexican scalped him. There were so many Indians that we decided to give up the chase and let them keep the horses.

This Indian raid put Yarborough & Sparks out of business for awhile, and they gave up the contract, so we went from there to the ranches of Col. Pickett, Dan Waggoner and Bill Chisholm, but made no trades and were directed to Fort Griffin. Here we bought 800 cows and beeves. Bob Sparks went on to Kansas with us, and had pretty good luck.

Jim White and I got an outfit together in 1871, and started on a buffalo hunt, locating our camp on the Saline River, about twenty miles from Ellsworth, Kansas, and went to killing buffalo for their hides, remaining there all winter and until the spring of 1872. Buffalo were on the range like herds of cattle, and when the north winds began to blow they would drift south in great droves. In March we left the Saline and went over on a creek called Saw Log, making our camp near the creek, never thinking of high water. About three o'clock

one morning while, I was asleep in the wagon, I felt
something cold and awoke just as the wagon was about
to float off. I yelled to Jim to get busy and we managed
to get all of our provisions out, but before we could get
everything the old wagon went down the creek and lodged
in a tree. Two of our horses were drowned in the flood,
which was caused by heavy rains above us. On this trip,
we killed hundreds of buffalo and made good money.
From there we went to Fort Dodge, then a very gay
western town, but soon the railroad was built up to the
Arkansas River and a small town sprung up there, Dodge
City. The first building to go up in the new town was a
saloon and dance hall, then a blacksmith shop and store,
then another saloon, and of all tough places, this was
the limit. All kinds of characters gathered there. Rail-
roaders, buffalo hunters, cowboys and gamblers—a mean
mixture. One night as I walked up to the front door
of the dance hall I saw a man standing with a gun in
hand. Inside two men had just stepped up to the bar to
take a drink, but he shot one of them through the head,
got on his horse and rode off. The music stopped until
the floor could be scrubbed and everything was going
again as if nothing had happened.

I came to Texas in 1874, and stopped in San Antonio.
Here I got acquainted with some of the leading trail men
of those days, and began to drive butcher cattle into
San Antonio from the ranches, getting several bunches
from the old Cortina ranch. Here I met Simps McCoy,
Duncan Lemons, John DeSpain and Jesse Laxson and
among others I had dealings with were Speicer, Ludwig,
Wm. Herpol, Mont and Cal Woolward, Billie Votaw, Lee
Harris, Oge, Captain Crouch, Steve Speed, Billie Slaughter and others. My business made me good money until
the railroads came through, then the stock yards were
put in and the slaughter pens were built. This made the
butchers more independent. Tom Daugherty was the
first commission man in San Antonio to handle butcher

cattle, and the next one was George W. Saunders, who is
still in business there.

In 1881 I married Miss Lucy Hall, but she passed
away within a year and a half, leaving me with a day
old baby boy, Chas. B. Vesper. I had no relatives in the
United States and I had a difficult time trying to raise
him, but he grew to be a big strong man and when he
reached manhood's estate he wanted to try his luck in
some other part of the country. I attended the Cattlemen's Convention at El Paso in 1903, where I met my
old friends, Mr. Moorehead and Mr. Newman, who I had
worked for in 1868 in Kansas. Mr. Newman had a son
who owned a ranch in New Mexico and he said if Charles
cared to try it there he would give him a chance. He
took the place and was manager for fourteen years. He
still resides in New Mexico, having married and settled
down, and is the father of two fine boys.

In 1884 I was married the second time, my bride being
the step-daughter of Chris Speicer, Miss Frances Bitter.
We moved out to the ranch which I now own, 5,000 acres,
and lived there thirty-two years, then moved to Big
Wells, turning over the ranch to my sons, J. H. and C.
F. Vesper. Have four children in my family, the three
boys above mentioned and one girl, Marie, now Mrs.
Y. C. Strait. On Christmas Day, 1919, my wife passed
away and since that time I have made my home with
my daughter and on the Strait Brothers ranch, nine miles
west of Big Wells. I am now seventy-five years old, enjoy the best of health, and can honestly say that I was
never arrested or had a case in court. Instead of driving cattle now I drive my old Ford car, with my little
granddaughter, Mattie Louise Strait, as my companion,
whose picture accompanies this sketch, and we don't
allow any of the young cowboys to pass us either.

MRS. IKE T. PRYOR

Mrs. Myra Stafford Pryor, wife of Col. Ike T. Pryor, of the Cattlemen's and Old Trail Drivers' Association, is a native Texan and proud of it. She was born near Columbus, in Colorado county, on her father's ranch. Her father was Robert Earl Stafford and her mother Sarah Elizabeth Stafford. Her father came to Texas in 1858 from Georgia, and when he had prepared a place for his family, Mrs. Stafford followed about six months later in 1859, with her two children and a few negroes, making the journey by water from Cedar Keys to New Orleans and from New Orleans to Galveston. Mr. Stafford met her at Galveston, and from there they went by railroad to Eagle Lake, thence by stage.

Robert Earl Stafford, who had learned the cattle business as a boy at his father's home in Georgia, on coming to Texas embarked in the cattle business as a matter of course. When the war between the States broke out he joined the Shropshire Upton Company—a part of Hood's Brigade, organized in Colorado county, and was in the war until the close of hostilities. After the war he returned to his home and re-entered the cattle business.

Earl Stafford drove up the trail for the first time in 1869. Mrs. Pryor's mother was a typical Texas woman, hospitable and patriotic.

Little Myra Stafford, with her sister and two brothers, enjoyed the usual wonderful life of a little girl on a big Texas ranch. There were horseback riding—and she does not remember when she learned to ride—and picnics at Eagle Lake and elsewhere, and all sorts of happy things occurring every day—and then, when Myra was thirteen years of age, she was sent to Virginia to finish school.

When she came home a sure enough grown up young lady, what a wonderful time she had on the old ranch and how glad she was to get home again.

The Stafford and Sam Allen families were old and intimate friends, in fact Mr. Stafford and Mr. Allen were long business partners and shipped cattle to Havana. Miss Myra often made long visits to the Sam Allen home at Harrisburg, and always had a splendid time.

Mrs. Pryor lived for twenty-five years at Columbus, but many of her old neighbors there have passed away or have moved to other cities. She loves the old Columbus oaks. There was one, across from her house, in which the wisteria had climbed, and when in bloom, mingling with the long floating grey moss, made a picture for fairy land. In Mrs. Pryor's opinion, the oaks of Columbus are unsurpassed in beauty and size.

Mrs. Pryor's father also owned a ranch in Wharton county, and she is familiar with all the small towns in those sections of the state, near her father's holdings. Eagle Lake was in those days a great resort, people would go to hunt and fish and picnic and have a great time. Alligators of all sizes used to inhabit the lake when she was a child and at times frightened the children by their roars.

Mrs. Pryor counts as one of her priceless relics an old flintlock gun used by her great-grandfather in the Revolutionary War. He, too, was a Robert Stafford. At the meeting of the Old Trail Drivers' Association she presented to Mr. Jack W. Baylor, an embossed leather belt ornamented with chased silver and gold buckle and side ornaments, and long worn by Brigadier General John A. Baylor, and presented by him, about 1885, to his old friend, Robert E. Stafford of Wharton and Colorado county. Mr. Stafford bequeathed it to his widow, who in turn left it to his daughter. Mrs. Pryor gave it to this particular grandson of General Baylor because he had always been kind and attentive to his aunt, Mrs. A. Burkes, who is a special friend of Mrs. Pryor.

Mr. and Mrs. Pryor were married in 1893, and moved to San Antonio in 1896. They were both elected officers

MRS. IKE T. PRYOR

of the Texas Historic Landmarks Association. They
have their home in the heart of the city and have taken
part in all public and private enterprises launched for
the good of San Antonio and Texas since their arrival.

MRS. GEORGE W. SAUNDERS

MRS. GEO. W. SAUNDERS

Mrs. Ida Friedrich Saunders, wife of Geo. W. Saunders, is always an interested and devoted attendant at the meetings of the Old Trail Drivers' Association.

Mrs. Saunders was a Miss Ida Friedrich, and was born under the shadow of the Alamo, and as a child, with her two sisters and four brothers, played around its sacred precincts.

Her first remembrance of the Alamo was with a feeling of awe about it, and that it was all fastened up securely. Then it was opened and used by Mr. Grenet as a grocery store, the Church being used as a warehouse.

She remembers interesting stories of the Indians as told to her by her mother, when they came in to trade at their store, and how frightful they looked with long rings in their noses, with knives in the legs of their high moccasins, and wrapped in their dirty blankets.

She also tells of the big spring by the Commerce street bridge, where many people went to get water for household purposes because the water was so cool and pure. The children used to fish there in the river and found it great fun.

As a tot she was always interested in the old Alamo ditch, it seemed to fascinate her, and she took advantage of every opportunity to investigate it.

Her parents, Fensel and Agnes Friedrich, came to San Antonio in 1854, and made their home on Crockett street, adjoining the Menger Hotel. The property remained in the hands of the family until a short time ago. Mr. Friedrich became known all over the United States for his horn furniture of all kinds. He had orders even from Europe. Their close neighbors were the Grenets, Stumbergs, Callahans and Kampmanns.

Miss Friedrich was married to Mr. Geo. W. Saunders in 1889. They have one child, now Mrs. Agnes Cannon.

COL. C. C. SLAUGHTER

The subject of this sketch, since early manhood, was identified with the cattle interests of Texas. He was born in Sabine county, Texas, February 9, 1837. Under the leadership of his father, George Webb Slaughter, he made a success of the cattle business and became a leader in his chosen lifework. He became an Indian fighter of note and was captain of the State Rangers for several years. His record in this re-

spect stands high in the annals of the state, and his courageous leadership had much to do with forcing the Comanches into paths . of peace, and in carving out a new home in the wilderness for the settlers that were to come later.

In 1861 Colonel Slaughter was married to Miss Cynthia Anne Jowell, of Palo Pinto,

COL. C. C. SLAUGHTER

and to them were born five children. Mrs. Slaughter died in Dallas in 1876, and in 1878 Colonel Slaughter was married to Miss Carrie Aberill, from which union there were four children. In 1877 Colonel Slaughter established the Lazy S Ranch, and for years grazed his cattle on the public domain in the Plains country of West Texas. At one time he claimed a section of the Plains 200 miles square or a total of 24,000,000 acres. Later he purchased ranch land, fenced it and improved it and at one time owned in fee simple more than 1,000,000 acres of land and was for years the largest individual taxpayer in Texas. There was probably more cattle bearing the Lazy S brand marketed than those of any other ranch in the world.

Together with Kit Carter, J. C. Loving and John N. Simpson he established the Cattle Raisers' Association in 1873, and was the second president of the organization. One of the great achievements in the life of Colonel Slaughter was the organization of the National Beef Producers' & Consumers' Association in 1884, which at one time had an enrollment of 60,000 members residing in all sections of the United States.

Colonel Slaughter's contributions to benevolent organizations have been abundant, his efforts in this line culminating in the building of the Baptist Memorial Hospital in Dallas, toward which he contributed more largely than any other individual. He was the president of the Confederate Veterans' Reunion held in Dallas in 1902. He won the title of Colonel for splendid service in the Confederate Army, where his career was marked for courage and patriotic devotion to principle. Colonel Slaughter located in Dallas in 1875, and from that time forward was prominently identified with every movement that had for its aim the upbuilding of that metropolis. He became one of the largest property owners there, and for many years was identified with the banking interests of North Texas.

Colonel Slaughter's children were George M., R. L., E. Dick, C. C. Jr., Alex A. Slaughter, Mrs. G. T. Veal, Mrs. G. G. Wright, Mrs. J. H. Dean, and Miss Nellie Slaughter.

M. HALFF

Mayer Halff was born February the 7th, 1836, in Lauterbourg, Alsace, France, and died in San Antonio several years ago. He came to San Antonio at an early date and established the well known firm of M. Halff & Bro., where they conducted a large mercantile business. M. Halff being a progressive business man, soon became

interested in the livestock business and forged his way
to the top of the ladder in that industry. Halff's ranches

MAYER HALFF

and trail herds, throughout
Texas, New Mexico and the
Indian Territory caused him
to be one of the best known
stockmen in the industry. He
was of a genial disposition
which made him a host of
friends. No old timer was
better known in the early
days than M. Halff. Always
loyal to his friends and state,
always ready to further the
interests of Texas few men
did more than M. Halff
towards the development of our great state. Long live
his memory.

DANIEL OPPENHEIMER

Daniel Oppenheimer was born in Bavaria, Germany,
November 22, 1836 and died
in San Antonio, December,
7th, 1915. He came to the
United States in 1853 and
worked for an uncle in Rusk,
Cherokee county, for several
years. In 1858 he formed a
partnership with his brother,
Anton Oppenheimer, under
the firm name of D. & A.
Oppenheimer, the well known
banking house of San Antonio which exists today. Both
brothers joined the Confed-
erate Army and served throughout the Civil War, Dan

D. M. OPPENHEIMER

Oppenheimer having been promoted to a Captaincy. The firm was the owner of several ranches and many cattle, their holdings being the well known Oppenheimer Ranch in Atascosa county amounting to 100,000 acres, which was sold a few years ago to C. F. Simmons. The firm was interested at one time in one of the best known herds of high-bred Angora goats, held on their ranch, known as the Fink Ranch, in Bexar county. This ranch was sold to the U. S. Government which established Camp Stanley on this property. Dan Oppenheimer was well and favorably known throughout Texas. His many good deeds will be long in the memory of those who knew him.

THE KILLING OF OLIVER LOVING

Charles Goodnight, Goodnight, Texas

Oliver Loving, Senior, is undoubtedly the first man who ever trailed cattle from Texas. His earliest effort was in 1858 when he took a herd across the frontier of the Indian Nation or "No Man's Land," through eastern Kansas and northwestern Missouri into Illinois. His second attempt was in 1859; he left the frontier on the upper Brazos and took a northwest course until he struck the Arkansas River, somewhere about the mouth of the Walnut, and followed it to just about Pueblo, where he wintered.

CHAS. GOODNIGHT

In 1866 he joined me on the upper Brazos. With a large herd we struck southwest until we reached the

Pecos River, which we followed up to Mexico and thence, to Denver, the herd being closed out to various posts and Indian reservations.

In 1867 we started another herd west over the same trail and struck the Pecos the latter part of June. After we had gone up this river about one hundred miles it was decided that Mr. Loving should go ahead on horseback in order to reach New Mexico and Colorado in time to bid on the contracts which were to be let in July, to use the cattle we then had on trail, for we knew that there were no other cattle in the west to take their place.

Loving was a man of religious instincts and one of the coolest and bravest men I have ever known, but devoid of caution. Since the journey was to made with a one-man escort I selected Bill Wilson, the clearest headed man in the outfit, as his companion.

Knowing the dangers of traveling through an Indian infested country I endeavored to impress on these men the fact that only by traveling by night could they hope to make the trip in safety.

The first two nights after the journey was begun they followed my instructions. But Loving, who detested night riding, persuaded Wilson that I had been overcautious and one fine morning they changed their tactics and proceeded by daylight. Nothing happened until 2 o'clock that afternoon, when Wilson who had been keeping a lookout, sighted the Comanches heading toward them from the southwest. Apparently they were five or six hundred strong. The men left the trail and made for the Pecos River which was about four miles to the northwest and was the nearest place they could hope to find shelter. They were then on the plain which lies between the Pecos and Rio Sule, or Blue River. One hundred and fifty feet from the bank of the Pecos this bank drops abruptly some one hundred feet. The men scrambled down this bluff and dismounted. They hitched their horses (which the Indians captured at once) and crossed the river where they hid themselves among the sand dunes and brakes of the river. Meantime the Indians were hot on their tracks, some of them halted on the bluff and others crossed the river and surrounded the men. A brake of carrca, or Spanish cane, which grew in the bend of the river a short distance from the dunes was soon filled with them. Since this cane was from five to six feet tall these Indians were easily concealed from view of the men; they dared not advance on the men as they knew them to be armed. The Indian on the bluff, speaking in Spanish, begged the men to come out for a consultation. Wilson instructed Loving to watch the rear so they could not shoot him in the back, and he stepped out to see what he could do with them. Loving attempting to guard the rear was fired on from the cane. He sustained a broken arm and bad wound in the side. The men then retreated to the shelter of the river bank and had much to do to keep the Indians off.

Toward dawn of the next day Loving, deciding that he was going to die from the wound in his side, begged Wilson to leave him and go to me, so that if I made the trip home his family would know what had become of him. He had no desire to die and leave them in ignorance of his fate. He wished his family to know that rather than be captured and tortured by the Indians, he would kill himself. But in case he survived and was able to stand them off we would find him two miles down the river. He gave him his Henry rifle which had metallic or waterproof cartridges, since in swimming the river any other kind would be useless. Wilson turned over to Loving all of the pistols—five—and his six-shooting rifle, and taking the Henry rifle departed. How he expected to cross the river with the gun I have never comprehended for Wilson was a one armed man. But it shows what lengths a person will attempt in extreme emergencies.

It happened that some one hundred feet from their

place of concealment down the river there was a shoal, the only one I know of within 100 miles of the place. On this shoal an Indian sentinel on horseback was on guard and Wilson knew this. The water was about four feet deep. When Wilson decided to start he divested himself of clothing except underwear and hat. He hid his trousers in one place, his boots in another and his knife in another all under water. Then taking his gun he attempted to cross the river. This he found to be impossible, so he floated downstream about seventy-five feet where he struck bottom. He stuck down the muzzle of the gun in the sand until the breech came under water and then floated noiselessly down the river. Though the Indians were all around him he fearlessly began his "get-a-way." He climbed up a bank and crawled out through a cane brake which fringed the bank, and started out to find me, bare-footed and over ground that was covered with prickly pear, mesquite and other thorny plants. Of course he was obliged to travel by night at first, but fearing starvation used the day some, when he was out of sight of the Indians.

Now Loving and Wilson had ridden ahead of the herd for two nights and the greater part of one day, and since the herd had lain over one day the gap between us must have been something like one hundred miles.

The Pecos River passes down a country that might be termed a plain, and from one to two hundred miles there is not a tributary or break of any kind to mark its course until it reaches the mouth of the Concho, which comes up from the west, where the foothills begin to jut in toward the river. Our trail passed just around one of these hills. In the first of these hills there is a cave which Wilson had located on a prior trip. This cave extended back into the hill some fifteen or twenty feet and in this cave Wilson took refuge from the scorching sun to rest. Then he came out of the cave and looked for the herd and saw it coming up the valley. His brother, who was "pointing" the herd with me, and I saw him at the same time. At sight both of us thought it was an Indian as we didn't suppose that any white man could be in that part of the country. I ordered Wilson to shape the herd for a fight, while I rode toward the man to reconnoiter, believing the Indians to be hidden behind the hills and planning to surprise us. I left the trail and jogged toward the hills as though I did not suspect anything. I figured I could run to the top of the hill to look things over before they would have time to cut me off from the herd. When I came within a quarter of a mile of the cave Wilson gave me the frontier sign to come to him. He was between me and the declining sun and since his underwear was saturated with red sediment from the river he made a queer looking object. But even when some distance away I recognized him. How I did it, under his changed appearance I do not know. When I reached him I asked him many questions, too many in fact, for he was so broken and starved and shocked by knowing he was saved, I could get nothing satisfactory from him. I put him on the horse and took him to the herd at once. We immediately wrapped his feet in wet blankets. They were swollen out of all reason, and how he could walk on them is more than I can comprehend. Since he had starved for three days and nights I could give him nothing but gruel. After he had rested and gotten himself together I said:

"Now tell me about this matter."

"I think Mr. Loving has died from his wounds, he sent me to deliver a message to you. It was to the effect that he had received a mortal wound, but before he would allow the Indians to take him and torture him he would kill himself, but in case he lived he would go two miles down the river from where we were and there we would find him."

"Now tell me where I may find this place," I said. Then he proceeded to relate the story I have just given, of how they left the Rio Sule or Blue River, cutting across to the Pecos, how the Indians discovered them and how they sought shelter from them by hiding in the sand dunes on the Pecos banks; how Loving was shot and begged Wilson to save himself and to tell his (Loving's) family of his end; how Wilson took the Henry rifle and attempted to swim but gave it up, as the splashing he made would attract the Indian sentinel stationed on the shoal.

Then Wilson instructed me how to find his things. He told me to go down where the bank is perpendicular and the water appeared to be swimming but was not. "Your legs will strike the rifle," he said. I searched for his things as he directed and found them every one, even to the pocket knife. His remarkable coolness in deliberately hiding these things, when the loss of a moment might mean his life, is to me the most wonderful occurrence I have ever known, and I have experienced many unusual phases of frontier life.

This is as I get it from memory and I think I am correct, for though it all happened fifty years ago, it is printed indelibly in my mind.

W. J. WILSON'S NARRATIVE

In the spring of 1867 I bought a bunch of cattle on the Clear Fork of the Brazos, started up the river with them and fell in with Charles Goodnight and Oliver Loving. They had had some trouble with the Indians, and we considered it safer to all travel together. We went on to the Pecos River on the old Butterfield trail. It never failed to rain on us every day until we reached Horsehead Crossing. The night we arrived at this crossing the cattle stampeded and all got away. Next morning we started to round them up. After hunting for three days we still had about 300 head of our big cattle missing. The rain had made all of the trails look old and we couldn't tell a new trail from an old one.

We concluded to go back to China Pond and take a circle from there and try to cut the cattle off. China Pond was about twenty-five miles back on the trail. So seven of us, made up from different cattle outfits, went back, and when we reached China Pond we decided to go east, and many miles out we found the trail of our cattle, and the signs showed that Indians had captured them and were driving them to their camp up the river. They had evidently expected us to come down the river looking for the cattle, and they did not discover us until we were within a hundred and fifty yards of them. Seeing we were greatly outnumbered, and as it was about sundown, we decided to turn back and go to our camp, which we did, arriving there the next day.

W. J. WILSON

When I returned from this cow-hunt, Mr. Loving asked me to go to Ft. Sumner, New Mexico, with him. We had a verbal contract with the people who were feeding the Indians there, and we wanted to hold that contract. The distance to Ft. Sumner was about 250 miles, and we were supposed to travel at night and lay up in the daytime so the Indians would not attack us.

The second day of our journey we stopped on a stream we called Black River, and stayed there two or three hours, rested up our horses, then concluded to go on to the point of a mountain where the road ran between the mountain and the river, and stay there that night. As we neared this mountain we discovered several Indians. They saw us about the same time, and we knew we were in for trouble, but we reached the river all right, and I picked out a little mound next to the river where I could see all around me, except one little spot where the polecat brush had grown up about three feet high, and that brush obscured my view of the river for a distance of about 100 yards. I told Mr. Loving if he would stay down at that little clump of bushes and keep the Indians from crawling up on us from the river I would keep them off from above. These Indians had increased in numbers until there were over a hundred of the red rascals. I think they had been hunting south of the river and were going back to their old ground.

After staying in the brush a little while Mr. Loving came to where I was, and I urged him to go back there and prevent the Indians from coming in on us from the river. He started back down there carrying a pair of holster pistols over his left arm. The bushes were about forty yards from where I was standing, and I kept my eyes on this spot for I knew if a demonstration was made from that direction the Indians would charge us from the hill. When Mr. Loving had almost reached the bushes an Indian rose up and I shot him, but not before he had fired on Mr. Loving. The Indian's shot went through Loving's holsters, passed through his wrist and entered his side. He came running back to me, tossed his gun to me and said he was killed and for me to do the best I could. The Indians at this time made a desperate charge, and after I had emptied my five-shooting Yarger, I picked up Mr. Loving's gun and continued firing. There was some brush, only a few inches high, not very far from where I was, and the Indians would run to it, crawl on their bellies, and I could not see them. I managed to get Mr. Loving down to the river and concealed him in a sandy depression, where the smart weeds grew about two feet high and laid down beside him. The Indians knew we were down there somewhere, and used all sorts of ruses to find our exact location. They would shoot their arrows up and some came very near striking us. Finally an Indian with a long lance came crawling along parting the weeds with his lance as he came, and just about the time I had determined to pull the trigger, he scared up a big rattlesnake. The snake came out rattling, looking back at the Indian, and coiled up right near us. The Indian, who still had not seen us, evidently got scared at the rattlesnake and turned back.

We lay there until night. Mr. Loving's wounds had thrown him into a high fever, and I managed to bring up some water from the river in his boot, which seemed to relieve him somewhat. About midnight the moon went down, but the Indians were still around us. We could hear them on all sides. Mr. Loving begged me to leave him and make my escape so I could tell his folks what had become of him. He said he felt sure he could not last until morning, and if I stayed there I would be killed too. He insisted that I take his gun, as it used metallic cartridges and I could carry it through the water and not dampen the powder. Leaving with him all of my pistols and my rifle, I took his gun and with a handclasp told him goodbye, and started to the river. The river was quite sandy and difficult to swim in, so I had to pull off all of my clothes except my hat, shirt and breeches. The gun nearly drowned me, and I decided to get along without it, so I got out and leaned it up against the bank of the river, under the water, where the Indians would not find it. Then I went down the river about a hundred yards, and saw an Indian sitting on his horse out in the river, with the water almost over the horse's back. He was sitting there splashing the water with his foot, just playing. I got under some smart weeds and drifted by until I got far enough below the Indian where I could get out. Then I made a three days' march barefooted. Everything in that country had stickers in it. On my way I picked up the small end of a tepee pole which I used for a walking stick. The last night of this painful journey the wolves followed me all night. I would give out, just like a horse, and lay down in the road and drop off to sleep and when I would awaken the wolves would be all around me, snapping and snarling. I would take up that stick, knock the wolves away, get started again and the wolves would follow behind. I kept that up until daylight, when the wolves quit me. About 12 o'clock on that last day I crossed a little mountain and knew the boys ought to be right in there somewhere with the cattle. I found a little place, a sort of cave, that afforded protection from the sun, and I could go no further. After a short time the boys came along with the cattle and found me.

Charles Goodnight took a party of about fourteen men and pulled out to see about Mr. Loving. After riding about twenty-four hours they came to the spot where I had left him, but he was not there. They supposed the Indians had killed him and thrown his body into the river. They found the gun I had concealed in the water, and came back to camp.

About two weeks after this we met a party coming from Ft. Sumner and they told us Loving was at Ft. Sumner. The bullet which had penetrated his side did not prove fatal and the next night after I had left him he got into the river and drifted by the Indians as I had done, crawled out and lay in the weeds all the next day. The following night he made his way to the road where it struck the river, hoping to find somebody traveling that way. He remained there for five days, being without anything to eat for seven days. Finally some Mexicans came along and he hired them to take him to Ft. Sumner and I believe he would have fully recovered if the doctor at that point had been a competent surgeon. But that doctor had never amputated any limbs and did not want to undertake such work. When we heard Mr. Loving was at Ft. Sumner, Mr. Goodnight and I hastened there. As soon as we beheld his condition we realized the arm would have to be amputated. The doctor was trying to cure it without cutting it off. Goodnight started a man to Santa Fe after a surgeon, but before he could get back mortification set in, and we were satisfied something had to be done at once and we prevailed upon the doctor to cut off the affected limb. But too late. Mortification went into his body and killed him. Thus ended the career of one of the best men I ever knew. Mr. Goodnight had the body of Mr. Loving prepared for the long journey and carried it to Weatherford, Texas, where interment was made with Masonic honors.

CYRUS B. LUCAS

Cyrus B. Lucas was born in Stratford, Canada, in 1857, and came to Texas with his parents in 1859, locating in Goliad county, where the father engaged in the mercantile and stock business, establishing the Fair Oaks Ranch which Cyrus B. Lucas still owns. Mr. Lucas' boyhood was spent on the ranch and after his graduation from college he devoted his time to the upbuilding of his business. In February, 1889, he was married to Miss Elizabeth Greenwood Scott, of Charco. To them were

CYRUS B. LUCAS

born two children, Richard Pryor and Lena Claire. Mr. Lucas served as commissioner in Goliad county for several years, and has been identified in politics and all movements that meant the upbuilding of county and state. He is recognized as one of the most progressive cattlemen of the Southwest. His Herefords, numbering several thousand head, rank among the best in quality in Texas. For more than twenty years he has used registered bulls in grading his stock. In 1894 he became a member of the Cattle Raisers' Association of Texas, and for several years was on the executive committee of that organization. He is identified with the Berclair State Bank, the Berclair Mercantile Company, The Berclair Gin Company, The Austwell Mercantile Company, the Commercial National Bank of Beeville, and various other enterprises in that section, besides owning three ranches, Fair Oaks Ranch near Berclair, embracing 58,-000 acres in Goliad and Bee counties; Buena Vista Ranch of 17,000 acres in Live Oak county, and the St. Charles Bay Ranch of 58,000 acres in Aransas and Refugio counties. He is also an extensive farmer, having 5,000 acres of land in cultivation on his different ranches, and when his time is not taken up with his extensive farming and ranching enterprises he is busy attending to the details of the other commercial concerns with which he is prominently identified.

Mr. Lucas and his family reside on the Fair Oaks Ranch in the summer, but spend the winters in San Antonio, where he has a handsome residence on Lexington Avenue.

JOHN J. LITTLE

J. J. LITTLE

John J. Little, one of the well known stockmen of Texas, was born August 8, 1860. His first commercial activity was in connection with his father's stock business. He went up the trail in 1879 for Captain Crouch at the age of 19, and afterwards he took charge of Capt. Crouch's sheep in Frio county. For many years he had the management of Schreiner & Halff Ranch of 68,000 acres in Frio county. He served as sheriff of that county, and has been identified in many ways with the upbuilding of that part of the state.

Mr. Little's wife was Miss Sallie Blackalle. Their home is at Pearsall.

WILLIAM HENRY JENNINGS

William Henry Jennings was born in Tippah county, Mississippi, and was the oldest son of a family of seven

W. H. JENNINGS

children. His parents, Joseph P. and Susan E. Jennings, moved to Texas in 1853, in an ox-wagon, and settled first on the north bank of the San Marcos River about twelve miles below its source in Caldwell county. Later the family moved to Lavaca county, purchased land and farmed there several years. Then moving back to Caldwell county the elder Jennings engaged in the cattle and horse business. In the late sixties cattle were cheap and plentiful, and Joseph P. Jennings was among the first to drive a herd over the trail to Kansas, trailing 700 old steers to Baxter Springs in 1869, where they were sold at a very good price. The subject of this sketch, William H. Jennings, assisted in gathering this herd and accompanied them as far as Austin. In 1870, when he was twenty years of age, he took part in his first trail trip, when his father and Colonel George Neil drove 1,800 mixed cattle to Abilene, Kansas. Working as a cowboy, he rode a little Spanish mule all day and herded one-third of every night. It rained a great deal during the trip and the work was exceedingly hard. In 1871 William Jennings became a full-fledged trailsman. He bossed a herd from Caldwell county to Wichita, Kansas, consisting of 2,500 mixed cattle belonging to his father, an uncle and himself. In 1873 he drove cattle for J. F. Ellison and J. O. Dewees, and from that time until 1880 he was associated with Blocker Brothers in buying and handling cattle. He made his last trip over the trail from Llano county with a herd of 3,500 two-year-old steers for Mat Murphy of Montana.

On December 3, 1878, Mr. Jennings was married to Miss Agnes Adelia Daugherty of Caldwell county. To them were born three children, two sons and one daughter. Mrs. Jennings died in 1883. The daughter, Willis Blanche and one son, Walter are also dead. After moving to Pearsall, in 1882, Mr. Jennings bought and handled fat cattle in Frio counties. In 1877 he became Assistant Livestock Agent for the International & Great Northern Railroad Co., working under Colonel Homer Eads. He represented the Gould system and the Chicago & Alton Railroad in South Texas when cattle went via St. Louis or Kansas City and on to Chicago. He bought many thousand of fat beef cattle on his own account and shipped them to market.

In 1892 Mr. Jennings, while associated with John R. Blocker, Jesse Presnall, Andy Armstrong, Sr., and W. C. Irvin, shipped 18,000 head of cattle from Frio, La-Salle, Dimmitt and Zavalla counties to the Ponca Osage Indian Reservation. The transaction turned out very disastrously, for in that year cows were sold on the Kansas City markets as low as sixty-five cents a hundred, and $2.50 was a big price for a good steer. Mr. Jennings acquired extensive ranch interests in South Texas and in Mexico, being associated with T. J. and John Blocker in the Piedra Blanca Ranch in Northern Mexico.

JOHN B. SLAUGHTER

John B. Slaughter was born in Sabine county, Texas, December 15th, 1848, and had a life of singular success and thrilling experiences.

His father, G. W. Slaughter, was of German-American ancestry and married Miss Sallie Mason, a young lady of Irish descent.

John B. Slaughter is a cattleman by birth and education. Born on the frontier in Sabine county, as soon as he could ride a pony, he was kept at work on his father's ranch, with occasional intervals devoted to rounding up

JOHN B. SLAUGHTER

cattle. This he followed until his seventeenth year when he went up the trail, driving for his father and brother,

C. C. Slaughter, and received $15.00 a month. This, with the little herd of thirty or forty head of cattle his father had given him, was his start in life. The trails to Kansas, the Chisholm, Dodge and Santa Fe trails, and the ranges of West Texas were his field, and the saddle and slicker his home. His father and brother located their ranches in Palo Pinto county in the days when Indian raids and outlawry demanded that every one should be a ready and fearless marksman and carry with him at all times sufficient arms to defend his life and interests. Encounters with Indians, who would swoop down like hungry wolves, were neither rare nor novel. Their desire for ponies was never satisfied, and a scalp now and then, as a trophy, was always in order. These were the dangers he had been born to and reared in, and the hand to hand battles and running fights he took part in in Palo Pinto, Jack and Young counties years ago, seem almost incredible. Where now are thriving villages and towns as well as cities, where a forest of oil derricks, highways, automobiles and rich farms cover the country, were once scenes of hot pursuits of marauding bands, or hasty retreats from overwhelming numbers of savages, in which he always took part.

In the spring of 1871, when preparing for the season's roundup with his father and other hands, the ponies were placed in a corral, an inclosure made of cedar pickets set close, to prevent Indians from stealing them. Going out into the corral before daylight to look after the ponies, he found a hole in the fence. At the instant he discovered the gap an Indian sprang up from the ground almost at his feet, and fired, the ball entering his right breast and coming out at his back. He did not fall, but ran back for his rifle, while the Indian joined his band which was near by, and escaped in flight. Though shot through the body, in six weeks he was in the saddle again and on the trail again with cattle for his father and brother, which were in charge of a Mr. Adams. At Victoria Peak, in Montague county, the cattle were stampeded by a storm and scattered all over the country. The following morning the cowboys set out in twos, to gather them up, Mr. Adams and a young man going west. At nightfall all returned except these two. As the Indians had, the day before, raided Bob Stevens' ranch at Victoria Peak near by, and stolen all of his ponies, the men believing Mr. Adams to be killed, after a short search, thought it useless to look further for him, but were prevailed upon by John and one of the hands to continue the search. John took charge of the herd, and three days later, attracted by a swarm of vultures they found the bodies of Adams and his young companion scalped and mutilated. The breast of one was cut open and his heart drawn out and laid on his stomach; the other had parts of his person cut off and stuck in his mouth. They rolled them in blankets and buried them under the bank of the creek where they had made their stand for life.

They were again attacked near Lookout Mountain, in what was then the Indian Territory. Fifteen Comanches stampeded their ponies, which were driven out in a separate herd, and ran them off, leaving them with 2,000 head of cattle to handle and one pony apiece. Yet they did it, arriving at Abilene, Kansas, on foot, where the herd was sold.

Returning the next spring, he went to Weatherford and purchased of Counts & Hughes $2,500 worth of ponies, and went with his men to Jack county to receive a herd of cattle his father had purchased of J. C. Loving. On the night of their arrival, while he and one of his hands were standing guard over the ponies, which had been hidden in a valley, were surprised by a volley of shots, yells and flapping of blankets. The Indians seemed to have come out of the ground, and, like a whirlwind, swept off every horse, leaving them on foot. He was almost in touch with the red brutes, shooting and being shot at. The cattle were scattered also and while they were being gathered he returned to Weatherford for a new supply of horses.

In 1877, he and W. B. Slaughter, with a combined capital of $6,000 entered the business together, buying steers and driving them up the trail to market, continuing until 1890, when he established a ranch in Blanco Canyon on Catfish River, on which he placed 2,000 cattle and remained five years. He then moved to Socorro county, New Mexico, and, in 1886 sold to an English syndicate for $125,000, and went to Utah, establishing a ranch on Green River, 30 miles east of Salt Lake City and remained there for two years. Returning to New Mexico he located near the Texas line and kept this ranch two years. In 1890 he moved to Glasscock county Texas, where he had a ranch of 160 sections, 6,000 head of cattle and 100 head of horses and was president of the Peoples' National Bank of Colorado City.

In 1898 he moved to Fort Worth, Texas, and built one of the handsomest homes, at that time, in the city. At about the same time he sold his Glasscock county ranch and leased ranches in Garza and Borden counties. This, being state land, was thrown on the market and in 1901 he bought the Square and Compass Ranch of 150,-000 acres from the Nave-McCord Cattle Co., at $1.60 per acre, together with five thousand head of cattle. Six thousand head of cattle were brought up from the Glasscock county ranch. After living in Fort Worth seven years he moved with his family to the ranch in Garza county and built one of the finest homes in West Texas.

In 1906 he sold 50,000 acres to C. W. Post, of Post Toasties and Grape Nuts fame, who was building a town and colonizing large tracts of land in Garza county. The town of Post, named after its founder, is the shipping point for the ranch and is located on the Santa Fe Railroad. The ranch as it now stands is amply watered with tanks, wells, and is fenced and cross fenced thoroughly, large branding pens with dehorning chutes, squeezers, dipping vats and is especially fine in that it has plains lands for summer range and brakes for winter range. The cattle brand is U Lazy S on left side, crop the left ear. The home is modern in every respect, having electric lights, hot and cold running water, electric washing machine, churns, irons, woodsaw, etc. A radio receiving station is installed which picks up the daily markets and evening entertainments all over the United States.

One special achievement of Mr. Slaughter's is the crossing of the buffalo with Brahma cows, which is readily done and is known as the "cattalo." Then he has succeeded in producing a second cross, which has been thought impossible, resulting in a large, heavy, thrifty animal known as the "Vernier."

He was married in July, 1880, to Miss Belle May of Dallas and they had three children, Mamie, J. B. Jr., and Louie, deceased. Mamie, the daughter, married Frank E. Lott, a real estate man of Kansas City, and lives there. J. B. Jr., is on the ranch with his father and mother having finished his education, graduating from Yale University in 1914.

John B. Slaughter is one of the best known cattlemen in the state and his superior judgment and thorough knowledge of the cattle industry has resulted in his success where others failed. He is loved by all his men and highly esteemed by all who have his acquaintance.

Although seventy-five years of age, every day except Sunday, which is vigorously held as a day of rest on the ranch, he will be found on his favorite horses riding over the range, looking after his cattle and inspecting windmills, tanks, fences, etc. This outdoor life keeps him fit and he is hale and hearty and can, as he says outride and outwork any man on the ranch today.

DENNIS O'CONNOR

Dennis M. O'Connor, the subject of this sketch, a son of Thomas O'Connor of Ireland was born in Refugio county, Texas, October 9, 1840, and died July 18, 1900. He received a fair education as he was growing up, but the Civil War coming on left his education incomplete. He entered the cattle business, assisting his father. Few men ever dreamed in the old c o u n t r y, where the elder O'Connor came from, of the possibilities for a poor boy that were possible in this glorious sun-kissed land.

D. M. O'CONNOR

Thomas O'Connor, the father, arrived in Texas from Wafford, Ireland, in March, 1834, and located in Refugio county. He served in the Texas War for Independence and was the youngest man in the battle of San Jacinto. After this war he returned to Refugio county and engaged in raising cattle on a small scale and also in manufacturing saddle trees and ox yokes. He invested all of his earnings in cattle and land and foresaw that those broad rolling prairies could not always afford free grass. He inclosed the first pasture in Refugio county, 10,000 acres, with wire, and continued to fence pastures until he had 500,000 acres under wire and stocked with cattle and horses, his lands lying in Refugio, Goliad, San Patricio, McMullen and LaSalle counties, its estimated value being $4,500,000 at the time of his death October 16, 1887. This property descended to his sons, Dennis and Thomas O'Connor, Jr. The mother of these boys came from New York with her parents, the Fagans, in 1829, and was married to Thomas O'Connor in 1839, the bride and groom riding on horseback to San Antonio, a distance of over 100 miles, to have the wedding ceremony performed.

SHANGHAI PIERCE

Of this remarkable character George W. Saunders says: "Col. Shanghai Pierce has a record in the cattle industry never surpassed and I doubt if ever equaled by any man. I spent ten years hunting his photo, and had about given up the search when A. P. Ward of San Antonio, a relative to Col. Pierce, suggested that I write to the Colonel's granddaughter, Mrs. Frank Armour, in Chicago. She directed me to write to her brother, Mr.

SHANGHAI PIERCE

Pickett Withers of that city and to my surprise and delight I received a good photo of Colonel Pierce just in time to get it in this volume of the Trail Drivers of Texas. Then it dawned upon me that I had no knowledge of where he was from, where he was born, or when he died, and I regret that I am unable to give this information at present. My first recollection of Mr. Pierce was just after the close of the Civil War when he bought fat cattle all over South Texas. I remember seeing him many times come to our camp where he had contracts to receive beeves. He was a large portly man, always rode a fine horse, and would be accompanied by a negro who led a pack horse loaded with gold and silver which, when he reached our camp, was dumped on the ground and remained there until the cattle were classed and counted out to him, then he would empty the money on a blanket in camp and pay it out to the different stockmen from whom he had purchased cattle. He would generally buy 200 or 300 head at a time. The cowmen would round up large herds at different times and Colonel Pierce would select what he wanted. We all looked upon him as a redeemer, and were glad to sell our cattle at any price as money was scarce in those reconstruction days before the northern trail started. Col. Pierce would sometimes stay in camp with us two or three days waiting to get the cattle shaped up. He was a great talker and would keep all the boys awake until midnight, laughing at his thrilling stories. He owned a large ranch on the coast, but his cattle were not fat and he would buy beeves to ship to Cuba, New Orleans and St. Louis, and he often came to Goliad, Bee, Live Oak and many other counties to get fat beeves. He kept this up until 1867, when the trail started north, and he became one of the biggest trail drivers of Texas, and became nationally known. During the money panic of 1873, which all old timers remember and but few operators survived, Colonel Shanghai Pierce pulled off some stunts that baffled the Yankees. He sent many herds up every year for several years from Matagorda county ranch in his straight mark and brand. His coast steers became known from the Rio Grande to the Canadian line as Shanghai Pierce's sea lions. Mr. Pierce was a loud talker, and no man who ever saw him or heard him talk ever forgot his voice or appearance. He was a money maker, empire builder, and a wonder to his friends and I believe to himself. His old ranch is now stocked with one of the best herds of Brahma cattle in the state, and is operated by Mr. A. P. Borden.''

J. D. HOUSTON

J. D. (Dunn) Houston was born November 18, 1850, in Dewitt county, Texas, and died in San Antonio a few years ago. He was raised in the cattle business and knew it thoroughly. During the trail days Mr. Houston drove many herds to different northern markets and became well and favorably known from the Rio Grande to the Canadian line. He owned large cattle ranches in Gonzales and other counties in Texas. For many years he owned and operated a large ranch on the Pecos River. At the time of his death he was a large stockholder in the Lockwood National Bank of San Antonio. It would require volumes to describe Mr. Houston's ex-

DUNN HOUSTON

tensive operations and great achievements. No one man has done more for the development of Texas than Dunn Houston.

BOB HOUSTON

BOB HOUSTON

R. A. (Bob) Houston was born April 25, 1849, in Dewitt county, Texas, and died February 1, 1895. He was raised on a cattle ranch and followed the cattle business all of his life, becoming one of the large trail drivers and sending many herds to northern markets, during the time maintaining large cattle ranches in this state, mostly in Gonzales county. All who knew Bob Houston liked him, for he was of a mirthful nature and could pull off more stunts purely for fun than any man in the country.

Seldom it is that when a bunch of stockmen congregated that you can't hear something recalled by them that Bob Houston said or did. He was the life of his company, at the chuck wagon, on the road, up at the branding pen, on the trail, at the markets, at Bank directors' meetings, or weddings, balls and at home. He left a host of friends.

JESS McCOY

Jess McCoy was born in Mississippi, July 27, 1841, died March 12, 1920. He came to Texas with his parents in 1848, settling in Gonzales county, where he lived all of his life. After serving four years in the Confederate army, Mr. McCoy entered the cattle business and was among the first to drive herds to Kansas. He followed the trail for many years and became well and favorably known on all the northern markets and all over South Texas. Jess McCoy was one of the most honorable and substantial stockmen of his section, and his many good deeds will be remembered by those who knew him.

JESS McCOY

ON THE FORT WORTH AND DODGE CITY TRAIL

T. J. Burkett, Sr., Waelder, Texas

While stationed in a line camp on the south line of the R2 Ranch in Walbarger county during the month of May, 1883, a message came stating that I was wanted to go up the trail, and at once to go to the R2 headquarters situated on Mule Creek, a tributary to Red River. Within three days every employee and the herd was ready to hit the Fort Worth and Dodge City trail. The herd was owned by Stephens & Worsham, and was bossed by Daniel P. Gipson. The first night out a thunder storm came up and the cattle stampeded and we ran them all night. I held between 400 and 500, and Billie Gatling held about 600 until after daylight, when several of the boys helped us bring them back to camp. We had 1,800 steers in that herd and it took several days to gather all of them up.

We crossed near Doan's, where the Dodge City trail crosses Red River, and resumed our long and tiresome journey in the direction of the north star. Hour by hour, step by step and day by day we pursued our way, not knowing the hardships that were in store for us. We had from one to three rains a week. Our route lay through the Indian Territory, where the range was a paradise for the long horn. One night we had a stampede in the Wichita Mountains, and when the sun rose on the bedground the next morning there was not a steer in sight. After three days' hard work we again had them ready to wend their way to a distant clime beyond the sands of the Cimarron.

One day Quannah Parker, accompanied by another Indian came to me and wanted "wohaw, plenty fat, heap slick." I pointed to Gipson and told Quannah he was the wohaw chief, but the little Indian shook his head and said Gipson was "no bueno." Gipson told me to ride into the herd and cut them out a yearling, and they went off with it. There were about 500 Indians camped near the trail, and nearly every herd that passed gave them a beef. Hundreds of cowboys knew Quannah Parker, and he had scores of friends among the white people.

After we passed out of the Indian Territory we soon discovered that we had arrived at a Sahara in America.

The grass was burned to a crisp, stock water was scarce, provisions were high and everything in the vegetable line was scarce. Irish potatoes the size of a hickory nut were $2.50 per bushel. Sometimes the boss had to pay $10 to water the herd. People there informed us that it had not rained there in seven months, and it looked to me like it had not rained in seven years. Holding one foot on the Kansas soil and the other on Territory soil was like having one foot in the submerged alluvial soil of the Nile and the other out in the desert where it had not rained enough to wet a pocket handkerchief in a hundred years. The cool nights and almost unbearable heat in the daytime about got the best of the cowboys.

Two days after we struck camp southwest of Dodge City several of the cowboys were excused by the boss to go to town for supplies. Soon after they arrived there they began to "tank up" on mean whiskey and proceeded to shoot up the town. As they came out at a high rate of speed one of them, John Briley, was killed by the marshal of Dodge City. I was in Dodge City the next day and saw that he was buried. Associating with bad company has cost many a man his life.

Man dieth and goeth to his long home, and the mourners go about the street. At the cemetery in Dodge City I noticed a number of fresh mounds, and I said to the sexton there that an epidemic of some kind must have struck that place, but he said the graves were those of desperadoes who had died with their boots on. While looking around I noticed on a small tombstone the following inscription: "Here rests Mary Hamilton, aged 14." Then came the following lines:

"Weep not for me my parents dear,
I am not dead, but only sleeping here.
I was not yours alone,
But God's who loved me best, and took me home."

Before we reached Dodge City Mr. Gipson received a message that Stephens & Worsham had 1,500 steers on the trail and to wait until they arrived, as they wanted to put both herds together. When one herd was made out of the two, making 3,350 head, all of the scrub employees were turned off and all of the stout, able-bodied men were selected to go on with the herd. Mr. Gipson returned to Texas and Frank Watson took charge of the outfit, and we proceeded on our way. An old trail driver told me that after a herd crossed the Arkansas River they would never stampede again. I was only pleased to find that his statement was true, for they did not stampede again. Solve this mystery if you can.

After we crossed the Kansas and Nebraska line we had a lovely range and plenty of water through Nebraska. When we crossed the plains of,that state, for a distance of 75 miles we did not see a stick of timber as large as a hoe handle and there was not a single house on this immense domain, not a creek or a river. Luckily for us heavy rains had fallen over the entire plains, and we had water. Old cowmen claim that on this stretch of plains the mercury often drops to thirty degrees below zero, and it is snow-bound for several weeks at a time. During severe winters it is impossible for anything to live there in the open.

After leaving the Nebraska line we crossed over into Colorado, and there had the pleasure of feasting our eyes on the most beautiful range that was ever beheld by a cowboy. The gramma grass was half a knee high, and was mixed with nutritious white grass that was waist high, waiving in the breeze like a wheat field. We drove up the Arickaree, a distance of about 100 miles, and had a picnic along this bubbling stream every day. The Arickaree was a tributary of the Platte River. We delivered our cattle near Deer Trail, Colorado, fifty miles southeast of Denver, and sixty-five miles east of the foot of the Rocky Mountains, on September 25th, 1883, to a man named Fant, who had bought them on the trail a few days before their arrival. After four long and lonesome months on the trail we at last reached our destination safe and sound, and after spending three days sight-seeing in Denver we pulled out for our homes in Texas. The old R2 boys are scattered today from the Black Hills in Dakota to Buenos Ayres in South America.

Gone to rest beyond the stormy seas,
To mingle with the blest on flowery beds of ease.
This world is but a bubble, there is nothing here
        but woe,
Hardships, toils and troubles wherever we may go;
Do what we will, go where we may, we are never
        free from care,
For at best this world is but a castle in the air.

CHARACTER IMPERSONATION

Among the different forms of entertainment provided for the Old Time Trail Drivers at their reunion in San Antonio in October, 1922, the character impersonations by Miss Elizabeth Slaughter were considered the best by the old cowboys in attendance. Miss Slaughter is a granddaughter of Mr. and Mrs. W. B. Slaughter, and as an entertainer she capped them all when she appeared before the audience garbed as a cowboy and recited a poem entitled, "The Chisholm Trail," from John A. Lomax's book. She gave the gestures and the emphasis necessary to make it true to life, and did not hesitate to use the cowboy slang wherever it occurred in the poem. Another rendition by Miss Slaughter was a blackface sketch, "Husbands Is Husbands," wherein the young lady appeared before the audience as a negro washwoman. The "Chisholm Trail" sketch follows:

MISS ELIZABETH SLAUGHTER

As a Texas Cowboy   As a Negro Washwoman

"THE OLD CHISHOLM TRAIL."

Come along, boys, and listen to my tale,
I'll tell you of my troubles on the old Chisholm trail.
Coma ti yi youpy, youpy ya, youpa ya,
Coma ti yi youpy, youpy ya.

I started up the trail October twenty-third,
I started up the trail with the 2U herd.

Oh, a ten-dollar hoss and a forty-dollar saddle—
And I'm goin' to punchin' Texas cattle.
I woke up one morning on the old Chisholm trail
Rope in hand and a cow by the tail.

I'm up in the mornin' afore daylight
And afore I sleep the moon shines bright.
Old Ben Bolt was a blamed good boss,
But he'd go to see the girls on a sore-backed horse.
Old Ben Bolt was a fine old man
And you'd know there was whiskey wherever he'd land.

My hoss threw me off at a creek called Mud,
My hoss threw me off round the 2U herd.
Last time I saw him he was going across the level
A-kicking up his heels and a-running like the .devil.
It's cloudy in the West, a-looking like rain,
And my damned old slicker's in the wagon again.

Crippled my hoss, I don't know how,
Ropin' at the horns of a 2U cow.
We hit Caldwell and we hit her on the fly,
We bedded down the cattle on a hill close by.
No chaps, no slicker, and it's pouring down rain,
And I swear, by G—d, I'll never night herd again.

Feet in the stirrups and seat in the saddle,
I hung and rattled with them long-horned cattle.
Last night I was on guard and the leader broke ranks,
I hit my horse down the shoulders and I spurred him in
      the flanks.
The wind commenced to blow, and the rain began to fall,
Hit looked, by grab, like we was goin' to lose 'em all.

I jumped in the saddle and grabbed holt the horn,
Best blamed cow-puncher ever was born.
I popped my foot in the stirrup and gave a little yell,
The tail cattle broke and the leaders went to hell.

I don't give a damn if they never do stop;
I'll ride as long as an eight-day clock.

Foot in the stirrup and hand on the horn,
Best damned cowboy ever was born.
I herded and hollered and I done very well,
Till the boss said, "Boys, just let 'em go to hell."
Stray in the herd and the boss said kill it,
So I shot him in the rump with the handle of a skillet.

We rounded 'em up and put 'em on the cars,
And that was the last of the old Two Bars.
Oh, it's bacon and beans most every day—
I'd as soon be a-eatin' prairie hay.
I'm on my best horse and I'm goin' at a run.
I'm the quickest shootin' cowboy that ever pulled a gun.

I went to the wagon to get my roll,
To come back to Texas, dad-burn my soul.
I went to the boss to draw my roll,
He had it figured out I was nine dollars in the hole.
I'll sell my outfit just as soon as I can,
I won't punch cattle for no damned man.

Goin' back to town to draw my money,
Goin' back home to see my honey.
With my knees in the saddle and my seat in sky
I'll quit punching cows in the sweet by and by.
Coma ti yi youpy, youpy ya, youpy ya,
Coma ti yi youpy, youpy ya.

MY EARLY DAYS IN GOOD OLD SAN ANTONIO

John A. Miller, Bandera, Texas

My parents, John G. and Katherine Miller came to
San Antonio in 1848, and I was born September 10, 1851,
where they first lived on Main Street and a ten-foot alley,
now West Commerce and Navarro Streets. They lived

there but a few years, then moved east on Main Street near the graveyard and powder house, then used as an arsenal. One of my childhood pleasures was to go to

JOHN A. MILLER

the powder house and watch Mr. Lollard, the caretaker, make paper cartridges.

In those days all of the ditches were full of running water. The ditch west of San Antonio River ran down North Flores Street part of the way, turned east and then south and ran on the west side of Main Plaza in front of the Southern Hotel. There were two ditches east of the San Antonio River. The first one ran back of the Alamo and under the Menger Hotel. The other ditch was farther east on what is now called Water Street. Most of the houses were built on the river and the ditch convenient to water.

At the river crossing on Commerce Street there was a very low bridge, and somewhat of a hill to pull on the east bank. There was a large spring on the north side of the bridge on the east bank, where all the neighbors procured their water. Houston Street had very few houses on it then. The Mavericks had an orchard fenced with cedar pickets, where the Moore building now stands and it ran up to the present location of the Gibbs building where Mr. Maverick lived. He had one of the finest pecan trees in his yard that could be found anywhere, and there were some large cottonwood trees back of the Alamo, which gave that historic building its name, as Alamo means cottonwood in Spanish.

The plazas were like duck ponds as the water would stand there for days after a rain. The old pioneers who I recollect were Messrs. Lewis, Maverick, Menger,

Grenet, Muncey, and many others who were men when I was a young boy.

In 1857 we moved to the Salado on the Austin road, and lived there until 1859, then moved to Selma on the Cibolo, where my father kept the store, post office and stage stand. The old time stage coach was the only way of carrying mail and passengers from San Antonio to Austin.

From 1866 to 1869 Riley Davenport and I sold beeves to San Antonio butchers. They were William Heffling and his slaughter house and pens were where Muth's Garden is now on Grayson Street. Loesberg and Speicer had their pens on the Alazan west of town. There were two markets in San Antonio then, one was the old market house on Market Street, and the other was in the middle of Alamo Plaza, south of Crockett Street. We delivered about forty head every two weeks. The prices we received were six or seven dollars for the first beeves weighing from 900 to 1,000 pounds, and if they kept it on hand until it got thin they would turn it loose and go out on the Salado, in the range, and get a big fat steer in its place. Sometimes we would sell them the same steer two or three times, but they were never short any steers.

In 1870 I went to Brownsville with Capt. W. L. Smith after horses which we brought to the Pettus ranch in the San Antonio River and sold most of them to the United States government on Col. Ed H. Cunningham's contract. Then we went back after 300 mules which we took to the Brazos River, sold some and worked the balance on the railroad for two years.

In 1873 I gathered what cattle I could, about 900 head, and drove to Wichita, Kansas, found the market dull and sold on a credit, for which I realized mostly experience. Some of the boys who went with me were John Davenport, Bob Murchison and Mike Connor. John Davenport now lives in Bandera county, Bob Murchison lives in El Paso, and Mike Connor died at Uvalde several years ago.

When I was 22 years old I bought a small place on the Cibolo, in Comal county, and improved it. I afterwards sold this place, and in 1881 bought 3,500 acres of fine land near Bandera, the old James ranch, and moved onto it in 1882, and still live on this ranch. I quit the cattle business in 1876 (at the wrong time) when I sold all I could gather, about 700 head, to Jesse Evans of Lavernia, and have not raised many cattle since, but have devoted my time to stock farming on a small scale.

I was married February 26, 1878, to Miss Jennie C. Davenport, who has been a faithful helpmate to me during the long span of wedded years. We have one daughter, Miss Minnie Miller. My wife's father was Captain William Davenport, a well known pioneer who lived on the Cibolo. He was captain of a ranger company which operated against the Indians in the early days. Captain Davenport died several years ago, but his widow, now eighty-five years old, still lives at the old home place on the Cibolo.

I have two brothers, W. F. Miller of San Antonio, and George Miller of Marathon, and one sister, Mrs. C. Y. Myer, who lives at Belton.

CAPTAIN A. C. JONES

By George W. Saunders

Captain A. C. Jones of Beeville, Texas, was one of our most widely known and popular men in Texas. He was a self-made man like so many of the sons of Texas, having no advantages in early life. His success was due to his unaided efforts, a keen business sagacity, and a prompt and decisive way of taking hold of things. He was born in Nacogdoches county, Texas, in 1830, and reared on the very borders of civilization, his boyhood being spent among scenes of privations and dangers.

Captain Jones began as a farmer and stockraiser with a capital of $2,500.00 at the age of 22. During the 70's and 80's he had invested in business, lands and cattle more than $100,000.00. He removed to Goliad county in 1858 and in 1860 he was sheriff of that county. He was later treasurer of Bee county, Texas. In 1861 he enlisted in the Confederate Army as a private soldier in Company E, Waller's Battalion, in General Dick Taylor's Command. After 18 months' hard service he was promoted

CAPTAIN A. C. JONES

to a captaincy and remained in the army until the last gun was fired. Captain Jones took the lead in all affairs pertaining to the upbuilding of the county in which he lived and in this he was backed by his entire community. Capt. Jones was never a trail driver but was a pioneer ranchman, merchant and farmer. He died several years ago, leaving a large fortune to W. W. Jones of Corpus Christi, who owns the Nueces Hotel there, several hundred thousand acres of ranch land, 13,000 head of cattle and a million dollars loaned out. W. W. Jones was the only son of Capt. C. A. Jones and is a member of the Old Trail Drivers' Association and promised to furnish a sketch of his life and his photo for this book, but, like many others, has neglected to do so. His greatest worry today is the income tax. I know he is honest, as last year he paid a forty-year-old $20.00 gambling debt which he lost when sowing his wild oats, but of course he has not gambled any since then. The party was threatening to charge compound interest on the $20.00 for forty years but Jones pleaded limitation. I have known W. W. Jones from childhood, have kept close tab on his operations through all these years and I pronounce him a wonder as a financier. He is very popular with all who know him, loyal to his country and his friends.

A. C. Jones, Jr., son of W. W. Jones, is a popular young ranchman of the Hebronville section, and is following in the footsteps of his father and grandfather, the latter remembering him in his will.

CAPTAIN HENRY SCOTT

By George W. Saunders

Captain Henry Scott, who died in Corpus Christi on February 27, 1891, and was interred at Refugio, Texas,

CAPTAIN HENRY SCOTT

his old home a few days later, was born in the state of New York in 1830. Two years later his parents moved to Mission, Refugio county, Texas, where a small body of intrepid Irishmen had established a colony. Captain Scott was raised fighting Indians. At the time Ward and his men were massacred near the Mission, Captain Scott, a small boy at the time, was one of the survivors. Soon after this came the massacre of Fannin and his men at Goliad. Such times as these made a deep and fearful impression upon the mind of young Scott, who was destined himself to play an important part in the history of Texas. When ten years old he accompanied his father on an Indian expedition, and in battle with the Indians, on the ground where Brownsville now stands, his father was killed, young Scott was captured and taken 250 miles into Mexico. One night, finding all the guards asleep, he mounted a pony, and after wandering through the wilderness many days and nights, living on berries and roots, he

finally reached a white settlement where he found shelter
and rest. Scott's account of the battle of Refugio in 1836
as given to Col. John S. Ford is recorded in Texas History by L. E. Daniel. Scott was young at the time but
those horrors were deeply impressed on the boy's mind.
He spent most of his life in Refugio, Goliad, Bee, San
Patricio, Aransas and Nueces counties to protect the border against bandits from Mexico that were stealing stock
and murdering our citizens. This company was in action
the majority of the time and for two years the value of
its service to the State could not be estimated. Mr.
Scott followed one of the Swift murderers into Mexico
and had him put in jail, paid $1,000.00 out of his pocket
to have his captive delivered to him in Texas and brought
the Mexican to Refugio where he was hung to a tree in
the yard of the Swift family where he helped to murder
Mr. and Mrs. Swift, four miles from Mission, Refugio
county, Texas. Few men in the state did more than Captain Scott towards the development of our great state.

OSCAR J. FOX, COMPOSER OF COWBOY SONGS

OSCAR J. FOX

Oscar J. Fox, of San An-
tonio, Texas, is winning fame
as a composer of cowboy
songs. Mr. Fox was born in
Burnet county, Texas, in 1879.
He went to Europe for his
musical education, and also
spent several seasons in New
York. He has just completed
arrangements with G. Schir-
mer and Carl Fisher, music
publishers of New York, for
the publication in concert
form of two cowboy songs,
"A Cowboy's Lament," (Oh, Bury Me Not On The Lone

Prairie) and "Rounded Up in Glory." Both of these songs were taken from John A. Lomax's "Cowboy Songs and Other Frontier Ballads," published by The Macmillan Co. of New York.

A. W. BILLINGSLEY, WIFE AND SON

Reading from left to right, Sergeant A. W. BILLINGSLEY, Jr., MRS. A. W. BILLINGSLEY, A. W. BILLINGSLEY

Mr. Billingsley, Sr., was born in Bee county in 1854, and was for many years a well-known cowman of Southwest Texas. He is now engaged in the dairy business in San Antonio. The young man in uniform in this picture was first sergeant in the 344th Field Artillery, 60th Division, and saw active service in France during the World War.

JOHN AND THOMAS DEWEES

By George W. Saunders

John O. Dewees was born in Putman county, Indiana, December 30th, 1828. His father moved to Taswell county, Ill., in 1832, located on Fox River and laid off the village of Dundee, Ill., engaged in farming and established the first planing mill erected in that section. At that time there were few white pioneers west of the Mis-

sissippi. Sioux and other tribes of Indians were camped
near the little pioneer village. The Indians were treated
kindly and made good neighbors. Mr. Dewees worked
on his father's farm and hauled produce to Chicago, 30
miles west of Dundee. At that time Chicago was a government post containing about 300 inhabitants. Mr.
Dewee's father moved to Texas and settled near Bastrop
in 1849, engaging in farming and stock raising. At the
beginning of the Civil War he owned 1,600 cattle. In
1862 he joined Company B, commanded by Captain E. B.
Millet, 32nd Texas Cavalry and served throughout the

THOMAS DEWEES   JOHN O. DEWEES

war and engaged in many battles and skirmishes. At
the close of the war he gathered what cattle he could and
started anew in the cattle business. He started a ranch
in Wilson county, Texas, bought land and cattle and in
a few years he owned 60,000 acres of pasture land in Wilson, Karnes and Atascosa counties. He began driving
cattle over the trail in the early 70's, formed a partnership with Col. James Ellison and this partnership lasted
many years. During this time the Ellison and Dewees
cattle were thick on the northern trails. For many years
they sent from 20,000 to 40,000 cattle per year. A long
time the firm filled Indian contracts and sold to ranch-

men to be delivered at different points all over the Northwest. Mr. Dewees died several years ago, leaving a large fortune and a host of friends. His widow and grandchildren are conducting the estate profitably.

Thomas Dewees, a brother of John O. Dewees, was a large cattle operator on ranches and on the trail. We are unable to obtain his history but it is similar to that of his brother. He was well known and very popular. He did several years ago and left considerable property.

CAME TO TEXAS IN 1838

Mrs. H. C. Mayes, Carlsbad, Texas

My father, William Rodney Baker, moved from Terre Haute, Indiana, to Austin, Texas, in 1838. I was then six weeks old. My brother, Nelson Baker, was the first white child born in Austin. Father moved from Austin to a place ten miles south of the village on Onion Creek. On February 1, 1842, father and my uncle, Silas Sherman, 17 years old, went out after the milk cows and never came back. Next morning they were found dead and scalped by Indians. They had cut out father's heart and badly mutilated his body. From the signs found there a desperate battle had taken place. Broken arrows were scattered about, the bark knocked off trees, and father's gun barrel was bent, showing that he had used it as a club against his foes after he had exhausted his supply of ammunition.

I am now eighty-four years old, and have lived in Texas all of my life. My husband, Hollen C. Mayes, came to Texas in 1850. He was in the Ranger service, and also served through the Civil War in the Confederate Army. He died August 5th, 1921, in his 86th year. We raised eight children, six boys and two girls.

A LONG, DRY DRIVE

The following story appeared in a booklet issued a few years ago by Joseph A. Spaugh of Hope, Indiana, telling of his experiences in Texas. Mr. Spaugh lived with the family of Silas Hastings in Wharton county, and went up the trail with one of the Hastings herds, but in his narrative he does not give the year. It is as follows:

JOSEPH A. SPAUGH

"One evening Dan Smith said to me, 'Get your traps together for in the morning we start for Llano county to round up a herd of cattle and go North.' If I were to tell you all that happened between the time we gathered those cattle on the Gulf of Mexico and the time we delivered them to the purchaser in Abilene, Kansas, it would be more than you could bear. I will only describe the outfit and relate our experience. The crew consisted of fourteen men and boys, eleven hands, the overseer, the scout and the cook, two yoke of oxen, thirty-five saddle horses and eighteen hundred stock cattle. The scout was a Mexican called Don. It was his duty to ride ahead of the cattle and look out for grass and water, kill game and furnish the outfit with meat. At night the cattle were rounded up and two men were put on guard. One man was riding one way and one the other, while the cattle were lulled to sleep by the cowboys with a low, weird strain, a song of peculiar charm, which quieted the cows when sung by the cattlemen.

"This year had been a very dry one. There had been but little rain and water was scarce. One evening after

we hit the alkali country in Central Texas, we were encamped near a small chain of lakes. Don had ridden
farther in advance of us than usual that day. He knew
that country, having been over it before and when he rode
into camp that evening he reported to Smith that he
found very little water in the Brazos country. He said
that ten or twelve miles out the trail forked and the prong
that the cattle had used this year bore to the West. The
other one, the way the cattle had gone the year before,
had not been used this year and it was his opinion we
would have to follow the west prong for water. Smith
said, 'That is the wrong direction, and if you keep turning this outfit from its course you will land us back where
we started.' Smith talked loud and I watched for the
blue smoke which could be seen on such occasions. It
did not come but some of the older hands said that unless
he took the advice of the Mexican it would materialize
a little later. And it did. We moved the cattle up to
the forks of the trail and camped again for the night.
Don advised the following of those who went before but
Smith said he wanted to take the cattle to Kansas and
did not want to keep them in Texas. Dan Smith, to his
sorrow, forgot the rule of life that to cope with those
who cut across, we must sometimes go around.

"The next morning before starting out every man filled
his canteen with black coffee for we could not drink the
alkali water as it made us sick. It had rained just a
little in the night and Smith was encouraged and said
he 'would drive those cattle over the old road or drive
them to hell.' So we were off. One day out and no
water. Two days out and no water. It was burning hot
on the plains and oh, that terrible alkali dust. I put my
red cotton handkerchief up under my hat and let it hang
down over my face to keep that awful dust out of my
nose. Talk about nothing to drink and a dry country,
that was surely the place. Three days out and no water.
The third night it took all the force we had to hold the

cattle. Range cattle possess a peculiar instinct whereby they can smell water and tell in what direction it lays. All through the long night those cattle would throw up their heads and sniff the air. I tied my broad brimmed hat down over my ears to partly shut out the sound made by those poor cattle dying for water. They could no longer bellow but continued a pitiful moan or lowing. The scout had reported that evening that there was some water twenty miles ahead so we got up and made an early start next morning, expecting to push ahead but when the sun came up it seemed to shine down on us with renewed power. With the glaring sun above us and the burning sand beneath us and no water in sight we were in a terrible strait. Now and then we would pass a cow that had dropped out of the herd and lay prostrated in the trail. That morning the cattle had been walking in a 'mile string.' Sometimes those eighteen hundred would be stretched out for two miles. About nine o'clock the cattle began to drop back and finally the leaders turned back. We made an effort to get the animals in bunches in order to check the backward turning movement, but it was of no avail. Seemingly the word to retreat had been passed along the line from the leaders and every cow in that herd turned back and went in the opposite direction. We had orders to stop the cattle and in an effort to obey we rode back and forth, whipping them over the head with our quirts. Dan Smith pulled his six-shooter and fired into the herd until it was empty. The fact was soon evident that we had lost control over the animals which would blindly walk right against us. It is well known to those familiar with cattle that cows dying for water go entirely blind. All our efforts to stop those foremost in the herd only gave those in the rear time to catch up and help form a solid, impenetrable line of surging, maddened animals which kept steadily advancing in defiance of every obstacle. Seeing that their efforts availed nothing, the men withdrew to one side and formed a little group, every member of which, except the Mexican, proved to be greatly excited. He sat on his horse perfectly calm and self-possessed saying not a word. Dan Smith in his rage, was the last one to ride into the crowd. When he rode up no one spoke and taking off his hat he threw it on the ground and began to pour forth such a torrent of profanity as was never heard before. He cursed until he was exhausted, and then, talking in a whisper, stood up in his saddle stirrups and swore if he owned Texas and hell he would sell Texas and move to hell. I realized that the cattle had a leader but we had none. Smith said every one of the cattle would die, but Don spoke up and said, 'No, you will have a loss in them but they won't all die.' Smith said to Don, 'You got us into this trouble and now you must get us out. What shall we do?' According to the opinion of the Mexican there was only one thing to be done and this is what was done. Riders were put out to throw in the stragglers and gradually work the cattle back to the lakes. Ten days later we took the west fork of that trail, being on a strict count thirty-five cattle and five horses short. After following the Texas steers on the cattle trail for five months we arrived at our journey's end and the cattle were turned over to those who had purchased them.

"The Mexican killed Dan Smith at Abilene in a drunken brawl. Someone else was put in charge of the train. More mules and wagons were bought and the journey southward and was continued, but I had given them the slip and worked for a time in Kansas, then came to Indiana where I have since lived."

CHAPLAIN J. STEWART PEARCE

Chaplain J. Stewart Pearce, First Infantry, Camp Travis, is always present at the conventions of the Old Time Trail Drivers' Association. He is the son of a cowman, and is himself a former cow-puncher, and is chaplain of the Association. On one occasion, during the annual memorial service, Chaplain Pearce, with feeling said of the departed trail drivers:

"Their language may not always have been couched in terms accepted of the church. Their prayers may not have always been as dignified, or their hymns as pure in tone as they might have been, but within the breasts of the men who braved the hardships of those early days beat hearts as true as those which beat within the breasts of any of God's children. I was reared in San Antonio. I knew most of the men whose names have been read in the memorial resolution. Some of them many a time have spent the night in my father's home. And I know that the cowboy frequently was not all he should have been. Many of you have wondered why San Antonio's streets are so crooked, and that's the reason. The boys came in straight but they went out crooked. But whatever they may sometimes have seemed to be on the surface, down beneath all that they were true blue. Uncle Ab was my first boss. Uncle Ab used to let his mouth run wild sometimes, as we have all have done on occasions. But whatever Uncle Ab's language may have been, he had a heart that was pure and good and beautiful. I remember one time we came into a border town with a herd of cattle. And you know what happens when cowboys come into town after six or eight months on a ranch. But Uncle Ab came to me and said, 'If I were you, I wouldn't go across the river with the other boys tonight.' He knew I had just joined the church.''

MARTIN AND JOE O'CONNOR

Martin and Joe O'Connor, of Victoria, Texas, are sons of the late D. M. O'Connor. They own and operate large tracts of land in Victoria, Refugio and Goliad counties on which they graze thousands of fine cattle, following in the footsteps of their illustrious grandfather, Thomas O'Connor, and are among the most worthy gentlemen of their section.

FATHER RECEIVED A PREMIUM FOR BEST CORN

C. E. Austin, Nixon, Texas

My father came to San Antonio in 1854, and at the fair held there that year he received a silver cup as a premium for the best corn raised in Bexar county. The cup was made by Mr. Bell, the jeweler there. My maternal grandfather received a premium for the best yoke of oxen at the same fair. We afterward moved to Karnes county where we raised cattle and hauled freight from Powder Horn to San Antonio, Austin and other points in the state. I was on my way to Brownsville with cotton when the Civil War ended. John Western, my brother and I were driving my father's wagons. There were about twenty teams in our crowd, and we were turned back after four days out of San Antonio. I was very young then, being only about twelve years old. We continued to haul freight until 1869, when father took his family and started with a drove of horses to East Tennessee, arriving there about the first of September of that year. I came back to Texas in 1873, and have lived in or near San Antonio ever since.

SON OF A TRAIL DRIVER

Harry H. Williams, San Antonio, Texas

I value my membership in the Old Trail Drivers'
Association very greatly, and it was very considerate of
you to invite me in to the association by virtue of my
newspaper work in behalf of it. And I was very glad to
join as a regular member by reason of being the son of
a trail driver. Also, as a boy and young man I often
made short drives with herds over the country, usually
in delivering a herd to some congregating point.

My father and his
brother drove a small
herd of East Texas
steers to Vicksburg im-
mediately following the
Civil War, in late '65 or
in '66. The drive began
from Cass county, and
the steers were gathered
in Cass and adjoining
counties. My father was
22 at the time and his
brother was 20, and each
had served the full four
years of the war in the
field. My father was
Henry C. Williams, born
at DeKalb, Bowie coun-
ty, 79 years ago, dying in
Milam county, 26 years
ago. His brother was
William W. Williams,
two years younger, now
living in Houston, Texas, at 136 Rosalie Street. My

HARRY H. WILLIAMS

grandfather was J. J. Williams, for many years at Doug-
lassville, Cass county, where he is buried.

I remember hearing my father tell incidents of the
trip to Vicksburg, one of which was that when the herd
was swum across the Mississippi River, there was one
steer, unusually vigorous and ambitious, that swam
circles around the herd while crossing. I don't know
how large a force the two brothers took along, but do
know that they had a cook, wagon and camping outfit, for
just a few years ago in Austin I met the man, who, as a
young boy, himself just out of the Confederate army,
went along in the capacity of cook.

Later, on returning home, my uncle was elected sheriff of Cass county, at 26 years of age. My father married
in Mississippi, returned to Texas, and principally reared
his family in Stephens and Eastland counties.

In my work as livestock representative of the San
Antonio *Express* I have repeatedly tried to make known
my great appreciation of the usefulness and value of the
Old Trail Drivers' Association; still, I cannot forego the
pleasure of again saying that Mr. George W. Saunders'
work, and the work of others whom you have enlisted in
the cause, in preserving the history of the old cattle driving days, is one worthy of the highest commendation.

MORE ABOUT THE CHISHOLM TRAIL

Charles Goodnight, Goodnight, Texas

I do not look at a trail as being an honor or a dis-
honor to anyone, but I see no reason why they should be
named for people who did not make them.

On page 289 of the first volume of this book is given
an article by Fred Sutton of Oklahoma City, in which
appears this statement: "This trail was started in 1868
by John Chisholm (Chisum), who drove the first bunch

of cows from San Antonio to Abilene, Kansas, and for whom the trail was named.''

Now, the facts are, John Chisholm (Chisum) followed the Goodnight & Loving Trail up the Pecos in 1866, reaching Bosque Grande on the Pecos about December, wintering right below Bosque Grande, with 600 Jingle Bob steers. We wintered about eight miles apart. In the spring of 1867 he disposed of those steers to government contractors, and returned to his Colorado and Concho ranch and began moving his cattle west. In 1860 I formed a partnership with him on the following basis: He was to deliver to me all cattle he could handle at Bosque Grande on the Pecos River, I allowing him one dollar per head profit over Texas prices for his risk. During this contract or agreement, he lost two herds by the Indians. I handled the rest of his drives from Bosque Grande west, disposing of them in Colorado and Wyoming. This continued for three years, and I divided profits equally with him. These profits enabled him to buy the 60,000 head he once held on the Pecos.

Chisholm (Chisum) never drove a herd north, and never claimed to have done so. He did drive two herds to Little Rock at the end of the Civil War, less than a thousand steers in all.

John McCoy conceived the idea of the Texas cattle trades going to Abilene, and sent scouts down to meet the herds and drive them through the country after they had passed Red River, at the place known as Red River Crossing.

Chisholm (Chisum) moved the herds before spoken of en route to Little Rock by what was well known as the Colbert Crossing, following the old U. S. Road the entire distance. In conversation with me he said one Chisholm, in no way related to him, did pilot 600 steers from the Texas frontier to old Fort Cobb, and he presumed that this was the origin of the name of the trail, although no trail was opened.

Chisholm (Chisum) was a good trail man, and the best counter I have ever known. He was the only man I have ever seen who could count three grades accurately as they went by. I have seen him do this many times.

I estimate that he delivered to me 15,000 or 16,000 cattle in the three years mentioned. I drove the last of his cattle in 1875, being two herds of big steers, and I took them over what is known as the New Goodnight Trail, leaving the Pecos River above old Fort Sumner to Granada, Colorado. I think W. J. Wilson, known as "One Armed Bill Wilson," will remember Chisholm's reaching the Pecos in the winter of 1866. As I remember it, he had passed up to the Colorado in 1866 with Mr. Loving with the stock cattle of our first drive, and he and Mr. Loving met me at Bosque Grande on the Pecos, I think, in February, 1867.

As above stated I positively know no trail north was made by Chisholm (Chisum) but the first herd driven north out of northwest Texas was driven in 1858 by Oliver Loving, leaving Palo Pinto and Jack counties, thence north to Red River, crossing Red River in the neighborhood of Red River Crossing, and striking the Arkansas River near old Fort Zarah, then up the Arkansas to just above where Pueblo now stands. There he wintered the herd. In 1859 (spring) he moved them to the Platte River near Denver and peddled them out. He remained there until the Civil War broke out and had much difficulty in getting back home, but through the assistance of Maxwell, Kit Carson and Dick Wootan, he was given a passport and afterwards delivered beef to the Confederacy during the war, which completely broke him up. He joined me in 1866 on the Western trail, and followed this until his death. Part of these facts were given me by Mr. Loving himself.

NOW A MEMBER OF CONGRESS

Claude Hudspeth, El Paso, Texas

I was born in a little log cabin that stood on the banks of the Medina River, one mile below the town of Medina, in Bandera county, forty-four years ago. I worked as a cowboy from the time I could sit in the saddle and whirl a lasso until this present hour, having just returned from my ranch on Devil's River, where I rounded up and delivered in person a herd of steers at the railroad station at Barnhart, some distance from my ranch.

My father was a frontier sheriff. He was away from home a great deal of the time running down outlaws and cattle thieves who infested that country in the days when the good right hand was the chief protection that was afforded the citizenship of that country, exercised by efficient peace officers of that day. I worked for some of the old-time pioneers of that section, namely John R. Blocker, Eugene McKenzie, and many others.

I have held the offices of State Representative, State Senator, District Judge, and am now serving my second term in Congress.

In my early life my principal job was a cook in a cow camp where cowboys will testify, some of them that survived, "that I cooked things that nobody could eat." The boss, wishing to promote, and also to prevent indigestion among the men, elevated me to the position of horse wrangler. There was hardly an old-time trail driver that I have not met up with, and for whom I hold the highest esteem, love and friendship.

My education consists of three months in a log cabin out on the banks of the Medina, where I thoroughly mastered the contents of Webster's Blue-back speller and reader combined. This constitutes the curriculum and the extent of my literary studies.

June 19, 1922.

CAPTAIN MIFFLIN KENEDY

Captain Mifflin Kenedy was born at Dowington, Chester county, Pennsylvania, June 8, 1818, and died at

MIFFLIN KENEDY

Corpus Christi, Texas, March 14, 1895, aged seventy-six years. Early in life he became a seaman and followed that line of work for many years. In 1842 he went to Alabama and during one season on the Alabama River served as clerk of the *Champion,* a boat running from Mobile to Montgomery. The *Champion* then proceeded to Apalachicola, Florida, and ran on the Apalachicola and Chattahoochie Rivers until 1846. While thus engaged in Florida he met Captain Richard King, then a river pilot and in after years his partner in steamboat operations on the Rio Grande, and ranching in Southwest Texas. In the early part of 1846 Captain Kenedy was placed in charge of the *Champion* and ordered to take her to Pittsburg, Pennsylvania. Upon his arrival at Pittsburg, he met Major Saunders, an engineer in the United States Army, and a friend of his, who was sent there by General Zachary Taylor to obtain boats for the use of the army on the Rio Grande. Major Saunders purchased the *Corvette, Colonel Cross, Major Brown, Whitville* and other boats for the service. Captain Kenedy was made commander of the *Corvette* and directed to proceed to New Orleans and report to Colonel Hunt of the Quartermaster's Department, U. S. A. The appointment was confirmed and Captain Kenedy enlisted for the war, as mas-

ter, and was ordered to proceed with the *Corvette* to
the mouth of the Rio Grande and report to E. A. Ogden,
assistant quartermaster, U. S. A.   One of the reasons
for selecting him for this work was his experience in
conducting light boats over the Gulf.   He reached the
station at the mouth of the Rio Grande in June, 1846,
and from that time until the close of the Mexican War
transported troops and provisions to Matamoras, Rey-
nosa, Camargo and other points on the river.   After the
victory of Buena Vista, and while moving on Vera Cruz,
General Winfield Scott stopped at the mouth of the Rio
Grande, desiring to consult with General Worth.   Captain Kenedy's vessel, the *Corvette,* was selected to take
General Scott and staff up the river.

Captain Richard King joined Captain Kenedy in May,
1847, and acted as pilot of the *Corvette* until the close
of the war, in 1848.   Both were thoroughly experienced
seamen and rendered their country good service.   At the
end of the Mexican war, Captain Kenedy, Samuel Belden
and Captain James Walworth bought a large number of
mules and wagons and a stock of merchandise and started
for San Juan, is the state of Jalisco, Mexico, but sold
their outfit at Zacatecas and returned to Matamoras
where they divided the proceeds of the trip and dissolved
partnership.   Captain Kenedy immediately purchased
another stock of goods and, with his merchandise loaded
on pack-mules started for the interior of Mexico.   At
Monterey he sold out and returned to Brownsville, reaching there in the spring of 1850.

Seeing the necessity of good boats on the Rio Grande,
he then formed a partnership with Capt. Richard King,
Captain James O'Donnel and Mr. Charles Stillman,
under the name of M. Kenedy & Co.   The firm's purpose
was to build boats and run them on the Rio Grande and
along the Gulf Coast to Brazos, Santiago.   Captain Kenedy proceeded to Pittsburg, Pa., and built two boats, the

Comanche and *Grampus*. He bought Captain O'Donnel's interest in the business during the following two years, and in 1865 the new firm of King, Kenedy & Co. was formed, Charles Stillman having retired. The two firms, during their existence, built and purchased twenty-six boats for trade. In 1874 the firm was dissolved and divided assets. During this time Captain Kenedy served under Major Heitzleman, in the U. S. Army, during the Cortina raid and was Captain of Co. A., 1859.

Captain Richard King established the Santa Gertrude ranch in Nueces county, Texas, in 1852, and Captain Kenedy bought half interest in it in 1860. They dissolved partnership in this undertaking in 1868, taking share and share alike of cattle, horses and sheep. Capt. King, by agreement reserved Santa Gertrudes ranch, Captain Kenedy buying from Charles Stillman the Laureles ranch consisting of twelve and a half leagues of land, 10,000 cattle, and many horses and sheep, and he moved thereto at once. After the Civil War so many thieves, marauders and outlaws remained on the frontier that Captain King saw that the only effectual way to protect their cattle interests was to fence. Captain Kenedy enclosed 132,000 acres of the Laureles, and Captain King enclosed his pastures. They were the first cattle raisers in the state to fence large bodies of land. Captain Kenedy remained on the Laureles ranch until he sold it in 1882 to Underwood, Clark & Co. of Kansas City, for $1,000,000 cash. At the time of the sale it contained 242,000 acres of land, all fenced, 50,000 head of cattle and 5,000 head of horses, mares and mules.

Colonel Uriah Lott projected the Corpus Christi, San Diego & Rio Grande narrow gauge railroad from Corpus Christi to Laredo in 1876, and with the assistance of Captains Kenedy and King built the road and sold it to the Mexican National Construction Company in 1881. Captain Kenedy also supplied the money with which

Colonel Lott built the San Antonio & Aransas Pass railroad, a distance of 700 miles, in 1885.

In 1882 Captain Kenedy established the Kenedy Pasture Co., the ranch lands lying in Cameron county, and being thirty miles in length by twenty in breadth.

April 16, 1852, Captain Kenedy was married to Mrs. Vela de Vidal of Mier, Mexico, the wedding occurring at Brownsville. Six children were born to this union, only one son surviving, Mr. John G. Kenedy, who is now president of the Kenedy Pasture Company.

Captain Kenedy was a believer in State rights and was a staunch Confederate. He and his friend, Captain King, assisted the Confederacy in many ways. They handled their own and Confederate cotton, and lost heavily when their cotton was denounced and seized by General Banks.

JOHN G. KENEDY

John G. Kenedy was born in Brownsville, Texas, April 22, 1856, and was educated at Spring Hill College, Mobile, Alabama. After leaving school in 1873, he accepted a position with Perkins, Swenson & Co., bankers and commission merchants at New Orleans, where he remained several years. In April, 1877 he started on the cattle trail from Laureles, his father's ranch, to Fort Dodge, Kansas, acompanying 18,000 head of cattle. He remained two months at Fort Dodge, drove a herd of 2,000 cattle from there to Ogallala, Nebraska, and then returned to his father's ranch. Six months later he went into the sheep business, which he sold to Lott & Nelson in 1882. After the sale of the Laureles ranch in 1882 Mr. Kenedy became secretary of the Kenedy Pasture Company, which owns 600 square miles of pasture lands, all under fence.

In 1884 he became general manager of this company and

JOHN G. KENEDY

took entire charge of La Par-
ra ranch, located six miles
from Sarita, Texas. This
ranch has 160 miles of fencing, a water front on Buffalo
Bayou and Laguna Madre of
sixty miles, seventy live ar-
tesian wells, and is stocked
with about 25,000 head of cattle. Mr. John G. Kenedy
married Miss Marie Turcotte
of New Orleans January 30,
1884, and has two children
living, John G. Kenedy, Jr.,
and Sarita Kenedy East. Mr. Kenedy is now president
of the Kenedy Pasture Company, and his son, John G.
Kenedy, Jr., is manager.

FELIX M. SHAW

Felix M. Shaw was born in Travis county, Texas, in
October, 1860. His parents were Mr. and Mrs. J. H.
Shaw, who lived "by the side of the road," near Austin,
and were truly friends to trail drivers. The subject of
this sketch had just entered manhood when trail driving
was at its best and there was no more beautiful sight
to him than to see Del Valle Flat covered with herds.
The fascination was more than he could resist, and
although his father needed and depended upon him to
help at home, he just had to go up the trail, and three
seasons found him with John Blocker's outfits en route
to Montana. Felix M. Shaw was married in October,
1896, to Miss Ella Matthews of Austin, who, after a short

and happy married life, was called to her reward. In 1895 he married Miss Florence Terry of Eagle Pass. To their union were born three daughters and one son, all now living in San Antonio. Mr. Shaw died and was buried at San Antonio July 17, 1908.

A LOG OF THE TRAILS

George W. Saunders, San Antonio, Texas

The question of the log of the Chisholm and other trails leading to the Northern markets has more versions than any question connected with the early trail days because no one, it seems, gives this phase of the game more than a passing thought. Most everyone has heard of the Chisholm Trail, the Goodnight Trail and the Loving Trail but as a matter of fact most of the trail drivers did not care anything about the name of the trail they were traveling, as they were generally too busy to think or care

GEO. W. SAUNDERS.
40 Years Ago.

about its name. In conversation I have heard men say: "I took the Chisholm Trail at Goliad, Lockhart, Corpus Christi, San Antonio, and many other Texas points." Some of the Sketches in Volume One of the "Trail Drivers of Texas" speak of the Chisholm Trail starting at San Antonio, Texas; some at other places. The writers of these sketches were honest. They had probably heard this and had not taken the trouble to investigate the real routing and commencing point, until after the organization of The Old Trail Drivers' Association in 1915. At that time our Secretary was instructed to write to old trail drivers all over the country for information on this subject. We received many letters, each one giving his version, which differed somewhat. W. P. Anderson, who was railroad agent at Abilene, Kansas, in the late sixties, and had to do with the first shipments of cattle out of that place, gives us a satisfactory description of the Chisholm Trail, laid out by Jesse Chisholm, a half-breed Cherokee Indian, from Red River Station to different points in Kansas. Quoting from Mr. Anderson's letter to the Secretary, which is recorded in the minutes of the first reunion and to be found on page 13 of the first volume of "The Trail-Drivers of Texas":

"In reference to Mr. Goodnight's allusion to my 'blazing' the trail for the Joe McCoy herd, my recollection of the first herd that came to Abilene, Kansas, was that of J. J. Meyers, one of the trail drivers of that herd now living at Panhandle, Texas. A Mr. Gibbs, I think, will ascertain further on the subject. The first cattle shipped out of Abilene, that I recollect, was by C. C. Slaughter of Dallas, and while loaded at Abilene, Kansas, the billing was made from Memorandum slips at Junction City, Kansas. The original chapters of Joe McCoy's book were published in a paper called 'The Cattle Trail,' edited by H. M. Dixon, whose address is now the Auditorium Building, Chicago. It was my connection with this publication that has probably led Mr. Goodnight into the belief that I helped blaze the trail with McCoy's cattle herd. This was the first paper that I know of that published maps of the trails from different cattle shipping points in Kansas to the intersection of the original Chisholm Trail, one from Coffeyville, Kansas, the first, however, from Baxter Springs, then from Abilene, Newton, then Wichita and Great Bend, Dodge

City becoming so famous obviated the necessity for further attention in this direction.''

One of the greatest developing projects ever known in the United States was done by this industry in taking the wilderness from the Indians and wild animals, stocking, peopling and developing sixteen states and territories in 28 years, namely; Western Indian Territory,

CROSSING AT RED RIVER STATION

Western Kansas, Nebraska, Montana, North Dakota, South Dakota, Colorado, Idaho, Nevada, Oregon, Washington, New Mexico, Arizona, Wyoming, Utah and Northwest Texas. We all know that this entire domain was a wilderness in 1867 and only a few trappers and miners had penetrated them. However, the Government's Immigrant California Trail crossed this wilderness, as did a few prospecting expeditions, but up to this date habitation was confined to a few trading posts and forts. Compare this condition with the condition in 1890. All of the Indians were on reservations, the millions of buffalo were replaced by herds of fine cattle, horses, sheep and hogs; the iron horse rumbled through these lands, bringing happy, prosperous people, who built towns, schools, churches and tilled the rich soil that was waiting for them. The government and other interests did their part and did it well, but to the old trail drivers belongs the glory and honor for having blazed the way that made this great development possible. They did more towards development in twenty-eight years than was ever previously done in one hundred years by our ancestors. The trail to the North from Texas was started in 1867 and closed in 1895, but most of this great development was done in twenty years, from 1870 to 1890. It is conservatively estimated by old trail drivers that there were 98,000,000 cattle and 10,000,000 horse stock driven over the Northern Trails during the 28 years of trail days and that there were 35,000 men employed to handle these herds. Many of them are dead. Those surviving are identified in all lines of business, from high finance to day laborers. The majority of them belong to Texas. One thousand and two hundred of them belong to the Old Trail Drivers' Association which holds its annual re-unions in San Antonio in October of each year, when they live over the bygone days.

From Red River to Abilene, Kansas, as I remember, the streams in 1871 were: Big and Little Washita, Turkey Creek, South and Northern Canadian, Cimarron, Bluff Creek on the line of Kansas. Here we found the first civilized settlement of English-speaking people. The next streams were Pond Creek, Salt Fork of the Arkansas, North Fork of the Arkansas, at Wichita, Kansas. The next town, Newton, Kansas, was a railroad camp as we went north and a big town when we came back through two months later, that being the terminus of the railroad at that time. Next stream was Smoky River, on which was located Abilene, Kansas, the great Texas cattle market at that time. My experiences at Abilene, and full details of this trip from Texas and return over the trail in 1871, and my trail experiences up to 1886 are fully described in volume one of "The Trail Drivers of Texas."

Some herds left the main trail in Wilson county, passed through Bexar county via San Antonio, to get supplies, then through Comal county, intersecting the main trail in Hays or Caldwell counties. All of these trails zigzagged and touched lots of adjoining counties not mentioned in my log.

The thousands of herds that were bought at Abilene, Wichita, Dodge City, Ogallala and other markets were driven to ranches all over the northwest, some as far as the Canadian line.

Here is a correct log of the cattle trails from Texas to Kansas and the Northwestern States and territory beginning at the Rio Grande in Cameron county and giving the names of all the counties in Texas these trails passed through: Starting at the Rio Grande, the trail passed through Cameron, Willacy, Hidalgo, Brooks, Kenedy, Kleberg, Nueces, Jim Wells, San Patricio, Live Oak, Bee, Goliad, Karnes, Wilson, Gonzales, Guadalupe, Caldwell, Hays, Travis, Williamson, Bell, Falls, Bosque, McLennan, Hill, Johnson, Tarrant, Denton, Wise, Cook, Montague, to Red River Station, or crossing where the Texas trail intersected the Chisholm trail. In the late 70's it became necessary to move the trail further west, as the old trail was being taken up by farmers. The trail was changed to go through Wilson, Bexar, Kendall, Kerr, Kimble, Menard, Concho, McCulloch, Coleman, Callahan, Shackleford, Throckmorton, Baylor and Wilbarger to Doan's Store or Crossing on Red River. Later on the Southern herds quit the old trail in San Patricio county and went through Live Oak, McMullen, La Salle, Dimmit, Zavala, Uvalde, Edwards, and intersecting the Western trail in Kimble county, from where all followed the well defined and much traveled Western trail to Doan's Crossing on Red River. As I remember the trail to

Dodge City from Doan's Crossing it passed up North Fork Red River, Croton Creek, crossed North Fork Red River at Wichita Mountains, up North Fork to Indian Camp, Elm Creek, Cash Creek, Washita, Canadian, Sand Creek, Wolf Creek, Otter Creek, Beaver Creek, Wild Horse and Cimarron where Red Clark conducted a road house called "Long Horn Roundup," on up Bear Creek, Bluff Creek, at Mailey's road house, Mulberry Creek and Dodge City. Now, my gentle readers, you have the log of old Northern cattle trails, through Texas, and by looking at a map of Texas you can locate any part of the trail by the counties touched, but remember several of the Texas counties were not organized at that time and none in the Indian Territory. You will recall it has been fifty-five years since the trail started and twenty-four since it closed. I personally drove over all these trails described and there are hundreds of men yet living that will vouch for the correctness of this log.

John Chisum of Denton county, drove lots of cattle to the head of the Concho in the late sixties, and on to the Pecos later. Oliver Loving, Chas. Goodnight, John Gamel, and others drove some herds from the head of the Concho to Horsehead Crossing on the Pecos in the sixties, on up the Pecos to Fort Sumner and on to Pueblo, Colorado. There was a trail called the Goodnight Trail that went from the Pecos by way of Tascosa to Dodge City and other Kansas markets, but I have been unable to get a true log of that trail.

For the information of readers who are not familiar with geographical Texas and its cattle industry, I will state that herds starting from ranches in all parts of the state would intersect the nearest of these Northern trails, coming in from both sides and I doubt if there is a county in the state that did not have a herd traverse some part of it during trail days.

Some of the sketches in both volumes of the "Trail

Drivers of Texas" report trouble with the Indians on the trail and others report no trouble. For your information I will say the Indians were not always in the same mood, as sometimes they would leave the reservations on hunting expeditions and change their plans to murder and stealing from the trailers, emigrants and settlers. They were always ready to steal but they were not fond of the Texas cowboy's mode of dealing with them and were very friendly when there were several herds near each other on the trail, but a lone herd was most always imposed on. Few herds passed through the Indian Territory in early days without some trouble with the Indians. I have gone several trips without any trouble more than having them beg for a few animals and some provisions; at other times I have had them steal horses, stampede the herd and molest us in every possible way, but the best remedy for them was to stand pat and they usually came to our terms.

The publication of this, the second volume of "The Trail Drivers of Texas" will complete a work I started many years ago, beginning with the agitation of, and the final organization of the Old Trail Drivers' Association. Collecting data for the two volumes was a task that would have tested the patience of Job. I was like Davy Crockett —I knew I was right—and I went ahead. The work was tedious and slow, but I enjoyed it because I knew the organization should exist, and the books would be very interesting and would give facts that the rising generation should know. The general matter of which these two volumes is made up depict a life of which the present generation knows very little. They deal with actual happenings that occurred in the days of trail driving, and these facts are much stranger than fiction. I started a campaign to raise $30,000 to build a monument in Brackenridge Park at San Antonio, on the old trail, to perpetuate the memory of those noble old trail drivers.

Donations are coming in regularly, and I believe we can build this monument in 1924. When it is completed my work is done.

The cowboys, or cow-punchers, sometimes called "waddies," were men who did all kinds of ranch and trail work with cattle. Whether he was a ranchman, owner of trail herds, son of a cattle king, or just a hand, his occupation gave him that name. Right here I want to defend the cowboys, or cow-punchers, against the so-called "Wild West" fiction stories that purport to link them with elements of bad men. There was a very small per cent of them went wrong, as the temptations and influences they met at the northern markets after a long, lonesome, tiresome journey, could not be resisted and entrapped some of them, but no larger per cent than would have fallen from the same number of college students. It is not fair to besmear the name of the cowboy with the deeds of every outlaw in the country. I know the majority of these cowboys made the best citizens of Texas. It is true they were light-hearted and care-free, but they never forsook a friend, or failed to respond to the call of distress. Woman's virtue was their highest ideal, and their respect for womankind was unbounded. These cowboys stood the acid test, and I do not think a nobler set of men ever lived.

In this volume there are about 200 pictures of representative trail men. I claim that 100 of them and their connections handled fully 75 per cent of all the cattle and horses that were driven out of Texas to the Northern markets during the trail days. I am proud to say I was personally acquainted with 90 per cent of these noble-men. They are passing away fast, and I fear there will never be another set of men with such traits of character, home-loving, straight-forward, and God-loving, as the old trail drivers were. They have all stood the acid test, and their memory will stand as a lasting monument to their many deeds and great achievements. And here again I want to take occasion to pay tribute to the pioneer women of our state, without whose aid and help the early cowmen could not have endured the hardships incident to frontier life. The most appropriate and fitting tribute to these noble women is given in J. M. Hunter's book, "Pioneer History of Bandera County," which chapter is here given in full:

"It is pleasant and right to recount the noble deeds of our fathers, but far more pleasant to say something in praise of our gentle sisters, the heroines of the pioneer; she who rocked the cradle bed of childhood; our first, last and faithfulest friend. We would feel remiss in a chivalric duty did we fail to note her share in the great work of discovery and improvement, and it is only proper that we should record some encouraging word to her aspirations and advocate her claims to a just and proper place in the history of our great state. The trophies of the years that pass are a few immortalities gleaned from its sepulchre. Epochs, events, characters, that survive; oblivion is the common goal of the race. Whatever has contributed to human weal has been remembered, memorialized by cenotaph and mausoleum and remains with us on History's page. Their deeds shine on the pages of history, like stars blazing in the night, and their achievements have long been celebrated in song and story. Romulus and Remus founded an empire and their names are immortal. Columbus discovered a new world and he stands unique in the sublime faith and courage which impelled him over an unknown sea. Honor has been rather partial in bestowing her gifts and fame has placed her laurels chiefly on masculine brows, forgetting the countless heroines who were worthy of recognition. It is with great pride that we call attention to the fact that the pioneer women of Texas have proved themselves competent to fill positions other than presiding at the

festal board, or beating out the rhythm of their blood with
sandaled feet on polished floors, or strewing flowers in
the path of the conqueror as he returns from the bloody
carnage; for many noble names have swollen the list of
those who have proved to the world that women can be
true and great even in arduous duties incident to pioneer
life. Bravely has she gone to the unprotected frontier,
with no shelter but the crude cabin, the dugout or open
camp, where winds whistled, wolves howled, where Indians yelled, and yet within that rude domicile, burning
like a lamp, was the pure and stainless Christian faith,
love, patience, fortitude and heroism. And as the Star
of the East rested over the manger where Christ lay,
so, speaking not irreverently, there rested over the roofs
of the pioneer a star of the West, the star of Empire, and
today that empire is the proudest in the world. The pioneer woman, though creature of toil and loneliness and
privation, she endured it with a constancy as changeless
as the solitude and danger about her. She has borne
her part in all the vicissitudes incident to the outposts
of the borderland and her hands have assisted in kindling
fires on the confines of civilization to guide the wheels of
empire outward, onward. Of necessity, the pioneer
woman sacrificed more than the pioneer man, the finer
texture of her being was less adapted to the rugged environments of pioneer life. However, as the tides of ocean
are forever faithful to the mysterious attractions of the
moon, so woman has followed man across seas, over
mountains and into deserts to witness his adventures and
share his achievements. Those who lay the foundation
of empire and extended the outposts of civilization are
worthy of all honor, and especially is this true of the
frontier women. If Texas today boasts of statesman or
warrior, of patriots and freemen, of a civilization and
social fabric into which is inwrought the elements of per-
manency and progress, she owes it largely to her pioneer

women who founded the first homes, worshiped in the
first humble chapels erected to God on these western hills
and boundless prairies now crowded with temples and
churches and schools and institutions of learning, while
the multitudinous tramp of a million feet are still heard
in the distance coming this way to enjoy what these pioneer mothers purchased by their sacrifice and privation.
It was not given to many of these leaders to enter into
the fruits of their labors. This splendid civilization we
enjoy today, the social vines that shelter us, the civic
boughs whose clusters feed us, all spring from seed sown,
and the harvest of tears reaped by our pioneers, our old
settlers. These pioneer women were familiar with much
that has passed with the years, so rapidly have conditions
changed. Be it said to their honor that in humble homes
and with few advantages she did her part well; there was
something in the lullaby that she sang to her children at
twilight, in the sublime simplicity of her teachings that
fostered a sturdy manhood and patriotism which was
inwrought into the stalwart republic, the precursor of
the Lone Star State. She has been scalped and tortured
by the savage, and her blood has reddened these plains
and valleys as an oblation on the altar of empire. Her
life and the tragic scenes through which she passed are
each a romance whose daring and adventure and sacrifice
are the chief actors on its eventful pages. All that is
noblest in man is born of woman's constancy and deathless devotion to him. Knighthood found its inspiration
in the pathos of her love and the charm of her smiles.
Woman loves man, is jealous of his freedom, his liberty,
his honor, and for him she sacrifices all. Heart and soul
are the smallest things she immolates on any altar. The
pioneer women of Texas robed themselves out in drudgery and toil that their beauty might reappear in the
structure their devoted hands built to liberty and progress. They buried themselves in these western solitudes,

that from these living sepulchres might come the great pulse-beat of a mighty nation, buoyant, chivalric, progressive civilization. They gave up the comforts and pleasures of society, severed the tenderest ties of the human heart, home and kindred, the old altars where they prayed, the graves of their loved and lost, these the dearest things to a woman's heart, that we today might enjoy in their fullest fruition what they lost. We may well be proud of the temper of these Texas heroines; their dear old hearts beat the prelude to the grand march of the empire. Their feet beat out the trail over the trackless prairie and across rugged mountains which has since widened into the great thoroughfares of commerce and travel; their tender hands planted the first flowers on the graves of those whose bones first reposed under Texas soil. God bless you, our dear pioneer women. We treasure you as trophies fresh from the field of victory; may your declining years be rewarded with the gratitude and appreciation of all who enjoy the blessings, and privileges of this great country; may your last days be as the calm eventide that comes at the end of a quiet summer day when the sun is dying out in the west. We believe and admit it today that woman is heaven's 'ideal of all that is pure and ennobling and lovely here, her love is the light of the cabin home.' It is the one thing in the world that is constant, the one peak that rises above the cloud, the one window in which the light burns forever, the one star that darkness cannot quench—is woman's love. It rises to the greatest height, it sinks to the lowest depths, it forgives the most cruel injuries. It is perennial of life, and grows in every climate, neither coldness nor neglect, harshness nor cruelty can extinguish it. It is the perfume of the heart; it is this that has wrought all miracles of art, that gives us music all the way from the cradle song to the last grand symphony that bears the soul away on wings of joy. In the language of Petronius to Lygia, 'May the white winged doves of peace build their nests in the rafters of your homes,' may the gleams of happiness and prosperity shine on the pathway of your remaining days, and may the smile of an approving God be a lamp unto your feet and a light unto your pathway, guiding you safely across the frontier of time to a safe place beneath the shade of the trees on the other side.''

THOMAS H. SHAW

T. H. Shaw was the son of Mr. and Mrs. J. H. Shaw, and was born in Travis county, Texas, September 27, 1856. He was a natural cowman, and from the time he was a mere boy he loved the work, the camp fire, the chuck wagon, and all the paraphernalia of the cowboy. For several seasons he went as far as the road was cut, from Texas coasts to Wyoming and Montana. He encountered Indians, had thrilling experiences, and had many narrow escapes. At different times he was interested with John R. Blocker. In 1886 he was married to Miss Nannie Blocker and to them were born two sons, Tom H. Shaw, Jr., and Blocker Shaw of Fort Worth. Mr. Shaw spent several years ranching and farming in Runnels county, where he made many lasting friends. In 1907 he moved his family to Fort Worth and entered the live stock commission business, in which he was engaged at the time of his death, November 17, 1912.

The picture on the following page shows George W. Saunders' Stock Yards in San Antonio in 1888, at the time when John Rutledge penned his 3,500 cattle there to allow his cow-hands to stop over and see the sights of the city. The cattle and horses in the pens can be plainly

time Houston Street was only a road through mesquite and huisache brush. In 1864-65 I attended the St. Mary's College and here I was taught those Christian principles that ever remained with me and encouraged me to overcome many temptations in after life. In 1870-71 I again attended this college after my return from my "spin" over the range in the Southern and Eastern States as mentioned, and on this "spin" I rode with the Klu Klux Klan in Tennessee when there was no other law to protect Southern homes against the ravages of freed Negroes urged on by the carpet-baggers and protected in their nefarious practices by Federal bayonets. In 1866-67-68, when not attending school I was working cattle for my father in Live Oak county branding, gathering and driving to Bexar county, where we were then living on the Olmos Creek, five miles north of San Antonio. In 1876 I left Dimmit county, where I owned a small bunch of cattle, which I sold, and started to Arizona, stopping awhile in Menard county where I had a sweetheart and here I joined Thomas W. Swilling to go with him to Arizona. We left Menardville early in September, 1876, and pulled out via Ft. Concho, fifty miles north, where we laid in a supply of grub, enough to last us until we reached Roswell, New Mexico, and again "hit the grit" for Arizona, every mile of it over an uninhabited country, infested with hostile Indians. At Centralia, which was a stage station on the high plains guarded by negro troops, we left the stage road and followed the old Butterfield route to Horsehead Crossing on the Pecos; thence up east of Pecos to New Mexico. The Indians were raiding the country when we left and we saw their trails and camped on them quite often from Fort Concho until we got to Seven Rivers in New Mexico. About twenty-five miles west of Ft. Concho we met a company of cavalry escorting the telegraph operator at Ft. Concho, a Mr. Milburn, who had been out repairing the line between

Ft. Concho and the Pecos River on the stage road, about three miles of which had been cut and destroyed. Mr. Milburn, whom I knew when operator at Ft. Duncan, advised us to return with them to the fort, stating that the country was "lousy" with Indians, and we would not be able to get through. At Centralia the negro sergeant in command of the guard advised us to go back. At the rifle-pits we nooned where the Indians had camped the night before; at Castle Gap the Indian trail split, the largest party keeping the trail westward and the smaller party going northwest. The large trail was mostly horses and was about forty in number, no doubt going to the Mescalero Agency at Tularosa, New Mexico, crossing at Horsehead and thence northwest through the Guadalupe Mountains with a bunch of stolen horses. Another trail came in from the north and crossed our trail near Castle Gap, going southeast toward Camp Lancaster, at the mouth of Live Oak Creek. There were about ten on foot and three horses and they crossed the trail we were on about five hours before we came along. We traveled until about midnight, hoping to strike the Pecos at Horsehead, water and get away in the dark hours as it was a bad place for Indians, but being sleepy and tired, we left the trail and went about two hundred yards south and lay down to sleep, staking our horses on fine grass. About five o'clock a. m. we saddled up and pulled out before day and reached Horsehead about nine o'clock, not many hours behind two bands of Indians. About three o'clock the next afternoon we a saw dust ahead of us and not knowing but what it was Indians I sent Swilling with the pack horse into the cane brakes of the Pecos while I maneuvered up the river to see who was coming and found out that it was two white men, a Mr. Pearce, and Nath Underwood, driving a small bunch of cattle from New Mexico to Ft. Stockton, Texas. They let us have a little corn meal and some "jerky" from their meager supplies and we went on about five miles

to Pope's crossing on the Pecos, where we watered our
horses and filled our canteens, then crossed our trail and
went behind a butte about one-half mile from our trail
and camped. Pearce and Underwood went about two
miles farther on their road and camped, making the distance between our camps about seven miles. They hobbled two saddle horses and one pack-horse and staked the
other pack horse, which was a beautiful black and white
paint. The Indians had no doubt spotted them before
we had met them and had gone under the banks of the
Pecos and hid until they went into camp and some time
during the night went after their horses, knowing that
they had four and only finding the one staked and seeing
the trail of our three horses naturally supposed that it
was the other three belonging to the cattlemen going on
the back track, which they followed and ran into us just
at daybreak. It was misting rain when we got up to
make a fire next morning and we had rolled our shooting-
irons in our bed to keep them dry and we did not see the
Indians until they were very close to us, nor could they
see us until they reached the top of the butte. We saw
each other about the same time and they fired only one
shot with a carbine and ran back towards the Pecos.
When I got my gun they were one hundred and fifty
yards away and I fired four shots, wounding one horse
and killed one Indian and wounding one. They changed
their course, going south down the river a half a mile,
then turned east and went up on another butte about
three-quarters of a mile from us and buried the dead
Indian, then went north parallel to the river and crossed
it next day where they were seen by a cowman. We then
made coffee and packed up and were about to leave when
Nath Underwood rode into camp on their trail. I told
him about seeing them with his paint horse. Two Indians
were riding him. There were seven Indians and four
horses, three horses carrying double. (Nath Underwood
now lives in San Antonio and I had the pleasure of meet-

ing him at the Old Trail Drivers' Convention in November, 1921.)   Next day we got to Pearce and Paxton's camp and got enough "chuck" to last us to Seven Rivers. After resting our horses a few days, Mr. Paxton wanted me to locate land at Rattlesnake Springs, near the Guadalupe Mountains and he and I went to see it, leaving Tom Swilling in camp with the others whose names I do not remember. We pulled out early in the morning, crossed the Pecos, then on up Delaware Creek, on which we nooned, then went on to Rattlesnake Springs, only to find it in possession of other parties, three Jones brothers, with whom we spent the night, and started back next morning. At noon we camped in the deep bed of the creek and while there we heard a racket and in peeping over the bank we saw ten Indians driving about twenty-five horses about fifty yards distant right on the trail. The loose herds ahead had obliterated our trail, but they were liable to see it any time and return to investigate. When he got back to Paxton's camp that night we found all well, but next day one of the Jones boys came to camp and reported that the Indians had passed their ranch just at night and next day they were afraid we had been killed and came to investigate. Tom Swilling and I continued our journey to Seven Rivers (Beckwith's ranch) where we met John Slaughter's outfit returning from a cattle drive up in New Mexico. When we arrived at South Spring, the headquarters ranch of John S. Chisum, we camped on the ground where the Slaughter outfit had camped a few days before and saw where a Texas cowboy had been shot from his horse by one of Slaughter's men as he rode into their camp, his congealed blood lying in a pool on the ground where he fell and died. His name was Barney Gallagher, and I knew him at Carrizo Springs in Dimmit county. He was generally known as "Buckshot," a typical cowboy character of those frontier days.

Chisum was putting up two herds of cattle when we

arrived and we went to work gathering a mixed herd for Nebraska and one of wild old "moss-horns" for the Indian reservation at San Carlos, Arizona, John Chisum having the contract to furnish the Government beef for over seven thousand Indians on this and its sub-agencies. While working the range, which included all the country from Anton Chico on the north to Seven Rivers on the south and the White Mountains on the west to the Canadian on the east, which John Chisum claimed as his range and over which grazed approximately 100,000 head of John Chisum's "rail" brand and "Jingle-bob" ear marked cattle, we had some tough work and adventures. Two men were tried by "Judge Lynch" and executed; one at Bosque Grande ranch, for murder and hung, and one near Narvo's Ben Crossing while bringing a herd down the river to Headquarters ranch, for murder and shot. Both of these were for cold-blooded murder which was witnessed by other cowboys who immediately arrested, tried, convicted and executed the murderers, and went on with their work as if nothing of so grim a nature had just happened. The law of the range was "forget it" for discussions were likely to lead to trouble. In those days, cowboy law was enforced and every cowboy knew it, and I never knew of the subject again brought up around the campfire. After the Nebraska herd had been gathered, cut and road-branded it took the trail via Trinidad, Colorado, with Si Funk in charge, and in about a week we were ready to hit the trail for Arizona with 4,000 head of wild "moss-horn" steers and 150 head of horses, including the wagon, teams and some private stock belonging to the boys.

It was now November and the weather was getting very cold. We had, as near as I can recall, twenty regular men in the outfit, the "big boss," "Big Jim," the negro cook and the secretary; our night reliefs of four men three hours each and one man on relief three hours with the remuda. The men had running guard relief and sometimes were justified in reducing the force on relief and at other times reinforcing it according to the fore-seen danger of Indians, trail robbers, or weather stam-pedes.

We camped one bitter cold, sleety night on the summit of the White Mountains and were to pass through the Mescalero Indian reservation next morning. We had grazed our herd that day in the mountains where the grass was good and protected from the snow that had fallen heavy the day before and the previous night, and we thought that they would bed easily, but they were restless and wanted to drift, which necessitated putting on double guard and bunching the remuda under close guard, for we believed the Indians would try to stampede both cattle and horses as they were mad at Chisum's men, who had killed some of them the previous year on the reservation. Every man not on duty that night had his horse saddled and tied up, as Chisum told us on the trail that ever since the Indians had been located on the Tularosa, through which his cattle trail led, that as toll, they would cut twenty head of the best beeves each trip, and they do the cutting themselves and they would not take "drags." Every man in the outfit except "Old John" and old man Northrup, his private secretary, had a pow-wow and made "big medicine" and did not intend to let "big Injun" have any beef on this trip. There were with us 21 well armed men, with the cook, and over one thousand fighting Apache "bucks" five miles ahead of us, whom we had to encounter manana, unless we submitted to their insolence. We knew Chisum's men just a year before had ridden into the reservation after stolen stock and on getting no satisfaction from Godfroy, the agent, they attempted to drive the stock away and were attacked by the Indians and some of the Indians were killed and all driven into Ft. Stanton; that now they were not on Government reservation, having left it after the cowboy raid above mentioned and took refuge along the

brakes of the Tularosa and Lost Rivers on the west side
of the White mountain, therefore had no right to demand
toll and we believed they would not attack us if we refused
their demand for beef, we resolved to refuse and fight
if it became necessary. At 3 a. m. the cook was roused
and told to "rustle chuck." We were not long in getting
on the outside of some hot coffee, "pone" and "sow-
belly" and at daylight every man was in his saddle at
the herd. The remuda was now thrown in the herd and
we were looking for "Old John" to come and start the
cattle, when old "Solomon," the Mescalero chief, and
twenty painted warriors, well mounted and armed, came
towards us. Frank Baker (afterwards killed by Billy
the Kid) and I rode out and met him and he not seeing
Chisum whom he knew, ignored us and attempted to pass.
I signaled him to halt and with a scowl on his face he
said "Captain Cheese-om? Queremos baka-shee," (all
the Apaches called beef or meat baka-she, pronounced
bah-cah-she. The northern Indians called it wo-ha). I
replied "yo soy captain; ninguna bakashee por usted.
(I am captain; no beef for you.)" My back being turned
to the wagon, I did not see Chisum leave camp, but one
of the boys rode up and informed me and I signaled the
chief to remain where he was. I rode back to meet Mr.
Chisum. He was very angry and wanted to go to the
chief and I asked him not to interfere and to go back.
I called Bill Henry who was near by and told him to
tell the boys if they saw Mr. Chisum and me ride back
to the chief to surround the Indians and if I fired
a shot not to let an Indian escape nor an Indian
horse get back to the agency; that if Mr. Chisum
interfered I would shoot the chief. Henry went off in
a gallop and "Old John" being thoroughly convinced by
this time, turned his horse and started back to the wagon,
which had gone up close to the herd. I returned to the
chief who sat on his horse with a sullen look on his face
and I pointing in the direction of the reservation said,

"vallese bakashee nada." He grunted and offered me his hand which I refused to take, knowing that if I did so every one of his warriors would offer their hands and he and every buck would want to shake hands with every man of us and thus get to the big boss, which I did not want to occur. He wheeled his paint mustang and took the back trail at a fast gait and every buck formed in single file and followed him. We had no more trouble with them and when we got the lead cattle to within a mile of the reservation Frank Baker and I were sent ahead to see that the Indians were kept back so as not to stampede the herd. Godfroy, the agent, had a confab with Solomon, the chief, through the interpreter, who gave orders and our way was cleared. Here I was shown the Indian whom I shot and wounded at Pope's Crossing in September. He was convalescing, but as poor as a snake, my bullet having struck him in the back, passing through the right nipple. I told him I shot him and killed one and a horse. Several stood by him who said they were there and all seemed pleased to see me and shook hands and asked for "el otro?" (the other man). I told them he was with the herd and they said "bueno," and rode to meet the herd. We watered at Lost River and started over the long trail of sixty miles over the "white desert" to San Augustine Springs, where Shedd's ranch was located. It took us nearly thirty-six hours to reach there with the lead cattle and the tail drags were forty-four hours in getting in. When the lead cattle got to within five miles of San Augustine, they were held back and allowed to go in slow, the drag end was twenty miles behind, which meant a line of cattle twenty miles long. The remuda had been sent in to water and back twelve miles the evening of the second day to enable the line men to change mounts and send their jaded ones to water. This drive was the worst of the whole trip but we did not lose a single head. Chisum said it was the first drive he ever made over it that he did not lose cattle, both from exhaustion and cattle thieves who would cut the line between the riders, who were often necessarily several miles apart, and get away with them as they were never followed on account of scarcity of men. These thieves were generally Mexicans, but sometimes Indians and white men. When we reached the Rio Grande we laid over a couple of days to rest and graze, while some of the boys were sent down the river to Dona Ana and vicinity, to pick up stolen cattle he had previously lost. For some reason or other I was generally made "side boss" on these trips, so taking four men we left early in the morning and began to round up at Dona Ana in the afternoon and we had picked up nearly fifty head, nearly all work oxen, and started back with them when we were followed and attacked by a bunch of Mexicans. We had seen them coming and rode back to a gully where we dismounted. They could see us and came at us on a charge, yelling and shooting. Our first volley scattered them and drove them back. It seems that some soldiers from Ft. Sheldon were with the Mexicans and two of them got hurt or were killed, for the next day an officer and ten men came to us while we were crossing the river to inquire into the occurrence. He was shown the cattle we had brought in, all bearing the same brand and ear-mark as the balance of the herd and informed that they were stolen cattle belonging to Mr. Chisum, with whom he had been conversing. He said that after the fight it had been reported to the post commander that it was cattle thieves who had taken the oxen and the Mexicans had followed to recover them when they were attacked and seven killed and two soldiers badly wounded. The soldiers had no right to be with them, but were courting some Mexican girls and were induced by the Mexicans to go with them, not thinking of having a fight.

I quit the outfit when we reached the San Simon in Arizona, thirty-five miles from our destination, which was Croton Springs, in Sulphur Springs valley, and where I again worked for Chisum in 1878, "circling and signing" and guarding his range from the point of Pinal Mountains on the north to about where Pierce is now on the south, from the Dragoon Mountains on the west, to the Chiricahua Mountains on the east. It would require too much space to relate the incidents that transpired in connection with our lives the short time I worked there, but all will be told in detail in a book I hope to have published in 1924.

In the latter years I served as a special ranger in Companies D and F, Texas Frontier Battalion, and U. S. Deputy Marshal and also deputy sheriff and other official positions on the frontier. This service was from 1881 to 1889. I have met most of the so-called outlaws and bad men who ranged in Texas, New Mexico and Arizona from 1865 to 1890 and never knew but one but what had some good traits about him. On the other hand I have known some so-called good men and officers with some very bad traits about them. I married in San Antonio in 1885 and have two boys and a girl dead and three daughters living. They are, Mrs. William E. Lea, of Sanderson, Texas; Mrs. A. M. Preston who was with her husband in France and Mrs. Robert C. Courtney of Del Rio, Texas. Now at the age of sixty-eight years I am still hale and hearty and square with my fellowmen, but owe much to God for keeping me and mine.

GOT A TAIL-HOLD AND HELD ON

R. F. Galbreath, Devine, Texas

In 1873 I helped to drive the second herd of cattle out of Medina county for Lytle and McDaniel, from Haby's ranch above Castroville to Ellsworth, Kansas. We crossed the Guadalupe at New Braunfels, and went

on by San Marcos, Austin and Fort Worth, crossed Red
River at Red River Station,
and on to Pond Creek, where
the Indians killed a man
named Chambers, who was in
charge of a herd belonging to
Jim Tucker, of Frio county.
I and Jim Neal, Hyge Neal,
C. K. Perkins and others
helped to bury Chambers at
Pond Creek. Then we drove
on up to Russell, Kansas, on
the Smoky River above Ellsworth, and from there I went
with another herd to Chey-

R. F. GALBREATH

enne, Wyoming. We were near Big Spring on the Platte
River when Sam Bass and Joel Collins made the big
haul in a train robbery there. I knew them both well.
Collins and another of the robbers were killed at Buffalo
Station, in Nebraska, and Bass was killed at Round Rock,
Texas.

Our outfit consisted of Bill McBee, Quiller Johnson,
Bill Henson, Jim Berrington, and three negroes. All are
dead now except Bill McBee and myself. Bob Trimble
was our boss. He was killed a few years afterward by
Joe Cordova, who was hanged in Bexar county jail for
murder.

In 1877 I helped to drive a herd to Dodge City, Kansas, for Lytle and McDaniel. James McClusky was our
boss. On that trip I met up with Mack Stewart, who
served ten years in a Mexican prison, and afterward died
near Dallas.

In 1895 I helped to drive a herd from Garza county to
Wyoming for A. J. and F. M. Long of Sweetwater. John
Goggan was our boss.

On the first trip mentioned in this story Quill Johnson, Bill McBee and myself crossed Red River on a ferry

boat. Tony Williams, a negro, was riding a mule, and swam with the cattle to point the herd. The waves were so high Tony was swept off his mule, and we thought he was gone, but in a little while we discovered him holding on to the tail of a big beef steer, and when the steer went up the bank Tony was still holding on and went with him.

THE POET OF THE RANGE

C. C. Walsh of San Angelo, Texas, is known all over the southwest and western parts of Texas as the poet of the range. When he meets a man whose character impresses him he studies the man and the man's character. Idiosyncrasies of his speech, peculiarities of expression, distinguishing facial features—all of these are within the purview of the studies of Col. Walsh, the banker and student of men. Then he writes the man he has studied into a poem and poems he has written will preserve a race of men rapidly passing from the range and from existence.

The West Texas cowman's folk life is a hobby with him. He believes the Texas cowman to be one of the noblest American type. Their brogue, their mannerisms, their ideals and their shortcomings are his study book and he has faithfully incorporated them into poems, one of which follows:

THE OLD "SQUARE DANCE" OF THE WESTERN RANGE

Imagination—onc't I had!
I hain't got none no more.
It wuzn't like we used t' dance
Out on th' old dirt floor—

With cowboys thar in highheeled boots,
   A kickin' up, my law!
While that old fiddle played, I think,
   'Twas "Turkey in th' straw."

That old square dance we used t' see—
   With fiddle er guitar,
Accordeum an' tambourine,
   While folks frum near an' far
Cum driftin' in fur miles around,
   Th' tops of all th' herds,
All laughin', happy, bright an' gay
   An' full o' pleasant words.

The glow of health, an' pride of strength,
   That grace which nature gives,
Unto them rugged boys an' ghels
   Who clost to Nature lives,
Wuz somthin' grand to look upon
   When tha cum on th' floor—
An' danced th' graceful minuet
   Which all seemed to adore.

The old square dance of Airley Days
   Wuz unsuggestive, Bill,
Thar wuz no vulgar stunts pulled off—
   But, like the laughin' rill,
Which flows through pleasaint shady dells,
   An' sparkles in th' sun,
'Mid innercence an' purity,
   Tha danced each merry run.

Bill, sumtimes, when I shet my eyes,
   It all comes back onc't more.
I see ole "Uncle Jimmie" Jones
   A comin' thru th' door.

His violin within its case,
  Which he removes with care;
I see him rosum up his bow
  With artist's skill most rare.

Ole Uncle Jimmie, praise his name,
  An' rest his soul in peace;
Wuz known all over the Western Range;
  His fame shall never cease.
Th' music which he played, I know,
  May have been cor-do-roy;
But it wuz jist th' kind which pleased
  A country ghel an' boy—

His rep-er-tore wuz circumscribed—
  In keepin' with his skill.
But everything he tried to play,
  Wuz done with right good will.
That "Ar-kan-saw-yer Traveler" chune
  Wuld allus head th' list—
No cowboy dance would be complete
  Ef this one chune wuz missed.

It mattered little what tha danc'd—
  The Ole Virginia Reel,
A polka, Schottisch er a waltz—
  It was th' same old spiel.
In sets o' four, in sets o' eight,
  A one-step er a two,
That "Ar-kan-saw-yer" chune wuz play'd
  Th' blessed evening through.

'Mong other chunes were "Money Musk,"
  "My Sailor's on the Sea,"
Er—"The Old Fat Gal," an' "Rye Straw,"
  "The Fisher's Hornpipe"—Gee!

Of course—with "Turkey in the Straw,"
  Er "Bonapart's Retreat,"
Th' "Ole Gray Eagle" soarin' high,
  We got thar with both feet.

Thar also wuz another man
  Who made himself a name
Which may sumtime be posted up—
  Within "Th' Hall of Fame"—
It wuz Ole "Windy Billy" Smith,
  A waitin' with a grin—
"Official caller" at the dance—
  In whom there wuz no sin.

Yuh couldn't call him hansum, Bill
  He wuz no cherum fair,
He had a long beak fur a nose
  With carrot reddish hair,
His eyes wur like two small black beans,
  His mouth was one long slit,
Then he wuz kinder lantern jaw'd,
  An' stuttered quite a bit.

But when he stood up fur t' call
  Th' changes in the dance,
His stutterin' 'ud disappear;
  Th' creases in his pants
Caused by them short bow laigs of his'n
  Wuld make you laff an' grin
Until th' herd commenced to mill!
  As "Windy" would begin.

Th' fiddle now is chunin' up—
  As Jimmy draws his bow;
While he begins to plink and plonk
  Th' folks git in a row.

Then as he plonks and plinks and plunks,
 An' tightens up his strings,
The boys and ghels form into squares
 An' sich delight it brings.

Ole "Uncle Jimmy's" now chuned up—
 He draws his bow at last.
Ole "Windy Billy" takes his stan'
 He'd sail'd before th' mast.
His voice rings out upon th' air
 Like sum clear bugle call,
While all now liss'n fur th' words
 Which opens up th' ball.

"Gents: Hang your hats out on a limb,
 This one thing I demand.
 Honor yer pardners—right an' left."
How pompous his command!
"Heel an' Toe—lock horns with yearlin's.
 Now chase 'em round an' round,
That fiddle's goin' mighty fine—
 Now both feet on the ground."

"Gents to the center—How are you?
 Man! Hear that fiddle play.
Th' ladies do-ce—how de de?
 Now hip! hurrah!! hurray!!!
Right hands across—chase yer squirrels.
 Th' gents will do-ce-do.
Now swing six—when you reach th' line—
 My! see them yearlin's go.

"Do-ce—ladies—Th' 'culls' cut back,
 Just see that 'dogie' trail.
Everybody dance—now you go—
 See that one steer 'turn tail'—

Salute—pardners—promenade all—
  Steve cut th' pigeon wing.
Swing on the corners—mill th' herd.
  'Dock' dance th' Highland Fling.

"Tie yer hats fast to yer saddles,
  Now, ride to beat th' wind.
Every gent salute yer heifer—
  Show how th' baboon grinned
All th' ladies to th' center;
  Cow punchers, stake yer pen—
Play that tune a little louder—
  Now russel 'em like men.

" 'Hog-tie' pardners, swing on corners—
  Swing across—now swing through.
Elbow twist an' double L swing
  Do-ce-do, tight as glue—
All big steers do th' 'buck an' wing,'
  Young steers 'double shuffle'—
Honor pardner—all-a-men left—
  'Big Boy' do that scuffle.

" 'Eight pretty Herefords, form a ring,
  'Slough foot' in th' center.
Twist th' grapevine round his horns—
  Let no Mavericks enter.
All hands up a rarin' to go
  Jake—don't brand that sleeper.
All promenade around th' pen—
  Catch your heifer—keep her.

"Boys —chase that 'rustler' frum th' camp—
  Th' hon'ry 'ball o' hair.'
The ghels all form a ladics chain—
  Of 'Bowleg Pete' take care—

Now then—reverse men—try yer hand,
    Corral 'em in th' trap;
Then swaller fork, an' do-ce-do,
    Uncinch that broken strap—

"Walk th' huckleberry shuffle—
    Do th' Chinese cling—
Long Simpson, lead th' trail herd,
    An' git 'em in a ring—
Gents purr round yer purty pussies.
    Now rope 'em—balance all,
Some dance 'clogs' an' sum dance th' 'Tucker'—
    Ride in an' top th' hall.

"All hands up, an' circle around,
    Don't let th' herd stampede.
Corral 'em on th' open ground
    Then drift 'em in t' feed.
Do-ce, ladies—Salute your gents.
    Lock horns—now—arm in arm—
Start up th' trail—drift—two—two by two—
    Refreshments have their charm."

'Twas thus we'd dance th' night away—
    In those old days of yore—
Sumtimes we'd set a number out
    An' then, our minds 'ud soar
Away out in th' realms o' space—
    Whar smilin' cupids dwell;
Er sumtimes wander near th' brook
    Down in th' moonlight dell.

Then as we wandered, hand in hand—
    Sumtimes our eyes 'ud meet—
We'd feel a twich of th' heart
    Which was so awful sweet—

We culdn't tell you how it felt—
   Fur it jist felt so good,
It culdn't be described to you
   Jist like I wish'd it culd.

Alas! them good ole days air gone—
   Gone air them good ole times—
When "Windy Billy" call'd th' dance
   In good ole-fashioned rhymes.
When dear ole "Uncle Jimmie" Jones
   Sat with his trusty bow,
An' played upon his violin
   Th' chunes which made us glow.

For both ole "Uncle Jimmie" Jones
   An' "Windy Billy" Smith
Have drifted up th' Silent Trail,
   A huntin' fur thair kith—
Which have been losted frum th' herd,
   Upon th' range so wide;
But tha will find 'em I am sure,
   Across th' Great Divide.

I look back on th' yesterday,
   With pleasure an' with pride,
While calling up familiar names
   With whom I used to ride,
In going to a country dance
   With sum sweetheart o' mine,
When—Oh! such pleasant times we had
   In days of "Auld Lang Syne."

JAMES B. GILLETT

Recently there appeared a book, *Six Years With the Texas Rangers,* recounting the experiences of James B. Gillett, Ex-Sergeant of Company A, Frontier Battalion, which should be in every Texas home. James B. Gillett

was born at Austin, Texas, November 4, 1856. He worked
with cattle for several years, and in 1875 he joined Captain Dan W. Roberts' company of rangers at Menardville, and engaged in the work of running down outlaws,
fighting Indians and ridding the border of undesirable
characters for a long time. Mr. Gillett writes interest-
ingly of those early days, and tells of many events that
are found on the pages of history. In his book he graphically describes cowboy and ranger life, gives the names
of his comrades and associates, relates thrilling anecdotes
of battles with Indians and desperadoes, and keeps the
reader interested from start to finish. He served as city
marshal of El Paso for several years when that town was
considered the "toughest" frontier town in the United

JAMES B. GILLETT

States. The lawless element
held full sway there for a
time, killings were of almost
daily occurrence, and it required an iron hand and a
steady nerve to cope with the
situation, but Jim Gillett was
equal to the emergency and
helped to make the Pass City
a decent, respectable place in
which to live.

Mr. Gillett, after so many
years of strenuous duty, during which time he had many
narrow escapes from death, retired from official duty
to accept a position as manager of the Estado Land and
Cattle Company, which owned large ranch interests in
Brewster county. He had previously purchased a small
ranch of his own and had acquired a number of cattle.
He was manager for the Estado Company six years, during which time the herd had increased from six to thirty
thousand head. His own bunch of cattle had also increased to such numbers that demanded his attention,

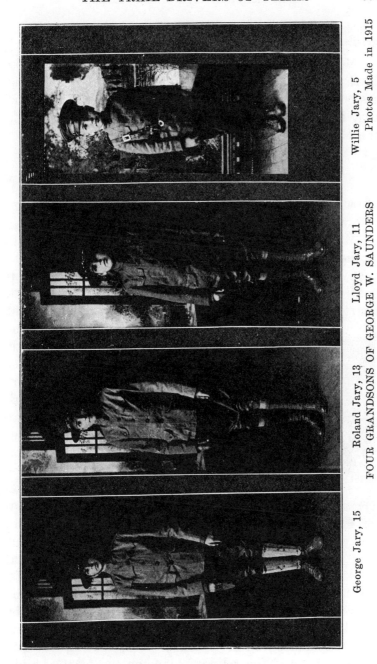

George Jary, 15   Roland Jary, 13   Lloyd Jary, 11   Willie Jary, 5

Photos Made in 1915

FOUR GRANDSONS OF GEORGE W. SAUNDERS

and he resigned to devote his time to his own ranch near Marfa, where he lives today.

Mr. Gillett donated fifty copies of his book, *Six Years With the Texas Rangers,* to the Old Time Trail Drivers' Association to be sold and the proceeds to go to the fund that is being raised for the erection of a monument to the old trail drivers.

A FEW BARS IN THE KEY OF G.

Reading Before the Old Time Trail Drivers' Convention by
Miss Marian Elizabeth Jennings of Devine, Texas

Miss Marian Elizabeth Jennings is a popular favorite at the reunions of the old time cowboys, and she is generally called upon to give readings at the annual conventions. Her renditions are always good and meet with hearty applause because she brings the sentiment right home to her hearers. The following, by Clifton Carlisle Osborne, was recited by Miss Jennings at the 1921 Convention of the Old Time Trail Drivers' Association in San Antonio, and when she had finished many of the Association's members came forward to express their appreciation and tender their congratulations:

MISS JENNINGS

"Two o'clock and time for the third watch on the night herd. Disentangling himself from his damp blankets, John Waring groped for his boots, and unrolling his 'slicker' which had served temporarily as a pillow, he enveloped himself in it and went out in the drizzling rain. For the hundredth time within a week, Waring had condemned himself for relinquishing the comforts of civilization to become a cow-puncher among the rock slopes of Colorado. He wondered if she felt the separation— if she cared. How happy they had been, and how much he still loved her. But the memory of that last day was still too clear in his mind. The words she had spoken in heat of anger had burned themselves into his soul. In hot rage he had come out here to plunge into the perilous life in a vain effort to forget. His thoughts strayed to the strange postal he had received the day previous, and he began to puzzle his mind to decide who sent it, and what it could mean. For the communication was composed not of words, but of music—four measures to the Key of G. He hummed the notes over and over, and they had a strangely familiar sound; he could not place the fragment. Abandoning the riddle as he rode around and around the cattle, he began to sing to pass the time. Suddenly in the midst he stopped short. He was singing the notes on the card. It came to him like a flash. He tore open his coat and drew out the postal. There was no mistake. He had solved the mystery. With a wild shout, he wheeled his horse and rode furiously to the camp, and reached Coberly, the boss, in two bounds.

" 'I must be in Denver tonight,' he said. 'I want your best horse quick. I know it is a hundred and twenty miles to go, but it is only sixty to Empire, and I can get the train there. It leaves at one o'clock, and I can make it if you will lend me Star. I know he is your pet horse and you never let anyone ride him, but I tell you, Mr. Coberly, this means everything to me. I simply must get there tonight.'

"Mr. Coberly scowled. 'You ought to know, Jack, that I won't lend Star, so what's the use of askin'? What in thunder is the matter with you that you are in such a confounded rush?'

"Waring thought for a moment and then, drawing the boss beyond earshot, spoke to him earnestly, finally

handing him the postal card. Coberly scanned it in-
tently and a change came over his face. 'Why didn't
you show me this at first? Of course you can have the
horse. Hey there, some of you boys! Round up the
horses and rope Star for Mr. Waring. Jump lively
now!'

*   *   *   *   *   *

"Eight o'clock found twenty-three miles behind Star's
nimble feet, and the Bar Triangle Ranch in sight. It
lacked twenty minutes to ten o'clock when Waring drew
rein at the foot of the great divide, the railroad station
still fifteen miles away. He unsaddled Star and turned
him into a corral for an hour's rest to put new life into
him. At a quarter past ten Star, refreshed by rubbing
and water, was carrying him up the road. Up, up, they
went, mile after mile, towards the snowy summit of the
pass. Two miles from the top Waring dismounted and
led his panting horse along the icy trail. He still had
twelve miles to go, seven of which were down the steep-
est road in the state. Could he make it? He must. He
stopped and anxiously examined his horse. He had
plenty of life and energy yet. Waring was again in the
saddle and racing down the dangerous path. Almost
sitting on his haunches, Star would fairly slide down the
hill, and recover his footing at the bottom. At last they
came to a level road. A horseman approached and
whipped out a six-shooter. 'Hold up there. I want to
talk to you. I'm the sheriff and I want to know what
you're doing with Joe Coberly's horse.'

" 'Why, I've been working for Coberly, and he lent me
the horse to ride over here and catch the train.'

" 'Hold on there, young man; that air won't do at all.
I know old Joe, and I know he wouldn't lend that horse
to his own brother, let alone one of his cow-punchers. I
guess I'll have to lock you up till the boys come over.'

" 'Look here, Mr. Sheriff, I'm telling you God's truth.
Coberly let me take the horse because it was the only one

that would get me over here in time to catch the train. Look at this postal. That is my reason for haste.'

"As the officer read the card his face lighted up. 'That's all right, youngster. Sorry I stopped you. I don't wonder Joe lent you the horse. I hope you won't miss the train.'

"Waring rode forward, the town before him a half mile distant. The train was at the station. The black smoke began to come in heavy puffs from the engine. A quarter of a mile yet to go. The line of cars moved slowly from the station. Then Star showed the spirit that was in him. He bounded forward and swept down on the town like a whirlwind. Thirty feet—twenty feet —ten feet—he was abreast of the platform. Swerving the flying horse close to the track, Waring leaned over and grasped the railing with both hands, lifted himself from the saddle and swung over to the steps of the car. After congratulations of the passengers, Waring dropped into a seat and was soon lost in thought. Suddenly he remembered he had left his money in the bundle attached to Star's saddle. There was nothing to do but throw himself on the mercy of the conductor. He whispered in his ear and showed him the postal, and the conductor's expression softened. 'I reckon I'll have to fix it for you by paying your fare myself and you can send me the money.'

"The car wheels were still turning when Waring strode through the station at Denver. Jumping into a carriage he was driven to the nearest drug store where he consulted the directory. 'Number 900 S. 17th Street,' he cried. Arriving there, he sprang up the steps. The butler ushered him into Mr. Foster's presence. 'Mr. Foster, you are the president of the Denver National Bank which handles the Western interests of the Second National Bank of Boston. I have an account at the Second and want you to cash a check for me. It is after banking hours I know, and even if it were not, I have no immediate means of identification. It is of the greatest importance that I make the Eastern express tonight or I would not come to you in this irregular way.'

" 'It must be an urgent matter that requires such haste. Really, Waring, I must positively decline to do anything for you.'

"Then Waring told of the card. The banker said: 'Let me see it. From what was it taken, did you say?' Hearing the answer, a bulky musical score was laid upon the table before him, and turning the pages carefully he compared the music on the card with that of the printed sheet. Then he said in a kindly voice: 'I will assist you, Mr. Waring. It will, of course, be a purely personal accommodation; I cannot resist such an appeal as this. What amount do you require?'

" 'A hundred dollars.'

"The banker wrote a check for a hundred and fifty, saying, 'You can cash this at the Brown Palace Hotel. I envy you with all my heart. You have my best wishes for a pleasant journey. Goodby.'

"Waring ran down the steps with a light heart. 'Telegraph office,' he shouted. Ten minutes later these words were speeding over the wire:

" 'Postal received. Arrive Boston Friday night. See Luke 1:13.—Jack.'

"When the Chicago Limited pulled out of Denver that evening, John Tarbot Waring was standing on the rear platform, humming a fragment from the great oratorio, 'The Messiah.' There was a tender look in his eyes as he gazed at the postal card and the words he sang were:

" 'For unto us a child is born,
" 'Unto us a son is given.'

"At the same moment, two thousand miles away in the East a young wife was holding a telegram close to her lips. Turning softly on her pillow she glanced lovingly at the dainty cradle, and whispered as she glanced at her open Bible:

"Thou shalt call his name John."

THE MORRIS FAMILY

G. W. MORRIS and his manly sons, of Devine, Texas, who are: G. C. Morris, T. H. Morris, G. W. Morris, Jr., J. E. Morris, L. C. Morris. There are also two girls in the family, Misses Pearl and Minnie Morris, and two sets of twins

ONE TRIP UP THE TRAIL

B. D. Lindsey, San Antonio, Texas

I was born in Union Parish, La., January 21, 1856, and came to Texas when I was 17 years old, with my uncle, who located near Waco. I assisted him on the farm for awhile, then went south intending to become a cowboy. I had bunked with Ad Lindsey that winter, and he had been "up the trail" and I had caught the fever from him. In the early days of February, 1874, in company with Neally Cone and Bill Foster, I left Waco and traveled south on the Austin road. We had provided ourselves with a good supply of brandy peaches, a concoction sold in those days. That evening late we landed at the Westbrook ranch on Cow Bayou. Mrs. Westbrook kindly consented for us to stay overnight and directed us to the barn. Just about that time Mr. Westbrook appeared on the scene. I shall never forget him. He was a small sized man, wiry, spare build, about 30 years of age. With a firm look in his eye and a steady voice he said. "Boys, I see that you are drinking and I had rather you would ride on." We did. We crossed over the bayou and stayed over night. The next night we stayed with a Swede farmer six miles north of Austin. There were very few houses along the road in those days. We reached Austin the next day, remaining there only a few hours, then pulled on for San Marcos. When we got to the Blanco River our money was getting scarce so we sought employment. My first job was planting corn two days for Billie Owens, who now lives at Sabinal, Texas. My next work was for a Mr. Cochran, who owned a farm on the cattle trail. He paid me 75c. per day. Herds were passing daily, and one rainy day I saddled my horse and drifted with a passing herd. In conversation with one of the boys he asked me if I had ever been up the trail, and when I informed him that I had not, he said I should claim that I had as I would be paid better wages. I kept this information for future use, and when I learned that a herd was being gathered in the neighborhood, to be in charge of Sam Driskill, I made up my mind to go with that herd. I hailed Mr. Driskill as he was passing one day and asked him for a job. The first question he fired at me was, "Have you ever been up the trail?" "Yep" I replied, right off the reel. Two days later he sent for me and put me and Eberly Peters, who now lives at San Marcos, herding about 400 mixed cattle. We were both green hands, but we came in with all the cattle for two days. We held them bunched as though they were in a corral. The third day we moved out to the Perry Day ranch, near where the town of Kyle is now situated. When we stopped at noon my troubles began. I was left in company with wiser ones, and my idea was to not let any get away, so I kept butting them in. John Rutledge, one of the boys, cussed me for being a fool, and proceeded to give me my first lesson in handling cattle. When I went to the chuck wagon Pres Horton, a typical cow-puncher, constituted himself a court of inquiry and began plying me with questions. He asked me if I had ever been up the trail, and who I drove for. I told him I went up the trail the year before, and drove for Chisholm. I had the idea that Chisholm owned all the cattle in Texas. Then Horton asked me where I drove to, and I told him Wichita. Next he asked me where I crossed the Brazos, and I said Fort Graham, and that I crossed the Red River at Red River Station. When he wanted to know what river Wichita was located on, I had to study for a moment, then said "Arkansas." By this time I was growing nervous. He was also stumped, for he could not figure out how it was that I was so well posted. The fact of the matter is Ad Lindsey, who had been over the route, had told me these things, and I had not forgotten. For a little while Horton let up on me, but finally came back with the question: "Where does the bridge cross the river at Wichita?" This was a stunner, but I said, "Kinder toward the lower edge of town." He had me, as there was no bridge there at that time. Of course, I thought it was back to the farm for me, but Sam Driskill, the boss, who had heard the whole discussion, came to my rescue and said, "Kid, I had discovered you were a green hand in this business, but I see you are willing, and I had rather have one willing hand than one too lazy to perform his duties." I was much relieved and right there I determined to give the best service I was capable of giving. We remained at the Day ranch about two weeks, and then moved on to the Baggett ranch, near where Temple is now, for our next and last stop. We completed our herd there and started on our long journey. Jess Driskill and Dock Day were the owners of the herd. Jess Driskill built the Driskill Hotel at Austin.

An incident occurred at the Baggett ranch, which while a little personal, I think is worthy of mention, as it will show how green and foolish I was. A down-

easter, whose name I have forgotten, had been employed.
He was about thirty years old and weighed 230 pounds.
Aside from being a greenhorn he was really too heavy
for trail work, and the bunch wanted to get rid of him,
and set about to do this very thing, while I was made
the "goat." The boys began to carry news to him of
talks I had made about him, and from him they brought
yarns to me. Of course neither of us had said anything
about the other. We all carried the old style cap-and-
ball navy pistols, as was the custom in those days. One
evening while I was holding the cattle, the evening relief
came out and this big 230-pounder made straight toward
me, saying that I had talked about him long enough and
he was going to put a stop to it. I had been told by the
other boys that the trouble was coming, and to open up
on him when it started, which I proceeded to do. I shot
at him six times as he was coming toward me, aiming
at his paunch, but he did not fall. Now mind you, the
boys had previously extracted the bullets from my pistol, and I was shooting only wads, but I did not know it.
The wads set his clothing afire, and also the sage grass,
and it took us several hours to put out the prairie fire.
The "wounded" man ran off, left his horse, went to
camp, got his time, and quit, just what the bunch wanted
him to do. The boys told me that I would be arrested
when we got to Fort Worth, and advised me to go to
the boss and get a horse and leave the herd, scout along
in the neighborhood for a few days, and fall in again.
I took it all in like a sucker, until I asked Sam Driskill
for the horse. Sam told me then it was all a put-up job,
and to pay no attention to them. From that time on I
got along very well. When we arrived at Hayes, Kansas, 500 beeves were cut out and left there or driven to
Ellsworth and held for a time. John Driskill was left
in charge of the beeves. He now lives at Sabinal, Texas.
There were twenty-three men in our outfit, but I can
remember only the following: Orland Driskill, Sam Dris-

kill, Dallas Driskill, Tol Driskill, Pres Horton, Charlie
Raymond, Eberly Peters, John Rutledge, Tom Evans,
Mills, one of the cooks, and Bill Hicks, my guard mate.

Near Fort Hayes we rested up on the Smoky River
two weeks. A storm there stampeded our cattle and
they mixed up with six or seven herds camped there at
that time, and it took us several days to separate them.
We traveled a northwest course from Hayes to Platte
River below Fort Sidney, and went to a point about forty
miles this side of Cheyenne, Wyoming, and on to the
Snyder Ranch near the foot of the Black Hills, where we
delivered the cattle to the new owners. I was offered
employment on this ranch at $40 per month, with the
privilege of investing my savings, but that country was
too cold for me. I was told the snow remained on the
ground seven months in the year. Some of us came
back to Ellsworth, Kansas, where I helped John Driskill
hold beeves for a month, then I took train for Texas,
well satisfied that I had enough trail driving. While
this is the only trip I ever made up the trail, I have seen
much of the old trail drivers, and my hat is off to them.
A truer type of manhood never existed in this or any
other country. I now live at 3020 West Commerce St.,
San Antonio, Texas, where I own a comfortable home.
I married Miss Ella Michell of Uvalde, November 8, 1888,
and we have four children living. Our oldest child died
August 8, 1912.

NO FRIENDS LIKE THE OLD TRAIL DRIVERS

G. M. Carson, Rocksprings, Texas

I was raised in Blanco county, Texas. My father,
John Carson and Mary Jane, my good Christian mother,
who have long since gone to their reward, moved from
Mississippi in the early 50's and they settled in East
Texas for a few years, then moved to Blanco county,

and settled a ranch about four miles east of Blanco City, on the Blanco River, with a small bunch of horses and

G. M. CARSON

cattle. In 1861, father joined the Confederate army and when he returned in 1865, broke and no market for cattle until 1870, he sold 200 aged steers to Tom Johnson. His ranch and branding pens were where the town of Johnson City now stands.

Father went up the trail with this herd to Abilene, Kansas, in 1878. I went on the trail with one of John R. Blocker's herds. A short sketch of this trip is in the first volume of the "Trail Drivers of Texas."

I moved with my family from the old home town in 1904 to Rocksprings, Edwards county, where we now live.

There are no friends like
  The old time Trail Drivers,
We greet them when we meet them,
  As roses greet the dew,
No other friends are dearer
  Though born of kindred mould,
And while we prize the new ones
  We treasure more the old.

There are no friends like
  The old time Trail Drivers
In lands beyond the ocean
  Or near the bounds of home,
And when they smile to gladden
  Or sometimes frown to guide
We fondly wish these old friends
  Were always by our side.

There are no friends like
   The old time Trail Drivers,
To help us with the load
   That all must bear that journey
O'er life's uneven road
   The weary hours invest
The kindly words of Old Trail Drivers
   Are always found the best.

There are no friends like
   The old time Trail Drivers
To calm our frequent fears,
   Through life's declining years
And when our faltering footsteps
   Approach the Great Divide,
We'll long to meet the Old Trail Drivers
   Who wait on the other side.

DOCK BURRIS WAS WELL KNOWN

The following article was written by J. B. Polly of Floresville, Texas, and published in the San Antonio *Express,* July 17, 1910:

The old settler of Karnes county that did not know Dock Burris was himself unknown. As a cowboy, Texas Ranger and soldier in the Confederate Army, none was ever more expert, adventurous and gallant. The bronco he could not ride and tame was never foaled, the cow or steer he could not rope and tie down never roamed the prairies of West Texas, and the Yankee soldier that, given any chance at all he could not outwit, never drew a bounty during the war, nor has drawn a pension since. Mr. Burris related the following incidents in his career:

"I was born on Galveston Island on August 24, 1840. In 1855, desirous of seeing more of life than I could while surrounded by salt water, I went to Karnes county and found employment as a cowboy. I continued in that business without let-up until the fall of 1858, and during the time thus engaged, hunted cattle and horses with and for almost all the old settlers west of San Antonio River. Among them, I remember, were Munroe Choate, John Pascal, John Talk, Capt. John Tom, Billie Ricks, Pat Rose, Walker Baylor, Bill Bishop, John W. Baylor, W. G. Butler and many others. In the fall of 1858, and until the next fall, I drove a freight wagon for Levy Watts between Indianola and San Antonio.

"In October, 1859, I enlisted in Capt. Bill Tobin's company of Rangers, which was organized for service on the Rio Grande, where the notorious Cortina had inaugurated a small war of his own against the Americans living west of the Nueces River, under the claim that all the country between the Rio Grande and the Nueces belonged of right to Mexico. I enlisted with John Littleton, who was recruiting for Tobin's company, and became one of its lieutenants. Tobin and the larger part of his company went on ahead and we recruits overtook him at Banquette. Thence we started on a forced march to Brownsville, but some of our horses gave out and we had to stop at King's ranch to exchange them for fresh animals.

"I was with the advance scouts when we arrived at Brownsville, about 12 o'clock on the night of the third day's march from King's ranch. I remember that we were fired into by the Mexican guards stationed on the Matamoras side of the Rio Grande. In the reminiscences of Capt. J. T. Hunter he fails to mention a number of incidents that occurred during the campaign. One of these was the capture by members of Capt. Pete Tumlinson's company of a notorious Mexican bandit and adventurer known as One-eyed Trevino. This scoundrel was given but a short shrift and was hanged. Another was the capture of a Mexican at Los Cuevos. As his captors were not prepared to hang this man, he was tied hand and foot, and thrown into the river and given a free swim down to its mouth. But he was not a good swimmer, and a few days later his body was found lodged against a boat. Another Mexican who was captured at the fight of Rancho Davis stepped into the Great Beyond from the back of Capt. Tumlinson's saddle horse, and a fourth one was hanged from a large root that projected from a bluff bank out over the waters of the Rio Grande. Each one of these men richly deserved the fate that befell him, for there was not a crime of which one or the other had not been guilty.

"Captain Hunter also failed to mention a fight that took place at Mule Shoe Bend, when Cortina and his men tried to capture a steamboat laden with gold and silver, whose passage down the river the Rangers were protecting. The Greasers were stationed in a jacal surrounded by a picket fence and were so busy watching the boat that they did not know until it was too late that Tumlinson had led a part of his company over into Mexico and was coming up in their rear. Tumlinson whipped them to a finish, drove them into flight and captured all their horses, as well as their supplies of ammunition and provisions. Such terror, indeed, did Tumlinson's men inspire in the minds of the Mexicans there that they never rallied again, and always afterwards spoke of the Americans as being 'muy diablos.' I was lucky enough to take part in that fight, having been, a few days before, transferred to Tumlinson's company, in which I had a brother, J. B. Burris.

"After this fight I went home on furlough and while I was away the company was disbanded. The first I knew of its disbandment was when on my way back to rejoin it I met the boys returning to their homes. Never having been mustered out myself and never from that day to this have I received any pay from the state for my services, I still claim to be a Ranger.

"In 1861 I joined a company of cavalry that was or-

ganized in Gonzales county by Mark Evans and which
later became Company C of the Terry Rangers, or
Eighth Texas Cavalry. We were mustered into the Confederate service at Houston with the understanding that
we were going to Virginia. Upon our arrival at New
Orleans, though, our colonel received orders to report at
Bowling Green, Ky., to Gen. Albert Sidney Johnston.
In accounts they have published of their experiences
during the war quite a number of my Ranger comrades
placed themselves under a fire from which it seemed impossible for them to escape alive and unhurt. I was in
many such places and I should wonder now that I escaped alive were it not that I am just enough of a hard-
shell Baptist to believe in predestination. That doctrine
comforted me mightily during the war; that there was
virtue in it is shown by the fact that often as I faced
danger and its close companion, death, I was wounded
but once, and then received only a flesh wound. That
was at Murfreesboro. My first experience under fire was
at Woolsonville, Ky., and then in due order came Shiloh,
Perrysville, Murfreesboro and Chickamauga. When
Captain Shannon was given command of a company of
scouts I was a member of it.

"One of my Ranger comrades, telling of how Forrest
captured Murfreesboro, says there was no Federal cavalry engaged. He was either sadly mistaken, or my distinct recollection of capturing that morning in a tent
where they lay asleep nine cavalrymen and all their arms,
is a mere dream. They surrendered the moment I threw
my gun down on them. Why my comrade did not see
the cavalry I cannot understand. The first camp we
went into was a cavalry camp. To one of the Yankees
captured that morning I was afterwards indebted, I
think for my life. Very shortly after Shannon's scouts
had captured three negroes and two Yankees and were
in the act of plundering a house and after killing the
five of them, had placed their bodies in a pile with the

negroes on top of the two Yankees, I was captured and placed under guard in a prison pen in North Carolina. When it was learned that I belonged to Shannon's scouts the Federals guarding the pen, taking it for granted that I was concerned in the punishment of the five men, determined to take me out and hang me. But when they came for me the Yankee we had captured at Murfreesboro interposed, saying that he would shoot the first man that laid hands on me and that he had been captured by the Rangers at Murfreesboro and had been treated kindly. It was only this man's courage that saved me.

"When General Bragg marched his army through Kentucky, Wild Aaron Burleson and I were one day on picket together at a point about six miles from Green River. Between sunset and dark the Yankees rode up on us, fired a few shots at us and retreated in the direction of Louisville. Next morning Captain Shannon sent the two of us on a scout to locate the Yankees. We rode six or seven miles without coming in sight of the enemy and finally down to a bridge across Green River that the Yankees had burned down. Just beyond the bridge they had planted a Federal flag and Aaron and I resolved to get that flag. Hitching our horses we swam the river, and pulling down the flag, brought it back to our horses and started to make our report to Captain Shannon that no Yankees were in sight.

"We had gone but a short distance when we met an old gentleman, a citizen, who not only showed us a place where we could easily ford the river, but also told us that there was a sutler's store on the other side of the river a short distance below the bridge. Needing clothing and a whole lot of other things, too badly to object to buying them from a Yankee sutler, Aaron and I lost no time in showing up at the store. Hitching our horses, we entered and commenced buying and quite soon had each bought so many things that we needed saddle bags to carry them in. These being in stock, we each bought

a pair, stuffed our plunder in them, and hanging them
across our saddles, came back to settle our bills. Of
course we had no money except Confederate, and when
we offered that to the sutler, he no sooner looked at it
than he handed it back to us, saying it was no good.
'Well,' said Aaron, pocketing the wad returned to him,
an example which I immediately followed, 'that is too
good money for us to refuse, and as we have no other
kind, all we can do is to thank you for the goods we
have,' and off we rode, each pair of saddle bags packed
so full that we could hardly find room in our saddle for
ourselves.

"When Rosecrans' army was advancing on Murfreesboro, Col. Tom Harrison sent me and Wild Aaron
Burleson to the extreme left of our skirmish lines. We
found the Yankees forming in line of battle to come in
on our left and, thinking to stay them awhile, we dismounted, tied our horses behind a hill and went forward.
Getting within easy range of the Yanks, I dropped down
behind a stump about fifty steps to the left of the one
Aaron had pre-empted, and both of us began firing as
fast as we could. Aaron's position proved too exposed
for comfort and he changed it, without notifying me of
his intention to do so. In fact, it was some little time
after he left me before I discovered that I was fighting
all by myself and without any support. I fired in all
about twenty rounds at them while they were getting
into line, and I kept up my fire until they were within
twenty steps of me, coming at full charge. Then I broke
for my horse, mounted him, I might say, while still running, and ran as fast as he did when once on him, for
the Yanks by this time were on each side of me and
behind me—those behind shooting at me and those on
either side calling on me to surrender and trying to knock
me out of the saddle with their long sabers, but not
shooting lest they fire into each other. But as both my
steed and myself combined our efforts, we soon forged

to the front and outran them. Just at that moment, though, that I got out of the range of small arms they turned a cannon or two loose on me, and a shell struck a mudhole off to my left and spattered mud and water all over me. Before that my horse and I must have been making at least forty miles an hour, but when that mudhole was torn up by the roots and flung at us and over us we turned on enough power to carry us at the rate of a mile a minute.

"In Middle Tennessee one day, while I and six others were tearing up a railroad, an old citizen rode up and informed us that a fellow would soon come along riding in a buggy with a lady, who, although dressed in citizen's clothes, was really a Yankee soldier. It was hard lines on him to be taken from the company of his handsome companion, and he pleaded hard not to be and when we insisted he got mighty mad about it. Three years later, down in North Carolina, he was one of the Federals who captured me, he himself taking the butcher-knife I carried in my bootleg from me and saying to me, 'One of you rangers took my coat off my back when a lot of you captured me in Middle Tennessee, taking me out of the buggy in which I was riding with a lady, and if I knew you were the man I'd cut your throat with your own knife.' Naturally I did not care to acknowledge just then that I was even with the party that captured him and, as I kept my face turned away from him, he did not recognize me as spokesman of the party.'

"While we were around Rome, Ga., a party of Yankees were out a mile or so from town trying to round up a bunch of cattle. To catch them, Captain Shannon left me and Bill Lynch at one end of a lane while he went around to the other. As the Yankees entered the lane Bill and I charged them, our object being to drive them into Shannon's clutches. But they did not drive. Instead they turned on us and shot Bill Lynch off his horse and left me for a minute or more not only alone but considerably demoralized. Luckily, though, Shannon heard the firing and came down the lane upon the Yankees. I was mighty glad he came, but while the fight lasted I was in as much danger from his bullets as from those of the enemy, and it was a wonder that I was not killed by one of them. One of the Yankees dismounted to let down the fence on one side of the lane and through the gap his comrades all escaped. As for him, I was at his side before he could remount and he surrendered. Bill Lynch owed his life to a gun strap that deflected the bullet.''

Comrade Burris was telling the old vets that gathered at Confederate headquarters in San Antonio about that pony of his and how intelligent he was. His story started a long conversation about horses, during which Buck Gravis told of two cow ponies he used to own— one a dun, the other a bay.

"Why, gentlemen," he said, "when my crowd in the old days had rounded up a herd of cattle and wanted to cut out our own from the herd all I had to do was to read a list of brands we wanted to that dun pony and, durn me, if he wouldn't go into that herd and cut 'em out without a bit of help. He would drive 'em out of the main herd and that bay pony would take charge of them and hold 'em out."

"Yes," said Comrade Briscoe, "it was really astonishing how sensible and trustworthy some of those old-time cow ponies were. When I used to live down below Goliad my cattle got in the habit of crossing to the west side of the San Antonio River and mixing with Tom O'Connor's cattle. But I had no trouble in getting them back whenever I wanted to. All I had to do was to lead a little brown, gotch-eared pony that I owned across the stream and, turning him loose, saying 'Seek 'em Gotch, Seek 'em!' and he'd trot away and pick out my cattle by the flesh marks and drive them one by one to the place where I and a lot of lads were waiting to hold them in the herd. And something more singular than that was that after Gotch had done this about three times my cattle would no sooner catch sight of him trotting around over the prairie and looking like he meant business than, as if by one accord, they would detach themselves from the bunches with which they were grazing and come lowing toward the herding place. As it was only when we turned Gotch loose that they did this, I am satisfied every one of them felt it was no use to try to sneak away from him.''

''I never had a cow pony as intelligent as either of those you fellows have told about,'' said Hart Mussey, ''but I did have a smart dog when I was ranching on the Pecos. One morning he went nosing around a steel trap I had set for a wolf and got the end of his tail caught, and what do you reckon he did?''

''Just turned around and bit his tail off,'' suggested Buck Gravis.

''Just pulled up the stake the trap was tied to and dragged it, trap and all, to the ranch,'' suggested Briscoe.

''No sir,'' said Hart, ''he didn't do either of those fool things.''

''What did he do then?'' asked Gravis and Briscoe.

''Why he did what any other sensible dog would have done,'' said Hart. ''He just set up a howl and kept it up until I heard and went out and released the poor brute.''

WAS IN CAPTAIN SANSOM'S COMPANY

J. W. Minear, 140 E. Cincinnati Ave., San Antonio

In 1870 I joined Captain John Sansom's company of Rangers, stationed at Camp Verde, Texas, and in the spring of 1871 we went to Fort Griffin on the Clear Fork of the Brazos, where we were told that 400 colored soldiers had been driven into the fort by Indians only a short time before. After reaching Fort Griffin and resting our horses for a few days we went on a scout for several days, thoroughly combing that region. While in camp on a little creek Frank Kiser was taken ill and Captain Sansom left seven or eight of us to stay with him while the main command continued scouting. They were gone several days and succeeded in killing two Indians. On the lance of one of the fallen braves were six notches, our Tonkaway guides saying that each notch represented a white person that particular Indian had killed. The same dead Indian had a long braid of woman's hair fastened to the top of his head.

The Tonkaway Indians were very superstitious. When Kiser was sick, two of our rangers roped a wolf and brought it into camp. The Indians told Captain Sansom that if we should get into a fight with the Comanches, the men who killed it would be slain in battle. They begged so hard that Captain Sansom prevailed on the men to turn the wolf loose. When the two Indians were killed, the Tonkaways held a council and smoked a pipe, and because the smoke floated in the direction of Fort Griffin they wanted to go home. On the way to the fort we killed some buffalo, I bringing down a bull four or five years old. I killed four others in Kansas.

In 1873 I helped to drive a herd from Bandera to Wichita, Kansas, for Schmidtke & Hay. In the fall of the same year I went with cattle to Creston, Union county, Iowa, and to show how easy it is to drive cattle at times, will state that while camped at Wichita, the boss took several hands to Cow Creek and cut out some cattle to ship, leaving me with 400 head, and saying he would send a man to help me drive them to Sexton's house, twelve miles west of there. I got the herd strung out and by riding up and down the line, got along very well. When I reached a spot where the grass had been burned from the ground they needed no driving. Finally

Henry Fick overtook me and we made it all right. He said the boss got drunk and failed to send me the help promised, so he volunteered to come to my assistance.

While on our way back to Texas, and not far south of Caldwell, Kansas, Frank Jureczki and I, while driving our loose horses, saw two men running a buffalo cow, and I roped her for them. They hauled her home in a wagon, and said they were going to raise buffalo.

AL. N. McFADDIN

Al. N. McFaddin is the owner of 50,000 acres of land near Victoria, Texas, and is a promoter of agricultural prosperity and developer of the State's natural resources. Mr. McFaddin is the eldest son of James Alfred and Margaret E. McFaddin, and was born on a ranch near Galveston. He has lived in Refugio and Victoria counties all of his life, and has devoted his attention to cattle raising a n d agricultural pursuits. He is past-president of the Texas Cattle Raisers' Association, and during his term

AL. N. McFADDIN

of office did valiant work in behalf of general betterment of the cattle raisers' interests throughout Texas. He has been associated prominently with the Texas Sanitary Commission, and gave freely of his best thought and effort in the furtherance of their policies. Mr. McFaddin is an able man, whose work is ably accomplished along lines that devolve in betterment of public and private good.

IRA C. JENNINGS

Of the death of Ira C. Jennings, which occurred December 27, 1922, the San Antonio *Express* in its Cattle Clatter column had the following to say:

"All that was mortal of Ira C. Jennings was laid to rest Friday in the old Humphreys cemetery at Martindale in Caldwell county, and in his passing there is a distinct loss to the ranks of the big cattlemen of Southwest Texas. For twenty years he had ranched in Zapata county, holding extensive acreage and specializing in the raising of cattle, rather than in buying and selling. Always he was the cowman of the family as differentiated from the steer man. Every year he had for sale or to keep a crop of calves. Born in Hayes county, removing to Guadalupe county, where he grew to manhood, he lived for a time at Pearsall, then in La Salle county. From La Salle he went to Zapata. His ranch lay about 30 miles east of Laredo, and in that city he had for years maintained a home, and there he died. For about three years he had been in poor condition following a stroke of paralysis which came up on him while branding calves one hot summer day. He liked to 'run' the brand on the calves himself, and fell in the branding pen with the heated iron in his hand. His condition had become so bad that he was confined to his bed for about three months before the end. In his youth he drove the cattle trail to Kansas, and while passing through the Indian Territory had an adventure with the redskins in which he won by getting more speed out of his horse than the band of pursuers could get out of theirs. He was a member of the Old Trail Drivers' Association, and two years ago was able to attend the meeting in San Antonio, although in failing health. He is survived by his sons, T. C. and Roy, and a daughter, Mrs. J. W. Neal of San Antonio, whose husband is a conductor on the I. & G. N.

Railway. Also he is survived by his two brothers, W. H. and R. H., both well known to all the cattlemen of the country. His wife died in 1911 and he was laid to rest beside her in the country graveyard where his parents and four sisters are buried. W. H. and R. H., the two brothers referred to above, are all that are left of the family of seven children. The great Mystery came upon him at 7:20 P.M., Wednesday, in the 65th year of his age, and those who know him best, say he left none but friends to grieve for him, having no enemy at all. Nothing finer could be said."

A TRIP TO KANSAS IN 1870

W. R. Massengale, Rio Frio, Texas

I went with a drove of 700 big steers, about the first of April. We put the road brand on them at the Strickland ranch, a few miles east of Helena, on the Yorktown road.

The first night it came a little rain and wind and hail and the cattle not being used to herding out we had one of the worst stampedes I was ever in up to this time. We only had a small opening to hold them on and it was very thick brush all over that country so in less than twenty minutes they were cut up in five bunches and running as if they had tin cans tied to their tails. We crossed the San Marcos River below San Marcos town; there we met

W. R. MASSENGALE

with John Campbell. He was bossing a herd for Choate & Bennet, and we camped close together that night. He penned his cattle. We herded out that night and had a bad thunderstorm and hard rain, but we held our "old mossy heads," all right till about one o'clock. It quit raining but the lightning kept up and the whole herd went to grazing and scattered all over the country, so Mr. Drake sent word to all hands to come in and let them alone. W. H. Mayfield was owner of the herd.

Just as we were all getting together a Mexican rode up and asked for Spencer (one of our men). Spencer asked what he wanted and the Mexican told him that his brother, Ran, was dead, so we all turned and went to Campbell's camp. We found Spencer sitting against a tree, his head drooped down just like he was asleep. We got down and took him to a nearby house and laid him out. A young man by the name of Fly had his head on Spencer's legs and was struck also, but did not die until next day.

We crossed just below Austin where we had to rope two and drag them up the bank and roll them off in the river. It was about half bank full. One of them got half way across and turned back, so when he came where we were we turned him back, and I turned my horse over to Vicento Carvajal and got the old scalawag by the tail—well if you never saw an old steer scared in swimming water you have no idea how fast one can swim. After we got our cattle broken in I think we had the best herd on the trail. We had a very good time. At Austin was the last ferry boat so we had to cross all the streams without a boat. At Belton we took the "New Chisum Trail," went by the way of Fort Worth, which was a small village of one or two small business houses, a blacksmith shop and I think a school house and about 20 families. The Indians were bad in that section and we had a double watch on every night which made it hard for us. Some nights the cattle would run the first watch and maybe we would be up all night. I have gone three days and nights without sleep, on the same horse, and with very little to eat.

FROM THE "HISTORIAN OF THE PLAINS"

The following letter was written to George W. Saunders, president of the Old Time Trail Drivers' Association, by William E. Hawks, of Bennington, Vermont. Mr. Hawks is the acknowledged "Historian of the Plains" and is collecting true data of the early days. He says:

"I want to thank you, for myself, and for every old timer who is lucky enough to get a copy of your book,

W. E. HAWKS, "Historian of the Plains"

for staying with the old timers until you got those letters and then having them published. I have spent thirty years gathering true data of the good old days, when men were men, and would offer you everything they had, even to their lives, and they thought it was right. I worked out on the old Overland Stage Coach and Pony Express trail long before Root & Connelly published their book, which is an epic. The Chisholm Trail, the Old Shawnee Trail, Middle or West Shawnee Trail from Red River north to Abilene and Baxter Springs. The Southern Texas Trail extended from Red River to the Coast. Joe McCoy started his yards at Abilene, Kansas, July 1, 1867, and sent W. W. Suggs down to pilot the herds to the new shipping place. The first herd to cross the Nation on that trail was Wheeler, Wilson & Hicks of 2,400 head bound for California. This herd drove within thirty miles of Abilene and stopped and were later shipped from Abilene. The second herd to cross the Nation and drive direct to Abilene was owned by Mr. Thompson, who sold them in the Nation to Smith, McCord & Chandler, and by them driven to Abilene and shipped. The first cattle shipped out of Abilene was on September 5, 1867, and there were 36,000 shipped from that point during the balance of that year.

"The Chisholm Trail is said to be named after a semi-civilized Indian who broke the road for government supplies to go to Fort Cobb from the Arkansas River.

"I have never seen but one of Joe McCoy's books and that is owned by Harvard College. Have been there and read it through several times. It names Wm. Perriman, James Ellison, J. M. Choate, James Daugherty, R. D. Hunter, George R. Baise, Hough-Reeves & Co., John Salisbury, W. H. Kingsbury, Holmsley, Ran Nichols, White, Allen & Co., R. C. White, Hunter, Patterson & Evans, L. M. Hunter, J. B. Hunter, Noffiner & Co., Tom Bigger, W. H. Winants, Noah Ely & Co., D. W. Powers, Joe Tanner, John Hittson, W. K. Shaeffer, G. W. Groves, Pedro Armego, Chas. Goodnight, D. Sheedy, Albert Crane, J. S. Driscoll, H. M. Childress, E. B. Millett, J. J. Myers, J. W. Tucker, Willis McCutcheon, J. H. Stevens, J. D. Reed, Seth Mabry, W. F. Tompkins, J. M. Day, Shanghai Pierce, Jonathan Pearce, J. T. Alexander, Tom Allen, J. S. Smith, Andrew Wilson, J. D. Smith, Rogers, Powers & Co., and others. I have pictures of

Chas. Goodnight, Oliver Loving, J. W. Poe, Pat Garrett, "Billy the Kid," Tom Ketchum, Big Foot Wallace, Wild Bill Hickok, J. S. Chisum, J. B. Dawson, E. B. Bronson, Clark Stocking, Cal Joe, Jim Bridger, Jim Baker, Calamity Jane, and hundreds of others. I gather only true data, and hope to live long enough to publish some of it for the benefit of the old boys who helped to make it possible for the punks to occupy the whole West.

"You can take a hackamore on your arm and you can't find in any place west of the Old Muddy, five people who know what it was used for. The only use I have for the West is the old timers and I don't want to be the last one to go.

"I hope some day to attend one of your old timers' reunions and shake with every man there. I sure know the pleasure of it."

THE TRAIL DRIVERS OF TEXAS

Maude Clark Hough, Chairman Literature Committee,
Texas Club of New York City

In giving you a word that's true
About this book, both fine and new,
I want to say there's more to do,
Than just a simple, short review.

The book itself, is good, well done,
And takes us back where cattle run,
And each day's descending sun
Sees fame, success and virtue won!

The men who helped to build our Texas
And wrote this book, don't mean to vex us,
But answer questions that perplex us,—
How Mexico's tried to annex us.

Here we can see the progress made,
And how their plans were straightly laid,

In order that a hero's shade
Should fall wherever the sunlight played!

Through "Trail Drivers" president,
George W. Saunders, high intent
With much of time and effort spent,
This book was made, and forthwith went

Out to tell the world, and you,
Facts that may be old or new,
But which are absolutely true.
Stories that will help you to

An understanding of their hope,—
To build a monument, so they who grope
In the future, for symbols, trope,
To make more plain all the scope

Of Texas men, and land and lives
Will thereby know that daughters, wives
Had done their share! That Texas thrives
Not alone on gun and knives.

But there dwelt in the heart of each,
A hope both high and hard to reach—
But which the wide prairies teach,
And Texas sunshine lights, "Free Speech."

The book has naught of vain conceit,
Is fine and plain; and I entreat
That no one here will make retreat,
But rise in patriotic heat,

And promise me to buy a book,
To read in some nice shady nook
This summer; or by prattling brook,
While they are seeking fish to hook!

MADE EARLY DRIVES

D. H. Snyder, Georgetown, Texas

My brother, J. W. Snyder, and myself made our first drive of cattle to the Northwest in 1869. We bought our cattle in Llano and Mason counties, and received them on the Llano River above Mason, paying $1.50 per head for yearlings, $2.50 for two-year-olds, $4 for cows and three-year-olds, and $7 for beef steers. We bought all on the credit, giving them our notes payable in gold coin. That country above Mason had plenty of range hogs in it and they were all fat in the spring on the dead cattle that had been killed and skinned for their hides. It was said that thousands of these hides were sold in Mason, Fredericksburg getting the largest share.

We drove from the Llano, where we received our cattle, to the Kickapoo and Lipan Springs and on to head of Main Concho River. Here we laid up two days doing all of our cooking and parching coffee to do us for our trip across the plains, ninety miles to Horsehead Crossing on the Pecos River, without water. This drive we made, driving day and night, in seventy hours. John Chisum was the first to cross the plains on this route in 1868. His herd was all captured by the Indians except seventy head of cripples and tailings, up above where Roswell is now situated. Chisum, John Hitson of Palo Pinto county, Rube Gray and White, his brother-in-law from San Saba county, John and Tom Owens of Williamson county, Martin Cosner of Llano county, and our herd are the only herds I remember crossing that route in 1868, with no settlements of any kind on the route from head of Main Concho to Bosque Grande, the Apache Indian reservation this side of Las Vegas, New Mexico. These Indians were moved from the reservation here to Arizona in the spring of 1868.

We drove on from Horsehead Crossing to Bosque

Grande, Las Vegas and Fort Union, a government post. At Fort Union we sold our beeves at $35. We met Chas. Goodnight and Old Han Curtis between Fort Union, N. M., and Trinidad, Colorado, sold them our yearlings at $7, the balance of the herd at about the same rate without tallying. We then went on to Trinidad and Pueblo, Colo., then went down the Arkansas River to Bent's old fort, Santa Fé, N. M., crossed the Arkansas River, and took the stage to Fort Wallace, then the terminus of the Kansas Pacific R. R., thence by rail to Brenham, Texas, thence by land home, Round Rock, Williamson county, Texas. Here we sold our currency exchange we got for our cattle in Austin for seventy cents on the dollar for gold.

In 1869 we drove a beef herd from Llano county to Abilene, Kansas. I can't recall the name of the Red River crossing at that time. The Indians came on us in the territory and drove off 140 beeves, which the Government paid us for after a long fight. We sold out at Abilene, Kansas.

In 1870 we drove 5,000 head of cattle, the first herds that crossed the Kansas-Pacific R. R., and went on to the Union Pacific at Schuyler, Nebraska, seventy-six miles west of Omaha on the main Platte River.

In 1871 we drove the first cattle on to Cheyenne, Wyoming, and continued to make Cheyenne our headquarters until 1885, our last drive.

In 1872 we sold a herd to John Tierman, Ingram & Co., of Salt Lake, and delivered them on Goose Creek in Nevada.

In 1873 we ranched a part of our drive on the Sobiel near Ft. Loring in Wyoming and also drove 400 head to Idaho and ranched them near old Ft. Hall reservation on Snake River. The market went to the dogs in that country and we sold our stock cattle the next year and drove our beef cattle to Cheyenne and got a fine price for them.

In 1877 I contracted to Mr. J. W. Iliff of Denver, Colo., 17,500 two- and three-year-old steers, which we delivered in June and July, 1878, at Julesburg, Colo. Mr. Iliff died in February, 1878, and at the earnest request of Mrs. Iliff we took charge of the entire cattle business of the estate and wound up the estate part in three years and we bought the business in connection with Mrs. Iliff, D. H. and J. W. Snyder & Company, which we maintained until 1887.

We adopted three rules for our cowboys to be governed by on our first drive in 1868, as follows:

First: You can't drink whiskey and work for us.

Second: You can't play cards and gamble and work for us.

Third: You can't curse and swear in our camps or in our presence and work for us.

These rules we kept inviolate as long as we were in the cattle business.

I am past eighty years old and have been blind more than eight years. If I had my sight I could take time and make this much more interesting and give much more information.

Georgetown, Texas, December 27, 1913.

RATHER CONFUSING

According to George W. Saunders, there was a certain Texas cowboy boarded a train at Denver, Colo., after having driven trail from Texas to that salubrious clime, back in 1880, or thereabouts, says "Cattle Clatter" in San Antonio *Express*. He walked into the sleeper with a bundle of blankets and asked the Pullman conductor if there was any place where he could bed down. The conductor said sure there was; the cowboy could have either upper or lower. The cowboy said any place would do for him, not knowing what was meant by the upper or lower. The conductor continued, saying: "The lower is higher than the upper. The higher price is for the lower. If you want the lower you will have to go higher. We sell the upper lower than the lower. In other words, the higher the lower. Most people don't like the upper, although it is lower on account of its being higher. When you occupy an upper you have to go up to go to bed, and get down when you get up. You can have the lower if you pay higher. The upper is lower than the lower because it is higher. If you are willing to go higher it will be lower.'' When the conductor looked around the cowboy had spread his blankets down in the aisle of the Pullman, using his boots and pistol for a pillow. He ordered the conductor to stop talking, as he did not understand his chin-music anyway. The conductor fell in a faint, the cowboy went to sleep, and Mr. Saunders left the train at the next station—which was a peculiar thing to do, considering the fact that he had no business there.

All manner of persuasion has failed to induce Mr. Saunders to reveal the true identity of the aforementioned cowboy.

JAMES WASHINGTON WALKER

J. W. Walker, who lives on Laxson's Creek, three miles east of Medina, Texas, was born in Grimes county, Texas, December 25, 1847. His father, Jesse Walker, a San Jacinto veteran, died when the subject of this sketch was quite small. Sometime in the 50's the family moved to Gonzales county. In 1862, when James Walker was fifteen years old, he came to Bandera county and worked for Berry C. Buckelew, herding cattle for $7 per month, which place he held all winter, then went to Camp Verde where he had two brothers in the Confederate service. He tried to enlist at that time but Major Lawhon, in command of the troops stationed there would not accept him because he was too young. Sometime later, however, he succeeded in getting into the service, and a few days after his enlistment four of the companies at Camp Verde were transferred to South Texas, leaving only a few men to garrison the post and look after the camels there. Henry Ramsey was in charge of the camels at the time and young Walker was put to herding them. He says the animals, numbering about 75 head, were a source of great annoyance and trouble. They ate but little grass, and could not get up the rough places to get to brush which they had to eat. Through the winter they were fed on corn that had to be brought from San Antonio. Mr. Walker now has a bell which was used on those camels, and prizes it very highly as a relic of those frontier days.

At the outbreak of the war between the states, Camp Verde was taken over by the Confederate forces under Gen. Ben McCulloch, and remained under the Confederate control until the war ended, when the post again passed to the United States, and a small force of Federal troops were placed there.

In 1869 Mr. Walker went to California with a herd of 1,500 mixed cattle belonging to Damon Slater of Llano, Mr. Slater being his own boss. Those who went on this trip were Jim and Charlie Moss, Jim Walker, Alf Anderson, Bill Denison, a man named Perryman, John Dupont, John and Riley Billings, Billie Click, a German named Mahaley, Jack Hamilton and Damon Slater. They took a route up through the Concho country to the Pecos and crossed at Horsehead Crossing, out by old Fort Stanton, through Tularosa Valley, across Sacramento Mountains to the Gila River, crossing the Colorado River, passing Tucson and Fort Yuma, and went on to the Winters Ranch in California where they delivered the herd. On the trip they had some trouble with the Indians, particularly with some of the Pima tribe who were trying to run a bluff and secure some cattle from a herd belonging to a man named Crockett Riley.

Mr. Walker and several of the Slater hands went to Riley's assistance and found him surrounded by about 80 Indians. They were off their reservation, and did not really want a scrap, so when they fired into them they hastily retreated. Mr. Walker killed the chief's horse at a distance of 500 yards. He was later arrested by the Indian agent, and Slater gave the Indians five head of cattle to satisfy their claims for loss of the chief's horse.

After delivering the cattle at the Winters Ranch the cowboys scattered, and only two of them, Billings and Riley, came back to Texas together. Mr. Walker went to Los Angeles and San Francisco and struck up with a man named Jacob Sanders who was from Ohio, and they decided to go to New York. Accordingly they secured passage on a steamer, the *Golden City,* which sailed one Sunday morning. On the following Tuesday the steamer was wrecked in Mexican waters and the crew and 450 passengers were forced to take to lifeboats and landed on the barren coast. In company with a guide the shipwrecked people walked a distance of twenty-five miles to a cove, and were there taken aboard a vessel that carried them back to San Francisco. While on the coast they were without food and had but very little water from Tuesday until Saturday. As Walker and Sanders paid transportation to New York, the steamship company allowed them passage on another vessel and they again started. He says they crossed the Isthmus of Panama, and took a big steamer which carried them across the Gulf of Mexico and ran direct to New York. Arriving in that city, Mr. Walker decided he had seen enough of the world and immediately started back to Texas by water, reaching Key West, Fla., and from there proceeded to Galveston and when he hit land again it was to hike straight for home. He had been absent one year and four months, and came back rich in experience, but mighty poor in pocket. On the same day he was shipwrecked off the Mexican coast, February 22, 1870, his brother, Riley Walker, was killed by Indians on Bell Mountain in Llano county.

On February 10, 1864, Mr. Walker was happily married to Miss Melvina Bandy of Bandera county. To them have been born 13 children, 11 of whom are still living: Thomas Walker, Mrs. Ada Moseley, Mrs. Alice Smith, Jeff Walker, all of San Antonio; Jim Walker, killed in Oklahoma by a falling tree; Jesse Walker, died in infancy; Mrs. Ida Fines of Tuff; C. C. Walker of Caddo, La., R. L. Walker of Medina, Mrs. Mary Davis of Vanderpool; Miss Myrtle Walker of Medina; Mrs. Ruby Neely and Charlie Walker of Yoakum.

In 1895 Mr. Walker located on his present homesite, where he has resided all these years, quietly following farming for an occupation and raising his sons and daughters to be useful men and women. He has had an active part in the development of the country, and recalls many intresting events that transpired in his section.

ANDREW G. JONES

The Jones family has been one of the solid, representative and substantial families of Bandera county since the early days of settlement. "Uncle Andy," as he is familiarly known, is one of the best citizens Bandera county has ever produced, and his sons and daughters are numbered among the quiet, thoroughly honorable and upright citizens of the county. He was born in Bexar county, February 24, 1853. His father, John A. Jones, true type of the Texas pioneer, came to Bandera county in 1864 with his family, and located on Myrtle Creek, Mr. Jones dying there in 1895, and his good wife, Mrs. Mahala Jones, surviving him until 1920, when she died. There were eight children in the family of John A. Jones, five boys and three girls, namely: Sam Jones, deceased; Jim Ike Jones of Parker Canyon, Ariz.; Ranse Jones, deceased; John L. Jones, for many years sheriff of Kimble county, now deceased; Andy G. Jones, the subject of this sketch, Mrs. Margaret Stevens, now deceased; Mrs. Mahala Brown, deceased; Mrs. Eliza Brown, lives on the Nueces River.

Andy G. Jones was a small boy, about 11 years old, when his parents moved to Bandera county. He grew to manhood, married and raised his family here, and to-day lives on a beautifully located ranch not far from the location made by his father in the early days. He went to school in a little clap-board shack with a dirt floor, which stood at the forks of Bandera and Myrtle creeks.

In 1874 Andrew G. Jones was married to Miss Anna Stevens. They had six children, five of whom are yet living, Mrs. Dora Duncan of Medina Lake; Mrs. Lelia Emsley, died in 1910; John Henry Jones, lives in Kerr county; Lou B. (Baker) Jones, lives on Bandera Creek; George Jones lives near his father; Mrs. Noma Smith, lives near Camp Verde. Mrs. Jones died in 1889. Mr. Jones next married Miss Laura Nerthlin, and to this union were born six children, as follows, Florida, Pink, Virgil, Gervis, Manila and Salome Jones, all of them being at home.

In relating some of his frontier experiences, Mr. Jones said:

"I was a member of Robert Ballentyne's company of minute men, organized for the protection of the frontier. We had to scout twenty days in each month, and our pay was $20 per month. We furnished our own grub and mounts, while the state supplied us with guns and ammunition, and gave orders how we should take care of our horses. When in camp we had to stake and side-line each animal and put out a guard. A Mexican named Manuel, who had been an Indian captive for fifteen years, was our trailer and guide, and he was a good one. He knew just how to follow all signs and trails, and he thoroughly hated an Indian. One day we struck an Indian trail on Mason Creek and followed it to where the San Antonio road crosses Privilege Creek. Here the trail led up the creek, and we found a Mexican that had been killed by the Indians. The Mexican was at work building a fence when he was attacked, and when he was struck with a rifle ball he ran and took refuge in an old chimney which was standing where a frontier cabin once stood, and there he died. We found his body in this chimney in a sitting posture, with his pistol in hand ready to shoot. From there we went on and came to a house which the Indians had pillaged. They carried off a number of articles and trinkets, some of which we picked up as we hastily followed the trail. We then found where they had stopped and painted themselves, preparatory to an attack on Jim and John Scott, who were clearing land, but they probably discovered our approach and fled, scattering in several directions, so that we could not successfully follow their trail. We then went to the Bladen Mitchell ranch and decided to go over to the Casey ranch on the Hondo and try to intercept the Indians as they came out of the country. We patrolled that region, two men each twenty miles apart scouting and observing signs, but without success. Then we crossed over to West Prong of the Medina, and here we found a bunch of wild beef steers. Our captain told us to kill them and we shot eight of the big fellows, and as wild as cattle ever got. Taking a supply of the beef we went on to head of the Frio, Tom Click and I patrolling. We found a place where the Indians had left fourteen Indian saddles, and also where they had made a great many arrows and mended moccasins. We stayed there four days expecting the Indians to come and get their saddles, but as they did not show up we burned the rudely made saddles and left there.

"I remember when the Indians killed Mr. and Mrs. Moore on North Prong of the Medina River. We took their trail the next day and followed it across the mountains. They went into a dense cedar brake where it was impossible for more than one or two men to go together. F. L. Hicks was with us on this scout and when we came to the dense cedar brakes our captain said it was unsafe to go in, and several of the men turned back, but Mr. Hicks said to me: 'Andy, let's go in; we can whip every red rascal in there,' so we went. It was a risky thing to do, but Mr. Hicks was a man absolutely without fear and when duty called he was always ready to respond. It is said that Indians will not kill a crazy man, so I guess they thought we were crazy for entering that big thicket.

"The next scout we made we hired old man Smith with his three yoke of steers and went to the Frio Water Hole, where we built a good pen, and then we went to Bull Head on the Nueces and gathered 400 steers which we intended to bring to Bandera and sell to Schmidtke & Hay for $2 per head. We appointed Sam Jones as our boss on this mavericking expedition. While on the Nueces we captured two government horses on the range with halters on. They had escaped from some post months or years before and had become wild. We brought the steers into the pen as we gathered them, and one night they stampeded and seventeen of them were killed by running against cedar stumps which had been left in the pen. About ten miles this side of the water hole was another pen which was called Post Oak, and we brought our steers to it. Four men had to stay with the wagon, and as we were coming to the Post Oak pen, Jim Brown, Jim Gobble, Lum Champion and myself intended to reach a spring at the head of the hollow. There were some Indians there, but I suppose they heard the wagon and hid out, as we did not see them. Near the spring I picked up a pair of moccasins and a small mirror which had been dropped by them. Leaving Champion and Gobble with the wagon, Jim Brown and I scouted around the spring to try to locate the Indians, but without success. We found where they had killed a cow just a short time before and taken some of the beef. They were afoot, evidently coming down into the settlements on a horse-stealing expedition. When we reported our discoveries to the captain he said we could not leave the cattle to follow the Indians, but to guard against attack. That night old Manuel and I stood guard around the horses, and at different times during the night the horses showed signs of alarm and we made ready to secure an Indian scalp, but they did not come. We delivered our steers in due time and received $2 per head for them, and also received $50 for the two government horses we had captured, and we thought we were making money. Somebody reported that we had gathered the 400 steers, and our arms were ordered to be returned and we all got fired from the Ranger service.

"When I was a boy on my father's ranch the government kept a lot of camels at Camp Verde. One day we hobbled three or four of our horses and turned them loose near the house, and fourteen of those old camels came lumbering along. The horses took fright at the sight of them, and we did not see those horses again for many days. My brother and I penned the camels, all of them being gentle except one. We roped the wild one, but never wanted to rope another, for the old humpbacked villain slobbered all over us, and that slobber made us deathly sick. We had a jolly time with those camels when we got rid of the foul, sickening slobber, and as we often rode broncos and wild steers we rode those camels too. The camel has a swinging pace and is easy to ride when you catch the motion of its gait. They could easily travel 100 miles in one day. The Indians seemed to be afraid of the camels and, of course, never attempted to steal any of them."

FOUR BANDERA PIONEERS

Bandera county has become noted for its extremely old people. Living in that county are many pioneers who came when that region was a wilderness, among those we mention Amasa Clark, now 96 years of age; George A. Hay, aged 87; W. D. (Seco) Smith, aged 87; and Ben Batot, aged 83.

AMASA CLARK

All of these pioneers are actively engaged in some calling and are able to attend to their own affairs. Amasa Clark was born in New York State in 1828, and enlisted in the United States Army when just a lad seventeen years old. He saw service with General Scott in the invasion of Mexico, marched from Vera Cruz to Mexico City and was in all the desperate engagements that occurred along the way. Coming out of Mexico in 1848, he came to Texas, and to Bandera county in 1852, where he has resided ever since. His life story is full of thrills and reads like a romance. He owns a nice little farm five miles from the town of Bandera, and recently marketed a thousand bushels of pears which he sold at $1.00 per bushel.

George Hay was born in Scotland in 1836, and came to America while yet a small boy. He located in Bandera in 1854, and for many years was engaged in the mercantile business. He sent a number of herds up the trail during trail driving days, and is well known to all the old timers of southwest Texas. For the past few years he has held the office of Justice of the Peace at Bandera, and only recently r e t i r e d from that office.

W. D. (Seco) Smith was born in Mississippi in 1836, and located in the Bandera region in 1857. He was a noted scout and Indian fighter during the early days, and was a warm friend and admirer of B i g Foot Wallace. He now resides on a pretty farm near Medina City, in Bandera county, and looks after his crops and live stock personally.

GEORGE HAY

Ben Batot was born in Germany in 1841, and came with his parents to Texas to the Castro Colony on the Medina River in 1843. He lived in Medina county many years, but later moved to Bandera county, and now lives on his farm near the town of Bandera.

All of these old pioneers have raised large families, Amasa Clark being the father of nineteen children and Seco Smith being the father of fifteen.

IN CONCLUSION

It has been a pleasing task to compile this wonderful book, and I feel that something should be said of the efforts of Mr. George W. Saunders to "round up" all of the old boys and get their history in print so that the coming generations may read of the hardships and dangers they encountered and the splendid achievements of his comrades of days gone by. For years Mr. Saunders endeavored to interest men in the publication of this kind of a book. At the Old Trail Drivers' convention held at San Antonio in 1917 the first steps were taken in this direction when the cowboys there present each volunteered to write a sketch of his life and send to Mr. Saunders for publication in the Trail Drivers' Book. Some of them sent in the sketches in due time but some of them failed to respond promptly, and then the "round-up" started. Letters were sent out, phone and telegraph requests were made, and finally a sufficient number had been corraled to make an interesting book. Arrangements were made to have it printed. An editor was employed to compile the sketches and get them in shape, and the editor and printer were going to get them out for Mr. Saunders. Suddenly the editor "went all to pieces" with a nervous breakdown, and the printer closed shop and departed for parts unknown, taking along all of the manuscripts and letters that had been sent in. But nothing daunted, Mr. Saunders, set about again to roundup the old boys, and after two years' effort the first volume of the "Trail Drivers of Texas" was brought out, but it was incomplete, although it contained 500 pages. The old trail drivers were delighted with the book and decided to have an additional volume. It was my happy privilege to write, compile and edit the first volume, at the behest of Mr. Saunders, and when it was decided to get out a second volume he insisted that I take charge of the work.

I have been handicapped in several ways, chiefly because I never was a cowboy, never put a rope on anything larger than a milk calf, never rode a yearling, forked a bronco or adorned my boot with a pair of "cornbread" spurs, and only by accident am I entitled to membership in the Old Trail Drivers' Association. Some time in the remote past my father, John Warren Hunter, helped to keep up the drags with a herd going north, and thereby made me a son of a trail driver. My father was born in Alabama, but came to Texas when he was about nine years old. His father was a Methodist preacher, and settled near Sulphur Bluff, in Hopkins county, where he was living when the Civil War broke out. My father, being about fifteen years old at the time, was employed as a teamster to haul cotton to Brownsville, the only port open to the Confederacy. He spent the term of the war on the Rio Grande, where he became well known for certain daring feats. After the war he spent awhile in Lavaca county and returned to his home in Hopkins county to find that home broken up, his father dead and his brothers and sisters scattered to different parts of the country. He went to Tennessee where he was happily married to my mother, Mary Ann Calhoun, and went to Arkansas where he farmed for a season, but he longed to get back to Texas, and returned in 1878, and became a school teacher. For many years he taught school in Gillespie, Mason, Menard and McCulloch counties, being one of the pioneer teachers of that section. In 1891 he quit the school room to take up newspaper work, having purchased the Menardville *Record,* later moving the plant to Mason and establishing the Mason *Herald.* He was one of the fearless editors of that time and the *Herald* became known as an outspoken weekly. Oftentimes he had to back up his assertions with muscle and brawn, but he was of Irish descent and really enjoyed a fisticuff, and when the match had been pulled off he was ready to shake hands and make friends. He removed to

San Angelo in 1907, and for several years was connected with the San Angelo *Standard*. His death occurred January 12, 1915. For many years prior to his death he had been engaged in collecting historical data and manuscript pertaining to the early history of Texas, and became recognized as one of the leading historians of the state. Naturally I became interested in this kind of work and have tried to follow the same line, with the result that I fell right in when Mr. Saunders announced that he was going to print a book of reminiscence sketches of the early cowmen. I realized then that it would be a wonderful contribution to the historical annals of Texas, and that the time was ripe for its publication, as the older fellows are passing off the stage of action at an alarming rate and that within a few years not many would be left to tell the tale. I realized then, which fact has been made apparent since, that I was not qualified for the task that has been assigned me, but I have done my best, and that is all anyone can do. It has been a great pleasure to perform this task under the direction of Mr. Saunders, for he has been very considerate and patient, and left matters very much in my hands. The Old Time Trail Drivers, as well as the youth of Texas, owe him a debt that can never be paid for thus rescuing from oblivion and preserving this important link in the chain of Texas history.

J. MARVIN HUNTER.

THE END

INDEX